I0625523

My Life With Words

My Life With Words

A baby boomer journalist chronicles her journey
to professional success and personal peace

Barbara F. Luebke

Red Fish Books

My Life With Words © copyright 2024 by Barbara F. Luebke. All rights reserved. No part of this book may be reproduced in any form whatsoever, by photography or xerography or by any other means, by broadcast or transmission, by translation into any kind of language, nor by recording electronically or otherwise, without permission in writing from the author, except by a reviewer, who may quote brief passages in critical articles or reviews.

Red Fish Books

ISBN: 979-8-218-32585-5

Cover and book design by Mayfly Design

Library of Congress Catalog Number: 2023922493
First Printing: 2024
Printed in the United States of America

For you

For me

Contents

"I think we are well advised to keep on nodding terms with the people we used to be, whether we find them attractive company or not. Otherwise they turn up unannounced and surprise us, come hammering on the mind's door at 4 a.m. of a bad night and demand to know who deserted them, who betrayed them, who is going to make amends."

From "Slouching Towards Bethlehem" by Joan Didion

The words, in patterns
    on paper, flow again
The hour glass has been turned
The drought has ended
And thoughts/feelings are penned
    once more
The soul in me once more
    seeks escape
And in verbalizing I am again—
    whole

What forces now want out?
What brings on this renewal?
Why do I write?
Tho I know not why— I
    know I must— as if
    my pencil-fingers are
    guided by another face.
But, alas, I am . . .

Transcribed as scribbled
on a 4x6 notecard
Dated 2-24-73
Barbara F. Luebke

Author's Note

I offer these thoughts to enhance your reading experience.

▶ As a journalist, I am accustomed to using quotation marks to designate the *exact words* of a speaker or writer. As an academician, I am accustomed to setting off *long* quotations typographically (indented, single spaced). I follow both these conventions in this book, regardless of whether I am quoting my own words or someone else's.

▶ I use italics to express thoughts, usually mine.

▶ With some exceptions, I have used the full names of the people who play a key role in my story. When I chose not to, it was out of respect for their privacy or because I thought a descriptive word or phrase was sufficient.

▶ I read in a *Washington Post* story that as a Justice Department official, Merrick Garland urged the prosecutors in the trial of Oklahoma City bomber Timothy McVeigh, "Do not bury the crime in the clutter." I stuck a Post-it with that quote on my computer to keep me focused as I waded through my own ocean of source material. As I sought to balance the important and the interesting. Nonetheless, I have written a **long** book. When you find I have given you more than you need or want, I encourage you to do what I do in my own reading: Skim ahead.

▶ I have used Appendixes to share a few documents.

▶ I am fond of including information parenthetically in my writing, so I apologize in advance if the parentheses annoy you. (I and my editors removed many from one draft to the next.) You also will notice frequent insertions of observations, updates, commentary, etc. I identify these as "An aside" and put that text inside brackets.

▶ I am a journalist to my core -- committed to verifiable facts and, when offered, opinion(s) clearly recognizable as such. I have done my best to ensure the accuracy of what you are about to read, and I accept responsibility for any errors that snuck in.

Preface

I was on the cusp of my 72nd birthday when I first spoke these truths: *Words have been my life. Words are my life.* A few days later, after involuntarily and steadily mulling over those sentences, I refined them to specify *written words*. In the midst of months mired in memories, those truths emerged as I was describing my latest discoveries to Luise, my dear friend of more than 50 years. As the coronavirus pandemic wore on, our telephone calls had become more frequent. She was a lifeline. During one of those calls I struggled to express my joy at finding the brief speech I had delivered at my eighth-grade graduation. Certain that I had saved it, I had emptied all my storage containers without finding it. I was bereft. Then, one afternoon as I rifled through a pile of stuff, there it was -- tucked into a folder where it didn't logically belong! Two hundred and sixteen typewritten words on a yellowed sheet of paper. I was ecstatic about having early evidence of my writing and a foreshadowing of my academic success.

In October 2020, I self-published "Dementia's Unexpected Gifts: A memoir of stumbling into caregiving, then learning to live my best life." Along with my notes and stash of emails, that book was made possible by the seemingly unlimited cache of materials I discovered when I began to empty closets and basement of my partner's belongings. She had been in a nursing home since September 2017 and I was beginning to move forward. Along the way, I also emptied a few file-cabinet drawers of my own, but I set aside my boxes and giant rubber containers. What I discovered when I returned to them was that I had saved at least as much as she had. "If I had become famous, I would have been a biographer's dream," I joked.

I unearthed a treasure-trove of letters dating from my childhood to the present. I found my earliest diaries and a couple dozen notebooks chronicling -- generally in excruciating detail -- my personal and professional lives. I found every issue of my high school newspaper, the issues of my college newspaper during my editorship, scrapbooks of newspaper stories I wrote in college and as a young reporter. I found hand-written poems, short stories and the chapters of two "novels" I started writing in high school. All that and so much more.

I began looking at greeting cards (recycling most) and letters (keeping most to sort and read later). As I did so, ideas popped in and out of my consciousness. I was hungry for a project to help me manage the first winter of COVID-19, which kept me at home in Rhode Island instead of enjoying a third stay in southwest Florida. An idea would spark one day, then fade to be replaced by another awhile later, until it, too, faded. That conversation with Luise changed everything. My graduation speech, I came to understand, could be the cornerstone I needed to document the arc of my life in journalism, a life spent with words. It was the impetus to undertake a personal exploration of a life spent learning, doing and teaching journalism. I was further encouraged when I read the last sentences of Jill Lepore's introduction to "These Truths," her survey of U.S. history: "The past is an inheritance, a gift and a burden. It can't be shirked. You carry it everywhere. There's nothing for it but to get to know it."

The same could be said of personal history, I thought. Reflecting on my life as a not-famous female journalist and educator during the incredible decades of the late 20th and early 21st centuries could be instructive. Guided by a reporter's traditional "5 Ws" -- Who? What? When? Where? Why? (and How?) -- I set out to understand how my ethos developed, why I followed the paths I did, and what lessons I might be able to share. How had I made my way from the 1950s world of limited opportunities for girls and women to the world where I was able to live the life of my choosing? I had what I needed to tell that story, if only I could find the words. I long had abandoned the notion of journalistic objectivity, concluding instead that our goal ought to be telling stories objectively. Adverb instead of noun! I would allow my words -- journalistic and otherwise -- to speak for themselves, with me filling in blanks, offering commentary and providing perspective.

I soon understood that I could not tell the story of my career without sharing at least some of the story of me. I paused, unsure if I wanted to write a second memoir. Truth be told, if I had read Amy Tan's "Where the Past Begins: A Writer's Memoir" about then -- instead of months later -- I might have set this project aside. Passage after passage, Tan's words echoed those in my head. "Holy shit!!" I noted more than once. She, too, found that she had forgotten much: "[W]ithout conscious choice on my part, my brain has let a lot of moments slide over the cliff." She called her lifelong habit "wonderment"; I call mine "curiosity." She believes that "if I cannot write, I would have no further knowledge of myself." For me the same would hold true if I could not read. By the time I finished Tan's book, she had reminded me how fiction and nonfiction (for me, journalism) are different not just in content but in approach for the writer. We share techniques, and while the material used may seem to be the same, we work with it differently. Perhaps most importantly, in Tan I found the words to explain why I had decided to *not* give my archives to the project for which I had saved so much. "There is no symbolic immortality to be had" in doing that, she wrote. "It's perpetual misinterpretation."

As discouraged as I frequently am by the current state of American journalism and the behaviors of many who fancy themselves journalists, at the end of my exploration and reexamination of my career I was left with my most important truth: I was born to be a journalist. Two sentences from Adrienne Rich that I rediscovered mid-writing explain this book best: "I write for the still-fragmented parts in me, trying to bring them together. Whoever can read and use any of this, I write for them as well."

A scene from the workspace of a "memory archivist." I hope Nora Krug approves of me borrowing that term from her incredible visual memoir, "Belonging." I stumbled on it during the final stages of work on this book. I am in awe!

Prologue

English 76 — Feb. 4, 1969

A 5-year-old girl sits patiently on the couch while her father finishes the Sunday Sports pages. Then, not so patiently, the blue dress requests, "Hurry." Green Bay Packer news digested, the man begins with "Blondie and Dagwood," moves through "Nancy" and "Donald Duck," and completes the journey with "Priscilla's Pop" and "Beetle Bailey."

"I can't wait until I can read, daddy," the blue dress says. "Then I can do the funnies all by myself."

In a couple of years it comes -- C*A*T, D*O*G. It takes an hour, but the corduroy playsuit forges her way through the comic characters by herself. She can't read all the words yet, but the funnies don't seem to lose much in her translation.

More important than the understanding, a new love grows -- a curiosity for words sneaks its way into her mind.

Second . . . third . . . fourth . . . fifth grade. Year after year piles word upon word, meanings upon meanings in the pigtail's mind. Still, curiosity. And now, a new feeling -- a yearning for adventure and experience which sometimes only words could offer her young mind.

The blue jumper is in sixth grade now. A contest -- with a prize for the student who reads the most library books during the year. She wins. The contest rules were satisfied -- but more than that, her mind. Yet, it really wasn't, for she continued to read. Anyway, her first book of her own library. "Huckleberry Finn." It was of her own choosing and one to be paged many times hence.

High school now -- and the words became longer and harder -- the books more time consuming . . . begging for understanding . . . questioning.

But her appetite decreased not, but grew, becoming insatiable. A book a week -- and yet the "to read" list grew even longer.

Her first book club. Paperbacks now long forgotten or given away. But not regretted. Mother said "foolishness," but she saved her babysitting money.

So much in life to experience -- so much of it never to be hers. But books were hers and in them she could dwell. Escapism -- maybe? Perhaps, her own kind of reality.

The blue dress, corduroy playsuit and pigtails has grown up now. . . . On to college. Required reading which leaves little time for personal reading. From fiction novels to contemporary nonfiction and the classics. But still a questioning of the world -- a greater desire to live it to the fullest.

Other book clubs. Last dollars spent for a suggested paperback. Only to fall on the unread pile. Good magazines and respected newspapers.

And all the time a soul and mind questing for more -- reaching -- grasping -- trying to avoid the unavoidable realization that there are just too many things the semi miniskirt wants to read and never will.

CHAPTER 1

Family Tree

Memory has its limitations when documenting one's early years. The times before "real" memory often reside in family stories that, heard often enough, morph into memories accepted at face value. Besides, as a journalist I find memories not only suspect but insufficient. To find evidence of me I researched to uncover facts and specifics, to fill in gaps, to find "truths." I discovered that the particulars of my professional and personal lives are not discrete data points; many of the dots, as I have come to appreciate, meander and connect in ways that amaze, amuse, assure and anchor the early me to the me of now. So, in the beginning. . . .

Glenn Luebke of De Pere, Wisconsin, met Barbara Walker of Waynesville, Ohio, on Labor Day weekend 1947. He was in Ohio to attend a reunion with an Army buddy, who had enlisted his cousin Barbara to entertain Glenn. After he returned home, the pair corresponded and, according to a brief biography of our mother written by my sister, it was his daily letters that won her heart. That Thanksgiving, Glenn returned to Ohio for a visit. He made the trip a third time for Christmas, and Glenn and Barbara decided to get married. Immediately. Because of Ohio's three-day waiting period, they went to nearby Richmond, Indiana (no waiting period after blood tests and license). They were married by a justice of the peace on December 30. Glenn was 25; Barbara would turn 20 a couple of weeks later.

There was no honeymoon. There *was* subterfuge. Barbara was midway through three years of training to be a nurse, and the rules required students to live on site and forbade them from marrying. The newlyweds decided Glenn would return to his bookkeeping job in Wisconsin and Barbara would finish her schooling. They would tell no one about their marriage. The plan lasted just two weeks before Barbara arranged to join Glenn in De Pere. I joined them about a year later.

De Pere is in northeastern Wisconsin, a few miles south of a city well-known today for its football team, the Green Bay Packers. According to the 1950 census, De Pere (city) had a population of 8,146 and De Pere (town) another 891. There were 52,735 people in Green Bay, and in all the county -- Brown -- just under 100,000. In other words, my roots are small-town Midwestern roots, grounded in the post-war years of stability, prosperity and burgeoning consumerism. Along with the fear of communism at the heart of the Cold War, the seeds of the Civil Rights Movement, and a "woman's place is in the home" attitude.

My roots are also working-class. As my sister wrote about our parents' Wisconsin start: "Money was tight in the Luebke household. With no car or money to buy one, Barbara could not continue her nurses training and Glenn would need to rely on the bus or friends to get to work." Glenn was employed by a meat-packing plant. Bookkeepers in those days earned about $3,100 a year (about $32,500 in 2021 dollars). Like so many of their generation -- children of the Depression -- the couple were used to "getting by."

Glenn, whose paternal grandparents and maternal grandmother emigrated from Pomerania, Prussia, in the 1880s, was the fourth of six children. His father, Ernest, was an accomplished butter and cheese maker; his mother, Sophie (Sophia Anna Eulalia Wiedenhaft), a stern matriarch. (The slight smiles I see in photos from my first and second birthdays were rare, as I recall.) They married in 1912, just after he completed the butter and cheese course at the UW-Madison agricultural school. In 1915, he bought the Little Saumico Creamery Company. (One store reported selling as much as 300 pounds of its Billy Butter each week.) During the Depression, Ernest lost his business and he went to work for the De Pere Dairy. The 1940 Census listed him as working 10 hours a day, seven days a week.

Barbara was the fifth of eight children; her maternal family tree traces to the Mayflower. Her father, Frank Edwin, was in his late 30s when he married her mother, Martha (Smith). She was just 20 and was his third wife. He was a land surveyor. In 1934, when Barbara was 6, her father died of thyroid cancer. During his illness, several of the children had been "farmed out" to aunts and uncles for care because their pregnant mother simply could not manage. After her husband's death, she found work as a housekeeper, but neither she nor the relatives were financially able to care for Barbara and her siblings. Eventually they were placed in the church-run Otterbein Home. Barbara was 7, and the orphanage in Lebanon, Ohio, was her home for eight years. She was reunited to live with her Aunt Louise and Uncle Delbert Conger (she called them Mom and Pop) after her freshman year of high school.

[An aside: I was surprised to reread a 1995 newspaper story in which my mother reported "very fond memories" of her orphanage years. "We didn't run the streets, we always had food, and I was never mistreated," she told the reporter. She did say that as a youngster she didn't understand why her mother sent the family away. "But you learn over time," she said, explaining that "there was no Social Security, no help." Also, because children couldn't be adopted out of Otterbein at least the siblings could not be split up. What did not surprise me was her acknowledgement that "you just felt sometimes that nobody cared about you and some days -- if you [as an adult] get discouraged or are having a bad day -- that old feeling comes back." Then she surprised me again, describing herself as "somewhat introverted" and crediting her kids with helping her come out of her shell My memories of her and her memories definitely do not jibe on that score!]

The newlyweds lived for a bit with my paternal grandparents until they found their first apartment several miles away on the east side of the Fox River, which divides De Pere. It was to that apartment they brought me after my January 23, 1949, birth at Bellin Hospital in Green Bay on a "slippery, sleeting winter morning," as my mother described it in my "baby book." They had gone to the hospital at 8 a.m. Saturday and I was born at 5:16 a.m. Sunday. (It was not until my sister wrote about our parents not owning a car that I wondered, *how did they get to the hospital?* By then no one was alive who could tell me.) My mother wrote that I had "very black hair and blue eyes." (That was news to the brown-haired, brown-eyed me I have always known.) My birth certificate attests that I weighed 7 pounds, 13 ounces. There is no record of my length. My footprints (barely 3 inches long) and my mother's right thumb print on my birth certificate are faded, but 73 years later they leave me smiling.

I also was left smiling when I recently found "The Story Of Our Baby," with its pink sateen cover. I am sure it had gone unearthed and unread for decades. Today's digital documentation of one's children might be more extensive than the handwritten records by mothers of earlier eras, but I cannot imagine them eliciting the same emotions. For example, seeing in my mother's neat handwriting the observation that, "I think Daddy was more tired than mommie" after her almost 24 hours in labor. Or reading the page filled with my "firsts" and learning that "at 5½ months [she] got angry at herself because she couldn't crawl." It was touching to learn that "Daddy slept in Barbie's crib 27 years ago" and that Grandma Luebke had given the crib to me. And I was flabbergasted to read that my favorite toys included two cars -- "a red one from Daddy and a yellow one from Grandpa Conger" -- because to this day I love cars, and my first was red and my favorite was yellow!

My first years also proved to be well-documented in photographs; the first was taken by my father when I was 2 weeks old. The black and white snapshots were more numerous than one might expect given my parents' economic situation. In fact, it was photos that first alerted me to an early trip to Ohio. Notes and ticket stubs in the baby book confirmed I was just 6 months old when, as my mother wrote, a train took us "to visit Mother's friends and relatives." The list of my first outings also includes "Downtown in Baby Buggy" at 14 weeks ("Barbie likes her rides in buggy") and "to Abrams to visit great uncles" at 4½ months. Is it any wonder I grew up with a fondness for travel?

In adulthood, I regularly explained that I had been named after both my parents, my middle name -- Francine -- an homage to Frank, one of my father's middle names. But I didn't know this for a fact until I found what my mother wrote about my baptism: "Barbie was named for mommie and daddy." The church officially recorded my February 4 baptism; my mother recorded that it occurred "at home by Rev. Wegner" and I was "very quiet, never cried once." I owe my mother a debt of gratitude for not only preserving those details in the baby book, but also for organizing so many of my artifacts into a massive scrapbook that brings me to tears whenever I look through it. I smile to think that my lifelong "saving habit" might be genetic (although it is more likely generational). Thanks to that scrapbook, I know my baptism was followed on June 13 by my addition to the Cradle Roll of the St. John's Lutheran Sunday School. Two 14-by-11-inch parchment certificates and a pink satin ribbon attest to my successes in the September 1950 Better Baby Show and Festival. (I won Baby Countess in the Junior Class of the Royalty Division and earned 100% in the Health Division.) I acknowledge much more interest in these things now than ever before. Or should I write "astonishment" or "wonderment"?

It was written that I "was very spoiled when we returned from Ohio," and apparently I had my father at my beck and call. "Barbie cries at night before she goes to sleep if Daddy does not play with her." That no doubt changed in October 1950 when, three months before my second birthday, my sister, Christine, was born. (In her late 20s, she legally changed her name to Kris and that is how I will refer to her.) By that time, my parents had moved across the river to a one-bedroom rental at 450 Grant Street in West De Pere, just a couple of blocks from my grandparents. I cannot begin to imagine the noise and commotion in that apartment, with a toddler and a newborn. Dad was closer to work (still no car) and money remained tight. "I think we were happiest when we didn't have money," my mother told my sister. "We spent all our time together and never felt like we were poor." Economic circumstance led my parents to decide to limit their family to two children. They believed that with a small family, should anything happen to one of them the other could still manage. That plan, like the one to keep their marriage a secret, did not last, and in 1959 they adopted a son, the last of four foster children they cared for starting in February 1956.

It wasn't only in Ohio that I was spoiled; after all, I was the second grandchild and first granddaughter on the Luebke family tree. I also suspect I was a precocious child, based on two memories about my early years. One involves me proudly proclaiming to Grandma Luebke that I could spell, then rattling off B-L-A-T-Z to prove it. That is what the sign on the tavern across from our apartment had taught me. Grandma was not amused. The second story involves my pride in learning to read "by myself" at an early age and showing off with the "funny papers"

(Sunday newspaper comics). I don't believe it is a stretch to see these memories as the earliest evidence of what would be my lifelong love affair with reading, newspapers, writing and words. (Mom wrote that "[Barbie] talked at an early age and talked very clearly. Was making sentences by 21 months. Sometimes she had to stop and think *what word she wanted to use.*") [Emphasis added.] Visual proof is a photo from 1951 that captured Dad reading to me as I cuddled on his lap. My writing life began just a few years later, when I went to school. Sometime after that, my cousin Ed and I created a neighborhood "newspaper" that we printed on his toy press.

CHAPTER 2

School Days

I feel like a visitor in a foreign land as I revisit my first nine years of schooling. Everything about them, it seems from the vantage point of 2021, was *so* different from what I have observed in the lives of my grand-nephews and grandnieces. But regardless of the educational philosophies and practices that shaped me, those formative years steered me toward a six-decades-long journey in journalism.

Surely Mom walked me to my first day of kindergarten to meet my teacher, Mrs. Flaherty. It was Wednesday, September 8, 1954. I was an eager pupil; I already had been attending Sunday School for two years. Mom recorded that I "enjoyed it very much and learned quickly. Kept wanting to know when it was Sunday again." The first thing I remember about kindergarten is the walks to school with my cousin Ed. I remember that there was a "nice old lady" along the way who sometimes gave us cookies on our return trip in the afternoon. I remember that now and then we detoured to visit Grandma and Grandpa Luebke. Our small-town world was safe, our route to school familiar because walking was how we got around. If our mothers were anxious about the freedom their 6-year-olds had to get themselves to and from school, we didn't know it.

Our family of four had moved a year earlier into a house about a half mile away from Nicolet High School, which housed the kindergarten and elementary classrooms. By today's standards, our 900-square-foot abode on Lande Street was tiny, dwarfed by the Sullivans' house on one side, the Bushmakers' on the other and our uncle's behind us. When we moved in, it already was 53 years old. It cost my parents $5,900

($59,877 today) and beginning in October 1953 they paid $50 monthly ($507 today) in principle, interest and taxes. (An online real estate site told me that house last sold in early 2018 for $78,000.) Amazingly, when my parents were not able to get a Veterans Administration loan to buy the house, their banker personally loaned them the money. Later they earned extra money cleaning his bank on weekends, and one Christmas some of our gifts were pass-alongs from him. I learned about saving at his bank with my 10-cents-a-week Christmas Club. Aunt Florence, who eventually became the bank's vice president, often was the teller accepting our dimes. I also remember standing in line at the bank to meet Santa and get a goody bag that always included a very dry popcorn ball wrapped in colored cellophane.

From my most recent drive-by, the Lande Street house looks about the same on the outside. Interior photos from the real estate site suggest many changes. Give me paper and a pencil and I can easily sketch the layout of "our" house: Front door opening directly into the kitchen, with a tiny bathroom off to the left (on holidays the bathtub sometimes doubled as a dish-washing space). A trapdoor in the bathroom floor opened to a dirt-floored, cobweb-covered space where at least once we took cover during a tornado. The kitchen included a narrow pantry with a counter; Kris and I learned to bake there, following recipes from our "Fun To Cook Book." Dad and Uncle Edwin -- beer bottles in hand -- once hid there from their mother. Through the kitchen were the furnace and water heater, and behind that the bedroom my sister and I shared. Go up a step on the right side of the kitchen and you were in the living room. Our parents' bedroom and closet (the hiding place for Christmas gifts -- and once for a neighbor running from her abusive husband) were off the living room; a curtain separated the rooms. A porch ran along the Third Street side of the house. Eventually it was converted into a bedroom for our brother.

My elementary school world was small, too. Uncle Edwin and his family lived kitty-corner behind us; a path through hedges joined our backyards. Our playmates came from the houses nearest us; an empty lot was our baseball diamond, football field and hockey rink. Walk north on Third Street or Fourth Street a few blocks, turn onto College Avenue and our grandparents (along with Aunt Florence and Uncle

Roland, neither of whom married or moved away) lived in the middle of the block. Our holidays were often spent there with as many as 14 Luebkes. Children were not allowed beyond the landing on the stairs that led to Florence's and Roland's rooms, so we sat there to spy on the adult table. I still marvel at the sumptuous meals that were cooked in a kitchen tinier than ours. I wish I could ask Grandma how she managed to roll her Christmas gingerbread cookies almost paper thin; I certainly never have been able to do it. I wish I could ask Grandpa why and how he ate peas using a knife.

Our church -- St. John Lutheran -- was two blocks from my grandparents. Stay on Third or Fourth for another block or so to Main Street and a downtown that included Stowe's drug store; the "family" bank; Van Dyke's Shoes and Clothing, where Roland worked; the "dairy bar" with its jukebox and cherry Cokes; various shops; and a few taverns (the staple of every Wisconsin town). About midway between our house and the high school was Micke's store, a modest neighborhood market that was the centerpiece of a nostalgic story I wrote for a creative writing class in college. The high school -- a three-story brick, Neo-Classical Revival style structure built in 1923 (and listed on the State and the National Register of Historic Places since 2015) -- was between the Main Street bridge across the Fox River and the St. Norbert College campus. Only in my imagination can I see myself in the kindergarten and first-grade rooms, the first of what for me would be classrooms too numerous to count.

I have no such trouble seeing myself in Lincoln Elementary School, which opened in September 1956. I can still name most of my teachers and tell you a little something about them. Without a doubt, the most influential was Mrs. Duquaine, my first-grade teacher . . . and my second-grade teacher . . . and my fourth-grade teacher. I loved her. When I found a newspaper clipping about her among my mementos, I teared up. I also cringed at the sexism exhibited in that story (centered on her French meat pie recipe), a sign of how times -- and I -- have changed. It was Hazel Duquaine who recognized a talent in me and nurtured it. I begin my author's profile on Amazon by acknowledging her influence: "I published my first story in the second grade, when Mrs. Duquaine hung the large sheet of lined paper with my printed sentences about the train that sped past our new school." She taught me phonics and the "times tables," both of which I appreciate to this day. She taught me to love words. And she nurtured my love of reading. A Wisconsin Young People's Reading Circle Primary Certificate, signed by her, indicates that by the end of first grade I had read at least 10 books, including "Day In and Day Out," "I Know a Story" and "Fuzzy Tail." A certificate from the De Pere Public Library records that in the summer before second grade, I completed "the prescribed Summer Reading Course." Mrs. Duquaine also signed my second-grade certificate, which awarded me a "testimonial of merit" for reading, among other titles, "Moon, Sun and Stars." I name that one because my adult fondness for suns and moons inspired the tattoo on my right forearm.

I don't know how much I *read* the summer after second grade, but I know I already was a letter-*writer*. That August, Kris and I were in Ohio with Grandma and Grandpa Conger (how we thought of our mother's "Mom" and "Pop"). I wrote at least four letters home, each a bit longer and more "sophisticated." The first, with its half-inch-high printing, was addressed to Mommy and Daddy. It included the news that "we are going to take a ride in the truck" and my promise to send a postcard, before ending with "Take good care of your selves." The last letter was to Mother and Father, and after the usual "How are you. I am fine." offered details about our activities. Spelling remained an issue, but my message was clear: "We are going to have corn on the cob for supper and had it for dinner. Granpa is making sement at Dale's. Grandma is going to sprinkel cloths. We may go over to Recca's for supper. Momma there was nine kids herh playing yesterday playing cowboys. Last letter we are writtig. We are shure having fun. See you soon." At the bottom of the paper, after two lines of X's and O's, was my 2-inch reminder: MUCH LOVE."

So much about my early experiences with education is defined by the times. For one thing, I attended an elementary school -- housing grades one to eight. It was the public elementary school for all of West De Pere. An overwhelmingly Catholic community, the city also had two parochial schools. After kindergarten I didn't attend school with many of those classmates again until we reached high school, although I did ride the school bus with some of them. (This included my cousins, who were raised Catholic.) The faces in my elementary classrooms didn't change much from grade to grade. Not a lot of people moved out of West De Pere, and not a lot moved in. Similarly, the only people I remember knowing from East De Pere were the couple who had lived next door to my parents in their first apartment and a family from church. My classmates were overwhelmingly White, with the exception of a couple of kids from the nearby Oneida reservation. (I do not recall knowing a Black person until college.) My classmates included more boys than girls.

I remember that we walked or rode our bikes the mile to Lincoln School. In the winter, when money allowed, we rode the school bus. Kris remembers that to keep warm we wore slacks under our required dresses. Lincoln didn't have a cafeteria until I was in the seventh grade. Our lunch boxes (along with our baseball cards and comic books) would be worth a lot of money today, if only we had them. Cheez Whiz on squishy white bread was a sandwich favorite, as were the hot dogs Mom put in thermoses filled with boiling water, which cooked them by lunchtime. Kris and I carried our milk money (chocolate was a rare treat) each week tied into a corner of our cloth handkerchiefs. We didn't have to pay for the "goiter pills" we received once a week (given out by a student no doubt being rewarded for good behavior). The pills were chalky-chocolate-tasting iodine pills intended to ward off thyroid problems. You either enjoyed the taste or found it foul. I enjoyed it and would take advantage of frequently being chosen to hand them out by allowing myself an extra pill.

Like many girls of the era, I kept a locked diary. My first, for 1959, was a Christmas gift from Kris. Its entries lasted just about two months, but three things stand out: I didn't pay much attention to spelling. My handwriting was atrocious. My entries were brief but generally filled with specifics. It is that last observation that I connect to journalistic writing. My January 1 entry, like every subsequent one, began "Dear Diary." (Always write for an audience, I would learn years later.) "We watched the Orange Bole on T.V. Okla. Won the game 21-6. We went out for supper, then I stayed over night at my friends house. We took or Christmas tree down. then we put it outside and put bread on it" [for the birds].

The January 4 entry (and many others) included my church activities and is a reminder that those things once mattered to me. "Today was Sunday. I sang in the Jr choir then I went to Sunday school. I came home and read the funnies. We had our friends in for supper. Judy, Barbara D. my sister and I ate on Tv. trays. Sandy and John ate at the card table. The parents and Timmy + Davy ate at the table." The friends mentioned lived on a farm across the river, and it was there that I learned something about the birds and the bees from watching their cows. I also learned to ride horses, bale hay, catch snapping turtles, shovel manure and play a lively, laugh-filled game of telephone after a hard-work-hearty meal. The ride from our house to theirs seemed *so* long, and I distinctly remember a left turn onto a gravel road. In reality it was maybe five miles.

Other diary entries offered details about my life in fourth grade. "We got right down to work" the day we returned to school after our two-week Christmas break. I had a microscope, which I brought to school. We had music and "Phy. Ed." (physical education) twice a week. I was competitive even then, as suggested in an entry about playing a game called Buzz. "Roy W. and I were last. Roy won the game because I forgot to say buzz." We had a geography test on my birthday. "I got 90/B. No one got 100." There also are plenty of details about life at home, especially the television shows we watched, the weather (28 degrees below zero one Sunday did not stop us from going to church, where "there was a bat in Sunday School") and snowfalls (never too much to keep us indoors). Our excitement at going to a television station in Green Bay one Sunday oozes through that diary entry. WBAY annually sponsored a telethon to raise money for cerebral palsy. Kids who collected money could bring it to the station, deposit it in the "fish pond" and meet visiting celebrities. I wrote that "we saw Doc and Miss Kitty from 'Gunsmoke' and Lt. Rip Masters from 'Rin Tin Tin.' And shook Hands With Rip Masters."

Some people were building bomb shelters in case "the commies" dropped "the BIG one." I wrote about being sad that we couldn't afford one. I also was sad because Mom *had* found the money to send Kris and me to dance lessons. I hated the frilly dresses and white gloves. She also managed to find money for music lessons. I tried clarinet, but my pinky fingers are crooked and wouldn't stretch to the lower keys. I switched to French horn, perhaps because it has just three keys. Or perhaps I had read it is the most difficult instrument to learn and welcomed the challenge. Although I did not realize it at the time, Mom's determination to expose us to culture expanded our world and laid the foundation for lifelong pleasures.

Being frightened about the possibility of an atomic bomb was one thing, but when a routine test for tuberculosis was positive, I really had reason to be scared. Hickory Grove Sanitarium, which had been housing patients with the dreaded lung disease since 1914, was about four miles south of our home. We regularly passed it on Sunday drives on Lost Dauphin Road along the Fox River. Thankfully, a second, more sophisticated test confirmed that I did not have TB. That led the family doctor -- a chain-smoking survivor of the Bataan Death March during World War II -- to determine that I was allergic to alcohol.

By the time of my diary for 1963, I wrote almost daily. My handwriting and spelling were noticeably improved, and entries focused on my first boyfriend ("I adore Dwayne"), several girlfriends, school activities, schoolwork, 4-H, my approaching confirmation ("We started back to catechism. It was dreadful as always.") and books ("I went to the library and got 3 great books including 1 on basketball."). Sometimes I included sketches related to an entry, such as the April 8 one of my graduation dress. I have only vague memories of that girl; re-reading her thoughts and opinions, I judge her a typical 1960s young teen.

I certainly was a toe-the-line, uber-responsible, over-achieving first-born. Habits I began to develop in elementary school have stuck with me throughout my life, and more than a few contributed to my successes in journalism. Of course, I know that only in hindsight. For one thing, I learned the importance of "showing up" and being on time. My first-grade report card records that I never was tardy. Interestingly, it lists the number of days present rather than days absent, so I can only speculate that I did not miss often. Starting in second grade, absences were recorded along with tardiness. My yearly absences ranged from five days to 13 ½ days, but I was late only once -- in the last quarter of eighth grade. To this day, I go out of my way not to be late and have little patience for people who are. (I attribute this to my father who, I like to joke, was early for everything, even church, where there never was a shortage of seats.) As a reporter, being early impressed sources and guaranteed a seat at the front of a room, all the better to hear and see.

As an editor, meeting deadlines -- being on time -- was of paramount importance and something I took very seriously.

I learned that hard work was rewarded, be it with a teacher's compliment, a report card peppered with A's, a certificate of accomplishment, a perk such as "clapping erasers" clean or helping a teacher distribute handouts, and the like. Eventually I learned that good reporting requires the diligence to go above and beyond and dig below the surface, and the bylines that mean the most are those on stories that were not easy to report or write. Eventually I learned that good editing polishes a reporter's work to make it the best it can be. And that good editors are rewarded for nurturing good reporters and other editors.

I learned responsibility. From the earliest days of doing my assignments and homework to being entrusted with the busiest intersection as a school-crossing guard, I took my duties seriously. And if, as my seventh-grade teacher wrote, I had "assumed too many responsibilities," he was spot-on in adding that "on the other hand she needs something to keep herself busy." Of course, I did have that oldest-child status going at home, too, which also instilled responsibility. In any event, at every step along the way of my journalism journey, my sense of responsibility generally served me well.

[An aside: That seventh-grade teacher, Don Binkowski, was my first male teacher. He eventually left education for broadcasting; he worked in television in Green Bay for years and among other gigs was host of WBAY's Northeastern Wisconsin Championship Bowling show, a family favorite. Decades later, while vacationing in Green Valley, Arizona, I perused the home-town list of residents in the back of the telephone directory. (I don't know when or why I developed the habit of paging through phone books.) Imagine my surprise at finding a Don Binkowski from Green Bay. I was tempted to stop at his house and introduce myself, but I let that small-world moment get away from me. When I noticed his name gone from the directory during my next visit, I searched the internet and found his obituary. I said a silent thank you for the role he played in my life all those years ago.]

I learned there is a connection between reading and learning. How to find answers. How to find information. How to explore the world. Even in reading for pleasure, I discovered, I was accumulating facts, vocabulary, opinions, attitudes and so much more. Equally as important, I eventually would realize, I was learning about writing. I trace my list-making habit to that first-grade record of books read and all the reading-program accomplishments that followed. Eternally grateful for the role books have played in my life, I wrote an essay about that in a little Blurb book I published, "Musings of a Newly Retired Professor." My most precious volumes include three from my elementary school years: "Heidi," a gift in 1957, and "Little Women," a gift in 1958 (both from Aunt Florence), along with "Huckleberry Finn," inscribed "To Barbara from Miss Kottke, for reading the most library books" during the 1960-61 school year. [An aside: Anna Kottke was a beloved teacher, and I looked forward to being in her class. Unfortunately, when I started sixth grade she was ill and we had a substitute for the first half of the year. I was amazed to read Miss Kottke's prescient comment on my year-end report card: "I am going to miss Barbara next year in giving news reports each morning, especially on sports."]

So it was that by the time I moved on to high school, where for the first time I would work on a newspaper, I already had begun laying a foundation for my professional self. That is not to say I knew it, because I am pretty sure I entered high school with only vague thoughts about my future work. I had many interests; as one teacher noted, I did not "concentrate on one thing, but [was] good in all phases of education." From the speech I gave at my eighth-grade graduation, it is clear that I had absorbed what our teachers had been preaching: the importance of education. Our class motto -- "The door to success is labeled push" -- could have been my personal mantra. In my speech, I asked my classmates, "Which path will we choose? The one leading to high school graduation or the one leading to high school but not to graduation." The decision, I added, "may be one of the biggest of our lives." I earnestly explained: "We will never get very far in our scientific world without working and striving for high goals. Why? Because now more than ever, we need high school graduates and those people who go on to still another path -- college graduation." Four years later, I once again would be a graduation speaker. And by then my vision of my future was a bit clearer.

CHAPTER 3

A Mighty Phantom

Barb Luebke is pursuing a literary career. She has received her Masters in English from Brigham Young with an extensive study in Elizabethan Drama. Barb is currently employed by MGM where she is the head writer for Class B Movies. They always said experience is the best teacher.

Class of 1967 Prophecy
West De Pere High School

For my classmates and me, high school was very much about growing into our teenage selves, and at graduation beginning lives that would be "better" than our parents'. It was social as much as academic as we wished ourselves from adolescence to adulthood, guided by our class motto: "Don't be afraid to fail, be ashamed not to try." As I wrote at graduation, "We evolved from wandering freshmen into Seniors with an aim and purpose in life." What we prophesied for one another, having spent four (and in many cases 12) years sharing classrooms, gymnasiums, playing fields, parties and more, was silly with a dash of reality. The fortunetellers did not mention journalism for me; what stood out to them was my "literary" work. Mining my cache of high school memorabilia reminded me that what I had developed over those four years was interest and practice in writing over many genres. The occupations I chose to explore one Career Day were social work, teacher, politics/

the law. By graduation, my love of reading and writing had me thinking about being an English teacher and school newspaper advisor.

I see in my high school experiences how those habits I began developing in elementary school evolved, and how others were born. Hindsight allows me to chart my continuing growth and development -- personal and professional. Re-examining those four years reminded me how I inhabited my environment and the times, and how I was fortunate to outgrow/escape that small world. At the same time, I was buoyed whenever I found something that allowed me to think, *Ah, here is the first time I.* . . . Understanding my eventual career in journalism requires more than a cursory look at me from 1963 to 1967.

The summer after eighth grade was one of family, 4-H, babysitting and carefree fun (especially during a cottage rental "up north"). It included an event that years later was disputed family lore, but I found the evidence in my diary. My mother, brother, sister and I had arrived in Ohio on June 17, after a 13-hour train ride. "Was it ever hot," I wrote. (Fascinating coincidence: The diary stated it was Bunker Hill Day in Boston. Meant nothing to me, of that I am certain. Decades later I was working in Massachusetts, where it is a state holiday that gave me a day off.) We were excited to be with Grandma and Grandpa Conger. The visit allowed us to spend time with our favorite cousins, who figure into the story documented in my June 26 entry: "Today they took us swimming at Mason. We went at 10 a.m. Aunt Jane [and Mom] went to Dayton and was going to come back and pick us up about 1 p.m. We didn't get picked up 'til 5 p.m. Did I ever get sunburn and does it hurt." Kris and I also remember that we wore only our swimming suits and had just our towels and a dime each. The adults never admitted to having forgotten about us.

We spent a month in Ohio. Although I still had my eighth-grade boyfriend, Dwayne, the "relationship" was waning. My goody-two-shoes self had had second thoughts about attending his graduation party after I learned several kids were going who "have a dirty reputation." I fretted, "How can I say I don't want to go?" I couldn't, but my diary shows how "straight" I was: "I had fun but to those other kids it was a kissing party. It made me sick." I noted that the boyfriend and I "danced but mostly sat around and talked. He had both arms around me but if he would have tried to kiss me he'd be black and blue." It seems all those sermons and Sunday School lessons, cemented by my May 26 confirmation ("I am so happy."), had taken hold.

Also taking hold were life skills being developed by participation in 4-H. Having recently expanded beyond the farm with its focus on the personal growth of club members, 4-H was a highlight of my teenage years. To this day, my sister and I have fond memories of our leader, our projects and the many activities that membership afforded us. There is no doubt that I owe some of my sense of civic responsibility and social awareness to 4-H. Indeed, I would so impress my freshman civics teacher that he wrote on my report card (addressed to my father!): "What a girl! She is tremendous. When you kick her out she can move in with us. It is a pleasure for me to have her in class." I also credit 4-H with lessons about public speaking that have served me well for decades. *Tell them what you are going to say. Say it. Tell them what you said.* Further, 4-H taught me the useful journalistic skill of thriving under deadline. This was the summer that I frantically sewed to complete my entry for the 4-H Dress Revue, held just nine days after our return from Ohio. I remember well that shorts, blouse and jacket set, which despite my low expectations earned me a blue ribbon. I had my photograph taken for the Green Bay newspaper, too, and was disappointed to learn that "If I would have been 14 by Jan. 1st, I would have been able to try for STATE FAIR."

By the time high school started in late August, I was ready. I had exasperated my father by spending countless hours helping my beloved 4-H leader, who now lived around the corner, prepare for her wedding. (My youthful desire for fairness and sense of outrage are well represented in diary entries offended by how she was being treated for converting from Catholicism to marry a Lutheran.) My mother exasperated me: "Mother insisted I wear a dress all day so I didn't do much." The boyfriend had been reduced to postscript status in my diary. "He hasn't called. I don't know why and I really don't care." Truth be told, were it not for the diary entries I would remember only two things about that boy: Kris and Tim teasing, "Dwayne the bathtub, I'm dwowning" and a long telephone conversation during which I agreed with every opinion he expressed, regardless of what *I* thought, only to hang up and quietly chastise myself for surrendering my identity.

On August 28, I wrote that "I got my first real taste of high school. I went until 3 p.m. from 9:00 a.m." I noted that I had physical education (we called it Phy Ed) at 8 a.m., so I probably wasn't happy about that. My entry the next day was two sentences: "Went to school all day. My algebra class is kinda boring." After the third day, all I wrote was, "I like high school." That conclusion held up for four years. My report cards show that I never was "tardy" and had just six absences, the first not coming until the second quarter of my junior year.

In preparing this chapter, I eventually arrived at a number of observations that I connect -- directly and indirectly -- to my life in journalism. Taken together, I think they also represent how I fit into high school and how high school fit me. Supporting "evidence" was plentiful because school news was published regularly in the local papers, and I taped every clipping mentioning me into a scrapbook.

I was a leader -- in my class and in the school -- although my record of losing elections wasn't broken for about 30 years. (I fared better at vote-getting outside of the academic setting, be it 4-H, a sports team, a church group, etc.) On the day we voted for freshman class president I wrote, "I doubt if I'll win." The next day I noted that "I didn't win president but I really don't care." That wasn't quite true, I suspect, because my next sentence was, "I still might get it though because the guy elected is accused of getting into trouble at school." As a freshman, I also was "chairman" of the Texas delegation for our mock Republican convention. In another mock campaign, I was the Democratic candidate for governor. I served a year as president of the Future Teachers Club.

I had a streak of rebelliousness. After the school band played at the city's dedication of a new post office, during which "we had to sit right in the sun. Hot!" I wrote that "next time I'll have to be dragged" to do it. Further, I chafed at what I perceived to be unfairness: "I babysat from 8:15 to 2:00! Only made $1.50. Chris babysat less time and made $2.00 What a racket!" Another time I wrote, "Well, I knew it would happen. 2 boys got student council representative."

I had high expectations for myself (and others), regularly recording test results, grades, bowling scores, homeruns hit and basketball points scored. I could be my own harshest critic, but I also could pat myself on the back. A diary entry in mid-October stated, "Boy did we have a Latin test today. I know I didn't get an 'A' but I hope a 'B.'" That same day "we got back our Civics tests and I got the only perfect paper in our class." I missed the mark in predicting my Latin grade; a week later I learned I got a "D," "the first I've ever gotten." I probably vowed to not let that happen again. It didn't deter me from being eager to receive my first high school report card.

I planned ahead, whether it was finishing my Christmas shopping a month early or carefully plotting how to persuade my parents to let me do something. On summer days when I was bored, I would think about the next year's newspaper and how to make it better.

I was reflective. My December 31, 1963, diary entry provides early evidence of this. I wrote: "1963 was good to me. I think I grew up some and I know I've learned alot [sic]. I've made new friends now that I'm in high school. 1963 was good to our nation too although it took from us many great people. Some unneedingly [sic]. I only hope and pray '64 will bring the world closer to peace."

My girlfriends played a more significant role in those years than did boyfriends. I finally cut loose my eighth grade "love," and on October 3 wrote: "You'll never guess what I did today. Yup, I finally tore up all the notes D wrote me when I liked him." I would not have a steady boyfriend again until my senior year, but I remained close to girls from elementary school, made new friends among the freshman class, and even added a couple of sophomore girls to my inner circle. Feminism wouldn't be in my vocabulary for some time -- and all my writing used male pronouns -- but I was beginning to recognize the limits placed on girls. [An aside: The lack of a junior-year boyfriend did not keep me from attending our prom, but the invitation came in a most untraditional manner. One day in class my chemistry teacher asked who did not have a prom date. Several hands besides mine might have been raised; all I remember is him pointing to John Heugal and instructing, "Why don't you ask Barb." And he did! I am sure the next year I was relieved by a conventional invitation from my boyfriend to the Senior Prom.]

I wasn't afraid to criticize -- often only to the diary pages I kept locked away -- and I could be an edgy commentator. I took issue with a radio commercial that referred to white as a flavor of milk. I wrote to the offending station, WDUZ, and the station manager wrote back to tell me that I was "absolutely correct in your criticism of the Goal commercial and the reference to 'white' as a flavor has been dropped." Another time I was a guest at a Lions Club meeting. "What a riot," I wrote in my diary. "Never saw such silly men in all my life." (I would have a similar response when, as a young reporter, I attended another Lions Club gathering.)

I was goal- and detail-oriented. Not only did I tell my diary about every babysitting job, how long it lasted and how much I earned, but I always seemed to have something planned for the money. For example, when saving to buy my first golf club I wrote about other things I *wasn't* spending money on. Most entries contained specifics, such as the time I got up or went to bed, the movie I saw or TV show I watched, my bowling scores, the color of a sweater or slacks I bought, a list of gifts received. This habit of being specific was vital to the reporter I would become. Two entries jumped out at me. The first recorded our 4-H leader's wedding; a decade later I would write many such stories in my role as society editor of a small daily newspaper. The entry spilled over from its dated page to both sides of three additional tiny notebook pages:

Today was the day of J's wedding. I washed my hair this morning. I didn't get up till 8:30 and all I thought about was J and how she was being treated.

Aunt Florence went to the wedding with us. We got there about 1:45.

The bridesmaids were dressed in simple gowns of a pink-red with shoes to match.

J had a real pretty white floor length gown. R and his attendants had white jackets and black pants.

I felt so sorry for J because she had to walk down the aisle alone. The whole ceremony took about 25 minutes.

It went real smooth except J had a hard time getting her gloves off and she and R got their right hands mixed up. It was a double ring ceremony. None of J's close relatives were there. . . .

We got to the reception about 5 but there was no one there yet.

She had the most beautiful cake. It had a book which said "J and R, Sept. 14, 1963."

Then J and R and their attendants got there. They brought J's picture and was it ever good.

One of J's sisters was at the supper. . . . We didn't get to talk to J much but she said she liked my dress.

The supper was delicious. We stayed for about 45 min. of the dance but Elaine said the wedding dance wouldn't be until 9:30 so we left. . . .

I couldn't sit at home and know my daughter was getting married and not be there. J never did one thing to hurt her family and I don't see how they could hurt her so.

I wish them all the luck and happiness in the world.

The second entry (three days' worth) is an accounting of President Kennedy's assassination. I kept each day to a page, but my script is tiny and neat, maximizing the amount of information I recorded. Like the wedding entry, these were a mixture of facts and personal feelings:

November 22: This is hard to put into words but our president of the U.S., John F. Kennedy, was assassinated in Dallas, while he was on tour. I heard about it in Latin, about 1:10 p.m. when the speakers in school came on. He was shot about 12:25 our time and died about 35 minutes later. They have caught one man and have charged him with murder. I can't put into words how I feel but it isn't a pleasant feeling. I still can't believe it, it just doesn't register; it's more like a nightmare. We are going to have a 30 day mourning period. My sympathy and prayers are all for the Kennedys. Much stuff has been closed down and postponed.

November 24: We went to church today and will attend a special service in honor of the late John F. Kennedy. But something else happened today only 48 hrs. and 7 min. after the presidents [sic] death. His accussed [sic] assassin was shot and died in the same hospital, only about 10 ft. from the room Mr. Kennedy died in. Today his body, in a closed, flag covered casket has been in the capital building and people will pay their respects to him till 10 a.m. tom. Mrs. Kennedy made one last, unnoticed visit yet tonight. I can understand why. It is becoming easier to believe, and there is a feeling like part of me has died. I only pray that God will give strength to Mrs. Kennedy and her family and the family of the late president and to Mr. Johnson, our new president. One sad time for me was today when just before the casket was brought to the capitol, Hail to the Chief and The Navy Hymn was played.

November 25: We attended a special service for the late president Kennedy. All morning, till we went to church we watched the procession from the White House to the Capitol, where the body was put on the horse drawn caisson. Then it went back to the White House, and from there everyone walked to the church. After the mass the caison [sic] led procession went to Arlington National Cemetery where the president was buried. An eternal light was lit by Mrs. Kennedy, Robert and Ted, his brothers. This light was requested by Mrs. Kennedy. I don't see how she possibly held her emotions as good as she did the whole time since Fri. I feel sorry for her and imagine during her private period of mourning she will be able to shed some of her spent up tears. There were oh so many dignitaries from all over the world. Mrs. Kennedy was also given the flag which had draped the casket. God Bless Them All.

We returned to school on the 26th, "but things were still kind of solemn," I noted, adding: "I guess Mrs. Kennedy did cry but not till she had left the grave. I bet she goes there often. I know I would." Ironically, I grew into an adult who is definitely not a cemetery person, but I took advantage of an opportunity to visit JFK's gravesite in December 2017.

My interests were wide-ranging. Reading continued to feed my curiosity. I absolutely loved the De Pere Public Library and frequently studied there. One of my happiest days had been when I finally was allowed to select "grown-up" books from the shelves behind the librarian's counter. I could be a critical reader, too. New-freshman-me started one diary entry with "Boy is the Odyssey ever gruesome and morbid." I was introduced to SQ3R in freshman English, and to this day I easily remember "Survey. Question. Read. Recite. Review" and greatly appreciate all that reading-comprehension method taught me. Outside the classroom, my father's interests spilled over into my life. He not only taught me to fish and bait my own hook, but how to catch nightcrawlers in the yard to use for bait and how to scale and gut fish like a pro. He taught me to paint; I ignored his advice to do it in the shade, thus enduring more than one serious sunburn. As an adult, I came to realize how important it was that he never said, "No, girls don't do that." If he did not directly teach me a skill, he instilled in me the confidence to try just about anything. He also insisted that I take high school bookkeeping because "you never know when you might use it." Turned out I was pretty good with numbers. Commenting on my "A" grade, my teacher wrote, "The #1 in the class. (I'm wondering if some of the aunts' and uncles' aptitude in accounting has inspired her!!!!) Father too????"

Sports were important to me. I was a tomboy in elementary school, and my love of sports and competition dates to then. I honed my skills in the empty lot across from our house, where neighborhood games matched the season. Kris and I played in a parks department softball league as soon as we were old enough. High school offered an opportunity for organized sports, though for girls that was limited to the Girls Athletics Association intramural teams. Basketball rules annoyingly still differed from the boys. My diaries lists the points I scored each game, and in my mind's eye I see myself making three baskets from the corner to seal a win. My senior-year team won the GAA championship. Photos from volleyball show my good form -- and the silly one-piece gym uniforms of the day. My sophomore team won the class championship. Badminton was fun and square-dancing was familiar territory to those of us in 4-H. I had begun bowling with my 4-H club, and it was the focus of many, many dates. Bowling scores are peppered throughout my diaries and numerous newspaper clippings document competitions. In high school I was captain of the freshman girls team. As a senior, the "mixed" team that included me, my best friend and my boyfriend won it all.

More than any of the above, however, I fancied myself a writer -- in school and out. Looking back on the work I saved, I am able to enjoy it as well as evaluate it with a critical eye. Unfortunately, not everything is dated. But I am amazed that five decades later I recall details about writing many of those pieces -- and have *no* memory of others.

I have only a few examples of my written classwork. One, titled "It Won't Happen In My House," has a few comments in red -- including "Tense consistency needed" at the top of the page -- but no grade. My best guess is it was an assignment for sophomore English, requiring us to respond to an article written by a Mr. Wylie. Over two handwritten notebook pages, I offer my opinions about "being overrun by armies of frozen, dried, and instant foods" that were turning us into "an increasingly dull society." How judgmental I was! TV dinners, I wrote, "have won their battle. We now can lounge around all day with our eyes glued to the 'idiot box.'" My concluding paragraph included a bit of wordplay: "We cannot surrender -- but fight on like Custer(d). It wasn't a mix, by the way." And although my last sentence reflected the times, today its sexism makes me shudder: "So ladies form ranks -- real potatoes, cows milk, your own homemade bread and cakes, a homemade four course meal and left face."

[An aside: I think it was my sophomore English teacher who embarrassed me in class with a snotty comment after I assumed she had misspelled COLLEGE on the blackboard. She had printed COLLAGE, a word I did not know. Her lesson about not assuming stuck -- but so did the hurt inflicted by her criticism.]

The only mark on a second essay, written in January 1966 for English 3, is the "A" on the cover page. Like the assignment above, it responds to another's writing, but my presentation and prose are more formal. (I had taken a typing class during summer school between my sophomore and junior years, and regularly put it to use.) The article I wrote about was "Interracial Marriage and the Law" by William D. Zabel, published in the October 1965 Atlantic Monthly. I long remembered writing about miscegenation, and when I saw the movie "Loving" in 2017 I immediately thought of this paper. A couple of things jumped out at me when I reread it. For one thing, the topic seems "foreign" for a class in a school without a single Black person. I don't know, however, if I chose it or if it was assigned to the class or to me. Regardless, it is clear that the SQ3R lessons guided the structure of my essay, and techniques important in journalistic writing are evident. I made good use of quotations, paraphrasing and attribution. I paid attention not only to transitions between paragraphs but also between sentences. Only at the end does my opinion creep in, and even that could be called evaluation: "Mr. Zabel is discussing a very delicate subject and his report is obviously biased. His views are backed with sound facts and statistics, which fully support his beliefs. This article definately [sic] gives one a reason for more thought on the subject of interracial marriages."

The reason I kept a third written assignment is obvious; neatly written in red across the top is "You have a talent!" The untitled, typed page was written in the fall of my senior year. I was fortunate to be selected to enroll in English 101-Composition at nearby St. Norbert College, for which I would earn credit for senior English and three college credits. I loved that class; the tough-as-nails professor both intimidated and inspired me. She sat on the desk at the front of the classroom, legs crossed, chain-smoking as she guided us through the demanding works in "Tragedy/Plays, Theory and Criticism," then taught us how to write formal analysis. One such paper of mine was titled "Mrs. Alving and Othello: A Comparison of Two Classical Tragic Heroes." What I notice now is how meticulously she commented on the essay, including its bibliography. *Ahhh, I thought, she was my first role model for taking time when grading students' work.* To this day, I consult the other book she required us to buy, "The Complete Stylist." If I was disappointed by the "B" I earned, I left that course prepared for the rigors of college thinking and writing. (In the spring, I continued at St. Norbert with a history class, Western Civilization to 1500. All I remember is that the professor was boring and uninspiring. He wouldn't be the last.) What surprised me when I found that "Talent" paper (for which I earned an "A") was its topic: newspaper headlines, "the words with which newspapers speak." Besides the topic, I was struck by the sophistication of my writing, whose sentences mirrored the brevity required of headlines. Little could I have imagined that in a few years I would be writing headlines or that one day I would publish an article about stand-out headlines.

Outside the classroom, I found an outlet for my creative writing in the first *A Phantom Odyssey*. With its bright orange cover and pretentious illustration featuring Shakespeare, this was the school's "attempt at compiling an anthology of the literary efforts" of its students. The advisor, who also was the newspaper advisor, further explained in the Preface that "the papers have been selected by a special committee" from those submitted by the English teachers. Ads from 20 local merchants made possible the high-quality paper and professional typesetting. It was my sophomore year, and I had been asked by that advisor to work on the publication. I also was a contributor, with this short piece.

Rays shine from the eyes of the specialist as he shows a young mother how to care for her toddler so he may grow strong and maybe someday lead his people.

Versatility is the first name of this light. A petite young thing may drive a tractor, plow with a water buffalo, or shear sheep. A strapping athlete may bake a cake, bathe a baby, or clean a native hut.

Love is the middle name of this light. Again, this same athlete may rock a baby, ill with malaria, or tenderly change a diaper. The girl may gently mend a wound or cut a fellow's hair.

Caring is the last name of this light. For they care — these people who are giving up part of their lives that the life of someone else may be better. Yes, they care or they wouldn't be in the farthest corners of God's earth.

American Peace Corps is the full name of this light.

Barb Luebke '67

I was not on the staff of the Odyssey as a junior; by then I was busy with the school newspaper. Its second cover was a more subdued beige. Surprising to me today is that its illustration included lines from "The Creation" by James Weldon Johnson, the Black writer and civil rights activist. Once again, I had a piece selected for publication. Titled "Moment of Truth," it took readers to a surprise conclusion. By its third year, the "Odyssey" staff had shrunk to five and had a new advisor. The Preface ended with the hope that the volume would "direct your thoughts toward the future, and will give people a deeper understanding of youth today." Four of the first five entries were mine: three poems and a dark three-paragraph musing that ended, "With the heart of one man went a village, and with it the world."

Not all of my writing was school-related. Although there is much about my high school years that I don't remember, I retain a clear picture of writing a "review" of Truman Capote's "In Cold Blood" (probably in 1966, the year the book was published). I was babysitting. My charge was asleep, and I stretched out on the living room floor with a notebook and pen. Although I don't know what compelled me to review the book, I am certain it was not an assignment. It is clear I was familiar with the style of book reviews. I began: "Truman Capote has, I hope, opened up a whole new literary field, namely one of the non-fiction novel. His newest novel, In Cold Blood, is surely an excellant [sic] example of what can be done with non-fiction. It is a novel in which dryness, which is very often present in non-fiction material, is non-existent; yet not one bit of factual reporting has been overlooked." (I forgive my young self for the incorrect use of *novel*.) Two detailed paragraphs summarize the book, followed by my conclusion: "Let's hope that more authors follow Capote for the door which he has opened promises to lead to many exciting places, if only it is not slammed shut." I signed the review BFL. [An aside: Mimicking a teacher I admired, I was using my initials a lot. Over the years, my spoken name has been Barbara, Barbie, Barb, Little Barbie and Biffle, and my bylines have been Barb Luebke, Barbara Luebke, Barbara F. Luebke, Dr. Barbara F. Luebke. A couple of times I even used a pen name, Bobbie or Bobbi.]

In addition to the Capote review, I remembered starting a "novel" but I was surprised to find handwritten chapters for two in a folder. That folder also contained a very short story titled "A Decision," an untitled short piece, barely readable because of the pencil used, and two other untitled items. All had long faded from memory. What I observed when studying them was that I already understood the importance of revision. I routinely edited for word choice, grammar and punctuation -- and not often enough for spelling. I wrote strong opening sentences. I used similes. I alternated sentence lengths. I understood complex and compound sentences and knew how to punctuate them. I was fond of social commentary. I was not adept at dialogue.

Based on my handwriting, I believe the unfinished "Sweet Sixteen" was the earlier of my two novels. I have 15 notebook pages, written on both sides, and three chapters are titled. I have two versions of it; the first has numerous changes, including the name of one character. At the heart of the story is a girl about to turn 16 and her life the first few months after her sister goes off to college. I was a young girl writing about her real life jumbled up with a life she fantasized. Had I heard or read the advice to "write about what you know"? I used the first names of my 4-H leader and her twin for my main characters. When I named records, I used those of my favorite singers. I described meals of foods that my family rarely could afford. The characters drank pop. The father skipped Christmas shopping to watch the Friday night fights on TV. On that shopping trip, the main character spent much more money than I remember having as a teen. But her first stop was a book shop (so like me), and in another shop she bought handkerchiefs for her teachers and grandparents (so 1960s). She went to the "dime store." Sometimes the mother and father behave like my parents, and sometimes their actions are my wishful thinking. Nonetheless, "Sweet Sixteen" suggests a teenage writer comfortable with language, writing and storytelling. It shows me a writer versed in precise word choice, e.g., "startled," "scurried away," "mournful girl." A writer who built in two plot twists. One who in a margin scribbled "too much mother." But the young me, late in the manuscript, also inexplicably began referring to pop as soda. And I had the main character mailing invitations the day before the party. Finally, I cringe to read my representation of the traditional sex roles of the era. How it is the father who comes home and "settles things down" or says to his wife, "Speak woman, speak."

I describe my second piece of novel, "The Pedagogue," as social commentary woven into a story, but its goal remains fuzzy because of where I stopped writing. The theme is reaction by a variety of characters to a teacher holding an "experimental" literature class in his apartment. The title appears to have been added, given how it looks on the first page. Considerable revising on the first few pages suggests I rethought the beginning even as I moved forward with the story. Each chapter is devoted to one character. (Not surprising to me-the-editor, the first thing I checked was if I had written the chapters in the order the characters are listed in the beginning. I had.) As with "Sweet Sixteen," I was writing about a familiar topic. I was a student -- probably a senior -- becoming aware of social changes under way. I was crazy about an English teacher with unconventional methods. High school was beginning to feel constrictive.

I wrestled with ideas by writing that story. I "tried on" a bit of rebellion, even as I generally hewed to the straight and narrow.

Lastly, there are three pieces with one thing in common: they are darkly pessimistic, exhibiting the sort of angst I now know is often associated with adolescence. "Duck and cover," "better dead than Red" and fallout shelters were in my immediate past, after all. But if the tone in these writings now makes me wince, I also see more evidence of the editorial eye that eventually would define me as a journalist. For example, in "A Decision" my opening originally read: "The night was beautiful. It was warm but not too warm." I turned that into a single sentence: "It was a beautiful summer night, warm but not too warm." Several sentences later, I turned "all the men on earth" into "mankind." Because the story is written in ink and the changes are in pencil, I am comfortable concluding that I was self-editing. I also see that in another typed piece in which I had made changes so tenses were consistent.

High School Journalist

I didn't wait long to join the newspaper, the Le Fantome (the school's mascot was an orange phantom). The staff list for the Autumn 1963 issue includes B. Luebke. My first "story" -- bylined Barb Luebke -- was two paragraphs: a long one listing students nominated for class officers (including me for president), then naming those elected so far. A one-sentence paragraph followed and stated that freshmen sold "homecoming shakers." I took note of the story's publication in a p.s. to my October 8 diary entry. I only wish I had recorded *why* I joined the paper; I assume it was for the opportunity to write.

The paper, folded to 7 inches by 10.5 inches and center-stapled, looked more like a magazine. Stories were typed by a gaggle of girls and arranged on unnumbered pages by the editor, who used a light table in the school's darkroom and rubber cement to prepare the paper for the printer. Clip art, original cartoons and sketches, and a few small photographs were scattered throughout. The paper had no ads, but the back page listed 12 local businesses and their addresses, whose contributions "made the publication of this paper possible." Articles had simple titles, usually a word or two. A sample from that October issue:

Homecoming Festivities, Cheerleaders, Yearbooks, New Teachers, Teen Board, Future Medics, Assembly. Book of the Month summarized "Deliver Us From Evil" by Dr. Thomas Dooley who, a classmate wrote, told of his "fantastic experiences" as a Navy doctor "among the terrorized victims of the Communists." STUDENT FORUM allowed several kids to respond to the question, "Has the increase in enrollment affected the discipline in our school?" (Enrollment was 549.) Four stories over two pages reported on the football games played to date. One full page had a calendar of events for the month along with a description of important events in history. Another full page was devoted to HUMOR, best described as sophomoric and borrowed from elsewhere. Items frequently were altered to use names of students or teachers.

Mr. Barron [history teacher]: Who defeated the Romans?

Jim Hudson: I'm sorry I don't follow the minor leagues.

Little about my first year on the staff is noteworthy. My second story, "Civics Class" by Barbara Luebke, was a mere 81 words about class discussions. The Christmas Edition was my first with two stories: the unbylined two short paragraphs about SQ3R for Class News and, a few pages later, my short article titled "Freshman Representatives." Our Leap Year Edition, dated February 19, 1964, stands out for its cover. The illustration's only connection to the date seems to be the leaping fish, but more disturbing is another illustration that now -- I hope -- would be vetoed for its racial/cultural insensitivity. The paper reported on itself in that issue, naming section editors and noting that for the first-time student reporters would pay dues of $1 a year! I didn't have any articles, but I was named in two stories: as one of two freshmen earning straight "A's" and as captain of the freshman girls' bowling team, which won the class championship. The Easter Edition of March 25 was more of the same; my stories were unbylined news about the freshman class meeting and a bylined "short" about a student who ripped his pants at a basketball game. It is notable because I was able to "see" a story in the incident and write about it with a light touch.

I don't remember taking a break from the paper, so I don't know if my absence from the staff list for the first issue of my sophomore year was an oversight or I was late to rejoin. I am among the feature writers listed in the November paper, but I didn't have a bylined story until the April 20, 1965, Easter Edition. My concise diary entries for 1965 (it was a five-year diary that provided just four lines per year) suggest I was spending a lot of time producing the Le Fantome, not writing for it. For example, on Saturday, February 6, I was at school from 9 a.m. to 3 p.m., then on the 9th stayed until 7 to finish it. The next day the advisor told me I would be in charge of layout in my junior year and in my senior year would be the editor. But by early April, I seem to already have been handling some of the editor's responsibilities. I worked after school on the 12th and again on the 13th. "I even had to right [sic] the editorial -- wish the editor would get busy." I was back at it for the next three days, and when that issue came out, I wrote: "[It] looked real nice. I'm editor for the next addition [sic]."

That April paper included my bylined report on a student assembly; I noted that the "program was unique in that the [band] director . . . is an alumnus of West De Pere." At least a couple of stories each issue now had real headlines (perhaps in my production work I had begun this practice). Another of my stories (I penciled in my byline on my copy) had the headline: "Academy Awards" Night Climaxes Forensics Year. My first editorial was about responsibility and reading it now I suspect it was a passive-aggressive jab at the "lazy" editor. It referenced a book ("A Message to Garcia"), which I frequently did (do) in my writing.

As it turned out, my editorship started with my junior year and continued until my graduation. I lived and breathed the Le Fantome. My editorship earned me hall-roaming privileges that few students enjoyed. I spent all my free time and lots of weekends working in the darkroom cubbyhole.

Being editor required me to step in to do whatever needed doing in order to publish. When we lacked a photographer, for example, I took pictures. A diary entry records the time I was on the sideline for a football game and "almost got trampled" at the end of a play, "but I do think I got some good action pics." (The same thing would happen to me as a young reporter.) And I learned early on to roll with the punches when something went wrong. My November 1, 1965, diary entry captured one such episode: "Well, the paper is at the printers— what a great feeling. Time to start working on the Christmas edition.— Oh no— [the advisor] called about 10:00— the margins are ½ inch off. The whole paper must be reset and some typed over. That's Life."

More than 50 years later, after reading through "my" issues, I made a list of immediate thoughts:

My growth
My leadership
Left my mark
Those things that now make me cringe
How different the times were for content
Thinking on my years of judging high school newspaper contests
    decades later
Where were our issue stories?

Examining these is valuable in charting the evolution of my thinking and nascent journalistic sensibilities.

The conservatism of my first editorial certainly leaped out at me, as did its youthful righteous attitude. I criticized "those bearded 'don't know enough to come out of the rain' people who claim to be working for something good, but who instead are causing more trouble than they are worth." I was talking about college students protesting the war in Vietnam, and although I acknowledged their First Amendment right to do so, I judged that "it's being abused." Further, "If such actions as these continue, you can be assured that this freedom will soon disappear, closely followed by others." File this under cringeworthy. [An aside: More than once while writing this book I have thought about how the 1950s didn't prepare me for the '60s or '70s.]

I did not shy away from tackling big topics, nor did I lack a strong editorial voice. I wrote that Christmas "should not be the only time we give. People should be willing to give -- not just gifts -- but of themselves, 365 days of the year." I stated that students had many opportunities, but "when there is anything to be done, it's the same people who must do it." Finally, I argued that being "a good citizen and accepting the responsibilities of citizenship are only two of many ways to give." Another time I wondered if too much emphasis was being placed on grades because colleges were being more selective even as more people aspired to college. I concluded that "good grades are important, but even more important is that the student gets as much out of each course as possible."

I often found my inspiration in the words of others. In the Easter Edition, it was Thomas Aquinas. I seem to have edited text prepared for a forensics competition into a shorter editorial. "With every right there is a corresponding duty," I began. After describing four scenarios in which teens made bad decisions, I concluded: "Kids must realize that duties are just as important, if not more so, than rights; for if one does not meet his obligations, he can't expect to retain his rights." File this under self-righteous. And file that issue's cover under "naïve editor." In search of original art, I asked my boyfriend if he might provide something. He did -- a simple line drawing of a rabbit's profile, which we colored lavender. I did not know he had "borrowed" the Playboy bunny for inspiration! Then again, the paper's advisor never pointed that out, either.

At least the cover illustration on the last paper of the year was just a sophomoric drawing for the seniors who had made it to graduation. My editorial bemoaned the fact that "so many people decide their futures often having lived for only seventeen or eighteen years. . . ." The future, as I saw it, was that many of the new graduates "will be married by the time school begins next fall. Many will have found jobs in the area and there they will spend the rest of their lives." I imagine I already was thinking ahead to my own graduation, already was intent on fulfilling different dreams. "There is so much to see and do in this world that it seems odd for people to choose to be tied down so soon in life, without first experiencing life to the fullest degree possible."

I don't know what my classmates thought about the year's pontificating, but the faculty approved of my efforts inside and outside the classroom. I was named Student of the Month for April (the vote was unanimous, according to my diary). The notice in the paper listed my activities and included the fact that I had been elected to membership in Quill and Scroll, an honor society for journalists.

The cover of the Le Fantome for October 14, 1966 -- my first paper as a senior -- looked like any of the papers published over the seven previous school years. But I had made several changes inside. For the first time, pages were numbered. The typing was neater. The staff list was moved off page 2, replaced by an index. A page of "Tid-Bits" offered information not unlike the short stories I had written as a freshman.

(For the record, there were 563 students enrolled, including 135 in my class.) "Meet Your Teachers" required two pages to introduce seven new faculty members. Four pages were devoted to sports; football statistics were used for the first time. And there was a "FLASH . . . West De Pere Phantoms skin Bonduel Bears 41-0" about the game played just before publication. The staff list was on page 14; my cousin Ed was the new business manager. The guy could sell *anything*, and the paper now had 35 advertisers named on the back page.

My approach to editorializing had not changed over the summer; if anything, I wrote with more fervor and conviction. In this issue I begged for more student involvement. "Just what does it take to make you kids become active participants in the activities of WDPHS?" Perhaps I was thinking of myself when I wrote the last paragraph: "We are all freshmen at one time, and it takes guts to join an organization of all upperclassmen, but join! Believe it or not, you are needed and wanted. Your present participation will help shape the future of West De Pere High School."

I continued to put my own stamp on the paper with the Thanksgiving issue. I editorialized with a poem by Helen Hunt Jackson. In it she observes that even in the darkest of times there is cause for Thanksgiving, if only because "things are no worse." I wonder where I dredged up that poem, why I used it, and what my classmates thought about reading it in their high school paper. [An aside: When I Googled her name, I was amazed to learn of her book "A Century of Dishonor" (1881), an exposé that led to the founding of the Indian Rights Association. *We were soul sisters*, I thought. More about that later.] Other changes: More photos, including a page devoted to pictures of students at work and at play. A small illustration that we hand-colored before the paper was distributed. A page of classified ads and our first display ad. "Fantom Flashbacks" from 1962 and 1963. Although I had not written an editorial, I published two stories under the byline Bobbie (perhaps I thought it ill-advised for the editor to include her own bylined work). One, titled "Oops," was a tongue-in-cheek tale from girls bowling about low scores, falls, dropped balls and forgotten street shoes. The other was my first "Sound Off" column, this one an attempt to find humor in four-day school "vacations" that proved anything but leisurely.

With no diary entries for fall 1966, I was unable to find anything describing why the format of the Le Fantome changed dramatically between November and December. In my first month as editor in 1965, I had written a diary entry bemoaning the paper's lack of money and stating that it might be necessary to change to a "cheaper" format. "I hate to do that," I had added. For whatever reasons, we had not. A year later, my very brief editorial in that December 20 paper did state that "the idea behind this [format change] is the hope that the student body's interest in and response to the Le Fantome will be greater." I referenced the need to "reach more than twenty per cent of the student body." It must have surprised students and teachers alike to see a newspaper that looked like a newspaper. There was a stylized flag, complete with a drawing of our Phantom in one ear. There were columns and column rules. Typewritten stories were replaced by professionally set type. To distinguish it, a la "real papers," the editorial was set two columns wide, in italics. Many more stories had headlines, not just labels. The few "fillers" were like those seen in newspapers of the day -- item for sale, a quotation and the like. Gone were the random hand-drawn illustrations scattered throughout. My "Sound Off" column tried for humor with its asides about the "languages" I heard in the hallways. A sample paragraph: "Fourth hour I think it's fun to listen to the band members talk about 6/8 time, fortissimos, and pianissimos (two pianos?). Along with this, the auto mechanics classes bury one in talk of combustion, carburetors, and cams (past tense of comes?)."

Subsequent issues of the paper that year tweaked the format, but the content remained familiar. My editorials continued to preach. In February, with first-semester tests and report cards now history, I urged students to remember that "the nine weeks ended only with promises of another one soon to come; so buckle down and get what needs to be finished, finished!" I appear to have been too busy -- editing the yearbook, rehearsing for the class play, filling out college applications, bowling on a successful "mixed" team -- to write my column. In March, that bowling team made news, complete with photo, for winning the championship. In my editorial, I once again opined on the value of being open to new experiences. "We can better choose how we want to live, what we want to be, what philosophy we want to live by, if we have experienced life to the fullest. We must possess an empathy for the entire world, not just West De Pere."

And then graduation was upon the Class of 1967. One hundred thirty students would receive their diplomas on June 8. The final issue of the Le Fantome under my leadership was published on June 2. During my two-year editorship, I had transformed the paper from amateurish to more polished. I also had transformed my own journalism. In the beginning, I had written simple stories about mundane school activities. Eventually I penned editorials that sought to be erudite and columns with a voice. One of my editorials even was used in the Teen Times section of the Green Bay Press Gazette, which headlined it "Education Right Tool." I had learned to write with confidence and righteousness -- and now and then indignation. Some of my classmates probably found my attitude "holier than thou," and they might have been right. How easy it was at 17 or 18 to be cocksure of one's position on *everything*. My final editorial, however, was one of gratitude to "everyone who in any way made this all possible." The "this" was our transformation to "a full fledged newspaper in newspaper style." After describing our production process, I wrote that "each edition got better because each time the staff worked more and more as a team." I ended by quoting Red Smith (the renowned sportswriter who I somehow failed to identify): "Writing a daily column is easy. All you have to do is sit at a typewriter until small drops of blood form on your forehead." My parting observation: "The same is true when putting out a school newspaper." I could not know it at the time, but I was not finished with school newspapers.

And I was not quite finished offering advice to my classmates. WDPHS did not name a valedictorian and salutatorian, but I was designated to be one of two student speakers at graduation. Because my grades were tops in the class, I got to choose opening or closing, and I opted for opening. As with my eighth-grade speech, I concentrated on looking ahead and offered my thoughts about our "Broadened Horizons." Talking about change as "an integral part in the life of modern man," I referenced something familiar to me -- the news. "Each day headlines and newscasts scream at us with reports of advances in technology and the world." I asked my fellow graduates to "consider this somewhat frightening statement: 1/2 of today's jobs will be obsolete in

10 years." I posited that "such constantly changing situations demand that we be equally flexible, able to adopt and adapt." Not surprisingly, I believed that our education had prepared us to fulfill our responsibility "to meet the world head-on. We must be able to adjust and to make correct decisions accordingly. We must rely on our intelligence and the amassed intelligence of others." That meant, I continued, that "we must be an individual in the world of the party-man; a non-conformist in a world of conformity." Recognizing that it might seem difficult, I reminded my audience that law and morality could guide us:

> Although we have immeasurable freedoms, there are certain laws by which we must abide but which can also serve as guideposts for us. These are laws established for the good of society -- a society of which we are a member. We also have basic moral concepts to direct us. These would include the laws of God and those of personal integrity. We will not be respected if we do not respect and have pride in ourselves and our actions.

Law and morality, I concluded, "are the foundation for the unchanging conscience of man." Finally, as I had been taught to do for my 4-H speeches, I circled back to my beginning to end this way: "We graduates may, then, not only meet the challenge of a world overwhelmed with constant change but realize the opportunities of this world -- a world of broadened horizons."

When I walked out of the school building that late-spring night, I left with more than a diploma, dreams and self-confidence, however. I also left with a secret, one that took decades for me to understand, share and eventually make peace with.

Snapshots

Glenn Luebke and Barbara Walker, Thanksgiving 1947, Ohio.

april 3, 1949

Earliest photo of me with Mom and Dad.

Storytime, March 1951.

When I got a bit older, I regularly could be found standing on an axel while Grandpa Conger drove.

Ken Loehlein Ed
Barb Luebk

Off to kindergarten with my cousin and a neighbor.

I got an early start on my lifelong habit of record-keeping.

Dad was usually behind the camera, but Mom recorded this birthday celebration in our tiny Lande Street kitchen.

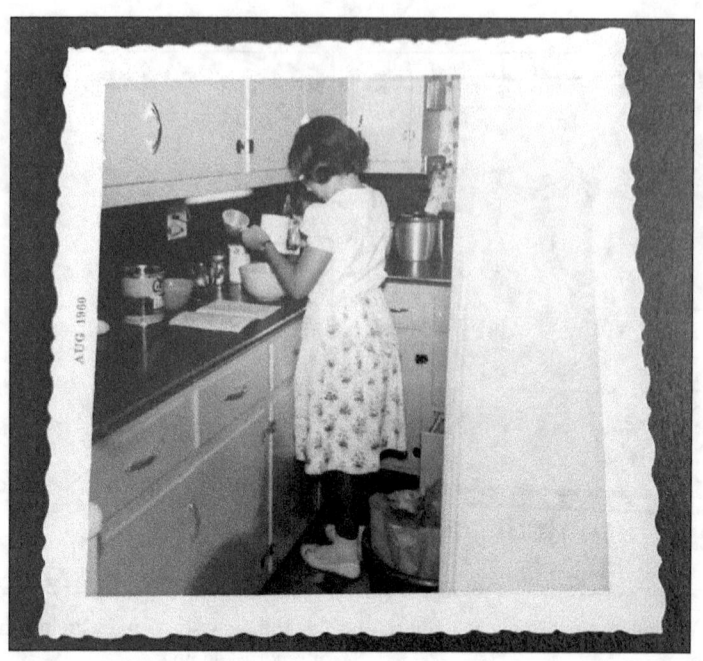

The 4-H recipe book instructed that muffins should have "tunnels." I was making a batch to enter in the county fair. August 1960.

We became a family of five with Timothy Glenn's adoption in 1959.

My eighth-grade graduation portrait.

R-i-p

by Barb Luebke

Anything can happen at a basketball game, and it did at the Algoma-Kimberly game. A fan from East De Pere found the bleachers full when he arrived, so he decided to sit on the temporary bleachers on the stage. Everything went all right until half-time when he decided to get up. Then..... you guessed it, he ripped the leg of his pants. This incident brought on much laughter from those of us on the stage, but we laughed harder and longer when he borrowed Mary Laurent's manicure scissors and made bermudas out of his one-time slacks.

My first byline.

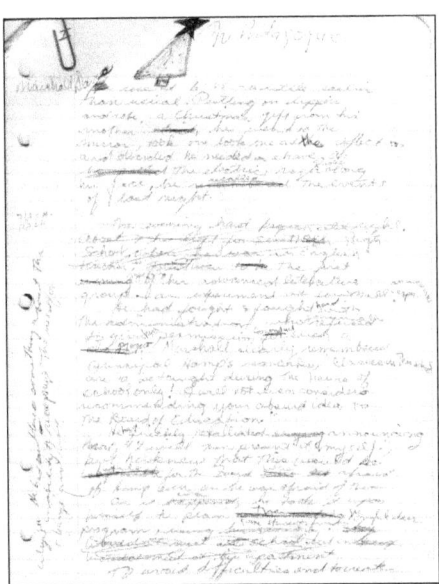

The first page of one of my teenage "novels."

I engineered format changes that made our high school newspaper look like a newspaper.

Attending football games with my high school girlfriends was a staple of our weekends. That's me at the far left.

June 1967, with Dad and Mom.

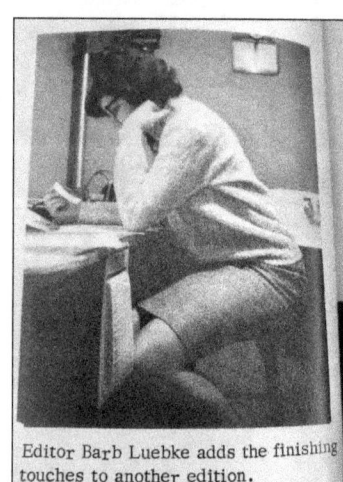

Editor Barb Luebke adds the finishing touches to another edition.

From the yearbook.

CHAPTER 4

Becoming a Blugold

The summer of '67 found me academically confident, eager to move on, and both curious and scared by the prospect of once again being an academic newbie. My last high school report card reinforced my belief that I was prepared for college work. In comments, my teachers had written that I was "well organized," "one of the most mature students I have ever had" and had "superior ability but . . . never relaxes her personal effort and is never satisfied until she really understands and can apply a principle."

On a typed (and doodled on) copy of my "Education as Tool" editorial the Press-Gazette had reprinted, I found an all-caps statement appended: "I think what I am trying to project here is the hope I have for myself; the way I want to live my life; the desire I have to know as much as I possibly can, to experience as much as I possible [sic] can, and then to give these experiences to people through literature." The larger world beckoned me daily, with news of race riots (including in Milwaukee, just 115 miles south of West De Pere), hippies, Haight-Ashbury and the war in Vietnam (at least six classmates enlisted after graduation). My favorite song was Scott McKenzie's "San Francisco" and I dropped plenty of coins into the jukebox at a dingy tavern where my boyfriend and I hung out (the drinking age was 18). Heading 200 miles west for college would start my journey through the larger world, I imagined.

[An aside: Mom and Dad allowed us carefree summers by not pressuring us to find jobs. After graduation, however, I was desperate to earn money to help with my college costs. I was elated when a cannery in Green Bay hired me and undaunted by the 3 p.m.-midnight shift because the money was good. Years later, an article in New Times magazine brought back such vivid memories of that experience that I wrote a letter to the editor with this brutal assessment: "I lasted one night. I was assigned to picking 'garbage' off a conveyor belt of green beans. Among my awful memories are the stench, the noise and the other women, whom I remember as all being fat. Worst of all was the utter boredom that overwhelmed me." I further observed that "I would have gone mad had I worked a second night. I wonder why there cannot be a more humane way."]

Only a handful of my classmates went directly from high school to college. As I recall, I had applied to three of what were then Wisconsin state universities and Luther College, a private liberal arts school in Decorah, Iowa. (At the time, the University of Wisconsin in Madison seemed too big for this kid from little West De Pere.) I didn't think of any of those as "safety schools"; if that concept existed then, I don't remember hearing the term. They were just schools that interested me. In 1965 I had gone with the forensics team for a meet at the state university in Oshkosh and noted in my diary: "Boy, is that a neat campus. I won't mind going there." I guess by application time I had decided that at 50 miles away it was too close to home. Eventually I ruled out one state school because, in my mind, it graduated "too many farmers." Another, in the far north of the state, I deemed "too cold." And Luther, when all was said and done, seemed "too churchy" -- and was probably too expensive. Mind you, I didn't visit any of these in advance of making my decision; that practice had not yet become the norm. So I first saw the campus of Wisconsin State University-Eau Claire when I arrived for summer orientation.

[An aside: Using the pseudonym Bea Effe, I later included the ride to orientation in a 1,200-word piece about Greyhound bus riding I titled "WAITING: A Simple Narration." I described a friend and me as "quite alone in the world, more than a little apprehensive about what would happen once we got THERE, and definitely not prepared for the five hour trauma that lay ahead." I explained:

> It was a Tuesday in June, hot and humid. The bus was nearly empty. The last passenger got on and took [a seat near the front]. He was tall, dressed in baggy corduroy pants and a wrinkled white shirt,

wearing cowboy boots and carrying a guitar. He was also very visibly carrying a pint bottle in his back pocket.

Soon after our journey began, he took off his boots, took out his bottle, propped his feet up on the seat in front of him, and began serenading the rest of the bus. His music was country-western. Kind of. His Texan-accented words were slurred. It was obvious that he'd done his waiting in the bar near the bus depot.

The passengers gawked. My friend and I whispered. The driver could at least stop the bus and throw the guy off. After all, the sign up front did say "no alcoholic beverages." And the driver wasn't exactly a 90-pound weakling. But [the driver] simply told the guy to "keep it down." To our chagrin. And suggested he "put away the bottle." Little chance of that. So, naturally, the further we went the rowdier things got. Our songster began to make regular and frequent trips back to the john. I was glad I had a window seat.

During our half-way stop, the "gentleman" stepped across the street to refuel, and only just made the bus's departure. To our dismay. He was unbelievably quiet for a while. Then he decided he didn't like the way the driver was driving and wanted to take over the wheel. The driver threatened to throw him off. That didn't work.

The fellow became angry and obnoxious. He threatened the driver. Challenged him to a fight. "Stop the bus and let's us get out. I'll beat the shit out of ya." Promised to kill him. "Come on. Stop the bus. I got a knife here says yer chicken. I'll kill ya."

I don't know about the driver, but we were scared. Every mile seemed like ten and every minute like an hour. There was no fight, however. And when his whiskey ran out, the cowboy's threats slowed down. He dozed. And in a little while the bus made its final stop. The cowboy sauntered-staggered into the depot. I guess he spent the night in jail, 'cause the last thing I heard was the desk-man calling to have the "live one" removed.

I swore I'd never ride a bus again. Except the next day I had to get back home and I had the other half of a round-trip ticket in my pocket. . . .

In my four years in Eau Claire, I made that bus ride often enough that I could recite forward and backward the trip's 10 stops.]

My parents first saw the campus when they dropped me off for the start of school in September. The two classes I had taken at St. Norbert's had given me a taste of college classrooms, college teachers and college students. Sharing a room with my sister (and a bed until we finally got "twins" about 1963) and bunkrooms at sleep-away church camp prepared me for a roommate. Nonetheless, I was a nervous first-generation freshman about to embark on an adventure into the unknown.

Eau Claire transformed me.

Eau Claire set me on my life's professional paths.

Eau Claire offered me a world of famous and infamous speakers, of music of every variety, of foreign films, of brilliant thinkers, of art and artists, of literature and writers, of independent-minded classmates, of serious partiers, of change makers, of professors dedicated to peace and justice as well as their disciplines, of administrators willing to listen.

I found almost no tracks to follow when I began to write about my freshman year. I don't seem to have kept a diary, nor had I saved many letters. I was mostly left to memory jogged by research. But I can state one thing with certainty: My transformation started on one of my first days on campus, when I walked into Schofield 26 -- the school newspaper's office -- and asked about joining the staff of The Spectator. I was appointed the copy editor! How on earth did a neophyte become an editor? I imagine I mentioned my high school experiences and that was enough for the staff-starved editor in chief. Besides, I think "copy editor" meant I would read stories for basics such as grammar, spelling and punctuation. I was in no position to question content. But just like that, I was a member of the team.

To be a college freshman in the fall of 1967 was to be caught in the shifting sand of an hourglass turning from calm to turbulent. At WSU-EC, freshmen were initiated by traditions such as two weeks of wearing "beanies" in the school's colors: blue and gold. As the yearbook reminded me, when a sophomore asked us to "beanie," we were required to stand and recite the freshman poem, then give our name and address. Fortunately, it noted, sophomores could not make freshmen stand on chairs or carry their books. A photo from the Freshman Forum in a packed gymnasium shows nary a bare head, although the yearbook records that a few rebels protested by hanging the sophomore class president in effigy.

We freshman also had mandatory Saturday-morning classes to keep us on campus and "in loco parentis" to keep us in line. Our well-being was overseen by a dean of women and a dean of men. He was also the basketball coach, known for encouraging us to drink milk and reminding us of the need for "a sound mind in a sound body." Girls in the dorms had sign-out procedures and a strict curfew. Boys seldom were allowed in, and then only into the dorm lounge, where everyone had to keep one foot on the floor at all times. We were required to "dress up" for Sunday dinner in the cafeteria; we were assumed to be returning from church, I guess. Class attendance was required; "cuts" were recorded, and more than a couple reduced one's course grade.

I found a Mid-Semester Evaluation for that fall among my mother's things. The envelope, addressed to my father, also contained an explanatory question-and-answer memo from the director of counseling services. (Dad also was the addressee on the letter with news that I had been included on the Dean's Honor List for the fall.) With so many of us the first in our families to attend college, our parents likely were as adrift as we sometimes felt. *What can we as parents do to help our sons or daughters improve?* The thoughtful answer: "Offer them encouragement and understanding. Suggest that they distribute their time more wisely while on campus. Suggest that they seek help from their professors when needed and confer with their advisor or counselor regularly." The memo concluded:

> In summary, your son or daughter has received a copy of this evaluation prior to the mailing of this one to you. We feel that responsibility must be given before it can be assumed. Each freshman has a professionally trained counselor available for advising. It is the student's responsibility to see his advisor. We are helpful only when given the opportunity to help.

I could only chuckle at the convoluted "Slight Correction" tucked into the memo:

> The descriptive code from the instructor is to the <u>left</u> and not to the right of the grade. If the instructor made one comment, that code is located approximately 1" left of the grade for that course. A second comment, if any, is about 3/4" left of the grade. If the student has been absent, the number of times is listed about 3/8" left of the grade for that course.

My dorm, Governors, was on the upper campus, 234 steps up "the hill" from the lower campus, where academic buildings, student union, fieldhouse and the like were located. (That top-of-the-hill location did have one advantage; in winter we could watch nearby ski jumping.) It was not unusual for me to trudge up that hill several times a day. In addition to my classes and Spectator duties, as a freshman I also played French horn in the marching band and orchestra. In my first high school music competition, along with critical comments such as "tone is extremely pinched," the judge had noted "some very nice musical moments" and concluded, "Wonderful potential here. Has the makings of a horn player." That's why at college I braved the audition process and surprisingly made the cut. One early evening, rushing down the hill for a concert, I tripped and pitched forward on the pavement, tearing my pantyhose and badly scraping a knee. Bloodied, but without time to return to my room, I limped to the concert hall. The show must go on, after all. It was not the last time I cursed the hill, and I never did join those residents fond of sliding down it on cafeteria trays after a snowfall.

As I remember it, my first semester was ordinary. My roommate was from nearby Menomonie and, like me, had left a steady boyfriend back home. My best friend from high school lived a floor below us. I attended classes and took lots of notes during the day, and at night I studied. I got used to standing in line for my meals and hanging out in PJs in someone's room to gab before "quiet hours." Mail call brought joy or despair. My roommate went home most weekends, so I cleaned and read when I did not have to march at a football game. Photos document that I had decorated my side of the room with reminders of home, including a No Parking sign the boyfriend had filched, a bowling pin, beer bottles, a Packers banner and a framed print of old boats on a shore. Other photos show us "girls" wearing our hair rollers, gathering for slumber parties or partaking in tomfoolery. For Christmas my roommate and I assembled a cardboard fireplace, which turned our room into holiday central.

Truth be told, I had arrived on campus more politically and socially conservative than I like to admit. But the news that I immersed myself in daily ever so slowly began to cause fissures in my world view. A poem suggests my evolving social consciousness (and careless typing).

```
bfl
  fall 1967


                    THE GREAT SOCIETY


        Zing...Zing...
   The bullets fly
        And
          men
            fall.
   The ground is covered ⱷⱵⱵ/Ɏ
        with blood
            and human flesh.
   Some white, some black,
        some the enemy.
   But flesh none-the-less.


        Shhh...Shhh...
   The feet shuffle
        And
          men
            carry sighns.
   The grassy slopes give
        evidence of the youth
            of the contry.
   Some white, some black,
        ALL the enemy.
   But Americans none-the-less.
```

I started college as an English major with a Journalism minor whose plan was to be a high school English teacher/newspaper advisor. The introductory Journalism course, Mass Media, was included in my first-semester schedule. The only other course I remembered before looking at my transcript was Greek I. My reason for choosing it to satisfy the language requirement reminded me that I was determined to chart my own course, to explore. *I don't want to do Spanish or French like everyone else*, I smugly declared at the time. It was a lesson I would try to impart years later when, as a professor, I advised freshmen. As an advisor, I also would speak from experience about dropping a course, as I did Zoology. I disliked the course and the professor's teaching style. I needed time for band and The Spectator and my other classes. And I wouldn't be "behind" because of the six credits from St. Norbert's.

I found only one academic artifact from that first semester: ten 4-by-6-inch handwritten index cards, each summarizing and commenting on a magazine article related to journalism. I imagine that we had been instructed to find the readings as a way of learning how to use the library, how to find information about the media, how to summarize/paraphrase/identify passages for quoting directly in preparation for writing. In choosing our own articles, we might also express something about our interests. In those pre-internet-search-engine days, we relied on "The Reader's Guide to Periodical Literature," a handy reference to articles in popular and academic publications. Among my selections -- all written by men (including one who I eventually taught with) -- were: "The Racial News Gap," "Why Radio Is Here to Stay," "A Warning to Young Men" and "Women in Journalism: Threat or Promise." The publications I cited included the then-popular Saturday Evening Post, the then-influential Saturday Review, and journalism-related titles I would come to know well over the course of my career, including the one I misidentified as Editors and Publishers.

By my second semester, I had switched to a Journalism major with an English minor. My grades suggest where I concentrated my efforts; my only A was for News Reporting. I saved some of that work in a folder labeled Public Affairs Reporting, and from it I realize that course is where I learned about covering a community -- in general its government, police and courts, and specifically in Wisconsin. Two exams tested our factual knowledge; I am struck by how my "short answers" were written as complete sentences and begin with a rephrasing of the question. From an answer on the first exam, I know I had been assigned the city council beat. After detailing specific information about it, I concluded: "It's an interesting beat but I wouldn't want to spend too long there, although it is the center of a community and its news." Little did I know that in my first reporting job I would cover that beat. The second exam tested our knowledge of court reporting, including plenty of precise terminology. From the few assignments I saved, I know I attended at least one council meeting and at least one court session. But what really astounded me was the complex story I wrote about the city of Eau Claire's bond issue. How foreign that must have seemed to me at the time; indeed, I would be hard-pressed to tackle the topic after decades of being a taxpayer.

In February, a motion was made and received by the Eau Claire City Council. The motion was passed and started the wheels that will eventually turn some three million dollars over to the city for various improvements. This motion involved the decision to acquire the necessary 3.5 million dollars through a bond issuance.

Despite that weakest of leads, the story earned me an A and the brief comment "good job on a difficult subject." What I see now as particularly deserving of praise was how my last paragraph connected back to that lead.

> And thus the wheels are now spinning rapidly. Only the printing, delivery and receiving of the check are yet to take place. Construction can soon begin. All that will remain of the 3.5 million dollar bond issue by the city of Eau Claire for 1968 will be the re-payment plus some 1.5 million dollars in interest.

I had not been taught that technique -- except through "osmosis" from my newspaper reading.

News Reporting introduced me to Eau Claire beyond the campus, but it was during that second semester that the Spectator offices started to become my home away from home, the center of my campus universe. The offices were in the basement of the administration building, adjacent to the yearbook offices. A hallway tunnel allowed convenient access to the student center. That meant it was easy to bring drinks and food to the office. Serious work on the paper happened at the beginning of the week. Frantic work happened in the hours before it was delivered to the off-site printer, for distribution on Thursdays. As the copy editor, I spent a few hours a week in the office correcting stories. I quickly learned that the pressures of producing a weekly were unrelenting, that planning and meeting deadlines were essential. I quickly discovered that everything about the process was always exciting and often fun.

Somewhere along the way I was told to save all my published work in a "clipbook" that I would need when job hunting. Not that I was thinking yet about a job in journalism. But more than 50 years later, it was amazing to find my first "real" published stories. I wrote 10 stories that spring. All were straightforward "preview" stories for the arts and entertainment section; none merited a byline. They demonstrated my ability to write a standard "inverted pyramid" story, however, and when I began my sophomore year, I had been appointed editor of that section. The lesson I was learning was one I also heard in my reporting class: This is a business where "you work your way up by paying your dues."

The early months of 1968 were tumultuous, off and on campus. On my birthday (January 23), North Korea captured the Navy intelligence vessel USS Pueblo and held its 83 crew members hostage in a prisoner-of-war camp. A week later, media coverage of the Tet Offensive brought home the horrors of the conflict in the jungles of Vietnam; it marked a turning point in the war. At the end of March, President Lyndon B. Johnson announced that he would not seek re-election. Martin Luther King was assassinated on April 4. Student activism was fomenting around the world. Particular attention was paid to a sit-in at Columbia University, where angry students protested the war and that university's plan to build a gym on public land in Harlem.

I searched in vain for evidence of my social/political self that semester. Paging through the 1968 yearbook suggested that our campus was generally quiet, with students engaged in the "benign" and "mundane" activities with rich histories, such as Homecoming and Winter Carnival. Two photos, however, were prominent in the yearbook's introductory pages. One was captioned "Eau Claire students marched for peace in Vietnam." It is impossible to tell from that photo how many students marched, but it doesn't appear to be many. It was raining, and the photographer focused on two guys in suits and ties. One of their signs is visible; it said simply "Negotiate NOW." A few pages later, the second photo has two guys, one smoking a pipe, posing in front of a box labeled "PAPERBACKS For the Boys in Vietnam." The caption explained that the Veteran's Club was collecting the books. Minnesota Sen. Eugene McCarthy, seeking the Democratic nomination, spoke on campus in February and advocated an end to U.S. involvement in Vietnam. I don't know if I attended that speech; I do remember a Spectator staff member who was "Clean for Gene" and worked on his campaign. In March, Republican hopeful Richard Nixon drew an overflow crowd of more than 4,000 people. I know I attended that speech. I am embarrassed to acknowledge I cheered.

CHAPTER 5

Finding My Way

In late May 1968, after one year of college, I returned home to West De Pere a bit less naïve (not least because of Martin Luther King's assassination), a tad more worldly, somewhat awakened to liberal politics and committed to being a journalist. A few days later, Robert Kennedy was assassinated and the world felt even darker. It became darker yet when I went to church with my family on June 9. We had just learned that my neighbor/high school classmate Mikal Sullivan had been killed in Vietnam. I remember struggling to hold back tears, struggling even more to make sense of the senseless. Mike had enlisted in the Marines and was off to boot camp shortly after our graduation, which at the time I thought was admirable. His death proved to be more of the string unraveling from my ball of high-school convictions. By August, when Chicago Mayor Richard Daley's police thugs responded violently to anti-war protesters at the Democratic National Convention, I was a changed young woman. And I was more than ready to be back on campus -- especially back with my Spectator pals -- where I thought I would not feel so alone with my evolving views.

My clipbook is better organized for 1968-69. For one thing, I carefully dated my published stories. There were a lot more of them, too, but for the most part they were similar to those of the year before. On October 10, my Homecoming preview topped Page 1. Still no byline, though. The first of those came a week later, under a two-column headline: "Norse Cryptograms Explained At Leif Ericson Day Banquet." That all-caps style -- with each word capitalized -- looks foreign to me now. I began my story with a quote, which I came to learn (and teach) was seldom the best way to start. I jammed a lot of information into my twelve paragraphs.

A month later, the front page carried my "News Analysis." In that story, "Women Students Given Chance to Decide on AWS," I questioned the need for a new organization called Associated Women Students. I started this way: "With the movement for student power, black power and even Tower [a dorm] power, the women of Wisconsin State University-Eau Claire will soon decide whether or not to accept 'women power.'" I then used several paragraphs to describe what AWS had done on other campuses and quoted local organizers about their hopes and plans. My take on things: "The steering committee seems to assume that because AWS has been effective on other campuses it will be effective here." I was not convinced, asking, "Is this valid or reason enough?" I suggested that women students were already served by existing organizations and administrative structures. "The total implication of AWS seems to be that it will simply be the 66th chartered organization on campus; nationally recognized; sponsoring social and cultural events, attempting to be budgeted, at least in part, by the senate, and offering 'identity' to its 4,000 members." In conclusion, I asked, "Is it really all necessary?" Who would have guessed the skeptical writer of that piece would eventually serve as the AWS executive vice president? I certainly could not have imagined that she one day would be a vocal feminist marching for adoption of the Equal Rights Amendment, doing research on women in the news media, teaching Women's Studies courses and co-authoring a book about Women's Studies graduates.

I continued to crank out arts and entertainment "previews," but increasingly I was covering other news. Many of those stories were ones I had written for my News Writing class, including one about the visit to campus by Gaylord Nelson, who was seeking re-election to the U.S. Senate. It was a traditional "speech story" in which I alternated summary statements with supporting quotations. I didn't remember the Nelson speech or writing that story. Robert Theobald, on the other hand, made a big impression on me. The British socio-economist visited the university just before Thanksgiving for its Forum speaker series. Over the years, that series brought incredible thinkers to campus (and to this day continues to do so). As a freshman, I attended because, as I recall, it was required. Then I attended as a reporter. Eventually I went because the series presented opportunities too fabulous to pass up. Theobald's presentation led me to buy and read his book, "An Alternative Future for America," which remained on my shelves for decades. Rereading my Spectator story, I see why. Indeed, what I reported him saying then seems prescient: "The problem in America today is that we all disagree about what is going wrong. . . . Furthermore, we have radically different views about what we ought to do to put things right. . . . We must be willing to listen to everybody who has ideas about what ought to be done. . . . The fragmentation of society is frightening."

Having a class assignment published in the paper was not unusual. Most Spectator staff members were journalism majors (there were a record 125 of us, up from 88 my freshman year), so we shared many classes in addition to our Spectator work. The department had added a fifth faculty member -- another man. Students chose from "tracks" in news-editorial, advertising, education and electronic media. It is not a stretch to say that fifth professor single-handedly nurtured many of us to reach limits none of the other faculty members could have fostered. The university's motto is Excellence, and that teacher, Leslie D. Polk, took it to heart. The son of a North Dakota newspaper publisher, he arrived on campus with a bit of high school teaching experience and a whole lot of first-rate journalism experience at The Wall Street Journal. He came to us from the East Coast, drove a Volvo (a "foreign" car I dare say none of us had seen) and commanded our attention from day one.

I remember my initial disappointment at finding him at the lectern in my News Writing class. I had expected the instructor from my freshman-year reporting course who, although I found him dull, was at least familiar. My disappointment did not last long. I might not have remembered the Spectator stories that originated as assignments for Mr. Polk's class, but I remembered -- and treasured -- the comment he had written on the back of an early story: "Gosh, you've got a talent and mind for this work." The story only earned a B, but the rest of his comment propelled me to work my butt off. "Basically this is very good," he wrote, "but I want very much for you to perfect your writing style into real professional quality. Watch some points I have made and plse, if any ?s, come see me and I'd like to explain my comments." I did. He did. And until I graduated -- and forever after -- I did everything I could to produce work he would judge worthy. As a journalism professor, I emulated his rigorous standards and, I hope, his nurturing of talent.

Looking through my folder of work from that News Writing semester, I was surprised by the number of assignments and the variety of stories we wrote, in addition to the in-class writing that ranged from "ledes" to single-paragraph briefs to a story with multiple updates. One of our first assignments demonstrated that we always would need to be on our toes. Mr. Polk walked into the classroom, climbed atop the desk -- which he told us was the roof of a seven-story residential building in Greenwich Village -- and began emptying his wallet and pockets. He tossed out money and coins, and ripped a piece of paper, declaring "That was me." Then he jumped. And told us to write the story. I misspelled Mobil, from the credit card found near "the body." I have not made that error since. I hedged on the dead man's identification, but in my last, highly problematic paragraph provided a name. Lesson No. 2 learned. As for my writing, "Style interesting and unique. Shows distillation of ideas and organization." Lesson No. 3: News writing need not be formulaic.

If I weren't busy enough with classes and The Spectator, that fall I also helped create and was the editor of a newspaper for my dorm. There is a backstory: Our academic calendar did not end with the Christmas break. We returned to campus for a last week or so of classes, followed by final exams and another short break before the start of the spring semester. By the end of our first semester, my freshman roommate had decided to leave school. I was told I would not get a new roommate because the vacancy occurred so late. As much as I liked my roommate, I was excited to have a room to myself for the first time. Things did not work out that way, however. When I returned to campus after the January break, I was surprised to find the other half of "my" room occupied. My unexpected roommate was a sophomore transfer student from Milwaukee named Luise Forseth. We couldn't have been more different, and we got off to a rocky start. Didn't much like each other. Eventually became friendly. Both of us returned to Governors Hall the next year, but to different wings. Somehow we became good friends. Then roomed together off-campus for a year. And remain loving friends to this day. It was Luise who, as dorm president, asked me to start the "newspaper." We settled on the name GNU (after the gnu, an animal someone knew about, which could also represent Governors News for You) and I was its editor for the three issues produced in fall 1968. My initial editorial explained its purpose: "Hopefully, it will serve all of you -- to inform, to advertise, to provide a means of communication between the residents of the dorm and to make you laugh a bit." Today it is a technological dinosaur, mimeographed on gold paper and stapled, with handwritten headlines, its two-column format meant to look like a newspaper. "Classified ads" were two lines for 10 cents. Residents were referred to as girls, the head resident as Miss Maulfair (no first name). There were a few cutesy touches, such as the headline written as a reflection, unfilled spaces labeled "for autographs" and hand-drawn cartoons.

Like the university, The Spectator also had an unusual calendar, with a new editor-in-chief appointed to serve January to January. The January 9, 1969, paper had a front-page story announcing the new staff and explaining that the associate editor position had been eliminated. The "chief" now would be responsible for the Editorial page in addition to overseeing the staff. No. 2 on the masthead would be the news editor -- me. The yearbook described my job this way:

> The news coverage and layout of the paper were delegated to . . . sophomore Barbara Luebke. BFL [by now, almost everyone called me Biffle] instituted a "beat system" -- where a reporter is assigned to a specific department and checks there every week -- that had been long in planning. She was trying for more efficient news coverage. But it was the page layout that was different. "Say Dick," she'd say to photo editor Richard Hayward, "Do you have any one-column-by-six-inch feature pictures?" And Dick would moan. So she'd change the page design.

Mind you, I had yet to take a course in newspaper layout. But I had been reading newspapers forever, so I knew how they looked and began to teach myself how to make that happen.

The new-staff photo accompanying the Spectator story, and a similar one used in the yearbook, showed the "girls" in dresses (me in a suit) and the "guys" equally spiffy. We look so ordinary, so wholesome. But the social changes under way on the coasts were afoot on our Midwestern campus, and The Spectator was beginning to report on them and become a part of them. My unbylined story about WSU-EC's first "teach-in," which I believe marked a turning point for the campus, captured this new mood. I wrote about that all-night event for the December 5 paper. My story -- its staccato style anything but a traditional "inverted pyramid" news story -- summarized a "night of talk, thought, listening and discovery." I described the teach-in's impact this way:

> But to the sensitive, the searching, an autumn that began with Charles Evers, brought along 'Carmen,' Whitewater Falls, Robert Bly and, finally the thinker Robert Theobald, then Roach and Forum and 'ban the bomb' had done something. . . . Unshaven, straggle-haired, blood-shot eyed, the 'survivors' left [the teach-in], hoping the sparks set off that shortest of all long nights would stay, linger and have, hopefully, positive, long-range effects for WSU-EC now and for classes yet to come.

A couple of months later, the climate on campuses around the state was explored in an Associated Press series written by student journalists. In its introduction, the AP stated that "the series embraces the full range of campus life as the students seek to shed light on the conflicts and contradictions comprising one of the major continuing news stories of the decade." The second installment, about WSU-EC, was reported and written by me and three fellow journalism majors. It was my first professional byline, and among the newspapers publishing the story was my hometown Green Bay Press-Gazette. Of our campus, we concluded:

> The atmosphere is not yet that of a Madison [University of Wisconsin]. The [high school] football supremacy debates are still essential to some; organizational power and prestige are primary for others; the social milieu is vital to another segment of the enrollment. But, the nihilists, or activists, concern themselves with the upheaval of the institutional structure, and hopefully regard other students as potential fuel that could be ignited by a radicalizing experience -- like being clubbed on the head by an enforcer of the law.

My spring 1969 semester was incredibly full. I seem to have been determined to pack every waking hour with meaningful activity. The demands of my new Spectator job notwithstanding, I enrolled in five courses, at least two of them writing intensive. My friend and freshman colleague David Gunderson (GunR to us) and I created and self-published a "rebel" literary magazine. I attended lectures, concerts, films and basketball games. I regularly partied with journalism students and Spectator staffers, who included Ann Devroy from Green Bay, the city of my birth. Ann would go on to an incredible reporting career, including White House correspondent for Gannett and USA Today and, from 1989-1997 for The Washington Post. Andrew Rosenthal of The New York Times, who was her main competition, reportedly described her as "the scariest and most generous reporter I've ever known. She would kick your butt 24 hours a day." Tough as nails, nose to the grindstone -- that's the Ann I remember, the Ann who mentored us and who hosted the best soirées, generally lasting into the early morning hours. (Our paths came close to crossing again when I invited her to speak one spring at my university. She explained in a note that "the first six months of a new administration are total chaos, and I've done little but work and travel with [President] Clinton. Trying to juggle this job with my life as mother of an 8-year-old is a joke!") Ann's death from cancer in 1997 was a shock. Periodically since then, I have wondered how she would have reported a story. At no time did that happen more often than during the circus that was the Trump presidency.

One of my writing-intensive courses, "Advanced Composition," included a requirement that we keep a daily journal, which we periodically submitted for critique. Not surprisingly, my entries frequently were about The Spectator or journalism. They are a reminder of how much time I spent thinking about the news, reporting and reporters, and the "big questions" of the day. I can't explain why I abandoned capitalization for most of that journal (which autocorrect would make unbearable today), but back when news stories were typed and "30" was used to mark "the end," it was easy.

a call from madison came to the spectator office this afternoon from the [WSU-EC] senators who are down there for the budget hearings. one of the comments was a question as to whether or not eau claire had the monopoly on concerned students.

and all this while we thought the campus was apathetic.

-- 30 --

I wrote an entry about the Spectator work cycle as a freestyle poem.

```
                        2-7-69


    thank god it's friday.
        the end of another week is come,
        except our week doesn't end.


    tomorrow it is in to sit behind the desk;
        layout the pages--at least make a noble beginning;
        take some feature photos--
                        see that guy slide down the hill.


    but, tomorrow night, "rippled" up, we will forget there is
        a tomorrow and a tomorrow
                        and a production night.


                        -30-
```

Nice word choice

Another entry was "philosophical." It was a Monday, and "we are all very, very busy" with Spectator work, I wrote. "so, i think i'll just put down a Thomas Jefferson quote oft used by people in journalism but seldom in its entirety." After Jefferson's statement about the importance of newspapers over government, I added questions posed by Edward P. Morgan in a Playboy (!) article titled "Communications." It began this way: "Would Jefferson sleep better tonight if -- in the place of government -- the [conservative] Chicago Tribune dictated American foreign policy or if William Loeb's vitriolic antisocial Manchester, New Hampshire, Union Leader were running the Department of Health, Education and Welfare?" His questions continued in that vein; my conclusion suggested my answers. I wrote, "i would venture to guess that thomas j. would turn over in his grave."

Spectator editors were paid a stipend, as my 2-11 entry reminded me, but clearly we weren't in it for the money.

2-11-69

    it's 4 a.m. now, and all is quiet on the campus. in each of the seven dorms, in the rooms, two beds are occupied with sleeping students. but, in five rooms, there is life. the _spectator_ has gone to bed for the night, finally, and the last remnants of the staff just finished trudging up the hill.

    schofield 26 is dark and quiet. no more than 15 minutes ago there was laughter and joking, and a bit of swearing. in fact, there was quite a bit of swearing. things just weren't going well. there was too much copy and not enough space. so much of the copy wasn't in the basket. it had to be written, written over, or edited. and in the end it was the five muskateers who stuck it out--those same loyal kids trying to hack out the headlines.

    but, come june 1, they will be reimbursed--to the tune of 13 cents an hour.

-30-

Two days later I mused about words.

```
                        2-13-69

        "ain't got the bread."  boy, is that an open statement.
    to the guy sitting over at that corner desk, talking to our
    features editor, it means one thing.  you see, he is from
    biafra and is attempting to instill into diane the empathy
    she is going to need to write his story.  or the story of his
    country.  "ain't got no bread."  nothing to eat, starving
    children with distended bellies.  thousands dying each day,
    and no food...no help.
        but to the guy sitting here on the corner of my desk, the
    statement means no money to go skiing this weekend.  no money
    for a good time with his girl.  "no bread" to him means that
    he may have to spend the evening in his apartment tonight
    without a six pack.  or he'll have to borrow the money from
    one of his roommates to throw his share in the "grits box."
    But there will be grits.  and somewhere he will get the beer
    and somehow he will find a way to take his girl on a date.
        i guess it only goes to show how important semantics and
    context and the speaker are.  in other words, COMMUNICATION.


                            -30-
```

The further I read into that journal, the more I thought about how important such pondering (some might call it pontification) was to my development as a journalist. How important it was that I spent time thinking about the profession. How time spent chatting -- in the Spectator office, around a table in the student union or at breakfast after a long production night -- was one bonus of having found like-minded compatriots early in my college career. Indeed, I described one such moment in an entry reflecting on our attendance at a journalism conference. Several of us had gone to the state university in Oshkosh for a gathering of student newspaper staffs. It was an awful experience, so many of our fellow journalists seeming oblivious to the turbulent times. Afterward, I wrote:

We had a mini-teach-in today in the Blugold [student union]. Eight of us, not all students, sat for well over an hour drinking cokes and kicking around the idea of whether or not recruiting of any kind should be allowed on a university campus. And what is education -- and training. And what are we really here for.

And all this time I couldn't help but think it would never happen in Oshkosh. And wishing that we could have had a microphone connection to all nine universities so they could hear the kind of things that are happening at wsu-ec, because things really are happening. Even Jean Houston [a Milwaukee Journal editor who had recently spoken at a special Forum about "The New Consciousness"] noticed it, and she was here only 24 hours.

Comments on my journal entries, coming as they did from my favorite English professor, reinforced my developing style and challenged me to work at it. For example, a series of entries elicited this critique: "Good work. Your experiments are interesting. Your use of detail and your sensitivity to concrete imagery show good writing sense. Let some of these things develop more. Also try evaluating some of your material -- word by word." It was advice as applicable to my Spectator stories as to my other prose. A journal entry from early March seems to have been written to explore the oft-offered advice to "show, don't tell." I introduced it with "just for the heck of it, express concretely the following abstract statements." Among them:

... the wind is blowing
... the wind is out of the southwest at 15 miles an hour
... he began to take pride in his appearance
... his hair was combed now, and his shirt tucked in
... he is lazy
... he seldom helps with the chores

My almost universal use of "he," although standard at the time, today causes me to wince. In an entry described as a "concluding paragraph," even as I alluded to my aspirations to be a good reporter there was not a *she* to be found:

Thus, one sees that although the elements of a good lead paragraph(s) for a news story have always been the same -- get the 5 W's and H in the first paragraph and you've got it -- more is required of the good reporter. He must evaluate the importance of each element and determine in which order to present them. He must decide which details to include, and how to present them. And he must decide on a lead which will attract the interest of his readers. Furthermore, all this must be taken into consideration in the minutes before the reporter turns his notes into news copy.

Surely one motivation for so often writing about journalism was convenience. It was easy because so much of me was invested in the topic. That also explains why I "double-dipped" at least once for a "Literature of Journalism" assignment. Among other tasks, we wrote several columns. Mine was called "from where i sat," and my topics included the university's first Black Culture Week, "obscenities" in campus newspapers and an updating of several Ben Franklin adages. Being able to express an opinion was heady stuff for a young reporter; who didn't dream of earning columnist status?

The instructor for that course was the department chairman, who also was advisor to The Spectator. He was a straight-as-an-arrow, military-grade flattop, ill-fitting-suit guy who the staff took issue with more and more as student activism grew and we exercised our independence. He had little real journalism experience, as I recall, and we found it difficult to take his comments on our work seriously. A review of the spring-semester Spectator shows our commitment to covering the campus, and we did it so well that 50 years later the issues are a valuable time capsule, that "first rough draft of history" that is journalism. Throw in the ads to really walk down memory lane. Pay attention to the newsmakers, the language, the activities for a reminder of the sexism of the time.

As news editor, I seldom wrote. My clipbook holds just three bylined stories, all from late in the semester when, I suspect, the staff was stretched thin. Instead of writing, I spent my time helping to direct news coverage and then fitting stories and photos onto the front page and several inside pages. In the last paper of the academic year, a Page 1 story reported the results of an "impromptu poll" of the staff to identify the "best" news stories. Those featured under my watch included the financial crisis precipitated when the legislature cut funding for state schools. (It would be far from the only such crisis of my career.) As the Spectator detailed on January 30, WSU-EC President Leonard Haas addressed a special rally of students, faculty and others who packed an auditorium. Typical of his leadership, he calmly and carefully outlined the severe repercussions if the cuts were enacted. Today a reporter might describe his "transparency." He appealed to students to write their legislators about how they would be affected individually and collectively. The Spectator followed the story as students undertook their letter-writing campaign and the Student Senate president testified in Madison. One legislator commented, "How come Eau Claire has the monopoly on all the concerned students? Are the other state universities just sifting and winnowing?" Campus activism was picking up steam. Among the other significant stories of the spring that emerged from the poll were: a second teach-in, the first Black Culture Week, the abolition of Freshman Forum, the opening of a new physical education center and the Faculty Senate approving the right of each dorm to establish its own visitation policy.

When I read through the papers five decades later, many things caught my attention. They are noteworthy on different levels and for different reasons but taken together they are a reminder of how different from today college life was in the late 1960s. They also reminded me that a key to The Spectator's success -- acknowledged by its frequent "All-American" status -- was that it treated the campus as a community and in its news coverage saw itself as a community newspaper. My 2021 self was especially drawn to stories such as these:

▶ Beginning in fall 1969, long-distance telephone calls will be possible from dorm rooms, as each will have a telephone and a distinct number. (No more sharing a hallway pay phone.)

▶ **Mrs.** Janice Washburn is named the new coordinator of the **women's recreation** program (emphasis added).

▶ The Board of Regents approved a new bachelor's degree in **Physical Education for Women** (emphasis added).

▶ This cutline: "The practice session looked familiar -- but women, not men, were shooting basketballs. These **girls** (emphasis added) were practicing for final cuts in the newly-formed women's university basketball team, which opens its season at River Falls tonight. . . ."

- ▶ The story headlined "Hitchhiking Dangerous, Illegal, Fun"

- ▶ A rare Page 1 "Interpreting the News" story. (The practice of a reporter offering perspective and personal opinion was an emerging trend in professional newspapers.)

- ▶ A letter to the editor proposing that "Physical Education should be dropped from the list of required courses." The writers were two freshmen who were mothers! A few weeks after the letter was published, the paper included a two-question survey about the requirement. That led to a story about attitudes toward it. [An aside: I found the requirement silly. I put it off until my senior year, when I took Golf (I had been playing since I was 16) and Bowling (all the while thinking of my high school trophies).]

- ▶ A first-person story about unrest on the Madison campus by a Spectator staff member.

- ▶ Headline: "Nurses Elect Male Leader"

- ▶ A story on underground campus newspapers

- ▶ Approval of the school's first Black literature course, described by the English Department as "an experiment." That was because "the class will be largely discussion, with students having a voice in how it is run," including deciding what they would read. (I took that course.)

- ▶ The addition of a Black history course and a journalism course on the "minority press."

- ▶ A long feature on the Campus Crusade for Christ organization

- ▶ A visit to campus by the Journalism Advisory Board -- 15 men!

- ▶ A photograph used as an editorial, with the cutline "Isn't it ironic to note on this envelope from the Selective Service a postmark that says 'Pray for Peace?'"

- ▶ A story about food stamps for students

- A feature on "sensitivity groups"

- A paragraph from the story about the new "chairman" of the Physical Education Department, Dr. Ida Hinz. "Dr. Hinz, who is single, said she has no new policy ideas of her own; she only wants to carry on where Olson left off . . . such things as a physical education major for women, a major and minor in health education, and a major and minor in physical education for the handicapped."

- A faculty resolution supporting "a student-faculty exchange program with a black college or university."

- This lead on a front-page story about my dorm having no hot water for about five weeks: "Women of Governors Hall have not been dreaming of castles, kings and princes lately. They instead dream of hot showers and demonstrations."

- The lead on a story about the Class of '69: "Among the 545 students to receive diplomas . . . will be a soldier serving in Vietnam, a handicapped gymnast, a blind girl, two four-point students and the first male student nurse."

I add my bylined stories that spring to this list. The headlines were "Teach-In Follows Confrontation," "Draft Information Center Results in Senate Debate" and "Liberalization of women's standards approved by Haas; effective next fall." Reading about the teach-in now suggests how the campus balanced burgeoning activism with Midwestern manners (remember the protestors in suits and ties?).

Teach-In Follows Confrontation

By BARB LUEBKE

It began at 10 a.m. Monday when teams of black and white students entered some 20 classrooms, unannounced, for a "black/white confrontation."

The mood carried through the afternoon, into the evening. The action began again at 10 p.m. when students gathered in Davies Center to take part in the Spring Teach-In.

IT DIDN'T COME easy, the right to carry out the morning confrontation.

On March 6 the Faculty Senate passed a resolution after some debate, which allowed for the confrontation. The debate centered primarily around student and faculty rights. Some argued that students have the right to know ahead of time what will be taking place during a specified class hour. Others argued that such a confrontation would infringe upon the rights of the instructor to choose a guest lecturer and the topics to be discussed.

The debate continued. A petition with about 100 faculty signatures asked for reconsideration of the resolution and forced a special meeting of the faculty.

THE COMMITTEE for the Concerned, who planned the confrontation and the teach-in, withdrew their request for the confrontation. They had several reasons. Two stand out: "a possible inability to provide sufficiant resources for all classrooms involved" and the fact that the "petition might jeopardize future opportunities for meetings of this kind." That's how University President Leonard Haas explained the action to the faculty.

Still, debate continued. But the faculty, by a margin of less than 10 votes, accepted a substitute resolution allowing for the confrontation. And the date was set.

The approaches Monday morning were all different. Directly confront, accuse or question. Detailed preparation or play it by ear. But each team entered classrooms with the same purpose in mind — confront WSU-EC students with the black-white situation on campus. Stimulate minds into thinking about the situation and persons into doing something about that situation. Awareness.

THE RESPONSES were as varied as the approaches.

The late evening-early morning teach-in carried things one step further. It dealt with specific questions directly related to the black/white situation. And in the Maple, Spruce and Walnut Rooms, discussions centered around academic freedom, religion, student power and sex.

And in the Cabin, original poems and ad-libbed songs and Cohen music, all part of the Happening, were like the reactions most everywhere else that evening — spontaneous.

The information center -- a symbol of increased attention to the draft by the Student Senate -- required authorization from President Haas. Also debated at that meeting was the more parochial issue of student-vehicle registration. To my mind, the most dramatic changes were two affecting women living in the dorms. The Parent Overnight Weekend Permit was eliminated, and women no longer would need special permission from the dean of women for "extended weekend leaves." On the other hand, women still would need to sign out when leaving a dorm at night and still would have a curfew. The times were changing but change had its limits. No matter. I would be living off campus when I returned for my junior year.

I also was changing, as a *lengthy* letter to my parents documented. (Thanks, Mom, for saving it!)

2-16-69
10 p.m.

Dear Mom & Dad –

I finally am getting a minute to write. I am sorry it has been so long and hope you didn't mind the phone call but I knew it would be a while before a letter. Some day I'll call for free from the office with this special long distance # we get— and can use to call home about once a month.

A lot has been happening around here and we have been kept hopping. Just finished Black Culture Week— as you probably saw in the Spectator— and now Winter Carnival is in full force. And it is only 6 weeks until Easter, so time is passing swiftly. Most days I go down the hill at 8:45 a.m. and come up again at 10:45 p.m. It sure is nice to be able to eat on lower campus. But hopefully, if I ever get organized at the Spectator, I won't have to spend so much time down there. But the trouble is I love it— and the people. And then just about every night I'm going to something. In the afternoons there are Arenas of Ideas where they bring in speakers on all sorts of subjects who speak from 4-5:30 or so. Then Monday nights is pure <u>Spectator</u>, and sometimes to the pizza hut for smorgasbord and if we work late to the Crossroads for breakfast. Tuesday nights I have a class and more <u>Spectator</u>. Wednesday nights are open— usually— but many times there are speakers or other things. On Wed. afternoon 5 of us & Mr. Polk get together for a Lutheran journalists discussion in the Blugold. Thursday nights I am taking part in a "Decent Society" discussion which is sponsored by the Cooperative Campus Ministry at the Newman house. And then the weekend begins. But I feel like I am getting so much more out of school than ever before. And I love every minute of it.

The wedding reception was really great yesterday. It was about a 50 minute drive to Baldwin and it was held at this real swanky place called The Coachman. The reception began at 2 and there was all the champagne you could drink. There were to be only sandwiches we thought— but they had a big meal— turkey, ham, potatoes, gravy, etc. And it was delicious. We left about 4:30 I think— none of us had watches on. Well, we were going to go to Minneapolis— about 40 miles— but decided we didn't have too much money between the 5 of us. So it was back to E.C. We went to the basketball game and then Tom & I came up to the dorm. But at midnight we were both so sleepy we called it a day. But what a fun day it was. [I had been dating the *Spectator* editor, a senior, since the fall. "I've never kissed an Arts and Entertainment editor before," he told me early on.]

Did you hear any comments on our newspaper article. I have a copy of it from the Racine paper and Wausau. By the size of the by-line in Racine's, I sure hope Aunt Pearl saw it. Phi Beta Kappa isn't everything. [I was tired of her bragging about my oldest cousin.] Am enclosing a couple of copies from the E.C. paper— I have one.

Thank Kris for the Valentine. I will try and write her soon. I also got one from Sue and must find a minute to write her. There just are not enough hours in the day. And Luise is so busy with homecoming I haven't seen her for days. But she'll probably pop in around midnight tonight.

I bought some acrylic paints Friday and am doing some stuff on poster board. They aren't very good but they sure serve as a good relaxer to paint for an hr. now & then.

My stipend check is supposed to come Thursday & so I'll endorse it and mail it to you. I would like it put in my savings. I plan to live on my $44.60 income tax [refund] until Easter. By the way, for this semester I should get about a $180 stipend.

As far as interning— I wrote to De Pere, Clintonville, Sturgeon Bay and Beloit. I have not heard from Green Bay or any of the others except St. Bay— and they were looking for a photographer so that left me out. But Ann Devroy had been offered a job at Beloit & turned it down & Mr. Karwand (J. dept. chrmn) said I had a pretty good chance for that one. I am not going to sign the [Park Department] contract because Les said last year 1 kid did and wanted out— they let him but said they could take it to court. I don't plan on taking any chances.

Oh yes— if you have not mailed a care package— you can add hair spray— And any other goodies your heart desires. As for a birthday gift— you can forget the Sister Coritta book 'cause that was $20. I would like a blouse with the big collar— but I don't know what color.

Maybe blue. Plain. And a neck scarf to go with it. Kris can help. Otherwise wait and I can get something for spring.

Well, I guess I'll close for now. Don't faint over the length of the letter. Write soon as I like Mail.

I signed off, Love Barb. Then drew a dotted line across the stationery. Under that I wrote "This part of the letter is separate from above:"

Dear Mom & Dad –

I've been wanting to write this for a long time and just had not time & wasn't quite sure what or how to say it. (No I'm not pregnant or getting married.) It concerns our plans to go to New Orleans at Easter [spring break]. Now please don't take a negative view— but hear me and my leaky pen out. I wish I could explain it in person— but I can't— and so a letter will have to suffice. I realize you are against the trip so I want to try and have you see my side of it. I hope— and I think I can understand your thinking— partially. I am your oldest child and for one thing it's hard for you to see me grow up— to realize I am a grown woman (almost?)— and to realize I am becoming independent. Then too, you are worried about my safety. And my fellow travellers. And the cost. So I'll look at each of these from my side.

As far as growing up— I have little to say about that. But I do consider myself a woman. I am 20 and mature. Not in all ways, I know, but do any of us grow up entirely. And it's not that I am anxious to untie the apron strings But that's life. You say one more summer working at home— but will you ask this again next summer? You say I can travel after I'm out of school and working But, life is now and here— and the opportunity is here. It won't— and can't be the same in 2 ½ years. These are the people I am with 15-16 hours a day— the kids I go out with— and party with— and have bull sessions with— go to class with— learn with. And they are a terrific bunch of people. I am dating one of the guys, and having a good time doing so. For the most part these are the persons who make life up here liveable. And I hope you trust my judgement in choosing friends. I know you do. I haven't really failed yet, have I.

As for my safety. Well, we live in the atomic age and any day we could get it— or hit by a car— or plane. I have faith that when it is my time to go I'll not have much to say about it. And if it's to be it's to be. That's in God's hands. And from a different angle— Tom and Ed are both good drivers, and I'm sure would take no unnecessary risks.

As for the money— I don't expect it from you. I can either take out a short term loan here— to pay back within 3 months, using my stipend or can use my $80. Tom has joined the standard oil travel club and they will plot the route. He has figured $15/person for gas. There will be ten of us going. Any other expenses will be what we make them. We are taking 2 tents and the travel club will locate camping sites for us. Many other details are yet to be worked out.

All in all, it would be an experience— a learning experience— a fun experience. I see it as an opportunity which just can't be passed up. Can't you please see it like that. I never really asked for much before— I'd beg for this if necessary. It's hard to explain— even for a journalist— but this trip means a very lot to me. Please think it over good.

All my love
Barb

I remember the rest of the New Orleans story this way: My parents finally gave their OK in time for me to tell them the trip had been called off.

In mid-May, Mr. Polk was hospitalized. I shared the news in a long letter to my parents dated 5-14-69 8:30 p.m. I wrote that "I really believe I've grown up a lot these past couple of days. Under the circumstances I'd prefer not to have." Just before that, he had joined my pal GunR and me when we drove to Chippewa Falls to pick up the copies of Outlet, our literary magazine. We three then celebrated at "a coming out party for it at MacDonalds." Privately, GunR and I shared how we didn't want to lose him because, as I explained in my letter, "for the dept. he's the best thing that has happened in 10 years, and for some of us, too." I warned my parents that I might not write for a while and asked them to "understand the bitterness and adultness you are likely to notice. It's all part of life— my life— and right now I'm not necessarily enjoying it." I instructed them that I would be ready to leave campus mid-morning on the 28th. I already had finished a term paper, but "next week will be hell. I have a final exam Tuesday p.m.— a major exam Wed.— a major exam Thurs. and a final exam Friday. Then finals next Mon-Tues & Wed. Real fun!" I don't know what I was thinking when I also shared that there was going to be a "Big Spectator beer bust sponsored by the editors Friday. I don't know yet if

I'm going— probably will." Finally, I asked if they would "please consider allowing me to stay at the farm [which my father had inherited from his uncles] . . . for 2 or three days after the weekend. I really could use the time alone & rest."

What I thought today after I wrote about my "adultness" was that cliché warning: *Be careful what you wish for.*

CHAPTER 6

The Summer of '69

Internships have long been a staple of journalism education. Back in the day, the "real world" experience they offered -- most often without pay, sometimes with academic credit -- typically happened between junior and senior year. They were a rite of passage, providing evidence of one's readiness for the (usually) lowest rung of the professional journalism ladder. Eager to hone my reporting skills, I decided to pursue an internship after my sophomore year. I got mixed messages from my advisor (the department chairman), who had said it would be highly unusual for a sophomore to get an internship, then told me I was a strong candidate for one in Beloit. I thought one back home, which meant the De Pere weekly or the daily Green Bay Press-Gazette, might happen. To be on the safe side, I eventually decided to return to my job of the previous summer: staffing a neighborhood park. My high school friend Les VanVonderen and I had supervised kids at play, taught them to weave lanyards and such, and generally kept them occupied and out of trouble. I also coached a girls softball team. The days had been long, but it didn't feel all that much like work, and I was ready to do it again. Until the Press-Gazette offered me half an internship. Would I be interested in working the second part of the summer? You bet I would! If only I could talk the Parks Department into hiring me for just the first half of the summer. I pulled it off, and for five weeks I was "Barbara Luebke, Press-Gazette Staff Writer."

Actually, my first published story -- a lengthy (and dry) account of a hearing before the Wisconsin Employment Relations Commission -- did not carry a byline. I'm sure I was disappointed. I obviously was bored by the hearing because I wrote this poem during it.

There's safety in numbers:
Unionize.
Trouble with your employer?
Don't worry—
A "nice," all expenses paid lawyer
will out talk the opposition,
and prove unfair labor practices
(no employer has the right to fire
a union man— it wasn't REALLY a blacklist, anyway—
just a list of non-U employees)
while your third-shift coworkers
cheer silently,
hiding their white socks and bluejeans
in the last row.

I also did not get a byline above the story that resulted from the reporting coup of my career. A week or so into my internship, I found myself parked at a microfilm reader with reels of the old Green Bay Advocate. It was, I thought, the sort of intern's nightmare I had been warned about: busy work. In November 1967, a diver trying to free fishing nets had discovered a shipwreck off Chambers Island, west of Wisconsin's Door County Peninsula. That diver, Frank Hoffman, and a team were now getting ready to raise what had been dubbed the "mystery ship," and my editor assigned me to search for its identity. The clue: It was a schooner that Hoffman believed sank in a storm in 1864. I don't recall how long it took me to find the stories describing a vicious storm and the sinking of the Alvin Clark. I wish I could write that this research led to my first "scoop." Instead, the editor handed my information to a "real" reporter, who wrote the Page 1 copyrighted story -- without a byline. That struck me as odd, and I was disappointed that the story used a lot of the details from the Advocate without explaining how the paper -- that is, I -- got them. A couple of weeks later, however, I was rewarded with a Page 1 byline when I wrote the story confirming that Alvin Clark was "as close as we are going to get to the true identity" of the ship. My source was the Green Bay museum director who had worked closely with Hoffman. He acknowledged the two had early on suspected the ship was the Alvin Clark but kept that secret until they could find confirming evidence. [An aside: In 1981, the Coast Guard's Merchant Vessel Documentation Division declared the Alvin Clark the oldest Great Lakes ship in existence and the oldest known floating merchant ship in the world. Unfortunately, it was demolished in May 1994 because it had decayed beyond repair.]

Several years later, that museum director married one of my college friends, a Spectator staffer and longtime journalist. That wasn't the only "small world" moment that surfaced as I reviewed my internship. Newspapers then routinely monitored police and fire scanners for newsworthy activity. One morning an editor was alerted to a barn fire several miles away and instructed me to go with the photographer. I dutifully grabbed a notebook and went dashing out the door with him. I quickly learned that news photographers tend to be fast -- and slightly wild -- drivers. It took a few minutes, but I realized we were heading toward the rural area west of my hometown. We turned onto a familiar road. Then, as the fire came into sight, I realized the barn was on the farm of my high school best friend. Upon arrival, the photographer began shooting and I hung back, unsure of how to behave. I spotted my friend and gave her a bear hug. I felt awful for her and was on the verge of tears. *Is this all right for a reporter to do?* I wondered. I understood that I needed to do my job and gather information, so I did. The ride back to the office was less frantic. The editor ended up using only a photo from the fire, and I provided information for the cutline. Years later, when I taught reporting, I drew on this experience to talk about objectively covering news even when we find ourselves *in* it.

My reporting experiences that summer offered other important lessons. One that stuck with me, and which I also frequently used in my teaching, came from a reporter I shadowed on an assignment that took him to "the Reformatory." Then officially called the Wisconsin State Reformatory, the big stone structure was familiar to me because it was on the bus route between home and Green Bay. Before the reporter and I entered the facility, he counseled me to "remember, everyone in here is innocent." In other words, don't take an inmate's story at face value. It was good advice with far more general application. A couple of months later, when studying editing, I would hear the equally valuable,

"If your mother says she loves you, check it out." In other words, verify everything.

Another lesson from my internship, buttressing what I had been learning, was the need to be able to quickly prepare to report on unfamiliar topics. The corollaries: Don't be afraid to ask questions of sources. Don't be afraid to follow up if you are writing and find yourself confused. In addition to that Employment Relations Commission hearing story, my published work included an examination of the increase in seafood sales over the three years since the pope had lifted the ban on Catholics eating meat on Fridays; a survey of disaster resources by the Army; local budget increases; declining meat prices; city ordinances on bike ownership; observations from a St. Norbert College professor recently returned from three weeks in the Soviet Union ("no generation gap . . . no hippies or long hair . . . females all in dresses . . . the cleanliness of the cities unbelievable"); and Farm Progress Days. Of all my leads, the one for the FPD story speaks volumes about a change in journalism -- and me -- since I wrote it.

> Husbands taking in Farm Progress Days are likely to wander off among the latest in combines, tractors, milk coolers or barn cleaning equipment.
>
> But wives need not tag along.
>
> A program of demonstrations, displays, exhibits and a fashion show has been planned for members of the fair sex -- be they rural or urban homemakers.

Had I remembered that story, it would have found its way into my teaching and research on stereotyping.

Most of the subjects I wrote about that summer, my clips showed, were unfamiliar to me. Each story added to my knowledge bank, to my reportorial "bag of tricks." My internship may have been only several weeks long, but I headed back to The Spectator and the classroom better prepared because of it.

CHAPTER 7

Junior Achievement

Returning to Eau Claire for my third year moved me along the path toward independence. I was excited to be living off campus, although only a couple of blocks away. I had been selected, along with 10 other young women, to live in a house sponsored by the Cooperative Campus Ministry's "Faith and Life Community." We would be the companion house to one of 12 male students established a year earlier. A story in The Spectator described the community as "for students who can no longer ignore the crucial questions about life's meaning." Its sponsors said the intent was "to prepare students to be informed, articulate, concerned Christian laymen who as parents, churchmen and citizens can make a vital and relevant witness to the issues of the 20th century." Participants would get together weekly to share a meal, Christian fellowship and guided discussion. I had been attracted to the opportunity when it arose the previous spring, even though I found myself feeling more and more distant from my Lutheran upbringing. Indeed, I attended the Sunday guitar Mass at the Catholic chapel on campus more often than a Lutheran service. When I attended church at all, that is. Over the summer, I had expressed my disillusionment in the poem "UNCLE ROLAND."

> You are a hero -- a real Christian
> in their congregational eyes:
> -direct the choirs
> -serve on the council
> -tithe weekly
> -give of your time willingly, asking nothing in return.

Surely, they think, you are heaven bound.
"You should have been a minister."

Don't they see, any of them,
the hypocrite:
-knows all the latest nigger jokes
-voted for George Wallace
-rejected his own brother

Heaven demands more than deeds. . . .

By fall 1969, I was not at all sure the housing arrangement would be a good fit. Our first challenge of moving into the house was cleaning up after the previous residents: college guys. I have not been able to use Janitor in a Drum since then! My next challenge came when we were expected to take part in a retreat to prepare us for the year. I wanted nothing to do with sitting around and sharing feelings with strangers, so at the last minute I decided not to go. I also failed to tell anyone about my decision. Somehow I talked my way out of being tossed from the community. In my heart, I knew that what living there really meant for me was proximity to campus and The Spectator office. That was especially important because I was enrolled in seven courses for 19 credits. I would have had a 4.0 GPA for that very busy term -- if it weren't for the C that I earned in "Photography" and an F in "General Psychology." (I quit going to the latter class after failing to drop the course on time, then blew off the final exam by being high when I took it.)

It was during that term that I discovered my professional loves: editing and non-mainstream journalism. Editing was a required course, I believe; the course called Minority Press in America was having its test-run as an elective. Mr. Polk taught both. Count me among the students who after one course with him had decided to take anything he taught. (I treasure the handwritten, "very personal" list he had prepared for me during that first course, after I asked for reading suggestions. Three were marked +++ (Dietrich Bonhoeffer's "Letters and Papers From Prison," Truman Capote's "A Christmas Memory" ("what prose," he stated), and the poet Gerard Manley Hopkins. Mr. Polk was demanding and he didn't suffer fools or foolishness, but he was an excellent, accessible teacher. And oh-so-smart. Those were the days when office hours were appreciated and plentiful (and might spill over into the student union). A professor who had something to discuss instructed a student to "come by during my office hours." And you did. If you had a question, needed a form signed, wanted advice (course-related, professional or even personal) -- that's what office hours were for. If eventually you made a special connection with a professor, you always were welcome to "shoot the breeze" during office hours. Many journalism majors learned at least as much from Mr. Polk during office hours as they did in his classroom. I was one of them, and one who earned the right to call him Les (outside the classroom, of course). On October 2, doodling during a literature class, I wrote this, titled "for ldp— a person, real":

You are	You are
One	a person
To whom I can turn	real
When	alive
All	partaking of life
Others turn their back	to the fullest
When	yet
I	giving
Need	fully of yourself
Need	and caring
Need	about others.
Someone	
To talk to	
Who will listen — understand	

It was just his second year on the faculty, but Les already was respected in The Spectator office -- and around the campus. He was fond of dropping by to share a news tip, a criticism, a compliment, a student's story he thought merited publication. His voluntary, red-pencil critiques of an issue meant something to the staff; those offered by our advisor not so much. Perhaps when I recently looked again at the year's newspapers it was through a haze of admiration, but I easily saw his influences. I also saw my continued growth as an editor and writer.

An advertisement in the school year's first issue suggests The Spectator was short-handed. Nonetheless, we produced a 16-page paper for

September 11. The one significant news story reported that a new student constitution was ready for a vote. Over two pages inside, we published its entire text. We also ran an editorial urging its approval. The rest of the issue was mostly short items related to the start of the year, including sports. One of those stories was about the library buying $5,000 worth of materials for the Black Studies program but deciding it would not get its own section. Interestingly, it was students who proposed the purchase and who advocated for the section. The decision prompted cartoonist Jon Hannafin to draw.

Jon's biting, often satirical, commentary reflected shifting attitudes on campus. The previous semester, for example, the first in a four-part series based on two surveys of students had carried the headline "Student Apathy Changing to Campus Concern."

It was also in that first issue that I made my debut as a columnist under the title "specks in my eye" and the byline B.F. Luebke. As I would do almost every week during the semester, I offered brief commentaries on whatever I wanted. As I had done with my high school column (and would do in my professional career), I frequently referenced something I had read. I clearly read increasingly varied and less parochial publications, such as The National Observer (a weekly general-interest newspaper), Crawdaddy (a rock music magazine) and The Distant Drummer (a Philadelphia underground newspaper). Along with exchange papers from campuses around the country, the office also received Notes from Cuba and Granma International, the weekly version of the Cuban newspaper published in English. Reading them felt rebellious. The staff's request that the library begin subscribing to The Village Voice, the "underground" Los Angeles Free Press and

Rolling Stone was a public service. Nonetheless, the first observation of my first column was campus-based and used word play to take a jab at Prophet, our food-service company.

> I guess the faculty here can't be trusted. In the past, when they bought a cup of coffee and doughnut in the Flambeau Inn it was done on an honor basis. There was a box into which they threw their money and took change, such as the case was.
>
> Now a cash register and cashier have been installed.
>
> Wonder what the effect will be on Prophet?

Another time I offered my critique of campus "improvements."

> I sure hope Claire Bailey's gang in Auxiliary Services runs out of blue and gold [the school's colors] paint soon. First it was fire hydrants and now it's the doors on Governors Hall, the tops of two chain spikes in front of Brewer Hall, and who can guess what else.
>
> I am anxiously waiting for blue and gold chalk boards, sidewalks, classrooms, toilet paper. . . .

A week later I had an update: "I understand those doors . . . are color coded -- the blue ones are for men and gold ones are for women. That still doesn't explain the . . . fire hydrants." In a couple of weeks, I followed up once more: "Governors Hall residents have initiated a petition asking the doors of the dorm to be painted one color. An alternate solution was attempted over the weekend when some unidentified person(s) painted polka dots onto the doors." A common complaint about journalism is that too often stories are dropped, developments are ignored. At least with this one, I didn't let go.

I didn't shy away from snark, either. An example:

> If your organization is looking for a money-making project this fall, why not try selling piggy banks. All the mickey-mouse with change in the Blugold and bookstore caused by the new four-percent-on-everything tax is making for some coin-laden pockets.
>
> Just think, you could be doing a public service, which is more than can be said for the legislature.

Then there was the item I started this way: "A Haight-Ashbury physician and two teenage ex-drug addicts will be in Eau Claire October 6 to rap about the use and abuse of drugs." Although the items I chose leaned decidedly left, I did once include an announcement from Young Americans for Freedom, the largest organization for conservative youth. The group had launched a campaign asking North Vietnam "to renounce military victory in the South," and I noted that "anyone interested in circulating such a petition" could get a copy in The Spectator office.

I think anyone would be hard-pressed to describe that WSU-EC school year as a sea change; it was more akin to a snowball gaining size and speed as it rolls downhill. The Spectator of fall 1969 -- its news coverage, its language, its advertisements -- in many ways reflected tradition and change coexisting, and a "balance of power" shifting. For example, the lead story of the second paper of the semester was headlined "No action taken by senate on petition to end beanies." In four short paragraphs, a story at the bottom of the page concerned another tradition: Homecoming. Next to it a large photo accompanied a story about Marine recruiters being presented with a coffin during a silent protest. The photo showed a "one-legged demonstrator" stepping out of the coffin. Inside pages included stories about a forthcoming speech by the leader of upstart Students for a Democratic Society, the first in a series of anti-war films to be shown, and a speech critical of Cold War policy by the chairman of the philosophy department.

As news editor, I seldom reported stories. When I did, I don't remember whether it was out of choice or necessity. One such story topped Page 1, and when I first looked at it again I saw not my byline but the layout, which used four wider columns rather than our standard five. This was also the issue where I realized we had abandoned (several papers earlier, it turned out) all-caps headlines for the then-in-vogue upper/lower case (only first word and proper nouns capitalized). The alternative column width, along with the story's position on the page, was designed to call special attention to the story. In this case, I wrote in detail about long-range development plans for the campus. The plans had been revealed at a joint meeting of the University City Liaison Committee and the Advisory House Committee. Several stories I had written for my internship certainly had prepared me to report and write this one.

Other changes to the way the paper looked became commonplace. For the most part, The Spectator's nameplate appeared at the top of

Page 1 and was the width of the page. Newspaper design was modernizing, however, and I began placing the nameplate elsewhere on the top half of the page and altering its width. Inside, we added a calendar of events for the week, which allowed for a lot of information in a small amount of space. We also were using more and bigger photographs. On October 9, I chose a photo whose news value was its composition, not its relationship to an event. That was rare, as was its size; it took up the bottom third of Page 1. That paled in comparison to the photo we used to tell the story of the October 15 Vietnam Moratorium March in Eau Claire. No cutline was needed; the marchers with their "Peace" hands raised, one holding a sign saying simply WAGE PEACE, spoke volumes. A short story -- without a byline -- added details and color. Les had cranked out that story for us; I know because I have the original. It was a wonder that we were able to publish anything, because the march happened on a Wednesday night, when the paper was printed.

A bit of background about that is in order for 21st-century readers accustomed to instant information. When I joined the staff in fall 1967, production of The Spectator involved our typewritten stories being hand-delivered to an off-campus printer, where a linotype operator turned them and their headlines into the lead lines used to create a page galley for printing. It was time-consuming, as was the process of readying a photograph for the galley. [An aside: Henry Beetle Hough, in "Country Editor," wrote this lyrical description of how a linotype worked: ". . . words and ideas, on the one hand, and an alloy of lead, tin and antimony on the other, were combined in a somewhat mystical union to form type, eloquent type." Today I think how sad it is that we have more or less lost an entire vocabulary of printing.] We also provided page layouts indicating what was going where. Eventually a staff member "proofed" pages, looking for typographical errors, misplaced items and the like. Making changes to a page was neither easy nor quick. By fall 1970, production deadlines shortened a bit when we transitioned to the new technology, offset printing, but they remained a challenge. Still, the tedious process of producing a paper that could be delivered around campus each Thursday had for some years provided access to an important tool -- a university vehicle. A couple of privileged staff members had authorization to "sign out" a car; they were on a first-name basis with the employee overseeing the fleet. We were required to be traveling on Spectator business and to track mileage so our budget could be charged. Let's just say that an editor or two managed now and then to need a car over a weekend and knew just which side streets offered parking away from prying eyes. Those editors deserve credit for creatively enabling spirited get-togethers that raised staff morale -- without ever once getting caught.

Now, back to that moratorium march. In addition to the problematic production deadline, many Spectator staffers, including me, were among its participants. We marched in order to report and photograph, but we also marched to protest the war. I like to think that we talked about the ethics of being involved before we decided to be involved, but I don't remember. I do know that the WSU-EC march garnered attention from the national press, including Time magazine, because it included the son of a high-ranking public official. One of our classmates was John Laird, son of Defense Secretary Melvin Laird (previously a longtime Wisconsin congressman). The Spectator had published a letter in which John explained why he declined an invitation to speak at the rally before the march. In his letter, he also offered support for the moratorium and urged others to do the same. "I feel that the Vietnam War is grossly immoral and it is time for the end. As concerned students . . . we have the power to control our future and it is time to grasp this power. A march brings attention, but revolution brings action." It is not an exaggeration to say many student journalists shared his sentiments.

Still, The Spectator was a campus newspaper, not one of the growing number of radical "underground newspapers" on campuses around the country. So, while the moratorium dominated the front page, inside the 16-page paper readers also found a page of photos from Homecoming and stories about the first Forum speaker of the year, problems with the new campus phone system, a review of the Fifth Dimension's Homecoming performance, and the university's rental of a Burroughs 3500 computer for instruction and data processing. The calendar listed a performance by the Alvin Ailey American Dance Theater scheduled for the next evening. That was significant to me because I had a ticket and was eager to attend. Unfortunately, my parents chose that weekend to visit. They were concerned about my growing activism, political views clearly out of sync with theirs, and an independence that increasingly seemed to be shutting them out. I decided they would not be interested in the Ailey performance, but I could not bring myself to attend and leave them at the Howard Johnson's Motor Lodge. I probably pouted.

My second bylined story of the semester was a follow-up on the moratorium. The headline -- "Oct. 15 'successful' . . . focus shifts to November" -- didn't match my lead, best described as drawn out, or the story. I reported with my eyes and ears as much as I quoted what others had to say. I started this way:

> An estimated 100 persons gathered in front of a television set in the Davies Center lobby to watch the Mets and the Orioles. The chairs in the barbershop were filled with regularity; purchases in the bookstore were comparable to those on other days. And in the Blugold, crowded conditions persisted, although a table or two were available on the East end throughout the day.
>
> So it seemed to go Wednesday, Oct. 15, as business continued pretty much as usual on the WSU-EC campus on the day that had been set aside as a national "moratorium on business as usual."

I further observed that the success of a boycott of classes and programs scheduled for the day was difficult to judge. I remember walking the hallways and peering into classrooms. "Some classrooms appeared emptier than normal, while others were filled because instructors had designated Wednesday an exam day. Some instructors, on the other hand, met their classes but discussed the war, as the moratorium committee had urged." I practiced attendance-estimating skills I had learned in News Reporting and wrote:

> A crowd of about 600 filtered in and out of the University Arena where a debate was going on during the morning hours. At one time a random head count showed about 40 faculty members in the audience. The Davies Center Southwoods Room was filled for the noon-hour rock concert and the rap sessions were attended by enough persons to warrant a plea for volunteers to leave and start other, smaller discussion groups.

The evening, I reported, drew an estimated 2,500 people, who "braved cold rain to take part in the march-rally. There were a few parents with their children and some local clergymen, but the majority of the crowd were members of the university community. The moratorium was directed to encompass the entire community. But organizers termed it successful anyway." After quoting one of them, I transitioned to writing about what was ahead: ". . . Oct. 15 is history. And what this community will do in November, when two days of moratorium activity have been called for, is now the center of attention."

What came next was an all-night teach-in. I reported that story, too. Along with pen-and-ink drawings by a staff member, it filled the front page.

After three introductory paragraphs of observations, my story took a turn to the first-person. Writing as "I" in 2021 wouldn't raise an eyebrow; in 1969 it was the exception to the rule of "reporters don't belong in the story."

> I was not up for a teach-in that night. It had been a bad day, tragic and shocking. A friend's father had been killed. I was thinking. But I didn't want to think aloud for I had not yet sorted my thoughts. I could not share them. And it was cold outside, terribly cold. I had an early ride -- didn't want to have to take the late walk.
>
> I had debated with [one of the organizers] ... before the teach-in. For some 45 minutes we had thrown out ideas about why teach-in and why now and the prospects for success, however measured. He was convinced it was a "social phenomenon." I was convinced it would be a flop.
>
> So the assemblage Wednesday was somewhat of a surprise. The crowd was estimated at between 1,200 and 1,500. . . .

I then wrote about what I had seen, heard and experienced. I quoted lots of people from lots of sessions. The last student I cited said, "It wasn't as good for me [as the previous teach-ins] because the subjects just didn't appeal to me." Playing off that, I ended my story: "I agreed. And I had experienced two. My thoughts still needed sorting . . . the type possible only in some quiet corner. So I called it a night." It was 4 a.m.

What readers found when they turned the page -- a full-page political cartoon with the caption "Effete snobs: clip and save" -- surely surprised most. The rest of that issue's content was pretty standard fare. I had a story about an Arts and Sciences faculty meeting. Results of the Student Senate elections were reported, as was the news of a change in leadership for the moratorium committee. Student reaction to a ban on the artificial sweetener cyclamate was mixed. A new science building cost more than expected and likely

would remain without some equipment for years. Seniors selected for a "Who's Who" publication were named; a fraternity housemother was the subject of a short feature story. A sports story was headlined "Women's athletic stigma dying," but women quoted still had a "courtesy title" attached to their names and the male athletic director did not. (We couldn't seem to get out of our own way on the topic. An earlier story about powderpuff football included the headline "Girls successfully invade male domain" and a cutline reading "Seldom do football players face opponents as attractive as Margaret Langlois, a quarterback. . . .") The semester's final four issues continued in this newsy vein, including a four-part series about over-30 students. At least one story signaled that the spring semester's Spectator staff might face new challenges, and that was the draft lottery of December 1.

Even 50 years later, my fall 1969 is memorable for a reporting "first," notable for a plan that never came to be and remarkable for a Spectator-related trip. There was also the early Christmas present I received while home for the holidays and the significant announcement made on January 8, 1970, in the last Spectator of the fall semester.

In mid-November, with the lead story about academic calendar reform, for the first time in The Spectator I used the byline Barbara F. Luebke. Under consideration on four state campuses, including ours, was a move from semesters to what was dubbed 4-1-4. It would have two 14- or 15-week semesters with a 3- or 4-week "interim" between them. Yet again my internship assignments had provided me guidance on how to read documents, figure out the questions to ask and who to interview. I also now had considerable experience organizing a "long" story. (I suspect its complexity and length were why I wrote no column that week.) A couple of weeks later, I sold a version of my story to the St. Paul (Minnesota) Pioneer Press, which curiously attributed it to the "Pioneer Press News Service."

Despite our ambitious intentions, a second issue of Outlet, the independent literary magazine David Gunderson and I had created, was not to be. Outlet had been born out of our disenchantment with the campus publication, which we continued to see as "elitist." Our first volume essentially committed to publish whatever was submitted, which we had done. In preparation for the second, we advertised for contributors, and The Spectator ran a story. The reporter referred to us familiarly as Barb Luebke and Dave Gunderson, but once again the anachronistic style subsequently referred to me as Miss Luebke and him as Gunderson. That's the last information I found about Outlet, except for a handful of unused sketches and writings among my files.

As for that remarkable trip: Spectator editors enjoyed a few perks, one of which was the annual Associated Collegiate Press convention. In 1969 it was held in Miami Beach, Florida. In November. For cash-starved college students from chilly Wisconsin, this was an amazing opportunity. It was my first airplane travel, and back in the day that meant wearing one's Sunday best. It meant meals on china with real silverware. It meant smokers. The convention was held in the Americana Hotel, on the beach, and we were treated royally. When I returned to campus, I breathlessly described the experience in a letter to my parents.

> Sitting here in photo class listening to a boring lecture— so thought I'd use part of the hour to get a quick letter written to let you know we made it back to E.C. OK. Arrived about an hour late Saturday night— but other than that all went on schedule.
>
> I must say we were not too impressed with Miami— it rained 6 inches Wed & Thurs & the humidity was about 90%. The wind blew at about 30-40 mph & the waves on the ocean were really high— made Lake Michigan look calm. The hotel was kind of a rich man's "Picasso Plaza" (Oshkosh)— and everything was so damn expensive. We were given $25 for 10 meals— I had 3 and spent $30— and everywhere you went you had to tip somebody— they'd actually ask for one. This I expected— but it is definitely no place for college kids. We made it to downtown Miami— 15 miles from the hotel— Thursday in the rain— but found little except expensive stores aimed at tourists. It was interesting in "Little Havana"— everywhere you went people were speaking Spanish— and in the 2 newsstands we found there were a great number of Spanish papers and magazines.
>
> At the hotel— it was almost like one continuous party— especially at night— and even we didn't take part in much of this— we had our own and some good gab sessions. Friday night 7 of us went to the floor show and dinner in the hotel— ran up a bill of $145 — including $25 in tips— But it was fun and a good experience.
>
> The hotel was built to give the impression of wealth— a sign in

the lobby informed that gentlemen were required to wear ties and jackets after 7 p.m.— And everything we had brought just didn't seem to be dressy enough.

The plane ride was great— I loved it— and we had good weather both times. Chicago at night from the air was really beautiful & exciting. When we were leaving O'hare— just boarding the plane— a piece of machinery ran into our plane & punctured the shell— we had an hour's wait while they changed planes— but we all got a free drink— It is impossible to believe the flying time— 2.30 from Miami to Chicago and 35 minutes from Chicago to Eau Claire. Just can't adjust to this.

A couple things for Kris to remember [she and a friend were planning a trip to Florida]— be sure and bring cash or travelers checks, preferably the latter. But don't expect to cash checks. Also, when there keep track of money & plane tickets— either with you or lock in your train case when you leave room and take keys with you. Cause a lot of people have access to your room. Also, be sure to have something very dressy for evening wear. Nothing else I can think of now—

One good thing about the convention was it was a good vacation— which it should be called anyway. Got a chance to catch up on my sleep.

Got a letter from Dave last week— and he should be home [from Vietnam] for Christmas and is going to pick me up here. For Thanksgiving, I'm not sure yet. I have been invited to Luise's, and am considering this. Also may stay here— I can't leave until Wed p.m. anyway— and have so much I could get done on campus Fri and Sat— like my independ. Study and a philosophy term paper. I'll make up my mind soon— one of the other girls at the house may also stay here— we are going to discuss it.

Got a philosophy test back today— an A— that is two A's and we have 2 tests left and our paper— so I really want to spend time on it. Thursday we go to Minneapolis to see a play for Black Lit— we finished our presentation on underground papers for Minority press and I turned in my content analysis today.

That's about it for now. Class is coming to an end.

(I wonder now how much my parents understood about the specifics of my class activities, but I seem to have regularly shared those details.) It is a good thing we enjoyed ourselves so much because, as luck would have it, the next year's convention was in Minneapolis, just a

90-mile drive west of our campus. All I remember about it is that we were in the audience for the premier of "The Sterile Cuckoo" starring Liza Minnelli.

I definitely remember the first -- and only -- telegram I received. It was December 19. The hand-delivered envelope contained a page with strips of words pasted on it. It was the "instant-messaging" technology that had been in use for more than 150 years.

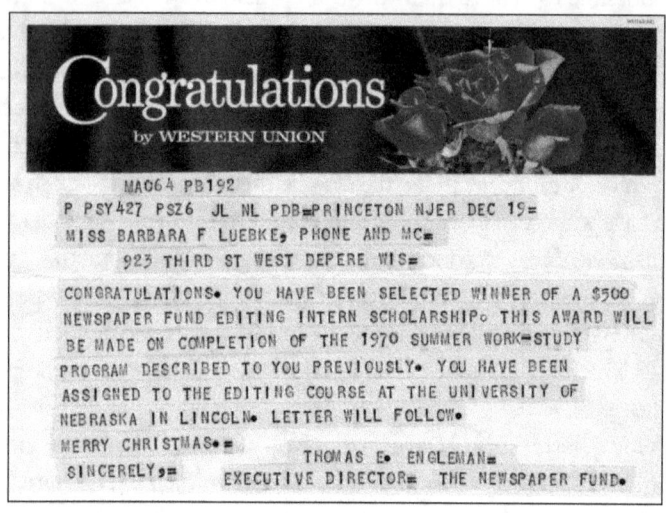

My Spectator work and my Press-Gazette internship certainly had made me a competitive candidate. I had scored well on the test of my knowledge of grammar, spelling, AP style and news writing. But I think Les Polk's recommendation carried the most weight. After all, he had worked for Dow Jones, which then owned The Wall Street Journal, whose editors founded the Newspaper Fund (now called the Dow Jones News Fund). Over the years, countless of his Eau Claire students would become Editing Internship alumni. Coincidentally, I would one day help run one of the program's campus-based training programs.

In January 1970, the campus learned what I had known for a little while. I had been named editor in chief of The Spectator and GunR would succeed me as news editor. I was about to lead the staff for what would prove to be a year of challenging news coverage. In the story about our annual reorganization, I noted that my old position of arts and entertainment editor was being eliminated, along with that of features editor. "To better facilitate news assignments," I explained, "all news except sports will be handled through the news desk." Other changes were in the works, including moving the editorial page to Page 4. Such changes were not happenstance; a favorite pastime when staff members hung around the newsroom or the student union was fantasizing about how we hoped to one day own a newspaper and how we would run it. Our rehearsal, if you will, was about to begin. I couldn't wait! A 21st-birthday poem from Les cautioned me not to lose "the spark of youth/the little zing/that once gone is gone."

Spring 1970

As editor in chief, my challenge was to continue the good work of my predecessors. The Spectator consistently earned "All American" status from the Associated Collegiate Press. In April we learned that our fall semester was the fifth in the last six terms to get that rating. We had received "Marks of Distinction" for content and coverage, writing and editing, editorial leadership and photography. I was fortunate that much of that accomplished staff remained, including the previous editor in chief, Dave "Rock" Hass. He, GunR and I had become pretty much inseparable, so the Spectator offices would have felt weird without Rock.

From my first issue as editor, there was no shortage of significant news. And as often happens for a weekly, the timing of the most important stories tested our abilities to produce under severe deadline pressure. It was the semester of Kent State, Jackson State, a student strike, Earth Day, another teach-in, debates over ROTC and beer on campus, appearances by Margaret Mead, Jesse Jackson and David Dellenger, and national success for men's basketball. And so much more. Rereading the papers, I quickly concluded that we did a hell of a good job. Our coverage was broad, our reporting solid, our news judgment sound, our design respectable and often creative. I also saw how much our work benefited from Les, who had introduced new courses and new ways of thinking about journalism -- and challenged us to settle for nothing less than our best. For example, although we had eliminated the arts and entertainment editorship, we published lots of such stories. In addition, we had a music critic and a film critic; their often-controversial opinions generated more than a few letters. Incorporating arts criticism was a natural, because Les was teaching Critical Writing that semester. News and sports reporters also benefited from a couple of semesters of his courses, and our editing and page design reflected his influences.

Times were not easy for campus newspapers that dared to challenge authority, to test the limits of their independence. Across the country, administrators clamped down and student (and faculty) readers often had different ideas about the role of the student press than did the editors. After all, many papers, including ours, were funded at least in part by student fees. My first editorial, on January 29, abhorred the WSU-La Crosse president's decision to put that school's paper under control of the Mass Communications Department.

4 • Thursday, Jan. 29, 1970

═══════════ Editorials ═══════════

Unhealthy precedent set with Racquet decision

The recent action by WSU-La Crosse President Samuel L. Gates, which put the school newspaper, the Racquet, under the auspices of the Mass Communications department, is to be abhorred. The situation, no matter how one looks at it, is regretful.

A newspaper's objectives are to present a truthful, comprehensive account of the day's news and to responsibly interpret this news. The newspaper may state an opinion, but this is always to be labeled as such and is usually reserved for the editorial page. In attempting to meet these objectives, no newspaper can satisfy all readers.

THE JOURNALISTIC SIN the Racquet committed when printing the "Contingent in Solidarity with the Vietnamese People" article was failing to identify the source — Liberation News Service. In printing "Student as Nigger," an article a couple of years old, the staff could have, as did the Lakeland College paper last year, censored the article by blacking out the four-letter words. The Racquet editors obviously decided there was some value in printing the article as it had been written.

University faculty newspaper advisers serve one purpose — to give consultation when requested. But La Crosse reportedly wants to hire a part-time "faculty superviser" to read all copy to check for libel, content and language. He would also review the paper's makeup, organization and style. Thus, the adviser takes on the responsibilities of the editor. And this is, whether officially or unofficially labeled, censorship. Conceivably, anything the "supervisor" did not approve of or was told not to approve of could be omitted from publication.

More importantly, though, the action by Gates could set an unhealthy precedent for the rest of the newspapers at schools in the state university system which offer journalism programs. If any type of support is given to Gates' decision, it might encourage other administrators to consider a similar course of action when they, from their non-journalistic positions, believe a newspaper has gotten out of hand.

A week later, I reprinted an editorial from Editor & Publisher, the weekly bible of the newspaper business, under the headline "Campus papers need autonomy." A couple of weeks after that, a letter writer took issue with our news judgment. As I had learned while arts and entertainment editor, individuals and groups seeking publicity generally were hard-pressed to understand how that differed from news. In this case, the writer was upset about what she saw as inadequate attention to "the largest college and high school jazz festival in the history of Wisconsin." I suspect she had been the person who submitted "an article and picture to . . . The Spectator office, on time, to be printed." Instead, the paper used it as the source for a brief story with all the pertinent details. In light of that news judgment, she urged us to reevaluate our "position as a 'campus newspaper.'" Another time our coverage of Winter Carnival was challenged by writers who objected to the "slight" attention paid to fraternities and sororities. And so it went.

Although I believed the more letters to the editor the better -- the paper was being read! -- by the middle of March I had decided it was time for a journalism lesson. My editorial was a more mature statement of the case I had made about my high school paper.

4 • Thursday, March 12, 1970

Editorial

The Spectator's role is not...

A university newspaper is not many things. It is not a political propaganda publication for the left or right. It is not a publicity agent for university organizations. It is not a house organ for the administration. It does not exist merely to train student journalists.

Lately, several members of the WSU-EC community have attributed one or several of these qualities to The Spectator. Thus, we believe it is necessary to publicly interpret our function.

WE EXIST INDEPENDENT of control or censorship other than that which is self-imposed. All matters of policy are formulated by an editorial board, consisting of the seven editors, which meets weekly. Opinions expressed in the paper, except for the "editorials," are the views of the writers, not necessarily the editorial board.

The Spectator operates under and interprets its function in the light of several basic principles: An attempt is made to present a comprehensive account of the news to the university community. There is a conscious endeavor to fairly report all developments on campus or those which affect the campus. When necessary, an interpretation of the news is presented. A clear distinction is made between news and opinion columns.

A university newspaper is unique in that its administration changes frequently (yearly with The Spectator), and what was policy one year may be disregarded the next. Each staff must examine its role, then try to do its job most effectively. But the basic premise always remains the same — present the news comprehensively and fairly.

The Spectator has changed — because its editors believed a change was necessary. Its role is seen not as a bulletin board but as a newspaper. We are attempting to function accordingly. And last year's policy will not be maintained simply because it was policy.

A couple of weeks later, I offered another view of the power of the student press, reprinting an editorial from the The Western Courier from Western Illinois State University. ". . . [Y]ou [students] are freer because we are here," it stated, arguing that "even if you cannot agree" with all the paper publishes, it deserves support. "All power to the students. All power to the people."

I enjoyed writing editorials. Our editorial board hashed out policies and positions, which I turned into what I hoped were cogent arguments in support of informed opinions. We published 25 editorials that semester; all but a handful were WSU-EC related. I wrote (twice) in favor of proposed changes to the Student Body Constitution. I urged students to vote on a referendum about beer on campus so the outcome would be meaningful. In light of criticisms around campus, I declared Black Culture Week successful and called the Senate's expenditure for it worthwhile. I wrote about the need for follow-through on the "call to action" of the Earth Day teach-in. I advocated changes to Winter Carnival "or it will lose all meaning for WSU-EC students." I cautioned the Senate not to fall prey to a spring lull but instead continue working on issues. I took issue with the campus moratorium committee's strategy of "fusing . . . the issues of the war in Southeast Asia and ROTC on campus" as "an unwise means of revitalizing the war protest." I congratulated the NAIA tournament-bound men's basketball team (in the language of the day, the headline was "Right on, Blugolds"); the outgoing Student Senate president, whose "homework on issues" was at the heart of his successes; and the university president for a decade of "thoughtful, progressive leadership necessary at a rapidly expanding university." I remain particularly fond of the tone I achieved in a short editorial critical of students after a "pie fight" at the Hilltop Recreation Center.

Beer and pie - no!

One of the reasons given for pushing for beer on campus was that it would help socializing by boosting on-campus activities.

If the pie fights in the Hilltop Center last week (the participants had been socializing at a Sand and Graveller) are any indication of the kind of social drinking WSU-EC students partake in, perhaps non-acceptance of the proposal would be wise.

At least one person has found some optimism in last week's melee. Student Senate President Bob Jauch said the incidents could perhaps strengthen the Beer Committee's argument that "the atmosphere in which you drink will be instrumental in attitude."

If nothing else, he proposes, beer on campus may teach students how to drink and socialize.

Obviously someone should.

But it is the editorials published before and after the May student strike that truly resonate with me. Perhaps that is because May 4, 1970, when four Kent State students were murdered by Ohio National Guardsmen, was a seminal moment in my life. I wish I could say the same of May 15, but that would be dishonest. The killing that day of two Jackson (Mississippi) State College students and the wounding of 12 others by city and state police was no less egregious but much less in our consciousness.

"Call to Action," the editorial we published on Thursday, May 7, was written in response to President Nixon's April 30 announcement that he was ordering U.S. troops into Cambodia. "On college campuses across the nation, protest actions are being organized. Many are calling for a nationwide strike for peace. We add our enthusiasm for such a strike. And we urge students on this campus to consider the events of the past 10 days (including the deaths of four Kent State brothers and sisters). We trust their consciences will dictate what must be done." Only in a note at the end was it explained that the editorial "was written Monday night, before any formal plans for a strike on the university were formulated. The Editorial Board decided to publish it as a public statement of position." That note was necessary because most of the front page was taken up by a photo and story about strike activities that had begun at noon the day before. An estimated 3,000 people gathered for the kick-off rally, and that night 2,000 people marched from the upper campus to the U.S. Army Reserve Center about two miles away.

Much of the following week's 12-page Spectator was devoted to stories about the strike. Our challenge was to provide full coverage of the historic events -- now more than a week old. Indicative of the seriousness with which we approached our task was a boldface note from the sports editor: "In conjunction with the events of the past week, I . . . think it inappropriate to publish as if nothing had happened. Therefore, after much soul-searching, I have decided to attempt to make this paper as relevant to the current situation as possible. For this reason, only scores of last week's campus sporting events will be carried." His page included an editorial, "Athletic isolation criticized," and a commentary, "Competitive role needs reevaluation." On the news pages, there were photographs and stories from the campus, a first-person account of the strike at UW-Madison and a poem. We published two editorials, seven letters and one incredibly controversial cartoon.

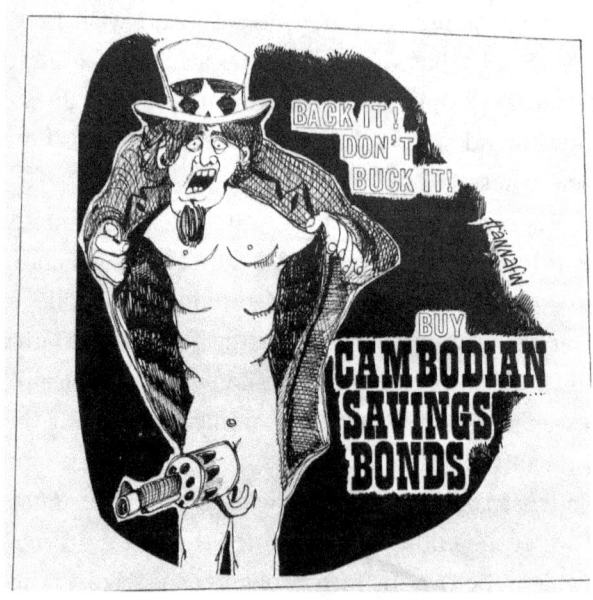

Without a doubt, Jon Hannafin's cartoon caused an uproar. Actually, that was nothing new. His paneled cartoons, "t.f.'s bush," often provoked letters, and his stand-alones frequently were used as editorial cartoons. The May 14 cartoon was prominently placed on Page 3, rather than on the editorial page, and that is the only mistake I now think we made in using it. We editors certainly discussed/debated before voting to publish. As I remember it, we believed Jon was expressing the widespread outrage at government policy that we shared. And we believed in the shock value of his cartoon. No doubt we were naïve in not anticipating the shockwaves to follow. One letter writer stated it displayed "an adolescent immaturity" and several faculty members signed a letter objecting to its "extraordinary vulgarity."

Our concerns quickly focused on threats to the paper's independence and funding. I remember contacting my constitutional law professor about our rights and asking him about reaching out to the American Civil Liberties Union. I wondered if I might be stripped of my editorship or expelled from campus. I remember the Spectator advisor berating us and suggesting in no uncertain terms that we had been irresponsible, at best, in not consulting him. In the end, calmer heads prevailed, which is to say that although we were called on the carpet by the president, he listened to us. Nothing else happened. And eventually everyone moved on to other issues. As for the cartoon, I framed the original and for years hung it where at least I could see it and be reminded of the importance of fighting for what one believes in.

I wrote two post-strike editorials. The first, reflecting on campus events, began:

> Many individuals struggled through intellectual gymnastics sessions last week in their own quest for the truth. At least we should hope so if we plan on entertaining any semblance of optimism for change. If the world-view perspectives of most people were not at least somewhat challenged by recent occurrences, then we will have to resign ourselves to an increasingly dogmatic world where issues do not predominate as much as Machiavellian power.

Even as we praised campus efforts, such as a boycott of classes "to change the normal procedures, to emphasize the urgency of the situation," we took issue with others. "[S]ome of the little revolutionary 'games' played by self-described radicals in rhetorical glass houses are questionable." In particular, we thought that using a log -- instead of "cause committed bodies" -- to block a road was ill-advised. "The tactics must be believable if we are to be successful in our attempt at persuasion." The editorial ended with a call to "remain conscious of our goal and seriously pursue such objectives without submitting to a passivity that strengthens the status quo, or a frolicking that is analogous with some sorority-fraternity functions."

Our second editorial wondered, "Where do we go from here?" It concluded: "One thing is clear: Commitment, no matter to what cause, is not measured by days or hours, but by continued work for success of desired goals. Last week's activities must not have been in vain." Running through each of those editorials was at least a strain of cautious optimism about continued student activism. My final editorial of the semester, published May 21, echoed that.

> ... To debate theory with those in agreement with us is easy. But it is rather useless. To confront strangers is not quite so easy. But it seems obvious this is what must be done.
>
> There are elections in the fall. There are candidates who need campaign workers this summer. We must work to elect those who can best represent us. But we must remind Richard Nixon, Spiro Agnew and all of Capitol Hill that they were elected by us to rule [I wish I had written "govern"] for us. If enough of us continue to talk, continue dialogue, they will have to listen.

My journalistic writing that spring was not confined to editorials. I had two bylined news stories and a book review, and although irregularly, I continued to write a column, the latest called "specks in my eye," (yes, all lowercase). Outside The Spectator I tackled a wide variety of the arts for "Critical Writing" assignments and learned to love legal research and legal-brief writing in "U.S. Constitutional Principles." My 16 credits also included plenty of reading for "American Renaissance" and slide-viewing for "Introduction to the Visual Arts." My schedule was rounded out by a second semester of Editing and news photography.

The first of my news stories was a front-page review of the president's first 10 years, written in advance of a dinner honoring him for that anniversary. One of the privileges I enjoyed as editor was a regular one-on-one with the president. Our conversations helped each of us. He was committed to keeping open the lines of communication between students and administrators and understood that The Spectator was a vital link. I had a direct line to the man in charge, with no subject or question off limits. In turn, this gave Spectator staffers access to other administrators and campus officials. I can say that, as a rule, we benefited from the generally accommodating people in offices across the campus. Even as a freshman editor, for example, my frequent appointments with the director of student activities had made covering arts and entertainment easier. By graduation, I was on a first-name basis with him.

The headline over my story about the president said it all: "Hass -- a decade of flexibility." I crafted the bulk of the story from an interview in which I asked him about presidential leadership, student governance, challenges and the like. But from the first sentence, I reminded readers of how the campus had changed under Leonard Haas. The story started this way:

> In the fall of 1959, 1,700 students were enrolled at Wisconsin State Teachers College at Eau Claire. There were approximately 100 faculty and administrative staff members. Lower campus was the campus. . . . The physical plant was valued at about seven million dollars.
> Leonard Haas was 44 years old in 1959. Photographs indicate he was a bit stouter than today; his hair was graying, not yet white. And it was shorter. The glasses were wire-rimmed.

He assumed office on January 1, 1960, and was inaugurated on May 25. The position, he said in his inaugural address, was "an honor that I covet. But I assume these responsibilities in a spirit of humility, too. . . . I have one main objective, to work with the college to make this institution second to none, one in which all of us can be proud." He certainly did that.

After six paragraphs describing the campus and student culture of 1970, I mused about why Eau Claire "has not suffered from the violent protests which have plagued many campuses across the nation. She has evolved, though some would contend too slow. She has survived, the lines of communication still there, though many would content they are clogged." [Whatever prompted me to refer to the campus as "she"?!]

Before sharing the president's thoughts, I continued: "Why? It's hard to say, and no one would be foolish enough to try to weigh one element against another. Leonard Haas has been here 10 years. He's been through it all and instrumental in much of it. He attributes WSU-EC's stability to many factors."

One he identified -- and the one that fellow alums I have reminisced with over the last 50 years always cite -- was a commitment "to hear students." He valued the role of student government, which under his early leadership grew beyond a concern with social matters, and supported the delegation of "advisory power to the students to make recommendations with varying degrees of finality so long as the faculty agrees." Beyond that, however, was his open-door policy for students; "anybody who wants to see me won't be denied." Eventually, I became a faculty leader and university administrator. Among role models, I count Leonard Haas as the first to offer nothing but positive lessons about leadership. (I was honored when The View, the alumni magazine, reprinted my story.)

My other bylined news story appeared in the last issue of the school year, when I reported on the campus' response to the deaths of the Jackson State students. A fair question today would be why that story was on Page 3 and not Page 1. I have no answer. It would be reasonable to speculate that because the events had taken place a week earlier, other news was seen as more timely. But the lead story -- the faculty's vote against ROTC -- involved action also from the previous Thursday. In addition, the bottom one-third of the page was a "timeless" feature story and photo about the campus laboratory school. Whatever the reason for its placement, the Jackson State story today makes me smile because of its abundance of declarative statements and its use of sentence fragments. As a teacher, I was fond of telling students that "there is nothing wrong with a simple declarative sentence." Or *purposely* using fragments. I was a product of plenty of instruction in grammar and diagramming sentences; I did not realize how those lessons had stuck. Here is the last paragraph of my story:

> And with that the crowd broke into smaller groups. Questions were asked. Answers attempted. Occasionally, a temper flared. But only occasionally. Topics varied. The questions were many. The spirit

was of communication. Dialogue. Some went on until 6 p.m. Some went home with the participants. Some, perhaps, to be further transmitted to friends and neighbors.

Also of note -- especially to me -- was the news on that May 21 front page that the Student Assembly (the renamed senate) had voted to allocate "a maximum of $475" so six students could travel to Washington, D.C., to testify at a congressional hearing. An ad hoc House committee, which included several members of the Foreign Affairs Committee, had been formed to elicit "Student Views Toward United States Policy in Southeast Asia." I was one of the members of the Eau Claire delegation. It was pretty heady stuff for all of us.

Before we left, Les slipped a note under my office door with details on a couple of Washington contacts, including "a good solid capitol secretary who could be of help in anything Capitol-ish!" He ended by urging me to "Have fun and work for PEACE, LOVE AND JOY." We drove to Washington nonstop in the university's minibus and, as I recall, squeezed into one hotel room to save money. Our plan was to contact as many congressmen as possible to explain WSU-EC students' concerns and problems. Among those we met with was our own congressman, Republican Alvin O'Konski (who, by the way, was a co-author of the GI Bill). At the hearing, he mentioned having spent about two hours with us the day before. I vaguely recall being paired up and visiting congressional offices. I definitely remember O'Konski taking us to lunch in the Congressional Dining Room and arranging for us to tour the White House. We toured Georgetown on our own to partake in its nightlife.

Eau Claire's testimony was scheduled for 12:45 p.m. on the second day of the hearings. I doubt it started on time. Reading the printed report of the proceedings, I saw that we were tucked between Muhlenberg College (Allentown, Pennsylvania) and Colgate University (Hamilton, New York). Randy Surbaugh, vice president of the Student Assembly, read our statement and answered questions, but we all had pitched in on the content. Its tone, even today, clearly reflected a campus spurred to action and committed to nonviolent protest. The number of students visiting with congressmen and administration officials "provides evidence of a new student commitment to change through channels," Randy said. He enumerated several concrete steps that could be taken, then said: "It is time for Congress to assert its powers in determining policies of this country. All power to the people can be accomplished if Congress reassumes its position as representing the people on all issues." I like that we asserted, "It is not strictly the American Government that is involved in Vietnam; it is the American youth." As for dissent on campuses, the statement explained that our experiences had been "completely nonviolent," in part because rally organizers worked diligently to keep participants in check and local police had not reacted with undue force. In fact, during the Q&A after Randy spoke, Congressman O'Konski noted: "I might mention that the college newspaper, The Spectator, complimented the police of Eau Claire for their tolerance and for their good behavior as a whole" during campus demonstrations. I wonder if I had pointed that out to him.

I had grown accustomed to bringing information to people's attention. With my "specks" column, I continued to share tidbits that tickled my fancy; even today, many of those items still do. This one, for example, reminded me of faculty behavior when, decades later, I chaired a Faculty Senate:

> The Faculty Senate is in a bit of a tizzy. It seems they have so much work they may have to meet twice a month. Yet, with the amount of "pressing business" to be handled, they spent at least 15 minutes of their last meeting discussing the proposed methodology for a mailbox vote.
>
> "Each faculty member will receive a ballot, a blank envelope and a second envelope pre-addressed to the elections committee chairman. Each faculty member will then mark his ballot, seal it in the blank envelope, and sign his name in the return address area."
>
> In part, that is how the resolution read. The senate then took about five minutes demonstrating how the three-envelope system would work. They then discussed, at some length, the validity of the system and wondered aloud if it was really necessary to use three envelopes, or if they couldn't work on the plan a while longer and shorten the process.

Another time I shared this story from the Distant Drummer, the Philadelphia underground newspaper that we had gotten the library to subscribe to. Change the commodities and it reads like a stock report mixed with a CDC warning.

> GRASS: Prices are being lowered on the West Coast and a lot of good weed is expected soon . . . Prices should drop somewhat in the coming months.
> ACID: Purple tabs, quantity 85 cents to $1.50 per hit . . . A lot of "clear dot" around . . .
> Beware of medium yellow tabs with a few orange dots being sold as Mescaline. It is strychnine cut acid.
> A good quantity of psilocybin in soon.
> Meditation experiment: Picture yourself on a mountain; fall off and die.

For students who felt put-upon by required class attendance and end-of-semester official reports on absences, I shared this from an issue of the Faculty Bulletin:

> Members of the faculty are reminded of the statement on pages 67 and 68 of the Faculty Handbook pertinent to the absence of faculty members. It is particularly noted that all absences should be reported by faculty members teaching University classes on a form provided by the Dean of the School.
> . . . A record of all faculty absences, regardless of reason, is maintained by the Dean in each School for the use of the Dean, in order that the Vice President for Academic Affairs might be kept informed, and so that appropriate reports may be sent to the Board of Regents.

I clearly got a kick out of taking pokes at bureaucracy. Consider an entry I drew from "Order of the Regents of the University of Wisconsin [Madison] Amending and Creating Rules," which included this: "The presence of dogs, cats and other pets is prohibited in all buildings, except when their presence is necessary for research or instructional purposes. . . ." I wonder if I was thinking of cat dissections I had been told about? Another time I found a way to get around one of the paper's own rules. The lead item in my column after Earth Day started this way: "Last week's . . . activities have received all types of comments and criticisms. The following thoughts came across my desk as a letter. They were unsigned, though, and thus could not be published." I thought the anonymous "Everybody's Uncle" had written something "worth sharing," however, and I took advantage of my column to publish that letter.

My weekly column by now was irregular, and I suspect that was because of my duties as editor in chief and the paper's space limitations, along with the substantial writing I was doing for classes, including "Critical Writing." If ever a journalism class pushed me out of a comfort zone, that was it. In an end-of-the semester "letter" to students in the class (mimeographed but individually signed), Les referred to watching us "grow, change and become more cautious in criticism, more concerned with finding solid criteria for judgment, less hasty to dismiss an artist's work as you realized your own failings in having solid background for judgment." I know I experienced that as I learned how to research and report *before* critiquing. I know, too, that the possibility of a larger lesson "for us [he included himself]" that he posited hit home. "Something like 'don't leap to judge' -- the arts -- or any man -- or any thing until we really know -- REALLY know. Keep our minds open, feed them constantly, expose our minds to the arts -- and to life -- to learn to live with it and to grow and then, perhaps, just someday, somehow, we will be able to 'judge' critically."

I was bowled over when rereading my folder of reviews ("The Manor" by Isaac Bashevis Singer; a poetry anthology created for us by Les; Gilbert and Sullivan's "Ruddigore"; the movie "Bob & Carol & Ted & Alice"; Les' personal art collection; a concert by the WSU-EC jazz ensembles; a faculty art exhibit; a concert by the Minnesota Orchestra; and Joni Mitchell's album "Ladies of the Canyon"). I marveled at the range of work. I was incredulous about my confident pronouncements. I distinctly remember the effort that went into the jazz ensembles story. I wish that I had done more such work in my professional career. And I see the roots of my own approaches to teaching in Les' creative assignments, detailed comments on our stories, and reporting/writing challenges.

From our first assignment, which had us describing arts coverage in a publication (I got the London Spectator), he edited our work as if preparing it for publication. His comments typed at the bottom of that assignment anticipated my reaction: "Before you weep over the editing done, realize teach has dedicated himself, as much as possible, to work hard on the copy of students in this class as it is a WRITING class. OK? You must become more economical, get rid of some of your folksy phrases that are from your oral tradition, obviously. . . . So -- chop down the chaff and keep the grain strong and rich."

I seem to have been fond of parenthetical addenda at the end of my reviews, almost as if I were trying to explain their shortcomings in advance of Les' grading. After the Singer review, for example, I wrote (in lower case; ugh!): "i must admit this has been one of the hardest things I have faced writing in a long time, if not ever. i realize there are multitudionous (sic) shortcomings, and hope by June I can look back and exclaim, 'my god!'" He wrote: "Your comments [in the review] too often point right back to YOU and, to some readers, could show your weak points or lack of wrestling with the [book]." Bingo! This English minor had gaps that required filling. And The Spectator editor, he wrote on another paper, needed "to edit [herself] a bit more at times to make style concise as possible, if you want that."

Eventually, I hit my stride with the jazz concert review, which Les wrote "should be printed. . . . Your review would make those who missed it <u>miss</u> it. That is something a critic should do. . . ." I especially liked/like the extended lead because the "history" I cited provided important context.

Three years ago, the Wisconsin State University-Eau Claire Jazz Band's audiences filled Schofield Auditorium each time the group played a concert. Their music had an appealing rhythm and a hand-clapping beat. And it was loud. Director Joe Casey liked his jazz loud; musicianship was secondary.

Last night the WSU-EC Jazz Ensembles appeared in the University Arena. Their crowds had grown too large for Schofield Auditorium, and about 1,000 persons took advantage of the move. Again, it was the music which attracted many who don't like "serious" music. But something else had happened in two years. And that was Dominic Spera -- a director who insists upon musicianship and gets it. The ensembles overcame the acoustics and tuning problems of the un-concert hall and hot, humid weather, producing their best concert to date.

The highest praise, I had come to learn, was "publishable." That did not mean perfect. I have no idea how I got away with turning in a handwritten movie review, a detail Les did not mention. Instead, he called it "a cool, analytical approach quite thorough in its treatment with many good points of detail that aren't always evident to everyone. I like it and believe it to be quite publishable." In my own teaching, it is only fair to point out, I don't think I ever accepted a handwritten newspaper story.

CHAPTER 8

City Girl

The summer that provided my first taste of urban life began with a couple weeks at home in West De Pere. My parents had bought the house across the street from my childhood home in 1968. Its owner, a widow who craved less space, had offered to trade, but for legal reasons money needed to change hands. For one dollar my family had upgraded to a four-bedroom (all small) house with room for a big garden and a lot that ran down to the Fox River. I shared the upstairs with my brother (no door between us), and what I most remember about my room is the alcove that held the writing desk I had "antiqued" while in high school. I remember typing assignments there when I was home on college breaks and writing letters to a pen pal serving in Vietnam. I saved hundreds of letters over the years, but none he wrote from Southeast Asia, which might have provided some additional context for my 180-degree change in stance on the war. Or perhaps they would have revealed the political me at odds with the personal me.

I also didn't save my work from my two semesters of Editing; I remained more committed to reporting and writing. And yet here I was, one of 60 college students selected from more than 200 applicants for the third Editing Intern Program supported by the Dow Jones Newspaper Fund. Credit Les Polk for preparing me and another WSU-EC major to join students from 47 other universities, most of them in the journalism school big leagues. Arriving at Eau Claire, Les had insisted that a classroom be equipped with a horseshoe-shaped copy desk like those used in professional newsrooms. He saw to it that the room had an Associated Press teletype machine that gave us access to "live" copy.

He required us to buy editing pencils, pica poles (printers' rulers; I still have mine), proportion wheels for "sizing" photos and rubber cement -- tools of the trade now long gone from newsrooms. One semester he taught us to edit copy, which included AP Style tests, current events tests, spelling tests (I still think *rumrum*, its backward spelling, when I write *murmur*) and all manner of exercises filled with "problems" to trip us up. We learned to always do the arithmetic to double check ages in obituaries because grieving families often get them wrong. We learned that if a story stated, for example, that "six people did thus and such," we must always count the names to make sure the numbers matched. We learned that "hard" and "difficult" do not mean the same thing, and to save "still" for writing about moonshine. On and on they went, the lessons on language and libel and context and readability -- and so much else. The following semester was more of the same, with page design and newspaper production added. He required us to work in teams to produce mock newspapers and defend our decisions on everything from story selection and placement to typefaces and head-line sizes. In other words, we practiced the skills used to make a daily newspaper, and he graded our work with the expectation that we were capable professionals.

Those classroom lessons, along with my Spectator experiences, are what I packed for my three weeks of pre-internship training. I had been assigned to the University of Nebraska-Lincoln, and I was both confident and intimidated when I arrived on the campus. Each "crash course" was designed to ensure its 15 participants were similarly pre-pared before we left for our newspapers. What I remember is: Nebraska is HOT in June. The university had more and bigger and fancier frater-nity/sorority houses than I ever had seen. Man-made lakes are glorified mud holes and not that great to swim in. After Lincoln, I was off to join the copy editors on "the rim" of the "telegraph desk" at The Milwau-kee Journal. My first order of business was to find housing. Five poems scribbled on yellow notebook paper make it clear that my city life got off to a shaky start. "A PERSONAL NARRATIVE in Poetic Form" car-ries the date 6-29-70, which was a Monday, so I must have written it after-the-fact. Here are excerpts, exactly as penned.

YWCA Take I

Feet tired—
Afternoon of 'home' searching
with no luck—
Mind discouraged—
(They said it would be easy) . . .

Solution— for the nite anyway—
is Astor Hotel ($9/per and 40¢ call)
Again,
Or, try to break the "Y" wall
Previous nite impregnable— glass partition—
"You need a reservation"
(Could it have been alcohol on breath
Or traveling companion?)
But Try Again— JOURNALISTIC CURIOSITY!

219— And that will be $6—
Lobby empty— and
God— I'm ALONE— cut off . . .

YWCA Take II

A struggle ensues—
luggage & elevator incompatible—
But human muscle overcomes—
Dim hallway— here's 219—
Key in
Turn— no luck—
(It's not my day)
Another struggle— Another win

It's not home— But . . .
a bed-desk-sink-
signs on john door—
And the CLUE
"No food or candy— Let's starve them out"
(cockroaches) . . .

Exhausted body in bed
to read a minute—
But the Newsweek is old

so sleep— to prepare for
Sunday— Oh God—

Tossing, turning— hair rollers
(Look like a lady— at least)
make sleep difficult

But restless mind is worse—
Cockroaches— YWCA— Milwaukee
what am I doing here—
I don't really think I
belong— And I almost
want to cry (And I don't
Cry much)
so— self revelation— I
ain't what I - - -
      And didn't I always
      know it . . .

YWCA Take III
      Sun— 10 a.m.
      Knock on door
      A maid— Door Opens
      ("Don' bother— I's jus'
      checkin' the room— You
      stayin' tonight")
      Instant decision—
      "Uh— Yes"
      Pessimism

      1 p.m. phone rings— friend arrives
      world is brighter—
      sun is shining—
      Lake breeze—
      (How does it feel to be a babysitter?)
      Then - - - -
      A series of coincidence
      And a "home" is in sight . . .

YWCA Take IV
    Goodby—
    Brownstone sanctuary
    for Young Christian Women.
    $18.15 for services rendered.

As a college student, I had not yet developed a taste for posh accommodations, and so was happy to rent an attic room and dogsit for a professor leaving town for several weeks. The house was on a bus line and a short walk from the University of Wisconsin-Milwaukee campus, which offered a library and beer in the student union. I made it all work -- until late in the summer when the dog ran away and I had no idea how I was going to break the news to his family. Lucky for me, he returned several days later, just before they did.

I quickly adapted to commuting to the Journal by bus, and it did not take me long to fit in on the desk, which processed wire-service copy. There were practical lessons, such as seeing my fellow "rim rats" (and they were, as I recall, all men) work with rolled-up sleeves, thus minimizing pencil and ink stains. There were lessons about the Journal's idiosyncratic style rules and shorthand ways of identifying headline styles. And there was a lesson I don't think I recognized or appreciated at the time: The few women in the newsroom had to be tougher and work harder than their male counterparts to even have a shot at advancing. The term "glass ceiling" had not yet been coined to refer to barriers to professional advancement for women and minorities, but journalism had one. At the Journal, I learned this by observing and listening. I thought the woman who sometimes sat in the slot, reading back copy and approving it, was harder on me than on the other editors. In hindsight, she was modeling success. It was the first time I had a female editor, and although she was no more demanding than Les, I often felt picked on. That was my problem, of course. Despite that, I know I worked hard to please her, and in doing so contributed to the quality newspaper we offered readers.

I got along well with the men around the rim, although one irritated me from the beginning, and near the end of my stay I committed him to a poem.

Stuart
is a scared sonofabitch.
He thinks you can't tell
because he is so sure of himself.
He has all the answers for you:
How the NEGRUS can't squawk,
they are a lot better off than they ever were;
How the revolution will never be,
'cause the revolutionaries can't see past their noses.
He can cite all the sources—
The bible, and stuart, and history.
Damn, but he's big on history.
And he speaks with such authority.

But he's damn scared,
the copy editor with glasses sliding down his nose,
White shirt, rolled-up right sleeve only
and pants with cuffs and a narrow belt.
He just doesn't understand,
and he never will,
Unless he learns to LISTEN.

My scrapbook includes four pages of clippings from my summer's work. I kept the "sampling," as I labeled it, in anticipation of job-hunting. I jotted a few comments, focused on the headlines, but the range of stories I edited also was represented. One page is devoted to "22 and 33 heads— the 'lighter' news with a 'bright,' attention getting head— the kind I found most difficult." One of the typographic styles common then was called a "hammerhead," which placed a couple of words in large type above a smaller main headline. For a story about a New York bar opening to women for the first time in its 116-year history and within a couple of hours having a male patron pour a beer on a "women's liberation" advocate, I wrote:

Liberated Zone
Women Can Belly Up to the Bar, Fight, Too!

For another story, about the use of Ms., I wrote:

Name Game
When Is a Miss or Mrs. a Ms.?

Other such stories had more traditional headline treatment, such as the one I wrote for a story about a banned rock-music festival in Connecticut:

Music Turned Off,
but Not the Crowd

I was surprised to find that early in my internship I had handled the story when Britain's Prince Charles and Princess Anne visited the United States. My scrapbook annotation: "their 1st visit to the U.S.— wire services were pumping out 100s of inches of copy— problem was to get some worth reading, then do an original head which hadn't been said in all the tons of preview copy." Newspapers sometimes used different colors of paper for the transmissions from different news services, and when piecing together a story from them (cut and paste with rubber cement) the result was what I called a rainbow. That is what I did for my 12-paragraph story. My headline:

Charles Tackles 898 Steps,
Anne 'Doesn't Give Interviews'

As a rule, stories were distributed to the next copy editor available, but the telegraph editor also had a good feel for matching stories to editors' interests and expertise. I worked on more than a few stories about women's liberation and my generation's culture. But if I was "up" and it was an Indochina or Middle East story, for example, the editor would send it my way. Among the stories I saved was one from the front-page of the States Edition of August 11. Its 60-point main headline:

Equal Rights for Women
Wins Approval of House
Amendment
Now Goes
To Senate

A couple of weeks later I had another top-of-Page-1 story:

Women Across US
Strike for Liberation
Some Battle,
Others Love
Man's World

I also saved two long Sunday feature stories I handled: "Student Activism Shifts to Politics" and "When Is Flag Waving Flag Tromping?" But the jaw-dropping find of my saved work was the story written by Leroy F. Aarons of The Washington Post about Bob Hope, with the headline "Hope's Political Conscience Forces Him to Speak Out." Jaw-dropping in 2021 because in 1989 I worked with "Roy" Aarons and a journalism instructor to analyze data from the first survey of gay and lesbian journalists in the United States. The study had been commissioned by the American Society of Newspaper Editors, and Roy presented our findings at the group's 1990 convention. Four months later he and six other journalists launched the National Lesbian and Gay Journalists Association.

Almost as surprising as that connection was finding the lengthy memo I wrote evaluating my internship. Amazingly absent from my narrative was any mention of the situation that confronted me before I set foot in the Journal building for the first time. I vaguely recalled crossing a picket line but could find nothing to support that -- until I turned up a Miami Herald story from Sunday, June 28. Headlined "Strike Slows Milwaukee Newspapers," it reported that 17 electricians had walked off the job the previous Thursday and set up picket lines around building. The story stated that several hundred employees from other unions chose not to cross them, but the evening Journal and morning Sentinel managed to publish abbreviated editions. When I arrived on Monday, feeling I had no choice but to go into the newsroom, I kept my head down and nervously tried to ignore the strikers.

What I did describe in my memo was how I found the summer profitable and exciting -- both as a journalistic experience and as a living experience. . . .

From working, listening and watching, I believe I have acquired much insight into the inner workings of the newspaper. I saw things I did not agree with, things I did not like. But for the most part the experience has made me even more idealistic about this field of communication we are involved with, has made me more vehemently believe in some of my own theories, has drastically altered others.

I described the newsroom as "a very pleasant place to work, the people good to learn from. Everyone was friendly, anxious [I should have written eager] to help, willing to take the time to answer questions and offer pointers." I also wrote that I "was most impressed with the fact that the 'pros' treated me as another rimman [Argh!], not just a summer intern. I felt respected as a professional, the same things were expected of me, and my opinions were listened to. . . . I soon felt most competent in my job. I didn't feel as if I was slowing down the copy flow. . . ." As an example, I noted that when I worked the later shift, "often the third edition banner would be a late breaking story that I was forced to handle. . . . I don't think anyone ever wished one of the more experienced desk men were there to do it." At the beginning of the summer, I added, "I had not expected that."

Although I was used to working under deadline, "the thing which had scared me most about the summer was the fear of not being able to keep up, to be forced into editing quickly and therefore not thoroughly." What I found was that I "enjoyed the general pace" at the Journal because "there was nearly always enough of us on the rim so that stories could be given the attention they deserved" and there was enough time "to write something other than the run of the mill dry head[line]." I also found that editing wire copy was more interesting than I expected. "I think it is just important to remember the guy on the other end of the teletype is an ordinary reporter, and his copy must be examined in the same light as that of local reporters." By summer's end, I had concluded that I could not have taken "very many hours of [locally written] zoo stories, rapes, robberies, murders and cute little features."

My concluding paragraph reminded me that while I had not committed to copy editing as a career, I wasn't ruling it out: "I found I like the work, it seems compatible with me, I feel competent. More than ever I believe the copy editor has a real contribution to make to any newspaper. And though I'm not convinced I would want to do it for the rest of my life, I don't think my editing days are over." The paragraph also confirmed that I already was planning for graduate school, where I thought "a part time editing job would be in line."

That summer of living in Milwaukee also afforded me a taste of being a working woman. I enjoyed a new kind of independence, especially on my days off. Among my memorable experiences were two concerts shared with Les, who was "freshening" his skills with a couple of weeks in the Journal newsroom. It was the third year of Summerfest, a cultural festival staged at a former missile base along Lake Michigan. I doubt I would have ventured there on my own, but eagerly agreed to join Les to hear Sarah Vaughan, the jazz singer. She was fantastic. The July 26 performance by Sly and the Family Stone, on the other hand, was frightening. The night was hot and sticky, and Les and I were crammed in among more than 100,000 others, most of us sitting on the ground. A fence in front of the stage was knocked down during the opening act, and the crowd grew increasingly restless waiting for the very late Sly et al. I remember fights breaking out all around us, which is when we decided to leave -- no easy undertaking. The next day's paper reported that the group was on stage for only 50 minutes. Amazingly, the "almost riot" resulted in only a few arrests for disorderly conduct and "pot."

CHAPTER 9

A New Consciousness

After Milwaukee, I had just a few days of R&R at home before my parents drove me to Eau Claire for my senior year. Ann Gavin, a friend from the "Jesus house," and I were sharing a second-floor apartment a few blocks from campus. In return for reduced rent, we had agreed to do chores for the elderly owner. It didn't take long for us to realize that she expected us to be at her beck and call -- and to be unreasonably quiet at all times. Somehow, we would make it to the end of the fall semester. Anne was an Eau Claire gal; reluctantly she moved home. I had to scramble to find a room in need of an occupant and would end up with strangers (and mice) for roommates and a mattress on the floor for a bed.

The first issue of The Spectator hit the campus on September 17. The paper had undergone a noticeable facelift. A brief story on Page 8 explained: ". . . if it seems a bit uneven, it's because the staff is getting used to new type styles, a new publishing method and a new printer. Things should settle down in a couple of weeks, typographically at least." We had fully entered the offset printing era, which, among other things, would make the paper available about noon each Thursday instead of late afternoon. New to the paper itself were a front-page index and the location of the editorial page (the back page). We had editors but advertised for staff members. The university's enrollment was predicted to be up about 350 students, topping out at 8,200. The lead story described overcrowding in the dorms, with more than 100 students forced to live in lounges. The other story promised an eventful semester of speakers, including cartoonist Al Capp, feminist Gloria Steinem, consumer advocate Ralph Nader and environmentalist Paul Ehrlich. Inside, the 20-page issue contained a plethora of campus news. Advertisements, such as these on facing pages, were indicative of the "forces" competing to define students.

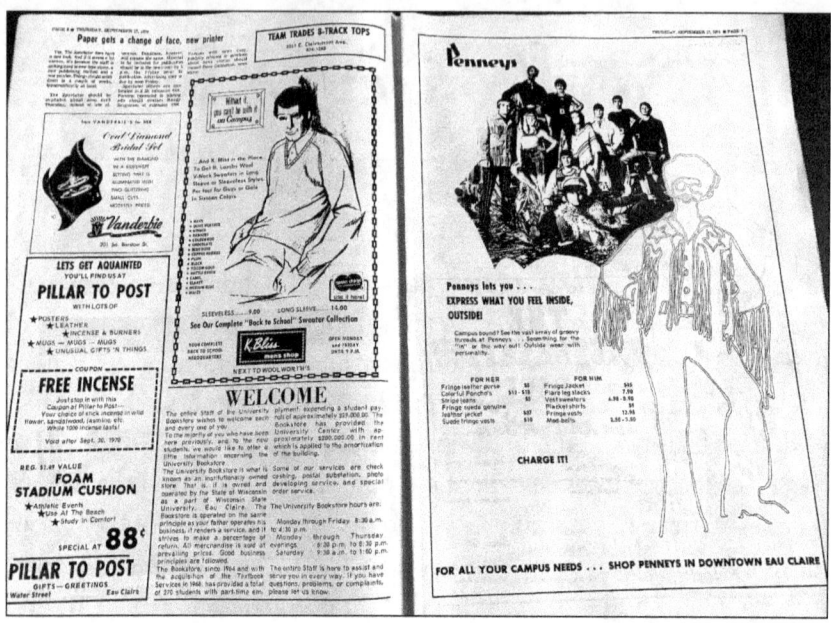

My lengthy editorial, headlined "'Cool' is today's necessity," expressed "a certain amount of apprehension" about the new school year. "Bomb scares two years ago were more or less a farce. Today, they are to be taken seriously. [The August 24 bombing of Sterling Hall at the University of Wisconsin, which killed one and injured three, was on the minds of most of the state.] A year ago repression was a word from the history books. Today, it is all too meaningful." Reminding readers that "last year, WSU-EC students showed a political activism almost foreign to the campus" and "demonstrated their concern in the ways they thought best," the editorial asked, "What now?" Believing that the Board of Regents and Legislature were "ready to jump at the slightest provocation," I wrote that "the wrong action at the wrong time could prove exceedingly harmful -- whatever the cause." Far from suggesting that we should not act, however, I argued that "positions must be cooly [sic] assessed from all angles; decisions reached only after all possible repercussions have been considered." The editorial then concluded, "At this time in our history, only the most thoughtfully considered protest will further the cause."

Looking back at the papers we produced during my second semester as editor, I see content that is more traditionally focused on campus news and events. I attribute this in large measure to the experiences many staff members had on their summer internships. Almost totally absent are stories of anti-war organizing and protests. A new weekly column, "Mastering the Draft," was authored by two young attorneys who directed the draft counseling center at New York University. But we also added a column called "Let's Live," written by a WSU-EC junior psychology major with an interest in health and organic foods. I no longer wrote "specks in my eye," but I did periodically contribute to its replacement. Called "pot boiler," it was fashioned after the Milwaukee Journal's "Accent on the News" column and featured staff members' observations and comments. In tone, it would be right at home in today's blogosphere. The first item published (September 24) came from my good friend and ace reporter/copy editor Laurel Mather.

> As the "hippie" phenomenon has reached epidemic proportions, the all-American businessman has profited from the whole scene. F.W. Woolworth here has joined these businessmen as they advertise "hippie wigs" on their sales shelves. Manager R.A. McNamara of the local store said the mangy looking things (that's my observation, not his) are being sold as Halloween costumes, although they've been on the shelves for a month now.

> McNamara said the store always puts seasonal things out early for shoppers, but he also said that other Halloween items just became available this week. Halloween costumes, you say?

> If, per chance, you buy and wear now, but trick or treat later, wear the wigs with few guilt feelings. Even GIs have donned hairier head-toppings to hide their real military haircuts.

> You might even start a new fad -- the weekend hippie syndrome. But then, what difference does it all make anyway? Some people feel that the real so-called "hippie" is just a costumed hunk of humanity anyway. Much adieu [sic] about nothing.

Considering that a couple of other staff-written columns appeared regularly, I think that fall we were as open to allowing staff members to spout off as we had been to letter writers doing so the previous spring.

By no means, however, did we shortchange serious news. For example, in a series that started with our second issue we detailed how the fees allocated by the Student Senate in May were being spent. I wrote the first story, about the campus art galleries, which operated solely with student funds. It was my only bylined story of the semester (indeed, it was the last of my Spectator career); it reminded me how far I had come from the freshman writing arts and entertainment briefs. There were plenty of numbers to explain the cuts necessitated by the $12,500 allocation (after a request of $20,740.94). There were details to show just how the art department-run galleries worked. And several "stakeholders" were quoted. The same can be said for the rest of the series, which delivered on its "kicker": Budgets in perspective.

I think I also delivered perspective in the 19 editorials I wrote that semester and the four I reprinted from other publications. As with our news coverage, my editorials were overwhelmingly campus-centered. Major events of the semester included release of a new calendar eliminating the "lame duck" weeks after Christmas; revisions to the general education requirements; the cancellation of Winter Carnival; the beginning of beer sales on campus; and the update of the rules governing women students. Other significant stories included the opening of a new Fine Arts Center; the beginning of construction on a library addition; and a plan to allow students to evaluate their professors. I presented the Spectator's position on many of these.

The new calendar emerged after the proposal for a 4-1-4 plan was nixed following almost a year of discussion. The paper had reported the story extensively and, on September 24, the day of yet another vote on 4-1-4, I wrote in favor of its approval. Honestly, parts of that editorial sound so much like faculty-leader-me decades later. I hoped that "each and every eligible faculty member would make every effort to attend this afternoon's meeting. A gallery of student observers would also be impressive." I hoped that when discussion ended, "Each faculty member will consider the weight of his [sic] vote -- not only what 4-1-4 will mean in terms of his workload, classroom hours or research time, but more importantly in terms of the students." Finally, I offered these thoughts:

> For 4-1-4, even with its shortcomings (and what system lacks them), seems to be the dynamic move that could be a real asset to this university -- would force a revamping of the general studies program so long in coming; would force a reevaluation of courses (necessary every so often, at least); would help pull the educational processes out of the dull doldrums they tend to fall into because of convention and tradition.

A week later, the top story on Page 1 reported that the faculty had voted its opposition to the proposal "at this time." The debate and the wrangling of the chaotic meeting described in that story sound like almost every faculty meeting I ever was a part of. My follow-up editorial argued that "students must act to keep 4-1-4 alive." Stating the obvious -- "We were disappointed by the outcome of the vote" -- I suggested it was time for students to assert themselves. "There are some 8,000 of us. Surely that must mean something." The editorial urged the Student Senate to "educate the student body on the 4-1-4 plan. Fact, not opinions are necessary. . . . Then, a petition must be circulated, and recirculated and recirculated until there are sufficient signatures to force the faculty to recognize the existence of student opinion on this campus -- be it for or against" the plan. As it turned out, 4-1-4 was dead. In early December the Faculty Senate voted for a proposed "experimental" calendar that ended the fall semester just before Christmas, followed by a three-week break before the spring semester. A couple of weeks later the Board of Regents accepted the proposal. And that was that.

Interestingly, despite my implied confidence in student leadership, a second editorial on October 1 asserted, "Student Senate President Bob Jauch and student senators should have their hands slapped. Jauch should be wary of overextending his powers, i.e. deciding a bill should not be introduced before the Senate." As for the senators, they should "be wary of wasting their time drafting legislation" already being worked on. "There is enough wasted energy in the senate." No doubt some senators thought that about The Spectator.

As I would come to learn in my own academic career (on five campuses), few curricular matters are more contentious than general education -- those courses or categories of courses required of all students, regardless of major. No sooner had 4-1-4 been dispatched with when the Faculty Senate scheduled a vote on a revised "gen ed" plan. As our lengthy October 8 story reported, although there was agreement on the need for changes, there was much debate over exactly what those changes should be. And this being academe, discussions had been ongoing at least since 1968 when an ad hoc committee was named to study the matter. My primary editorial that week expressed our support for the proposal. It would, I wrote, "require instructors who are imaginative, innovative and willing to experiment. The emphasis would be on breadth of experience with a de-emphasis on specialization." Speaking to those who argued there were not enough specifics in the proposal, "we would point to the fact that this is an all too familiar position." Referencing the faculty meeting that considered 4-1-4, I noted, "Departments seem unwilling to work on specifics until they are positive a proposal will be instituted, yet they say they cannot support a proposal because it is not specific enough." Once again advocating on behalf of student self-determination, I added, "To those who would argue that basic courses taught in their department are fundamental [for all students], we would say let the students decide. Give the student credit for having the intelligence and maturity to choose whether or not he needs history 1a or philosophy 50 in terms of his own particular future." Finally, to those advocating more study, we simply concluded that "now is the time for action."

A second, short editorial grew out of researching the forthcoming vote on the proposal. We wondered (1) if the parliamentarian should be a voting member or a "neutral" person; (2) if Faculty Senate members should vote "according to their own beliefs or according to the wishes of the department which they represent"; and (3) if 75 names (15 percent of the faculty) on a petition was "enough to warrant full faculty [re]consideration of Faculty Senate action." At one time or another over the years, I realize now, I asked similar questions. As it turned out, the general education debate was far from over, after the Senate voted on October 13 to send the proposal back to committee.

The committee was instructed to present the plan again on October 27 in "bite-size chunks" for further consideration. Finally, on December 1, the Senate passed a revision, detailed in The Spectator two days later.

Two social issues -- Winter Carnival and beer on campus -- were of special interest to students that fall. The Spectator had questioned the continued existence of Winter Carnival for some time, and we applauded its cancellation. "Three cheers for the Student Senate Social Commission! They finally had the guts, and the intelligence, to cancel Winter Carnival. There was little doubt, in our minds at least, that the event was an archaic one." We did not see the need for an "alternative activity," but hoped that "in the name of post-semester tensions and energy . . . serious thought is given to doing *something*." We previously had favored a "help" project -- community service, in today's terminology. We now added hope for a "big name" concert. "First, there is a need for exposure to good music on this campus. But more than that music is an essential part of our culture, indeed a focal point of expression. It can, and does, bring us together. And that, too, seems essential for a campus which grows more and more fragmented as it each year grows larger." Sounds downright prescient to me now!

When I began to page through the Spectators of my college years, I was transported back to a time when ads for bars and beers were commonplace in student newspapers -- at least in Wisconsin. The state's age for drinking beer was 18 (buying it off-site was 21), so college students were a ready-made audience. The notes I made as I read bear this out, and in late 1970 students were eager to have beer sold on campus. Eau Claire students had expressed their support at least three times: a referendum, a petition with 3,500 names and a survey. Our first issue of the fall included the news that the administration had submitted a plan for a pub to the Board of Regents. The plan included allowing students to decide the brands of beer to be served. Smile!

In the November 19 issue, our lead story announced that the Regents would consider campus requests for beer sales. The story also explained that Faculty Senate and Eau Claire City Council support were needed. Curiously, we did not offer an editorial opinion on the matter. We did report, on December 10, that the Faculty Senate had voted in support of "beer facilities" on campus. City Council approval came in mid-January. That merited a banner headline and story in our January 14, 1971, paper -- the last of my editorship. Again, however, no editorial.

Similarly -- and surprisingly -- I never wrote an editorial about the rules still in effect for women living in the dorms. Having arrived when "girls" living on campus were held to different standards than "guys," and having grown into advocating for change, I was particularly interested in how my papers covered the issue and others related to the burgeoning women's liberation movement. I also could not help but chuckle at the changing images presented in advertisements; my notes are peppered with references to them.

Discontent over the dorm regulations had been building for some time, and some women were "fired-up," as the lead on our November 5 story noted. "'We're sick and tired of these hours,'" said one young woman who came to rap [this verb was used a lot by reporters and headline writers] on women's standards and what could be done to change them." Another woman, "spunky . . . with fiery red hair, wearing blue jeans and a T-shirt had plenty to say." Twenty-two and married, with a son, she was living in a dorm until her January graduation. "Every weekend when my husband comes up, I have to sign a card saying I'm going to Howard Johnson's to stay with him," she told the group. A third dorm resident told of going to bed without returning her "out" card to the "in" box and being called to the front desk by the receptionist. She said that by the time she reached the lobby, she had been charged with five "late minutes." The unbylined story reporting on the gripes ended this way: "'We need support,' [one woman] said. And she wasn't talking about girdles." [An aside: Adjacent to this story was a Penney's ad, complete with illustration, to "Go natural. In our one-size bra and bikini set of soft Antron nylon/Lycra spandex. Just a little bit more than nothing at all in lots of pretty shades. One size fits 32-36, A, B, C; 32-40 hips. $5 set."]

A lengthy story (November 19) by News Editor David Gunderson attempted to explain the muddled situation surrounding potential changes to the standards. The headline: "Women's standards raise 'power' question." As the Student Senate president put it, "There are too many fingers in the bowl . . . and no real work gets done." As the dean of women put it, women had separate standards because "women have felt they want to establish the standards they'll live by." Further, the story paraphrased her thinking on this form of in loco parentis. She told GunR that having someone looking out for them continues for women later in life when they depend on their husbands. Some women, she added, like sign-out, sign-in procedures in the dormitories so they can be reached in emergencies. And parents also want someone to "keep tabs" on their daughters, she said. Oh my! [An aside: Under that story is a Sears ad for a "Perma-Prest bra, cut low in front. Perfect for holiday fashions. 32-38 A, B, C. Regularly $4; Thursday night special $2.99]

The editorial page of that Spectator expressed what some of us in the newsroom were thinking, but not via an editorial. A contrary opinion appeared under the headline "AWS shouldn't play politics," with the kicker "Comments of others" and the credit "Hints from Heloise, ASG newsletter, October 22, 1970." I cannot explain what was going on with that. I can only speculate that we found the argument compelling.

> ... In pre-liberation days women zealously [were] taught to identify as women, not students, citizens or humans. ... But today the prospects are encouraging. Women are redefining their roles in society and beginning to perceive that student power and people power are sexless. A student government that cannot speak for all students on issues like hours, visitation and judicial structure is not worthy of the title. ... The time is right to enlist the support of women students in the struggle to build an effective student voice.

Elimination of sign out/in and women's hours would not come until the spring semester. Coincidentally, the April 15, 1971, Spectator issue reporting the president's approval of the changes included a story on the opening of the University Pub.

When reviewing fall-semester papers, I zeroed in on other stories about the status of women, and many issues of The Spectator contained them. For example, the Physical Education Department had been trying for nine years to get a major for women, and in mid-October 1970 we reported its approval was "likely." A couple of weeks later, there was a story with this lead:

> The girls were dressed casually -- in jeans and faded workshirts. Some wore sweaters and tie-dyed t-shirts. Faces were free of makeup, bossoms [sic] were free of bras. They were meeting to talk about the women's liberation movement and whether it could find a place on the Eau Claire campus.

And then there was this sentence with its unenlightened attribution: "'I think we can do away with the stereotype of the liberated woman as an ugly, sexually-frustrated old maid,' a pretty sophomore said."

In early December, Kathryn Clarenbach, a specialist in women's education at UW-Madison, spoke on campus. Reading our story, I could not help but be reminded of how language and journalistic conventions contradicted the feminist messages being reported. Dr. Clarenbach was described as a former chair**man** (emphasis added) of the National Organization for Women. The story, in its second paragraph and apropos to nothing, noted that she was "married and the mother of three children." She portrayed herself as "of the branch of the movement which is not man-eating and [I] believe that men and women must make changes in society's attitudes together." She might have been a moderate, but I suspect more than a few audience members squirmed as she criticized American higher education for, as the story stated, pushing "women into prepackaged roles" and discriminating against them in college admissions policies. [An aside: Running next to the story was an ad for engagement rings, illustrated by a line drawing of a couple looking appropriately smitten.]

The Clarenbach story appeared on Page 15; the "double-truck" that followed had full-page ads from Penney's that serve as a stark reminder of the times. On Page 16, an illustration of a young white man in shirt and tie, hair neat, short sideburns, holding an armful of shirts and a sweater. "Instant gifts, pre-boxed. All you add is the card." He is positioned to face Page 17, with its trio of young white women, one in a "lace-banded sleepgown" and two in robes. "Ideas. Match up these gifts with the ladies on your list." These and so many similar ads make the one at the bottom of Page 25 that much more jolting.

Center Concert Hall. | John Berryman, 8 p.m., Davies Theater. | "We are essentially law clerks for Greenberg. We get the Facts, | danger rather than alleviating one."

Also jolting was an ad for "Abortion Counseling, Information and Referral Services" that caught my eye -- 50 years after it appeared in our October 29 issue and before the U.S. Supreme Court struck down Roe v. Wade in 2022. The display ad, from The Abortion Information Agency in New York City, explained that abortions up to 24 weeks of pregnancy were now legal in New York state. There were no residency restrictions; "only the consent of the patient and the performing physician is required." The ad advised: "If you think you are pregnant, consult your doctor. Don't delay. Early abortions are simpler and safer." It offered "immediate registration into available hospitals and clinics." A front-page story on December 17 reported on the legal question raised by the ad, published in a few student papers. An assistant state attorney general had issued an informal opinion that the ads were "clearly in violation of Wisconsin law." Our story explained that The Spectator stopped accepting the ad "after receiving a letter" with that opinion. The editor of the paper at WSU-River Falls, however pledged to continue using the ads if they were submitted for publication. The university president threatened to shut down the paper if that occurred. The Board of Regents reaffirmed its decision from August that stated the president is, in effect, publisher of a campus paper and thus has final say over news and advertising content. The editor, "Mrs. Judy

Heise," explained that "my reasons for accepting these ads stem in part from deep personal beliefs that abortions and contraceptives should be available to those who seek them, regardless of marital status." She also described the ads as "a public service."

Christmas vacation followed this news, and when we next published (January 7, 1971) I relied on reprinting excerpts from an editorial in the nearby Chippewa [Falls] Herald-Telegram to offer an opinion on the matter. Under our headline, "The Regents goof," that paper suggested that "a great deal more is at stake than the seemingly simple publication of a couple of advertisements." The editorial continued:

> At a time when we are saying that students must learn to take on responsibility, by the Regents' order the president at River Falls is saying that the students should not have the responsibility of running their own publication. [He] is also telling the newspaper what it can and cannot print, which gives him censorship over anyone's ideas -- and does not require that he stop at merely censoring advertisements.
>
> This is an intolerable situation anywhere in American society. It also does not allow the students to learn by making decisions, and then, if they are wrong, being called to account for them.

I want to believe that choosing to use a professional's words rather than mine felt as if it would have a greater impact. Certainly that last paragraph expressed my personal philosophy of free expression and personal accountability. In hindsight, I also know how lucky I was to edit a student newspaper on a campus with a president who was even-tempered, even-handed and extremely tolerant of young journalists.

A week later, my final editorial suggested, nonetheless, that optimistic/idealistic me was weary and had grown more than a bit pessimistic. I ended my Spectator editorship by sharing "some personal thoughts -- about the paper, what it is and is trying to be."

> We have tried very hard in the last year to do a number of things, not the least of which was offering you something you would want to read, would find worth reading. I think, occasionally, we succeeded.
>
> The names of some of our regulars . . . are more familiar to you, I am sure, than the names of the editors. They are to be commended for their work which, though many times made us cringe at the thought

of reader reaction, almost always provided food for thought. It was their controversial topics, their comments, their observations, that consistently brought a pile of letters to my desk.

The backbone of the paper, however, is in its reporting staff -- small but for the most part dedicated. They are the ones who weekly churn out accounts of campus politics and politicking, academics and weekly activities, the everyday happenings and issues which involve this university and you. These reporters don't always (if ever) get the glory, but without their work we could not be much of a newspaper.

The editors, who have spent much of their college career, especially their Monday evenings and early Tuesday mornings in the basement of Schofield, put it all together. They consistently take fragments and make a whole.

Editorially, it has been a rather slow semester. Some may criticize the paper for being editorially weak. But a tempered-by-experience belief that editorials change no minds, have little, if any, effect, has been supported by the fact that no one has criticized.

Still, when necessary, we have taken a stand, have publicly announced our opinions about an issue. Sometimes we were cutting, once in a while just congratulating or saying thanks. We tried always to act in the students' best interests. . . .

Several times I chose to reprint editorials from other papers -- professional and collegiate. An attempt at cross-fertilization of minds, of thoughts. A chance to see how others are thinking, are reacting, to identical or similar situations. A chance to view our own ideas from a different perspective.

For the same reason, I chose to continue a liberal policy of publishing letters to the editor. A paper has an obligation, I think, to be a forum for opinion exchange by its readership. And for that reason almost every letter coming into this office was (between five and seven a week) printed (generally, as received).

I have seen The Spectator in the last 3½ years become a more student-oriented, news oriented, issue oriented paper. The dream that has kept a lot of us going is that we could continue to improve in this direction. Now the Board of Regents has passed a resolution saying [we] are not a student paper but a Regent (through the president) controlled press. The future is hazy. And a controversy, such as the one which arose around a cartoon last spring, could mean the end of the paper. That cannot be. Communication is essential. But then, freedom of the press must be more than a sentence from the Constitution.

Power to the people.

My signature, a neat BFL by which the campus knew me, appeared one last time above my full name and title. A week later I received a congratulatory letter "on a splendid year" from Johannes Dahle, the director of Student Activities and University Programs. I had known him since my arts and entertainment days when he was a primary source on my beat. By my senior year, we never passed in a hallway without chatting. To this day, his words touch my heart.

> During the past several years The Spectator has evidenced a growing maturity which climaxed this year in the finest campus newspaper I have ever seen. We both know that keeping a balance between all of the forces on a campus is a difficult or perhaps impossible task. You have done admirably in this regard. Personally, I have enjoyed our relationship very much and expect that it will be some time before a similar one will exist between this office and The Spectator.

Without a doubt The Spectator had kept me busy. The December 10 paper was the largest in history. As we noted on Page 1, "[T]he 32 pages you'll read this week don't just nudge out the old records. It's a total wipeout. The record was 20 pages. And there have been very few of them. Until this year, that is. [This fall] started off with a 20 page paper -- unheard of for the first week of classes, when understaffed staffs try for a paper closer to four or eight pages." Further, we crowed, The Spectator had published 228 pages during the fall semester and "this issue marks a total of 244 pages" with three issues remaining.

In addition to my newspaper responsibilities, I carried 17.5 credits that semester (the half-credit for "Beginning Golf"). Included were "Shakespeare" for my minor and "Depth Reporting" with the ever demanding Les Polk. I did not neglect my studies. I earned my second-best GPA -- a 3.65; my best (by 0.02) came in my final semester (19 credits, including bowling), when a C in gen-ed Biology marred an otherwise perfect grade report.

"Depth Reporting" was an advanced reporting course just a bit ahead of its time in introducing us to techniques of the nascent New Journalism movement and investigative reporting as it emerged a few years later. I don't have the syllabus, but Les' aspirations for us are clear in the handout describing our final stories. By then, he expected that we would "demonstrate your journalistic abilities operating at their top level." His goal was "stories as near to publication standards as possible, with some of them ready for publication." For the grade conscious, he wrote "that will be readily satisfied by adhering to such standards." In short, he challenged us to "s t r e t c h your minds and talents." It took me awhile, but in my own teaching career I found publication-ready to be the most meaningful "grade." And, as Les had done, I wore "hard-ass professor" as a badge of honor.

A paragraph of that handout was devoted to the importance of "wide reading, varied reading to test your formula against that of the professional." The examples of "good Depth" he provided were numerous. He reminded us of the range of publications in his own library, and that reminded me of where I had acquired my own penchant for subscriptions and regular visits to the library reading room. I was not the only student to read from his list: Wall Street Journal, Harper's, Atlantic, Minneapolis Tribune, Milwaukee Journal, Minneapolis Star, New York [magazine], New Leader, Horizon, Atlas, Evergreen, Scanlan's, Chicago J Review, Columbia J Review. I clipped. I saved. I filed (and eventually hired a high school student to organize my piles of folders). I lugged those folders around the country for decades -- using some in my teaching and others in my research -- until finally tossing most in 2020. The first sentence of one saved story, from The Village Voice, still periodically pops into my mind: "I saw am seeing a girl murdered today."

Beyond reporting techniques and learning to "analyze coolly and critically," there was something else about "Depth Reporting" that inspired us. We were hungry to believe, as Les suggested, that "writing can be of some social value, can spark or ignite change." That it could, perhaps, "be read by 'the' citizen who'll take the ball and run with it and effect change." We, like Les, were "NOT satisfied with this world." We, too, hoped our work "can and does occasionally . . . perhaps stimulate thought and (who knows) even change somehow, as values and institutions are reexamined."

My first major story examined the United Nations Atomic Energy Commission, and Les ripped apart my 1,900-word effort with a single-spaced, full-page critique. That stung. I had the information, he observed, but "so much that I fear you lose me and any reader in it." This was followed by: "I'm a bit surprised, after a summer of editing, that your copy comes out so formal, so legalese, so governmentese, so dull and dry." And not very well edited, judging by *his* edits. Ouch! What he wanted, he wrote, was "a good, sharp, readable story . . . something that points out to me the value of this thing I've never heard of before. I want something that reaches me and this doesn't very well." He also offered me a personal challenge:

> [H]ere's your major problem right now and one you've had for some time, I fear. STYLE. Experiment with it a bit; have fun with it; joke with it; play with it; let me be the butt of seeing how bfl can do DIFFERENT things. One odd thing about good students -- they have a helluva time getting away from turgid prose cause somewhere some teacher told them this is how educated people wrote and thought. Uh uh. The educated KNOW it in their heads and don't have to prove it to 'teacher.' Or to their audience.

Again, his advice would find its way into my classrooms as I sought to encourage students to do better.

Rewrites not only were allowed but were expected, because in the real world stories seldom came off the typewriter ready for the printed page. Here is my original first paragraph and its rewrite, by way of example.

> While the possibility for all-out nuclear war hangs over the world like the Sword of Damocles, the United Nations agency charged with international control and development of the atom continues to be stymied by world politics. Indeed, its future effectiveness may rest on how it handles its most recent political situation.

—

In Hiroshima's Peace Park, on the spot where the first atomic bomb fell, an arch with the words "Rest in Peace, the Mistake Will Not Be Repeated" stands -- a monument to the desires for world peace. Another monument to the hopes for world peace is the United Nations. And from its beginning, fear of all-out nuclear war has led the world organization to work toward both nuclear disarmament and peaceful use of the atom.

My end-of-course project on national health insurance stuck with me over the decades. The main story and its sidebar reflected reporting in depth, for sure. Its drafts demonstrated my efforts to humanize my storytelling. Its last paragraph provided me an example I used in my own classrooms time and again -- about how history sometimes proves us to be very wrong. I optimistically had written:

> Whatever the case, it appears that former HEW secretary and Medicare architect Wilbur Cohen was correct when he said of national health insurance: "It's going to come. It may take two, five or even 10 years, but it's coming, and coming a lot quicker than most people realize."

My trip home for the Christmas break inspired the story I submitted just before final exams. Slugged "a new consciousness," it was a last attempt at showing Les I could "play" with my style as I reflected on Charles Reich's new book, "The Greening of America." Atop the story are several lines of a Bob Dylan song, beginning "If dogs run free/why not me. . . ." My extended lead connected the dots:

> When I climbed the steps of the bus that sunny Sunday morning and handed the ticket to the driver, I had only one thought on my mind -- to try to forget the long ride ahead which would take me home for a Christmas holiday. And a holiday it was to be. School would not exist. Nor required reading. Nor heavy thoughts.
>
> But then, somewhere between Cadott and Boyd (two of the one-minute seemingly unending milk run stops the bus was to make) that damn dog ran in front of the bus. And those lyrics from Bob Dylan ran through my mind. They were to haunt me for the next 15 days.
>
> I had with me the September 26 issue of the New Yorker, which contained a good portion [of Reich's new book]. . . . I had a vague

idea of what it was about, and I thought the Yale law professor might serve to reinforce some of the opinions I was sure to have to defend while home. I was wrong.

Because stretched out in my seat (for the first time in a couple of dozen such trips sharing it only with myself) I was challenged. Reich's theory of revolution fascinated me, and for some unknown reason Reich and Dylan made me wonder . . . would the folks at home buy this. . . .

As mile after mile of woods and fields and farms and an occasional small town rolled by at 50 miles an hour, doubt creeped into my mind. I wondered whether Reich's revolution was, or could be, spreading as fast as he implied. Did it, in the form he presented, even really exist? And if it did, does it permeat [sic] the entire younger generation or only select portions of it?

So it was that I found myself in search of revolution, beginning at the Green Bay bus depot. I described my reporting this way: "It was to be silent (much listening and subtle control of conversations). It was to be anonymous. The quest for information was on, but only I was to know it."

[An aside: Well after I had drafted my paragraphs about that Depth Reporting course I was stunned to find a big envelope from Les with a note dated June 25, 1986. That unexpected gift was his copies of the three stories cited above. He was sorting his old course files and had decided that "the teacher who continued to hang on to these papers was a bit daffy. It was 'sentiment,' pure and simple, I guess, but what a class. Anyway, here's some of your work for your review and your OWN files." I was particularly interested in the "consciousness" story because appended to it were my post-writing comments and a page of critique from a classmate (and fellow Spectator editor), who jotted his name and "St. Barbara" in the upper left column. **Appendix A**]

As different as my approach in "new consciousness" might have been, it was a piece of traditional journalism that thrilled me while on break. Ever since I had written about the "underground military press" for an assignment in "Minority Press" in the fall of 1969, I had been trying to get the story published. I was ecstatic when The Washington Post bought an excerpt, which appeared in the Outlook section two days after Christmas. I had made the big time; under the headline "GI Underground Press a Stubborn Bloom" was *my* byline! A check for $75 followed. I never did get the magazine-length article published, but because I tried I do have rejection slips from Playboy, the Evergreen Review, Saturday Review, The New York Times, Newsday and The Atlantic Monthly.

Spring 1971

During my book research, I stumbled on a journal entry, written several months after my graduation, that included this: "... even in the last months of the Spec[tator], tho not happy, it was still a 40 hr a week job -- and I'm really happiest when I'm busiest...." I had not remembered that unhappiness. I always have recalled my undergraduate years -- and my Spectator experiences in particular -- as among the best of my life. Reviewing the fall 1971 newspapers, I did notice a number of "house ads" seeking staff, which suggests our record number of pages was even more amazing. I mentioned in a "potboiler entry" that I was responsible for typing the weekly "official notices" -- a mundane, tedious task at best and not one *the* editor should have been saddled with. The prospect of losing our funding or independence lurked in the background. There also was my heavy course load. Not to mention run-of-the-mill "senioritis" and uncertainty about what might follow graduation. No wonder I was tired as the spring semester got under way. And yet, if grades are to be believed, it was a successful semester.

I know that I continued to hang around The Spectator office and to hang out with my newspaper friends, but I seem to have completely cut ties to the paper itself. At Les' urging, I was giving serious thought to graduate school. I already had sent a transcript to Ohio University in Athens, chosen for its journalism program and location near relatives. A "potboiler" nugget that I wrote in December hinted at another reason for considering graduate school: "The economy is tight. The unemployment rate keeps going up. The job market gets tighter and tighter, and for many ... things don't look as rosy as they did four years ago."

The volume of written work I have from my courses that spring suggests I was concentrating on academics. I had just one journalism class, the required "Press and Society." What really allowed me to spread my intellectual wings were: "American Novel," a semester of challenging reading; "Modern Near East history," which enlarged my world view; and "Urban Problems and Politics," taught by a young instructor who allowed us to grade ourselves. But most significantly, it was an Independent Study project supervised by Les that shaped one of my career-long research interests. [An aside: That young instructor's grading policy no doubt was one reason her contract was not renewed. She also was quite comfortable hanging out with students, including me and a male journalism student, in the bars on Water Street. Eventually he and I would drive her home to North Carolina, then road-trip up the East Coast and across Canada. It was on that trip that I first visited Ogunquit, Maine -- a town that came to mean the world to me.]

I took as many of Dr. Alan Jackson's English courses as possible. Now I see sexism in his handout listing "some American novelists of the Twentieth Century" (73 authors, just eight of them women); then I saw only a lot of authors and titles I wanted to read. [An aside. One of the women was Edith Wharton for "Age of Innocence." I have twice toured her home and gardens, each time buying that book and then never managing to get very far into it. Sigh.] I remain thankful to Dr. Jackson for introducing me to Thomas Wolfe, via "Look Homeward, Angel" (I have toured his home, too), and for encouraging me to read Bernard Malamud's "A New Life." About the latter, I wrote a paper arguing that he presented "a stereotyped picture of higher education." Amazing how being a student for four years made me an expert on the topic. Finally, I am thankful to Dr. Jackson for introducing me to the professorial shorthand PSM (Please See Me), which I borrowed when I began to grade papers.

My term paper for the history course was another reminder of how the women's movement had infused my thinking about the world around me. (A cherished memory from the spring was hearing Gloria Steinem and Florynce Kennedy at a University Forum.) And the comment with which I closed that paper, titled "The Emancipation of the Middle Eastern Woman," reflected how I was thinking about my own world: "[W]hile the crusade now centers on freeing women from certain traditional restrictions, ultimate success seems to also demand it move toward freeing women _for_ all opportunities."

For my "Urban Politics" project, I wanted to apply some of the political theory I had been studying to my own field. The result was a 29-page, 102-footnote exploration of the idea of a self-managing/employee-owned newspaper. My thesis was that "self-management of a newspaper (and of the press) is unlikely unless there are major conceptual changes about the nature of the press." By examining the newspaper as a place of work and focusing on the structure of decision-making, I was able to weave together what I had learned in my journalism courses, unconventional organizations such as France's Le Monde, and current events such as the underground press of the 1960s. Today, such an undertaking would feel at home in meeting a capstone requirement.

If I had not worn out a typewriter ribbon producing those projects, I surely finished it off with my Independent Study: "An Examination of 'Militancy' in Selected American Indian Tribal Newspapers." Again, such a project today would easily pass capstone muster, and I have read shorter, less well-researched master's theses. Not only did this project demonstrate how work done for one course (in this case "Minority Press") could be narrowed and mined to provide a deeper understanding of a topic, it also showed me the value of telling untold stories. I did not know it then, but the foundational bricks of me as a serious scholar had been laid. My work required not just reading and synthesizing, but also coding for my first stab at content analysis and creating simple tables to detail my findings. I did not know it then, but the roots of my master's degree work had taken hold.

For long forgotten reasons, graduate school at Ohio University was no longer an option by my graduation on May 29. Taped inside the program I saved is a newspaper clipping that mentions I would be doing graduate work at the University of Oregon. Financial considerations, along with encouragement from Les, who had earned his bachelor's degree from Oregon, sent me west. I got through Eau Claire without debt thanks to a small insurance settlement from an automobile accident, scholarships and Spectator stipends, but I had meager savings. At the time, Oregon charged in- and out-of-state graduate students the same tuition and fees. I figured I could find a way to scrape by there.

CHAPTER 10

Go West, Young Woman

Like other rites of passage that in the moment seemed unforgettable, my college graduation faded quickly from memory. All that remain today are the program, three photographs and the gift from my parents. The program allows me to write that the ceremony -- the university's 55th -- was held in the University Arena beginning at 9:45 a.m. That means we commenced and concluded our undergraduate years at the same spot. We had listened to many influential people speak in that arena; our graduation speaker was not among them. I wonder if any of us remembers even one thing the president of the University of Wisconsin said in his address, oddly titled "Don't Die on Third." Bachelor of Arts recipients included me and 16 other journalism majors. The photographs show me that the weather cooperated because the reception was on the lawn in front of Schofield Hall, in whose basement I had spent *so* many hours. The fuzzy photos are of me in my gown, me with my parents and me with Les. My parents credited him with helping them choose a special book for me -- "The Complete Poems and Plays, 1909-1950" of T.S. Eliot -- to mark the occasion. It has always merited a treasured spot on my shelves, even though I have yet to read much of it. I think I shall remedy that when I finish this book.

My summer plans did not include a job. They did include winding down with a road trip before returning to West De Pere. In the late spring, I had used my Newspaper Fund money to buy my first car: a used Toyota Corolla. Back then, Toyota was a "foreign" car and there were few options for servicing them (a detail that would become quite significant for me). It was red, and its standard transmission was connected to a long stick shift on the floor. I could not drive it when I bought it, but thanks to lessons from a very patient GunR, I learned. It was with supreme confidence in that newly acquired skill that one night over beers, my friend Ed and I volunteered to drive my newly unemployed political science instructor home to tiny Mount Olive, North Carolina.

That trip set the tone for my summer. I anticipated graduate school would be rigorous and demanding, and I hoped to recharge in preparation. It never occurred to me that starting with a 1,200-mile, follow-the-U-Haul drive would be its own kind of rigorous and demanding. I wish I had made notes and known enough to write a travel story about our trip. Or at least a cautionary tale about driving so long that flinging French fries at one another during a rest stop made perfect sense. Eventually we made it to Mount Olive, toasted the sunrise with a couple of fingers of Scotch while sitting in rockers on the porch, and then collapsed into deep sleep.

From Mount Olive, Ed and I headed back to Wisconsin the indirect way: up the East Coast to Canada, then west across Quebec and Ontario. Another 2,300 or so miles. Another missed opportunity to sell a travel tale or two. I could have written about the Mt. Olive Pickle Co. (I still love their Old Fashioned Sweet Bread and Butter Chips). I could have written about seeing the expansion-team version of the Washington Senators play during their last season at RFK Stadium. I could have written about how it was unwise to drive a car with no license plates (the bill of sale and other paperwork were in the glove box!). The Highway Patrol officer in Pennsylvania was more understanding than the small-town Maine policeman who detained us for a couple of hours and gave us a scare. (Les had handwritten two pages of "musts" for that town, Ogunquit, but I think in our eagerness to get away we skipped most. And from that day on, Ed tucked his '70s long hair under a hat.) I also could have written about managing to buy beer in a French-speaking market outside Montreal, then trying to pitch a tent after drinking that beer.

Once I was back with my family, re-entry had its uneasy moments. Four years of an increasingly independent life and liberalism, along with my stubbornness, made things uncomfortable. My activism -- especially since the post-Kent State strike, moratorium and teach-ins -- was at the root "of all the static," I once wrote. Overhearing my parents wonder "why is she doing these things" had added to my resentment. No wonder I often felt out of place. I missed my Spectator friends. I missed the stimulation of the classroom. I missed working with Les. Lacking written evidence, I will guess that I spent a lot of time reading and sleeping. I probably played some golf. I no doubt made lists of what I would need for Oregon. For sure I worried my parents with my determination to drive the 2,200 miles to Eugene. Eventually it was arranged that my slightly younger cousin Mike would drive with me, and I would pay for his flight home.

Because the U of O was on the trimester system, classes did not begin until late September. Of another road trip worthy of a travel story or two, I remember only an overnight in Bozeman, Montana; a short stop up the interstate in Missoula to visit my Governors Hall head resident; and some sort of car trouble. For two Midwestern kids, Bozeman felt like a real western town, the perfect spot to enjoy a beer or two in a "cowboy bar." That we did; I remember the building being narrow, long and dark with sawdust covering the floor. We got a room at the Hotel Bozeman, which the Bozeman Chronicle had described as "the most elaborate, complete and comfortable caravansary . . . in the state" when it opened in 1890. It was considerably less than that in 1971 (and by the middle of that decade it no longer was operated as a hotel), but it was a place to sleep. Fitfully. Especially when, after the bars closed, a drunk cowboy burst into our room and insisted it was his. We managed to convince him otherwise, but for the rest of the night propped a chair under the doorknob, as we had seen done in the movies. After another 860 miles, we arrived in Eugene on September 21.

bfl
9/24/71

OBSERVATIONS – DAY 1

Dogs run free
on the U of O campus
while zillions of 10-speed bikes
weave in and out
of people and cars.

Somewhere, someone draws a crowd
by making music

with a 6-string guitar, or flute,
or home-made dulcimer.

Craftsmen peddle their wares
(even organic apple juice)
and activists hawk their propaganda.

Tennis courts are full
of bodies in regulation white
using the newest in aluminum rackets. [sic]

Freaks play frisbee.
But few eat in the cafeteria
(unless they are new).

The sun shines,
so people soak up energy,
storing it for the rainy days ahead.

I have not met any Jesus people.
And I have not yet stumbled barefoot
through dog shit.

Among my artifacts were years of meticulously kept calendars, beginning with 1971. Thus I know that I took cousin Mike to the airport at 10 a.m. on Wednesday, September 22. The next day, at 12:30, I registered for my first graduate courses: "Magazine Editing," "History of Journalism," "Theory of Mass Communication" and "Community Politics." Choosing political science for my required secondary area of study proved fortuitous. The department was experimenting with five-credit courses, so I needed only three for my degree. I had chosen to live in the graduate dorm because that seemed easiest to arrange from a distance. Morton-Earle also proved fortuitous, especially because of its proximity (vital in such a rainy environment) to the student union, dining hall, journalism classrooms, tennis courts, and track and field complex (where I watched the legendary Steve Prefontaine race).

My assessment of my graduate school months (I finished my degree in nine, astonishing just about everyone) is that they were much more about personal growth than the advanced journalism education I expected. The journal entries I wrote almost every day starting on Halloween, along with pages and pages of letters I received, led me to that conclusion. Because I write knowing how the rest of my life has gone, I can connect important dots about my life and work habits -- and habits of mind. Some of my experiences are history lessons. Others are as relevant to ambitious young women today as then. That is the framework I am applying to this chapter. My "talking points" are personal expectations, handling change, managing stress, self-identity and achieving goals. Embedded along the way are periodic thoughts about journalism education, journalism and journalists.

When I started that journal, I had been in school a month and I was not happy. Yet again typing in all lower case and using ellipses for a stream-of-conscience, punctuation-and-typos-be-damned style, I wrote:

> i think im mostly frustrated. intellectually, i feel stagnant . . . certainly not challenged . . . the things i wanted most out of grad school . . . perhaps it is my fault . . . i know i have little to do and even with the 15 credits i have im not putting out 100 per cent . . . but there is no motivation . . . no les to please???"

What I expected were demanding courses. What I felt I was getting were more undergraduate-level demands.

> ive been going to class and doing all the reading . . . but something is lacking . . . the gears are still going . . . ive done much outside reading and would do even more if I had the money to buy the books and such . . . but I feel like im marking time . . .

I hungered for "something intellectual, or at least challenging my ways and beliefs etc, if ive got any . . . how else can I grow. . ."

In a three-page, single-spaced letter from mid-October, Les wrote: "Know you're a bit bored. You are taking 'classes' and not enjoying them. Getting this degree is a union card thing and a credential and something to get through. . . ." He advised me to "find a good course or two somewhere." I recognized the quality of my undergraduate degree; Les acknowledged the quality of my work. "I don't mean to flatter or BS you but I believe you were doing graduate level work in several areas before you ever graduated and that's just a fact of life." He urged me to "remember you have something to 'teach' there, too, so don't be in a personality shell and let out some of the info you have, some of the stuff you already have. . . . Don't be a shrinking violet, by any means. You've got too much to offer them." Because he knew me so well, another time he offered just the right words to calm me: "Keep . . . exploring in the idea world -- and you'll be OK."

The connection I had with Les predated the now-popular notion of mentoring, which is why I have not used the term. Over the decades he -- and his family -- came to mean so much more to me (the person and the journalist). By the time I was in Eugene, the richness of that connection was important, as Les wrote in the middle of what he called a "stream of consciousness" letter.

> . . . Where are you? Somehow, Barb, it's been difficult to say. You are here, in my mind, as friend, companion, helper, worker, friend, friend, friend, and someone unforgettable. I think it's a rather unique thing, our thing. [*What's up with this, editing teacher? There are no degrees of uniqueness.*] I've felt there was a rather mature young woman here -- one I could talk with, share much with, and didn't HAVE to say everything to sometimes. Just let it be -- let it be. I was pleased when you took the time to see my family before leaving here; when you sent a card to them, too. That meant something. I hope you will always be a part of our lives, somehow, in whatever way it works out. . . .

And then he gave me my marching orders by reminding me that "when you run out of work there's a critical [writing] book to be done. There's Minnie [Minority Press] who always wants attention."

Confoundingly, at the same time I fretted over not feeling challenged I also fretted about grades. Graduate-school rules required at least a C for a course to "count" and a minimum 3.0 GPA for continued study. In my first journal entry, I was anxious about a history exam that would be returned the next day, when I also would take a theory exam. I earned a B for the history exam "and my thots of flunking out (slim and airy as they might have been) have dissipated." I described the theory test as a

> whopper . . . kind of like the gre . . . 66 multiple multiple guess questions . . . I don't know what hes trying to prove or not prove . . . but he walked in and told us wed miss half of them anyway . . . which is

insane . . . testing is so invalid anyway . . . and then he pulls this out-dated trick . . . he didn't want to give an essay test cuz of the size of the class (about 45) . . . yet there are 125 or so in the history course and we had a short essay test . . . and he returned them in a little over a week . . . without the help of a ta

About seven weeks into the term, I was downright frantic, wondering "if id have the guts to drop this whole trip, and get a job . . . i sincerely doubt it." What had me tied in knots was the project for my political science course. I don't recall the particulars, but my journal is clear about the brick wall I hit. I considered dropping the course, having figured out that I could still finish in four quarters. "i guess that would be better than a 5 credit c." I wrote how "needing the 3.00 gpa . . . does weird things to one, ie. making one (me) who did not ever really worry too much about grades and even managed to accept an f and a number of cs really get uptight about making the grade . . . i don't like the feeling at all." I didn't drop out. I did change projects. At semester's end, I earned an A for those all-important five credits; indeed, only a B in Theory prevented a perfect grade report. I had exceeded my expectations and apparently the school's, based on a congratulatory letter from the dean in which he wrote that "I find you have done considerably better than most" other graduate students.

Lessons: Have expectations but be willing to temper them. Set high goals, but don't rush to judgment about your progress. Don't quit, pivot.

◇◇◇◇◇

Leaving the security of Eau Claire for the unknown of Eugene was more disquieting than I ever imagined. On my life's journey, it proved to be the first of many times when I leapt ahead without fully considering what I was doing. I longed for change, but I didn't adjust to it very well. I am not sure that even today I have fully overcome that tendency. I have known for a long time that I don't like being lost, so I have learned to carefully plot my routes. I have known for a long time that I don't do well in new or unfamiliar social settings, so I often avoid them. I consider myself an introvert, yet for the longest time fancied myself a reporter, which meant regularly interacting with strangers. By graduate school I considered myself a rebel, but I also longed to be accepted by fellow students I judged (often correctly) to be much more traditional.

I had learned about The Depression, but I didn't know about depression. Only a few pages into reading my Oregon journal, I said aloud, "*Wow, you were depressed!*" There is irony in my eventual realization that nine months after arriving in Eugene, I had birthed solid friendships (which I nourished for years) and increased self-confidence. Before that, however, there was much pain. A low point was missing my sister's wedding. It was set for three weeks after my arrival in Oregon, and when I had learned of her plan I told her I could not afford to fly home. We were not particularly close then, so it didn't feel like a big deal -- until it did, but then it was too late to do something about it. Thanksgiving break proved to be an equally low point, but the tide began changing with my two-week trip home for Christmas. The high points began in March.

On November 23, I anticipated a rainy Thanksgiving spent alone. It would not be my first Thanksgiving away from my family. In 1969, out of "stubbornness and resentment," I remained in Eau Claire. It snowed, and to pass the time Wednesday evening I shoveled the walk at the Jesus house. Then two journalism pals and Les came by to fetch me for conversation and beers. Along with one of those guys and a student from New York, I spent Thursday with the Polk family. Late into an evening of wine and talk, with everyone else asleep, Les began improvising on the piano, a "Sonata for Bernie and Barbie." It was magical. I felt more at home than I had in months. (Early in my own teaching career, I paid it forward by hosting holiday dinners for students unable to go home.) Turkey Day in Eugene was anything but magical. As I wrote, it was "watching football on tv, reading a bit, eating a cheeseburger basket in a fast service restaurant . . . more tv . . . not being asked in for a drink where everyone else is . . . then falling off to sleep early." Little wonder I felt sorry for myself. "What does one do with 4½ days of holiday and all the time it is raining and you aint got a lot of money. . . ," I mused.

My journal did contain hints of a more positive attitude, such as a long paragraph that today I would label a gratitude post. I clearly tried to see beyond self-pity, writing that "i guess ive been pretty selfish . . . cuz I don't really have it bad at all . . . I mean, ive got food and a roof and im getting an 'education' and I do have money and a car and all such 'necessities' . . . im healthy and have my parents and family and friends . . . so what have I got to beef about." A few days after that, an entry written as a poem conveys mixed messages (and errors).

> Today was
> Waking up with ahangover cuz of too much cehap white wine at a
>   birthday party across the hall
> realizing it was dec. 1 and being amazed there was no snow on the
>   ground
> a lousy glass of tang for breakfast
> trying to keep alert in classes
> hare Krishna chanters in front of the emu, abt six feet in front
>   of the campus crusade table
> a frizzy heared chick selling homemade gingerbread
> reading about the blugolds in sports illustrated
> finding twopages of recycling info in bullfrog
> steak for supper
> being lazy and not studying too much
> a long distance phone call
> a hot shower
> and
> insomnia.

But mostly it was too much time alone, too much beer, too little money and wishing for "someone to be able to be in my brain and thoughts so theyd know all the things that run thru me at a given time . . . so we could discuss them and try to put it all together." [An aside: I was living on my one and only student loan -- $1,500 -- which didn't quite cover three terms of tuition and fees. Eventually I added a loan from my Aunt Florence.]

Finally, it was time to travel home for Christmas. What I needed more than anything was an uneventful flight to Minneapolis, where my friend Luise would be waiting for me along with "hours and hours to share millions of words and thoughts." What I got was another test of my ability to deal with the unexpected (*change* in the extreme). The story is best told by my handwritten journal entry for December 16, written shortly after my plane took off.

I preview this by noting it's only 11:45 and I've already had 2 bloody Marys— Here's why. Damn Toyota blows another distributor on the I-5 at the Eugene beltline— and I <u>almost</u> breakdown and for a minute panic— what to do— damn car— have to get to Portland. It's 7:10 a.m.— wait several minutes— no help— light comes— hike to Shell station— 2 or 3 minutes— no good— to Arco station (Damn right-wingers I said I'd never patronize)— call tow truck— patron mentions he was screwed by Air West strike [yesterday]— driving to Portland airport— I speak up (certainly out of character)— chance for ride— he's nice, checks with wife— OK— tow truck comes— finally get things settled ["Just take it away and I will pick up when I return."]— Paulsons own several nursing homes— money— new cadillac every year— but they are nice— and I see the airport I'd thought was hopeless— but then those bloody Marys on an empty stomach— head's high— grooving on clouds and such— love to fly— dreaming

No surprise that the two-week break flew by. The conversations with Luise. "[B]eautiful reunions [over a few days in Eau Claire] with GunR and les and other friends looked up or stumbled on." A five-hour bus ride to Green Bay. "[H]ome was great . . . the food and lounging around and feeling comfortable again . . . a pleasant xmas day." In the middle of the second week, a 103-degree fever and the flu kept me in bed until it was time to leave for Eugene. The highlight of that January 3 trip was an upgrade to first class from Portland to Eugene; the lowlight was spending the long flight from Minneapolis sandwiched between "two very stout men." The break had done what I needed it to do. Back on campus for a six-month stretch, I wrote that I was

> not upset by the thot or frightened by it or uptight. . . . the road to the end at least appears much shorter . . . and the success of the grades has renewed my waning confidence in myself . . . and of course, as always, im excited by the new term and new courses . . . i got what I wanted and so far I like what I got . . . lots of reading I think but also a schedule which will allow me enuf time to work consistently on my thesis.

Lessons: Don't let the fact that change is difficult prevent you from embracing it. Recognize that you have the inner strength to handle change. Recognize that you do not have to handle change on your own; learn to reach out.

◇◇◇◇◇

Not all of the stresses of graduate school came from trying to adjust to change. Other factors included my meager budget, my living situation, my impatience with mediocrity and "laziness," and my alcohol use.

Although I did not have to pay an out-of-state tuition premium, I quickly learned that Oregon would be more costly than I anticipated. For one thing, I had not budgeted for (or expected) car repairs, which began even before I arrived in Eugene. (Once there, I assumed the car would mostly be parked, which it was.) My self-imposed $5 a week spending money didn't provide much wiggle room. I remember giving serious thought to working part time during the almond harvest but didn't follow through. My journal entries are peppered with references to not buying a book or album or taking advantage of all the campus and state had to offer because "I just don't have the bread." I at least once wrote: "thank god mom sent me $5 today . . . which is going to have to get me thru next week . . . no more beer I guess . . . or candy bars. . . ." And then there was this: "i hate this poverty level living and hassle about money and worrying about it . . . think I'll just quit the whole show and get a job and enjoy life a bit . . . bullshit. . . . "

I have limited memories of my dorm room. It was a single, and for weeks I spent a lot of time with my door closed. I also spent a lot of time lying on the floor listening to albums I had brought across country to play on the same portable stereo that had comforted me at the Jesus house. My memories of my dorm mates are limited to three women. Our friendships bloomed after Christmas, and by March we four shared a spring break trip. But throughout my stay, I struggled to find my place as a tug-of-war between my need for "authenticity" and a desire to fit in played out. The feelings I expressed in this journal paragraph were all too common pre-Christmas:

> this weekend was typical in its dullness . . . yesterday read a 400 page book and some other outside stuff for a class . . . and played soli-taire and watched one tv show . . . the girl across the hall had said

she might like to go for a beer with me, but then went and played bridge and never said another word to me . . . so screw her . . . cant say I didn't try.

It was more of the same in early January. I had gone to a "bigtime" basketball game (Oregon vs. UCLA) but "skipped the post-game dorm party (a) can't really enjoy socializing with any large group of people (b) esp. who I don't know well (c) couldn't dress as they expect, which is really no big thing (d) alcohol, even free beer, isn't terribly appealing— so there." The day before my birthday, I wrote how "the Snoopy poster on the door across the hall says 'We all need someone to kiss away our tears,'" then added, "I really dig it— I'm looking—" But I spent January 23 in a "bad mood— bitterness— and mostly feeling sorry for myself" after my mailbox held just one card, and the book my parents sent was one I had read the previous weekend. I "went to a double feature— alone— with enough blood and guts to last a year . . . then a McDonalds double cheeseburger— and now some scotch — still feeling low— Won't Somebody wish me Happy Birthday. . . ."

Nonetheless, offhand comments written now and then suggested gradual improvement. On February 2, I ended a poem titled "To The Party Across the Hall" by asking, "would it have been too much trouble to invite me? Probably." But the very next day I wrote about having supper with Ruth from down the hall. She read the draft of the editorial I had been working on and said my point came across. I clearly was pleased -- and encouraged.

> Perhaps it is just me— I don't know, but at least with Ruth and sometimes B.A. [Brenda Ann, across the hall] there lately seems to be more give and take— talk— reaching out to each other— working both ways. It's good. I need it— even with Beth— not sure I can explain it but I feel it — like noticing my hair was down tonite instead of usual ponytail— and commenting. I do have things to offer— and I want to share me— I really do.

A day later, I wondered, "Am I finally beginning to belong?? I hope so— and somewhat on my terms i.e. being myself." Increasingly I shared more of me. That led to more shared meals. Ruth taught me a new card game, and multiplayer Squeak replaced solitaire. I kept my door open much more often, and people stopped in to chat much more often. There were spontaneous outings and tennis matches. I cautiously reached out to B.A., telling her I would like her to read "some of my stuff," which I explained as "a sign of friendship." A few days later I gave her a folder of poems. In my journal, I wondered if doing that was "my ego trip or me wanting (trying) to let someone else know who I am? Hope I don't regret the move in the a.m.— or in 10 minutes." I must not have. On February 26, in the last journal entry I have from Oregon, I wrote: ". . . the best of last night was being asked to go to Victoria [British Columbia] over break with Ruth, B.A. and Beth— I shouldn't [because of finances] but must."

My quality of life improved after that invitation because I allowed myself to fit it. I joined dorm mates for dinners out and for the first time ate Chinese food that didn't come from a can. I started attending get-togethers of the grad students on my hallway. One of them was Hawaiian, and I remember the night he adeptly wielded a large knife to prepare fresh pineapple for us. Card games and late-night tennis provided welcome study breaks. Friday-night beers and burgers got me off campus, as did visits to a local ice cream parlor famous for its gigantic sundaes.

[An aside: Had I written a travel story about that spring break trip, I would have described the fields of daffodils along the way. I would have shared the tale of the border agent who insisted on searching our car, presumably for drugs. We were four young women in a Volkswagen Beetle, its every inch crammed with our necessities. *Where, we joked, could we hide anything?* I would have detailed high tea at the Empress Hotel and explorations along the rocky beach. I would have described sharing wine and the Wisconsin cheese that was my thank you gift to B.A.'s parents, who had embraced us all as daughters.]

Lessons: It takes time to forge friendships; be patient. (As Ruth wrote to me after we left Oregon, "Even with all of our bitching it was a good year . . . because of the people.") The first step in a new place is acquaintances; reach out. Realize that you can control how much of yourself you share; trust your gut on this. Figure out how to deal with rejection -- perceived or real.

◇◇◇◇◇

In today's parlance, I headed to graduate school comfortable in my own skin and with the cocky sureness of a 22-year-old overachiever. I was not a casual student; I was a scholar. I was a serious, voracious reader. I was politically liberal and socially progressive. I was committed to a career of my own, a life of my own. I had more or less settled on journalism but didn't rule out other possibilities. I was ambivalent about marriage but not about motherhood, which held no attraction whatsoever.

My successful first term fueled my determination to press forward in the classroom and to graduate in June 1972. Doing so would keep me *busy*, which I needed. I equated not doing anything with being lazy -- and to my mind that was unacceptable. Not the healthiest attitude, of course, but one that had been with me a long time and one I continue to struggle with. It is not that I cannot be inert, but that is a state that makes me uncomfortable. After skipping my journal for a couple of days, for example, I started the next entry with "bfl's getting lazy." Early in the second term, there was this:

> Today was a funny day— certainly not strenuous on body or mind— a little reading, some basketball on tv and tonite the ends of movies— one on Vincent Van Gogh very good— the movie itself almost had the texture and coloring of a Van Gogh painting— Enjoyed it much.
>
> I don't believe how non-uptight I am— Just sort of drifting along— it's nice for a change— no tension, I mean— But in the long run it is the tension which in me is productivity— which is another way of saying I'm letting my mind be lazy (note the passive tense— quite deliberately used).

That was about the time I took "the BIG step" -- seeing a professor about getting an appointment to talk about a thesis idea. I met with him on February 1, and in my journal wrote "a rejoicing from yesterday— thesis proposal has been informally accepted . . . a good feeling . . . which will be even better when I can begin researching." It was formally approved on the fourth! There would be little time for "laziness" now. I immediately sent a copy of the proposal to Les. It was his Minority Press class that had spurred my plan to compare two Navajo newspapers. After we discussed my ideas during our Christmas visit, he had offered an important concern about "the critical equipment we bring TO the study of another culture's paper." Our shared conviction that "we cannot study or assess properly the Navajo or any other peoples without some background, solid, about the actual culture of the peoples themselves" informed not only my thesis but much of my subsequent research.

If by now you are thinking I might have added *serious* in describing myself, I agree. There is so little levity in my journal that it deserves mention, if only to demonstrate I had and have a sense of humor. There is an entry written left-handed because "I have to occupy myself." Another time, I included two "jokes." The first stated that "typing 'it' tonite I inadvertently typed 'id' . . . is that a Freudian slip??????" The other wondered, "along same vein, two people talking about a guy named Lloyd the other day . . . one called him Floyd . . . is that a 'floydian slip'????" Finally, there was this poem -- which I titled "Exclusive" -- penciled on a notecard:

> Left side,
> slot 3 down.
> U of O J Dept
> reading room.
> The only place
> in the world
> where you can
> read
> The "Atlantic Constitution"

Lesson: Self-identity is a work in progress. Oregon tested the way I saw myself, especially the personal but also the professional-to-be. In doing so, it taught me to pay better attention to both. Honestly, though, it would take me a lot longer to learn how to truly practice that self-care.

◇◇◇◇◇

I did not need graduate school to teach me how to achieve goals; rather, Oregon proved to be another affirmation of my ability to do just that. What I began to discover on this particular journey was the importance of the *process* involved in degree-earning. I began to understand how "the game" was played, how "old white men" had created a system to initiate the young by mimicking their own experiences. (There were no women on the Journalism faculty!) I began to see who they overlooked, demeaned, devalued. Ingesting content mattered; any joy in doing so was a bonus. I learned to recognize how *learning* was different from fulfilling a requirement. I left believing that I could be responsible for both, that I could invest my heart and soul in learning while being OK with sometimes doing the minimum to tick off a requirement-box.

◇◇◇◇◇

After I successfully defended my thesis, I didn't hang around Eugene for the June 11 commencement. I had managed to apply for a few jobs while writing "Profiles of The Navajo Times and Diné Baa-Hani: A Preliminary Examination of Two Navajo Newspapers," but that effort proved premature. Ruth also finished her degree, and to avoid traveling alone we decided to tag-team east. We stopped in Wisconsin to drop off my car, then headed to her Oak Ridge, New Jersey, home (the Volkswagen once more stuffed). I spent a week with her family, during which, she later wrote, "I probably saw more of New York than I had in all my years of living here." That included a visit to Radio City Music Hall, where a "dirty old man" sitting next to me fondled my leg, which forced us to change seats in the middle of the Rockettes' performance. [An aside: In her book "The Barbizon: The Hotel That Set Women Free," Pauline Breen included an anecdote about a strange man putting his hand on a young woman's knee in a movie theater. That reinforced for me that I had not done anything to invite the pervert's attention. *Obviously, this went on!*] During our NYC visit, we also enjoyed cocktails in the Rainbow Room on the 65th floor of Rockefeller Center, but it was lunch at a cafe there that changed my life. Too embarrassed or too shy to tell the waiter I had ordered tea, I drank my first cup of coffee. Black. Never looked back.

Snapshots

My fall 1967 roommate and I dressed (as required) for Sunday dinner in the cafeteria.

The Spectator was always on my mind, as doodles in notebooks and on scratch paper confirmed.

A favorite Spectator staff photo. I am on the left, behind the dog; my good pal David Gunderson is seated at the far right.

Post-ceremony smiles with Les Polk.

I spent more of my time in the Spectator office than anywhere else on campus.

The wire-rim glasses and tie-dyed shirt I wore for my ID photo fit right in at the University of Oregon in fall 1971.

High tea at the Empress Hotel during spring break in Victoria, British Columbia, required more formal attire.

CHAPTER 11

A Professional at Last

I boarded a west-bound Greyhound bus at the Port Authority terminal in New York City in late June 1972, on my way home to an uncertain future. Luise was at her parents' house in Milwaukee, where she was completing the papers for her graduate degree in psychology. I planned to spend a couple of days with her before finishing my journey. My only other plans were job hunting and the July 15 wedding of my Eau Claire friends Laurel Mather and Bob Walker. I *needed* to be employed ASAP. I was *thrilled* that Laurel had asked me to be her attendant.

While in Oregon, I had gotten occasional tips about jobs. I also had scoured help wanted ads each week in Editor & Publisher, the primary source then used by newspapers. My sights were set on reporting or copy editing for a midsize daily paper. I didn't much care where, but I believed that my experience and internships merited that starting point. Waiting for me in West De Pere was another rejection letter, forwarded from Eugene. The managing editor of the St. Petersburg Times in Florida apologized for "the tardiness of my reply" and stated that he was offering the job to someone "whose background and experience seem to us to more precisely fit our needs." Competition for jobs was stiff, I was learning. And, as it turned out, classified ads were not nearly as valuable as personal connections.

One of my undergraduate classmates was Fred Berner, whose family had bought the Antigo Journal in north-central Wisconsin in 1901 and converted it to a daily in 1905. I don't remember Fred working on The Spectator, but we shared classes until he graduated and went off to edit the paper in Hartford, Wisconsin. He returned to work in Antigo in

1972. That spring the Antigo Daily Journal had moved into a new building and converted to offset printing. I probably learned through the Eau Claire grapevine that the paper was looking for a society editor/reporter. I applied, not certain that I wanted the job but certain I wanted *a* job. Marie Berner, the publisher and Fred's mother, interviewed me one July morning and immediately offered the position. The sticking point was salary; as I recall, she offered slightly less than or the same as I had made two summers earlier for my Milwaukee internship. I also wanted to start work after Laurel's wedding, which was not a problem. So remembering the advice offered early in my education about "paying your dues," I agreed to her salary offer and the job was mine.

The outdoor wedding went off without a snag on Saturday the 15th. On the afternoon of the 16th I drove the 150 miles from Merrimac to Antigo, where I moved temporarily into a motel. On July 17th, I began my career as a professional journalist (and almost immediately asked for a day off to attend the funeral of my high school newspaper advisor). I had a title -- society editor -- and, thankfully, responsibilities much broader than writing about engagements and weddings. I also wrote obituaries, covered the city council and school board, wrote feature stories, covered some high school sports, and edited and rewrote copy from "correspondents" scattered about the county. I often took my own photos, and sometimes even developed the film and printed the pictures. Sports and the police beat were handled by a man who pre-offset had been a linotype operator. The news editor, primarily in charge of wire copy and editing our work, was a dour guy who eventually warmed to me and my words. The gentlemanly, nattily dressed "editor emeritus" (who worked for the paper for 71 years before dying in 1984 at the age of 96) wrote historical articles. Ruth, the proofreader who seemed ancient to me, was smart and wise, and a fount of general and community knowledge. She saved me from errors more times than I could count, particularly preventing me from embarrassing myself by misspelling local names. The "paste up" people -- working without dummies for inside pages -- somehow fit the pieces together without getting flustered by looming deadlines.

As for Antigo, it was a small town and its population of about 9,000 accounted for slightly less than half of the overwhelmingly caucasion county (Langlade; population 19,220). A corner of the county abutted the Menominee Indian Reservation, which I frequently drove through but never reported on. Farming, especially potatoes, and lumbering were significant employers. I started work in Antigo more than a little jealous of GunR, who was interning at The Washington Post that summer. (His internship eventually turned into a full-time job.) I felt I had paid enough dues to be a small fish in a bigger pond, yet there I was about to put my degrees to work in the community-journalism pond. When I left the ADJ after 14 months, I did so with a better understanding of what it means to "serve your public." In those days, community journalism was a synonym for small-town journalism, and independent community newspapers were everywhere. Fifty years later, when that is so not true, I hope I have described my experiences through a lens that is more than just nostalgic for "the good old days."

My ADJ clipbook is stuffed with stories, the tape that once held them on the pages so brittle that I spent a couple of days redoing it before I could review my work for this chapter. On the night of my first day on the job, I attended a school board meeting. The next morning, I wrote the story, published that afternoon without a byline. The story was routine, with this mundane lead:

> "Housekeeping" chores and the opening of bids for L.P. gas, fuel oil, milk, and towel and laundry service for the 1972-73 school year were the main orders of business for the Antigo unified school district Board of Education Monday evening.

I don't remember if it was Marie or Fred who attended the meeting to introduce me to board members and school officials, but I appreciated the gesture. In rereading the story, I was fascinated to see that I described one of the new board members sworn in as "the first woman to serve on the board since Unified School District No. 1 was organized in 1961." Fascinated because a couple of decades later I would publish my research about "first-woman stories." Fascinated to see that a couple of weeks later my first bylined story was a profile of that woman. It's an informative feature, with lots of detail and lots of quotes. I wish, however, that the news editor had asked for a rewrite of my presumptuous first paragraph: "Mary Zelinski is 'no great advocate of women's lib.' She is not actively involved in politics, let alone a political activist."

School boards are a vital component of municipal government, and from that meeting on I was a presence, the eyes and ears of the mostly absent public. As any reporter can tell you, such meetings can be long and tedious, often boring but lively when contentious. For the most part, I enjoyed them. Not only did I get to watch government in action, but I was depended on to fully and accurately provide information to our readers. If they were informed, they could be engaged; if they were engaged, they might act. Journalism at this level had potential to be anything but passive -- and that was my kind of journalism. The same was true of my other beat -- the city council. My first meeting was my second night on the job, and I had to get up to speed quickly on an annexation issue the council had been working on.

Two days on the job, two night meetings. The wheels of government, it seemed, not only turned slowly, but they turned at night. And on an afternoon daily newspaper, that meant my wheels had to turn the morning after. No problem, though; new to town, I had no social life. Within a couple of weeks I did get out of the motel. There were not a lot of choices, so I considered myself fortunate to move into a second-floor efficiency apartment just a few blocks from the Journal building. My across-the-hall neighbor was Fred Berner. The 11-unit building was just 6 years old and compared to my graduate dorm and my Eau Claire apartments, it seemed luxurious. I was living the dream: employed, independent and without roommates.

My employment dream -- of this I am sure -- did not include writing obituaries. ADJ obituaries, for the most part, were formulaic. (Well after this job I would come to see the importance of writing about a person's life, not just a biographical precis.) For examples of that work in my clipbook, I included only an October 30 page with nine obituaries. I probably figured that was sufficient to show my mastery of the form. And form is the appropriate word, because the area funeral homes would provide me a pre-printed sheet with the facts filled in, and I would use that to write. I also frequently transcribed that information onto said form during a phone call from a funeral director. John Bradley and I spoke so frequently that I came to recognize his voice as soon as he said "Hello, Barbara." Then, in the spring of 1973, I found myself in the long line at the visitation for an employee of the local radio station who had died unexpectedly. When I finally reached the door, a man directed me where to go. "John?" I asked upon hearing him speak. "I'm Barbara Luebke." From then on, the telephone voice came with a face. It was years before I learned that modest John Bradley was a Navy corpsman who had helped raise the U.S. flag at Iwo Jima. A fact until 2016, when a Marine Corps internal investigation concluded it had not been him in the iconic photo that inspired the Marine Corps War Memorial in Arlington, Virginia. [An aside: That radio station was owned by the Berner family and Marie's son-in-law managed it. I prepared all obituaries and many news stories in duplicate: the original for publication and the copy that he would pick up each day to use on his noon news program. I never did like that practice!]

Even less a part of my employment dream than obituaries was writing wedding and engagement stories. Indeed, as friends learned of my job their first comment almost always included wonderment or mirth related to my society editor title. Throughout my career, I mentioned it because, after all, I had been an *editor* since my first job, but then I quickly rattled off my "serious" duties. I was so out of my element writing about wedding dresses and flowers and rituals that more than once I slipped up. Or left out a detail or two or three that seemed trivial to me -- and clearly weren't to those involved. The nastiest letters I got from readers were always about these stories. I wrote from information provided to me by people who expected to see, as one woman put it, "a real nice write up." I used that information like the reporter I was, and what I judged important or essential was sometimes challenged.

> All the most important points were left out. First of all you printed that each girl made their own dresses which was wrong, as the Bride made both dresses and also the suits for the Groom and Best Man, which wasn't as important to mention, as was the names of the two children who read the Scriptures in church. They worked so hard to prepare for that, and expected to see their names in the write up for their effort.

At least once, I remember, Marie called me into her office to chide me over carelessness. Point well taken. By the way, I saved not a single wedding story in my clip book!

Correspondence with my Eau Claire friends almost always included mention of their work, and today letters supplement my memories of what being a reporter was like back then. That is especially true in letters from Laurel, who was a reporter at the weekly Delavan (Wisconsin) Enterprise. In August 1972, she described being "really gung ho" on returning from vacation to do "some in-depth things." Instead, she "walked into a brick wall -- catching up on things not done while I was [away], and working on two special sections that take no brains but lots of time." One was the yearly back-to-school section and the other the county fair tabloid. Of the latter she wrote: "All PR pictures and copy, but it all has to be edited and most rewritten." Once that was done, she even would be doing the paste-up. Such special sections -- important revenue streams for newspapers -- taxed staffs. Not surprisingly, those tasks left Laurel fighting "the motivation hassle again."

Similarly, I hit motivational walls when I tired of doing the routine -- not just obituaries and weddings, but the daily transformation of press releases into stories and the numerous "shorts" we published about people, organizations and activities. And then there were the stories about annual events and the "check passing" photos that were de rigueur in community newspapers. I worked hard at catchy leads and photo angles that were different. Sometimes I succeeded. A few examples (which also exhibit the paper's unusual style on capitalization):

> "A dog fight, that is cool!"
>
> That, in a nutshell, is the way things usually go at a pet show. And things were no different at Antigo city park last week when the recreation department sponsored its annual pet show.
>
> But could anything else be expected at a gathering of 56 domesticated pets which included 30 dogs, a four-day-old pig, a goat, several cats, rabbits, hamsters and gerbils?
>
> ---
>
> Snow can be fun. To walk in on Christmas eve. To ski on. Or to snowmobile on. To build snow forts in. Or to sled on. But slush isn't much fun. Especially to hold parades in.

And while Friday in Antigo was a perfect parade day, Saturday was anything but. Still, participants and spectators alike braved the weather to help usher in the Christmas season and to officially welcome Santa Claus to the city.

—

Earlier this week, the prevalent color in Antigo was red, as the Antigo high school Red Robins prepared for the state high school basketball tournament.

Saturday, however, the prevalent color should be green -- in Antigo and everywhere else there are Irishmen, be they of true Irish descent or not.

Saturday is March 17. And March 17 is St. Patrick's Day.

I also struggled with feeling unproductive, that bugaboo I had grappled with in graduate school. It helped to learn that it was not just me feeling that way. After I mentioned one such week, Laurel wrote to acknowledge similar feelings. But it is what she understood about the process that explains why she remained a reporter and columnist for her career, and I did not. Unproductive weeks, she stated, "come and go no more than the really great ones. . . . [S]ome weeks I really feel totally useless, and wonder what a nice girl like me is doing in a place like Delavan. But then once in awhile I manage a good idea, a good story here and there. And then it helps for awhile." Even GunR began one of his missives from the Washington Post with: "I so much want to write an 'up' letter, but somehow, that would seem terribly foreign today. I'm not sure why I have the quasi-blues, but it has a lot to do with my job, which has been altogether boring and annoying lately. . . . I guess I'm silently rebelling to being a cog in Kay Graham's machine. . . ."

[An aside: I expect that readers who have known only email, instant messaging, texting and social media would be astounded by the volume of words we wrote back and forth to one another. I know that I am amazed by our correspondence. I was reminded during my research that airmail could be used for domestic mail, and GunR usually sent his letters from Washington that way. But what truly amazed me was our letters' lengths. The handwritten ones might run six or eight pages, sometimes on both sides of the paper. Typed ones routinely were at least three single-spaced pages; often there were handwritten postscripts in the margins. We were writers, so it is not surprising we wrote to one another. Besides, long-distance phone calls were expensive (sometimes we found a pretext for a short, free call from our offices). So, we mostly made do by conversing -- about our work, our lives, politics and so much more -- through our letters, including passing along tidbits about friends and acquaintances we had in common.]

I think now that many of us were struggling to find the sense of purpose in our early professional lives that we had felt so strongly in our college journalism. As Laurel wrote after stumbling across The Spectator strike issue, the one with the controversial cartoon, "We've just gotta save that -- show to our grandchildren some day." And I think aspirationally we had bought into the notion that success meant employment at a major metropolitan newspaper. I know that is what I thought as I toiled away in Antigo. I was just six weeks into the job when Les, who knew that I harbored thoughts about one day teaching, lectured me: "I'm absolutely convinced, more and more, that this is the sort of thing your career needs at this particular time. So you, as all good j teachers, will have a body of experience to draw on when you need it. Otherwise, classroom j teachers are a bit phony, methinx."

The stories in my clipbook demonstrate how broad that body of experience proved to be. My school board and city council stories were not just reports about meetings. I wrote about issues important to the community, such as elections and candidate profiles; debate about the need for a full-time mayor; industrial development; innovative teaching; and vocational education. I wrote countless stories previewing or reporting on the organizations and events that were the lifeblood of the town. I even initiated a regular (albeit short-lived) series of book reviews, which the paper promoted with display ads. Eventually, I was more than the Journal reporter; I became a member of the community. Several sources became friends. I remained close to the recreation director and her husband for years after I left Antigo, for example. There were Thanksgiving cards from David and Bernice Fromstein, who owned the men's clothing store. They were the first Jewish people I knew well; Bernice taught me to make authentic bagels. The head of the Area Association for Retarded Children persuaded me to coordinate its annual fundraising, 10-mile bike ride. (I had to buy a bike to participate, ordering it from J.C. Penney Co. and assembling it myself.) I played recreational volleyball for a local business and softball for a favorite tavern -- and convinced the sports editor to allow me to write about women's rec league games. I understood then that some might consider these relationships to present conflicts of interest. I did not -- and do not -- share that assessment. Becoming part of the community -- as all my Journal colleagues were -- provided me with important perspective, I believe, just as being a student editor and an involved student had done. Further, my ability to connect with readers-turned-sources helped me write some of my most memorable stories. Four stand out.

The first, two months into my Journal career, was an in-depth examination of why the Jaycees had closed the coffeehouse they had sponsored for four years. On August 14, the city council referred to committee a letter from the Jaycees noting they had closed the coffeehouse and offering to sell or rent the building. That sparked my story, which was published on the front page of the September 27 paper. Rereading the 75-column-inch story I marveled at its thoroughness and was amazed that the paper accommodated its length (and two large photos). I remembered doing the story, mostly because I always have been particularly proud of the lead. From somewhere in the recesses of memory I had dredged up an image from journalism history class, which I put to good use:

> The ad in the September 20 Antigo Journal said that "any bills pertaining to the Coffee House must be submitted by October 1st, 1972 to the Antigo Jaycees."
>
> It was outlined with a one-half inch black border not unlike the traditional notice of death. And that was more than remotely significant, for the statement did give public notice of the fact that Antigo's coffeehouse was dead.
>
> It had died a quiet death the week before, as Jaycee members boarded over what was left of the windows in the old Calvary Lutheran church building.

The next couple of paragraphs suggested the cause of death.

> ... [A] lot of Antigo's citizenry are happy. Or, perhaps more correctly, they are relieved. Relieved that the loud rock music of

amplified guitars is gone. Relieved that the squealing tires are gone. Relieved that the periodic influx of teenagers into the neighborhood is no more.

The Jaycees can breathe a bit easier now that they have taken the final step and closed the coffeehouse. . . . The complaints by angry neighbors should have stopped. But there are still the unpaid bills run up by the coffeehouse's youthful managers. However, once they are paid the Jaycees have expressed a desire to "let the sleeping dog lie."

In two paragraphs that would feel right at home in Wikipedia, I then explained the origins of coffeehouses in 17th- and 18th-century England, and how the contemporary "youth culture" had revived the concept. I noted one thing most coffeehouses had in common: "a quiet atmosphere conducive to conversation without hassles." I suggested that "if the Antigo coffeehouse had taken that direction, it might be operating today. But it evolved into a dance hall, and through that evolution came its eventual death." After allowing all the principal parties to have their say about what had happened and why, I offered my conclusions in the last paragraphs:

But all this is history now. The coffeehouse windows are boarded and the doors are locked. In many ways, the questions of "who is to blame" and "what went wrong" are academic.

Except for the fact that the failure of the coffeehouse project was not an experience unique to Antigo. And, unfortunately, it tends to leave one skeptical about other such community projects.

A second memorable story introduced a local woman who met the English pen pal she had been corresponding with for 10 years. I connected with the woman because I, too, had pen pal experiences, though mine were as a youngster and later as a young adult writing to a soldier in Vietnam. Those led me to write a five-paragraph introduction (a *very* delayed lead) before the real story started. Here's a bit of it, for flavor:

A short quiz. Have you ever had a pen pal? How long did your correspondence continue? Do you remember your pen pal's name? Does your pen pal remember your name? [That last sentence should have been edited out for obvious-to-me-now reasons.]

If you are over the age of 20, your answer to the first question will most likely be yes. As for the other three, I'd be willing to bet you would (as I do) strike out with three "nos."

Pen pals, it seems, are born of rainy summer days or snowy cold winter nights. . . .

[From a list of individuals looking for a pen pal] you find one or two that interest you and try your luck. . . . Occasionally there emerges the story of a real, live, lasting friendship carried out via the mails. Pen pals who really are (and have been, and will be) friends even though they have never met.

The rest of the story tells of the meeting between "the wife of a Wisconsin potato farmer" who quipped that she "never gets out of Langlade county" and her pen pal from Brighton, England, who said she got "the travelling bug" at age 18. Having explored Europe, she was in the United States for the first time -- not to be a tourist but to visit Karen McDougal and her family. What fun it was to interview those two women and share their adventures via my story.

Then there was my feature about "Mrs. John (Antonia) Novak Sr." I suspect that she *wanted* to be identified that way, apropos of her generation. Today, were that true, I would have included that detail. The hook for the story was that she had published a small book of poetry. During my interview I discovered a woman of many talents, which the headline captured: "For Starters, She's a Poet . . . ." My story leaves no doubt that I was captivated by her. It started: "Occasionally, one meets a person who is full enough of life for several persons, a person who truly lives and does not just exist, a person who has taken life by the tail and made the best of it. Such is the diminutive, gray-haired woman who lives in the little green house on highway C. Meet her once and one can't help but be impressed." Several paragraphs of supporting details followed, including this one: "Watch her sew doll clothes to earn enough money for a typewriter. Watch her pick at the typewriter ('I bought a book of lessons but I couldn't make my fingers go'), working until each page of her manuscript was letter perfect. Watch her sew more doll clothes to earn the $240 to print the book." *Wouldn't it be fun to be able to sit down again with her today*, I thought to myself as I reread that story. She was, I realized, a woman as committed to her writing as I have been to mine. [An aside:

After the story was published, she wrote to the paper, "sending a bou-quet to Barbara Luepke (sic) and your Antigo Journal for the extensive coverage you have given me. . . . It has brought me many new friends and promoted the renewal of many old friendships of the past. It has brought me happiness, and I am grateful."]

Without a doubt, however, the one story in my clipbook that I never have forgotten is the one about a local optometrist with a fas-cinating approach to working with children labeled learning disabled. The feature, complete with photos, filled a page of the January 10, 1973, Journal. At the heart of the doctor's work was the difference between "sight" and "vision." As he explained to me, the former relates to the eye itself, the latter with interpreting what the eye sees. As I reported,

> "Basically, what we have is a program of teaching children who are poor learners in school to perform better when their problems are visually related," he explains.
> After the third grade, 85 per cent of all learning is visual, he says. "In grades one and two, you learn to read. After that, it is reading for the sake of learning. The stress is on the visual system, and if that system is not ready it will not perform or it will break down," the doctor says.

He became interested in the specialized field, he said, after tiring of hearing others conclude "his vision is good; there is nothing we can do" about a youngster's subpar performance in school. He shared a case study, which I described at length to demonstrate a success story.

I still recall the doctor's enthusiasm and earnestness, which I sought to convey through my words. I recall him having me do some of the visual exercises he used, which allowed precision in my story and the cutlines accompanying the photos. I recall being able to watch him and an assistant work with a young client, which I captured in my photos. I recall the determination evident in that boy. And I recall being impressed with the outcomes the doctor described and wondering why more youngsters couldn't be helped.

In the course of reporting a story, I often walked away having learned something(s). That certainly was the case with this story. The doctor made me a true believer! Years later, when a young nephew was having problems in school, my mother remembered my story and gave a copy to my sister. The article, Kris reminded me, "turned us on to the problem and how to correct it," and they were able to find someone doing similar work to help my nephew.

The vision story got 1973 off to a good start. I was journalistically and socially settled. Out of necessity, I had a new car -- a purple Gremlin I took to calling the high-top tennis shoe. The dastardly Toyota had gotten me to Eau Claire for a December visit with the Polks, then died in their driveway. That was it; I was finished with used cars. One five-year loan later, I had reliable transportation, with an eight-track tape player to boot! In a March letter, Laurel commented that "your last letter sounded like you're really getting into the spirit of things at Antigo." A postscript on that letter brought me up short then and again upon reading it in 2021. "Why do you address my letters Mrs. Robert Walker? My name's Laurell!!!"

I must have been conveying mixed messages about my frame of mind, though, based on a letter from Les, penned in mid-January and signed "a friend/priest/uncle." It seems I had wondered to him about the worth of my work. His response was jam-packed with advice directed to me but, I believe, just as valuable for young journalists today. He started by telling me again about the important lessons I was learning "IF you are planning on a teaching career, which was once in your mind, and is still occasionally." Secondly, he wrote,

> We've talked about communication impact, theoretically. Sure, there's not much value to the average party story, bride, obit, etc. (or is there?). But, how about your vision story? How about if, because of your story, one or two more persons LIVE? Have you been productive, have you lived a life of value, of worth? How about, if after your [coffeehouse] story someone realizes that something new is needed for youth? Have you done something of value? How about after your city government or school story someone gets AWARE of the real problem, underlying gov't agencies. Have you been of service?

He went on to describe himself as a "hopeless optimist re communications in general." He elaborated:

I truly believe that it's possible thru the work of old average reporter to change one corner of the world. I believe it's possible for you to help, to aid, to educate Mossie. To perhaps show Mossie where she should have gone, and could go, for aid. Have you ever thot about that as a story? Hey, citizen, you with this problem (welfare, education, cripple, vision, medical, marital) -- you could have a whole series of social welfare articles pointing out who is where for whom. And if even ONE more person is aided, haven't you done as much as the preacher, teacher, doctor, lawyer???

He ended by suggesting that "your 'down' doesn't ring true" and reminding me:

You need always to keep strong and aware in your mind, a sense of real public service that can come thru your work. Without it, you will be on an EGO bit -- you'll be no good -- you'll do inferior wirk [sic]. With it, you'll turn up excellent stories that are excellent because you HAVE a mission idea in your mind, are searching for meaningful stories to aid the person in your audience -- and praying they happen to read it. Optimistic, fate, chance? Sure -- but what isn't.

His advice rang true then and rings true today. Subsequent letters from him and friends no longer referenced job dissatisfaction on my part. In late February I received a phone call from the managing editor of The Press in Binghamton, New York. I had inquired about a job as a copy editor before I left Oregon, but by the time I heard from him I had begun work in Antigo. He had promised to stay in touch, but his call caught me by surprise. I explained my reluctance to make a job change in a follow-up letter, written "now that I have my wits about me again." I told him I felt committed to Antigo for one year. But "after July 1 or thereabouts, changing jobs will become only a matter of a two weeks notice to my present employer. That I could do in all good faith and conscience." I added: "Small-town reporting is fine experience for a future copy editor and someday journalism instructor. But I think that a year or so is enough, and frankly I think that is about all I will be able to take." I never ended up working in Binghamton, but I used the anecdote many times as a professor counseling unhappy young graduates tempted to leave a job after only a short time.

In July, I made it to the one-year mark (an anniversary I didn't have to write about), which earned me a week's VACATION, as I penciled in red on a calendar. I kept three: I hung one in my apartment. I carried a Virginia Slims "Book of Days." And I had one on my work desk. Together, they chronicled busy months leading up to that vacation. Work included the usual meetings along with elections, proms, conferences and banquets, the county fair (including tractor pull and demolition derby) and a church dedication. Along with lunches and dinners with friends, I enjoyed volleyball (except for the tournament we lost because we were committed to using everyone in the title game, including our most inept player) and softball (my hitting prowess got my name in the paper quite often). My friend the recreation director, her husband and I went trout fishing on opening day -- when it snowed. They took me tavern-to-tavern snowmobiling, fed me my first venison and taught me to eat smelt (the tiny fish are deep fried "as is" and you eat them whole). I agreed to go rafting with my friend the cooperative extension agent, then in a hungover panic stood her up. Mom and dad came for an overnight visit; I cooked stroganoff for the first time. A couple of weeks later, the former Spectator editor I had dated on and off since freshman year visited. I met Laurel and Bob in Eau Claire for Journalism Alumni Weekend but could stay for only one night because I had the ARC bike ride to manage.

In mid-August, I made a quick, secret trip south to Madison for dinner with Daryl Moen, a 1966 Eau Claire graduate who was managing editor of the DeKalb (Illinois) Daily Chronicle. I did not know him, but I knew of him, and I knew he had hired my friend Dave "Rock" Hass to be his city editor. Now he was looking for a copy editor. Rock had written me at the beginning of the year about his job:

> We have many more murders, nastiness, etc. here than [at his previous job] so life is generally more interesting. We've got a young, almost totally new to Illinois and fairly talented staff so I enjoy it most of the time. Our product is heavily community-oriented, so that national news usually suffers. Like any situation the newspaper has good and bad points, but good experience for me.

I didn't have many specifics about the copy editor job, but by the time I drove to Madison I was determined to persuade Mr. Moen that he should hire another Eau Claire graduate.

CHAPTER 12

Editing in Illinois

I generally have thought of DeKalb as the place where I began doing the journalism I thought I wanted -- editing. Preserved in more than three notebooks and dozens of letters are thousands of words that illuminate that reality. On reflection, however, those 11 months proved to be more consequential than I ever have given them credit for. I discovered that as I transitioned from age 24 to 25, I continued to be professionally and personally conflicted, regularly waffling about where I belonged. True, the tug of war between on-the-job insecurity and confidence, between loving my independence and wondering when or if I might find a relationship, did not resurface immediately. The move south also quieted my restlessness -- at least for a while. In these ways, I suspect, I was like many young career women in the early-1970s.

I remember leaving Madison, having immediately accepted the job Mr. Moen offered, and the next day giving Marie Berner my two-week notice. The days and nights between then and starting work in DeKalb on September 4 were filled with work and goodbyes amid choked-back tears. Just before then, Fred had been on vacation, so in addition to my usual meetings I handled photography. My clipbook has several pages of photos annotated "Prtd" (printed); thank goodness for Bob Smith's photography courses at Eau Claire, even if he graded my work average, i.e., worth a C. I closed out my ADJ tenure with the usual municipal meetings, obituaries, weddings and whatnot. My final byline appeared August 28, 1973, over a story about improvements to the local school lunch program. Also running that day was my brief story from the previous night's school board meeting.

Even today I marvel at the variety of people I connected with in Antigo. The softball team's going-away party at "our" bar included more than a few toasts to my hitting (and jokes about my sluggish base running). There was one last dinner with the Fromsteins and a final lunch with the mayor and my friend Mary, the recreation director. There were thanks and handshakes at that last school board meeting. Although I was the youngest person in the newspaper building, over time I had come to care for all my colleagues. I am especially proud of how well I got along with the "backshop" folks. (I like to think it is because I treated them with respect, talked their language and met my deadlines.) To this day, I treasure -- and use -- paste-up-Linda's going-away gift: a recipe notebook. "Knowing what a busy girl you are," she inscribed, "I thought you might enjoy some of these quick recipes. Some are not so quick but good. Perhaps when making some of these from time to time you will think of the old Antigo Daily Journal gang." The first recipe, untitled, calls for:

½ c friendship
1 c thoughtfulness
Cream together with a pinch of powdered tenderness.
Beat very lightly in a bowl of loyalty along with 1 cup of faith,
    one cup of Hope and 1 c of Charity. Be sure to add Gaity
    that sings and the ability to laugh at little things.
Moisten with Sudden tears of heartfelt sympathy.
Bake in a good natured pan.
Serve repeatedly.

I believe I have lived this recipe and, in my own ways, honored the role models I found in Antigo.

I resumed journal writing on September 1, when I detailed "the ultimate moving day." The red-covered, spiral "theme book" that cost me 49 cents was the first of at least eight I filled over the next several years before transitioning to fancier journals. Mary and her husband, Mike, had volunteered to drive me and my paltry possessions the 255 miles to DeKalb. We got an early start, "me wishing I had had a few less beers and a few more hours of sleep." I have no memory of how I had arranged for an apartment, but we arrived about 1 p.m. to find "all was set." After we showered and devoured Kentucky Fried Chicken, Mike put my bed together and hooked up the cable TV (that technology a first for me). Mary napped. I unpacked boxes. After we watched "a very goofy horror movie," they left. "The farewell was hard— very hard. There are tears in both our eyes; Mary sez she'll be down soon. And I express the hope to make Antigo before winter. I really hope we are both able to do so— tho I suspect such promises are the things of all good-byes, although those 2 words are never spoken." When I went back into my apartment -- which, unlike Antigo, had real rooms -- I assembled an end table. I needed to be busy. I feared "the long, lonely Labor Day weekend" but I was "ready to go to work and that challenge excites me."

Sunday was, indeed, "very long." There was "so much that could be done" but I "did not have a lot of initiative to do it." After breakfast, however, was "a mind blower— Imagine me reading the Sunday Chicago Tribune?" I had learned about the paper's conservative bent in college, which was enough for me to pay it no heed. On my first full day in Illinois, I found it "not all that bad, really, if one skips the editorial page." More to my liking was the weekly National Observer, and I had several past issues to read, which is how I started my afternoon. I took note of "an excellent article . . . on devil worship— every other word a 50-cent word." I also paged through a new magazine, Singles, "which I found more or less revolting."

I tried not to think about Antigo, "but that is hard cuz that place is still me and this is not— at least yet." I wrote about how "maybe more than ever" I had come to realize "how much people do mean to me— perhaps something I'd never have learned without a year of being a reporter— And which I wonder how much I'll miss." Clearly in a pensive mood, I concluded:

> Being here on this long weekend, talking only to the [supermarket] check-out clerk, reminds me somewhat of Milwaukee— I can't really recall first days in Antigo, tho I'm sure they were the same— Everyone we come in contact with touches our lives in some way— Wonder why it is— or how it is [that] certain of those come to mean more to us— And how do we mark that point in time when a relationship moves from the casual to something more?

Five decades later, I continue to wonder.

Even before I walked into the Daily Chronicle building for the first time, I knew of differences that would have an impact on my working life. Perhaps most important was that the Chronicle was part of a newspaper chain, as opposed to the family-owned ADJ. [An aside: When researching my story, I learned how long that paper held on to its independence. Fred Berner sold it to the Adams Publishing Group in June 2019. Sadly, early in the morning of November 25, a week before he was to retire, Fred died at his desk. His mother had died in 2011; at age 98, she was still active in the newspaper business.] In the mid 1970s, collections of newspapers generally were referred to as a "chain," and for many that was a pejorative. Eventually the term grew out of favor, and we who used it were corrected; *call it a group*. I called that a euphemism then and I stand by that now. The Hagadone Newspaper Co., which owned the Chronicle when I worked there, was headquartered in Coeur d'Alene, Idaho. That's all I knew in the beginning, and what I came to learn was seldom positive.

A second difference from Antigo was how the Chronicle was organized. Because it was a somewhat larger daily, it had more staff for each of its divisions -- editorial, advertising and production (composing and printing) -- and distinct lines of authority. Daryl, as managing editor, headed the editorial section. It included me, the city editor, the sports editor and an assistant, the family-page editor, the state editor, five reporters and two photographers. Because most were early-career journalists, I immediately felt at home with the staff. It was not long before the newsroom felt like that of my college days, with the potential of a ready-made social circle. As the copy editor, it was my job to edit stories; choose and edit wire-service stories; fit stories and photos onto the pages; write headlines and cutlines; and work with the composing room to ensure everything was where it was supposed to be. Most important: I had to meet deadlines. In other words, I was a magician. I also took a turn writing a column for the editorial page.

That first day -- "more or less a crash course" from Daryl to prepare me to run things the second day -- quickly showed me what else the job entailed and some of the things that made the paper unique. I realized I had some "unlearning" to accomplish. I wrote:

I suppose that until one does change jobs like this he [sic] doesn't realize that although both Antigo and DeKalb put out offset papers from new plants . . . how different both are and how different the components that accomplish the job. Tis exciting. And I even do such things as clean and ready the photo machine— stock the paper for the wire printer, etc. A continuous learning process.

For example, I learned that my mornings would be long -- from 7 a.m. until about 12:30, when pages 1 and 2 were completed. My afternoons were for "doing some of the next day's inside pages and other goodies." I began to acquire a new vocabulary, too: HTK copy (stories I edited in advance and had typeset, with "headline to come"); "early run" (special sections and papers with a second section required a late-afternoon press run); "timeless copy" (stories, usually features, that I edited and banked for unexpected holes). I also acquired a new skill: winding the "tickertape" for a story in a figure-eight around my hand, then using a clothespin to attach it to the corresponding story from the United Press International news service teletype.

I survived Day 2, "and a long one it was" -- up about 6 a.m. and home about 4:15. The early alarm would take some getting used to, as would the pace of my often-nonstop mornings. "Exhaustion" appears frequently throughout my journal entries. What I wrote of Day 2 was that

I didn't wreck the photo machine— refurbished paper on the puncher [it spewed the ticker tape that coded wire stories and allowed them to be turned into type]— and made my deadline at 12:10, with quite a lot of help from Daryl. . . . I think I already realize the nightmare of my job— being hurried, missing a "big" story and not finding out until it's too late, i.e. on the 5:30 news.

I soon realized that it "doesn't matter how light the [news] day, all hell breaks loose from 11 to noon." On a day when the paper was just 10 pages and "all I had to fill was 1 and 2 and about 1/8 of another page it was really rush-rush at the last minute to get it all done. And believe me, once that is done, I'm drained— emotionally and physically." Reporting seldom had that effect on me. Then I was responsible for a story or two; now I was responsible for so much more.

My learning curve wasn't limited to my job; it wasn't just big city "career girls" (I idolized TV's fictional Mary and Rhoda) who confronted obstacles. After learning I could not get my telephone installed for two weeks because of a fall-semester influx of Northern Illinois University students, and realizing how few people lived in my apartment-complex building, I wrote: "Things to remember choosing next apt: check air conditioner covers to know which apts are occupied— make arrangement to get phone hooked up on day 1."

By Day 3, I wrote that "I'm getting the hang of it— at least today went smoother— front page went up about 11:45— and paste up went okay." That entry also marked the beginning of a job-long habit of writing not just about my own job but also including observations and commentary on newspapers and the news media. I believe my generation of journalists thrived on thinking and talking about journalism. We believed we could make journalism better not just by doing better journalism, but by critiquing journalism. Of my own work, that day I wrote:

> I realized in watching them paste up page 2 that my headlines are usually one size too small. Something Daryl later pointed out. Glad I had noticed it [first]. While I didn't totally do page 1, I did most of it, and feel more confident that it won't be long until I can get it all— and be creative and effective. I realize I must pick up speed, but can feel myself doing so already.

My broader critique started with the observation that "a person in my position has real power, as I see it, in the newspaper world." I explained:

> All the words read about gatekeepers never really were more than theory— until one is a gatekeeper. It also became apparent to me while watching Walter C. [Cronkite] tonite that some of the misgivings I was having about getting wire copy— more than in digest form— in our paper are probably needless. We really, really go overboard to get local copy first and then what space is left over goes to wire. And why not— cuz at 5:30 the others are all there— complete with photos. What we offer is unique— and the rest is up to the reader.

I ended the entry with two more observations, both of the sort that were a constant during my stay in DeKalb. The first was how September was going to be "a tough month for money, but things after that look manageable." The other judged the episode of "The Waltons" where John Boy taught a black woman to read and write "so good— even the second time around— and shows . . . what TV fiction can be."

As it turned out, I didn't have to wait long to see my friend Mary. After my first DeKalb Friday, which hinted at their easier pace and included my first solo front page, I was home in West De Pere by 5:15. That allowed me to attend a cousin's wedding, where "the kid [me] overdid the champagne." I met Mary the next day, in a town halfway to Antigo. She and Mike lent me their television. "Such good friends and such a nice thing for them to do. Everyone needs 1 such person in their life." Once back in De Kalb, I pledged to give up driving for a couple of weekends. (I worked every other Saturday.)

With each passing day, I felt more settled into my job -- even as those days often revealed something new about the work. On my first day "with no Daryl [in the office]," I was pleased that "things didn't fall apart. Matter of fact, I was quite pleased with my first— totally done by me— front page." I even coped with a couple of "emergencies" -- a quarter-page hole to be filled and a missing headline on Daryl's editorial page. A week into the job, it dawned on me -- while reading Ms. magazine -- that other than the family-page editor and her reporter, I was the only woman in the editorial department. I had replaced a guy and wondered "if there was any hesitation in hiring me that might later come out. I certainly feel competent. And of course I suppose my interest in and knowledge of sports doesn't hurt." My competency was confirmed for me more than once, but never more so than when I overheard the production manager tell Daryl: "She's 10 times as good as [my predecessor]. Damn, you never realize it . . . ." That night in my journal I wrote how I was embarrassed for overhearing them, "but I felt so good. Such added confidence about what I am doing and what I am capable of doing."

As I think now about how my time in DeKalb unfolded, I wish that as an educator I had returned to my journals and used them to write a guide for interns and young professionals. My entries were chockablock with useful information and, dare I say, wisdom. I remain enthusiastic about what I wrote, even as I recognize that today much of it is perhaps best characterized as historical. So, in no particular order, I offer a taste of my professional and personal lives for those 11 months. I believe the morsels are representative; I certainly have tried to share the essential along with the tastiest.

"Chain Gang"

At the Antigo Daily Journal, my publisher owned the paper. Her office was not far from the big open space housing the newsroom, composing room, and advertising and business folks. The publisher was accessible, though not always approachable. If her first priority was advertising revenue, producing a newspaper that served the community ran a close second. In DeKalb, we had a publisher, Ray, but he didn't own the newspaper; he answered to the head of the chain. And it was painfully clear that Ray's only priority was profits. That trickled down, too. When a staff member's fiancée interviewed for a job in the classified ads department, the manager told her: "This paper exists only to make money. There are some people 'over there' [in News] who think otherwise, but it's not so." Another time, when we had an early deadline, all was OK until Ray went ballistic because there was no "house ad" on the front page promoting a special section. He actually ordered the presses stopped -- 2,000 papers already had been printed -- and instructed me to redo the page. I had made a note to myself about needing that ad, but somehow overlooked it. "Oh well," I told someone in the backshop, "I'll never be a publisher because I think about news and not promotion."

I realized almost from Day 1 how little respect Ray garnered from the news staff. One Saturday morning he was in the office and I watched him go up and down the rows of desks putting things into drawers. Then he straightened every typewriter and desk pad. Who could take seriously a man who insisted that before we left the office each day our desks and typewriter tables be cleared off (reporters are notorious packrats and pre-internet editors required all manner of reference materials and tools to do their jobs)? All that could remain, according to a memo, were a calendar pad, tape dispenser and ash tray! "Plus of course your phone and typewriter." He also wrote that "on Oct. 1, 1973, the janitors have been instructed to throw everything out on the desks except the items mentioned." On October 4, he wrote to tell us that "housekeeping has improved considerably." But he remained upset that "there are a few that continue to leave odds 'n ends on the desks," and he gave them until the next day to change their ways. "I don't know what motivates the guy to come to work each day," I wrote. "He certainly has nothing to do— or does nothing. Friday when I was so swamped, he came by and asked if I needed help. I wanted to ask him what he thought he could do."

More of a mystery to us was the owner of the chain, Duane Hagadone. His holiday message in the company newsletter stated, in effect, *We are making a lot of money; let's keep it up*. He visited once during my tenure; the joke around the office was that we would not be able to put out a paper that day because our desktops would have to be empty. I described his visit in my journal: "Mr. Big (Duane) was here, tho he didn't meet— or speak— to us underlings. Met all a.m. with Ray, which at least gave Ray something to do. Guess D.H. has something about closed doors cuz even the lunch room and [wire service-] tape-room doors were kept shut while he was here."

Not surprisingly, Mr. Big abhorred lawsuits. The scuttlebutt around the office was that the Hagadone chain enforced a dictum that anyone responsible for a suit against one of its papers would be fired automatically. "Nice to know management stands behind us," I wrote. Near the end of my stay in DeKalb, an old lawsuit against the Chronicle finally went to trial. Ray didn't get the call requiring him to attend until the day before. He was upset because he would miss the Western Open golf tournament.

Mr. Big tried to motivate the 14 papers in the chain with a yearlong contest to identify the best based on performance in all phases of the publications' operations. Scores were tallied; there were 47 categories related to the reporting of local news, by which editorial staffs were judged. What got our attention were the cash awards that came with winning. At the end of December 1973, our editorial department was in second place by a couple of points. When the competition ended the following June 1, we were on top along with the production and business departments. Our checks paled in comparison to the all-expenses-paid 30-day trip around the world for Ray and his wife, and the paid vacations to Spain for the other bosses. But who was keeping score? (For the record, Duane Hagadone died in April 2021. He was 88, and one story reporting his death described him as a megamillionaire.)

Location, Location, Location

DeKalb is in northern Illinois, about 60 miles west of Chicago. With about 33,000 residents when I moved there, the city was almost four times as large as Antigo. The county, which encompassed the Chronicle's circulation area, added another 38,000 or so. With 14 cities and towns, and another 16 populated locales, we had plenty of datelines in our pages. Among them were Sycamore, the county seat; Genoa, settled by a Revolutionary War soldier from Ohio and named after a New York town; Cortland, also named after a New York town; Hinckley, site of the Harlem Globetrotters' first road game, in 1927; and Sandwich, which bedeviled headline writers, including me. (How else to say Man Dies in Sandwich, for example.)

Raised in dairy-farm country and having lived in potato-growing country, I was now ensconced in corn country. DeKalb AgResearch's flying-ear-of-corn logos were planted in fields throughout the county -- and the country. The company's hybrid corn was the most-planted brand well into the 1970s. I edited my share of corn- and farm-related copy, and in doing so added to my knowledge base and vocabulary. DeKalb also was renowned as the birthplace of barbed wire because in 1874 one of its residents patented the double-strand variety, which remains in common use around the world. We observed that centennial with a special section.

Lightning Bug vs. Lightning

I am fond of the Mark Twain quote "The difference between the *almost right* word and the *right* word is really a large matter. 'Tis the difference between the lightning bug and lightning." Precision with words and accuracy with facts are essential in journalism, as is attention to detail, and as copy editor I was generally the last line of defense. The Chronicle office was home to a desktop statue of a golden turkey, which was bestowed on a staff member when she or he made a major error or did something else "shameful." The recipient was required to display the turkey until the managing editor (or other department head) awarded it to someone else. The first Golden Turkey I made note of in my journal went to the family editor, who had published a story about a long-married couple and misnamed them. Ouch! Within a couple of weeks, that turkey sat on my desk in recognition of this headline: Man charged / with battery. I brushed it off, at least in my journal. "Oh well, can't win them all— Personally, I find my heads better than D's— at least in terms of no splits, good division [of lines], etc." The second time I got the turkey was also for a headline: Baker described / 'missing piece.' That's what was printed after I had to turn a four-column, two-line headline about Tennessee Sen. Howard Baker into a two-column, two-liner. The double entendre "didn't jolt me at all until the paper was out and somebody [joked] about it."

Thankfully not all my errors earned the turkey. Many humbled me, however, and each reminded me of the need to concentrate, pay attention and double-check the little things. Had I done so, for example, I could have avoided:

▶ The wrong date on the nameplate. "Thought I checked it, but then I sometimes can't remember the date."

▶ The headline that said Oct. 9 above the story that said Oct. 4. "I have got to slow down. No matter how hectic things get around deadline— I've got to be a careful, accurate editor. It is so easy to be sloppy."

▶ The headline ("thank god it was a small one") where I had someone *stabbled*. "How can something look right at paste-up and turn out wrong. Carelessness is the only answer."

▶ Designating a story for Page 1 and forgetting to send it to the composing room. "Caught it quick, tho, so no disaster."

▶ "A big goof" when the story across the bottom of Page 1 didn't wrap correctly "and was quite a challenge to read." I knew why it happened: "We were rushed and neither [the composing room guy] nor I checked the wraps, as we usually do." Yet again I concluded that "the incident was necessary to wake us up."

Current Events

As I've noted, the Chronicle's focus was local and regional news, but we could not overlook major news stories. As an afternoon newspaper, however, that often meant a "second-day" story adding to what our readers had learned the night before from their favorite news anchor, especially Walter Cronkite and John Chancellor. We also could -- and usually did -- find a local angle or two to report. One such story came early in my tenure, and for a couple of days I devoted my journal to describing how we handled the resignation of Vice President Spiro Agnew.

> October 10— My God, Spiro Agnew resigned this afternoon . . . and at the office the reaction was light. I immediately said "the chicken." Someone else said the only one to succeed him would be Donald Duck. Such a reflection on the times— not unexpected— he did some dirty things and got caught. Is anyone "clean"? Now the heat's off Nixon and he should be happy, but shouldn't he also do the same thing? How effective can that damn man be?

When the news about Agnew came over the wire -- a FLASH (so rare that I saved it) -- our press run was finished. The Hagadone paper in Beloit, Wisconsin, called to say they were replating. I agreed with our decision not to. "Considering the electronic media's speed, I don't think we were out anything." Instead, we immediately began planning the next day's local sidebars. That paper would be big -- 28 pages -- and I relished the challenge of doing justice to the Agnew stories. "This business can be dull— it can be routine— but it can also be terribly exciting— and I hope I always find it as much 'fun' to go to work as I most days do."

I called October 11 "probably the biggest news day I'll come across in a long time" and bemoaned the menstrual cramps that made me miserable. "But I survived the day— and we put out a good paper— considering all there was to get in." We had a main Agnew story, two local sidebars and a wire-service sidebar on Page 1, along with two major local stories. "Watergate and Mideast war had to go to Page 2— and I spread a lot of Agnew stories inside." I had counted 22 UPI photos concerning Agnew -- "of which we used none; did use a pix from when he was in the area recently, tho." I also wrote about "never trusting UPI again. On Friday [the news service] moved a story about Nixon's p.m. speech, noting VP was big secret but it definitely would not be [Gerald] Ford. So we started a pool and none of us voted Ford. . . . So much for speculation!!!" A couple of weeks later I was in Eau Claire for a weekend of catching up and relaxing with my "other family." Les, Ruth Anne and I were enjoying a leisurely Saturday evening of television when CBS broke in with the news that President Nixon had fired Watergate Special Prosecutor Archibald Cox and accepted the resignations of Attorney General Elliot Richardson and Deputy Attorney General William Ruckelshaus. I couldn't help but wonder what the "Saturday Night Massacre" would have me editing on Monday.

Another significant news story during my time in DeKalb was the energy crisis that followed OPEC's 70 percent increase in the cost of crude oil and embargo on oil from the United States and countries it identified as supporting Israel during the Yom Kippur War. Those actions came in October, and I first mentioned energy in my November 7 journal entry: "Nixon on tv tonight re: energy crisis— and now says he has 'no intention whatever of walking away from the job I was elected to do.' BASTARD!" On November 13 I recorded that the "way was paved for Alaskan pipeline today— and so the energy crunch most likely is major reason the environmentalists lost this one. Each day it seems rationing is more and more likely." I wondered about "where it will all lead" and concluded, "Obviously all is not prosperity in the land of prosperity."

By December 18, eager for my trip to Wisconsin for Christmas, I could get only 10 gallons of gasoline at my neighborhood station. A few days later, on the drive north, I reduced my driving speed (then recommended, soon to be mandated), "not minding it much at all— really felt more at ease and in control of the car— arrived home in only about 30 min. more time than usual and not any more tired than usual." To reduce energy consumption, daylight saving time went into effect on January 6, and for me that meant getting up at 6 a.m. "would be a bummer" because it wouldn't be light until well after I was at the office. The energy crisis had another direct impact on my life. I had been casually dating Brad, who had moved into the apartment next to mine. He traveled the Midwest as a snowmobile salesman, and a few hours before we went to see the movie "Papillon" (which I judged "disturbing, to say the least") he learned he had been laid off. He "was in fairly decent spirits" and I promised to cook him dinner when he returned from snowmobile races in northern Wisconsin.

My continued ambivalence about a relationship had prompted me to write in late September about "some days [when I] almost long for different— Different in that there would be someone to come home to— someone to talk with— and to do things with— to have me love and to be loved by." But even on those days, I wrote, "I need my independence. I dream of a relationship that would give me both— and wonder if it ever will be— cuz I'm not sure I know how— or want to— let it happen." Tom, the one guy I dated at Eau Claire, had given up journalism for the Marines and flying. We saw each other when circumstances permitted and corresponded, too. When I mentioned him in my journal, I usually wondered "if I see him as my safety net." Brad, it had seemed, might be a good fit. We continued going out until he found a new job in Ohio. I saw him for the last time by accident, when I ran into him at the post office. That night in my journal I mused: "People move in and out of our lives constantly— all touching us in some way— which makes life worth something, I guess." [An aside from my small-world life: While I was in DeKalb, Tom was writing me from Marine Corps Air Station Iwakuni in Japan. As I write this, my youngest nephew, a Navy aviator, and his family are living on that base, home port for the USS Ronald Reagan aircraft carrier.]

Increasingly I wrote about my own energy-crisis problems. People afraid of gas shortages were causing a run on service stations and long lines were becoming common. Anticipating a trip to Antigo, I noted in late January that the "gas situation in Chicago is being reported as really tough now and through the weekend. Hoping it won't be too bad here. I'll need a couple of gallons on Thursday, but thank goodness mine is only a ½ tank trip." Just two weeks later, I could only get $3 worth (at about 39 cents a gallon). To conserve gas, the staffers with whom I socialized generally kept our weekend road trips short. One Saturday morning in March, those of us working had decided to go to a shopping mall in nearby Rockford -- until one of us suggested going into Chicago instead. He planned to shop for a camera case and the rest of us thought we'd enjoy walking around the Windy City. The result: "shoes for Eleanor— cigars for Rock— a book for me— a camera strap for David— ice cream for all of us." It was my first trip into the city; I hoped to see a lot more of it.

In my experience, there is much truth in the stereotype of hard-working/hard-partying journalists who are drawn together by the crazy, unpredictable hours of their jobs and shared world views. Most of us at the Chronicle were not that far removed from college weekends, so as usual we had planned a get-together for Saturday night. After Chicago, we returned to my apartment and "the party got going about 9— chicken was fantastic (in the crockpot about 13 hours)— beer— some cheese and hard rolls— basketball game on tv— music— some good grass and lots of talk" until about 2 a.m. The following weekend, Rock, Eleanor and I shared a drive to Wisconsin and our individual destinations. Our plan was to be back in DeKalb by early Sunday evening; I, for one, had a column to write. Alas . . . it was St. Patrick's Day weekend, so we stopped for more than a couple of green beers in Oshkosh (the college town then notorious for its raucous celebration). We continued south, and by Columbus we agreed it was time to stop again. Ditto for Madison (where hot cherry pies at McDonald's hit the spot) and finally Janesville. Feeling no pain, we arrived in DeKalb about midnight. Needless to say, I didn't get my column written.

Another Saturday outing that has stuck with me over the decades was memorably macabre. Part One of the story: I had no plans to go out but showered just in case. I had given up on an invitation and had started making popcorn when Rock called. We joined another staff member and his fiancée. Eventually we found ourselves at a favorite bar in downtown DeKalb, but we left before closing. Part Two of the story: Before I left work Friday, I kiddingly had told Daryl I hoped he'd have a murder or two on Saturday (because all the weekend excitement seemed to happen when I worked). It wasn't until I met Rock that I learned there *had been* excitement. A 22-year-old -- the proverbial innocent bystander -- had died in a bar we frequented. Apparently her jugular vein was cut by a shard from a broken beer bottle thrown during a fight. If that weren't enough to keep Daryl busy, the body of a gunshot victim was found near Sycamore.

What Might Have Been

Sports-related comments are sprinkled throughout my DeKalb journals. Reading them, I was reminded that at one time I thought I would be a high school physical education teacher, but misguided adults deemed me "too smart for that" and steered me away. While reading those comments it also dawned on me that I might have wanted to be a sports reporter -- if I had had role models. That is not a problem today; women are on playing fields and in press boxes. Not so in my formative years. While working in DeKalb, I satisfied my appetite for sports by watching them (on TV and in person), by playing them (rec league), by reading about them (in magazines and books) and, most important, by talking about them. To this day, my range of sports knowledge creates a comfort zone with male colleagues and friends in a way nothing else can.

Billie Jean King vs. Bobby Riggs -- On September 20, 1973, I wrote about the "big TV extravaganza" taking place. I described it as "more show business than sports . . . and quite fantastic cuz at this point she is whipping the ass of that arrogant SOB— and keeping me up late." I critiqued the event the next day:

> All in all I think ABC blew it in the end when . . . immediately after the match ended, it cut out for [the TV show] "Streets of San Francisco." Only planning on 2 hours for a best of 5 set match was dumb— especially when the first 30 min was garbage— and there was no room at the end for interviews. I was mad! And this a.m. discovered a real group of chauvinists at work— male and female. Putting down Rosie Casals' comments— caustic, but honest, I thought. If it had been Howard Cosell, I told them, they wouldn't have said a thing.

Football pool -- Most of us in the newsroom tossed in a dollar a week for the privilege of predicting NFL-game winners. I made note of my performance most weeks, and so I know I won for the first time in early October. Sadly, four others had the same record and therefore I took home a whopping $3.60. Throughout the rest of my career, I almost always found a football pool to join; a couple of times I even was in charge.

Sports Illustrated -- A few years ago, I resisted canceling the magazine primarily because I had been a subscriber for so long. I never was certain of how long, however, until my journal told me it had been a gift for Christmas 1973. For decades, I read it cover to cover each week -- often the day it arrived. I marveled at the quality of the writing, which consistently hooked me into reading stories about topics I did not think I was interested in. I marveled at its photography. I rejoiced when at long last it allowed me to *not* receive the swimsuit issue. Sadly, however, the media revolution of the internet age changed SI into a publication I no longer recognized. Issues sat unread for weeks, until it felt absurd to keep the no-longer-weekly coming for the sake of nostalgia. In 2018 I made the difficult phone call and said "cancel." Remarkably, some weeks later I received a refund for the unused portion of my subscription. Classy, I thought, but I still don't like what it has become.

A streak ends -- On Saturday, January 19, 1974, I spent a miserable three hours at work, then returned home to my couch for the rest of the day. I was recovering from a bad cold -- and I had worked every weekend since Christmas. At least I had the Notre Dame-UCLA basketball game to watch, and so witnessed UCLA's 88-game winning streak come to an end. My journal comment was a simple "Cool."

A record is broken -- On April 4 I penned a long entry, having not written for several days. Near the end was this: "Hank Aaron hit #714 today [tying Babe Ruth's legendary record]— first game of season— first at bat— 3 & 1 pitch. What a shiver that sends up one's spine." At some point I wrote a marginal postscript: "TV guy just notes he played in Eau Claire!" Coincidentally, I would leave for a weekend there after work the next day. Catching up on that getaway, on April 8 I wrote "while watching Atlanta vs. L.A. and Aaron's try for 715." After 13 paragraphs, I ended the entry: "Hot damn— Henry Aaron just hit #715 off Al Downing— 1-0 pitch on second at-bat with man on first. We are watching history — and for first time in a long time it is good— not assassination or scandal." I vividly remember jumping for joy and tearing up as I watched a childhood hero round the bases. On July 5, I was lucky enough to see Aaron play in person at Wrigley Field. Baseball heaven times two.

Playing games -- In the spring of 1974, I found relief from the stresses of editing on the softball diamond and at the driving range or golf course. Unlike Antigo, where the paper paid scant attention to women's rec league contests, the Chronicle regularly published not only stories but box scores. In my journal I commented frequently on games, once acknowledging that "I'm a horrible loser" prone to reliving bad games. (Still am). We "blew it last night— lost to a shit team," I wrote midseason. "A 7-run inning and we just couldn't rally." I also critiqued my performances: "I played OK; 2-4 at bat. Made some good catches— but not too good on the bases." "I still run like shit," I had observed another time. But I could hit; I have the box scores to prove it. And when out of necessity I was given the opportunity to pitch, I wrote about the "ecstasy" of my team winning in the first round of a tournament. "I pitched well— 4 or 5 strikeouts, including 2 straight with 1 out in the 7th and us with a 2 run lead. Six straight pitches. I couldn't believe it. And overhearing a teammate say 'She should have been pitching all year' made me feel great." I struggled to describe "that fantastic feeling I have." I settled for "I'm on cloud 9— or 900— or whatever— HIGH— knowing I came in, put in a clutch performance, and did a damn good job."

Rock's fiancée, one of our photographers, was assigned one of my games to get shots for a photo page. "She really doesn't have an eye for sports— or knowledge of the game," I wrote, declaring that she had missed the best photo -- a collision at home plate. "And then she didn't take photo of the downed player cuz she felt sorry for her. Ugh!!" I wrote the story -- more like a love letter -- for that photo page. I did *not* write the headline:

Women!
There's a diamond for everyone

I ended my story by declaring:

So, take me out to the ball park. No, let me take myself. And as long as I can hobble from first to home, roam the field and handle relay throws, I want to be ON the field. Munching my gum. Shouting encouragement. Sharing an experience.

And when I can't do that, I'll coach from the sidelines.

And when I can't do that, I'll be in my grave.

Despite those sentiments, my softball-league days ended in DeKalb (although I did write a never-published humorous column about the game **Appendix F**).

Golf, by contrast, remains an important part of my life. One advantage of the hours I worked at the Chronicle was that I often had time in the afternoon for other things. With pleasant spring weather, I found myself hitting balls at a nearby driving range. By early summer, golf was a regular activity. Sometimes I played by myself, sometimes with Rock. Once, after a trip to the bank, I wavered about playing. "Thank god I did— such beautiful weather. And tho I played alone and on a shit course, it was fun— not at all crowded and took only 1+ hours [nine holes], so I plan to do it more." I did.

Reporter and Columnist

I was surprised to be assigned an occasional news story and interpreted that as a vote of confidence in the skills I had honed in Antigo. Even Ray, the clueless publisher, once told me he liked my writing and wanted "to put your talents to better use." There also was the letter-to-the-editor that contained this: "Thank you . . . for writers such as Barbara Luebke." I have no idea what prompted the anonymous subscriber to mention me and follow it with "Thank you God for the talents you give to light the way in a somewhat darkened world." I simply figured that continuing to polish my reporting and newswriting skills could only make me a stronger candidate for my next job, whenever and whatever.

My first reporting assignment was routine; I covered a meeting of a minor municipal committee for a vacationing reporter. The next was meatier: a series of articles on self-defense for women. After my first interview for that, I was confident about "a good series." It was refreshing to get out of the office, to be reporting again, a reaction that surprised me. "I really learned to enjoy it [in Antigo] and have conquered much of the old fear." I observed that while "my interviewing technique may not be the greatest, it works for me." I favored preparation and "a basic idea of what I'll need" over a long list of prepared questions. I believed I was "quick witted enough to work from that." After all, time and again I read how the best interviews were *conversations*, and more often than not I found that to be true.

I ended up writing six stories for that series, which ran under the kicker "Protect yourself!" The first -- an overview of rapes and sexual assaults in DeKalb -- was planned for Page 1; the others were to run inside. I was pleased with that first story; what pleased me even more was Daryl's decision to keep the series on Page 1 "because of the widespread interest in the subject." Stories that make an impact are my kind of stories. With the second installment, "Officers say definitions important," I was particularly proud of "getting around overuse of legalese quite handily." That reflected me the *copy editor*. And *columnist* me already was thinking about how I would "try to milk [the topic] for a column."

After a scary storm blew through DeKalb County I got the opportunity to write a first-person story -- rare back then. A tornado seemed likely, but eventually the official determination by the National Weather Service was "straight-line winds" that reached 85 miles per hour.

'I know what it's like to be frightened'

6-21-74

By BARBARA F. LUEBKE
Copy Editor

I know now what it is like to be frightened. This morning, in the aftermath, it seems weird. Not quite funny -- but I can laugh.

Last night, I couldn't.

When I heard that Civil Defense alarm, shortly after watching the sky turn as black as the ace of spades, I remember thinking, "My God, what do I do."

I had no basement to go down into. Quickly, the boots and typewriter and vacuum cleaner were tossed out of the closet along the inside wall. I left the kitchen chair. To protect my head, just in case, I thought.

I wasn't sure where else to go. I knew only that I had to go somewhere.

And I was alone. For a minute, I longed desperately for somebody to hold my hand. I have been frightened before. A head-on collision at age 12. A Palm Sunday tornado. Driving to work in an icy Midwest blizzard.

Nothing, though, compared with last night.

The worst seemed to be over very quickly. The wailing of the alarm continued, pierced occasionally by sirens. And

the wind blew, bending the small trees in front of my apartment building almost double.

I know, because in the midst of it all, my journalistic curiosity got the best of me.

I had prayed ... hard ... and a new kind of prayer. Not the nightly "thank you for life" words, but a scared kind of prayer ... a "keep me alive" and "protect me" kind of prayer.

Still, I had to know what was going on outside. If there was a twister, I'm not sure I wanted to see it coming. But I remembered Reg Murphy (kidnaped editor who kept his cool, helped himself, and got a fantastic story) and I wanted to see and feel and smell and touch the flavor of the entire event.

I heard voices in the hallway, sounding, at least to me, as upset as I was.

I saw cars continue to drive by. To pull into the parking lot, drivers scurrying out of the torrential rain and wind and into "safety."

I watched the lights in the car wash across the street go off, flicker on, then go off for good. My little piece of world became even darker.

I puzzled over the continuous traffic into Convenient Mart.

I worried about friends also alone this night.

Peeking out of my closet, I saw the sky lighten. But the wind continued and I could hear it howling under my door and through the vent above the stove. The rain pounded against my windows.

I wondered when I would know it was safe to come out. I didn't know, of course, so I'd duck back into my closet for a while, until I just had to SEE what was happening.

Eventually, I did leave my "shelter," and until it got too dark to do so, I watched the outside world. I didn't have enough candle power to do anything else. No electricity. No radio.

The traffic continued. So did the lightning -- horrible yellow and salmon-colored bolts. And the thunder.

Business at Convenient Mart continued to be brisk, it appeared. The winds continued to blow hard.

Apartment dwellers came and went. I continued to hear the sirens, so I knew things were bad elsewhere.

I fell into an anxious sleep. And hoped morning would come early. I knew there would be nightmares. And I was anxious to get the story.

195

I told another story -- how we met the challenges of covering the storm -- in a lengthy journal entry. The power out, I had gone to bed about 9, only to be awakened an hour later by my ringing phone. (It was so dark I had trouble finding my way out of the bedroom to answer it.) I was told to go to work early in case we were forced to print in Beloit. I arrived at a dark office about 5:15, "in grubby clothes and [with] fresh OJ from my thawing freezer." I was lighting candles for my desk (on hand because of a previous power outage) "so I could at least type my narrative" when the power was restored. Rock and I immediately took charge. We sent the assistant sports editor to buy the Chicago and Rockford morning papers. I used them and limited wire copy to get wire pages filled early -- in case of another power loss. We had a photo page planned for the day, so I devoted that to storm coverage. We also decided to use only storm stories on Page 1. It was all hands on deck.

> Kent came in and contacted his correspondents. Betty, who was to be off, called and said she'd be in. We put her on a summary of area stuff gleaned from papers and calls. David gathered county info. Dan got NIU and a sidebar there. I did my narrative. And Rock got city stuff and an interview sidebar. Finished processing the last copy about 12:15— but unbelievably we made deadline out of the backshop.

> Compliments on coverage from people in back, and even Ray said it was a good job. We were all very tired by lunch, and only minimal work was done in the afternoon. But it was all very exciting— challenging— and showed just what we could do.

A week after the storm, a Hagadone executive sent Ray a note to share with the staff. He had found a grammatical error in one of our storm stories. "My god," I wrote, "if that was the only error we made that day, we were lucky— And it wasn't— including things like the Y roof and the people burned out, etc."

I was happy about being included in the rotation as a columnist. I was no stranger to column-writing, having produced one weekly for a few semesters in college. I relied on that experience to guide me. My topics -- often stumbled on or sprouting at deadline -- came from my reading, current events, my job, personal experience and my political/social outrage. A few had a single focus, but I favored sharing what I once described as "a collection of tidbits and trivia" (related or not). All told, I wrote 22 columns -- including the one that grew out of my research for the self-protection series. I commented on pet cemeteries, asking "What is happening to our sense of values?" I commented on advertising, intrigued by how *"causes* and *products* get married," then concluded that "most make strange bedfellows." I devoted an entire (funny) column to Wacky Packages, the trading cards for cynics. I quoted Yeats. I handled Christmas by using the "recipe" from Antigo as my wish for readers. I challenged a fellow columnist who had written about "reformed male chauvinists." I described collecting newspaper "missteps," such as this headline from the Louisville Courier-Journal: "Pope blames priest shortage on laymen's misconceptions." I used an item from Ms. magazine about childhood aspirations to mention my own -- including playing for the U.S. women's Olympic basketball team, which at the time did not exist -- and then asked readers to share theirs. (I was disappointed when I got no takers.) One column that stood out upon rereading was about the disgraced and disgraceful former vice president.

In my opinion 12-12-73

Agnew, the job hunter

Reliable sources, who asked not to be identified, report that Spiro Agnew pounded a lot of pavement before Eva Gabor's husband decided to take a chance and hire him.

That source, with some ingenuity, just happend to have the offices of a small newspaper in Iowa under electronic surveillance when the nation's most celebrated unemployment statistic stopped in. The following conversation between a secretary in the advertising department and Mr. Agnew was recorded:

S—Yes sir, may I help you?

A—Are you in charge of hiring?

S-Not exactly; he's out with a bug. I'm his secretary. What can I do for you?

A-My name is Agnew. S. Theodore Agnew. I'm looking for a job.

S-Oh, I see. Well, I can't hire you, but I could interview you and pass the information on to my boss.

A—Well, let me ask you first, are there any positions available?

S-Nothing on top. You must understand you can't start out as top dog. However, I do hear we are planning to add an assistant to our assistant class. man. (that's shop talk for classified advertising salesman.)

A—Well, well. I have a lot of class. Note my Brooks Bros. suit. I have a closet full of them. They are an integral part of my lifestyle.

S-That's nice, very nice. Shall we get down to the nitty gritty? I need some background information for our files, but first tell me, Mr. Agnew, why should my boss hire you?

A-I'm not exactly a household word in the area, miss, but I assure you, once this face is seen around town, the money will come rolling in – through the mails, over the counter and

By
BARBARA
F.
LUEBKE
Copy Editor

under the table.

S-I see. All right, then, date of birth?

A-Nov. 9, 1918.

S-Marital status?

A-Married. You know that old American cliche, behind every good man, i.e. me, there's a good little woman.

S—Any children?

A-a few.

S—Mr. Agnew, what jobs have you held for the last several years?

A—Ah...(short pause) ...I was in Washington for the past, oh, five years or so. A government job. Before that, I was employed in Baltimore, Maryland. That was a government job, too.

S—May I ask why you left those positions?

A—Ah ... (longer pause) ... the pay wasn't too good. I just couldn't seem to make ends meet. The bills ... always the bills. Judy always seemed to need a new gown and the rent kept going up. I just had to get out.

S—Do you have any areas of specialty or expertise that might help you in advertising.

A–I know a smattering of Greek.

S—Oh, that's good. We've never had a Greek

working for us.

A – I also know a little Latin, such as nole contendere.

S – That's good too. I hear Latins are good lovers. You might pep things up a bit around here.

A – I can also turn a dandy phrase or two. I'm sure I could write a good copy block. How about these: "Attention, nattering nabobs of negativism", or, "Do you have an effete snob in your family?"

S—That's not bad, Mr. Agnew. You sound experienced.

A – Oh, I am, I am.

S – Can you give me the names of three or four personal references we might contact?

A – Let's see now. You might try to find F. Sinatra. He's probably in Palm Springs or Las Vegas. Then there are Allen Green and I. Hammerman. They are in construction in Maryland.

S – Are these your former employers?

A – No. I'd rather you didn't contact them. You see, when I left, well, they were disappointed that I left the team. They might hold grudges. I wouldn't want to throw salt in old wounds, if you know what I mean.

S—Right. Now to money matters. May I ask what you'd consider a fair commission?

A – Let me see. I'd say 25-25-50.

S – I don't understand.

A – That's 25 per cent for you (if you see that I get the job),25 per cent for your boss (if he'll send the choice accounts my way), and 50 per cent for me, of course.

S – Thank you Mr. Agnew. I guess that's about all. Oh, by the way, don't call us. We'll call you.

Reading my columns again for the first time in five decades, I swelled with pride. They unearthed the roots of the writing style I continue to call mine. They demonstrated how my eclectic reading interests were put to good use. But mostly they reminded me of my 20s and how, had I chosen to, I might have been a columnist for real. I regularly shared my work with Les in Eau Claire, who flattered me after getting a batch by asking, "Have you ever thought of a little syndicating of your column?" He called it "bright, sound, thoughtful, varied." His suggestion: "You already have a possible market thru Antigo -- thru places your classmates work. And you write it well. . . . Like Shana Alexander -- Flora Lewis -- only this is uniquely BFL."

Leadership

It is not uncommon to become at least a bit disenchanted with one's boss after the hiring honeymoon wears off and the *real* workplace reveals itself. That did not happen with Daryl. There wasn't time. A few days after Thanksgiving he told us he was leaving at the end of the year. I was surprised but not shocked by the news he was heading to the University of Missouri to be managing editor of the city daily published by the School of Journalism. "It sounds like a good deal," I wrote, "and obviously there must be something drawing him after only being here a short while." He had hired several of us and, I wrote, the staff felt "very close" to him and "respected him very much. He truly shapes the content of the paper."

He certainly knew how to work with young journalists. I described a long staff meeting a couple of weeks before he left as "a good exchange of ideas and plans— and enthusiasm. And guidance from Daryl, but not heavy-handed. We all got our say, we discussed ideas among us, and made decisions together." Another time I overheard him quietly suggest to a reporter that instead of saying to sources, "I wonder if I might have your reaction," it would be more forceful if he said, "I would like your reaction" or "What is your reaction?"

His expectations for solid reporting and engaging writing guided the staff. His record of cutting-edge design inspired me. I appreciated his leaving me alone to do my job, and how he seemed to know when

I needed him to step in and help. I appreciated the fact he gave me a month on the job before dropping a written critique of several papers on my desk and promising to go over them the next day. I appreciated that on the alternating Saturdays he did "my job," he seldom left me Monday-morning surprises. I appreciated his offer of a nice lunch if I quit smoking for a month, and although I backslid after earning that lunch, by the time I left DeKalb I had quit the Virginia Slims habit for good.

From the day of Daryl's announcement, I began thinking about "who (what) they'll get— and how it will affect us all." The staff would have no say in the matter, which was par for the course. Indeed, the December 11 announcement that the new managing editor was coming from the Hagadone paper in Beloit was how we learned a decision had been made. We ferreted out that he had been an "award-winning reporter" before being promoted to city editor there. It didn't take long for us to discover that when it came to being a managing editor, the guy didn't have a clue. The months I worked with him were a lesson in how *not* to run an editorial department.

Frank first appeared in the office on December 27, but he was not introduced to us. Instead, we were told to clear our desktops because the publisher would be inspecting them the next day. A week later, although he had not officially started work, Frank sat in our staff meeting about an energy crisis project. My first impressions: He "added some worthwhile stuff. He seems okay." But I also wrote that I "had to feel sorry for him . . . sort of lost and nobody quite ready to let go of Daryl." He left before we finished the meeting. A couple of days later he told the city editor and me about some changes he wanted to make: reducing the amount of copy from correspondents, tightening our writing and publishing more feature stories. All good, I thought, until he made an unusual comment to me as we talked about wordy copy. I said I wished he would point out examples to me because it was my job to fix them. He replied that on a paper our size editors don't have time for such things and reporters should clean up their own copy. "I have to think about that awhile," I wrote.

I wanted to assess him fairly, especially after a coffee-room conversation during which he expressed an understanding of my job and noted that contrary to what some in the building seemed to think, it was "not the easiest job on the paper." I did like his idea of rounding up items about Scouts, 4-H, the Grange, etc., once a week because that would be easier to edit and to process. "Maybe I haven't given the guy a chance," I wrote. "Hell, I've only been here five months; how can I have anything 'old' to cling to." Then I returned from a weekend away to find chaos -- and "many people glad to have me back." I learned Frank had been an hour late with Saturday's paper! He had to work Sunday in order to finish things for Monday and then "mucked up" the early copy he processed for Tuesday. "I really don't think that the guy is organized enough to be an M.E.," I concluded. When I was out sick several days later, my colleagues declared it "a fiasco." My growing sense of his editing incompetence was shared. "From talk, it sounds like none of us on the news side are overly impressed with him," I wrote.

One thing that upset us was how Frank wasted our time. A staff meeting scheduled for 30 minutes lasted 90 -- "with not a hell of a lot accomplished" -- because of his inefficiency. He didn't seem to believe we had work to do. He was dismissive of reporters. He kept telling me to "put in your two cents worth" about style issues; but when I did "I got shot down." I concluded that "although he heaps on the compliments about how well I am doing, I think he is 'afraid' of me." My colleagues agreed. Griping by journalists is nothing out of the ordinary. We are, as a rule, a cynical bunch certain that if left to our own devices we could produce a far better newspaper. At happy hour one Friday, a group of us were "hashing over Frank" and the "mutiny" that seemed more and more inevitable. We agreed "our staff, our paper" had changed. There was "an entirely different feeling" in the newsroom, where "the good 'vibes' are not as apparent."

The situation became so unsettled that Rock, a reporter and I met to discuss two stories we didn't want Frank or Ray to "get wind of" until they were finished "for fear of interference or having them quashed." One was an examination of gambling in local private clubs; the other was about "a judge who's a loser." We three also agreed that as long as Frank would not critique and guide us, we were going to help each other. We would, we decided, organize our own staff meetings. "This should be interesting," I wrote. I wondered "what will come of it and out of it." We dubbed ourselves the "Ted Baxter Bitch Club," after the bumbling anchorman on "The Mary Tyler Moore Show." As dissatisfaction grew with Frank and what we felt was a general disregard for the editorial staff, more colleagues joined our club. We tossed about words such as union, solidarity and rights. "I don't know what will come of things," I noted, "but talk is getting heavy— and the situation at work gets no better."

Up to that point, we had managed to keep our discontent under the radar. That changed when one of us got angry about something and in a conversation with Ray told him how upset and unhappy the news staff was. The publisher began calling us in, one by one; but only four staff members were in the building. Then he called in Frank, "giving, if nothing else, the impression that the 4 of us were the only unhappy ones . . . a bad scene all around." Ray and Frank met about two hours, and "since then Frank has been terribly friendly. God only knows what will happen next." At a staff meeting the next day, he said he would try to be more accessible and open communication lines. I grudgingly admitted that he "handled it very well— with only passing reference to his time with Ray." Then he told us we must begin to list our actual hours worked on our timecards instead of just writing 40 hours. *Grumble. Grumble.* We also found it curious that Frank did not take issue with Ray's declaration that none of the rest of us were editors -- despite our titles. Frank, he said, was the only editor; the rest of us were reporters.

It wasn't long until we had another staff meeting. It started routinely enough but soon became more contentious because we finally voiced our concerns about how the editorial department was being treated. We objected to ads on Page 1 (rare in those days). We offered example after example of how advertising took priority, too often resulting in unpredictable news holes. In today's jargon, we felt "disrespected." That feeling only grew after Frank shared another dictum. Each week we would be required to provide him a schedule of our hours for the upcoming week, "to get us all close to 40 hours," he explained. We thought that "it comes off like Coeur d'Alene doesn't trust us or believe the hours we do work."

Things came to a head when "the gang" quickly turned lunch into another gripe session. David, the feisty reporter, wanted action: union, strike, something. Rock, the city editor and "logical one," noted we were a small staff, easy to replace. "We will never cause changes in the chain," he added. "Besides, we won't be here forever." He favored working for ourselves and trying to roll with the unpleasant punches. That settled us down, although I did boldly suggest that "we should buy our own paper -- and then run it our way." One thing was for certain: We wouldn't comply with the request to "sandbag" stories in order to have entries for all the categories in the chain's contest. That idea "is a bunch of BS," I wrote. "No regard here for product— Just sell ads and do whatever will get 5 pts in the contest. Few here think *news*paper. How sad it is, especially for the citizens of 'Chronicleland.'"

Unlike Daryl, Frank did nothing to help me when there was too much copy for one editor to handle. I beat that horse to death in my journal. But it was his editing of one of my columns that erased any shred of respect I had for him. Accustomed to working best under dead-line, I usually wrote at the last minute. As often was true, my inspiration on this Friday came from the news, in this case ERA (Equal Rights Amendment) Week in Illinois. My opening paragraphs brought me to "the most flagrant and obscene exploitation of women that I have come across in some time." It came from a United Press International story about a bar owner in Des Moines, Iowa, who advertised that the "girl with the largest breasts wins a door prize." I offered my thoughts on how that was discriminatory and degrading. "Just as, I might add, it would be discriminatory and degrading to draw patrons by advertising a door prize for the man with the largest penis."

I didn't see the column again until I got home to my Chronicle on Monday night. I was furious to read that penis had been changed to "greatest physical endowment." I could not stop fuming about how Frank's editing altered the tone of what I had written. I finally wrote an angry letter to the editor, which I put on Frank's desk Tuesday morning, "knowing I won't be able to escape his reaction because of the proximity of our desks." Eventually he arrived and promptly opened the envelope, read my letter "and shortly laughed in that obscene way of his." A bit later he threw the letter in his trash, which prompted me to suggest it was meant to be taken seriously. He got defensive and declared, "Well, that's where it's going to stay."

After a bit, I reiterated what my letter had said, that the change had destroyed my argument. He countered that he had made the change because he didn't want "to ruin" the column, then said he was told to make the change, which I challenged. "Does Ray read all our columns?" I asked. "Of course not," he replied, curiously adding that "this isn't a college newspaper." To which I responded, "Damn, I know that." Once again I protested the change -- and not being consulted or informed about it. At that, he told me to "grow up." I realized the hopelessness of saying more and went back to work, eager to get out of the office and away from my boss.

Amid all that horror I got a call from Binghamton, New York, the Gannett paper whose earlier interest in me had come with bad timing. The editor said he was updating his files and had "traced" me to DeKalb. Was I editing? Was I still interested in Binghamton? I was, I said, but once again I needed to complete a year of employment. I said that "in July or so" I would be interested in talking about something specific. "He seemed super optimistic" and asked about salary. When I told him what I was making (by then I had received an $11-a-week raise, to $181), he said they would be in the ballpark. I also expressed a desire to "go management." He promised to be in touch. "All of which really brightened my day. Going east, going bigger, Gannett. It's something to look ahead about."

Media Critic

In the 1990s I began teaching a course on media criticism, but I had been a critic of the news media since my undergraduate days. Then, it was "bull sessions" around a table in the student union, The Spectator office, a bar or late-night eatery that fed our appetite for idealism-inspired opinions. In the pages of my DeKalb journals and in the many long letters I exchanged with my journalist friends, I found a steady diet of commentary -- about my newspaper, our profession and the varied media outlets I consumed. It's not that we wanted a different profession; more than once I wrote something like, "I wouldn't be in any other business for all the money in the world." But we thought our profession needed to be different. Better. Here are a few examples from my journal.

▶ A thought on the craft: There can be no pat definition for "news." News stories may have certain elements in common— but it seems to me that news is more than anything else defined by geography. I mean, what has been "news" in Green Bay, Milwaukee, Eugene, Eau Claire, Antigo, DeKalb— all has been different because of the uniqueness of each of those places— their size, their composition, the presence of other media. So in a class, don't we need to discuss this, realize our roles, though always as communicators, will be altered by our environment?

▶ I firmly believe that on newspapers the size of ours, there should be someone on the advertising staff capable of performing some "editorial functions." I say this becuz I spent all afternoon— and must go back later tonight, and will work some tomorrow— on filling a Xmas advertising supplement with editorial matter. Granted, this consisted mainly of taking pre-print pap and puffery, writing headlines, and matching copy with holes. But it's time consuming— a waste of time, really. Wonder how many will read it.

▶ Another excellent piece by Studs Terkel in today's Trib. God, but he is good.

▶ Can't get over how much I enjoy the Sunday Chicago Tribune. . . . If ever I teach, I'll not [belittle] the Trib— not without thorough examination of it. Still can't buy its editorial stance all of the time, but journalistically it does some good stuff.

▶ UPI has named Helen Thomas White House reporter— a first for a woman— and Nixon congratulated her on his tv press conference tonight.

▶ Really enjoying [Hunter Thompson's] "Fear and Loathing [on the Campaign Trail] ." He's far out, but damn perceptive.

▶ Proud because I managed to keep April Fool's Day off Page 1 today. "It's not a national holiday!" I said to photog, who couldn't come up with a pix idea.

▶ Editing some Copley copy yesterday and it dawned on me how regularly horrible it is— both the bureau chief's stuff and the gal working out of the office— real crap I wouldn't accept from a student— and they get paid. We need less mediocrity, and here they perpetuate it.

▶ TV2 (WBBM) newsman has been named newsman of the year by Northern Illinois University. Frank saw the news release today and scoffed "entertainment medium." While I agree, I don't think anyone could argue that Walter Jacobson is not a damn good newsman who does one hell of a job.

▶ Reading thru my editing text tonight— looking for stuff for my stylebook. And food for my brain— to help me do better.

▶ Today's paper really looked great. Think I've hit on some answers with my Faces in the News, State News Briefs and At a Glance.

▶ Woman [is] one of anchor persons on tv 2 news tonight and she's a no-nonsense type re: lib. Asked where she does her sunbathing, she asked [co-anchor] Bill Kurtis, "Where do you do yours?"

▶ Networks were given some trouble in trying to file reports from Russia today. All were censored— plugs pulled when they tried to show films of or talk about dissent and dissenters. An interesting, to-the-point comment on press freedom or as CBS News president Richard Salant was quoted as saying, "What it's like when the government controls the media."

Moving On

A week after the dust-up over my column with Frank and the "you still interested?" call from Binghamton, I received a "disturbing phone call— pleasantly disturbing." It came from Daryl. Would I be interested in a spot on The Missourian? *Would I!* The details were sketchy, but my primary responsibility would be "slotman" on the copy desk. I also would teach a course and have time to work on a Ph.D. "It sounds too good to be true," I wrote in my journal. He said he would be in touch before the weekend. That night— May 5— I hardly slept. "I'm exploding and can't tell anyone," I wrote the next day. "And I'm trying not to 'count my chickens'— but things are looking up. Hot damn, I am excited!!!"

My interest in college teaching was nourished in DeKalb, where I spoke a few times to classes at Northern Illinois University and had feelers from contacts there and at Kishwaukee College, a nearby community college. Over the years that interest had been fed by encouraging words from Les as I continued to assist with research and ideas for his minority press and critical writing courses. Clippings I sent him sometimes got turned into editing exercises. Clippings he sent me often came with instructions, such as "You must read— and save for some future lecture or something." After Minority Press was included in Eau Claire's new interdisciplinary program in Native American Studies, he wrote me: "That, friend, is a tribute to your work and digging and research." When health issues sidelined him during the spring 1974 semester, I was enlisted to help with grading editing projects and to tape several Minority Press lectures. And as the department added faculty, he floated the idea that "with a couple more years of experience Elwood [Karwand, still the department chairman] would welcome you as a job candidate."

A couple of days after Daryl's initial call, the Journalism School dean called to request a resumé, which I airmailed that evening. "I think I want the Missouri thing more than anything yet," I wrote in my journal." I am pretty sure I did not know it was the oldest school of journalism or that it considered itself the world's best. Eventually I was formally invited for interviews the weekend of May 24. With no Google to help me learn about the school, I concentrated on mapping my route, deciding what to wear and hoping I could sell myself without coming off as overly eager.

It was a long weekend. I left the Chronicle office about 11:30 Friday morning and arrived in Columbia after an eight-hour drive. What I most wanted was a shower and dinner. Instead, Daryl brought me to the newsroom for a couple of hours before he remembered I had not eaten. Saturday began with a 9 a.m. meeting with the professor who chaired the Editorial Department in the school. (Faculty in the newsroom, I had learned, straddled the worlds of traditional academe and daily journalism.) A meeting with Dean Roy Fisher followed. Once editor in chief of the Chicago Daily News, in 1971 he had become dean -- and Missourian publisher. I never have forgotten one of his questions: Who do you admire? My answer was cheeky! Ho Chi Minh for his poetry. And reporter Nina Totenberg, I quickly added, citing the recent New Times article in which she identified "the 10 dumbest members of Congress."

I thought the interviews went well, "though it is difficult to assess such things. I wasn't nervous— not at all— felt very at ease at all times." I concluded that "whatever happens will be for the best, I suppose." Before I left Sunday morning, Daryl told me he would call early in the week with the "unofficial" word. As I wrote after I got home, "There apparently is much red tape involved because of Affirmative Action. If I were a black woman I'd have it made, but being a woman does help because they are losing four. As it is, the school must prove they have made all efforts to seek out blacks."

In mid-June, I got a note from Daryl saying the dean wanted to wait a bit longer before hiring someone. Daryl was optimistic that I would eventually be offered the job. *You must be patient,* I told myself. I did my best, and on July 7 I was able to write that "dreams do come true— perseverance pays off— all those clichés run through my mind. I have been offered the job at Missouri, and when [department head] Ernie Morgan calls tomorrow or Tuesday I will accept it." The details: several shifts overseeing the copy desk of The Missourian and helping teach an advanced editing seminar. Most daunting was that in order to teach students to edit on a video display terminal -- the latest technology -- I would quickly have to learn to do so myself! I would earn $11,000 for a 12-month contract. Daryl explained the holdup had been deciding whether to hire somebody "permanent" or someone like me, who eventually would earn a Ph.D. and leave. "I can get some roots again," I wrote, because it meant a five- or six- or seven-year job for me. "Unless I bomb— and I don't see why I should."

I immediately called home, but my brother was the only one there. Next was Les, "who sounded so excited and happy for me." Because I didn't want to risk losing my vacation or a chance at the $500 bonus that winning the Hagadone contest would bring, I told only my family editor colleague and friend, Eleanor. We celebrated by using her free tickets to see Rosemary Clooney at a nearby dinner theater. I confessed that the thought of moving and readjusting again to a new environment and job and people "doesn't thrill me. I know it will be difficult." But I had a feeling I would be too busy to notice.

Busy certainly described life in the three weeks before I gave my notice and made my leaving official. There was softball. There were 24- and 28-page papers with big news holes. There was vacation, which started with a nonstop drive to Abrams, Wisconsin, where my parents had recently moved. (My father inherited the house and land my great-uncles once had farmed. Icky family drama ensued among the Luebkes.) Mom and Dad were hosting her family's reunion; the front yard soon looked like "tent/trailer city." Lots of golf. Lots of drinking (and only one bathroom). Lots of eating. Lots of catching up with Mary and Mike, who came over from Antigo. That "in a way saved me. I'm not too good with groups of relatives who are much like 'strangers.' I feel terribly uncomfortable— like we have nothing to say or share." I was a snob, and my journal reminded me that I knew it!

Midweek, I drove to Antigo for a few days. Ran into many acquaintances but it became "apparent that time and distance" had come between us and there was little to talk about "except maybe the past. And that can be a bummer." I spent the tail end of vacation in Eau Claire, and that proved to be "everything I knew it would be— wanted— and needed." There was a bottle of champagne to toast my new job, and Les told everyone we ran into, including UWEC President Haas, of that job. I blushed. "Why do you do these things to me," I asked. "Because I'm so proud of you," he answered. I was touched by his congratulatory gift -- a first edition of "All the President's Men." Finally, on Monday morning I saw Ruth Anne off to work, packed my car and waited for Les to return from his cardiac exercise program (two heart attacks had changed his ways). He, "little brother" John and I shared breakfast. Les was riding with me as far as Madison, so Ruth Anne popped home to send us off. It was a treat to have company on the long haul back to DeKalb. The talk was good, "nearly endless, touching on so many things." I managed to navigate us to the depot an hour before Les' bus to Milwaukee. Saying goodbye was "SO hard— wondering when we'll see each other again. There will be calls and letters, of course, but that *contact* is most important." Would I join the family on a winter holiday some time, he asked. Of course, I said. "Then there was a hug and a kiss and a few tears— and off I went."

My return to DeKalb was immediately hectic because I only had time to unpack and shop for supper before I was off to softball practice. The team had gone 1-1 in my absence, and we needed to win on Wednesday to remain tied for first place. The news on Tuesday, my first day back in the office, was crazy too. The repercussions of the Watergate break-in -- way back in June 1972 -- reached a tipping point when a unanimous U.S. Supreme Court ordered President Nixon to release the complete transcripts of his no-longer-secret recordings. A bomb scare that morning delayed the House Judiciary Committee's impeachment hearing. Vacation was a memory. Although the team had scheduled batting practice for 5:30, I figured no one would be there that early so news-junkie me stayed home to watch impeachment news on CBS. Surprise. I was the last to arrive at 5:45. Despite "practicing hard and an inspiring pep talk," we lost.

On Friday the 26th, I told Ray and Frank I would be leaving in two weeks. Before I could tell others, I learned that several people already knew because Eleanor had not been able to keep a secret. I didn't care. When I met with Ray, and before I shared my news, I got him to commit to printing the Chronicle stylebook I had been assembling for months. It was difficult to judge his reaction. I did explain it was what I really wanted, and he asked (no surprise here), "Then it isn't the money?" I noted I would be making more, but answered "no." As for Frank's reaction, I wrote that "I'm not sure if it was pleasure or panic in his eyes."

My fascination with the impeachment hearings continued. "To see Congress at work . . . a great lesson in civics." I explained further:

> I am totally intrigued by the televised Judiciary hearings— I mean, really and truly engrossed in what is going on and being said and procedures and all. Watched them until late (for me) last night— and this a.m. and all afternoon. The "reward"— watching history and seeing the committee vote "aye" on the first article of impeachment.

(Flash forward to the two Trump impeachment hearings, of which I watched zero minutes.) I had little time to continue my TV viewing, however, because of all I had to do in preparation for moving. I lamented having to spend $8 for packing boxes. At least I had decided to entrust the actual moving to professionals. [An aside. It was amusing to read my frequent mentions of money over the years. The one that made me smile most broadly was from DeKalb, when I observed that after buying stamps for Christmas cards, I was left with 18 cents in my checkbook and 35 cents in my wallet!]

I shared my going-away luncheon with a long-forgotten departing reporter, and it turned out to be "not at all weepy but rather fun." I used the cash in my staff-signed card to buy "Go East, Young Man: The Early Years," by Supreme Court Justice William O. Douglas, who was one of my heroes. By August 6, the big news was widespread speculation about Nixon resigning, despite his declarations that he would not. On the 7th, I wrote I hoped that "if he resigns, it is while I still am working. I couldn't stand being on the 'outside' with such a story breaking. I'd want to be where the action is— at the desk." We formulated plans for a post-resignation paper, "knowing our forte would be lots of local reaction." We made assignments. We had a headline ready to go. We planned for an 11 a.m. press run, but at deadline Nixon was still president. I continued to believe he would resign, and selfishly wished for "an evening thing that would be to our advantage. Anything near deadline, although we would replate, would leave us more at the mercy of UPI. . . . The excitement/anticipation is unique."

As the hours passed the next morning, resignation continued to seem only a matter of time. By deadline, our lead quoted an unnamed aide saying Nixon had told Vice President Gerald Ford that he would resign. We hedged our bets and went with a page-wide, 96-point headline reading "Historic decision tonight." We stuck with our plans but expected a regular noon deadline -- until the circulation manager told us he had prepared the carriers and drivers for another 11 a.m. deadline. We decided we'd work late to get local copy finished once the "inevitable" occurred. In the meantime, I designed a picture page "of historical shots, etc." I waited for UPI to move background stories, which I edited and fit on inside pages. That left me with about a page for "hopefully, the speech, reaction stories from elsewhere, and jump(s) of Page 1 copy. Also an inside page for other news."

Late in the afternoon, I went to my packed-boxes-filled apartment; I planned to return to the office to coordinate things after the speech. Shortly before 8 p.m. Central Daylight Time, I recorded my thoughts in a journal entry that reminded me of writing in my diary as a high school freshman after President Kennedy's assassination.

> In about 15 minutes, Richard Nixon will be on tv to address the American public— and it's almost positive that he will be President for only a few moments more— not even for another 24 hours. Tomorrow, I put in my last hours at the Chronicle. I will write of President Nixon— and when I am at the Missourian, it will be President Ford.

> I cannot put a finger on my mood now. As a newsperson, I am fascinated by what I watch, excited about what I have done today and will do later tonight.

> Seeing Walter C. and Eric Sevareid back from vacation to cover yet another BIG story. And thinking of myself, that this may be the Biggest story I'll work on. And glad it is happening now so I can work on it— be a part of it— a part of history.

> Still, I am sad— sad for the human Mr. Nixon— for his family— those who have believed in him, stood by him. I have never been a Nixon fan. Never could stand the man. And as a student activist I picked on him and attacked him with furor. But he is my "brother."

Adrenaline-fueled, I wrote again at midnight. "It's over. . . . He gives up the reins at noon CDT tomorrow, just when we are to go to press. For the last several hours, I have read thru copy relating to local reactions. Very mixed. A lot of disinterest. . . . Making you want to scream out: 'Look, people, it's history, affecting you and your life'—" I was back at my desk by 6 a.m. Friday "and worked my ass off. Thank god Frank did little to try to interfere. It was, if few knew, my show. And I was proud of the effort. A once-in-a-lifetime sort of thing."

I didn't expect to see our "historic" front page for several days, however. After a late breakfast (and lots more coffee) with several staff members, I made a quick stop back at the office for one final look through my desk before quietly leaving. "No goodbyes to everyone. I could not have stood that." I did promise Rock I would call when I returned to DeKalb. On the first leg of my journey to Missouri, I pointed my Gremlin north toward Abrams. At about the same time, private-citizen Richard Nixon boarded a Marine helicopter for the first leg of his journey to San Clemente, California.

Snapshots

As I had been taught, I saved my Antigo Daily Journal stories and photos in a clipbook.

ELEANOR M. HOERMAN
City Clerk
ROBERT E. MARX
City Treasurer
and Assessor
RICHARD T. WINTER
City Attorney
JAMES D. NOVAK
Inspector

CITY OF ANTIGO

EUGENE J. PREBOSKI, MAYOR

DR. J.E. McKENNA
Health Officer
KENNETH SCHLEINZ
Superintendent of
Parks and Cemeteries
GARY A. RADTKE
Director of Public Works
MARY A. CHERF
Recreation Director

ANTIGO, WIS. 54409

October 9, 1973

Ms. Barbara Luebke
220 E. Hillcrest Drive
Apt. B103
DeKalb, IL   60115

Dear Barbara:

I would personally like to take this opportunity on behalf of the members of the Antigo City Council and myself to express our gratitude for your contribution to the city. You exhibited a professional capacity for undertaking and reporting city business and council proceedings.

At our last Council meeting the aldermen unanimously approved a motion made on the floor instructing the Mayor to relay to you their appreciation and their compliments for you were truly an asset to our community.

Our sincere best wishes for continued success and prosperity.

Sincerely yours,

Eugene J. Preboski

Eugene J. Preboski
Mayor

EJP/ab

Community journalism in the 1970s proved to be a rewarding start to my professional career.

Editing during a power outage at the DeKalb Daily Chronicle.

```
FLASH

        WASHINGTON-Agnew

resigns as vice president.

    UPI
    141p


    482T
          7 1 1b weeee veep R 10
              BULLETIN
    WASHINGTON UPI  - Vice
    President Spiro T. Agnew has
    resigned, a White House official
    announced today.
          _____


    481T
          7 1 1zteeee Corrn R 10-10
    087
```

A wire-service FLASH, announcing what the AP Stylebook once described as "a transcendent development," was rare, so I saved the first one I handled.

CHAPTER 13

Becoming a Teacher

The "inverted pyramid" news story dominated newspapers (and journalism classrooms) for decades. Such a story starts with the most important facts, then relays the rest in descending order of importance. Thus, a person reading only the lead paragraph(s) still gets the news. A "suspended interest" story, on the other hand, is more like telling a joke, where the point of the story is revealed at the end. Such an approach was used sparingly because an editor who needed to trim a story to fit the space available on a page could not just cut from the bottom, which the inverted pyramid allowed.

In writing about my life and career, I so far have favored the latter approach and tended toward a chronological telling. That developed organically as I began to write, and I stuck with it. But looking back on my move to Missouri brought me up short. It did not make sense to write about the year that started my teaching journey without first offering a frank summary of it. Here is my inverted pyramid lead for the story about that pivotal year.

> The 25-year-old woman sat transfixed in her glassed-in office, stunned as 50 neophyte reporting students poured into the newsroom. She was a newly minted instructor in the School of Journalism at the University of Missouri. At that moment, she wondered if she belonged there. A year later, contract renewed, she was a baby step closer to believing that she did.
>
> That woman was me.

◇◇◇◇◇

I was smart enough for the job. Of that I was certain. And I was a skilled copy editor. Of that I also was certain. But was I truly ready to instruct editing students at the world's oldest school of journalism? Had I been hired because of connections, not accomplishments? Staring into a newsroom like no other, I conjured confidence before I headed out to the copy desk. *No time like the present to make my presence known,* I thought. It was August 26, 1974, the first day of the fall semester, and I was settling into my third new job in as many years. Also my third new city. The two weeks between leaving DeKalb and officially beginning work at the University of Missouri on August 19 had been a whirlwind of activity. As it turned out, those weeks paled in comparison with what was to come.

Exhausted when I exited DeKalb for my parents' home, I was forced to stop for coffee after only 75 minutes. Then I didn't stop again until I reached West De Pere, where Mom was working. (She had taken a job as a clerk at the local department store. When I learned of it, I teased her that she "was liberated.") I shopped a bit before joining her for dinner and then driving the last 25 miles to Abrams. I planned an early bedtime; instead, I drank beer with Dad and later talked with him and Mom until 2 a.m. After lunch the next day, I was off to Antigo. As I drove, I couldn't help thinking about the timing of yet another call from the editor in Binghamton, New York, which had come the day before I left Illinois. I don't know if he was going to invite me for an interview, but he responded positively when I told him about my new job. He asked me to get in touch if I had copy editor prospects. "There will always be a special spot in my heart" for that paper, I wrote in my journal.

I had scheduled 24 hours in Antigo. My friend Mary and I had planned a round of golf, but it was raining. Not surprisingly, we found ourselves at our favorite tavern, where we drank and talked until 1 a.m. Our conversation was "frank, open, honest" (uncharacteristic for me, which explains why I wrote that description), and we agreed our friendship was stronger than ever. Sunday, we were able to get together with the mayor before it was time for me to return to Abrams. (I was fond of the mayor. Today I chuckle over him setting me up with one of his mayor friends for the city Christmas party the year I left Antigo.)

As we had done when Mary and her husband moved me to DeKalb, we never said goodbye. She said it seemed "just like you are going back to DeKalb," and she talked of coming to Columbia in November. During my drive back to Abrams, I realized that I was, as I wrote, "anxious to see how things progress through time and across the miles. My guess is that the tie will grow."

On Monday, I organized boxes of possessions and "packed books— more than I ever realized I had." This move was different from others because I did not leave pieces of me behind. Somehow, we managed to get everything onto the truck that my parents were driving to DeKalb, and by 7 a.m. Tuesday we were on our way south. After an uneventful trip, they stayed only long enough to transfer everything from the truck to my apartment. I didn't record the emotions of that parting. I spent the rest of the afternoon and well into the night packing, with more of the same Wednesday morning. After the movers picked up 2,300 pounds of my worldly goods in the afternoon, it was time to "clean— and clean— and clean until about 6 p.m." Moving out of a real apartment was a lot more work than leaving my Antigo efficiency!

I had decided to spend the night at a nearby Holiday Inn, hoping Thursday morning's apartment inspection would be perfunctory and I would get back all of my badly needed security deposit. It was; I did. I was on the road by 9:30, every inch of the Gremlin filled. The day was hot and the drive was long, but I arrived safely about 5 p.m. I checked into the Ramada (where I had stayed the weekend I interviewed), "gorged myself on a $10 meal" and called Daryl at the Missourian office. He invited me to come by for a bit of acclimation.

I awoke early on Friday, "still not able to sleep well for about the fourth night. Guess it is the anticipation/tension/anxiety of getting settled." After making calls in search of an apartment, I decided that if the available one was "at all decent" I would take it for nine months. It was. I did. With two bedrooms, it was a step up in space from DeKalb. Until I could move in on September 1, I had arranged to stay with "the girl" (I really did call her that in my journal!) who was one of the city editors. I returned to the Missourian, where I met the other new copy editor, then found my way across campus to get my faculty ID and parking permit. Whew!

Thankfully, Saturday was a "lazy day— a little more 'indoctrination' at the office, getting acquainted with [my temporary host] Martha [Allen], the 31-year-old city editor." I observed that "we have similar professional backgrounds. She is very personable. And the arrangement should work out well." I left the Ramada for her apartment and on Sunday was at last able to sleep late. I missed reading the Chicago Tribune, "settling for" the Kansas City Star. I read all afternoon while Martha sewed. After a supper of Kentucky Fried Chicken, she showed me a bit of Columbia before we went to see "Chinatown." I already had seen the movie but judged the second viewing "worth it."

Finally it was Monday, August 19 -- my first official day as an employee of the University of Missouri School of Journalism. The school was founded in April 1908, and that September the first class -- 58 men and six women -- began studying journalism. From the beginning, the school's philosophy was one of learning by doing (contemporarily referred to as The Missouri Method), and what was then called the University Missourian was the laboratory in which students learned to produce "a well-rounded newspaper" under the faculty's supervision. The practical courses included "Copy Reading," where students learned to edit stories. By the time I arrived, the newspaper was called the Columbia Missourian and the school also operated a public radio station and a commercial television station.

Besides me there were three other new Missourian editors (all with degrees from Missouri): George Kennedy, a city editor, who came from the Miami Herald; John Rawlings, the sports editor, who had worked in Texas and for the other Columbia paper; and Brian Brooks, the news editor, who came from the Memphis Press-Scimitar. The paper ran a story introducing us. It included our photos, and I notice today that we all smiled broadly, except Brian. (I went to Missouri assuming Brian was a copy editor like me. It was an error that ended up causing me anguish; most, I realize now, of my own making.) My responsibilities and my schedule became clearer as I settled in. The paper -- the first morning newspaper I had worked on -- was published Tuesday-Sunday. Morning newspapers are produced in the late afternoon and evening, so my copy desk shifts would begin at 3 p.m. I would have Mondays and Fridays off, along with Sunday. (I got stuck working Saturdays because

Brian was a *serious* Mizzou football fan and season-ticket holder.) I also would supervise the production of special sections. It wasn't long before I learned that although "off" meant I wasn't working on the copy desk, it by no means meant I wasn't working.

Because the paper published year-round, students were needed to staff it even when the university was not in session. My first week came at the tail end of an "intersession," and this first Monday was primarily about watching and listening and learning. There was at least one light-hearted moment that day, when Brian's discarded cigarette started a fire in a wastebasket. There also was an early lesson about the dean who, I learned, was "very autocratic . . . delegates no authority. He even must assign offices." Because I was temporary until after the intersession, I had no office and "couldn't even kill time settling in." I was surprised to learn that when the semester started there would be about 200 students in the beginning editing class, which did not involve The Missourian. Brian would handle those lectures. Students in Newspaper Editing/310 would have a weekly lecture along with their "lab" hours on the main copy desk, the Sports copy desk or the People (lifestyle) copy desk. Students who moved on to Advanced Newspaper Editing/311 would be similarly assigned.

The copy desk operation worked this way: The faculty member on duty supervised three shifts of editing students and a teaching assistant. Beginning students edited stories and wrote headlines; advanced students (or the TA or the faculty member) designed pages. The faculty member and TA also monitored the wire services for stories and photographs. Daryl, as managing editor, convened an afternoon news conference of the faculty editors, and decisions were made on content and story placement, especially for Page 1. On the copy desk, my teaching involved approving student work or returning it for "fixing." I also was responsible for working with the composing room (backshop) during the production process to ensure everything fit, headlines had no errors and, most important, our deadline was met.

My journal entry, written early Wednesday, captured me doing the job alone for the first time on Tuesday.

It has been a long day— I woke up at 8 and the next thing I knew, after reading one article in Sports Illustrated, it was 10:30. Now, after my first night in the slot, I must try to unwind.

In many respects, this job may be "lonely" like DeKalb, in that, at this point, it looks as if I'll most often dine alone, because what is convenient for me won't jibe with others. And I'll stay late and probably miss beers, which is OK because I'm not anxious to get into that habit, for several reasons.

Meals, it seems, will most conveniently be taken at a nearby place; tonight, for instance, a club sandwich at the International House of Pancakes. Once in my own apartment, I think I'll try brown-bagging it. Cheaper— more nutritious— better for the figure. Today, though, dinner was my only real meal; but that's not a good practice.

Coming home at 12:30 is weird and I find it frightening. Hopefully I shall conquer that.

I think I shall enjoy this job. So far I get along fine with the few students (all men) on the rim. TA (teaching assistant) is fine, helpful; and I'm catching on to the mechanics of the system. Tho it seems strange not to be writing the heads. And I must be patient (without prodding) of those who seem so slow.

No real problems tonight, as I see it. Tho we were not out as early as we probably should be. But of course real test is Daryl's critique— which he does daily and in depth. That's good, and I expect to learn as much as the students. Only hope I always keep my wits about me and don't do something for which I'll really get chewed out.

As I observed in my next entry, my crew and I had done OK, with "no real gripes on the 'Good, Bad, Ugly' [critique]." I also was optimistic about the paper we put out on my second shift. I noted that I had "managed quite well myself and with only an occasional question [for the TA]. Should be 'faculty wise' by [next] Tuesday," my first day with fall-semester students. The third time was not the charm, however. I called it "not an especially good night." For one thing, the physical copy desk was being rebuilt, forcing us to set up temporary headquarters around some tables. Then nothing seemed to fit and there was lots of late local copy with difficult headlines required. I did not leave until 12:30 a.m. "Really could have used a beer— but no idea where Martha and the others went, so I came back to [her] apartment for orange juice and peanut butter toast." I already felt that "in many respects, it seems like I have been here longer than one week."

Finally, after some shuffling of newsroom offices, I was assigned a small corner space, not at all convenient to the copy desk. It had a table for my ancient typewriter, but no bookcase. I immediately hung a couple of posters to cover some of the glass, thus providing me a bit of privacy. The Editorial Department chairman stopped by for a chat that left me thinking I would have most of the responsibility for the lecture portion of 310. That was not the vibe I had gotten from Daryl, and over time that would cause me some consternation. Thinking it over now, I wish I had realized *not* having many classroom duties was a blessing in disguise for a newbie. I also would become frustrated that although I worked on the desk two-thirds of the time, Brian was "in charge," as Daryl put it.

Because a couple of things done under my watch had ended up on the "bad" list, that Friday I decided I would do my own critiques, as time permitted. I would red-pencil the paper for headlines and style. "Even though there will be different kids each day of the week, I think such efforts will be worthwhile." I also had become "more aware of culling and clipping examples of really good things [from the Missourian and elsewhere], particularly headlines." Already I had begun to expand my notion of teaching beyond the bounds of my weekly contact with each shift of students.

My first Saturday on the desk was notable for two experiences that would reverberate over the months to come: (1) an uncomfortable exchange with the night city editor and (2) personal insecurity combined with too much alcohol. The day started with what the TA described as a typically slow Saturday. There was little hard news and little space, so by 8:30 p.m. our work was essentially wrapped up. Then a local story broke, which I decided we would put on the jump page -- until, just as I was preparing to leave, a call came from city editor G. Thomas Duffy. Mr. Duffy, as I referred to him as long as I knew him, was a newsman straight out of central casting. He had come to the School of Journalism in 1961 from the East St. Louis Journal, bringing with him a reputation as a fearless, hard-driving reporter and editor. I did not know that night, but was soon to learn, of his penchant for leaving early on

Saturdays to, wink-wink, "unwind" -- with frequent calls to hound the newsroom. Earlier in the day, I had been caught in the middle of a minor disagreement between him and the photo editor, but his call to insist that we put the late-breaking story on Page 1 took me by surprise. Intimidated, I did as he instructed. Later I realized that I should have contacted Daryl, as I had been instructed to do before making any changes to Page 1. My own "unwinding" that night was not planned. When I finally did get out of the newsroom and back to Martha's, she was entertaining friends from Iowa. I will let my journal tell the rest of the story:

> I, of course, felt a little uncomfortable. Work had upset me. And I quickly guzzled four cans of beer. Then, at 1 a.m., I went with Martha to a party a few grad students were having to celebrate the end of intersession. Well, next thing I know it is 7 a.m. and we are eating breakfast at some all-night restaurant. Needless to say, I didn't get out of bed until 2:30 this afternoon and then only because I had to wash my hair.

One week in and I already was beginning to realize that one didn't decompress after a crazy night in the newsroom by going home to drink a glass of warm milk and read a magazine!

The real semester started for me when I greeted my first students at 3:30 Tuesday afternoon, followed by two more shifts. I quickly tired of my introductory pep talk -- and I would need to give it nine more times! Although I thought things had gone "fairly smoothly," I learned an important lesson: the need to balance the workload and keep students busy while also making sure our production deadline was met. That day, I had pushed too much copy early and left the second shift of students with "quite a lull, and nothing to do." (I can't imagine any of them cared.) The next night's students were, as my TA put it, "singularly inept." In my journal, I wrote that some of them were "not even able to deal with basics" such as knowing what a "downstyle" headline was or what headline instructions (e.g., 1-24-3) meant. "Many, many headlines were rewritten more than once." At 12:15 a student still was struggling with a Page 1 head, which I finally wrote. "Not a great head," I told my journal, "but it got the job done."

I left the newsroom feeling "the first-bad-day blues." I wondered "how the entire system can ever be made to work." Of course, it had worked for decades, and I was eager to see that happen, especially as the week went on and I saw more students who left me wondering how they ever had passed the basic editing course. "We have 16 weeks to work on them," I wrote, "and it has to get better." I didn't like how many copy desk items had been making Daryl's "Ugly" board. I accepted some blame: "Headlines have been giving us some problems, and part of it is a failure on my part to at least glance at leads and heads on all pages— and to read and check all on Page 1."

Outside the newsroom, I was struggling with the "work-sleep-work-sleep routine," which had become very real. I found it "scary, but things must get done." As determined as I was to do my daily critiques, I had not figured out how to find the time. "These 12-hour days are horrid!" Unfortunately, the plans I had to do laundry on my first day off were postponed when I learned that we all were expected to attend a faculty meeting. I found it to be "a joke." (The first of countless times in my career I would use that description for such meetings.)

> I think "we" are snobbish. I know I felt awfully insignificant when I heard my background [described] vs. some of the others. For one, Brian got his M.S. in 1969— two years before I even got my B.A. I guess I really am lucky to be here. For however long the experience lasts, it will have been an EXPERIENCE.

> Lots of mickey-mouse and petty politics very apparent. Didn't take much to see the tensions— divisions. And the predominantly male faces. I'm on the Library Committee. Whoopee!

The meeting did include news that enrollment in the School of Journalism continued to grow with the wave of post-Watergate/Woodward and Bernstein interest in journalism. At Missouri, students had pre-journalism status for two years before they could apply for admission into the J-School. A committee was considering ways of tightening requirements, and one idea was raising the minimum grade point average to 3.0 "Ugh!" I wrote. "I couldn't have made that at the end of my sophomore year, I don't think." (Actually, that was exactly my GPA.)

My insecurities and social awkwardness show up in journal

entries far more often than I remembered, but perhaps I should not have been surprised. After all, I was a young woman in what was at the time a largely male environment. The numbers of women studying journalism were on the rise, but those students were at least a half generation behind me. To date my role models were women I read about, not women I knew or worked with. In one early entry, I wrote about how

> my "old self" was showing tonight [a reference to Oregon, I suspect]. While finishing up work, Martha mentioned a group was going out for beer. I said I'd probably go along. A little later, I stood around talking with her, just shooting the breeze, and she said something to the effect that what I needed was a beer. Which I took as being "you go— I'm waiting for someone." So I went home.
>
> That is one of the kinds of things I'm trying NOT to do. Not to get in that mindset. [I want to] "let go." Obviously, though, it comes hard. Boy does it ever. Why am I so damn private? Sometimes I want to be, but certainly not all the time. And I take little things so personally sometimes. Read so much into things. My insecurity.

I had to bury that insecurity as best I could because my job required me to be decisive and in command. I realized that on the first weekend of the semester. Thankfully, there was no football game, when news deadlines were earlier than usual -- especially for home games. It seemed that we would be short-handed, and it was up to me to get a student who was scheduled to work 2-6 to leave and return for the 6-to-closing shift. No one volunteered, so I chose the person whose last name fell in the middle of my alphabetized roster. That student had a legitimate excuse for not working later, so I chose the last person who had signed up for the shift. Turned out he had planned to leave town the night before but had stayed only to work in the afternoon, then leave. He was not happy with me. I didn't like it, either, but I needed the body. As it turned out, a student came in to make up a missed session (I didn't know she was coming) and I suddenly had too many editors. For a while there was nothing for Unlucky Guy to do, and I felt guilty. At least the news got exciting, and I kept him busy.

That exciting news came near the end of the night -- of course -- and tested my decision-making. We got word of a possible shooting that we soon learned *was* a shooting. Information was sketchy at first; then we learned it was a domestic dispute. The consensus of me, TA and city editor was that we didn't have enough information for a Page 1 story. About 11:30 we learned we had a photograph. I called Daryl and described the situation. He said to put the package on Page 1, even though the printing plate had been made. This required some juggling; luckily we made it work. In my journal, I questioned what we had done. "I sure would hate to turn to my Sunday paper at breakfast and see that. Not in poor taste, body under a sheet, investigators in background, but I wonder if it really SHOWS anything. Adds anything to our paper/story."

My second week of work was more of the same -- with the added chores involved with moving into my apartment. I didn't expect that to take so long. I checked in with the movers on the 31st, only to learn it would be at least a week until my things were delivered. I didn't want to wear out my welcome with Martha but staying a few more days seemed necessary. Finally, before my shift on September 5, I eagerly moved everything from Martha's to my new digs. I had water, gas and electricity but no furniture, so I slept on the floor. I used my free Friday to clean and shop for necessities, including "a delicious pizza for today's meal." (Little did I realize how much pizza I would eat in the weeks and months ahead.) No television set made for a long day, so I went to a movie, "Death Wish," which I judged to be "a Grade B movie that painted a horrible picture of living in New York City."

Money -- specifically a shortage of it -- had been a constant during my first two years as a working woman. I thought life would improve with my new salary, but at least in the beginning I fretted a lot over money. As if it weren't challenging enough to be paid *monthly*, I had learned my first check would be delayed because the paperwork had not been processed. I was incensed. (As it turned out, the delay was until October 1, and I was not paid for the two weeks I was under contract in August.) Deposits on utilities and other expenses had significantly depleted my new checking account. I asked my parents for a loan and was relieved to know that $200 was on the way. One bright spot was the percolator I had purchased because I now had time to make and enjoy "real" coffee. (I was hardly a coffee snob then; I most certainly am now.) Doughnuts and paper cups meant I could enjoy "brunch" without going out.

On September 10, I still was sleeping on the floor -- and making phone calls from my office. On the 11th, I couldn't decide if I was getting sick with the flu that seemed to be going around. "In my normal forceful manner, I put off calling the movers— saying I'll do it tomorrow for sure." I did and was told to expect the truck the next afternoon, by which time I also was supposed to have a working telephone in my apartment. "It's back to civilization," I optimistically wrote. Left unstated was how relieved I would be if those two things happened. They must have, because on the 15th I wrote that it was "good to have furniture; living room looks great." I did wonder where my many magazines were being sent, when I would find the time and energy to unpack the boxes stacked everywhere, and what I might use to hold clothes until I bought a dresser.

At least I had begun to receive some personal mail at the office. Nothing brightened my days more than going to my faculty mail slot to find such treasures among the pink campus mail envelopes and school-related documents. Letter writing is in my DNA, evidenced by the treasure-trove of postcards and other correspondence I have been privileged to read from at least three generations of relatives. As I wrote this book, I often thought how useful it would be to have some of the letters I wrote over the decades, but at least I had bagsful of those I received.

Mary, true to her word, made sure I had a letter waiting for me at the office when I officially arrived for work. She wrote while attending a city council meeting and filled me in on news and gossip from Antigo. I was amused to read that the local gadfly was still harping about fluoridation, which I had heard him do at countless meetings. Mom came through with family news a couple of days later, and a few days after that I heard from Tom, the off again/on again man in my life. The Marine Corps was paying for him to attend graduate school and he had landed at the University of Wisconsin. He regaled me with the horrors of apartment living and included two hand-drawn maps for "The Big Picture" of his location, in hopes that I might visit. I found his closing paragraph most interesting. He wrote that he would welcome "good thesis ideas or maybe a few various and sundry re-search papers" because "after five years away from the game this stuff isn't coming natural anymore." His final sentence affirmed my neg-ative impressions of the military: "I've had to resort to something I haven't made use of for quite a while -- thinking." Used to him signing off with "Luv, Tom" I immediately noticed this letter said "Love." Not long after, among a list of one-liners in my journal, I asked, "I wonder how Tom defines our relationship?"

Another relationship I was interested in figuring out was that of the dean as the leader of the School of Journalism vs. the dean as the functional publisher of The Missourian. (The legal publisher was and is the Missourian Publishing Association, which empowers the dean.) I had my first unpleasant interaction with Publisher Dean on just my third weekend, a day that prompted me to write, "If all Saturday nights continue to be as hectic as the last three, I may decide to hang it all up." I was "initiated into the way Roy Fisher runs the ship— and what a scenario . . . what a fiasco." It was an unusually active Saturday, and we processed a lot of copy between 2 and 6 p.m., including most of that for Page 1. But we couldn't finish because we needed the dean's approval on a story. I am going to let my journal fill in the details; it is the sort of behind-the-scenes look into the business that people seldom get. (At least that was true in the "olden days.")

Went to my office early to write a couple of letters. Found a note that said [Dean] Fisher wanted to see me— wondered about what— soon found out. He didn't like a headline from Friday's paper. [Keep in mind I had not worked then.] "Black solons blast/law school dean." [The short "solon" was headlinespeak for legislator.] Thought the headline too strong for story. And didn't like organization of story, for which he had been the tipster. Also, he likes to be told of and to hear/have read to him "controversial" stories. Anyway, we had a little "session" on the headline/story and what should have been done, me mostly meekly listening/nodding. He's the publisher, so guess he can do what he damn well pleases.

Anyway, today we had another story on the subject— law dean's response, etc. For which Fisher ordered Page 1, above the fold, more than a 1-column head. Ruined our page 1 plans. Also, we felt he should hear the rewrite before publication. Problem came when we could not/never did get ahold of him.

Meanwhile (as the plot thickens— and note should be made that Daryl was out of town for day and evening) Duffy has gone home . . . [and soon begins] calling every 15 minutes or so. He likes one version— then wants it rewritten— then wants to know how it is going to be played— then wonders if headline is "positive." All this time the teaching assistant and I agreeing decision is the dean's. Yet we can't reach him. And we both WANT him to decide. Eventually we go with what Duffy wants. And if we are called on it, the buck will be passed.

A couple of days later I was summoned to Fisher's office. Instead of quizzing me on Saturday night's events, he asked what I thought the paper's position should be on the pardon of former President Nixon. I silently wondered what the hell was going on when he abruptly switched topics to the Missourian's design. After we discussed design, layout and headlines for a while he asked if I had any problems, then assured me that I was doing a good job. I walked out of his office even more puzzled than when I walked in.

Having ruminated on those interchanges, I asked myself, *If I knew our publisher to be as autocratic, stubborn and illogical as has come out in the last few days, would I have taken the job?* We followed up on Saturday's story with another, more detailed story. I believed it should top Page 1, given that it included a report alleging blackmail. "Instead, we are told to not put it on top. No reasons why, just what Fisher told Daryl, and he told us. Apparently, Daryl didn't put up much of a fight." I recorded that Martha, the city editor who handled the story, "was pissed as hell and muttered about 'getting out.'" The teaching assistant suggested that someone should do an article for the Columbia Journalism Review about this episode and others. I wondered

why— why top-notch, go-get-'em reporting— a real 'scoop'— NEWS— LOCAL— ends up like this. What do students think when we teach one thing and practice another. In this case, we seem to be more an example of chicken-shit journalism than Washington Post Watergate journalism. And our Big Man from Chicago is convinced he knows it all.

I might not do verbal outrage, but I could express it in words!

But wait . . . there is more. Once again, it was a Saturday, this one complicated by Missouri playing its first football game of the season -- in Mississippi, at night. That required us to have all our copy moved by 10:30, freeing the composing room to do the Sports pages. If need be, however, we could take the "Saga" story late. My copy desk had no trouble meeting our deadline and I was prepared to handle "Saga," which was being written. Andy, the reporter, read the dean the first page of his story about 10:45, at which point Fisher decided it would not be an "Insight" story, as planned. He ordered it be placed above the fold with a 1-column headline.

> That, of course, threw a wrench into everything. Luckily, we had an Insight in type, so used that, but then had to juggle some to get Saga on the page as ordered. And that meant juggling on the jump page and Records page. We managed, though visually both pages went to hell.

> Fisher wouldn't hear the story in takes, and about 11:20 the city desk couldn't get him on the phone, so they drove to his house and were not back until midnight. By the time we got the story, got it in type and the pages finished, it was 1 a.m.

> Only comment from the reporter was he felt, at this point, "like a whore." I asked him if this was the last of his Saga copy and he said, "Not for the reason you think." I answered, "I understand." Roy has made it very clear he doesn't want the story pursued further.

> Naturally, we are all angry, puzzled, tired.

It was too late to go to the party Brian was hosting, so the reporter, TA and I went across the street for a beer. Just as our pitcher arrived, Martha stormed in. She had been at Brian's and heard something was up, so she came looking for the reporter. She was furious. I finally got home about 3 a.m. and fell asleep thinking that Monday "should be interesting." It wasn't. Daryl asked only, "After all the juggling, what time did you finally get out?"

This sort of disillusionment shared the semester with moments of calm resolve about finding ways to do my job well and even a few of pure euphoria. I was determined to connect with students as Les Polk had connected with us at Eau Claire, and I held firm to my belief in the need to help shape a new generation of journalists whose calling was to "comfort the afflicted and afflict the comfortable." (My poster with those words hung in every office I ever occupied.) I wrote about wanting "to try to meet the needs of each student, to a certain extent, because I know each of them has his own expectations and needs."

At first, connecting did not come as easily as I expected, but over time most of the student editors (most just a few years younger than I) learned that my bark generally was worse than my bite, that I was approachable and that I wanted them to end the semester doing their best work. Those were messages I tried to convey during one-on-one conferences, which I offered regularly. For the initial meetings, no doubt to establish my credibility, I wore a skirt to work -- for the first time. The conferences challenged my stamina. There were three straight nights on the desk, each followed by getting up at 9 and being at my office by 11. I saw students until 2, then jumped right back into desk work or assisting students who asked for extra help. Another time, on a day off from the copy desk, I met with students from 11 a.m. to 5 p.m. because it was the only way I could fit in everybody. Many that day were my "poorer" students, and I wrote about hoping that I "could handle them well— can be honest, but not discouraging, except with one or two who may need to be discouraged." As I wrote that, I thought back to talking about my students during a conversation with "little brother" John Polk. "I can't believe you really are a teacher . . . and you sound just like my dad," he had said. I agreed and took that as a compliment.

I don't know if "dressing up" helped, but I judged my first 15-minute sessions "basically okay." I called one day "enlightening," and made note of "one gal who worked on something else during the entire time" and the guy "who's in journalism because he thought it was as good as anything else and because he had 'aced' an early course with no work." Thankfully, there also had been one student "who wants to go into editing and wants to do more work." Another time, a "hapless but genius grad student" missed his appointment, which was my last of the day. By then I was tired and did not wait around long, "which maybe was good because he is a special case." I tried to be patient with him, to put up with his apparent eccentricities— until he failed to show up for a Saturday shift. I called him in to ask why. I suggested that adults don't forget such things. He interrupted: "But I'm not a mature adult." I kept talking and said that if he had called in sick, I would have understood. His response was, "I am ill; mentally ill." I didn't know how to handle that, other than to say if he "forgot" again I would be forced to flunk him. I also learned that expecting graduate students to be qualitatively different from undergrads was problematic. For example, near the end of the semester another instructor and I were exchanging anecdotes. He told me about the number of graduate students in his introductory course who continued to misspell Kissinger, which astounded us. Later that afternoon, a student gave me a headline with Kissenger. "God help us!!" I wrote.

The new teacher was learning -- as she had hoped she would. One student from that first semester who I have never forgotten was Lucy, a graduate student with cerebral palsy who used a wheelchair. Her limited movement and speech could not hide that she was bright and determined to succeed; working with her challenged me in good ways. I wrote, "I certainly do better with her than I do with this jerk grad student from Texas with a shit-eating grin and a horrible attitude problem." I also never have forgotten about running into one of my graduate students, a New Yorker, at a laundromat. He seemed as surprised to see me as I was him, before he laughed and commented, "It was never like this as an undergrad, doing your laundry alongside your instructor." Indeed!

Affirmation that I was teaching in a way that worked came with my first evaluations by students, a sampling of which I recorded in my journal. Was it lingering concerns about being compared to my much-loved predecessor that led me to include a negative one first? "She is gruff and doesn't seem well adapted to working with and teaching students. Glad she wasn't here during my first year at J-School. Get someone like [previous copy editor] back." Two other negative ones I included were more helpful to me. One person thought I was "too hard in grading" (I saw it as having high standards.) and "was not always clear in explaining what the student specifically was doing wrong." (I worried in my journal about not always being able to translate what I had known "forever.") The other student wanted "a little positive reinforcement now and then." (I couldn't argue with that.)

Not surprisingly, I was reassured by the positive comments, which were in the majority. I was not surprised that I had labeled this one my favorite: "She's professional, a strongly liberated woman, young acting, hip, easy to relate to. She compliments a job well done, freaks out over stupidity." Among the others were these:

▶ She knows her shit. She was helpful, easy to get along with. I hope she doesn't change into a typical deadwood J-School prof. [I didn't want that, either.]

▶ Shows great deal of patience even when under pressure. Very even-tempered— never too busy to help. [I didn't always feel this to be true.]

▶ Calling her Barb. She is on friendly, one-to-one basis with students. Easier to see and talk to than "professors." Understanding about late assignments, etc. Not interested in "shafting" students. [The gulf between classroom teachers and newsroom teachers was mentioned often.]

▶ She's professional. . . . Easy to talk to, friendly, but will not hesitate to drive and push the student to higher achievement. [Bingo!]

▶ She's willing to teach if you're willing to learn. [Always a challenge when teaching editing, especially to students with no interest in editing.]

▶ Initiated conferences when she felt students need additional guidance. Encourages creativity. Generally helpful. Not enough faculty are.

▶ Looks unfriendly even though, after getting to know her, you find she's not. [I always have struggled with this.]

After reading my evaluations, I concluded: "I'm not trying to win a popularity contest, but I think I'm becoming the kind of teacher I want to be."

As for the me outside of work, I have only journal entries and letter fragments to remind me how much I struggled. Giddy pronouncements -- "I am not sure I believe my life has taken the turn it has; I can't believe I am here. . . . It is such a dream. I love it, every second, even when I complain" -- were sporadic. Adjusting to life outside the newsroom elicited more angst than joy, and my journal entries included a confounding mix of stressing over being single, making too many bad choices about food and alcohol, and ruminating about my place in the world. What seems clear to me now -- that there was a degree of inevitability to such personal developments because of my age and my professional environment -- was for decades mostly unexamined. Perhaps writing now of those struggles is my way of showing what is possible when reflection meets the past. Or perhaps it is an unburdening necessary to make sense of the decades that followed my first teaching job.

◇◇◇◇◇

I was not new to being geographically unsettled, but I seemed to have forgotten about my difficulties in the early months at Oregon (depression), Antigo (hectic pace) and DeKalb (colleagues as my only social circle) and their lessons. I can't imagine I was alone in feeling lost, but I often felt singularly alone and socially awkward -- despite whatever public face I presented. Thrust into a job with almost all male colleagues, working nights, maintaining a frantic schedule, and teaching students just a bit younger than I proved to be a peculiar recipe. I did not have a spouse to go home to, to kvetch to or to share chores (the latter admittedly a pipe dream for most women in the mid-1970s). My only experience working nights was sorting green beans on a canning-factory conveyor belt, and because of mind-numbing boredom I had quit after one shift. I had enjoyed personal connections with several faculty while in college, and my primary role model in that regard was Les Polk. I am not now surprised by how I acclimated, but in my maturity I also can see situations that were problematic.

I certainly was fortunate to share the newsroom with Martha and fortunate that I lived with her for a few weeks, which allowed us to become acquainted more quickly than otherwise might have happened. That we were like-minded about journalism was a bonus. There was never any doubt about where she stood, and she could shout instructions and cajole reporters with just the right measure of tough love. She saw the dean for what he was. When she eventually learned about pay inequities and confronted him, it cost her her job. For me, she was a model of how important it was to find a way to hold my own in the newsroom. As such, I summoned Martha's mien when I realized that I needed to convince one of the night city editors to teach his reporters "that when [Barb says] it is time to quit writing, that means finish the sentence and that is all." Although we occasionally socialized outside of work, however, that first year Martha and I were friendly more than friends. My few real friends lived elsewhere, and it is they who are mentioned in my journal, along with several students who I came to regard as friends.

At first I welcomed going home to the quiet of my apartment. After the noise of the newsroom -- "the people, teletypes, hustle and bustle" -- the peace was relaxing. I enjoyed getting into my robe, taking something out of the freezer for lunch the next day, "succumbing to a snack." I always had my music and something to read. Sometimes I did "really wish there was someone to come home to," but most of the time I was "not at all conscious there isn't." As the weeks progressed, though, I increasingly put off returning to that quiet apartment until "last call" forced it. One night, for example, the plan was for a couple of beers with "a German grad student, a married grad student, a city-desk assistant and a black TV newsman." I didn't get home until 2 a.m. The intersession between Christmas and the spring semester was "drinking every night after work— getting home about 2 and sleeping until nearly noon. Then going to work— and repeating the process." Yet another time, after we were 15 minutes late despite it being a slow news night, the city editor, sports editor, my graduate assistant and I went out and enjoyed ourselves -- until almost 3 a.m.

The camaraderie around the copy desk (and at the city desk, too), especially for the students working the late shift, lent itself to pizza and beer after the paper was "put to bed." The Greek man who owned the restaurant across the street from the J-School accommodated our schedules. More than once we knocked on his locked door. He welcomed us in, then joked with us as he made our pizzas and we complained about whatever had made us miss our deadline. Did we even think about him risking his license to serve us pitchers of beer after hours? When we staggered out at 2 a.m. -- or 2:30 or 3 -- did we acknowledge what a long day he also had endured? I hope we tipped him well.

Were it today and not the mid-1970s, the sometimes-blurry line between faculty editors and student journalists might charitably be judged unprofessional. More likely, it would not be tolerated by the powers that be. Having lived it, I know that shared time involved a lot of teachable moments, not unlike those my fellow journalism majors and I had benefited from in Eau Claire. Throughout my teaching career, I was least happy when I was unable to replicate that environment of working *with* students to do journalism. And I was happiest when I felt needed, when my opinions were sought. That happened most at Missouri, but of course I did not realize it in the moment.

My crazy schedule was very real, as supported by the Faculty Activity Survey that showed I averaged 76.4 hours a week during the fall. I was absolutely thrilled to have a traditional Saturday-Sunday weekend for the new semester. I especially valued lazy Sunday nights that allowed me to mentally prepare for the week ahead. Yet with my goal of being a "human faculty member," I could not be angry about a Sunday night call from an upset student I had come to know a bit away from the copy desk. It was early in the semester and she was, as I wrote, "overwhelmed already by work" and wanted to drop her business writing course. I wondered if she was asking for advice or just needed someone to support her feelings. We talked quite a while before I suggested that if she did not need the credits to graduate, why not drop the course. I pointed out that her career goals didn't demand what the course offered. "My thinking was [for her] to loosen up, have some fun during her last semester, spend time and efforts on fewer things." She came by to see me on Monday "and we rapped a while." A couple of days after that it seemed "all has worked out," although I did not make note of what that meant.

That Monday was, I wrote after work, "rather overwhelming, and rather fantastic." It also had included an office visit from Jan Winburn, who at my urging (and with my strongest recommendation) had applied for a Newspaper Fund Editing Internship. I still have the note she slid under my office door in December to let me know she had been accepted. On this day she wanted to tell me that she had been assigned to the pre-internship boot camp at Virginia Commonwealth University. I never had heard of the school, I told her. (But then, I had not heard of the Missouri School of Journalism until Daryl took his job.) She was excited, which I found "fun to see." I secretly hoped she would do well "or my credibility will suffer." After Jan, a student working on the latest of the special sections I was overseeing dropped by with questions. This project was a biggie, and the copy we had to process and our deadlines were never far from my mind. Other inquiring students followed, and every now and then my grad assistant popped in for something. The downside of my open-door policy, "which I do enjoy," was frequent exhaustion. Such "merry-go-round" days left me "unbelievably drained by nightfall," and even if I went straight home from the office, I often did not sleep well.

A self-imposed deadline I had was getting myself into a Ph.D. program. I had been assured of a contract for summer school and the 1975-76 academic year, and my department chairman told me I would not be pressured to finish my degree quickly and move on. But I knew I needed to get cracking. The problem was I had been vacillating between political science and journalism. My New Year's Day journal entry recorded that I had decided on political science. Why? "I think once I get started I'll be better off— and meeting new people. Also will be good to begin thinking again." This last sentence hints at negative views about advanced degrees in journalism that I had heard and read. I was prepared for a year of preparatory political science classes if need be. "I think that would be rather fun." After meeting with an administrator, I was left to decide whether I wanted to earn a Master of Arts degree before entering their Ph.D. program. "My tendency" was "to go for it, with summer 1976 as M.A. target."

With intersession under way after Christmas, I had written to Les for advice ("Still can't make those decisions alone, I guess."). As he so often did, he challenged my thinking (and while typing took liberties with spelling, capitalization and punctuation).

> WHY is it you're rejecting a mass com or J degree with phd? I'm not quite sure of that. I'm not quite sure it's the right thing to do. I can think of many things in J that you're eminently qualified to research, to do original work on, to come thru with some fine materials. I rather reject as not being sound argumentation the thoughts that upper level J research isn't vital. Not that I'm hostile to ur idea: I just

want you to be very very sure that you're doing the right thing. Your field is mass com, it's journalism. You would have a life of working with it. By studying it at the top level, you wud be encouraged and would stuff your mind with more ideas; question some of the concepts and thots of youth and come up with new thinking, I'm certain, about much of the whole thing. You have further contributions to make. Your undergrad work, your MA work shows that. NOW: do you forsake that for the "new" study of Political Science which, in some ways, to me doesn't seem as much the academic discipline as J does. J is a new study, too, but there's so much uncharted territory to study. Just Think, Barb, of the areas you and I have approached, tentatively. Think of all those courses, and studies, you've assisted with. Do you leave that? Could you not find something combining your political interest— as a minor, perhaps— with some of those areas? I wonder. Just want to slightly challenge your preliminary thinking here. It seems a bit of a waste to have to take another 15 to get ANOTHER ma. Truly, doesn't it? Somewhat of a time and commercial waste. What's wrong with OUR field. The one we're in???

Don't accept my word as the mt. sinai voice . . . but I want to be certain you think this thing thru, all the way. An academic program is something u live with many, many yrs.

Think it out more. and consider . . . just as tho we were batting it around in the living room. Hey, you didn't even take note of the new floor lamp at end of couch, did you????

To get a journalism administrator's point of view I asked my department chair which degree would be viewed more favorably for a career in teaching. He said he leaned toward political science because there would be "more prestige," but either one "would do the trick."

Eventually, I chose to pursue a Ph.D. in journalism. But before I finalized that decision, I had a birthday to celebrate. "One would think that by 26 the 'fun' might go out of these days that come once a year. Not so for me. They are a big deal." I resisted opening the package from my sister and brother-in-law until *the* day because I had a feeling it would be the only one. It was, and I was delighted with the "nifty wall clock." (A ditzy houseguest, the friend of an Antigo friend, had turned on my toaster oven without removing the Christmas-gift clock sitting on top. It was still wrapped in its plastic and, needless to say, had been ruined.) Before going to work I waited for the mail. Late, of course! But my parents' card included a check to buy the beanbag chair I wanted.

I recorded two birthday surprises in my journal. The first was flowers from Mary and Mike in Antigo. It was the first time I had received flowers, and I wrote that I "would love to have seen the expression on my face when I opened the door" to the delivery man. Surprise No. 2 was a book of poems by Anne Morrow Lindbergh from a student I had recently "counseled." The poet was new to me; I found her work "very nice, mellow." The student inscribed her thanks and wishes for a good party. Yes, I threw myself a birthday party. Two days after the fact -- a Saturday! My journal reminded me that after work on Friday I had stayed out until 3 a.m., then was rudely awakened at 10:30 by loud music from the apartment below me. Somehow I found the energy to hunt unsuccessfully for the beanbag and shop for the party. I said yes to a call inviting me out to dinner; we didn't make it back to my apartment until 9 -- just before my first guests arrived. The last did not leave until 4 a.m. Sunday. When I wrote about it, I concluded:

> It was a good night. Not everyone invited showed up . . . but that was OK. There wasn't much room left on the floor. And the good people were here. Think all had fun. I know I did. Lots of good talk— Real— Am sure I . . . got philosophical, as I usually do when I drink. But I don't feel bad.

I had said "no gifts" but I know there was at least one: a red-glass-pig bank. To this day I use it as a doorstop. Its pennies can only be released by breaking the glass, and I have no intention of doing that.

One of the challenges of publishing The Missourian was the need to start over every semester, when many new students joined the staff and others moved into new roles. That challenge was especially acute for me in my "freshman year" on the faculty. My winter intersession shifts, despite a few nights of "incompetence on the rim and panic in the slot," generally had gone well. Now I had to tamp down expectations and ramp up supervision. I quickly discovered one reason for the poorly edited stories that discouraged me. The first style test I gave was a disaster! Of the 42 errors to be corrected, most students missed at least 10. I decided on the spot that I would give them the same test in a week. I also was incredulous that a college student could forget to put his name on his quiz, and doubly incredulous about the graduate student who didn't realize there were three pages to the quiz — even though it was stapled. Another challenge was the number of student copy editors I supervised during my four nights on the desk. My first one-on-one conferences, in mid-February, meant seeing about 65 students over eight days. "That will cut down on afternoon socializing," I wrote, then added, "Wonder if I'll discover anyone worth knowing." I later observed that although I had a good rapport with most, so far I had not come across anyone as interesting as in the previous semester. "But then, [that group] was special because they were my first class ever."

After the conferences, my office returned to being Progress Edition Central for students working on that massive special issue. One day had four of us crammed in and working together for about five hours. "A good time and quite a bit of work done," I wrote, then added:

> Even got to use the listening ear a bit, for Rich who was a bit "down" because he got stood up by a date last night. And for Barb who was angry because of working on an editorial all morning only to be told it could not be run, and has vowed to quit working so seriously. And for Sydney who called and was on "take 12" of a story and had not seen C. yesterday to give him his Valentine gift.

If only I could have connected that way with my parents. That night, I received my first call (no letters, either) from them in about three weeks. "And it was painfully obvious we had little to say to each other— little to share. Our worlds are so far apart— separated by more than miles." I had returned to Wisconsin for my 10-day holiday break and in the days before my flight had expressed excitement about the trip. After it, without referencing specifics, I summarized my uneasiness:

> Have this very deep feeling of how little I have in common with parents. How little communication there is. Interests so different. Backgrounds so different. Time with them often is tense, strained. Not sure why. Being there just is not all that great. Can I help how I feel about it?

I contrasted that with my "opposite feelings being with the Polks." I had squeezed in "five very brief hours" with them (including me treating everyone to lunch), Mary and I having driven over from Antigo. In Eau Claire, I found "talk, THINKING, ambition— future— fun— intelligence— class— much more my kind of atmosphere." On our return drive, Mary didn't react much to the visit, but when we talked later she was puzzled by trying to reconcile my adoption of "the Polk lifestyle" and our friendship. How to account for *our* differences? I had no answers.

The relationship with my parents was the tip of the angst iceberg that I increasingly bumped into. I regularly wrote about personal failings, including controlling my weight. As I wrote at the beginning of the new year, "If I regret anything about my life to date, it is that I was born fat. And . . . I am finding my willpower waning. Now more than ever, I need strength. Question is, can I muster it." It was a familiar question. My January 1, 1963, diary entry had included the fact that "Mom and I started are (sic) diet. I want to lose 20 lbs. and get to 110." I didn't write much more about it, although on January 6 I recorded that I had lost 4 pounds. "Mom didn't think I could stick, but I am." Seems she must have been right, based on my March 10 declaration that "I am going back on my diet tomorrow." Another time I mentioned how Kris, Mom and I agreed to diet and the first of us to lose 10 pounds would treat us all to pizza! In college, I had a prescription for "diet pills" that I stopped taking after a couple of days because they left me shaky and unable to sleep. (Can you say amphetamines?) In DeKalb I had some luck with Ayds, the "appetite suppressant candy," but found it expensive. In Missouri, all I could think of was willpower to handle my crazy meal schedules and calorie-laden food choices (Jack in the Box, IHOP, pizza, burgers and fries). I regularly berated myself. "Fat pig" in one journal entry was followed by one raving about an outing to St. Louis where "this really fine restaurant offered a $5.25 Sunday smorgasbord that included duck with orange sauce." When I went to see the movie "Front Page," the line I remembered in my journal was, "I don't want to end up like you guys— fat slobs on the copy desk."

I also ruminated about my "singleness," which I saw as another personal failing. As much as I enjoyed/needed time "home and alone and lazy," at other times I longed "for something more— someone more." I wrote about "a feeling of wasting my life— of the days and hours passing without me really using them— a feeling of cheating myself— a feeling that it all could be better if only I would go out THERE— let the real me out a bit and not be afraid of life." Not long after that, I bemoaned the reality that there wasn't much to my life "except my work and those people associated with it." That had been true in DeKalb, too, but now it scared me. "I don't want that— Damn it. I have other interests— other talents— things to share— And I do nothing." Another day I was feeling sorry for myself, not just because I had been sick and still was not up to par but because I was "very lonely" and struggling with my feelings about

> the Independent me, making it on my own and wanting it that way, feeling I don't really need any other kind of security than I am offering myself— content with my life. Then there is a part of me longing for someone to love, to love me, to share life with— to make love with— someone to compliment me now and then— someone to want me— for whatever it is I am.

It frightened me that I didn't "know how to go about it," that I harbored a "fear of some unknown that I cannot put a finger on" and had not dealt with. "So I laugh it off and pretend to be happy or joke about it— when really and truly a date would be damn nice for a change— would make me feel human— would reinforce my self-image and my respect for myself as a woman." I even framed my decision to begin going to church again with, "Maybe I'll find something— or someone." I described a brilliant former graduate assistant as "the one man I've met here who I could enjoy going out with, tho I think there is little chance of that." I labeled it "a school-girl crush, I think." Clearly my feminism was a work in progress. Another time I wondered

> if I am not a little bit mad— Friendless, alone, able to survive only because . . . I have my work and contact with people there. But at other times no one touches my life— no one touches me— And what is most frightening is that . . . I don't know how to find anyone who might want to be a part of my life. . . . So I waste away on my couch fantasizing and getting immersed in old movies.

240

I wish I could write that the pain of that spring was temporary, but it was not, as I learned when I snuck a look ahead into the journal of my second Missouri year. For now, however, I will note only that I found no written evidence that my rookie-year moods impaired my work. We finished the Progress Edition and six of us celebrated with a spaghetti dinner I prepared. The Missourian even came through with four bottles of wine for us, and there were positive comments from a number of faculty members. Now and then I worked four consecutive nights, which was physically draining, and I continued to be a hawk about our nightly deadlines being met so the presses could roll on time. I enjoyed the half of spring break I didn't work and Columbia's mild weather -- conducive to golf. Sadly I didn't play "because I don't even know how to find a golf partner." Instead I began writing recommendations for soon-to-be graduates (delighted to be asked), but the job market was bleak and even some of the "stars" were pessimistic or looking at options such as the Peace Corps. I took advantage of several opportunities to hob-nob with big-time journalists, who regularly were at the school for contests and workshops. I especially enjoyed an afternoon with some of the top women journalists who came for the annual Penney-Missouri Awards. There was no denying such perks, even if I sometimes went away feeling insignificant. (I also felt like that when the fall 1975 schedule didn't include me teaching a *real* class. "Another bruise for the ego," I wrote, followed by, "But what I do matters, right?")

Chief among the perks was the annual Journalism Week, highlighted by a banquet and presentation of the prestigious Missouri Honor Medals for Distinguished Service in Journalism. I was reluctant to attend my first one because tables were assigned, and I didn't like the idea of being tucked in with strangers among the 1,300 guests. Attendance by faculty was expected, however, so I eventually bought a ticket and "managed a good table (location) and several students with whom I shall have no problems." After the banquet in late April, I called it "not bad," although "the food was awful." I enjoyed wearing my dress from Laurel's wedding and "seeing everyone else gussied up." (Students who sometimes found me at work in jeans and a work shirt no doubt were taken aback.) The keynote speaker was NBC newsman Edwin Newman, who had the audience howling as he pointed out sloppiness in the use of English. "And if he read the Missourian the next morning he probably howled at the non-word in the headline over the story about his speech. Ah yes, the grad assistant let 'laxness' get through." If that weren't enough, there also was a factual error in a Page 1 headline and an incorrect identification in a cutline under a photo from Journalism Week.

Along with the perks, there were periodic problems. I found Brian "bossy" and privately speculated that he had his eyes on the managing editor position. At times I found him condescending; it especially irked me when he criticized work done by copy editors under my supervision. But most of the time we were amiable coworkers. I was amused to read a journal entry describing the time he volunteered to work so I wouldn't have to drive home at 1 a.m. and chance getting stuck in the snow after a blizzard. "I, being independent and totally equal, didn't hesitate to accept." I was not amused by an entry describing how he questioned my news judgment after I had not included a story out of Tel Aviv on a motel takeover by guerrillas. After asking him where he would have put it, given that the story broke late and I already had "butchered" almost every Page 1 story to fit things, I told him to take his complaint to Daryl. I evaluated Brian's reaction as "that typical journalistic reaction to 'horror' stories. Granted it is news, but not a lot of significance for people living in Columbia. And the stories we published were a lot closer to home. And to me [they were] what we really owed our readers." I didn't always agree with Daryl, either. As he second-guessed published headlines, I discovered we had "some philosophical differences in this realm." But more often than not I felt he had my back and supported my decisions. One time when he especially annoyed me involved grading. Students' performance in the classroom and on the copy desk figured into their course grades, and determining grades was a collaboration among Daryl, Brian and me. Daryl worked the desk for me a couple of days near the end of the semester (I was out of town) and had the gall to lower the grades of two students to C's. His reasoning surprised me about one student, but not so much the other. But that did not matter to me, because we already had agreed on grades. "But, of course, I didn't put up much of an argument, so how can I bitch," I wrote.

My confidence in myself may have been shaky at times, but I was confident in my news sense. I had been a news junkie for years, and I reveled in getting the first draft of history onto newsprint and into readers' hands. For example, I was working the April night that Cambodia surrendered. We had been pushing furiously to get the paper out early -- or at least on time for a change -- when, about 11:20, the UPI wire clanged five bells to announce a bulletin. The story followed in short bursts. The news required changing our front page, but we were lucky to have placed a Cambodia story across the top. I worked on a substitute while my graduate assistant handled other chores. We made our deadline! I did observe that the page was "rather gray and ugly." I also had to significantly cut an Insight story, and I was "sure Mr. Duffy is seething. But damn, I'm the one there at 12:15 and I have to make those decisions." As someone in the newsroom had said, "Cambodia doesn't fall every day."

As luck would have it, I was in the slot a couple of weeks later when the bells on the UPI machine again went off -- this time signaling a FLASH. The second of my brief career, it reported that Saigon had surrendered. The Vietnam war at last was over. It was a little after 10 p.m. in Columbia. I thought about all the "boys" who had died there, especially my childhood friend Mike Sullivan, and then I went to work. Daryl came to the office, and along with the graduate assistant and two students on the rim ("one of whom was totally useless") we put together a new front page. I finally left the office about 1:15 a.m., having been there since 11 the previous morning. "The very long day was worth it— compliments on the front page. I learn more and more each day to be a better editor. Look out 'real world.'"

In college I had developed a habit of scribbling snide comments on whatever piece of paper was at hand during speeches, presentations, meetings and the like. As I explored my storage bins later in life I found many such scraps. More than a few left me muttering, *You were such a snob.* I found similar asides about Missouri in my journals. For example, when I learned that I was expected to remove the headlines I regularly posted on my office windows I was incensed. The dean wanted them gone before the journalism-school-accreditation team visited. *Can't the dictator see these are a teaching tool?* I thought the team would be impressed by that. I didn't put up much resistance, though, and lost that skirmish. Another time, having gotten up at 8 a.m. to attend a meeting of the Associated Press, I judged it "a real bore" and described the attendees as "mostly men— mostly older— lots of short hair." Nonetheless, I made note of an anecdote told by AP science writer Alton Blakeslee about his late colleague Hal Boyle. On viewing skaters at Rockefeller Center, Boyle said something to the effect that "anyone can badass his way around a skating rink but few can deal lovingly with words." I guess that meeting wasn't a total waste after all. I found one particular faculty meeting to be "the same old bullshit. Old men worried about tenure and promotions and students on committees, etc." After a J-School faculty retreat, I opined that it "was not a complete waste of time, but the dean really runs off at the mouth— very preachy— closed minded." To be fair, I did find an anecdote about him that was positive. The paper's promotion for a story following up an expose on Columbia housing had prompted some local Realtors and landlords to threaten to pull their advertising if the story was published. I got to the office about 2 o'clock and was informed of the situation and told that we didn't yet know the status of the story. "The dean came down and we held our breath. But he must have gotten his dander up because of the threat. Order was to play [the story] big, which we did."

A few days after the AP meeting, I left Columbia for 10 days of vacation. My timing wasn't great; I would miss graduation. But I had been invited to participate on a panel discussion during Eau Claire's fourth annual Journalism Day, which I was excited to do. Daryl had been chosen for the Alumni Award, and I would accept it on his behalf. In the days before I left, I mused often about how I had "only a few days of contact left with people I have come to need." I anticipated my "ultimate test of teaching" would be whether I could "move on from these nine months to accept those [new students] coming in— to enjoy my time with some of them— and not compare them." It was an odd convergence of emotions: anticipation about reuniting with important people from my undergraduate days and anxiety about how I might be remembered by important people from my first year of teaching.

On the road to Eau Claire, I stopped for the night in Ottumwa, Iowa, delighted that "one of my small treats is being able to whip out the credit card and 'afford' to do this." At last, I felt no pressure to drive on or to check in with The Missourian. I reveled in "real time off"; only one person knew how to reach me for the next 10 days. Ahh, the pleasure of quiet life before cell phones and the internet. Ahh, the pleasure of having time to pay attention to the world around me as I drove. Following a detour on a state road, I saw an Amish man in a buggy, "which got me to thinking— and admiring them for surviving in modern-day America. Clinging strongly to what they believe, despite what others might say or do. More of us should be like that." At another point, in need of a break I saw a service station with a "Good Food" sign and took a chance on stopping. The two waitresses reminded me of the movie "Alice Doesn't Live Here Anymore."

Using stationery from my room at the Holiday Inn, I wrote about what I had thought would be a difficult leave-taking. "But as I heard recently, birds and kids have to fly, i.e. leave the nest, and with God's help I have come to accept that, to treasure the time I'm allowed to spend with all the people who touch my life— and to treasure those hours spent with the few I really can call friends." I mentioned Dona, the student who had called to tell me she had been hired as a sports copy editor by the paper in Bradenton, Florida. "I like to think . . . my recommendation helped." I mentioned being on my way to lunch with Barb, who I had recommended for my old job in Antigo (eventually offered but not taken) and who was one of two students invited to apply to edit "Scotty" Reston's paper on Cape Cod. (I kept a copy of my letter of recommendation, and in my journal expressed sadness but not surprise when the offer went to Dean Fisher's daughter.) I mentioned running into Jan, who assured me she would drop by on her way to her Newspaper Fund summer. And I mentioned the student who had dropped by my apartment just as I was about to leave for a movie. Instead, for the next two hours I talked with him because he needed someone to listen and he trusted me.

Eau Claire -- as always -- offered me exactly what I most needed. Quality time with Les and Ruth Anne. Good conversation. Intellectual stimulation. A chance to "shine" in front of other grads. Affirmation of me. It also provided a surprise. But first, the backstory. I was happy that Tom would be driving up from Madison and wanted to arrive in time for my panel Saturday morning. I saw him come into the room; he smiled and waved, and I reciprocated. "From that moment until about 4:15 Sunday morning we were together." Because there were no graduates from our years, we didn't hesitate to leave the event following a long and boring session after lunch. We headed to a favored haunt on Water Street, where we ran into Fred Berner from Antigo and a couple I had not seen in at least three years. "Lots of booze and good talk." By the time we left for the official cocktail hour, Tom and I had fallen into our comfortable pattern of "togetherness." We shared a dinner table with Les and Ruth Anne and a young man who was coming to Missouri in the fall for graduate school. *What a small world*, I thought as I talked with him. I didn't intend to name-drop but found myself doing so occasionally. (Les said he wanted to take second-hand pleasure in my Reston letter.)

I had persuaded Fred to stay in town, and a group of us ended up in his motel room, talking (and drinking). "Perhaps it was the booze," I later wrote in my journal, "but I like to think it was a new confidence I feel in myself that allowed me to point-blank ask Tom, 'Where is this relationship going?'" That took him by surprise, but his response -- more than once asking if I "wanted a position paper" -- floored me. Turned out that although I was "a nice girl" and there was no one else, his plans for the near future did not include any lasting relationships. He seemed uncomfortable or couldn't seem to understand when I said that was OK, that "I just needed to know." Driving to Antigo the next day, I felt "refreshingly free, like I finally had come to grips" with what Tom had been in my life. For years I had thought that if I wanted him I could have him. Knowing that was not true, I could quit kidding myself. Writing those last two sentences, I had an "aha" moment of realizing how often I had approached life that way, going after the next best thing without ever quite letting go of what I ran from. Tom was an early example; how helpful it would have been to know that.

Of course, starting over was part of teaching and being at The Missourian. Before my vacation, I had discovered that saying goodbye to favored graduating students could be gut-wrenching. Upon my return to Columbia, I discovered the me "fighting the fat problem again, and at the point of hating myself," the me who procrastinated, the me who called myself "lazy" if I was not *doing* something, anything. With no reason to go to campus on off days, I finally had time for my longtime loves -- golf (playing) and softball (coaching). I enjoyed time at the apartment complex's pool. I worked my way through a stack of books, reading for hours at the pool or on my tiny porch. I even picked at doing research for a new military-press project. At work, I got to do editing as much as teach editing because we were short-handed. I gladly helped out on the sports desk one night and filled in for the sports editor on another. When I awoke on May 30 to the news that University of Oregon track star (and Olympian) Steve Prefontaine had died, I was moved to write about my recollections of watching him run. I gave it to the sports editor, who used it as a sidebar in the next morning's paper. *I still had it.*

'Pre' – as much a showman as an athlete

"...Some races increase, others diminish, and in a short space the generations of living creatures are changed and like runners hand on the torch of life."

By Barbara F. Luebke
Missourian copy editor

Oregonians are obsessed with running. Few persons walk the streets of Eugene at night; they run. Wander the outer fringes of the University of Oregon campus in the early morning hours, and that fleeting figure ducking the raindrops is most likely a jogger, not a mugger.

It is no surprise to track aficionados that one of the Beaver State's native sons is the premier long-distance runner in the United States.

WAS the premiere distance runner. Now he is dead.

Following the career of 24-year-old Steve Prefontaine, "Pre," has not been easy since I left Oregon in the summer of 1972. Too many Midwesterners look upon track with disdain; football's the game, son. But there would be occasional notices of Pre's success, usually in Sports Illustrated's "For the Record."

He was a helluva runner to watch, as much a showman as an athlete. He made you want to sit all day in the stands at Hayward Field to watch him run laps. But then, the University of Oregon has no trouble filling those stands. The school has a long tradition of track and field excellence — and 18 Olympians.

Pre was special, though, and although his 5,000- or 10,000-meter races generally were the last of a day's events, no one ever left before the bell lap was run.

And of course, it was Pre leading the pack. Chances were he had lapped the slowest runners, and the partisan crowd was going bananas, on its feet, index fingers held high, madly screaming, "Pre, Pre, Pre."

He made it look so easy, with long, powerful, graceful strides. His warmup jogs around the track would tire we mere mortals; for Pre, they were a prelude of what was to come. Then, after pushing himself to another record or near-record, he would take that victory lap. Arms outstretched. Victory grin. Sometimes barefoot. And we wondered how he could run another step. Yet the victory

lap often became two. "So he won't tighten up," someone would mutter.

The Ducks hosted the 1972 NCAA track finals, and the overflow crowds cheered every victory. But no one was greeted with more insane enthusiasm than Pre, who didn't embarass the Green and Gold.

Then came Munich. Getting up very early on a Sunday morning to watch Pre. A disappointing fourth in the 5,000; no medal.

We knew he would be back, though; the magic Gold could not elude him forever. Now, he had had some European competition, and he had four more years to prepare.

Things were looking good, too. Hadn't he just come within 1.5 seconds of his own record for the 5,000?

But that was to be as close as he would get.

With the start of summer school, I was about to see if I still had it in the classroom. And with the start of summer school, I began juggling responsibilities that would over time exact a terrible toll on me -- body and soul. Of course, I did not know what lay ahead. What I did know was that I was eager to begin working on my Ph.D.

CHAPTER 14

Summertime... and the Living Wasn't Easy

Disappointed by the easy academic work that led to my master's, I had set my sights on a doctoral degree for the intellectual challenges I craved. It would be my Everest, and having Ph.D. after my name (or Dr. in front of it) would be validation of what I was capable of accomplishing. The degree was a goal of unknown origin and one without specifics until I found myself at the University of Missouri. Not only did I earn a salary, but I could get a faculty discount for tuition and fees. After I had committed to studying journalism, my understanding was that once accepted into the program I could begin taking classes in fall 1975. Turns out I was accepted for summer; on short notice I decided to take one course during the first four-week session, which began one day after Intersession ended. Summer school courses met daily, "but the brain work might be a nice new experience," I wrote, noting that I would be on the copy desk Mondays, Wednesdays, Thursdays and alternate Saturdays. Whew! Whatever was I thinking? After my vacation -- which included driving about 1,500 miles, visits in five cities and a wedding -- I had jumped right into Intersession.

My first reminder of why students get frustrated by registration was learning that of the two summer courses I was interested in, one was full and one had been canceled. "I guess I will try for an urban history course," I wrote without enthusiasm. The second frustration was learning that the paperwork needed for my tuition discount had not been processed. I decided to pay out of pocket and seek a refund, figuring the chances of that were slim. I had been in a foul mood for days, describing myself in one entry as "a second-class faculty member— all give and no get. . . . It would be nice, just once, to be recognized as a faculty member with some brains and talent— and not just cheap academic labor." Then a postcard from Tom, in Washington, D.C., for some reason, irritated me. "First time, really, he ever has taken the initiative to write. Damn him for doing it. Want to be rid of him— and don't want to be rid of him." And to top things off, when Brian handed me a long piece of text titled "Welcome to the copy desk," my first response (unspoken) was, "Damn, I run that desk four nights a week. Why can't my opinions be solicited <u>BEFORE</u> things are done?"

Perhaps I could have rolled with those punches if I knew what a marvelous, eye-opening course "American Urban History" would prove to be. The young professor was extraordinarily dynamic, which helped ease the two hours a day, five days a week I spent in his classroom for a month. The daunting reading list required me to take advantage of every free minute at work and at home. The learning was priceless. It was because of that instructor that, among other things: I finally read "The Grapes of Wrath" and saw the marvelous movie version. I read a critical examination of Walt Disney's world (probably Richard Schickel's "The Disney Version"). I learned how to look at photographs, illustrations and paintings of urban landscapes in new ways. I learned about the toll industrialization and "progress" had taken on American society. I learned about the horrific Chicago race riot of 1919. Absent my course syllabus, I cannot confirm but believe I also learned about Tulsa's Black Wall Street. I can confirm that in 2021, when the long-buried details of the massacre of its citizens were much in the news, I immediately thought of that urban history course.

I have sat in boring classrooms and thought of the line penned by George Bernard Shaw: "Those who can, do; those who can't, teach." And I have heard my share of people suggest teachers choose the profession to have summers off. Balderdash -- at least in my life. I had proved I could "do" journalism, and the nature of my teaching polished those skills nightly. As for summers off -- not when you are an instructor supervising a "lab" that is a daily newspaper. The journal entries for my first summer in Columbia repeatedly detail "non-stop hectic" stretches of days. Summer session started with a visit from "middle brother" Phil Polk, who arrived a day earlier than I expected. I worked that Monday night. After spending Tuesday morning in class, I treated him to lunch and a tour of the campus and city before we defied a forecast for rain and drove to Kansas City for a baseball game. It rained, they played, and we stayed because our seats were under cover. I was up at 6:30 Wednesday to feed him before putting him on a bus to Washington, D.C., where he would meet his dad's plane. It had been fun having another beating heart in the apartment. He was content to do his thing while I worked, and I found him to be quite a "thinking conversationalist." Not for the last time did I see in him and his two brothers many qualities I wished for in more of my students. Another time that summer I wrote about a day when I "should have done so much more— laundry, letters, more reading than I did." I described an arm tired from transcribing class notes and eyes tired from reading. With the prospect of the next four nights on the desk, however, I had allowed myself a TV-movie break. It was "good escapist entertainment, and I wanted nothing more than that."

I regularly was "seeing parts of the day I have not experienced much of for about a year." But although it was nice to feel the warmth of the sun at the breakfast table, "having gone to bed with the night owls" I would have preferred sleeping in. Instead, the alarm regularly was set for 7:30 because I had reading to finish before class. Then, too, there were "early morning" phone calls, like the one at 8:15 from an Illinois editor with questions about a recent graduate. I didn't remember the young man asking to use me as a reference, and when the editor wanted to know about his speed on the desk "I had to be honest in admitting that was his greatest weakness." I almost certainly had shared that concern (copy editors can't dawdle) with the student, so why would he want me to be a reference? And why on earth did the editor call so early?

The class/hour by the pool/work/sleep/class routine wore on me, but I thought I was "hanging in there, [even though] I'm seeing little of my apartment and nothing of the golf course." When I read a journal entry that stated I was "antsy," I was surprised. Was it schedule fatigue already? I made note of "some Kansas college" looking for someone to teach nine hours of basic journalism courses and supervise the yearbook. That and the academic year salary range of $11,000-$12,500 sounded good. My April vacation seemed eons ago; the vacation I was planning for July seemed far in the future. In the moment, my life was either "go-go-go or crash."

When my midterm exam (after two weeks! of classes) was postponed, giving me a rare three-day weekend to study, I rejoiced. I hoped for an A. "And here we go again, playing the performance game— striving to please/fulfill expectations of someone else [the instructor] and forgetting what learning is all about. Now I know how my students must feel." The counsel I had offered more than once over the previous months was beyond my own grasp. Thanks to *the radar of years* (Donna Leon's phrase in an early Inspector Bruschetti mystery), I today understand how dangerous expectations can be. How they set us up to be disappointed, to fail more often than succeed. At the same time, I also believe my persistent expectations for myself contributed to my successes. By the time of the final exam, our midterms still had not been returned. As I studied, I wrote that "I have qualms about how well I did [on it] . . . but am going to try not to worry about grades but revel in learning." In my mind, I tucked away the memory of such professorial negligence and vowed to always return exams and papers promptly.

My attitudes about how a student -- me -- "should be" had an impact on how I reacted to my own students. I wrote about disliking those "who play one prof off another, especially about grades." Performance on the copy desk was the most significant factor in editing grades. From the first day, I was confident about my ability to accurately assess the quality of work and assign a grade. One graduate student I wrote about was unhappy about her C. She first tried to persuade me that she was better than average. Unsuccessful, she then went to Brian. Thankfully, we agreed the C was correct. "Too many graduate students so obviously want to be coddled," I wrote. (Mr. Duffy quipped that the summer crew had too many graduate students "who couldn't write their names.") Another time, a student didn't get the grade point he needed to graduate and thus would be forced to sit out a year. He called to ask if I would consider changing his C to a B. I told him I'd sleep on it, which I did before deciding the answer had to be no. "He could have had the B but screwed himself with his classwork again. I like Steve, but standards are standards." Over the decades, I refined my grading but never wavered from my belief that grades reflect performance, not good intentions or hard work. Outcomes assessment, which was in vogue before I retired, came naturally to me because from my earliest days as a reporter and editor my outcomes (how well I had done my job) were assessed daily -- by my bosses and by our readers.

As for my assessment of my teaching, the summer brought several more examples of how I *was* having an impact. Such news generally tipped the scales to a good-mood day. One time it did not was when one of two students I had recommended for a job in Lincoln, Nebraska, was hired. As happy as I was for him, I felt bad for the other guy. He wrote me a nice letter, which he signed "proud to be your friend." What more could a teacher ask for? A letter from "my" Newspaper Fund intern in North Carolina reported that she was doing well and looking forward to a visit from me. When Rich was in town ("loving" his job in West Virginia), he stopped by the newsroom "just to see you." The Fourth of July found me dining with Sydney, in town for a week with the baggage of her "same old man problems," which we parsed over a long dinner and drinks. That night's journal entry was my last until July 31, when I filled several note-book pages with details about my vacation, including these statistics: gone 20 "marvelous" days; traveled 3,697 miles; passed through 12 states; averaged about 24 mpg." Before I left Columbia I had acknowledged sec-ond thoughts about the scope of my vacation plan -- after all, I was phys-ically and mentally exhausted -- but I stubbornly stuck to it.

First up was my mother's family reunion in Ohio. I was a star be-cause I brought several cases of Coors beer, at the time available only in a couple of states west of the Mississippi. No one complained that I had not been able to keep it chilled. Next came a drive with my 18-year-old brother, Tim, to the Dayton, Ohio, airport to fetch my college buddy GunR. (I have no memory of why he met us there.) We three made it as far as Corbin, Kentucky (amazing, given my hangover); dinner came from the original Colonel Sanders Café, which delighted us. We aimed to make Raleigh, North Carolina, the next day but did not. By then GunR had decided to fly the rest of the way back to Washington (his long legs and the Gremlin proved to be a painful combination), and Ra-leigh by afternoon the next day worked for him. After that airport, Tim and I found a motel and swam and sunned until Newspaper Fund Jan came by after work. We talked nonstop until 2 a.m. She had written me a long letter from Raleigh, so I knew she was doing well and "finally had gotten used to writing upstyle headlines." She regaled us with stories about the "Nuisance Observer" and newsroom characters, and I shared news and gossip from Mizzou.

For me, the highlight of the next day's sightseeing was a stop at the Joan Little trial, where we observed jury selection. The Chicago Tribune had called it the trial of the decade, but I found the selection process to be dull. How wrong I was! Years later I read that the case was renowned for its use of scientific jury selection. (In August 1974, the 22-year-old Black woman had been in the Beaufort County Jail in Washington, North Carolina, still awaiting a court date on a breaking and entering charge two months earlier. One night her 62-year-old white jailer went into her cell with an ice pick. He planned to force her into sexual acts. Little stabbed him with the pick, then fled. He bled to death. Her case was widely reported, not least because of its attention from civil rights and feminist activists. Eventually Little was acquitted, the first woman to successfully offer the defense that she had used deadly force to resist sexual assault.)

From Raleigh, Tim and I headed toward the coast so he could see the Atlantic Ocean. We hit Myrtle Beach, South Carolina, midafternoon on a Friday and drove south along a coastal highway that was not near the water, as I had expected. (Years later, I would learn how wrong I was about that.) We spent the night "in a hole of a city, Georgetown, where beer sold for $2.05 a six pack." We finally got to a beach near Charleston, me determined for Tim to wade in the Atlantic "since we drove a day out of the way" to get there. I noted how flat southern South Carolina was, "60 miles of nothing— and real southern poverty." I revised my opinion about that nothingness years later when, after only one visit, Hilton Head became my vacation destination of choice. Over dozens of visits, my explorations of the Low Country included Georgetown, though I had no memory of having been there before.

Our next destination was Lavonia, Georgia. I had made plans to meet up with Barb, the grad who didn't go to Antigo or Cape Cod. She was working in the Lavonia bureau of a nearby newspaper. She had written me after a week on the job and, like Jan, was happily settled in. "As far as reporting opportunities go, it's ideal. Lots of good stories. Lots of good features." Our timing was good; it was Barb's weekend off and the Georgia Bluegrass Festival was in town. We arranged to meet there. It was hot. I was tired. They didn't sell beer. Tim loved the festival. I got bored quickly; after a while all the music sounded the same to me. (Although I certainly appreciated the musicianship of Bill Monroe.) Tim hitchhiked back for more music the next day; Barb and I talked and talked and talked.

On the road again ("nice to be heading north"), Tim and I enjoyed "a different part of the mountains, having tackled the Smokies on the way down." After a night somewhere in western Kentucky, true to form I kept us "pretty much on schedule" toward Abrams. But unable to find a suitable motel on our stretch of U.S. 41 south of Chicago, we ended up in the tail end of rush hour on the Dan Ryan Expressway before stopping for the night in Waukegan. The next day's drive was "a piece of cake."

After a couple of days with my parents, I was off to Antigo and an eye appointment with the "vision guy" I had written about for the Daily Journal. He said my eyes were paying the price for "too much close work" and instructed me to take more breaks. Hah! I didn't have time to explain my work and schedule to him, so I simply ordered new glasses. There followed a couple of days with Mary and Mike and other friends (along with too much food and drink) before a long, hot drive with too many detours on the way back to Columbia. After one final motel stay, I arrived home. I wrote that it "feels in many ways like I never left. And already I am restless." After I typed that, I recalled how more than once I have been scolded with a version of, *You always want more. Why can't you be satisfied with what you have?* I am not sure that I ever have answered adequately. Even as I wrote about my vacation in a lengthy catch-up journal entry, I already had decided to "next year get a cottage for two weeks somewhere in the north and have a relaxing vacation."

That was 12 months in the future, however. My immediate future was August -- another Intersession on the copy desk -- and preparations for the fall semester. I also had to figure out how to manage my finances. It pained me that before vacation I had to withdraw money from my savings account to tide me over until my late-July payday. I viewed my savings as sacred, not to be touched. At the same time, I viewed the fact that I had savings as a "sign of my having made it" in the world. When I learned that I would not get a paycheck on September 1, because of how my contract was structured, I was upset further. I would need all my savings for living expenses. I called it "a real bummer" when I realized I would "have nothing left of my $11,400 salary. . . . I never anticipated this. Dumb on my part." I pledged to do better and planned to open a second savings account for summer and vacation money. With a raise of about $600 in my nine-month salary, the $1,650 I expected for summer and my car being paid off, I thought I would do OK.

There is no denying that Missouri taught me many of the money-management skills I continue to use. There also is no denying that as a single woman I had a lot to learn about wisely using my money. Chatting with Jane Clark, one of my few female colleagues, I learned that she had decided to buy the house she was renting. We discussed how women were not conditioned or trained to deal with mortgages, banks and finances. With a chuckle, she told me how at age 46 she still "must bug my 75-year-old father about money matters." That conversation left me feeling "less embarrassed at 26 about having to call on my parents when I get involved in money things."

As for work, it was more of the same -- with one milestone. On August 11, I "made history of sorts" when I laid out the first six-column Missourian. It "looked pretty good, too," I wrote. Of course, Brian had hung around all night "and more or less took over in the backshop." What was most annoying, though, "were a couple of brown-nosing students who kept asking their questions of him and not me!" I tried to not let petty jealousy ruin my night. (Not-so-subtle sexism was at work, I think now.) I reminded myself of the faculty member who recently had told me of a critique session by his editorial-writing class. When asked to identify one Missourian editorial page that was superior [in design] to others and better than ordinarily published, they identified one I had done the week teaching assistants took their comprehensive exams. Hearing that made my day.

As for me the student, it was all systems go, full speed ahead -- once I got registered. Finding courses that fit my interests, needs and schedule was frustratingly difficult. "Do I want that damn degree???" I wrote one day. Then, when I stood in the first of several lines to retrieve my registration packet, it was nowhere to be found. After a few trips to an office across the quadrangle, I thought to look under LEU, in case my name had been misspelled. Eureka! Although my name was spelled correctly, the packet had been filed incorrectly. Relieved when everything fell into place the next day -- two journalism courses and one sociology -- I recorded the cost ($124.50 plus books) and the fact the university paid $139.50. "Not a bad deal," I crowed, adding that the textbook for the required two-credit Research Methods in Journalism was "enough to scare off anyone."

My rookie year in Columbia was not quite finished. I had one more hat to wear: temporary hotelier. I had offered Mark (the new graduate student from Eau Claire I had met briefly in the spring) a bed when he arrived in town. I also had assured Crazy Ann (the "walking disaster" friend of a friend who had ruined my clock the last time she stayed with me) that if need be she could have my guest room until she could get into her apartment. For a few days, I would be the familiar face in town for two newcomers. Never did I dream that they would arrive on the same day. Because Mark was still apartment-hunting, it was fortunate that Ann needed a bed for only one night. Mark stayed a few days; remarkably, I found him an easy houseguest. It was weird to discover we had been in Eau Claire at the same time, until he transferred to UW-Madison. Although we had not crossed paths, we knew several of the same people and he was friendly with Les. We also had common interests: sports, movies, books.

I had started a journal entry shortly after vacation by asking, "What is the future of an overweight 26-year-old woman with a M.S. degree who, on a Sunday night in August and sans TV and money, is only resourceful enough to play solitaire?" A week or so later, I acknowledged that I remained unsure about "where I am going with my life— Even where I want to go." I used a long letter to Les to "think things out— soberly." I thought ahead to the start of the fall semester and promised myself that I would "try very hard to take each day as it comes— good and bad— and work to find the real me— and learn to like myself."

CHAPTER 15

From Settled to Unsettling

Familiarity can breed contempt, but it also can breed comfort, and I was comfortable being in the newsroom when the new wave of copy editors, reporters and photographers poured in for the fall 1975 semester. Unlike a year earlier, I knew to expect the chaos that three shifts of students brought with them, especially during the early weeks. I knew I could manage the deadlines necessary to get the paper published. I still didn't like it when work under my watch made Daryl's "bad" list, but I knew it wasn't the end of the world. I knew not to jump to conclusions about a new assistant city editor, a Missouri graduate now in law school. He seemed eager; I found the tobacco he smoked in his pipe quite noxious. I described our graduate assistants as "green, and if they don't come around [quickly] it could be a very, very long semester."

It was going to be a long semester no matter what. For one thing, I was running the desk four nights a week, despite having been told I would work three. And because it was football season, I once again was scheduled to work Saturdays. Then there was the matter of me being a full-time graduate student along with being a full-time employee. My "easy" day -- Thursday -- included my own 10:15 class and at 2:40 the editing lecture with about 125 students. (I was not the instructor of record, but I was expected to attend and would be responsible for some class sessions, assignments and grading.)

That long letter I had written to Les in the midst of late-summer despair (cause unknown; more puzzling because not long before I had wondered, "Could it be I really am comfortable here?") had elicited an immediate response. I really must have sounded out of sorts and confused. I seem to have found enough reassurance among the tightly packed paragraphs of his four single-spaced pages to begin the fall semester with optimism. (When, I ask now, did I begin to describe myself as a born optimist? My journals so far had offered little to support that characterization.)

Whatever I had written to Les, he stated that he found it "honest, forthright." What I intuit from his responses is that I remained mired in doubts about the value of my work and the continued loneliness I expected my even crazier schedule would bring. One comment I wrote to myself as I read his letter in 2021 was that it was probably the most important one he ever wrote me. After a couple of introductory paragraphs, he began:

> I think I believe, cornily, that we intellectuals, in journalism to be specific, have a job to do: That's simply to get minds to think, to get young minds disciplined, to help enlarge the scope of minds, to feel we have a ministerial "calling," if you will. . . . We cannot consider that we're in it for the fame, glory, or monetary values. We're not. . . . I suppose it's my seminary background, combined with the journalism, and an old J teacher . . . who was an idealist about it all. I inflicted upon me that idealism . . . who in hell is going to do some truth telling if we don't "sneak it to 'em" in the daily press that's the only thing they MIGHT happen to read cause they're too lazy to read anything else? I think it's our job. And I think in your position now, and in mine, it's a job that we have to consider as being a role somewhat removed, different and unique.

Certainly I would have taken comfort in being reminded of my friend GunR's situation. Les had spent time with him in Washington and wrote: "I'm aware of how much he makes; I'm aware, too, of his empty feelings, his loneliness, his own self doubts. [Working at the Post] is no perfect life." GunR and I had exchanged hundreds of words about this, but somehow I had overlooked that. In fact, Les continued, there is no perfect life. "One thing I've learned . . . is that geographical location is relatively meaningless; but the peopleness of the thing is the important thing. It's that ability to be out there, mixing, to be loved, and loving."

How astute he was to "wonder, in thinking of you, and other young women in the business . . . how life is as a woman alone. For a guy, I can picture it, I know it a bit. . . . . But I suppose there are social barriers, and bits that enter in [for women] that I could never comprehend." I must have expressed concern about relying on students as friends, based on what he wrote next.

> I only know that my life now is inextricably bound up with the persons I interact with in the classroom, and on campus, almost exclusively. And I don't mind that. I know that it's impossible, as a self-steward, to mix up life with too many others anyway. It would be too complex, too messy, and too time consuming. I guess one of the things [experience has] taught me is to take care of myself, selfishly, even, in rest, recreation, work and other things.

He was counseling me, I believe, to not worry so much that my focus on work and school might cut me off from the larger world. He listed activities he shunned so he might "keep my mind clear, crisp and clean." He wrote that he wanted "to be a teacher. A damned good teacher. I want to change the world, just a wee tiny bit in my own area (wherever that may be -- with persons who are in classes, who read me or somehow come under my hegemony or influence). A mission; a sense of calling." Bingo! Me, too.

Quoting snippets from my letter ("shy," "in sort of a shell," "reluctant"), he suggested that my "self-analysis isn't bad." Being otherwise, he wrote,

> requires lots of self confidence. It requires a feeling, I believe, that, dammit I'm as good looking, talented, bright, as the best of them. Sometimes it requires dropping a bit of old-fashioned Lutheran puritanism; Midwest pietism to meet people on their own ground. It requires, to meet people, just being really open.

Decades later, his declarative "Insecurity is a terrible thing to have hanging over one's head" feels obvious. Ditto his next sentence: "Insecurity about anything -- professional or personal -- needs to be rectified." Les wasn't telling me anything that I had not told myself, as so many journal entries demonstrate. The *how*, I recently discovered, continued to elude me, despite his reassurances and advice:

Professionally, you have no reason to [be insecure]. (Remember that first J banquet here? When you were so apologetic, really, to be ONLY in Antigo?) But now . . . no reason at all. Personally . . . maybe the shy bit is right. But you have to ask yourself, "shy why?" What's back there, causing that? Perhaps you need to know that there's someone there who's your special friend, who sees YOU as the only person in the world. That helps. But if that's not there, it's just a matter of remembering Thoreau: "If a person does not keep pace with his companions, perhaps it is because he hears a DIFFERENT DRUMMER . . . (you finish it)." But there are other different drummers around, too. Find one. Or two.

Laugh much; love a lot. Smile often. Buy that outlandish outfit that might change your identity, hint at a change, or "keep 'em guessing." . . . How about a "different" look, even to give you a different feel of the world about you. And don't closet yourself, friend. Sure we need to read, study, and reflect. But we need to share, exchange thoughts, and just plain gab a lot, too.

As I continued to examine my Mizzou artifacts, I noticed that my journal entries were more sporadic, one victim of a schedule I described as "merry-go-round living with no relief in sight." To make sense of things, I decided to organize my life into *segments*. They were interrelated, of course, connected to pieces of my past and foreshadowing pieces of my future. I am allowing this chapter of my story to go its own way.

Me in the Classroom

I knew from my graduate work at Oregon that I was not interested in qualitative research. The content analysis at the heart of my thesis had been interesting only because of what I studied: nontraditional, little-known newspapers (two Navajo papers). A rudimentary understanding of statistical analysis had been sufficient for that; mastering more complex analytical tools in order to eventually parse a narrowly defined research question did not interest me. I had no choice about those tools, however; two semesters of Research Methods were required of Ph.D. students. [An aside: I was not (and am not) the stereotypical math-phobic journalist. Other than high school geometry, which I disliked and found useful only for billiards, tennis, pingpong, racquetball and the like, I enjoyed mathematics. Indeed, as a freshman I ranked sixth among our 102 students who took a skills exam sponsored by the American Mathematics Association. The story in our local paper noted, "Particularly noteworthy is the fact that Barbara Luebke . . . has [had] only one semester of algebra."]

I had been told that to earn a doctorate -- and then to ascend the ranks of academe -- I would be expected to produce "new knowledge." For now, I had time to chart my course, but I was not interested in mining some tiny bit of ground or writing thousands of words that would do little more than collect dust on a library shelf. From the beginning I knew I wanted to write a dissertation that had something to do with the minority press. I also knew I wanted to tell an untold story. To do so, I first needed new knowledge of my own. The sociology course I enrolled in, "The Black Americans," seemed to offer learning that could be interesting and useful. Importantly, it was an upper-level undergraduate course approved for graduate credit. Even better, it met only once a week, which was a boon for my schedule.

I noted in my journal that the class had been canceled for the first week, then I drew a smiley face. (In my experience, students seldom complain about a cancellation. I once worked for a president fond of saying that higher education is the only enterprise where customers -- students -- are happy to get less than what they paid for.) After the first meeting of "The Black Americans," I started my journal by commenting: "I really am fired up today. I was happily surprised to find the course is being taught just not by a black but by a black woman. Wow. First black prof I've ever had and only fifth or sixth woman. And from brief discussion today course certainly will be relevant to what I'm doing." I also was excited by my third course, "Controls of Information," and ended the paragraph: "2 out of 3 for the semester isn't bad." Later in the entry, I observed that "sitting in Soc class today, I realize how much fun I find in learning. And for today I am happy with the way my life is going. Probably will stay that way as long as I am in the driver's seat. At least so far I have been lucky with the 'blind' choices [of courses] I have made."

As it turned out, the connection I made with sociologist Loretta Williams was among the few significant relationships I cultivated on campus. After an early semester visit to her office, I wrote that "the brief exchange was great." We talked about my interests in minority media and I asked about the possibility of her supervising a "readings course" for me. "She may prove to be the model/impetus that pushes me to do the degree— because I know I can get excited about learning, given half a chance." (My aha moment after reading that: How much easier the experience would have been if I could have seen the Ph.D. as merely a credential with requirements to be ticked off rather than expecting an opportunity to grow intellectually, to *learn* from the best.)

If there was a downside to my experience in Loretta's class, it was the pressure I put on myself "to do good [sic]— to do better than good" because the professor was someone I respected and liked. After one of her exams, I wrote about how I had been the first to finish "again. Always have been, since first grade. Guess I figure that if you don't know it, you don't know it. And when it's done, it's done." (That attitude, I must say, served me well as an editor. Overthinking the process of creating a daily newspaper can impede meeting deadlines. Not being able to let go of yesterday's decisions can impede doing today's work.) In November, I did indeed register for that "readings" course for spring and wrote about how much I was looking forward to it. "Loretta is challenging my mind and I need that badly." I also anticipated that the experience would give me the opportunity to know her better. In my last entry of the semester (also my last of the calendar year), written on November 30, I was "grooving on knowing" her; "not just her course, but her— exchanging books and mags and reading lists." She was, I added, the only person I knew outside the J-School, "but I want to change that."

I didn't write much about my other courses. I did mention cutting "Research Methods" once, when I was too tired and hung over to make the 11:40 a.m. class. I also mentioned a lot of time spent studying and once having to fit in an assignment at the computer center during a day packed with student conferences. I mentioned hating quizzes and singled out the one where the professor said that "no one will do better than 60 percent" before he gave it to us. "So why bother," I wondered as I gave myself a pep talk about "not worrying about grades." I wrote about a week with two exams, "both leaving me with the feeling of not being prepared." I wrote about being disappointed that my final-exam schedule would keep me in Columbia at least until December 18, then acknowledging that I needed all the time I could get to finish a paper on textbook censorship for my "Controls of Information" course. On November 16, "I finally got into the [law] library to begin [that] research. I love libraries, but I hate becoming familiar with them— trying to figure out the system and find things." Ever the deadline reporter, two weeks later I had not yet begun to write.

Of course, I finally wrote the paper and submitted it on time. My first journal entry of the new year documented that I had done a good job and noted that it "probably is going to be published; that would be nice." It proved to be my first academic publication: "Textbook Censorship: New Aspects," Freedom of Information Center Report No. 349, February 1976. That January journal entry also noted that I was "ready to study [again], prodded on by my 4.0 on this fall's work." Before classes started, though, I had lined up "much reading" to prepare me to write a proposal for an Honors College course on the minority press. The thought of "teaching for real" excited me. I don't remember being excited about the spring-semester journalism course I had enrolled in, "Proseminar in Communications," but am certain I was optimistic about "The Sociology of Power" and my "Readings" course with Loretta.

Me on the Copy Desk

Working the weekend after Labor Day was no picnic, but I was hopeful because of "an efficient early crew" on Saturday, with a student producing "one of the best first-day headlines I've seen." The story was about the men surveying the bus system for the city, and the student wrote: Mr. Payne, how do you (like, dislike) / taking this city bus survey? I had been collecting headlines on and off for years, always on the lookout for examples I could use -- good and bad. Many of the best came from the weekly National Observer, so I decided to write editor Henry Gemmill:

> I am preparing a lecture on headline writing. My thesis is going to be that we who teach editing could get along very well by using two "textbooks" -- The National Observer and Sports Illustrated. I am dealing with students who have spent one semester on the Columbia Missourian copy

desk. I think what we must do now is increase their confidence. Then they should progress from the mundane to the magical.

I told him my favorite Observer headline was "Sick Transit's Glorious Someday," for an article about efforts to improve mass transit. (As I wrote this in August 2021, it occurred to me that it was a headline appropriate for today's news.) A close second, I told him, was above an article about the sports commentator/Las Vegas bookmaker best known as Jimmy the Greek: "Odds, to a Grecian, Earn." (Note the importance of comma placement.) I asked Gemmill about who wrote the paper's headlines and how. On September 7, I was happy to find a large envelope from him in my faculty mailbox. Not only did he share memos from staff members responding to my questions, but he said he might write about our exchange in his weekly column. He asked for a photograph of me. "Freak out," I recorded in my journal. It was the second-best news I recorded that day, even though it preceded the truly joyful paragraph (in which I buried the lead): "Try to sleep late Saturday, but kids outside too noisy for the new aunt. Wm. Frederick Parmentier II born noon Friday (9-5-75). Dad called to tell me. I called Kris Saturday noon to congratulate. 7# 7oz. and healthy. Praise the Lord."

In the Observer published for the week ending Oct. 25, Gemmill did indeed write his column about headlines.

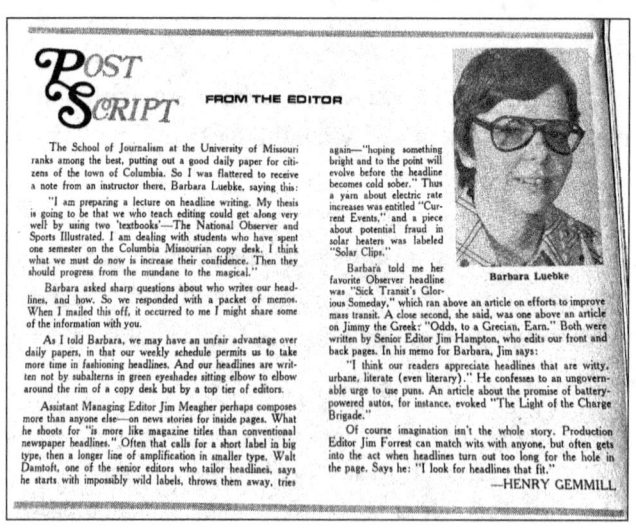

POST SCRIPT
FROM THE EDITOR

The School of Journalism at the University of Missouri ranks among the best, putting out a good daily paper for citizens of the town of Columbia. So I was flattered to receive a note from an instructor there, Barbara Luebke, saying this:

"I am preparing a lecture on headline writing. My thesis is going to be that we who teach editing could get along very well by using two 'textbooks'—The National Observer and Sports Illustrated. I am dealing with students who have spent one semester on the Columbia Missourian copy desk. I think what we must do now is increase their confidence. Then they should progress from the mundane to the magical."

Barbara asked sharp questions about who writes our headlines, and how. So we responded with a packet of memos. When I mailed this off, it occurred to me I might share some of the information with you.

As I told Barbara, we may have an unfair advantage over daily papers, in that our weekly schedule permits us to take more time in fashioning headlines. And our headlines are written not by subalterns in green eyeshades sitting elbow to elbow around the rim of a copy desk but by a top tier of editors.

Assistant Managing Editor Jim Meagher perhaps composes more than anyone else—on news stories for inside pages. What he shoots for "is more like magazine titles than conventional newspaper headlines." Often that calls for a short label in big type, then a longer line of amplification in smaller type. Walt Damtoft, one of the senior editors who tailor headlines, says he starts with impossibly wild labels, throws them away, tries

again—"hoping something bright and to the point will evolve before the headline becomes cold sober." Thus a yarn about electric rate increases was entitled "Current Events," and a piece about potential fraud in solar heaters was labeled "Solar Clips."

Barbara Luebke

Barbara told me her favorite Observer headline was "Sick Transit's Glorious Someday," which ran above an article on efforts to improve mass transit. A close second, she said, was one above an article on Jimmy the Greek: "Odds, to a Grecian, Earn." Both were written by Senior Editor Jim Hampton, who edits our front and back pages. In his memo for Barbara, Jim says:

"I think our readers appreciate headlines that are witty, urbane, literate (even literary)." He confesses to an ungovernable urge to use puns. An article about the promise of battery-powered autos, for instance, evoked "The Light of the Charge Brigade."

Of course imagination isn't the whole story. Production Editor Jim Forrest can match wits with anyone, but often gets into the act when headlines turn out too long for the hole in the page. Says he: "I look for headlines that fit."

—HENRY GEMMILL

Because I saved the page on which it appeared, I can write that the column was at the bottom and at the top was a story about a rodeo bull rider. Its marvelous headline: "A Good 'un Is When the Bull Is a Bad 'un." Positive feedback to Gemmill's column had me smiling for days. My new department chairman dashed off a note, "Good show. I'm proud of you," which I called "the most rewarding" of the many comments I got around the J-School. It "even made [a] chewing out from Daryl palatable." He was in a bad mood, I wrote, and took issue with an inside page and its headlines (ironically). "So much, again, for 'Monday morning QB'," I wrote.

Reactions reached me for months, as friends shared the column. Among them was my Eau Claire roommate Luise, who learned about it from Gini, our dorm head resident. Luise and I had not seen one another for some time, and it was just plain fun to have her describe me as "getting famous" and to remind me she had predicted it would be so. Equally fun was to read that Gini had called while Luise was writing to me and together they worked through a list of people they wanted to tell about the column. "So not only does the National Observer make you famous, there is the underground movement which are 'friends of BFL.'" It was always good to be reminded of that network.

I did get some mild criticism from a self-described "old fuddy-duddy" newspaperman who offered "what may be the outmoded conviction . . . that, generally speaking, the purpose of a headline on a news story in a daily newspaper is to give the reader at least an inkling of what the story is all about." He asked me to not overlook that and to not "put too much emphasis on 'the magical!'" What I most enjoyed was his postscript, in which he told of knowing a young woman reporter on a rival newspaper who became an instructor in the Missouri School of Journalism and ended up marrying the dean. "If you aren't married and if the present Dean is unattached, good luck!" he wrote. I chuckled over that for days.

I didn't write much that was new about work that semester. Thursdays were "my bad day." By then, exhaustion had set in "and I'm not as careful or patient as I should be." After only a couple of weeks, I described "desk people mostly at a standstill. Still slow, some trouble with basics." Too many low scores on a style and spelling quiz I gave supported my assessment. Back in the day, students were best served by memorizing basic AP style rules and knowing how to spell. Every minute used to consult a reference book was a minute not available for *real* editing of content. Today, computerized systems used by reporters and editors have the basics built in or enable a quick look up. And don't even get me started on those newsrooms where there is little to no copy editing. Or remote editing for all papers by a chain's centralized copy desk.

Nights when work went well must have been somewhat rare because I took note of them in my journal, e.g., "Work goes very well. I am able to leave at 10:30. Exciting, 'different' front page." A year earlier, when I wrote *at length*, I might have explained the how and why of that night. This fall, what I longed for was early release from the newsroom. More usual were hectic days, like the Saturday where I felt as if "I never really took a breather from 1 to 7" and had to go back to work after dinner, "always a bummer." That Saturday also had me wishing I could have been at the Missouri-Wisconsin football game. I settled for yelling "Go Badgers" periodically throughout the afternoon. (I wasn't a Tigers fan -- resentful about working Saturdays perhaps. But although I never attended the University of Wisconsin, I have followed the Badgers since I was a kid.)

I continued to look for ways to motivate students to become the best copy editors they could be, even though most expressed no interest in the position. Required conferences were one avenue. At other times, an unplanned conversation helped. One example I wrote about was a long talk with "a guy from whom I've felt some antagonism," a talk that left me "with a better understanding of him," I believed. He really made me think when he asked, "Exactly what is an 'A' copy editor?" I wasn't sure I had a good answer for him but realized that "I know one when I see her/him" was insufficient. Another time, a graduate student in economics who was taking journalism as "collateral" courses needed extra attention. His only background was the introductory "skills" course for graduate students, where editing was an afterthought. I found him eager to learn and master the skills of the copy desk, so my challenge was to figure out how to get him to competency. Another example comes from a discussion about layout assignments that my graduate teaching assistant and I squeezed in during a lull on the desk. I graded the assignments on a scale of 0-10, and Paul reminded me that he had gotten a 3 on his first one. Now he was a T.A. who, it turned out, had a natural feel for layout after a bit of instruction. From then on, I used his story to encourage others when they struggled. Finally, late in the semester I returned to the desk after dinner one Saturday "and had to try to convince a very talented young man who graduates in December not to get out of journalism." I diagnosed Senioritis. "I sure hate to see 'em go through it— but we all do, which is what I try to tell them—and help them through it." I advised Tom to get out of school and work and enjoy the paycheck for six months or a year. "Then, if you are still unhappy, get the hell out and do something else." I wanted him to at least try it, to use his talents. "I hope we can get him a damn job— take that [worry] off his back— provide him just a tad of security."

My Personal Life

Early in the fall 1975 semester, I went to the movie "King of Hearts," which I described as a black comedy. Afterward, my date and I went for beers. We ran into a couple of people I knew, and as I later wrote, "It felt good to be seen out with a man— and to see a movie with someone." I had taken a shine to this guy; our shared interest in sports took us to Kansas City for a Packers game, for example. But I found an early mention of him in my journal with "relationship" and "puzzling" in the same sentence. One night, six-pack in hand, he dropped by my apartment about 11 and we talked until 1. Then nothing for days. I fretted like a teenager— and I realized it. How could sharing be followed by ignoring? "It's not a lot of fun— at 26— feeling things so new, especially when you are me— a person not at all good at saying what is on my mind." He was on my mind, but "how to tell him without scaring him off," I wrote.

I certainly did not need more drama in my life— work and school provided enough of that. But one bad decision is sometimes all it takes to upend the equilibrium of one's life. I lived that. Knew immediately that "liberated or not," I wasn't into "messing around." The crush was not quite over, however. First there were a couple weeks of terror, then "joy in knowing I will not have to make the frightful decision." My own black comedy was over. I committed myself to never again settling. "Unless someone comes along and there is a long period of growing/knowing— I can say NO. I'm into my own thing now and don't have time to worry about someone else's hangups. I think Margaret Bourke-White was right re: marriage." I didn't explain that statement; I presume I had read about her life. A quick Google search revealed many quotations by her that would have resonated with me then, as they do now.

By that fall, I had settled into the creature comforts of my apartment and was happy to host visitors. Among them were my parents, who drove down for a few days around my father's birthday in late September. I even baked him a cake, writing that "domesticity (or lack of) shone through when I attempted to frost it." I, who hate shopping, roamed the mall with my mother. I took them out for dinner, and we enjoyed a movie together. After they left, I paradoxically wrote: "Guess we didn't see a lot but did have a good visit— But sometimes I just feel so remote from them." I take that to mean our conversations were, by my choice, superficial.

Several weeks later, Fred Berner (my Antigo colleague) dropped in for a weekend during his vacation. The weather cooperated and I took him on a long sightseeing drive. We talked nonstop, "and I think he enjoyed just being able to be out of Antigo and relax. Glad he felt he could come down here to do just that." A week later, I cooked my first Thanksgiving dinner -- for 14 people -- and a tradition was born. Because the Missourian needed to be staffed, and because so many journalism students were from out of state (and country), I issued an open invitation in the newsroom. I would make the turkey, mashed potatoes and gravy, and asked guests to contribute a side dish that would make the meal feel like Thanksgiving for them. Someone volunteered to make pies as long as she could do so in my kitchen. When the feast was over -- and judged a success -- I knew I would open my door for any holiday I was in town. And I did.

[An aside: I have a couple of vivid memories of that first Thanksgiving (one being a lot of wine bottles lined up and chilling on my porch), even though my journal entry was sketchy. One guest's name came to me immediately as I wrote this paragraph: Carrie Francke. She may have been the single most ambitious, hard-charging, tightly wound, accomplished young woman I have known. At the time, she was finishing her journalism degree and serving as the student body president. She already had completed a political science degree -- in three years. After graduation she earned a law degree. She was press secretary for a U.S. senator and an assistant attorney general for Missouri, and she served on the university's Board of Curators. Tragically, she died in a car accident at age 34. I often wondered if she had packed in so much because of a premonition of a short life.]

An important door also opened for me in the fall, when four of the seven women on the journalism faculty gathered one Friday evening for cocktails. When I joined the faculty, I had received an invitation to join the "Journalism Women" for a social hour. Turned out that group was essentially the *wives* of faculty members. If I attended that social hour, I know I never went to another. Talk about a fish out of water! But this was different; this promised time with like-minded professional women outside the newsroom. My mention of the evening in my journal was brief; I called it "really good." I noted that the other three attendees were older than I. And I recorded that I met Joye Patterson for the first time and "really liked" her. I knew of "Dr. Patterson" from several graduate students who were incredibly fond of her, so much so that she was much in demand as a thesis advisor. The "real" faculty members seldom ventured from their offices in Neff Hall to the annex that housed The Missourian, so it is likely I had seen Joye at faculty meetings, but that was it. I was disappointed that "I had to run off in the middle of good conversation" that night because of a previous commitment. I was hopeful the group would meet again and that my schedule would allow me to attend.

I had left that gathering to attend a one-woman theatrical performance. Independent women were much on my mind, and I wrote about that not long afterward. "I have been having some very positive contacts with women lately— single/divorced women who are doing well. It's refreshing and reinforcing." Among them was Ruth D'Arcy, whom the school had lured away from The Detroit News, where she had a distinguished 32 years as a writer, columnist and editor. She had helped transform women's pages (like the ones I had produced just a few years earlier) into "lifestyle" sections. At Missouri, she was in the newsroom as our People editor and directed the famed Penney-Missouri awards program. One weekend she had a friend visiting from Detroit, and I managed to skip out of the newsroom for a bit to share Saturday dinner. Lucky for me, I got to return to Ruth's on Sunday afternoon for coffee and more "chatting." I wrote about how Ruth "at 53 left the city where she'd spent all her life— to come down here— meet new people— do something new. A certain kind of adventuresome there." I added that I "liked her young Detroit friend, too— good head— fit right in."

I made it to the end of the fall semester, then enjoyed "a good two weeks in Wisconsin." I finally met my nephew, as a proud aunt and god-mother. My parents had a Christmas party that included Mary and Mike from Antigo. I saw Tom in Madison, on my terms. I spent 24 hours in Eau Claire, where "it was fun to spend $46" on dinner for four Polks and me at our "special-day" restaurant. I went to Milwaukee and re-connected with Laurel and Bob, "and in 30 seconds feeling like there had not been 2,000 miles and 2 years" since we last visited in person. When I returned "home" to Columbia, "I was ready for it— needed to be back to my own place— my own space." Waiting for me was "a giant stack of Christmas cards and letters" that caught me up on the news from friends from around the country. There were "new addresses for many— much friendship across many miles." On January 1, 1976, I cynically wrote that it marked "the year of the Bicentennial ripoff— 365 more days of it. Too bad we probably will not accomplish anything for the people of this country, let alone the world. A presidential year— but no new ideas." I didn't call it a resolution, but I wrote that "I want some things for this year. I want to give more of myself— get involved in some things outside J-School. One step at a time, but I'm going to try to reach out. . . . Look out 1976— I'm Ready!!!!"

A Rose Mary Woods Moment

My January 11, 1976, journal entry encapsulated the three segments of my "sophomore-year life," and I quote much of it because of that -- but mostly because it was the last entry I wrote until August 7. That gap, like the 18½ minutes missing from Nixon's Watergate tapes, was alarming. It was a puzzle I wanted to solve when I discovered it in 2021.

It all starts all over tomorrow and I really dread thoughts of the first week— 12 new shifts— new groups of students who are starting from Day 1.

Had Crazy Ann over for supper tonight. And she really is not too bad. Really going through a crisis as she is about to turn 30. But she is tolerable— and I've met a couple of other people through her— so that is good. . . .

Money a real problem this month. My ring got made ($22) and I've spent too much on food and drink this week. Now am on an austerity budget. Looks like a long month.

Saw Loretta briefly this week. She'll not start back until 1/26 and teach only one course and her Readings courses. She has cancer of some sort. I feel guilty about adding to her workload, but don't think it will be that much. And I do want to cultivate her friendship. Also have learned that woman (only one) from Political Science is teaching the minority politics course. Must talk with her about a readings course. And chances of getting one woman on my committee look good.

J-women dining at Ruth's next Sunday. Would be nice if we could agree to agitate for more women etc. Ruth is a real live wire/ forward-thinking woman who could be a mover.

I'm hoping to take in some of the Women's Center programs, beginning tomorrow. Should be a good way to meet more campus people— and I need that. And am ready for it.

Was the gap in journal entries because the promise I saw for the spring semester had not panned out? Had I found myself once again in that "dark place" referenced but not explained in an especially foreboding journal entry months earlier? Had I succumbed to a toxic mix of too much work, too little sleep, too much alcohol, dicey personal decisions and professional disillusionment? Was it an overstatement to describe my Missouri life as a cauldron waiting to boil over? Or was it merely that I was so busy with work and school that I no longer made time even for infrequent entries? I feared that I had no way to find answers, and if that proved true, I would have to figure out how to move my story forward. So, I stepped away from writing in fall 2021. The few clues I ultimately unearthed came from a handful of letters and a couple of documents. Here's what I ultimately verified about those seven months between entries:

- My spring-semester teaching workload was similar to previous semesters. My gradebook shows I had responsibility for numerous quizzes and layout assignments for the 91 students in one editing course, supervised two-thirds of them on the desk, and supervised about half of the 90 in the advanced course. I skimmed the names and found that I could attach memories to a few: Disheveled Joe (we connected over sports), who wrote me regularly for several years after he graduated. Bob, a graduate student who arrived with more debt from his Notre Dame undergraduate degree than I could imagine. Marie, a standout student and editor. Jim, one of the few Black men on the desk and an incredibly talented editor. Joan, who starred in helping produce two special editions. Paul, who eventually earned a Ph.D. at Missouri and went into university teaching.

- On January 13, I mailed my headline writing article to The Quill (the then-monthly magazine published by The Society of Professional Journalists, Sigma Delta Chi). In mid-March, the magazine's editor wrote to tell me my "fine article" had been scheduled for the April issue. He added, "Yours is one of the best how-to pieces I've seen in some time." "Sell the Sizzle," was published in the April issue. It was my first "practical" publication, which is to say it was "learned" but not "scholarly." In the academic world, it carried less weight because it was not refereed in the traditional sense of scholars reviewing another scholar's work. As I would argue later in my career, however, such articles had to pass muster with one or more editors, which ought to be considered refereed. And in the world of working journalists, "Sizzle" was *useful*, which is the kind of articles I liked writing. [An aside: Sigma Delta Chi was founded as an honorary fraternity in 1909. Its organizers were male DePauw University students interested in careers in journalism and upholding high professional standards. It became a professional fraternity in 1916 and a professional society in 1960. Women were not admitted until 1969. I boycotted the organization my entire career because when I had wanted to join, I could not.]

My article was well-received. A professor at the University of South Florida wrote that his news editing class was about to tackle headline writing and he was asking Quill for permission to mimeograph it for class use. He offered a couple of headlines for my collection, including one he had written for a wire story on the running of the bulls in Pamplona, Spain. A spectator whose first name was Juan had been nicked by a bull. The headline: "Bull Makes Hole In Juan." He explained that "the sad part about all this is that when I offer it to my students in a quiz on good and bad heads, about half usually reject it, preferring something like 'Man Hurt By Bull.' They tell me, 'Don't make fun of a serious accident.'" I was all too familiar with such students. The professor also shared a headline-counting guide developed for use by the student newspaper. (To this day, I can quickly count a headline as if I were checking its fit. Having a computer do the work is not nearly as gratifying.) The "witty" examples in that guide included: Shoppers Beef About Shortages, Irked Wife Breaks Up Hubby's Erector Set, and Lady Libber Singes Self While Burning Bra.

Tom Engleman, executive director of The Newspaper Fund, called my article "a gem" and said he was sending it to all 40 editing interns "so they will get in the swing of things early." GunR wrote to congratulate me and shared one of his Washington Post gems. He wrote it for an article on New York's perilous finances that included a "gorgeous" photo of the Manhattan skyline. The headline: Withering Heights. A letter from a senior editor at the Canadian news magazine Maclean's explained that he was responsible for writing the titles and captions, and he wanted "to expand a little on what you have written." He suggested that

the best . . . are those which create a bridge between something in the reader's own experience, and the article itself. Thus, the best title-writer -- and I think your examples bear this out -- have heads full of trivia: familiar lyrics, book titles, commercial jingles and gaga, commonly used Shakespearian quotes (and those of others), famous film dialogue, etc. And, of course, cliches and bromides -- there is nothing like a deftly-mangled cliché to attract a reader's eye and whet his/her curiosity.

However, he wrote, readers "will remember the story, but probably not the head." He concluded by writing that "it was nice to see that somebody actually teaches the subject, though I suspect that, like any other art-form, head/title writing cannot really be taught, only induced in people who have the ability and the perversity to begin with."

▶ I did submit a course proposal to the Honors College, which eventually approved "Black, Red, Brown: The Press of the People" for the fall 1976 semester. I would have needed my department chairman's approval before that, and I presume Daryl and I discussed what teaching it would mean for my Missourian schedule. Loretta left me a note saying she was "impressed!" by my syllabus. "(Probably 'cause I can see some of my influence!) No, seriously, I hope you get some older, self starter types. Your course sounds like one I'd like to take." Another time she alerted me to a publication she thought I would find useful for it.

▶ Loretta and I lunched frequently and socialized occasionally, and our "busyness" is clear from the notes we exchanged trying to arrange things. Once she double-checked my phone number, writing, "You're never there when I call— but then again I'm never here." Another time she "tried to catch up with you to go down to Faces to hear an incredible blues singer— Koko Taylor— fantastic!" Yet another time, both of us strapped for cash, she suggested a movie and asked, "What's the freebie at [the library] this weekend?" When she could not join me at a speech by Florynce Kennedy, the radical feminist, civil rights advocate and activist, she "had notes taken by 3 people. Less distressing that she's saying [the] same things; more distressing that both my classes were overwhelmingly hostile to her, her actions, suggestions, etc. I'm still upset over the conservativism amongst these 120+ students." We shared that wavelength.

▶ Daryl, Brian and I were successful with our second proposal for Missouri to be a new site for a Newspaper Fund crash course beginning in the summer of 1976. My calendar shows regular planning meetings and tasks. That had to have been time-consuming. In addition, the course would start just nine days after graduation. Whatever my specific responsibilities were, I worked them in around another Intersession on the copy desk.

▶ Thankfully, my Readings course met when convenient for Loretta and me. My "Sociology of Power" class, however, met MWF 10:30-11:30. That was brutal, but I found the professor to be another "winner," not least because he was outspoken, liberal and unorthodox. It was because of him that in April I had my first experience with political caucuses. I remember attending the local Democratic Party caucus and at one point crawling under a table to move my support from one candidate to another. I have absolutely no memory of which journalism faculty member taught "Proseminar in Communications." Perhaps a lack of interest explains my B grade to go along with A's for my sociology work.

▶ The first checkpoint on the road to a Ph.D. was passing a Qualifying Exam. For me, that involved taking the two-day Comprehensive Exam required of journalism master's degree students. The fact that I had a master's degree did not matter (although it did get me one year of residency credit toward the three required for my Ph.D.). The comps were scheduled for March 29 and 30, and until then I surely commiserated with more than a few of my graduate students who would also be taking them. Such high-stakes exams are anxiety producing for even the best of students, and certainly as a faculty member I felt added pressure not to fail.

▶ Before I threw out years of calendars, I took note of dates I judged important or interesting. As I drafted this manuscript, I was able to verify numerous dates, but I also was often left to wonder what I did *not* record. Still, looking at the spring 1976 semester, I had proof of increasingly busier months. Here is what I recorded for February, for example:

2— Lunchbag

5— Lunchbag

6— Meet re: Newsp Fund (have ideas)
    p.m. Movie w/Carol

10— Give 310 lecture

13— Lunchbag, meet Martha
    p.m. Arlo G. concert

18— Speak to WIC

20— Newsp Fund (specifics/examples)

24— Faculty meeting

29— Sydney brunch

March began with a spaghetti dinner at my apartment. Intersession/ spring break ran the 8th-13th and I worked the 8th, 11th and 13th. On the 22nd there was a Penney-Missouri Awards dinner, followed by a morning P-M seminar on the 24th and the P-M banquet on the 25th. Because of that banquet, I had to miss a National Organization for Women meeting. April included Journalism Week, which always was jam-packed with programs and speakers. I also spotted a new name that had begun to appear regularly on my lunch schedule as Robin. A botanist and wife of my newsroom colleague George, she and I became fast friends.

◇◇◇◇◇

My summer of '76 was far from carefree, but at least I took a break from my own studies. Surely I enjoyed working with the Newspaper Fund interns; incredibly, just a half dozen years earlier I had been one. (At least one wrote me from her internship in Albuquerque.) Surely I found Intersession as frustrating as ever. Surely I again took advantage of the swimming pool that came with the apartment I saw too little of. A letter from Les in early July mentioned that I had stopped briefly in Eau Claire and that he had spent time with me and Luise in Minneapolis. A long letter from a recent grad stated that "your vacation sounded wonderful. Something I'm sure you needed at the pace you keep." (I believe that vacation was the first Martha and I spent in Colorado.) However, I can document only two activities: (1) Teaching the introductory editing course during the second session of summer school. Eighteen students. Two A- and a whole lot of C's. (2) Dieting yet again and meticulously recording meals and calorie counts on my calendar.

On August 7, when I finally wrote in my journal again, I made no attempt to "catch up." Rather, I stated that this is my crisis book now. Need [to begin writing] to reinforce and scold. Got to fight Fat City again, and don't think it will be easy at all. Have backslid almost all the way. Don't like it, but now I'm part of that great statistic— people who "change" eating habits— drinking— etc. Lasts about two years. That's me. . . . Feel Fat and ugly, and sure don't need that. So here we go again, in an attempt to remodel BFL (body at least). Mind and psyche no doubt are beyond help.

Evolving as a Teacher

An early August night in the newsroom reminded me of how exciting -- and challenging -- it could be to be in a newsroom when there was breaking news. It was primary election day in Missouri. The Missourian had its skeleton summer crew, which added to the pressure to get election results into the next morning's paper. When news came over the wire that the congressman hoping to replace retiring U.S. Sen. Stuart Symington had died in a plane crash, we scurried to put together a story. I put on my reporting hat and marshaled background information from a variety of sources. Then I wrote while student editors provided me with details as they emerged. It was a team effort, and when we finished it was rewarding to know our readers were getting the most complete information we could provide. It was equally rewarding to know I had modeled how a professional can function calmly amid chaos.

When the new school year began on August 25, I think the merry-go-round must have reached break-neck speed rather quickly. After that determined entry earlier in the month, I did not write in my journal again until the middle of the spring 1977 semester. By then, I was banking on a new job that would put Missouri in my rearview mirror. I *was* able to piece together a few details about the fall semester. (1) I taught my Honors course. (2) My Missourian responsibilities changed. (3) I took three courses, in journalism, political science and sociology. (4) The Group, as I called us journalism women, met regularly, including for the first time at my apartment on Halloween. (5) I made a quick trip to Wisconsin for my brother's wedding. (6) I heard Julian Bond and Hunter Thompson speak, and I attended my first Judy Collins concert.

Although I had forgotten about that Honors course, in retrospect it represented the direction I found myself moving. More and more I wanted to be a "regular" faculty member, to teach not just "skills courses" but also those on the other side of the ledger. Normal hours and faculty duties were part of it, but more than anything I needed to scratch my intellectual itches. I did it first with "Black, Red, Brown." Its syllabus -- the first I ever prepared -- revealed links to my own studies and teaching approaches I would use for decades. It also answered a question that nagged at me during book research. The syllabus directed students searching for my office to look for the Sojourner Truth poster (with her "Ain't I A Woman" speech), a poster I remembered with fondness but couldn't pinpoint when I had it. Two other items on that syllabus jumped out at me. One was a paragraph explaining that because there was little research in the field of minority media, "there is a real possibility we can find a market for the best of your term papers." From the beginning, I wanted students to see that research was more than an exercise to earn a grade; it could be shared and potentially make a difference. Secondly, I wrote that "I do not think it would be of value for you to 'research' and write your paper one week before it is due." Instead, I devised a three-part paper that would be submitted in sections. That allowed me to critique each, return it with suggestions, and give students time for revisions. I wanted students to get feedback they could use to prepare their final papers, not just comments and a grade after the course was over. At the end of the semester, I was pleased to receive a letter from the Honors College director, who was "impressed" with the students' evaluations of the course. He encouraged me to "give every serious consideration to offering the course again (perhaps for three credits)" and alerted me that a formal invitation to do so would be forthcoming. "The Honors College seeks not only to find interesting new courses but to hang on to the good ones it has," he added.

There is little need to write much about my Missourian work that fall, which is a good thing because I have neither journal entries nor memories about it. A letter from a friend commented "only two nights on the desk. What a treat!" Before she signed off, she added, "Don't work too hard— a foolish thing to tell you." My sister mentioned in a letter that she "heard you are on days now. What does it seem like to sleep when most normal people sleep??" Reading that reminded me I had begun working at least part time with students assigned to the People pages. That was confirmed in a letter from a grad who asked, "How does it feel being part of a (snicker) lifestyles section?" According to my calendar, at least once I also helped out on the sports desk, and that must have been fun, and a Christmas card from a recent grad referenced my work as a part-time sports editor "after the quick exit of Mr. Baloney."

It is clear from letters that I was not the only one concerned about my work habits. My college friend Laurel, seemingly more settled than I, wrote to share news of changes to her beat, prefaced with "Yup, I'm still very satisfied and challenged at the [Waukesha] Freeman." She also filled me in on several classmates -- married, pregnant, changing jobs and more. She ended with the "hope you are taking it a little easier this term." Les suggested that I had

> often been a most vigorous workaholic. Ruth Anne and I have been concerned about it in the past . . . just about the fact that our dear Barbara MUST, while doing well in career, also give herself the chance to BE . . . to be woman, to be person, whole and rich, to develop all the "other" facets of the you that we know are there because we've seen them over the years. I think you come from a perspective of "having to succeed," very much. And you are doing exactly that.

I obviously had discussed my desire to change my focus in journalism education, to move beyond copy editing. "I agree that would be desirable," he wrote. "You're set as a copy editor, and can surely teach it. You may, at some point, even want to return to the business in that capacity," he added, citing a Stanford Ph.D. he knew who had done just that. "Don't lock yourself in, friend. And there's nothing wrong with reading a Harper's Bazaar or Glamour along with Ms. is there?" Truth be told, that last sentence probably never resonated with me; if I ever have read an issue of those first two magazines it was because that's all there was in a waiting room.

Several of my Missourian graduates kept in touch through regular letters -- commonly signing off with "Love" -- that shared not only news of their lives but comments on their work and our profession. I was flattered that they continued to ask me for advice or affirmation of a decision. Here was tangible proof of my effectiveness in the newsroom-as-lab setting, and in that I found support for broadening my reach. For example, in October Barb wrote from Jackson, Mississippi, to send a photo of her newborn son and bring me up to date on life. Her husband, a reporter, was getting restless and she thought he would appreciate hearing from me if I learned "of anything that sounds good." As for herself, she wrote that she was "happy with the mother-homemaker role for now" and "enjoying those things newspaper fanatics never have time for— the 'boring' things liberated women are supposed to scorn, like sewing and cooking." Before she closed, she noted: "I'm sure you're wondering if I'm starting the craving for newspaper fixes again. And the answer is yes, although I'm surprisingly indifferent to it all." There were days, she added, when she longed to be [back] in the newsroom "amidst all the action." But displaying wisdom for one so new to the business, she said that "at other times it seems so obvious that newspaper people take themselves much too seriously and there's so much more to life that they're obviously missing." I wonder now if she was giving me a not-so-subtle hint about my life.

That same month I also heard from Ann, four months into her job in South Carolina. Her opening sentence, penned inside a card proclaiming "Things are improving! It's Tuesday already" also was wise: "Somewhere between adjustment and acceptance is a long period of disillusionment." Her newspaper, she explained, had a new executive editor, no city editor and the state editor had dropped dead of a heart attack. Her disillusionment, she said, "had hit rock bottom." She was running the copy desk and "realizing how much I don't know." She didn't mail the card for two weeks, at which time she wrapped it inside a letter with updates. Particularly interesting to me was the paragraph describing the sex discrimination she felt. I presume we had discussed the topic before. She had heard that the layout for the lifestyle pages soon would be turned over to the copy desk, and because she was the only woman on the desk she believed (reasonably, I think) they would be assigned to her. In addition, "I have one man on the rim on Sunday that, despite all of his arguments to the opposite, doesn't cooperate with me much. I'm trying to determine whether it's me, my experience or my sex. We get along really well at any other time. Much to my dismay, I suppose it's my first, real honest sex discrimination. And it's a bitter pill to swallow." Indeed!

Then there was Jim's letter from St. Louis, written during his business statistics class. Married life agreed with him, he wrote, but "[graduate] school really sucks." And he hated his job as the night police reporter, "undoubtedly the most tedious, petty job" on the paper. "My nights are full of little crime stories, but I rarely see a byline. (I've only had 4 in a month.) The hours are terrible. . . . Between work, school and sleep, I have <u>no</u> time to myself or my wife." Although he didn't use Ann's phrase, "a bitter pill to swallow," the description of his job supported his observation that "I am even more jaded and cynical than when I left Mizzou." Over the years, his observations allowed me to explain to others that an entry-level job at a metropolitan daily newspaper might not be the best dream. To wit:

> Being a police reporter is terrible. I have an office at the City Police Station where I can't communicate with normal people, only pigs. I find the cops to be brutal, foul, vulgar, low-class, gross, despicable, and generally not-nice guys to be around. It was a rather rude awakening for a kid who used to watch Adam 12.
>
> Unfortunately, being a beat reporter, you have to grin and bear it, acting like you like the people, enjoy the job and ignore all the illegal shit the cops do.

After he provided me a detailed description of a deplorable incident he had witnessed, he wrote: "Not exactly the type of stuff they teach us in journalism school." In fact, it did provide me with important guidance.

Along with his scathing critique, Jim had asked me to track down a couple of addresses for him, including that of Mary Jo. Ironically, I found a letter from her that offered perspective from the opposite end of the job spectrum and proved particularly timely when I read it during the summer 2021 surge of COVID-19. She was a "paid-by-the-hour feature writer" for an "old and very small" daily newspaper in Arkansas. She described her "first big story" as an "in-depth look at the controversy, history and campaign against the poor little virus" called the swine flu. She told of taking my own personal survey today. Talked to 71 persons on the hoof, i.e. in person, and phoned an additional 79. Boy, am I pooped. I realize that 150 won't give me the same results as having contacted 700, but when you work alone, there's a limit to what you can do in one day! Besides which, how would you like to get appointments with 5 general practitioners in 2 days, not to mention a hospital administrator, nursing home heads, head health honchos at the state facility for the mentally retarded etc. etc. I'd sure hate to do this for a living!! (A bit of drollery to brighten your day.)

The [published] story will be an entire page with a large chunk devoted to answering the questions people raised when I asked them for (flu) opinions. Anyhow, it's been fun.

Misinformation, her letter reminded me, doesn't need the internet.

The physicians I talked to gave me varying responses. One clown told me people would get a mild case of the flu when they got their injections because the vaccine contained live virus. He was kind of—um— confused when I told him it was a killed virus vaccine and that (as state officials and vaccine information sheets told me) a person will not get the flu— only the symptoms!— and will not be contagious.

Another doc feared malpractice suits and would give the vaccine only to those patients with whom he enjoyed a healthy rapport (no pun intended). A third said he would not take the vaccine himself and would not recommend it for his healthy patients under 50. A fourth said he would take it and would give it. The fifth said he'd do what the state dept. of health recommended but would not take it himself.

In sum, a goodly number of those I talked to said they would check with their family doc before taking the vaccine. This will work fine until neighbors begin comparing notes— finding their docs differ greatly in opinion. An extra added amount of confusion will result. Life is hell.

After more specifics about her poll, she offered an assessment of her job that must have made me proud at the time; it certainly makes me smile when I read it now: "I must beg you to forgive my impetuous, naïve way of enjoying my work. I do so get a chuckle out of it. Being a mere snip of a J-grad, I still get a little twinge of excitement from the profession."

The many letters from around the country in which graduates described their jobs provided me countless perspectives I could share with students. Like the lengthy handwritten letters I continued to exchange with a few of my own undergraduate friends, such letters showed me the importance of human connection. *Dear Barb. Dear Miz Barb. Dear BFL. Dearest Toots.* Receiving those letters (not to mention birthday cards, holiday cards, vacation postcards, wedding invitations etc.) was so different from today's hastily written emails or text messages because I knew the commitment the writer had made to me. *Those letters took time, took genuine caring.* To this day, I am blown away by the fact that the handwriting on some decades-old envelopes remains immediately identifiable to me.

It wasn't just letters that reminded me of how I connected with some students. There was the heart-warming "Personal" included among the student newspaper's classified ads: "B.F. Luebke -- We Love you!" There was the story by Vicky, after she graduated and went to work for our competitor, The Columbia Daily Tribune. She featured me as the "Cook of the Week" with my recipes for spaghetti sauce and Cuban bread, which she must have enjoyed at one of my student dinners. [An aside: Credit the Eau Claire instructor I had driven to North Carolina for the bread recipe.]

Barbara Luebke

Tribune photo by Bill Marr

Cook of the week
Spaghetti artistry

By VICTORIA WIGGINTON
of The Tribune's staff

It seems just about everybody has a recipe for spaghetti. But among purveyors of pasta there are artists, and there is everybody else.

Barbara Luebke, 2012 W. Ash St., is not Italian, nor was she raised anywhere near the great Italian kitchens of the East Coast. She is, in fact, from Wisconsin. But heirloom spaghetti recipes have a way of working

1 bay leaf
Salt, pepper, chili powder and Italian seasoning to taste.

Brown meat in a deep skillet. Season with salt, pepper and chili powder. Drain. Stir in tomato sauce and pepperoni slices. Add drained mushrooms and olives. Toss in the bay leaf and add a pinch of Italian seasoning plus salt, pepper or chili to taste. Cook, covered, at least 3 hours over very low heat so that sauce barely simmers. Remove cover for last 15 minutes of cooking. Serve over

A month later, I was one of three individuals profiled for a Tribune Sunday magazine story on "Living Alone." A small photo captured me in my living room filled with books, record albums, wall art and plants.

Barb Lue
Missouri
says livin
'the key
success
Luebke

When I recently read that story, after a steady diet of words about discontent, I was taken aback by its ending: "Most of the time I am quite content to be where I am, doing what I am doing," I was quoted as saying. I was taken aback, too, by the realization that self-doubt continued to nag at me, even though my Ph.D. coursework, along with my professional work and words, gave me every reason to believe in myself. Although I do not have examples from the fall, two papers I wrote the following semester are representative of my classroom work.

I wrote "Covering the Busing Story/A Look at 12 Southern Newspapers" for a journalism seminar. I explained that along with an article by press observer Edwin Diamond, my study was prompted by my interest in "American minority situations" and recent events precipitated by government-mandated busing to desegregate schools. Further, I noted that the necessary limitations on the study "were predicated on the author's curiosity about a certain kind of newspaper: small, southern dailies in cities with considerable black population." I cannot recall a time when I did not believe that curiosity is a journalist's most important characteristic. And my own intellectual curiosity guided my academic work. For this paper, I hoped to gain insight into six questions, among them: the amount of space being given to the busing story, where and how the stories were "played," and what types of stories were being published. My methodology included a new tool I had learned about in my research methods course: Attention Score.

For my Sociology of Power class, I wrote "Some Thoughts on Media Power," a traditional, 16-page research paper with 67 footnotes and a bibliography with 22 entries. Its beginning sentence -- "Power and mass communication are terms that are used together often." -- dates it as a subject whose value is as a history lesson. The era in which I came of age -- the era of mass communication -- no longer exists because there is no longer a mass audience. Someone writing about media power today would be talking a significantly different language. I offer my paragraph-long thesis statement as an example of my mid-1970s thinking.

> Media observers have tended to focus on individual columnists, commentators, newspapers or stations in describing the power of mass communication. This has led to a false picture of media power. It is not that the mass media are less powerful than we have been led to believe. Quite the opposite: The media are more powerful than most of us might like to think. But that power lies in the fact that the media define many -- if not most -- of the situations that confront us daily and to which we directly or indirectly respond. As such, ALL media are powerful, an idea that under the common understanding of media power is laughed at: The New York Times has power, but the Podunk Gazette?! The distinction becomes that media have varying amounts of power, because of the particular environments in which they operate. And there can be overlapping spheres of media power. But the mere existence of a medium means it is a locus of power. It defines situations for its audience, and therein lies its inherent power.

Sometime early in the fall semester I learned (no doubt from Les) there would be a job opening at my alma mater for January. (The merger of the Wisconsin State University System and the University of Wisconsin System had been completed in 1971 and the school's name was changed to the University of Wisconsin-Eau Claire, aka UWEC.) In early November the chairman (still Elwood Karwand!) wrote that he was "delighted" to have received my official application. He said the search would close on December 1, wondered if I could get released from my contract and asked about my availability for an interview. In addition, he said a new staff position in news and public affairs reporting and editing was being added for fall, and he asked if I were interested in being considered for it. He said to expect to see it advertised in December, then ended with, "I keep hearing so many excellent things about you and about your work, and would be very pleased if we could work out matters so you could join our faculty." Ten days later I learned a few more details from Les, including that the as-yet-unadvertised position would be "Visiting," not tenure-track, at least at first. "Because they don't want to get overloaded for 1993 or something like that, when slow birth [rate] is supposed to vacate some jobs." And in a rewarding twist, he also asked if I knew of a photography instructor -- "a live, good, young, FEMININE (feminist?) one -- for heaven's sake direct their attention here when that ad comes out."

Full Steam Ahead -- and Then Some

I did not go to Eau Claire for the spring 1977 semester; they hired a man with no teaching experience. I did, however, switch jobs, moving full time to the Missourian People desk. Despite working days, I enrolled in four courses: three journalism and one political science. Whatever was I thinking? Probably that if I were fortunate to get hired by Eau Claire in the next round, the credits would allow me to fulfill the requirement for graduate work completed on campus.

The semester began on January 17; two days later my second nephew, Nickolas Mikail, was born. I wasn't writing in my journal; no doubt working with a new batch of students along with a new "boss" (People editor/ Penney-Missouri Awards director Ruth D'Arcy) and my own schoolwork left little time for reflection. From letters, I finally was able to piece together some details about "my head space" that semester.

I was disappointed that Eau Claire had not hired me, but I was alarmed when I learned what had gone on behind the scenes. It was my first exposure to lip-service affirmative action. It wouldn't be my last. I was well aware of the chairman's approach to running the department: top down and little, if any, collaboration. Although there now was a Faculty Personnel Selection Committee, it had not been involved in choosing finalists for the January job. Instead, Elwood gave the faculty a list of five individuals (all men) he had compiled. Apparently he had determined that I did not meet the requirement for five years of professional work. (He chose to count time in the way that supported him.) Further, despite instructions to all departments that the affirmative action officer be included in selection-committee meetings, she had not been. Les eventually filled her in, and thus it was that she invited herself to the meeting in early March to consider applicants for the fall job. As a result, deliberations were put on hold so *all* the dossiers could be provided to the faculty.

At the Missourian, I enjoyed the pace of lifestyle stories and editing. I worked with a strong graduate assistant, Carol Doup Muller, and enjoyed overseeing a smaller group of students. Most were young women, and a few were eager to make their mark as the world offered more and more opportunities to us. A couple developed into friends, none more so than Sue Littell. And yet. . . .

In an undated letter (March, I think) to Les that I never mailed, I opened by saying I had set my alarm for 6, hoping to catch three hours of sleep before writing the lecture I was giving at 10:30. Reverting to my no capitalization/no punctuation typing, I explained: "i guess i can wing it on editing out the isms. . . . i've enough examples of sexism to write a book. . . . but now i need to bounce feelings off you . . . and the hell with whatever." I clearly was unhappy.

> [T]he only bright spot in the last three weeks has been the offer of a part-time job at stephens college. . . . real classroom journalism at an all-women school with a fine woman [journalism professor]. . . . but I'm not ready to be just a poor person again. . . . i need my johnny walker red, now more than ever. . . . at least I know I have skills appreciated by someone/some institution.

I went on to write that at lunch with Loretta, "my closest friend here," I had learned she was about to have a second mastectomy. And to top it off, I had just spent 3½ hours with a

> student/friend who did not go to the washington post, and me trying to play— be— the person who has something to offer someone else whose head is screwed up. . . . damn, I can't even deal with my own

life and yet here i am forgetting me and trying to be something to someone. . . . hell, who do i lean on . . . who will hear me out . . . positive stroking has to come from somewhere . . . and it isn't.

I told him I didn't intend "a bitch letter," which may explain why I chose not to mail it. (But why did I save it?) It was just that it was midterm week and I had been "going non-stop for about 10 days." I dreaded a test on Friday and I was "restless and tired and scared and. . . ." I told him about spending a lot of time in the law library researching "an interesting paper on the legal definition of reporter . . . and another on extension of first amend. rights to adv[ertising]. . . . both of which have little or nothing to do with anything . . . but may get published." (They did.) I asked rhetorically: "do you realize if I had gone to law school I would have been practicing for three years already . . . and no damn foreign language [requirement] or dissertation or comps."

Shortly thereafter, I returned to my journal. "Why? On beer #7, I admit missing the nightly minutes spent with pen and paper. The recent hell is not recorded, but perhaps that is best. But the darkness must be realized and recognized and God willing it will not happen again, though I know it will." I continued to be the center of my own personal tug of war. Without missing a beat, I then wrote: "I have done well, I think, as the strong shoulder— and I suppose there is a certain amount of ego gratification in that— but more importantly, I have found recently people on whom I can lean, without giving up my strength— for they always seem to see me as the strong person." Wistfully I added, "But I'd sure like a little loving. And someone to carry out the garbage— or do the laundry."

I smiled when I read the journal paragraph describing "3 delicate white flowers on one plant— another preparing to bloom." The latter was my "begonia that wasn't a begonia. I should call it a memory plant," I once wrote. It was passed on to me by a student/friend from my first Missouri year when she graduated. I came close to killing it more than once and worked hard to revive it. "Amazed how I react to these— Tremendous pride— and love. Sorry I only recently have come to recognize this kind of living thing. And never again want to be without green around me." I never have been, either.

My letter to Les mentioned that I had met with a financial consultant and was confident that a tax shelter/annuity program would provide for me in retirement. ("Uncle Sam surely won't.") I was beginning to think like a working adult! That first journal entry, written March 26, offered further evidence of that. I wrote about buying myself a rocking chair. "I wonder, is this the ultimate sign of old age?" I described an outing to nearby Fulton (where Winston Churchill gave his "iron curtain" speech after accepting an honorary degree from Westminster College) as "playing— the first such day in years." Sue and I drove along county roads, with a stop at Antiques & Curios. There, Ethel Brown told us to call her Ethel "because I'm not important enough to be Mrs. Brown." I described her as "so open, so honest, in our brief conversation." After a quick swing through a furniture store downtown -- trying out each chair -- I chose one that, luckily, fit into my car. The timing of the outing was good for Sue, too. It was Mother's Weekend on campus and her mother had died 18 months earlier. I felt immensely privileged when she shared a collection of magazine articles her mother had written.

My next entry made clear how much I appreciated that new chair: "The rocking is soothing— the smooth waxed curves of the chair are nice to touch and pleasant to look at. I wait for the days when the warm sun will filter through the window. And I can sit and read or dream." That Sunday, however, was gray; but my play day and 11 hours of sleep had me feeling OK. "Three stacks of records— both sides" later and my law paper was typed except for the bibliography and footnotes. "So much for researching earlier. I'm a deadline writer I guess— and why not. I've been producing under deadline almost daily for six years."

I made note of an "appendicitis scare" and that I continued to deal periodically with some pain. I attributed it to "tension or nerves. Too much thinking. Got to learn to shut off the damn brain now and then. Too much going on up there for my own good." *If I had a dollar for every time I thought or wrote a sentence like that.* . . . With April approaching, I wrote that "we have survived another winter. I wonder what spring first found me saying that. I marvel now at the buds on trees. And eagerly await the magnolias. Remembering the February fragrances of Eugene. And nighttime tennis to relieve tensions. And knowing the ocean was an hour away." I concluded by judging it "a very quiet evening— feels good to be me tonight."

I long have self-diagnosed at least a mild case of SAD (seasonal affective disorder), and along with my "survived winter" comment, my March 29 entry supports it.

> How quiet the world was this morning, one of few on which I beat the sun— much to read and I find it a bit easier in the early morning. Today it was only the wind and the birds— blue sky so opposite from yesterday's rain-filled gray ones. The sun can do a lot for one's state of mind.

Springtime also turned my fancy to cars, and I was eager to buy a new one. I thought I could "swing it financially— so why not." Waiting seemed prudent, however, because I had been invited to Eau Claire to interview for the job— although not for several weeks— and feared making a hasty decision about new wheels. I also feared that I was "taking E.C. for granted" and hoped "that is not a fatal mistake."

I welcomed April with an almost-poetic entry. On a cool Saturday afternoon, I described:

> me with stereo headphones turned LOUD, wrapped in a patriotic red-white-blue Afghan [made by my mother, I am guessing]. I wonder what it would be like to have a You across the room, on the couch, sharing the day— the hour. We could share the pain of the week past or the fears of the week to come. You could hold me and there would be no reason to be scared. Or I could hold you and share my strength. Instead, I share the day with alcohol— And wish it were over— or dark— or something. Mostly, I want someone here to share the beauty of a flowering plant— and an empty bed.

The week ahead promised much law-review-article reading; the day's three hours had "barely put a dent in the list assembled for yet another paper I must write." It also promised to be "a pre-registration bitch." The week after that would be the always-busy, star-studded Journalism Week. And it was "finally starting to anger me that I've had to wait so long for [the Eau Claire] interview. Apprehension, I suppose. Wanting to be done. Life has to be better."

It didn't help that Ruth had begun to irritate me. I found her frequently moody and insulting, and I could not abide her habit of barking at me before I even had time to settle into my office. I could handle the criticism and the second-guessing; I could not handle being given no time to organize myself before being assaulted. Carol noticed it too, and we frequently commiserated. She had her own difficulties, agonizing for days over a job offer, finally coming to grips with her decision to try a commuter marriage (her husband was in medical school), then learning that the job offered was not what she thought it was going to be and not one she wanted. The last thing she needed was Ruth on a rampage. We both steered clear of her as much as possible, and I continued to count the days until my interview. I feared that "if my world crashes in on the 18th, I'm not sure I can handle it. . . . I'm afraid I've put all my eggs in the basket this time." Then I penned this poem:

> There are no Good Friday words in me
> No Easter words
> Or any other holiday
> I've lost the days— weeks— months
> And three years of my life
> Not wasted . . . completely
> But lost forever
> And there are plenty of Regrets
> Which is NO WAY to live
> Or, even
> Exist.

[An aside: In fairness, a short note from Ruth on March 28 accompanied the check for my Penney-Missouri critiques. She thanked me for "doing triple duty— for doing your own work on the Missourian, for doing my work on the Missourian and critiquing Section 1 of the Penney-Missouri workshop papers." Surely I must have felt good about her assessment: "You are a gem— a workhorse, but a gem. . . . I hope [the check] is enough to buy that rocker. Now, if people like Ruth D'Arcy would get off your back, you may have time to sit in that rocker and rock and rock and rock and dream pleasant thoughts of the fall."]

My former colleague Martha Allen, who landed on her feet as a reporter at the Minneapolis Tribune, annually declared Easter a "time of rebirth and renewal." In 1976, I had hung up on her after she said it for the umpteenth time. Despite the above poem, though, Easter 1977 at least found me renewed by the purchase of a canary yellow MG Midget. I had not waited. And not for the last time did I seek to buoy my spirits with a new car. This purchase was celebrated by an afternoon of beer on Harpo's sundeck, which left me with raccoon eyes and one very red arm. Joining me was Sue, whose reason to celebrate was a job interview in St. Louis. I offered to pick up the MG on Wednesday instead of Monday so she could drive my Gremlin to the city. "No matter," I wrote.

> I'm not at all sure the excitement of HAVING it can be any greater than . . . the act of actually going out and buying it. Not on true impulse, but with little fanfare. And when I remember 4-9-77, I'll remember how good I felt and what joy there was in calling home— and in calling Sue and hearing her good news— And for once sharing some good news with Martha.

There was a "literary" bent to more than a few of my journal entries going forward. I was reminded of writings earlier in life, where I played with language, narrative style, voice, words. An example:

> In the quiet of the morning, she was especially prone to fantasy. Alone in the big apartment, longing for someone with whom to share breakfast, she was like an actress in a movie— writing the script as she went along. Often, she never spoke out loud, instead silently mouthed each role.
>
> Scene: Smell of hot coffee— a quick whir of the blender and the orange juice no longer is frozen. Sun streaming in the East window. A new flower on the cactus. Noise of shower in the background. Lou Wood giving Sky Warn bulletins.
>
> She had no trouble setting the scene— the dialogue didn't come as easily. Too many news stories quoting others— and too little dialogue in her real life.
>
> H: Are you packed for tomorrow? You know you always forget your shampoo.

In red ink on a sheet from a yellow legal pad I wrote about overseeing my latest Journalism Week special section. I was on a flight to Eau Claire, via Minneapolis.

Egos— those very tender, touchy parts of us that make us— need massaging in many ways. Hers was especially fragile, tho she attempted to hide the fact and believed herself to be successful in the endeavor. However, after a week of work on the project, and the banquet drawing to a close, there was a gnawing feeling growing in the pit of her stomach that the Dean, per his usual fashion, had forgotten. The gavel would fall and the papers would remain bundled at the back of the gymnasium. It was an unexpected surprise then when he did not forget— moreover she could revel in 2 seconds of her own glory as he announced the distribution and gave her credit. Her name— amplified. And tho to many there it meant nothing, enough in the crowd knew her to make it a night to remember. She was not sure, but probably at that moment there was a sparkle in her eyes and the hint of a prideful smile. Moreover, her companions at the table exuded pleasure. And it was fun, in the proverbial sea, to for a moment be a big fish. And she had not even planned to attend the banquet. Those things have a way of working out.

Later in the evening, primed with cheap and expensive scotch and Missouri water— and over-intellectualizing— the two had another one of their incredibly intense and honest discussions. . . . There is a vitality to her life now that had been wanting. . . . She even had been able to admit her fears about the fragility of it all.

The dawn, on 3 hours of sleep, is annoying. The sun seems an intruder. The body rebels at tea— and Alka-Seltzer— hot water— and talk. Movements are in slow motion so as not to disturb some kind of warped equilibrium. Voice low and heavy; it's difficult to disguise the fatigue— the bone-weariness of running full-tilt for too long and realizing it is not yet time to stop. It is not a time for talk— tho there is some. The house looks like a tornado was through last night. Certainly nothing to come home to.

The air, heavy with cigarette smoke ("You must quit you know— Not for us but for you") is also heavy with words and emotions from the previous night. To leave the comfort and the safety of the place would be to imagine someone else's wall decorations.

The next day, on another sheet of legal pad, the entry written in my room at the Eau Claire Holiday Inn began: "I want to write a poem for [a Missourian colleague]. I'm not sure I have it in me at the moment. I want to write a poem for me. And I'm not sure I have it. What I really want to write is a poem that is not therapeutic. And I don't know if I can." As always, *words* were my refuge. I don't remember what prompted that entry. Until I read my journal, I didn't remember that Martha drove me from Minneapolis to Eau Claire. I didn't remember that we stopped for brunch and "plenty of good talk around a table at the old hotel in St. Paul where F. Scott Fitzgerald once wrote." *That was pretty darn cool!*

The Holiday Inn held no surprises: "One double bed. Gideon. The nice canned painting is above the bed, where you can't see it. The ugly one (still life bowl of plastic-looking fruit) is on the wall across from the bed." [An aside: No doubt I began noticing hotel "art" after my summer in Milwaukee, when one weekend my sister, Les and I hung out with a guy who made his living producing it.] I continued, "At least the mattress is hard— the spread looks new— the toilet runs unless flushed with care— phone is loud; sure to be better than an alarm when the wake-up call comes." Wherever and whenever I had learned it, I never forgot the lesson about the importance of details! I knew the telephone was loud because its ring had jolted me awake after exhaustion put me to bed early. It was Les. "You're supposed to call mommy and daddy," he said. "I'm trying to be . . . ," I answered. "You're doing a good job. How about a cup of coffee?" I was glad he made the move. I had promised Martha before she left to drive home that I would not spend the rest of the day worrying about the interview. That had not been difficult because "exhaustion is still the predominant emotion." I did hope sunshine would replace Sunday's grayness because "raindrops won't look good on a white suit."

I used my return flight to record the barest details of my interview day. I did <u>not</u> bury the lead: "To use a cliché, the ball is in my court now— which is what I wanted. The decision will be mine. I'm having a difficult time comprehending it as having happened. Or maybe I'm just over-thinking, over-feeling." I certainly didn't write about how I felt during my interviews, and I didn't write much about who I met with. I simply observed that it had been a long day with "a very different approach" from my Missouri interviews, where I "really was in town to be looked over. Here, they seem to have decided, and this is the formality." That meant "meeting with deans I once interviewed and sparred with. Both now promoted. Both good men." John Morris, now second in command, "was his usual southern gentleman." Between "asking first where the curls came from" and commenting that "I want you to know that suit is VERY sharp," he did ask about my teaching strengths and career goals. Before I left his office, he also noted that it would be good to get reacquainted. Obviously, the affirmative action officer still had work to do to raise the consciousness of campus leaders, but I am fairly certain I was flattered by his comments.

Before I left the campus, Elwood told me that a contract "should be in the mail in a couple of days." He was pushing for a $13,500 salary. "I could live with that," I wrote, "though I had hoped for a bit more." I took Les and Ruth Anne to dinner at our favorite restaurant (best popovers ever) "and it was good— food, talk, wine." As he drove me to the Holiday Inn, Les and I talked about me. "Ever since you were a little girl," he observed, "there has been a sensitive you, easily hurt." I countered, "I hide it well, though." To which he replied, "RA and I see through that." I got in the last word: "It's a good thing someone does." My journal makes it clear that I understood our relationship at times might be different if I returned as a faculty member. But "maybe not," I wrote. Ruth Anne had told me she looked forward to having someone to talk to, and the boys were excited. "You'd better let her stay here," they had said when told of my interview. I decided to tally "the good and bad about changing jobs."

> I'm not sure there is anything real bad. Missouri friendships will fade— or survive time and space. And perhaps we have little control over that. There will be new friendships in E.C. There are the Minneapolis people. And Les says one of these days I'm going to fall in love and fall hard. Soooooo.
>
> Luise, bless her heart, found me at the Polks. . . . Don't remember her exact words but they were to the effect that it is time we live near one another again, that it would be good. And I agree.
>
> Finally, I called Martha, who believes I ought to accept the job.

More than once, I had thought to myself that teaching at Eau Claire would allow me to pay back the university for all it had given me. Near the end of my journal entry, I put it this way: "To those whom life has given so much, to not give something back seems terribly, terribly selfish." Having flown home through the clouds— "black to gray to fluffy white" until we were above them and "among the lucky who today will see the sunshine; that is pretty damn remarkable"— I think my mind was made up by the time I landed in Columbia.

If I had harbored any thoughts of staying at Missouri, they were gone the next morning after Carol called to warn me that Ruth had been a terror the past two days. In retrospect I probably could have been more understanding of the pressure on her to do both her jobs. But I couldn't see past the demands of my own two jobs: teacher and student.

I had realized on my return trip that I needed to get "my head on straight" for the next few weeks. "I AM in school. I DO have a major paper to write and tests to take and a desk to run. I'd like to slow everything down to about half-speed (except me) and then, just then, there is a possibility I could make it."

Some sage advice in a letter from Sue (how could one so young be so wise?) helped. Referencing a phone call in which I had asked for "Luebke encouragement in reverse" before I committed to leaving, she offered these thoughts. Mind you, she made time to write despite being just one day into her new job.

> People is driving you ba-na-na, n'est-ce pas? It's getting to be a royal 'dwag.'
>
> School is easy for you— probably too easy, from what I understand (and by the amounts of our beer intake, I know I'm right).
>
> You're a restless person— Columbia gets old real quick.
>
> Les or no Les, E.C. is going to be an environment totally unlike MU's— the small classroom you dream and muse about all the time; potential mass rapport with a lot more kids who really need you out there.
>
> You won't be automatically tenured, so if you want to punt after a year, punt!

As I anxiously awaited word from Eau Claire ("I better take the job; seems [Missouri has] hired my replacement and word is around that I'm leaving."), I got some good news from my mother. A few days before I left for Eau Claire she had called to tell me about a grapefruit-size cyst. Surgery was likely, but first she needed some tests. Turned out to be "just" a fibroid tumor the size of a football. I could not imagine having something so large inside me. When I talked with her a couple of days later, she told me that prior to surgery, her doctor had thought she had a malignant tumor, although he told her otherwise. She said she was glad of that. His decision made me angry. "To encourage us all with the 90 percent chance fibroid shit— Had it not been, what a shock for all, even more so than the other. What right has he— an argument not unique to us, of course. Seems to me to be a real matter of medical ethics." Today it seems to me that despite not usually practicing what I preached, I believed in honest communication even when the message was difficult.

Elwood's "couple of days" to contract turned out to be 19 days! Its offer was immediately preceded by "a couple hours of despair" after Daryl told me the "promised" salary was an issue. He had contacted Elwood because he needed to know what was up so he could make an offer to someone to fill my spot, if need be. When my phone eventually rang, the brief conversation went like this:

ECK: I'm afraid I have some bad news. The best they'll come up with is $12,700.
BFL (a few seconds of thought, then): I guess that will do.
ECK (sounding surprised): You do— Well, that's wonderful.

And for the second time, he told me a contract would be on the way. It was not exactly the ringing endorsement or warm welcome I expected. Nonetheless, the return to Eau Claire that I had long dreamed of was going to happen. And yet I could not help myself; I acknowledged that "my apprehension is that it won't be what I want it to be— and I'll have to move on yet again." Five days later, the last item mentioned in my journal entry was the contract's arrival. "I'm a Visiting Instructor. Oh well, what are titles but ego trips any way. I'm teaching and that is what counts.!!!"

An Interlude

As I thought about what lay ahead, I noted that "I want to be able to write [and] I hope Eau Claire affords the time, once the hecticness [sic] of beginning is over." Today, I see that my journal already contained more and more writerly snippets along with details of my days and states of mind. Here are some that jumped out at me:

▶ Overheard in O'Hare [airport]: "Will the party meeting flight ### with the alligator please check at gate #." At least that is what I think I heard.

▶ Not even a proper burial for the bird. Looked newborn from the quick glance I gave it on the way up the stairs. On return trip I kicked it over the side. One flight down. SMACK. SQUISH. Wonder how long it will rot there. But at least I don't have to look at it.

▶ There have to be pauses in our lives that allow us to review where we have been and where we are going. It is the only thing that makes sense if we are going to view life as a continual learning process.

▶ Laundromats are very self-conscious places. You always feel eyes on you as you fold stained underwear/frayed bras/sheets with holes. No one ever sees the one really fine blouse you own. Fat man today with his wife— he sitting sullenly, elbows on table— while she did all the work. He didn't even help her fold the sheets. She didn't seem to ask, but. . . .

▶ Driving a sporty car leaves one prone to all sorts of drivers on macho trips who are out to prove to you their '68 Malibu can go faster. On the positive side, you feel a sort of affinity with all the other "class" cars on the road— and you seem to notice an awful lot of them.

▶ Mark Vonnegut p. 137— "How could I convince a man who drove Cadillacs, wore baby-blue alligator shoes, etc., that I was sane? Why should I have to?"

▶ Shadows on the stark white walls— my only roommates— mimicking my every movement— Except they do not answer my questions.

- The sun came up on life today.
  You walked in, agreed to share
  the time and space.

- A chill crept into the air— and into the house— even the sun on her back was not enough to warm her toes.

- Read into it what you will: First baby born here during Healthy Baby Week was deformed.

- Ironing the faded blue workshirt,
  short-sleeved remnant of radical days
  and Oregon rains,
  I realize it is big enough
  for a man.
  Now,
  I would not want to iron
  a lifetime of men's shirts,
  but there is time in my life
  for a man.

- Engagement we ran this weekend was a hoax— but not a child's joke. Parents brought it in. I guess because they want daughter to marry the guy— daughter does not want to. That is love?

- Brown bread— alive with green mold

- The gentleness in your face belies the toughness that makes you a survivor. And survivors are hurt deeply, too often it seems, but they always bounce back—

Moving on, but First...

As many of my students eagerly awaited their graduations and baby steps into the "real world," I prepared myself for "emotional upheaval, at the least" -- goodbyes, hellos and more goodbyes. If only I could make it through the extreme craziness that had come to define the ends of my semesters. Like my students, I had one last project to finish. After that would come two final exams before the 1976-77 academic year would be history. Having spread my research out around me, I waited for inspiration to get me typing. I needed to craft a catchy introduction for my exploration of the commercial speech doctrine. Eventually I powered through my writer's block and finished a draft, minus conclusion and with a couple of holes to plug. I didn't have the energy to drag myself to the law library, so I decided to edit it Monday morning before school and make a quick visit to the library. For sure, I would turn the paper in on time.

> Perhaps there is something to say for fatigue— the kind of fatigue that comes from pushing yourself as hard as you can, sans drugs, and realizing you have got the job done. I don't know how good my paper is— I never do when the time comes to commit the final draft to 20# bond— but it is done. Helped by lots of caffeine and only a couple of hours sleep— no speed— except my own will to do it. Finished tonight. And I relish the feeling.

Incredibly, two days after taking an exam I described "a Sunday in which I cleaned the house, including the floors— read two newspapers, several magazines, a lot of entries for the Penney contest— took a nap— washed the car— and felt bored." Perhaps I should have been studying, because as I noted on the evening of May 11, "At 7:40 tomorrow morning I can spit back the lists I have memorized [something I hated], provided I can keep them straight, and then I don't have to think about playing school for a full year." Some days later, after all my fretting and self-deprecating judgments about my academic work, I learned that my commercial speech paper was being fast-tracked for publication as a Freedom of Information Center Report *and* I was told by my law professor that my term project was by far the best he ever had read. When eventually my grade report arrived, I wrote: "It doesn't make sense, and I'm not sure I can believe it, but I got a 4.0!!! Which is a comment on something, though I'm not sure what." (I should have added that I had one grade outstanding because I had delayed completion of my Readings course. Eventually I earned an A for it, too.)

On to graduation. Not mine quite yet. Sue's. First in my heart among the many of my students who had made it to the finish line that May. After a spontaneous afternoon that ended with me cooking us dinner before we headed to a pre-graduation party, she remarked, "I'm glad the student-teacher situation is over." So was I, I guessed, but admitted I had not thought about it much. "Perhaps I should have," I later wrote. "But I can't measure people in those terms. And I wonder why I must." The journalism ceremony, held outdoors, was fun. Wearing my newly purchased master's degree hood, I marched with the faculty. "Three years and I want the Ph.D. blue and M.U. black and gold hood," I wrote that night. Only a week earlier, I had learned that some of my colleagues believed I would not finish my degree once I left Columbia. "Boy, will I fool them," I told my journal. When I mentioned the doubters to my mother, she surprised me by saying, "They don't know you very well, do they?" In that moment it occurred to me that there were times when she understood me better than I gave her credit for.

Two other memories from graduation Saturday endure: First there was Sue's father ("Mr. Littell") folding himself into my MG for a quick top-down ride. (Sue recently reminded me that he was helpless with laughter in being unable to extract his legs from the front seat.) Second was him commenting on "the mace" (carried for the processional) and me wondering why he mentioned pepper spray. (Despite my faux pas, I was told he found me "charming.") The evening began with an unexpected knock on my door. It was Sue and her friend Terry: "Can we use your shower?" I joined the group for dinner, after which we took Mr. Littell to some favorite haunts. After he called it a night, it was back to my apartment for "Saturday Night Live" and late-night conversation. We joined Mr. Littell for Sunday brunch at the Tiger Hotel ("or Hole, per the dean's Freudian slip yesterday"). When it was time for me to leave, Sue and I did not speak the word goodbye. I went home and put the Edwin Hawkins Singers on the stereo, "but nothing was quite right." I decided "to lose myself at a movie" that afternoon.

I enjoyed a few "leisurely" days before the Newspaper Fund interns arrived, with just the People desk to manage and last-minute exercises to create for the interns. One night Loretta and I celebrated (my new job and her sons being featured on Page 1 of the Missourian) "quite royally," starting with dinner and "a weird drink (Scorpion)" at a Polynesian restaurant. We must have been quite a sight in the MG, and she insisted on stops to show off the car to some of her friends. At a nightclub, we ran into some guys we knew and "got to dance a bit; fun." Two serious academics cutting loose for a change.

Our "crash course" for the interns also was a crash course for Daryl, Brian and me. Each of us played a role in getting the group of students from around the country ready to be entry-level copy editors. We pushed them hard. For example, I devised a three-minute-headline drill to force them to produce under pressure. They may not have liked it, but at least one intern later wrote to tell me how helpful it had been. I also concocted an editing exercise using two paragraphs filled with phrases from a "verbosity list" I had distributed. To fit in all my responsibilities, which included overseeing shifts of interns editing for the Missourian, sometimes I "graded" their work at home. On those long days, I worked at the People desk until 5:30 and then went back to help at the main copy desk from 7 to 10. I also taught the classroom portion of editing, and with "three quarters of them being grad students, it [was] not much fun." Their preparatory, no-credit reporting/editing course continued to be weak on editing, despite our complaints. There was little I could accomplish with them in five weeks, especially with page layout. "If I am lucky, this is the last summer I ever will HAVE to work— and won't that freedom of choice be nice," I wrote. Time would prove me to be a poor prognosticator.

In a twist that a fiction writer might fancy, my end-of-Missouri journal reminded me of my first weekend on the copy desk, when I kowtowed to city editor Tom Duffy. Eventually I earned his respect, and at Eau Claire I greedily mined his bag of tricks for teaching reporters to write feature stories. But he intimidated me— at least a little— until the end, and I never could bring myself to address him as Tom. This paragraph from my journal says it best: "Duffy to me this afternoon: 'Fussy (that's what he calls me; I don't know why), I wish you'd dress up once in awhile. (I was in jeans and a workshirt.) You're a good-looking woman.' I thanked him and walked on." A couple of days later, an entry harkened back even further, to my childhood. It was prompted by a television program recreating Thor Heyerdahl's building of the raft he used for an 8,000-mile Pacific Ocean voyage. I remembered reading his "Kon-Tiki."

Adventurers intrigued me then— in my days of wanting to dogsled to Alaska, etc.— when I wasn't reading about sports heroes. Wonder how much of my life has been spent reading— living life through the words of others. Tonight it was a dissertation on the press in Africa as I work (slowly) to take care of my Delay (for unfinished Journalism Readings course). Over lunch it was Lillian Hellman, and I suppose before bed it will be Gloria Emerson.

As the first summer session neared an end, Ruth went on vacation and the People staff smiled more often, no one more than me. As I wrote in a card to Sue, who had begun working in St. Louis: "Kind of fun with Ruth gone— since I'm making all the decisions, there's no waiting around— get done faster and so far no trouble keeping up." But my days *were* long. "I can tell by looking at the glows-in-the-dark calendar Crazy Peggy brought me. I kid you not!!" I did, however, have my weekends, and what a treat that was. My card to Sue, written in sections over eight days, mentioned time in the library. ("I stumbled across your brother John's thesis— Did you ever take time to read it?— Wonder if anyone in Oregon ever stumbles across mine.") It mentioned a trip to St. Louis for a party. ("I think I have the St. Louis-Columbia trip down to a science. . . . Thanks for another grand weekend— I really enjoyed the party— just the right size as far as I'm concerned— I don't know what I will do when we can't get together every couple of weeks.") It mentioned books read for pleasure. ("Finished Hellman. I must read more!!") And it mentioned lots of movie-going. ("Should have graded papers but took the night off to see 'Rocky.' Really enjoyed it— and it certainly puts the theme song in perspective— Saw 'The Late Show' with Art Carney and Lily Tomlin over the weekend. It's fun, too— Tomlin gets off some great lines. . . . On my way over to campus to see 'Play It Again, Sam.' It's free— tomorrow maybe I'll pay to see Fellini.")

The students on the People desk planned a party for the weekend before Ruth's return. They told me I would be the guest of honor, but they didn't tell me it would be a going-away soirée. Because of rain, we ended up at my apartment. There was a pony of beer on the porch and hot dogs cooked on the nearby grubby gas grill and garnished with ketchup and mustard packets from the People desk stash. And there was a framed so-long message.

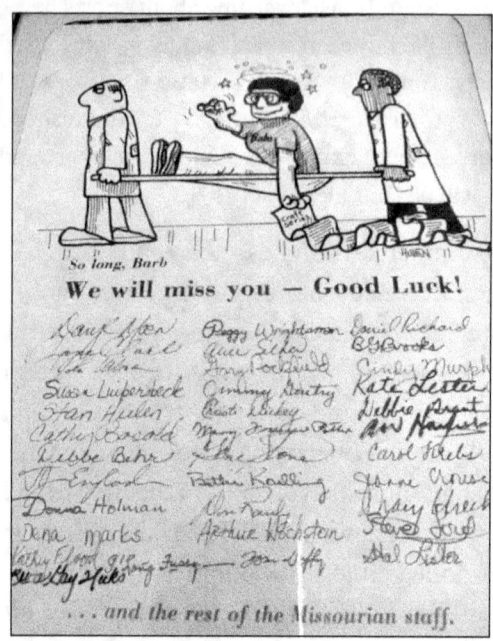

That party was the beginning of a "work-drink-sleep binge. A good way to end my Mizzou career. I went out in style."

Indeed. On Friday, July 1, I went to work with a hangover, my first full-fledged cold since the fall and several dozen doughnuts. I used my lunch break to buy Old Mizzou bourbon for my brother-in-law and do my banking. "Time after lunch spent mostly talking and laughing." I snuck out to the bookstore to get T-shirts for my young nephews and one for me. After a quick trip home to pack the Midget, I was on the road to St. Louis by 3. I had looked forward to a long weekend of fun with Sue and friends, but my cold turned me into a party pooper. "My weeks of play and boozing seem to have taken their toll on my resistance." The night before I was to leave, however, Sue and I "were like two schoolgirls who haven't talked for ages." We "laughed and giggled until midnight, and I'm not sure we would have quit then, except morning [and my 6 a.m. departure] was creeping closer."

When I left St. Louis it was already 80 degrees with high humidity. I was on my way to two glorious weeks in the Colorado mountains— by way of my parents' home in Wisconsin (where I was to trade vehicles with my brother) and Minneapolis to fetch Martha. That's right. The exhausted young woman who in August would have to pack up for a new job had a vacation itinerary designed to ensure she was more exhausted after vacation than before. Nonetheless, the vacation itself proved to be among the more memorable of my life.

I arrived in Abrams to find my brother and his wife already there because their house was infested with bats. My sister and nephews drove out from Green Bay. My mother worked only a half day. "It's like a zoo and you either step on toys, kids or dogs," I wrote. I watched soap operas, slept and learned about the orange Ford E-150 van (three speed "on the tree") I would drive west. Then I packed it, and on Thursday I was off to Eau Claire. The van was new, and in order not to use up the miles left on its warranty, I daringly drove without speedometer and odometer. I quickly learned to judge my speed using the tachometer. I missed my sports car but found that the van handled OK and was "pretty comfortable." Still, I already was tired of being on the road. I was a woman on a mission, however: find housing.

I was bummed to learn that the real estate agent I had been counting on had nothing for me. Settled at the Polks, I scoured the classified ads and eventually checked out two apartments. One rented for $175 but was "old and dumpy and small." The other, at $200, was "new and nice— but sterile" and I "immediately knew I did not want that one." By then I was hot and sweaty, and Ruth Anne's optimism as she sent me off for that evening's newspaper did not rub off on me. Eureka! There was a new listing that seemed perfect: near the campus, two bedrooms and a longed-for fireplace. At $250, it seemed more than I could afford, but Les told me to call about it and so I did. It turned out to be just a couple of blocks away. We checked out the exterior before I called again to make an appointment to see inside. Plans were made for later that evening, but first we three were off to our favorite restaurant for dinner. My gin-and-tonic and shrimp salad hit the spot. The apartment did too. "One look . . . and I know it is worth the extra bucks. Upstairs. Two bedrooms. Big living room and dining room with fireplace in blue marble. New kitchen. Hardwood floors. Can walk to school— to stores— perfect." I put down a deposit for an early August move-in.

The next morning I slept in and tended to Penny the beagle before heading to Minneapolis. I arrived in time to see Martha off to work; we planned to leave when she got home about 1:30 a.m. I napped, watched TV and made plans for dinner with Luise. Loretta called from Columbia to say she would not be able to join us in Colorado. Martha's workday turned out to be unusually tiring, so we agreed to a more reasonable departure. Our goal remained driving as far as possible on Saturday so that our Sunday journey would be shorter, which would give us time to shop for groceries in Boulder. Despite our weariness, after dinner in Lincoln, Nebraska, we set our sights on North Platte. It didn't take us long to realize we'd never make it. In Kearney, we tried four motels with vacancy signs— and all were full. "We must write their Chamber of Commerce," I declared. Ten miles farther, we found a dive in Odessa that had a room. "$14.25 for two— soft beds— noisy AC— receptionist with crying kid and tattoo— real Americana."

In the morning we learned that the threatening skies we had been driving under produced a violent storm during the night. I had been vaguely aware of it, but we both had been so road-weary that we paid it no mind. We had planned to be on the road again by 8 a.m., and miraculously we were. Our search for breakfast was quite the experience.

> A roadside truck stop/diner. It is packed. One waitress handling [all the] tables. An Indian who both clears tables and does dishes. Second waitress handles counter and register. People being pretty snotty, though "tables woman" seems to be doing best as she can, having only two arms and two legs. Food hardly worth waiting for. Eggs taste as if they are fried in fish grease— hash browns raw. Maybe the people ordering only Cokes and sweet rolls were better off.

Contrary to our hopes, Sunday proved to be a very long day. The weather was miserable: cloudy and threatening rain, then cloudless and hot. Western Nebraska seemed endless. After a stop for gas and ice, it was 40 miles before Martha remembered that she had not replaced the gas cap. We turned around, thus wasting the hour we had picked up when we changed time zones. We noticed a speed trap with at least seven cars stopped, "sort of assembly-line ticketing." Amazingly, back at the service station the gas cap was exactly where Martha had left it. We came upon another speed trap in eastern Colorado, which was helpful because by then the tachometer had quit working and we were judging our speed based on that of other cars. The scenery was bleak, but our spirits were raised by the first glimpse of the Rocky Mountains in the distance. (On each of our trips, the "game" was to be the first to spot the mountains, a tradition I carried on after trips with Martha and even when I flew.) "Finally, almost unbelievably, we make Boulder. About 5, I guess. We shop like zombies, wanting nothing more than to get up the canyon and settled in our cabin" at Arapaho Ranch.

That year's cabin was not on the creek, but we could at least hear it gurgling. There seemed to be kids everywhere, but we didn't much care. After unpacking, I downed a couple of beers and we crashed before dark. Twelve hours of sleep somewhat refreshed us. "I sure forgot how cold it can get at night and did not sleep well . . . but it feels good just to be here." With a pot of coffee and muffins, we enjoyed the late morning on our porch before driving into nearby Nederland. I needed to get a fishing license and we needed a few more foodstuffs. Afternoon naps came easily, given we were still recovering from the drive and I had enjoyed a few beers with lunch. It was campfire night, a gathering we had avoided the previous summer. I thought I might make an appearance because it was less than 100 yards from our cabin and our absence would be conspicuous. But after a couple of beers I decided I really did *not* want to socialize with strangers. So Martha and I talked and read our Doonesbury books until once more going to our rooms early.

The overnight wasn't nearly as cold and I slept soundly, which was a good thing because I planned to go fishing in the morning, and I knew the earlier the better. I was on the stream about 8. I longed to send my fisherman father a postcard regaling my success, but that was not to be. I had not fished in a while and my only time angling for trout had been five years earlier. My journal made clear my ineptness: "I get pissed early on when my hook keeps getting stuck and I lose bait on every 'cast' (the salmon eggs given me from a fellow fisherman who passes by). I quit after about an hour." My ego was bruised and my confidence shaken. A subsequent daytrip to Brainard Lake, where I fished as Martha hiked, proved to be the last straw. "Not even a nibble. I've had it. Not worth the frustration." On the way back to the ranch, we bought a steak to grill. At least, unlike the previous year's visit to Brainard, we had not found ourselves standing on snowbanks.

We did have a scare on our way up the mountain to Brainard, when the bolt holding the gear shift onto the van's steering column fell off. "A very sinking feeling when one considers the terrain." Hardly two helpless gals, once we found the bolt we figured out how to fix the problem. The only other frustration I recorded was with the bugs. One morning, as I sat on a rock in the creek and read Richard Wright, something stung my foot, and the flies seemed "to think my hair is a nest." I identified three varieties: "big and little pesky ones and very big ones that bite." As for the "ants that ascend my very hairy legs, I don't care." I tried using OFF! but, as I wrote to Sue, "I reacted to the alcohol with a cute little rash over much of my body." In addition, I told her, my "cold also is hanging on but I usually can breathe by noon." [An aside: I had been diagnosed as allergic to alcohol as a youngster. When I first began to drink, I ended up with rashes on my stomach. I outgrew them long before I outgrew alcohol.]

I used my new stationery for that letter to Sue (also a packrat, she returned the letter to me as I was working on this book). It was a newsy missive that included the surprising ("I have done about 2 rows of needlepoint— At least I remembered how.") and the mundane ("I had a good drunk yesterday and slept from 9 p.m. until 8:30 a.m. Drinking alone not much fun, tho— why don't you buzz out for the weekend."). In keeping with our habit of sharing details of our reading and making book suggestions, I noted that in less than a week I had "done all the Doonsebury books— Marvelous— finished Richard Wright— Powerful— and am midway into Brooke Hayward's reminiscing— it's okay, but not great." Ever the reporter, I described

a fascinating woman in the cabin down from us. She is from Indiana and does not like this place at all— Says there is nothing to do— she is depressing to listen to, but I suspect is representative of lots of American women. She complains that the beds are too soft and there are too many bugs and the roads are too curvy and everything is too expensive etc. etc. etc. I talk with her a lot because I'm on the porch reading much of the time and she walks by.

This was the summer of the power blackout that left New York City in darkness. A sidebar story in the Denver Post was promoted with "Little Effect on Denver Area." The obviousness of that made me chuckle. I did think it "would be weird to be in a city when 9 million are without electricity." I was amazed by a "marvelous [newspaper] photo of Statue of Liberty lit up (power comes from Jersey) and New York in background black." Vacation definitely did *not* mean ignoring the news, and I loved the opportunity to read and study newspapers from "away." I still do.

Martha had only one week of vacation, and just when we began feeling truly rested it was time for me to drive her to the airport. I looked forward "to the new company (Luise), tho I am not tired of the present." Martha and I were good vacation partners. The night before she left, we cooked trout on the Hibachi; "only could have been better if I had caught them." (They had been a gift from the man who had given me bait at the beginning of the week.) We pitched horseshoes, then sat by the stream until the cold drove us indoors. "The sky was beautiful; the Big Dipper and Milky Way seemed so close." We talked late into the night, never seeming to run out of things to say. I abstained from beer, deciding that I had "ingested enough to up the value of Adolph Coors' stock measurably." I was surprised to find that the clock in the cabin had gained almost 30 minutes. "A bit more time for us here, then. . . ."

I drove Martha to Denver on Sunday the 17th, and when Luise had not arrived by 7:30 that evening, I stopped expecting her. The alone time in my new cabin was nice. I had moved into No. 10, the last cabin at the bottom of a steep hill, alongside the creek. "I have found the cabin where I want to write my dissertation," I told my journal. Unlike the others, all the rooms in this one were "finished off." I was particularly drawn to a rocking chair and the big picture windows that I could look through while typing. I found the refrigerator and water heater to be noisy, and although there was no porch for morning coffee there was a picnic table. I was "going ape" over Tom Robbins' "Even Cowgirls Get the Blues," and the light in my new bedroom seemed better, allowing me to read more. That's what I was doing when, about 9:30, I heard, "Biffle, where is the front door of this place?" It was Luise, who had driven straight through from Minneapolis. She and her dog had dealt with 103-degree heat, car troubles and wrong turns, which made it about a 24-hour journey. Their arrival "was safe, if slightly manic," and of course we had to talk some before getting well-deserved sleep.

Much of our week together was spent indoors because of drizzle, rain, heavy rain and fog. When it was otherwise -- usually midmorning -- we hiked around the ranch or took long walks in the forest to collect pinecones for the Christmas wreath I wanted to make. Luise enjoyed reading on a log in the creek; I read indoors because doing so outdoors had been giving me headaches. To avoid the "international journalism crap" related to my delayed grade, I gravitated to anything else I could find: Anais Nin's diary volume 2 (because I couldn't find 1), Jill Johnston, a novel from Luise's bag, Ms. Magazine, and even several chapters in the newswriting textbook I would use in the fall. As always, our conversations "got pretty heavy in spots." (Evidence of how well Luise knew me was the book she brought for me, about better self-understanding through journal keeping.) One night we had a long discussion on sexuality. Later, I wrote: "I suppose I directed, consciously or subconsciously, the conversation that way— have been having thoughts for a long time on my own preferences (not sure I have any). Of course, nothing was resolved— at least if it was I don't recall (and that is why I must stop drinking— and not just beer)."

We lucked out with a sunny morning for the final day of our stay. That sent us into Nederland for souvenirs. Mine included a piece of Indian pottery to hold matches for my new fireplace and a coffee mug for my new office. We shopped for the repeat menu of Luise's first dinner at the cabin (steak, corn, wine)— "except it is better wine and we won't be up as late or drink as much." At least the afternoon thunderstorms cleared in time for me to cook. Early Sunday morning, we went our separate ways. After a week spent mostly in the cabin, which had me feeling "pretty squirrelly," I was ready to leave. I did not relish the long drive back to Columbia, but at least I had gotten the tachometer repaired. Long trips still made me anxious, but I had become a road warrior.

That Colorado vacation -- my second -- affirmed how much I loved being at Arapaho Ranch. I couldn't know then that I would return countless times, nor could I have known I would exchange Christmas cards and notes for years with its owner. A journal entry included this optimistic paragraph:

> It really feels good to be here. It will be a $500 vacation before it is over, but I feel I deserve it. Just as I feel I deserve the $250/month apartment I have rented. I'm starting a new life and I need it to be a good one, in ways the present one has not been. Hope to lose weight (where have I heard that before)— Sue and I have a bet beginning 8/22. She is going to stop smoking; I am going to quit beer and lose 20 pounds. And our reward will be New Years in St. Louis. And if we are lucky we will have dates. I want to be able to wear my slinky knit long dress again. I also want to begin getting furniture now that I have a home with character. I want to add to it. And if I budget well and pinch pennies wisely I can do it. RA will be a good model. I feel she and Les both think [this move] is good. And we can make it work, I'm sure.

A recent internet search confirmed that Arapaho Ranch is still operating and sparked a thought: *I should go back there one of these days.* I am, without a doubt, a creature of habit when it comes to vacationing, and I relish the idea of returning to Boulder Canyon. Not to try to re-create the past but to find new enjoyment in the present.

Snapshots

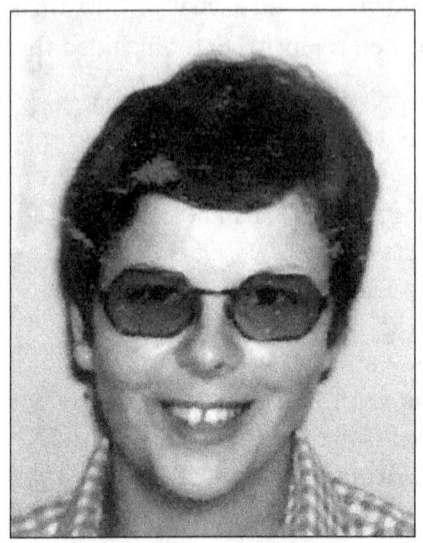

My first University of Missouri staff photo.

My love affair with technology began with the Video Display Terminals used at the Columbia Missourian when I arrived in 1974.

My favorite spot for reading during summer vacations at Arapaho Ranch.

Critiquing a newspaper for a 1977 Penney-Missouri Awards workshop.

My work-drink-sleep binge before leaving Missouri in 1977 started with the People Desk's going-away party.

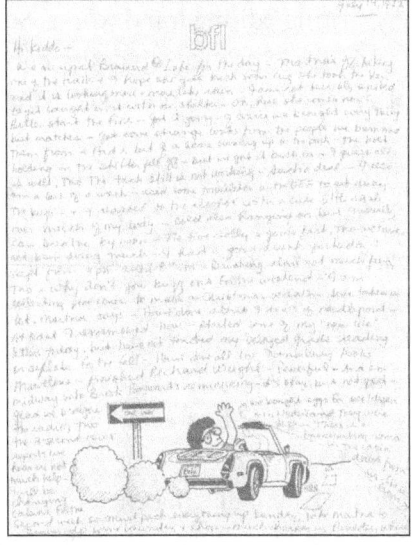

My student Stan Hulen created whimsical stationery for me, a prodigious letter-writer.

CHAPTER 16

A Wish Comes True

Challenging myself to use *one* word to describe my life from July 24, when I left Arapaho Ranch, to August 9, when I arrived in Eau Claire, I first scribbled several: whirlwind, blur, chaotic, unsettling, unforgettable, emotional. After considerable thought, I decided to use "whirlwind" -- until I consulted a dictionary; "a confused rush" was close, but "a violent or destructive force" didn't fit. What about "blur"? If I didn't have detailed journal entries, "something vaguely or indistinctly perceived" might have done it. So it went as I worked through my list and discovered imprecision or inaccuracy in each word. This is how my writing/editing mind works. Several days later, I noticed that I had overlooked "hectic," no doubt because it obviously applied to so much of my life over the previous many years. An "aha" moment followed: *Barb, hectic is precisely the right word. That was how you lived!* How I still sometimes live, I must acknowledge.

I left the ranch at 7:30 a.m., some 45 minutes after Luise's noisy departure. My timing was good; there was virtually no traffic heading down the canyon or through Denver, and once I hit I-70 East I often had the feeling I was the only person traveling in that direction. My goal was Oakley, Kansas, on the state's western plains. I promised myself I would not push it and figured if I was still feeling good I could continue the 88 miles to Hays. Breakfast was a sweet roll and iced tea at a Stuckey's along the interstate; lunch a cheeseburger on the Colorado-Kansas border. It was only 2 p.m. when I reached Oakley, but "it was at least 95 degrees and I was hot and weary." I snagged the last single room at a dodgy motel, but it was still being cleaned. After a milkshake at the equally dodgy restaurant across the parking lot, I settled in to watch television and read newspapers. An early dinner back at the "restaurant" was followed by my last two cans of Coors. A storm was brewing in the west when I set my alarm for 6 a.m. It was dark and rainy when it woke me, so I hit snooze and fell back to sleep. It was still rainy at 7, and I opted to eat breakfast before resuming my trip. Driving across much of Kansas under clouds felt effortless after the oppressively hot day before. Upon seeing a sign in late morning that said Kansas City 105 miles, I knew in that moment I would drive all the way to Columbia. I did.

I called my parents to let them know I was safely home. I called Sue with the same message and learned she had tickets for a George Benson concert. We agreed I would go to St. Louis for the weekend. *And why not*, I thought sarcastically, *I only have to pack the apartment and finish an Incomplete.* Exhausted, I fell into bed for a well-earned sleep. The rest of the week was a blur of packing -- including 15 containers of books -- until I ran out of boxes. I expected the movers between August 8 and 10, so I took a break. I was ready to leave, however. "Let's get out and on with it," I wrote.

> Have had my share of beer this week and will finish up in style this weekend, no doubt. But that is the end for a while. Am at 165 pounds and feeling very fat and ugly and I don't much like myself this way. Next week shaping up as a gorge-yourself time. Dinner with Ruth and some others set for Monday night. Lunch Wednesday with Vicky. John has promised me dinner, and I need to get together with Loretta. Then it is on to E.C.!!!

I was right about the week ahead but wrong about the move. Allied called Saturday morning (August 6) to change my pickup to Tuesday, with delivery in Eau Claire by Friday. At 7:30 a.m. Monday they called to say the truck would arrive shortly, with delivery in Eau Claire the next day. Yikes! I had been with the Journalism Women until about 1:30 a.m. and had planned to sleep in. Instead I busted my butt to complete last-minute chores. I called Ruth Anne, who said she could meet the movers in Eau Claire and let them into my apartment. "Good thing, too, because I knew I never could get there in time." As it turned out, I got out of Columbia a lot sooner than I anticipated. "In some way, too soon, because there wasn't even any [time] for good-byes. Just some nice memories of my last days in the city." Writing in my journal a few days later, I was "not sure if even today it has registered that I am gone."

Unbelievably, I arrived in my new city just several hours after the moving van. Ruth Anne and Les welcomed me with open arms, providing a first-night bed along with meals and advice and love. After a busy day of unpacking, my apartment looked livable, and I was happy to have them drop by. It was the first time since college that they had been to a place where I lived. "All is going to work out well," I believed. I had gotten a refrigerator (Italian made $286), I noted in my journal. My phone was to be installed the next day. "I have to buy a tv— and a dining room set. But financially that will have to wait." I didn't care. Life was "becoming ordered again" and I was eager to start my fourth year of teaching— *real* teaching at last. That wouldn't happen for a week, however. I described my first days back in Eau Claire as leisurely, but rereading my journal made them seem anything but. Realizing now my penchant for expecting myself to be busy -- with work or whatnot -- reminded me how perspective is everything.

I wrote about being ready for the "real structure" that the academic year would bring. I had not worked since July 1, and "mentally I was ready." My journal describes how I tended to my new environment and to myself, with scattered comments about preparing for school. And then there was this: "File for use somehow/someday. A story in this morning's [Minneapolis] Tribune told of a girl who was walking a dog with a metal leash. He pissed on a portable electric sign in front of a hospital and the current travelled up the piss and killed him and knocked her out." I had said I wanted to write, and here was an anecdote I might be able to use some day.

My brother and sister-in-law were my first houseguests. It was time to trade vehicles, and I was delighted to get my Midget back. Soon, I would discover the challenges of servicing a persnickety British car in northwestern Wisconsin, but for the time being I was happy just to be able to wash "it." My sister and brother-in-law ensured I would dine like an adult when they offered to sell me their dining room set for $250. "And they don't need the money all at once, thank god." I found a "12-inch TV for $98+tax— paid cash for that." I still needed to buy school clothes, but I was hopeful about saving most of the summer check I had not yet received from Missouri.

I didn't plan to buy many outfits, however. My game plan called for losing weight and I didn't want a lot of size L's hanging around my closet. Not for the last time, I was determined to "change some patterns of the recent past." Not for the last time, I gave up beer. "I really don't want to get into the drinking-at-home gig again; no one to drink with here; and [don't need] the calories." I also wrote about wanting to begin walking or running. My plan -- "and of course the problem is sticking to it" -- was to be 145 pounds by Christmas "and when I return to Columbia [to take summer school classes] to be 135 and running regularly." Hours after I wrote that, the lead item on the NBC news reported Elvis Presley's death at age 42. I should have pasted a photo of him, by then grotesquely overweight, on my refrigerator as motivation. Instead, I reminisced: "While I never swooned over him as many did, he is the first singer I remember 'liking.' And this was not in his early years, but his post-Army days, when he was making movies, and I don't think I missed many."

I never have enjoyed shopping for clothes (or anything else, for that matter), probably because of my poor self-image. Jumpers were in that fall ("nice for hiding fat," I wrote) and I bought a blue one -- "a nice safe color." I even wrote about its "nice material"; those 4-H sewing projects of my youth had some value! But that was "the last piece of clothing I hope to have to buy to hide something. After this I want to be able to show things." Today I am astounded that just a couple of days before my Eau Claire teaching debut, what I wrote about was my wardrobe -- and its cost: "almost $100 for pants-jacket-jumper and two blouses." Equally surprising was the attention I paid to my hair. For someone who to this day spends little time on hair care, I have always spent a lot of money on it. [An aside: My oft-expressed wish for reincarnation has been to be skinny and have hair with body.] I had my fingers crossed that the perm I had scheduled would turn out OK. "I sure hate changing women once you find one who does your hair the way you like. And I have a certain prejudice against anyone named Mary Sue. We shall see." (For the record, my stylist for the last 30 years has been John.)

I did find one mention related to school: "Strange sensation walking to office yesterday, briefcase in hand, down route I have taken so many times before. Real time warp. I'm one of 'them' now— part of the Establishment against which we rebelled so hard. Or am I?" The fact that I could walk to work (and elsewhere) was not lost on me. "I hope the novelty of walking does not wear off— or rather, that I do not let it." What was lost on me, until I turned the page in my journal, was the fact that 10 years had passed since I moved to Eau Claire to be a student. Surely, I think now, I must be a member of an exclusive club— undergraduates who returned to their alma maters as teachers. On the August 20 night when many of my West De Pere High School classmates reunited to party, I observed our reunion with "random thoughts."

> The foam on Shasta Diet Grape Soda is silver-blue, like the hair of old women.— I don't really like the watch I bought today and I am not at all thrilled about wearing one again.— The Packers won't be back this year; they looked atrocious vs. Tampa Bay.— Diet soda is no substitute for beer on a Saturday night, and I called Sue to tell her so, and we are to be part of a noble experiment on Wisconsin Telephone's claim of $1.65 for 10 minutes on the weekend, except we talk 20 minutes and I wonder what that does to my already high bill.— I found $75 extra [when balancing] my Columbia checkbook and should make it to payday without touching my meager savings.— I hope too much is not expected of me this first semester while I get my feet on the ground.— The Leader-Telegram is an incredibly BAD newspaper and it pains me to pay for it.— Why is it that fat seems to come on faster than it goes off?— I look forward to the Sunday morning ritual of multiple newspapers.

I *was* "a bit tired of talking to myself," but already Martha and I had plans to get together and I had sent a note to Luise asking if she wanted to join me for a Labor Day trek to visit my parents. "It is nice to have [Martha and Luise] near," I wrote, and I anticipated that "soon there should be people here" to socialize with. On the eve of the first day of my new professional life, I was "frighteningly content to be here. I miss Missouri people, but there are as yet no terrible pangs. Perhaps my head still just thinks it is on vacation."

A New Role for BFL

With rain threatening, I nonetheless enjoyed walking to my first-floor office in Hibbard Humanities Hall to begin the new school year. It was August 22. I think being in that building (opened in 1974) and not the one where I had spent my undergraduate years helped me internalize my new role. I was greeted by Journalism colleagues as they wandered by my end-of-the-hallway office. First on my agenda was new-faculty orientation, a nerve-wracking experience shared with a roomful of strangers, each of us wondering if we might connect with anyone. I described the morning's first session as "pretty boring for one who went to school here and knows all the administrative faces which, save for one death, have not changed. I forgot how impressive an extemporaneous speaker Chancellor Haas is— and he has aged very well." I sat alone, but at the coffee break met a woman from Sociology who had earned her bachelor's degree from the University of Missouri-Rolla. Amazingly, she knew Peter Hall of my Ph.D. planning committee. The second person I met, as it turned out, was also renting from my landlords. She was in Education and newly divorced. Debbie, the sociologist, and I sat together for the second morning session, which was "equally boring." I couldn't help but feel like an adult in the afternoon session devoted to staff benefits, which I had not thought much about at Missouri.

On my way into Hibbard on Tuesday morning I ran into a woman who had lived down the hall from me sophomore year. She was on campus for the year, on leave from a junior high school in Stillwater, Minnesota. I described her as "the most friendly person who I have met so far, but I must admit I have only vague memories of her" as a student. After a final "really boring" dose of orientation, I spent Tuesday afternoon working on my course syllabi. Wednesday was more of the same, and Thursday included several meetings. At Missouri I had heard the maxim that the fights in academe could be vicious because the stakes are so low, which I thought about that day. Les walked me to my first faculty meeting -- Arts and Sciences in the morning. "Lots of petty crap and politics," I wrote later. After lunch there was a department meeting, and it was clear Elwood had "not changed much in some respects, e.g.

he still preaches." The university faculty met midafternoon. I walked there alone but found my new acquaintance from Education and we sat together. "Which is nice because Les ends up sitting in the same row across the aisle, and I want/need to show I'm making it OK." This time, I found the chancellor to be long-winded and I was more than ready when the meeting finally ended at 5.

I was more than ready to begin meeting my classes, too, but had to manage those apprehensions until 1 p.m. on the 26th. My letter of appointment had spelled out my "specific duties and responsibilities" (and specified that my $12,700 salary would be paid in 10 monthly [again!] installments beginning October 1 and ending July 1, 1978). Typical of faculty teaching undergraduates, my course load would be "twelve semester credits or the equivalent." I also was expected to advise students and serve on departmental committees. For the fall, according to my gradebook, I had been assigned two sections of News-writing, two sections of Mass Media (for nonmajors) and a section of Editing. I began the semester with 97 students.

The dirty little secret of college teaching is that few of us were taught *how* to do it. Mastery of subject matter was expected; the rest might be learned at the feet of the wise men who oversaw our Ph.D. work. The lucky few received graduate teaching assistantships, but those typically offered little teaching and a lot of assisting with academic chores the professor could not be bothered with. My instructorship at Missouri had been a step up the academic ladder, for sure, but for the most part I had been left to my own devices to figure out teaching. I had proved myself enough to join the Eau Claire faculty, but I knew I had a lot to learn if I wanted to succeed at the front of the classroom.

A careless error left me red-faced in the opening minutes of my first class. As I carefully went over my Newswriting syllabus, a hand shot up. Brian rather reluctantly (it seemed to me) pointed out that the "weights" I had assigned various parts of the course totaled 105 percent. *Yikes. How had I done that? How had I missed that?* I thanked Brian, said I would share a revision at the next class meeting, and moved on. At least, I later thought, I did not "pull an Elwood." That's what we undergrads had called it after the Law class in which I pointed out that he had mixed up the arguments in a case he was presenting. He hemmed and hawed before saying it had been intentional; he wanted to see if we were paying attention. *Yeah, right!* we agreed after class.

In my journal I judged that my first two classes had gone OK. "I have a better feeling about the 3 p.m. group, which I did not expect because of the hour. But they seem livelier." Les and I had agreed to use the same exercises in our Editing classes and planned to meet weekly to coordinate. "How fun that should be." We shared a concern that his reputation for being tough might send students -- especially those less than enthusiastic about editing -- flocking to me. I was determined to be equally tough, so that the world would know that regardless of the professor an editing grade at Eau Claire reflected the same level of performance.

Ruth Anne had invited me to stop by on my way home, and both she and Les made a point of asking how day one had gone. "It feels right," I told them. After a Gibson, I continued to my apartment. I was tired and ready for a lazy weekend. That Sunday, a tradition of sorts was born. Les, Ruth Anne and I enjoyed a leisurely meal at our favorite restaurant, then went for a ride. "Airing my ladies," Les began to say of those drives. Somehow we three seldom ran out of things to talk about. Later that Sunday afternoon, I decided to skip the faculty reception on campus and watch "On the Waterfront" for the first time. "Love that cable! Enjoyed the movie. 'Rocky' seemed a lot less original now. I saw lots of it in Waterfront." Finally, I "messed with a lot of 'little' things," such as repotting a plant, carrying out the garbage and writing to Loretta, "who I really miss." With weekends free of the Missourian, no copy desk nights looming and no schoolwork of my own demanding attention, Eau Claire life already felt quite different from Columbia life.

For a while, my time at the office was generally without interruption. That allowed me to get my work done there. Never a slacker, I seemed to be "one of the first to arrive and the last to leave. And I certainly have not been staying late." Even after I finally got a telephone in my office, it didn't ring much. An early call came from "the Welcome Wagon woman," who arranged to meet me. In all my moves, I never had gotten such a call. "Does that mean I've made it?" I asked in my journal. *Talk about a blast from the past*, I thought when I found that tidbit in my journal. [An aside: A quick internet search reminded me how Wagon hostesses reached out to newcomers. Visiting in their homes, the hostess -- a woman, of course -- talked about her city and handed out gifts and coupons from local businesses. Marketing genius. Those home visits were stopped in 1998, when Welcome Wagon began outreach through the mail with a customized gift book.] At the end of the second week of classes, I quipped to Les that I was "having so much fun I shouldn't be paid. Then I reconsidered, remembering the paperwork [grading] that would soon begin." I also couldn't afford to work for free. Money was tight because I was three weeks away from my first Eau Claire paycheck and I panicked when I thought I had spent money I wasn't going to get from Mizzou. I was pleasantly surprised when I realized I had panicked needlessly.

Another pleasant surprise came late one night via a telephone call that startled me out of a deep sleep. It was Ann (Gavin) Meunier, an Eau Claire roommate starting with the Jesus House. I had written her one of my "new life letters" and she finally caught up with me. She and her husband were going to be in town in a few weeks. "God, what a reunion that will be. It will take hours to catch up. Annie— for whom I once wrote a poem. Annie— whose wedding I missed because the damn Toyota broke down in Kenosha. Annie— whom I feel very close to even though I haven't seen her for years." (My poem had been a birthday gift and it prompted Ann to write, "I'm happy our lives have crossed.") We have stayed in touch ever since, sometimes with letters, always at least a holiday card with a note.

Throughout the fall, those "new-life letters" also brought responses from many former students. Back-and-forth exchanges with several kept me up to date on gossip from Columbia and the comings and goings of faculty and students. I learned of hirings, firings, "betrayals," job searches, broken hearts, new loves, marriages, babies, toxic workplaces, rewarding workplaces, sexist workplaces, new apartments and used cars. And so much more. In short, friendships forged in the Missourian newsroom continued -- some for mere months, others for years, a few for decades. No one was a more prodigious letter writer than Sue, who often had me in stitches with her descriptions of life and work. The variety of ways she and others addressed me on envelopes make me chuckle today, and my heart smiles to see how often women and men alike signed off with "Love."

Other surprises led me to conclude that life in Eau Claire was good. I got to play "big sister" when Phil and John Polk were in town. There was the day John joined me when I took the Midget to be serviced, followed by a trip to the mall. "He sure got a kick out of driving back. I promised him he could do it again." One evening, when Les and Ruth Anne were at a university function, the boys and I shared pizza and beer. It was "the first time we all were adults," I noted. Another time they came to my apartment for beer and nachos. We hung photographs, listened to music and talked, and they volunteered to wash Midge the next day.

Of all the cars I have owned, the MG gave the most pleasure to the most people, and I never hesitated sharing. A favorite photo dates to that September, taken on my nephew Bill's second birthday. "He sure does like Barbie's car— and keys," I wrote. A painful memory also had its roots in that weekend. Luise joined me for the Labor Day weekend, and our drive to my parents' house went by quickly as we talked non-stop. My mother loved Luise and vice versa. Both loved to gab, so I was off the hook for that. My sister and brother-in-law had bought a house along the water in Green Bay, a 45-minute drive from Abrams. I saw it for the first time when we went there for Billy's party. It was a day of family fun, with good food and cake and, for some of us, more than a few adult beverages. A couple of months later Luise was back in Eau Claire. During a long conversation over breakfast, she brought up that party and my late-night, drunken drive back to the farm. "At that point, alcohol meant more to you than I did," she said. I knew she was correct. We talked about what I could do to get help, "and perhaps it was at that moment I decided to do it [stop drinking]— and do it myself." As I discovered in my journal, life had become less and less good in the weeks between the birthday party and Luise's declaration.

Lots of Work, Little Play

Looking back, I believe I underestimated the demands of my new teaching schedule and was unrealistically optimistic about the personal life I would lead. In addition, I had shed none of my workaholic and perfectionist tendencies. I never expected "dark days" like those I had experienced since Oregon. Today, I understand; back then, I muddled through as best I could.

I was excited to teach Mass Media for two reasons: it was a traditional lecture course and it was for non-journalism majors. I wanted to develop my skills at preparing and organizing material to present to a class. I wanted to learn how to foster discussion. I wanted to learn how to test students to measure their learning. I wanted to prepare students to be thoughtful media consumers. Like beginning on a bicycle with training wheels, teaching nonmajors could get me ready to succeed later -- in the non-skills-journalism courses I was sure to teach. A couple of weeks into the semester, I already was wishing "that I could get ahead with lectures." Furthermore, I often felt "as if I'm talking to walls." I remembered being an undergraduate interested in courses outside my major, but much to my dismay I was seeing little of that in my freshmen and sophomores. Of course, every lecture that I pulled from my typewriter -- often just minutes before class -- was new. I didn't have yellowing notes from the past to rely on. Besides, I was determined never to be that kind of professor.

Teaching News Writing and Editing presented different challenges, but as skills courses they at least felt familiar to me. I had done reporting; I had done editing. I had supervised reporters and I had supervised copy editors. I needed to translate those experiences, mix in material from the textbooks and concoct lessons that would move students along the path toward entry-level professionalism. That required lots and lots of grading. Imagine reading 30 stories written from the same set of facts and penciling many of the same comments on each. Imagine reading the same story edited by sixteen students and finding many of the same errors on each. Tasks daunting and tedious -- and too often discouraging. "Grading editing papers today was depressing. Mostly F's. . . . News Writing today was really hyper; need to tighten reins, I think." I tried to remember that progress could be slow, how it felt to *not* know how to do something.

By mid-October, I wrote that "life continues to move by so swiftly. Hours and hours of work. Little play. Students finally becoming recognizable people/individuals." Another entry began: "A dark, rainy, foggy night. And it has been productive. Think I got enough notes for two

Mass Media lectures on information control," all from a graduate course I had loved. "And I read about one-third of editing papers. All in front of a fire (less-than-roaring, but nice)." I reflected on how "I have only half a semester left with them [my students]— And then must wait to see if I've taught them anything." At least I had Les to commiserate with. Early on I wrote about how enjoyable it was "to have him in and out of <u>my</u> office and vice versa— someone to bounce ideas off of." I remember that interaction being a staple of my days.

Lonely weekends, on the other hand, were difficult. One October Saturday I set aside schoolwork and "hopped in Midge, top down, and drove for a couple hours, singing with Joplin. Then bought some new albums." (That entry reminded me how I enjoyed similar drives while in Antigo -- in the Gremlin, listening to John Denver, especially "Take Me Home, Country Roads.") The next day "I walked downtown for a film, then drove some and included a stop for magazines and munchies. And in doing so missed a call from the Polks to share dinner. But maybe that was better." I still wasn't sure where (how?) to draw a line between independent me and dependent me. For example, I bought a season ticket for the university's concert series, which I had so loved as an undergraduate, and then was ecstatic to find my seats were one row behind Les and Ruth Anne. I was equally excited the night I ended up dining with them and Pulitzer Prize-winning reporter Margo Huston of The Milwaukee Journal (1977, for breaking news reporting). I described the evening as "utterly delightful because MH is such a delightful <u>human</u>— someone I think I really could enjoy." A couple of nights later I was "off to dinner at 1435 [the Polks']— Partial payment I suppose for all the leaves I raked yesterday. Five hours' worth that left me exhausted and in bed at 8:30." I remember blisters, too.

I eventually took a step forward by reaching out to Debbie, the new Sociology faculty member I had met at orientation. Because she was married, I was not sure if socializing would work and had resisted calling her. After we met for coffee and conversation, I wrote that "there are possibilities there." Over time we did become friends, but it was a while before her name appeared in my journal again. Indeed, I quit writing for a few weeks, then wondered if it was "time to begin again— to catch some thoughts of the fall days, finally warm and sunny, before the REAL cold and gray of northern winter sets in. Time again to deal with unspoken loneliness, to confront unarticulated wonders about self and sexuality, future and futility, the possibilities of never being loved." Same old same old. Today, after decades of reading about the lives of other women, I know I was far from alone in those feelings. I also know I was luckier than some, whose stories ended without them finding a way out of the morass. "One minute alive, laughing, crying, breathing— and in a snap of the fingers you are no more," I wrote after learning of the death of a friend of a friend. "I don't want it to be me. I may have black days, but I can put up with them for all the rest of good days." I had developed a "deep-seated fear" that good would inevitably be followed by bad. I recognized that "my life has been more or less a piece of cake" and yet "I keep worrying about falling off the mountain."

Just two journal entries followed before another gap. One was a poem about the death of Grandma Luebke in a nursing home. I wrote how she "went from being mobile/to a withering woman/in a bed with protective rails./At Xmas I sent religious wall plaques/But hesitated to visit/And at the end she did/Not/even recognize me./Now she's dead/ And I've one grandparent left/of six." Finding that poem surprised me, but what surprised me even more was the accounting in its last line. Decades later I would write "Now We Are Four" after my father died, and at my mother's memorial service I talked about "us now being three."

When I resumed writing on November 13, it was to record how

the two weeks since [the last entry] have been different— and when the sun shines and I feel good, I'm sort of smug about not having put any alcohol into my body for 14 days— for having survived three situations in which I could have drunk. . . . No assurances this will last, especially with the holidays coming— But for ME I had to quit that putting away a 12-pack on a Saturday at home. Etc.

I had followed through with my decision to quit drinking after Luise confronted me.

Not that it is easy. I would like a drink— but once I start, it never is just one or two.— Something in me keeps going until I run out of booze or can't hold another drink.— I guess, for me, that is alcoholism— surely sickness— surely doing harm to my body— and my head. Luise says the personality change in me when drinking is something I'm also going to have to deal with. What I need to learn, I believe, is that there is no reason I cannot be the "fun" me sober as easily as drunk— And since my body and I cannot handle alcohol, I don't need to drink.

I finally acknowledged how my social isolation was "as much my fault as anything." I wrote about being invited to the Women's Association Christmas Ball and thinking "it would be fun to go. But with whom? I need to get my feet on the ground so I can find/make companions here. It's the same old problem— but I want to do it without alcohol." I resisted the strong urge to call Luise "and tell her of the last two weeks— not to brag, but to say I'm doing something. But what is two weeks? So I wait, and hope the next time she is here to visit Weird Harold, her chiropractor, we can have lots of time to talk and explore— without the crutch of booze."

Lest it seem as if my life was mostly despair, there were affirming moments, too. One occurred during a campus visit by members of the department's Advisory Board. I was "blown away" to learn that The La Crosse Tribune and its parent company, Lee Enterprises, were interested in me "in their desire to get women executives." In fact, I learned that my name had come up a few weeks earlier when the Tribune was looking for an editorial page editor. Never one to burn bridges, I told the Tribune editor to keep me in mind "because I don't know what the future holds." That connection, which dated to my undergraduate days, would indeed pay off down the road. I also was buoyed by the positive responses to the Alumni Newsletter I produced. Elwood wrote me a short note of congratulations, including, "You are contributing a great deal to the program." Les, who had been delighted to relinquish responsibility for the newsletter, cited my "fresh attack, your new ideas, your own perspective" as making it "fresh and vibrant." Another time, a cold but sunny Saturday -- "a day that demands aliveness" -- I walked downtown on an errand, then "popped into the floral shop" to buy mums. I also got some for Ruth Anne, which gave me an excuse (which I didn't need) to stop by. RA formally invited me for Thanksgiving, then added that she had assumed I was coming. I had been assuming that, too.

After a Saturday afternoon department meeting (*1:30 to 6 p.m. Who does that?*), I crashed. Although I was to be evaluated in my classes beginning Monday, I took Sunday off "to scream at the Packers as they lose again" and "<u>not</u> grade papers or prepare a lecture." The evaluations were required as part of the reappointment process. "I knew I was going to be under the magnifying glass . . . but I never expected Les to be one of the lookers. And so when he ambled into the room at 1, as only he can amble, it blew my mind. Tables are turned— the teacher, who as student evaluated him, was now colleague, being evaluated by him. Freaky!!" I could hear the nervousness in my voice as I lectured and wondered if the students could, too. My observer at 3 o'clock was the advertising professor, for whom I had absolutely no respect, so his presence didn't bother me. (He was fond of telling "pretty girls" that if they wore short skirts and sat at the front of his classroom they would do well.) "But for Les I had to be good— better than good. Had to please, draw praise— as always." Being a colleague had not changed that one bit.

The chairman's evaluation letter opened with him reporting that the Reappointment Committee "found your teaching performance during the fall semester to be adequate." Talk about tepid! Back in December 1977, I likely had been happy to read that the student evaluations "reveal a consensus that you were well prepared, conscientious and stimulating." I might have been surprised that "some of them found you to be somewhat stiff and strict but they also said you were fair and approachable." But I certainly would not have been surprised that "some thought the class material was too tough but I suspect they were reflecting the prevailing attitude toward [Editing] rather than an [sic] personal criticism." (I wonder if I wished then, as I do now, that I could have given him a lesson about run-on sentences.) Nor was I surprised to read that "there was some early concern" in the department "that you might become a carbon copy of some other instructors in the department [make that one instructor: Les Polk] but you have shown that you have a good mind of your own and are willing to stand up for your beliefs."

The weeks between being evaluated and reading that evaluation sped by, I assume. I've got just a handful of journal entries, several letters and some Christmas cards (more than one chiding me for not writing in a long time) with which to fill in the blanks. I found a reference to

> a non-stop day in a week filled with them just before Thanksgiving. Les was away at a convention, and one day I taught my class at 9, his at 10, ate lunch at 11, taught my class at noon and his from 1-3. Another day, I attended the Faculty Senate meeting with my News Writing students, who I had assigned to report on it. After dinner there was "one of the Les calls— no hello, no need for ID, simply a statement— a shared moment— and then a "be sure to watch Georgia O'Keeffe"— and I wonder, at this moment, if not for LDP would I even know who O'Keeffe is.

Another time I wrote about climbing into bed after grading a set of papers, with just "energy enough for a few pages of Doris Lessing."

When Martha and I arranged for me to visit Minneapolis for a weekend before Christmas, I had been eager to go; to shop, take in a ballet, spend time with her and perhaps Luise. The night before I was to make the drive, I was less eager but still willing, and I called Martha to check on the weather because a blizzard was possible. By Saturday morning, "I just felt too lazy— so I 'called in sick.' And after getting groceries and whipping up Rice Krispie bars, I settled in on the couch for one of my wipe-out weekends." Today I would label that a "therapeutic fib" done for my mental health; then I wrote: "Lying comes so easy for me. But it does not bother me— And I don't think I get caught often. Because people don't expect it. So it has become my way of dealing with many things." A couple of days later I was supposed to go to an open house for a new campus minister. But after a "lazy day spent inside at home," I wasn't eager "for an intrusion into my time— or to go out in cold and wind and meet new people." I knew it was a good opportunity, but "I don't want to. And wouldn't it be hypocritical— I mean, I don't go to church." I opted instead for "I, Claudius," the BBC series running on public television. I was surprised to read that a couple of weeks later, after giving my first exam, I went to the minister's house for a St. Lucia party observing the Scandinavian festival of lights. I suspect I chose to attend because one of the first stories I had written for The Spectator in 1967 was an "explainer" about the origins of the festival. Of the party,

I noted the singing of Advent hymns and recorded that I "felt awkward and out of place. Guess part of it was left over from church. . . . I chose to go but did not want communion— and was the only one who didn't. So obvious. That automatic flush of the cheeks— trying hard to be cool."

The reality of Wisconsin winters was in full force by early December. I was not the only one missing Columbia's generally mild climate. Midge needed a new battery and would start only intermittently. My landlord agreed to jump-start the car, but I had foolishly delayed doing it --until I had no choice. There had been more snow, the day's high temperature was unlikely to make it to zero, and I needed my car for holiday chores. I found myself "into Christmas for the first time in a long time" and was preparing to host an open house for my News Writing students. It proved to be the first of many such get-togethers, when I invited students to help me decorate my tree. In return I fed them homemade holiday treats, food I wrote about as "a gift of love." At least one student that year brought me an "ornament" -- a tiny, pink plastic airplane that I have hung on every tree since.

What I most definitely did not love was "the ordeal of giving grades." For the first time, I alone was responsible for determining the grades my students earned for their semester's work. Administering final exams, grading them and then calculating final grades that had to be submitted by the university's deadline made for "a pressure-packed, agonizing week." I couldn't help but "wonder if the students realize how hard it is for some of us. Trying to be fair in our assessment of their work and remain somewhat true to our standards. Ugh!" My gradebook confirms the complexity of my grading. How did I learn to assign such precise numerical values to activities, then attach a letter grade? It is clear that I believed an A represented excellent work. And, as I was fond of reminding students, I also believed "in the Honest C, which represents average work, and most of us are average." What also jumped out at me is how the few names I remember today are not necessarily those of the students who received the best grades. And although Missouri had provided me some experience dealing with students unhappy about a grade -- sometimes pleading, even crying, for a change

-- December 1977 was the first time I received a call *at home* from a complainer.

Not surprisingly, once I crossed the semester's finish line -- turned in the last of my grades -- I "really crashed." I hosted dinner for the Polks on the 22nd: "good meal, good talks, laughs." We exchanged gifts; mine was "a big basket for magazines" (picked out by Les and Phil on a Minneapolis trip; in continuous use ever since). The next day I was off bright and early, thankful to be driving to my parents' home in marvelous weather. "I sang carols all the way and felt good about the trip for the first time in years." I arrived to find Dad sick with the flu. That left Mom, Grandma Conger and me to go out for a perch fry (a Friday tradition in Wisconsin) and some last-minute gift shopping. I never got to deliver those gifts because on Christmas Eve we had a good old-fashioned blizzard. As it turned out, I never left the house again until my return trip to Eau Claire on the 30th. A "cold-flu combo" knocked me out, but at least it waited until after Christmas Day. It wasn't the first time (or the last) that work-related exhaustion sucker-punched me. By Tuesday the 27th I was moving from bed to couch (to watch TV) to bed. On Friday, although I still had a fever and was lethargic, I drove home because more snow was predicted for Saturday. (Smart me; we got 6 inches.)

That illness explained why I didn't write in my journal until New Year's Day. "Anyone who keeps a journal MUST have a 1-1 entry," I began. I had just finished "a good steak and potato salad meal," and the television was tuned to a football game. My tree was lit "so I can enjoy a few more days of it." Only a lingering headache spoiled the evening. "Hard to believe classes don't begin for 15 days yet. Love this academic holiday." Unfortunately, I didn't have money for travel. "Oh well, there is always next year." That I felt compelled to leave my parents' before I was well either spoke to how I could handle only a limited visit -- no matter how good -- or reflected my rigidity about plans and schedules. Or both.

Ups and Downs

As my semester break was ending, I described it as "slothful . . . this vacation of food and sleep." I suspect it was just what I needed to recharge for the upcoming term. [An aside: As was the case in Missouri,

Eau Claire also officially identified it as the winter semester. I found that depressing and chose to refer to it as spring.] My New Year's Day had not included "grand resolutions for the year (except to continue not drinking)." I wanted to use my free time to write letters, work in the library, go to Minneapolis, "clean a bit." Things "to get me out of the house and away from TV." After a couple of days, I wrote a description of myself that would be, in large part, accurate today: "While I can push like hell to accomplish something that needs to be done, I also can lie prone watching crap on the tube for days. I tell myself I'm storing energy for the push ahead, but now and then I think of all the minutes wasted and never to be recaptured."

And yet, reading my journal entries for that interlude suggested I was more occupied than I gave myself credit for. I know I read for pleasure, because one entry documented that I "gave up on Heller; sped through "Loose Change" and am now doing "Pentimento." (Later, with one chapter left, I mentioned being "enchanted by Lillian Hellman" and wanting to read a couple of her plays before moving on to another writer.) Although I may have spent time preparing syllabi, it is also possible that I waited because I was teaching the same courses as in the fall. I know I spent time worrying about money and how I could save for the two summer months when I would not get a check. "God, BFL, you are almost as poor at 29 as you were at 22," I wrote. After I registered to take a UWEC graduate course that I could use toward my Ph.D., I commented, "My god, it is January 4 and I have $35 in pocket money." I chose to pay for studying "Recent U.S. History" on the installment plan. I was particularly concerned about the high cost of heating my apartment, writing that the "damn fuel oil bills really make this apartment out of range of my income. Praying for big raise [next year]." The oil bills vexed me as long as I lived there; to this day, I believe "my" tank held the oil to heat the entire house.

My reaction to the news that a woman had been hired to teach typography was surprisingly snippy. "She's 24, I think, and completing her M.A. Will come for at least 18 months as a lecturer, which is lower rank than I. I believe she is coming sight-unseen." (Yes, that was done back then. It had not worked out well for the department before, by the way.) I wasn't sure about how I felt about the hiring. I did expect it would give me someone to talk to, "although it is silly to assume that gender alone provides that. And it is good for the department. But I'm also going to sort of hate losing the edge" of being the only woman. Then I got a call from Elwood asking me to "put her up" for a week or so, until she could get into her apartment. Of course, I said yes, just as Martha had done for me when I arrived in Columbia and I had done for newcomers there. Of course, I soon had second thoughts about sharing my space.

For the time being, however, that space sparked much joy. I could not bring myself to take down my Christmas tree. I loved the lights and their reflection in the window. I was housesitting for the Polks but chose to spend nights at home so I could light the tree. "I feel secure here, and with the tree I feel like a kid. It is my prize Xmas possession -- and it hurts to think it must come down; it has brought me so much happiness."

> Tree lights
> bright, bringing
> child-like wonder
> to eyes of one
> not yet too old
> to care.

I wrote poetically of getting "the same sort of feeling [of wonder] at night, after I turn the tv off and stare at the gray sky— the barren tree limbs make such marvelous art against the sky— all the feelings inside of me build up and I think how great my 'alone' life is." Nonetheless, once more I had begun to long for someone to share "what I'm doing and seeing and thinking." I posited that "I'm not sure continuous introspection as a birthday approaches" was wise. An important difference, I think, was that such longings were not expressed in alcohol-induced, barely legible entries but in moments of sober settledness. The day before the new semester, the Milwaukee Journal published a column that hit home. I taped it into my journal with the comment, "Never again, I guess."

Near Tragedy Ended
a Chain of Hangovers

By Bill Stokes
of The Journal Staff

When I was 14 years old I drank a bottle of beer at a neighborhood charivari. That was the first drink.

When I was 44 I drank a brandy on top of many others and then nearly killed myself driving home. That was the last drink.

In between those first and last drinks

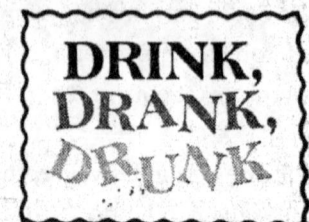

DRINK,
DRANK,
DRUNK

Friday the 13th marked the end of registration week, which was not busy for me because I still had not been assigned advisees. I did "a few unofficial gigs" and enjoyed exchanging greetings with familiar people. I "dished out a bit of TLC as needed," and agreed with Les when he said there wasn't enough of that in our department. "Perhaps that is one thing we females hand out better," I wrote. "I don't know. And while I'm not in the business of mothering students, I'm beginning to understand frosh better, and a dose of it now and then just shows somebody CARES." Over the years, I was party to this discussion many times. Women faculty, I found, often felt conflicted about the advising/mentoring role. With department chairs who had concluded we were better at it than our male colleagues, we found ourselves assigned a disproportionate number of advisees. Students who expected it of us could be unforgiving when they thought we were being "hard" or "tough" or "mean" or "unfair." That was in the "before times," when students and faculty members communicated face-to-face during office hours or chance encounters, a time when an advisor's signature was needed on so many official forms. What students generally wanted was someone to listen to them, and at the risk of overgeneralizing I think that in their experience that typically had been a female relative or female teacher. So they came to us, still a minority in most university departments around the country. Not all of us were mothers. Not all of us wanted to mother our charges, lest our hard-won professional status be diminished. Almost all of us, I think, did want to be empathetic *human beings*.

As for myself, when classes got under way I was trying to be understanding of my temporary housemate. I didn't see us growing into a friendship, as I had with Martha. I described Jean as a nice person, but she didn't strike me as an intellectual. She was "a TV addict worse than me. Doesn't even read. Lots of money. Nice Swedish Lutheran only child. Driving a paid-for Volvo station wagon. (Les: 'I didn't think there was such a thing as a paid-for Volvo.') Has an apartment of antiques and mother who sprung for the move." I wrote that the jury was still out on whether hiring her was "the right or best thing." Then I chided myself: "Be an adult BFL."

[An aside: I have a recipe for cranberry sauce that I clipped from the Christian Science Monitor "way back when" because it promised to keep the berries whole. I have used that recipe -- and shared it -- more times than I can count. With Jean in the house, I cooked real meals each night, a rare enough occurrence that I made note of it in my journal. "Even made cranberries, left over from Christmas bread, using a CSM recipe. I never cease to amaze myself." And now I know when I first made that recipe; it's the kind of detail I relish.]

Piecing together the details of my spring schedule before I moved forward with reading my journal left me breathless. My week: Mass Media 8-9 a.m. and 3-4 p.m. MWF; Editing 7-10 p.m. W; News Writing 9-10:15 a.m. and 2-3:15 p.m. TR. Granted I had taught all these in the fall, but each required some amount of updating, not to mention endless grading. Add the course I was enrolled in. Add department meetings and duties. Add professional activities. Add the unknowns. Squeeze in friends and social engagements. Writing in 2021, what I saw was a recipe for disaster akin to the one sparked by my dizzying days at Mizzou.

We celebrated Les' birthday on the first day of classes. We celebrated my birthday a week later. In between were the days of "new faces— people eager to learn" along with a couple of repeats/dropouts "who have chosen me" this time around. Starting over was both promising and challenging. Work down the alphabetized class list and begin to match names with faces. *How do you pronounce your name? Let me know if you use a nickname. Tell us something about yourself.* Distribute the syllabus. *Let me tell you something about me.* Carefully review course requirements. Point out important dates. *Here's what you need to do for our next session.*

I love serendipity, and it was at play as "volume VII" of my journal ended with my birthday-night entry. I wrote:

> I'm glad this volume, begun six months ago in Colorado, is concluded tonight as the last minutes of this birthday tick away. B'days . . . are very important to me, and for the first time in a long time I'm quite happy about this one. If I write less in here, it seems to be a sign of contentment, though I hope not complacency. I don't intend to ever stop growing and while I would like to share my inner self more openly, I'm not quite ready to give up the safety of this journal. There are some words and thoughts I just cannot bring my mouth to form even though I scream out inside. But I'm working on it—
> Life is love is life
> To be loved
> To love.
> BFL wishes BFL A very happy birthday!!!!

One of my reasons for returning to Eau Claire was to learn how to be a teacher, and that journey continued with my second semester. One stark difference from Mizzou was that not only was I working solely with undergraduates, but most were first- and second-year students. My primary frame of reference was myself and my own undergraduate pals— unrealistic and unfair to *my* students, I was realizing. As was my looking to the Polk boys for guidance; rereading their letters, I saw them wrestling with some of the same struggles as my students. But in them I also saw more intellectual curiosity and maturity. Today I am convinced that a developmental psychology course would benefit every college teacher. Such a course certainly would have helped me understand my own struggles, which today I clearly see revolved around my mental health. My journal entries during the semester charted the ups and downs -- or should it be downs and ups? There were plenty of both, which I am going to try to capture succinctly, but with enough detail to move my story toward its next chapter.

DOWN I had read about social drinkers. I thought I should be able to be one. I swore off beer -- again. For Les' birthday dinner, I brought a bottle of champagne ("California, $2.19"). I decided to join in for a glass and realized I could keep drinking, but I did not. I did have a "thimbleful" of liqueur at the end of the evening. I was "determined to teach myself to drink deliberately, if I want, on social occasions." For my birthday dinner with Les and Ruth Ann, I shared the wine I brought and could tell "it is still in me to get rip-roaring drunk." I did not, although I did also enjoy an after-dinner sherry. By my spring break visit with Sue in St. Louis I was drinking "a glass of wine now and then." In mid-April, I invited friends to my apartment for "happy hour" after work one Friday, and "I didn't have the good sense to quit drinking wine" as the evening wore on longer than I had planned. The next morning "I really was bummed out. My problem remains real— it is frightening. I thought I had gained a greater measure of control." On May 5 I got "stinking drunk." I had gone to a party with a liter of 7-Up, which I never took out of the car. "I remember it was dark when I drove home, but that's all." Saturday morning "I not only had a horrid, debilitating hangover but also a severe case of the 'guiltys.'" On Monday "I wasn't ready to teach and didn't want to, and didn't feel like dealing with people," so I called in sick. My semester was almost over; my resolve to abstain from alcohol definitely *was* over.

UP During the Christmas break, I had been excited to receive an invitation to conduct workshops on stereotyping in the mass media for the Iowa Conference on Multi-cultural, Non-Sexist Approaches to the Language Arts Curriculum. Specifically, the organizers wanted me to talk about the minority press and how K-12 teachers might use such newspapers in their classrooms. A professional connection made somewhere was paying off. In early February, as I began preparing for the conference in Ames, I began to get "I'm outclassed" jitters and my "usual apprehensions about travel and mingling." I worried needlessly. While in Milwaukee awaiting a late-night flight home, I made note of my reactions to "consulting gig #1." I started with "I survived!" followed by "I rather enjoy the briefcase look" and "The sessions went well; I received several compliments." It was the first time "outsiders" paid me for my "expertise," and that was a heady feeling. One important takeaway from that experience was recognizing that "the schedules in these things are so tightly packed you are left hoping for time to catch your mental breath." The more conferences I attended over the years -- as presenter or audience member -- the more irritated I became by the scheduling and the more willing I was to skip sessions. Increasingly it struck me that educators who harped on how students could not sit still and could not listen for an extended period inflicted considerably harsher conditions on each other. In Iowa, I also attended two workshops, including one on "Indian literature" that began with an excellent 30-minute slide show on stereotyping. I made a point of introducing myself to the presenter, who took my name (most faculty members were not yet carrying business cards). Finally, the conference left me with "really strong, positive feelings about professional women. Lots of good images. Intelligent, thoughtful, active women. Glad to be a part of it, although my own self-image is not quite as strong and positive." I did learn, I wrote, "that to be taken more seriously I have to be more forceful and outgoing. And dress better." I only hoped that "I get another chance to try it!"

DOWN One challenge of a college classroom is that it's inhabited by a random collection of individuals. Depending on the course, they may share a major, but even that doesn't mean much. They may not all be strangers to the professor, but they might be strangers to one another -- or not. For those the professor taught previously, it can be dangerous to assume you know what to expect. As is said about investing, "Past performance is no guarantee of future results." Looking back on my career, I can honestly say that I started most semesters optimistically -- hopeful that each would end with more than a few success stories. My spring 1978 classes disappointed me. Even as I wrote about giving an editing lecture that pleased me -- a lecture in which "I sermonized on words" and the students were "entertained by nonsense sentences, goofy syntax, etc." -- I bemoaned the need to entertain them. Another time I wrote about dreading my afternoon Mass Media section. It seemed to me that "most would rather be elsewhere" and "I just don't enjoy them." The course material that excited me seemed to bore them. I found myself feeling "very self-conscious and it's got to show," I wrote, adding that "I don't know why I'm letting myself be intimidated by 19- and 20-year-olds." After returning midterms in Editing -- 3 C's, 3 D's and 7 F's -- I couldn't help but feel discouraged. An assignment requiring students to analyze a newspaper wasn't much better. "These people sure need inspiring— sure are ignorant about the newspaper/media world around them." Later in the semester, one of those editing students got an F for his major project, which was "a real disaster." A senior, he was going to need a miracle to pass the course. Once we talked, he was more understanding than I expected. I could not say the same for one of my "afternoon smart-alecks" who had misspelled [Percy Bysshe] Shelley's name throughout his "pretty awful" paper. When he dropped by my office to dispute his F, he angrily complained about "having two English teachers." I told him that as far as I was concerned, he should have one in every course.

UP Reading -- widely -- continued to be a refuge. Even when I felt I could hardly keep up with my work, I found time for at least a few pages of someone else's words. For example, I was "enthralled by the [Will and Ariel] Durant dual autobiography" during one stretch of workdays that seemed endless. I was on a Christian Science Monitor kick, and although the newspapers might sit unread for days, I eventually worked my way through the pile. Same with the numerous magazines to which I subscribed; I added and subtracted titles freely. I remained an inveterate "clipper," often filing a story for potential use or tucking one into a letter to a friend. (Hardly a letter to or from Sue was sent without at least one clipping.)

UP I enjoyed cooking -- at least when the circumstances were right. I had developed rudimentary baking skills in 4-H and was comfortable following recipes -- the Betty Crocker sort, nothing fancy. I enjoyed having Les and Ruth Anne over for dinner, not just because it was nice to cook for more than one but because it felt like a gift to get her out of the kitchen. I very clearly remember one of those meals, when I showed off by serving tomato aspic (the one and only time I made or ate that disgusting dish). My tastes were generally more pedestrian and Midwestern. One night "I took real pleasure in tossing together leftover rice, broccoli, mushroom soup and some Cheese Whiz for a really fine meal." I spent the Saturday before Valentine's Day baking cookies for John and Phil (both away at school) along with a plate for Les and Ruth Anne. All things considered, I found the kitchen to be "a nice change of pace from the classroom."

DOWN Increasing tension in the department. After a "real knockdown-dragout" faculty meeting in mid-April, I wrote: "The troops aren't sitting still any longer for the dictatorial chairman tactics of ECK. How long will it take him to realize he must delegate authority and there are some of us willing and eager to share the decision-making?"

One thing we did at that meeting was refuse to accept his choice for an award; "the person a favorite of his— and only his." The faculty sent the matter back to the committee, "so Elwood is slapping our hands by having it meet at 4 p.m. tomorrow— Friday." I was on that committee "and normally I wouldn't bitch much," but I was driving somewhere and wanted to get there before dark. (I had not yet learned an important truth: Few things make faculty angrier than a late-afternoon meeting, especially on Friday.) Another reason for tension grew out of the fact that the faculty had become large enough for there to be factions. We were in the process of seeking accreditation, and Elwood brought in consultants to help us. I remember at least two, both visits including dreadful dinner meetings. At the first, one of my colleagues "made an ass of himself" by enjoying too many free drinks and rudely confronting the consultant. At the second, he obviously had been told to behave but still managed to fall off his chair. "It was wobbly," he said.

UP Family. I have written about frequently feeling emotionally distant from family members, but that no longer applied to my sister. When my brother-in-law, Fred, decided to quit his factory job and attend college in Eau Claire, Kris snagged a transfer to the Social Security office in town. Timing is everything -- but she was to start work in March. I offered to be the temporary solution to her housing problem; that is to say, she and the boys (sometimes I referred to them as "the midgets") could live with me. I cleared the arrangement with my landlords, not knowing until much later that when I talked about "my sister and the midgets" they thought I meant circus-type little people. Kris came in February to find day care; she and the boys returned in mid-March. "I give myself about a week and then my sanity will be gone— or I'll learn to have other people around," I wrote before the move. The first night "was quite an initiation. Billy was sick— and there was lots of crying and carrying on." Poor Kris in the room with two cribs! The following day "wasn't too bad— though maybe 'Aunt Barbie . . .' will eventually wear off." Naïve me seems to have expected the boys to have few problems adjusting to their changes, and I found the noise level "awful." Lucky for all of us, I had planned to spend spring break in St. Louis with Sue. Lucky for me, I returned refreshed. The remaining time we four lived together created lasting memories and treasured stories. None more so than learning that a hankering for pizza was no excuse to bring a toddler and an infant to an upscale, fern-decorated restaurant with long waits.

DOWN Foreign-car woes. Midge had generally been behaving herself, which I appreciated because I had just one option for service and even the most basic job was expensive. That was destined not to last -- and it didn't. Despite that 4 p.m. Friday meeting in April, I was on the road to Abrams by 4:40 and at the farm by 8:15. I planned to spend the night and drive to Appleton the next day, where I would meet up with Les and Ruth Anne and we would attend John's dance program at Lawrence University. Except for a brief stop for a soda and candy bar, I had driven nonstop on Friday. I arrived exhausted from the awful week at work and the drive, and when I discovered there was "nothing in the fridge" I turned crabby. It got worse. There was no door on the bedroom off the kitchen, so I was up too early with the noise. At least the weather was nice and I washed Midge before heading out. Circumstances continued to conspire to keep the weekend from being restful, although I did decide "to be decadent" and order a pot of coffee and sweet rolls from room service on Sunday morning. That afternoon, the Polks and I caravaned back to Eau Claire, at least until a gas stop. At that point, I wanted to enjoy an open window and the spring sun -- and a faster drive. Once home, I drove Midge into the garage, went upstairs and was in bed early. It had not been a restful weekend, but the worst was yet to come. In an attempt to catch up with paperwork, I worked in my office until 5 p.m. both Monday and Tuesday. On Wednesday a student broke down and cried in my office. I could have cried over another heating-oil delivery, but I just got angry. For one end-of-the week outing, my sister drove; for another, the weather was so pleasant friends and I walked to a restaurant. All week, then, Midge had remained in the garage. On Saturday, I was determined to put the top down to run errands before reading at the library. Midge had other ideas. She wouldn't start, "which didn't make a lot of sense since I hadn't touched her" since the previous Sunday. I was furious but decided there was nothing I could do that day. I went to the library but couldn't concentrate. I finally requested a service call, during which I learned that "it's probably the starter." I had to wait until Monday to have the car towed to the garage. "More money I don't have— Damn car."

UP A poet. "Robert Bly turned me on tonight— I heard him last time he was in EC, a long while ago, a different era it seems. Only anti-war poem tonight was by request; last time they dominated. Now he is caught up with sounds— a pleasant experience— a pleasant evening. And nice to see a couple of students and ex-students taking advantage, too."

> Tonight, Robert Bly (long vowel),
> you told us about diminishing rage
> that comes with age.
> You're not old enough, apparently,
> and have not reached the zero-point
> (Nor do I think you want to)
> Or would you label it something else?

	For R.B.	
Poet—	Poet—	Poet—
No pedestal.	No pretention.	Producing.
That's nice.	Nice, too.	Better yet.

Remembering, too, the night spent listening to Allen Ginsberg at the Guthrie Theatre in Minneapolis back in 1971. And while writing this, being able to go directly to the spot to pull two small tomes from a bookshelf in my study: Bly's "The Teeth Mother Naked at Last" and Ginsberg's "Kaddish and Other Poems 1958-1960." Very special Christmas gifts chosen by Les, with whom I had shared both experiences. The titles, he wrote, were "<u>most</u> deliberately chosen . . . 2 small, really, gifts— but large ones wouldn't mean any more— Just <u>lots</u> of Thanks for being you." [An aside: Poetry was a constant between us. In May 1971, Les self-published a small volume of poems titled "Dot and Dust." He inscribed my copy with "Your encouragement resulted in this— Thanks for three years of teaching one curious, interesting mind."]

UP/DOWN In order to meet the residency and continuous-registration requirements for my degree, I needed to return to Columbia for summer school. Missouri's academic calendar and mine didn't quite match, but I negotiated to leave Eau Claire early. Colleagues would administer my exams; the secretary would over-night them to me so I could grade them; I would call in course grades. Summer would be an expensive undertaking -- Eau Claire rent, living expenses in Columbia, tuition and books -- but I had no choice. Thankfully, my skills were in demand and I had left the School of Journalism on good terms. Daryl offered me a full-time position on The Missourian, which I declined because my coursework was my priority. When he said half time might be possible, I wouldn't commit until there were specifics. Eventually I signed on to be the assistant People editor for 12 weeks, 1-5 p.m. Mondays-Fridays.

Summer in the "Tiger Hole"

The Tiger Hotel, now a luxury boutique hotel, was anything but in the summer of 1978. When it was built 50 years earlier, it had been described as "the first skyscraper between Kansas City and St. Louis." With elevators and a circulating-ice water cooling system, it "set the bar for comfort and convenience." Its original rooftop sign remains a Columbia landmark. As I found it, its rooms tended toward shabby, the elevators were slow and the air conditioning unreliable. After I saw a cockroach scamper across the carpet in my room, I wondered what else might lurk in the cracks and crevices. But for me it had two advantages: It was cheap and it was just a short walk from campus, where I would be spending most of my time.

I left Eau Claire exhausted, and what I wanted most upon arriving in Columbia was a good night's sleep. Before my departure, I had taken an exam, endured an 8 a.m. meeting that was "a bit explosive" and an afternoon department meeting that was horrible. Ruminating on those meetings had kept me awake much of Wednesday night, and then Thursday I was up early to pack Midge for the journey. Thanks to the "good spatials" I often brag about, I got everything I needed for the summer squeezed into that little car. Ruth Anne fed me a substantial brunch before she and Les sent me on my way. I planned to spend the night about halfway, in Waterloo, Iowa. When I could not find a motel room, I pressed on -- so tired I was probably dangerous. Luckily, I didn't have to go far before I found a vacancy at a joint I would have avoided under different circumstances. It was quiet, but I still tossed and turned all night. Friday morning was so foggy that I didn't leave until 8:30. I endured a detour that took me at least 30 minutes out of my way. To top things off, I drove during a tornado watch for quite some time and in rain for the final leg of my trip. At least I received a warm welcome when I stopped in at The Missourian before checking in to The Tiger. Saturday morning I wrote:

> What am I doing back in Columbia, Mo., settling into Room 911 of The Tiger Hotel— 2 walls paneled/2 beige. I thought it would be bigger. And I sure hope not as noisy as last night. I could hear every word of the room next door— Guess I'll buy some ear plugs. Oh well, it IS cheap— even more so than I originally thought— now $125/month. Of course, that does not include food. I'm going to try 2 meals a day and even at that I must be careful not to let [expenses] get away from me. . . . Too much wine in the 3 Cheers Lounge before a very expensive fruit plate dinner in a deserted dining room (except for 2 very strange men). . . . At least there is a pool— and as soon as I get over feeling sorry for myself I'll make the best of it.

I skipped graduation because I wasn't up to seeing people. An afternoon nap, visiting with my friend Sue and attending a small graduation party where I drank only soda raised my spirits. So did Sunday brunch at a local diner followed by sun worshipping and conversation on a new grad's roof. My first impressions of The Tiger were not helped early that evening when I saw a police car pull up while I "dined" at the corner Dairy Queen. Walking past the hotel on my way to a movie ("An Unmarried Woman"), I realized there were two police cars. "Just what I didn't need— that and running into a weirdo on the elevator. I think he lives across the hall. Something to feed my over-active fictionalizing brain." I "enjoyed the flick" and noted it included "some fine scenes of women being friends," but I was ready for Monday. "It's nice to think that if I work hard, a year from now I could be ready to take comps!!"

I earned 12 credits that summer, all in journalism except for an Intellectual History course. In addition, I did the work for Advanced Research Methods -- independently -- but didn't register for it until the fall semester. I'm not certain about which I took when, but I commented on my graduate seminar in History and Principles of Journalism on May 16. It was taught by William Howard Taft, who in his 25-year career reportedly taught more than 10,000 students and directed 100 master's theses and

25 doctoral dissertations (including mine). I found him too old-school, too fond of exams requiring memorization and a less-than-inspiring lecturer. I tolerated him because I needed his support to pursue my dissertation topic. After the first class meeting, I observed: "Taft's history seminar is going to be painful. Promises to be anecdotes and prejudice and not much substance— from 8:40-9:40 every day for eight weeks. But probably no test and once paper topic is approved, should be okay. Besides, my research will be directed toward my dissertation, and that IS nice!!" In other words, I expected to be able to write a paper that could be a chapter -- or the foundation of a chapter -- in my eventual dissertation. After a week, however, I felt as if I were floundering with that project. "I just don't know where/how to go with it, and I doubt WHT will be of much help since guidance doesn't seem to be his bag."

I also was being tested by life in The Tiger, my journal comments running hot and cold -- and not just about my room's temperature. Making do on "two hearty meals a day" seemed to work, although "the variety is not great." Not too long after that, I tired of "throwing away so much [money] on food" and wondered if I could rent a small refrigerator. (I think I eventually did.) I was "not impressed with the way the air conditioning reaches the 9th floor— my room seems awfully stuffy." After a long, miserable Memorial Day weekend when I was mostly holed up there because the library wasn't open, I complained about the AC, but to no avail. Then, after yet another night when I hardly slept because my room was sweltering, I complained again. Vociferously. Insistently. Successfully. I got myself moved to the eighth floor; it turned out that the air conditioning on nine wasn't working at all. With conditions "more pleasant, my attitude seems improved. I'm really hitting the books."

For a while, my time at "The Hole" settled down. As the weeks passed, however, I was spending less and less time there because my classes, research and work once more were all-consuming. (My journal has revealing references: wondering if I were "on my way to a breakdown"; wondering "if I am short-circuiting.") I have a crystal-clear memory of walking from the hotel to campus with *Slow down, you move too fast, you got to make the morning last* playing in my head. To this day, whenever I hear "The 59th Street Bridge Song" I am transported to the summer of '78. Not only did I need to slow myself down; I also needed sleep. The former *felt* impossible; the latter *was* nigh unto impossible because of hotel noise.

In early July I wrote: "One thing I can't handle is people with no respect for other people— which is obviously true of the person in the next room who's playing music so darn loud [that] getting to sleep was a bitch." Several days later I wrote about being "so fed up with the noise from next door— have not slept through the night since I can't remember when." Earplugs kept "the noise out pretty well, but leave me feeling as if my ears are partially plugged. They also hurt a bit. So I guess they are not the answer." Two mornings after that entry, I found myself at the front desk complaining -- again. My description needs to be read in the context of the times: "There are Arabs next door. Calling home at 3 a.m. and such. And front-desk man figures they're smoking. Me too." I don't know what he said to them, but the next night, although I could hear the drag on their water pipe, the voices were quieter. I vowed that "the minute they get loud I'm going to bitch again." One night later, after stewing about the noise until 10, "when it was obvious the Arabs were going at it again," I went down to the front desk and said, "Look, give me a different room to sleep in tonight and move me tomorrow. But I've got to get some sleep." The manager came to my room a short time later to say he would move the men across the hall in the morning. He did. I think he also "must have asked them to cool it tonight because it is [now] quiet over there." Of course, I noted, someone else was "playing his television LOUD— but at least that comes to an end."

Uncertainty over my dissertation topic also eventually came to an end. I moved from the general idea of studying the American Indian press to a narrowed focus on the first Indian newspaper, The Cherokee Phoenix. When I learned the paper was on microfilm and the university library had those reels, "I flipped!" Shortly after that I refined my focus yet again. I wanted to write a biography of Elias Boudinot, the first editor of the Phoenix and thus the father of American Indian journalism. The paper I wrote for Dr. Taft's class would demonstrate to him that the topic was viable. I submitted that paper on July 27; it was 73 pages long. By then I knew I had earned an A on his midterm and was "psyched to try to get an A for the course, when before I was saying a B would be good enough."

Research Methods was an entirely different experience, one I thought "just might be the death of me." So much agony for two credits. How had I convinced the professor that I was capable of understanding the textbook without the benefit of lectures/discussions or that I could apply the lessons to research problems and demonstrate my competency? As the summer neared an end, that was the work that gave me nightmares. I was "using up so much psychic energy . . . the experimental stuff has me baffled. I wonder if I just am spinning wheels." When I finally managed to finish the research designs that were my homework, I wrote that "they certainly are not great, but can't say that I care. They are something to turn in." (I earned a B for the course; it felt darn sweet.) I was almost as jaded as I contemplated the final exam for my Intellectual History course -- "one of the last tests I'll ever have to take," I figured. I studied about 15 minutes. "Since I've done all the reading and been to all the classes, I'm not much worried, except he's given us 10 questions in advance and will ask 3, and we'll answer 2. So he expects brilliance in 60 minutes. So it goes."

From a personal standpoint, that summer in Columbia provided rewarding time with several friends, especially Sue, and strengthened ties with others, especially the Journalism Women. I even wrote about a meaningful exchange with a waitress. At dinner one evening she dropped by my table and asked, "Weren't you in here a few weeks back, reading 'A Woman's Place'?" It seems I had strongly recommended the book to her and she wanted to tell me that she had read it and "really enjoyed it." This was the summer that journalism professor Joye Patterson started to become a friend and brought me into a small social circle of successful women. Before that, an excerpt in the May Atlantic by Jane Howard, "an old favorite," had prompted a journal entry about families and friends:

> [Her] point here is that friends can (and must) be a family too. We don't just have blood families— something Les has long realized, of course. And I certainly depend on my clans for support and nurturing— through the mail— on the phone— in person. And as Howard

notes, these clans change, especially "friends of the road" who are "ascribed by chance." The others, "friends of the heart," are "achieved by choice." That's why moving is such a damn bitch— in the new place, for some time, you are left with only friends of the road and sometimes you need what only friends of the heart can give.

My longing to be someone's *best* friend continued to consume me. "No one needs me more, most," I once wrote. But it felt good to grow my clan a tiny bit. Evidence of that came from my history notebook, where I had doodled a dedication "for my Boudinot book, if it ever comes to be: To the women who have, knowingly and unknowingly, inspired me by their own achievements and sustained me with their friendship." After noting parenthetically that the "list is not finalized," I wrote the surnames of 12 women; all but three were Columbia friends. I was somewhat surprised to see D'Arcy on the list, until I found a journal entry explaining how that summer made me realize I had judged Ruth much too harshly during my first stint working with her. I wrote that I had been "grossly unfair in thinking she doesn't care— she does— and I value her friendship— her honesty and frankness— and willingness to listen when I needed listened to." I still didn't enjoy being "jumped on" the minute I walked in the door, but long evenings of far-ranging, spirited conversations both professional and personal revealed a woman I came to admire. She was someone I could trust "to set me straight." As was Joye, who had a knack that summer for knowing when I needed to put away the books and play. As I wrote after one such outing, "Thanks J. Today you were just what the doctor ordered!!"

The summer of '78 also was the summer that I again demonstrated I was a team player. I no longer recall the circumstances that led to me finish my Columbia stay working nights on the Missourian copy desk. Perhaps it was a "battlefield promotion," based on this anecdote from my journal: At noon of the day I was to begin, the dean sauntered into the newsroom, put his arm around my shoulders and thanked me for helping out. I told him no one ever really asked me. Ruth chimed in about my versatility. Somewhat amazingly, I wrote that I expected it "to be fun." And I told Daryl, "I'm obviously the one who can fill in on *all* the desks." That had me thinking that in the future "I probably could come and work summers if I choose." On July 10, my 12:40 a.m. entry began, "I haven't been up this late for a long time— and I'm hyper." I had made it through my first night in 18 months as news editor. I remarked on the small number of students and my irritation that one was a feature writer for the Tribune "who is [fawned over] by students all night." I was pleased to report "no errors of any proportion using the new editing system. It is super." I ended with, "I think the move was right." After writing that entry, needing to "unwind some way," I balanced my checkbook.

If only I could have found balance in my life. Despite periodic battles with my demons -- in particular alcohol, self-image and soul-deep loneliness ("I do have many people I consider friends, and I rely on some of them as _my_ best friends, but I am not most important to any of them.") -- I persevered through the relentless demands of the summer. Working nights again eventually took its toll, my sleep deprivation exacerbated by the never-completely-solved problem of hotel noise. Still I coped. Then something about being back on the copy desk caused restlessness to reemerge. I wrote about "some reluctance to leave" Columbia, then immediately equivocated. "But I don't really think this is the place for me." At the same time, I wasn't sure Eau Claire was, either, although it would be "at least for another year." My diagnosis: "I want life too fast. I know it." I also acknowledged that "it will go fast enough."

A possibility had burrowed its way into my consciousness, and I took note of it after the end of my copy desk tour. We had finished early and I was back at The Tiger before midnight. I referenced the final paragraph of my previous journal entry, which seemed to have "worked on my brain while I slept— sure woke up with goofy ideas." That entry had me musing:

> BFL— what does happiness mean to you? What EXACTLY is it you are working so damn hard for? Do you _really_ know? Or is your life one big fiction? Are you a phony? An intellectual phony . . . What is guiding your life? In what do you find meaning? Joy? What makes you laugh? Why can't/don't you cry? What are your real needs? Desires? If you had one wish. . . .

In hindsight, I see that I had allowed a tiny bit of ambivalence about earning a Ph.D. versus "doing journalism" get the best of me. I dare say that most graduate students at least once question the sanity of their Ph.D. work.

[An aside: When I read a 1974 journal entry from my earliest weeks of teaching that questioned if I belonged at Missouri, I thought immediately of "impostor syndrome." Curious about the term and when it first was used, I discovered it was introduced in 1978 by two female psychologists who had studied 150 high-achieving women. They characterized Impostor Syndrome as a specific form of intellectual self-doubt; many women were unable to internalize and accept their successes. Further, they found the women generally dealt with anxiety and often depression. Perfectionism was a third common characteristic. On the page of notes from that research, I wrote HOLY CRAP. Nonetheless, I chose to not use the term to describe my then-self, which predated the term by a few years.]

That questioning state of mind is what gave rise to a "goofy idea" -- applying for the Missourian sports editor job that was going to become available. And it wasn't enough that I was thinking about it; I also talked about it with several people. They included Daryl, "who I left quite speechless," and Ruth, "who does not think the idea at all crazy." So it was that when I pulled away from The Tiger Hole on Saturday, August 5, I was as exhausted as I had been upon arrival -- and even more unsure about my future.

> Everything comes so easy— I wonder if I'm still not looking for THE THING that will be a challenge for me? Or am I just getting weepy about leaving? Or fantasizing [about what could be]? Or what? I really wish I knew what the f*** was going on in my head. Oh well, [whatever it is] it is the future— And who knows where I will be— or if I will be —"

I had watched the sun rise over Columbia, "a deep pink with a church steeple off to the left," and even though my eyes were "still filled with sleep" it was beautiful. "Sun risings can be as nice as sun settings," I observed.

CHAPTER 17

Seeking Adulthood

As I drove to my overnight accommodations in Cedar Rapids, Iowa, I replayed my last summer day in Columbia -- "the best day of all." I had lounged on Joye's deck in the early afternoon sun until she returned from an unexpected meeting. The only Journalism Women in town were she and Ruth, so that would be my going-away get-together (and neither of us thought Ruth would leave work to join us). Joye and I had just popped open beers and were in the kitchen chatting when Ruth showed up. She actually played hooky and "I was so glad she cared enough to do so." Our "marvelous" conversations were all over the place. I found one of our topics worth recording in my journal. I brought up the "prevailing metaphor" idea we had closed my Intellectual History course with, i.e., what has guided your life, determined and influenced you? I did not record Ruth's answer, but Joye's was "the land" and mine was Vietnam. Then I asked, *What would you like to be?* I found the answers "really interesting: Ruth— ballerina, contralto. Joye— to write a sentence or two people would remember. Me— I had no trouble and I'm not quite sure where my answer came from— somewhere deep within, loosed by alcohol— but I said a Mr. Chips type teacher."

It was Joye who raised the matter of me considering a return to Mizzou. Once again, both she and Ruth were "so positive about it." Joye offered much good advice, including "thinking through and spelling out the conditions under which [you] would accept the [sports editor] job." I wasn't sure about whether I would apply, "but with friends like that to come back to, wow." Whatever hesitancy I might have had about applying I attributed to experience. "I think I have learned that I made my last move for personal reasons and the next time professional concerns must come first." Looking back, I think it would have been more accurate to write that since my first job in Antigo, my reasons for making a change were more complicated than personal vs. professional. I certainly did not foresee how my Eau Claire teaching career was going to play out.

Much To Think About

On paper, the conditions of my second-year contract were the same as the first -- with the notable exception that my salary increased by $1,110, "based in part upon an above typical merit adjustment." I felt I deserved every penny, and at the close of each year that followed I believed I had done more than my share to maintain the department's reputation for sending many first-rate graduates into the world. I also began to make my own mark as a teacher and a scholar. And from the day I got back into town (August 8), I committed "to be my own person . . . and not let myself be hurt by anyone." That was not the declaration of a mature adult, however. I was out of sorts when my homecoming "was less-than-spectacular." I thought my greeting from Les and Ruth Anne was "stiff and cold," so I didn't stay long. When I went to the office the next day, I only talked briefly with Les. Maybe I had expected too much; maybe it was all in my head. As usual I buried my feelings. I had felt very much the adult in May when I ordered china and stainless for myself. My sister, Kris -- best shopper ever -- had helped me then, and she and Billy shared my trip to the mall to claim them. I was not happy to learn the china still had not arrived but felt better after buying comfy chairs to place in front of my fireplace. "Think of it as a reward for a summer of hard work," I wrote about the expense.

On the one-year anniversary of my departure from Mizzou for UWEC, and before my return to work, I was trying to slow myself down by reading "A Sand County Almanac" by Aldo Leopold, a Wisconsinite. I expressed delight in once more being able to choose my book, albeit one from my Intellectual History course's supplemental reading list. I found it "a combination of philosophy and naturalist," and "even though

I probably don't completely appreciate it" its pace was helping. I copied an excerpt that seemed "apropos to the state of my mind lately."

> How like fish we are: ready, nay eager, to seize upon whatever new thing some wind of circumstance shakes down upon the river of time! And how we rue our haste, finding the gilded morsel to contain a hook. Even so, I think there is some virtue in eagerness, whether its object proves true or false. How utterly dull would be a wholly prudent man, or trout, or world!

I ended my entry with the observation that "I seem to do a lot of going and coming." And then I left for a couple of days in Minneapolis with Martha, newly returned from the Soviet Union and loaded with travel stories. I regaled her with my Tiger Hole tales. She encouraged me to write about them and suggested the Tribune might be interested in an article. I found no record of having done that, but I still have the lovely stole she brought back for me. And I did record that she was "a most precious friend whom I hope to see more of this year."

I was supposed to return to Minneapolis the following weekend for a concert that Ruth Anne had described as "a reward for your summer of hard work." The details of why I did not go embarrass me to this day, and my journal entry makes me cringe.

> My head is in one strange place— and I don't pretend to know what is happening. Just before I left Columbia I got a note from RA [about the concert]. I was elated, having heard so little from them all summer. Then there was the "cold" homecoming, though Les did tell me to reserve the 18th, "that is, if you like music"— a comment I found strange. Then nothing else was said; no plans were made. I saw RA yesterday and nothing was said, which pissed me off. So when the phone started ringing about 12:30 today I said "f*** it, I'm not going— and I'm not going to answer the phone." So I didn't— and I didn't— and I didn't. Though my reflex action was to jump up when it first would ring. But as I pondered it, I figured I might only be screwing myself and I certainly wasn't behaving like a 30-year-old; yet I didn't answer the doorbell, either. Well, my car was out— and assuming it was Les, I wonder what he thought. There have been no more bells. And of course I'm regretting the episode. I assume they have left, though it's only 4 p.m. and they wouldn't have to have. I probably have f***ed

up my life good, now. I'll fake forgetting the concert— but I wonder, why did I behave this way. Those are people I love— and if I am angry about the summer, is this any way to resolve it?

The piece of that story I did not commit to paper but which I vividly remember was rolling off my couch onto the floor, lest my presence be visible through a window (nonsensical given I was on the second floor). Could I have behaved more childishly?

Thankfully, school started and "after five minutes it was like I never was gone." My courses remained the same and once again involved teaching five classes; the difference was I had volunteered to teach the section of News Writing we offered for nonmajors. The result was I spent most of my time that semester teaching students who wanted to be something other than a journalist. I chose the section primarily so I would be free to enroll in a political science course. (I had been fortunate to get approval to substitute three political science courses to meet one of my language-competency requirements. "Change and Stability in American Systems" would be the last of the three.) I put off my plan to study Spanish because I didn't think "the strain is worth it this particular fall." I also took "one very small step toward shaping up— my morning mile."

My professional obligations increased, too, which I welcomed. I had not been elected to the Academic Staff Committee the previous spring, but in August learned that I would be appointed to fill the one year left on the term of the only teaching faculty on the committee. When I later ran into the vice chancellor, he told me to expect to be appointed to another committee, too. "Maybe these will make UWEC more of a challenge," I wrote, "but they also make thoughts of leaving more difficult." So did the good news that came two days into the semester. I had initiated the effort to secure a chapter of the journalism honor society Kappa Tau Alpha for the department. I had been inducted as a graduate student at Oregon and again at Missouri and thought KTA would be a feather in our cap and good for students. Besides, KTA was founded at the University of Missouri in 1910 and I was on good terms with its director. Once I got the call saying the draft of my petition looked good, I set about preparing the real thing. By the end of October, membership was a done deal.

I had more time for such endeavors because the scut work of teaching had begun to require less time. The first week where I had all my lectures and exercises ready on Monday morning merited a sentence in my journal, where I labeled the week "easy." So did the "high" of a Wednesday when my early morning newswriting class "went super and I bounced out at 9 a.m. on top of the world. Too bad it wasn't evaluation day." That came about a week later, but this time around I had "no worries." (Now that I think about it, how absurd it was to be evaluated near the *beginning* of the fall semester, with both instructor and students just finding their footing.) My classroom confidence had been bolstered by something Les said to me after I took him and Ruth Anne to dinner. We "talked long and hard and near the end" I shared my thoughts about a possible return to Missouri. "Not much reaction," but a couple of days later Les responded to a statement I made about how well I thought my teaching was going. "Then why don't you quit fighting it and let it happen," he said. To which I responded, "I didn't know I was fighting it." But he had given me something to think about.

Of course, "something to think about" remained dangerous for me. After reading in preparation for writing this chapter, I despaired over seeing my patterns of behavior repeated and repeated. Would the cycles, which I found increasingly painful to relive, end? Taking time out to contemplate -- yet again -- how to proceed, I began reading Colson Whitehead's "Underground Railroad." I was floored by this description of his character Cora as she tried to stop thinking about her life on the plantation: "Her mind was wily though, twisty. Thoughts she did not like wormed in from the sides, from beneath, through the cracks, from places she had battened down." That morning I understood that I cannot escape or ignore my ghosts. That my decision to relive my story -- and to generally tell it chronologically -- requires me to risk frustrating readers who may believe they already have figured out what I had not yet figured out. For example, there was a journal entry in which I stated, "In my sane and logical moments, I remain convinced there is relationship between the alcohol and my psychological well-being." I did not, however, describe any further attempt to connect those dots.

Understanding these things, my challenge was to move this part of the story forward with as little redundancy as possible. In many of the important ways, the final three months of 1978 were a lot like the preceding nine months or 19 months or 29 months; take your pick. I also identified things that made them different.

Classroom experiences. It was impossible for me not to compare each new batch of journalism majors to those who had come before. It was particularly unfair, I now think, that my gold standard was three years' worth of experiences with several hundred fanatically focused students driven to succeed at the world's oldest school of journalism. High standards are one thing; impossibly high standards are quite another. In addition, I had little patience for nonmajors whose enthusiasm for the subject matter didn't match my own. With rare exceptions, my journal entries for the fall recorded disappointments. For example, I wrote about lecturing my editing students, "who had totally blown last week's work." They reacted "by accusing [me] of trying only to 'trick' them and flunk them, etc." I wasn't surprised. My newswriting students were in store for a similar lecture the next day because "they really blew their obit assignment." Neither editing nor writing students could understand why certain mistakes were fatal. A misspelled proper name was an automatic F. So were careless errors such as a wrong address or miscalculating the deceased's age. Ditto for factual errors.

Another time, after grading just five analyses written by editing students, I had: B+, B, C-, D, F. That led me to comment how "they are so poorly prepared vis-à-vis their writing classes." One student, who I had in a previous course, "turned in a page of generalities." I anticipated that "when I return the papers I will be seen as the 'bad guy.'" By the end, I judged the semester "wasted." Editing, my professional love, hurt the most. The high grade on the final exam was D- (two of 12 students) and for the course it was C (two students).

No doubt I thought of those students during an end-of-semester "knock-down faculty meeting" when we debated whether a C- was acceptable in the prerequisite course for Editing. The idea of a less-than-average grade being good enough to move into Editing should not even have been on the table, I thought. At one point, fed up with the BS, Les walked out of the meeting. We who taught Editing and thus had to deal with the ill-prepared students were in the minority, however. The measure passed 7-3. I later wrote, "It's so hard sometimes to not feel like you are working with complete idiots led by the last of the authoritarians."

And then . . . on the afternoon I went to campus to administer my last exam I found a handmade wall-hanging from some of the students in my 8 a.m. newswriting class. Its message was one of appreciation. After seeing it, Les wisely remarked how the highs and lows of the classroom even out. "At least I left the semester with a nice warm feeling," I noted.

An awkward reconciliation of sorts with Mary, my Antigo friend. Late one night during what turned out to be my last visit, she had concluded that "we just have nothing to talk about." We who had talked and written endlessly and regularly confided in one another. The next morning, I tossed my stuff into the car, said I would be in touch and left. But I wasn't in touch, nor was she. Until that night a couple of years later when the phone rang and a familiar voice said, "Hello there. How are you?" After a few strained minutes, we continued to talk for more than an hour. Although she never explicitly gave a reason for calling, near the end of the conversation she commented on how she just had to let me know my "talk of [feminist] stuff now was making sense. How she was reading in the area— how Miss America *was* bullshit." (She had chosen that last night to have us watch the Miss Wisconsin pageant.) Several days after that call, I wrote that I was still "blown away" by it. I wondered "why— why now. And will it go anywhere? Mean anything? Or is life just playing cruel tricks again."

Family fun. Having Kris, Fred and the boys living in Eau Claire allowed my sister and me to continue working our way back to the closeness we had shared as youngsters. Our lives had gone in different directions but living near one another as young adults was in some ways magical. I loved being an aunt and I was maniacal about finding Billy and Nicky the perfect gifts. I chuckled when Kris told me she had to drag Billy off his Playskool desk (my gift) in order to get to the sitter's the morning after his third birthday. (It wasn't funny a year or so later when I volunteered to babysit and was told by Billy: "We don't have to do what you say. You're not our mommy.") I also introduced Kris and Fred to my sociology colleague Debbie and her husband, Dale. Along with my journalism colleague/temporary roommate, Jean, and David, the new photography instructor, we became a social circle. We spent many Friday afternoons at Walter's Brewery drinking free beer with the workers. (To be fair, Kris usually got left behind because somebody had to care for the boys.) I spent many summer weekends lounging with them in their backyard with a cooler of beer while Billy and Nicky washed Midge. It turned out to be the only time I lived in the same city as family, and it made possible all the sharing that has followed.

Martha and Luise. By the time I moved to Eau Claire, both friends were living in Minneapolis, so it seemed only natural to introduce them. Luise was known to drop in on me unexpectedly, and one of Martha's visits allowed me to share her with the Polks. Increasingly, my time away in "The City" included the three of us socializing. One weekend, for example, included dinner at a favorite Italian café, a production of "The Wiz" and Sunday brunch at the Art Institute. I didn't make note of who did what, just that "the expensive but needed" two days resulted in "lots of good times with Martha and Luise and the three of us." Another

Saturday had me going into the city to see "Hamlet" at the Guthrie Theatre. When my extra ticket from Les' class turned out to be two tickets, I called Luise. Incredibly, she was free and so joined me for the play, after which the two of us enjoyed a long dinner. Our time together was not always for fun, either. Given enough alcohol, I always had been able to tell Luise things I shared with no one else. After one such phone call, pre-Thanksgiving, I remembered

> babbling to Luise again about how unsettled I feel— about to reach 30 and so unsure about my life, in ways I never imagined. Example? Sexuality— I am so lonely— so in need of someone to care for me— to share me— and more and more I wonder if it really matters who. I think right now that intimacy could come from a woman— and I'd be ecstatic about it. Of course I'm not alone; piece on "The New Intimacy" reinforced my thinking. And a beautiful, touching tv movie on a custody fight by a lesbian added to my "why not"— Isn't what I want love, deep sharing/caring?

Special times. I missed hosting my Missouri Thanksgiving dinner, but I no longer had students far from home. I decided to put my efforts into my Christmas party. This year's would be in two parts: afternoon tree-trimming with students and an early evening open house for family and friends. The day before, "Sociology Deb" and I went out to cut a tree, which we lugged upstairs and got in a stand. "And a beautiful tree it is. My first Scotch pine. About 6 feet— full and wide." That evening John, Phil and Sylvia (Phil's girlfriend) came over and put on the lights. Fewer students than the year before dropped in the next afternoon for "Round 1" -- decorating the tree and eating homemade Christmas goodies. "At first I was down about that," but decided that I would "continue my tradition because I think they at least need the opportunity for a break." The evening festivities included Southern Comfort punch, "which was a hit, even though I used only about a quarter of the liquor the recipe called for." Later, I thought of that party as "my Christmas gift to my friends; next year I must phrase my invitation that way." Limiting it to 6-9 p.m. had been a good idea, I wrote as I reflected on the day.

> Like Mira in the "Women's Room" I'd like now just to sit in the dark and sip brandy— but I can't stand the taste of it. So I've flipped

one last Christmas album over one last time, and put on one dim light to write by. Then I'll just stare at my tree for awhile. It is that anti-climactic after-party time. All is clean but the floor. The fire is dying. And the guests are gone. I'm dead on my feet— and a bit let down. Why not? It's a long time planning for and a long time preparing for— and gone. But appreciated for sure. It was good.

A couple days later, at 8 a.m., I took my last-ever exam. "A one-hour, spit-it-all back essay test. I filled a blue book. Couldn't care much." Then I began my holiday in earnest, hosting dinner for Kris, Fred and the boys, and the Polks. It was a simple meal that introduced chicken booyah, a northeastern Wisconsin staple, to my "other family." I enjoyed getting Kris and Ruth Anne out of meal duty, and we all enjoyed seeing Les relaxed because he had finished his grading. We had birthday cake and presents for Sylvia, and Christmas gifts for one another. I hoped this tradition "would be enjoyed for these years we are together."

The next morning I filled Midge with gifts and and left for Abrams. I made good time despite the wind and drifting snow; Kris et al arrived a few hours later. My one clear memory of that Christmas is of Kris, Fred and I driving to Green Bay for last-minute shopping and lunch at Red Lobster. Among the activities I found worth recording in my journal were: Friday night fish. Plenty of beer. Dinner with our long-ago 4-H leader and her family. Christmas carols about 3 a.m. ("I was asleep and dead to the world.") A quiet Christmas Eve with "me in the doghouse" because I didn't go to church with Mom and Dad. I was in bed early "and fairly oblivious as various parts of the family return, play Santa, and fill every available bed."

Christmas Day was as one might expect, "with far too many gifts under the tree." But I also wrote how "even on the special days this family seems to have a knack for hurt. Grandma and Mom have words. Dad does a disappearing act. Grandma seems to need reassuring that her gifts to us are good." A photo taken by Fred became a treasured memento, capturing as it did a moment we seem to mention every holiday. Santa had brought "coaster sleds" for the boys, and Kris and I decided to try them out. We bundled up, grabbed our drinks and went out to the "hill" in front of the house. I daresay that was the most fun I had had in months.

One thing I discovered when rereading my journals was how frequently I mentioned needing a challenge. Once, after dinner with the Journalism Women during which the topic came up, I had written that I "never have found anything to <u>really</u> challenge me." Except life. "It is a challenge I have not been good at— or able to 'beat.' Had I become the chemist I wanted to be as a child, or the physical education teacher of my high school years, would it be any different?" I ended that entry by drawing my initials in block letters followed by a declaration:

BFL can help everyone but herself

Revelations

I have always found a special sort of feeling on a campus the first few days after an extended break. A cordial "glad to see you again" atmosphere. Walking across the open spaces of the UWEC campus in early January 1979, before classes resumed, it felt good to get back to work. I enjoyed tidying my office, filing stuff that had been piling up for months, tending to a stack of correspondence and advising a few students. I did not enjoy walking to my office in the cold, however, and made note of unseasonable heat in Hawaii -- "91 yesterday" -- which sounded like heaven to me. All in all, though, I was "feeling pretty good about things."

Writing about the first day of classes, I practically drooled over a "schedule so light I almost can't believe it." I was determined "to use my Fridays for writing or I really will be wasting precious time." Not only did I have just four classes, but my enrollments were reasonable. I started the term with eight in one News Writing section and 15 in the other; eight in Editing; and 26 in Mass Media. I was disappointed to have the journal Indian Historian reject my manuscript, with the notation that it "merely skimmed the surface of the Indian press." I didn't agree but planned to keep working. At the same time, the course about stereotyping I proposed for the interim term before summer school passed muster with our Curriculum Committee. I was optimistic that it would continue to wind its way through the approval process.

I was less optimistic about turning 30. After all, the counterculture of my undergraduate days had adopted the "Never trust anyone over 30" mantra, and there I was about to cross over that line. This was also the January of a milestone birthday for Les, who turned 50. My age engendered more introspection than usual; his required a special gift (cufflinks instead of a book). Writing for the first time in my fancy new journal (goodbye spiral notebooks!), I copied a passage from Jane O'Reilly from the latest issue of Ms. It was if she were inside my head.

> Well, let's see, what do I want? I want to share my life. I want to eat English muffins together on Sunday morning. Sometimes I want to have a place in someone's life, and to have him have a place in mine. I want stability, cooperation, and commitment.
>
> What I do not want: to be supported, to be given an identity, to have my dog walked. I don't need someone else to give me security.

That last sentence was not entirely true of me, but nonetheless I responded with a written fist-pump: "Yeah!!" A day later, at the bottom of my after-birthday entry, I taped the Ellen Goodman column that had been published in The Minneapolis Tribune on "my special day." Her reflection on "The '60s kids who dropped out of life" is haunting to read today. I wish I knew what I was thinking when I saved it, but I wrote nothing. Not long after that, I recorded that I was reading Charles Reich's "The Sorcerer of Bolinas Reef." I observed that "I keep mentally marking passages and then am not able to find them. What follows may or may not have been an original choice."

> There was nothing that I wanted to do that represented a true part of me. I had no interests or hobbies or pleasures that genuinely could be called expressions of myself. It did not really matter whether I stayed in the apartment or walked down to the shopping center or called up a friend or visited a married couple I knew or called a woman for a date. All of these would be as far from myself as just staying at the office. The truth was that there were parts of me I had left behind somewhere.

I would like to know now what parts of me I thought I had left behind.

Interestingly, I didn't consider myself officially 30 until February 4, when I received a copper candelabra from Sue and "re-celebrated" with Les and Ruth Anne. I loved their mix of gifts: a subscription to The American Scholar, a plate to add to my china and a book by Kay Boyle, "Testament For My Students and Other Poems." Les inscribed it: "The title poem. I know you had to have." I recently pulled the book from my shelves and reread that poem, which has 1968-1969 in its title. Boyle's word portraits of memorable students and acerbic skewering of a tone-deaf academic snob resonate as powerfully today as 40 years ago.

My new journal, embossed in gold, had been a Christmas gift from Sue. Her inscription stated that she hoped it would spark "one (at least) of the several books that are flying through your head. There are great works yet to be done." I hesitated to begin writing in it, noting that I was "afraid that my entries as of late have been without much creative merit . . . and therefore not worthy of a book given with the thought of spurring magic." The first poem I had written in ages, I explained, was penned "in a goofy birthday card" for 2-year-old Nicky. I don't think it was what Sue had in mind, but I copied it into the journal. (I went on to write many such doggerel for my nephews and niece.)

On the occasion of your being 2
I send a special card to U.
I.
From Aunt Barbie comes
A birthday wish that really humms [hand-drawn musical notes follow]
It's full of wishes and good cheer
which is all you get -- no beer
(p.s. It's fun having you here).
II.
During the year ahead
I hope you don't fall out of bed
Or hurt your head.
Instead,
Have fun
Playing cars and books and stuff
And when and if you get enough
of that
don't bat
a lash, just yell whee
It's time to be 3!

I do think Sue would have approved of me "journaling" with my new Cross pen. I found writing with it "almost a sensual experience, its thin gold form within my fingers gliding across a page." I was gobsmacked to read that description as I took notes in 2021-- using that Cross pen!

The words my pen committed to paper were increasingly the observations and concerns of an academic. This was the semester, I see now, when I really began to come into my own as a faculty member. Those entries didn't eliminate my musings about personal demons, but the frequency and thoughtful tone of entries about professional matters was noticeable. I wrote at length, for example, about the meeting where the Arts and Sciences Curriculum Committee considered my Stereotyping course. It was an experience that foreshadowed many similar encounters over the years to come.

> You would think that after 5 years of teaching, I'd be able to confront unfamiliar people with a certain amount of calm. Not so— my face still blushes (a response I can in no way control) and my heart pounds. Today was no exception. . . . Had no advance "warning" about what questions would be asked. I shouldn't have worried; after all, it was a solid proposal with an excellent reading list. But sitting and waiting until 5:20 was hair-raising (especially after an International Studies course took lumps as not worthy of academic credit and failed to get approval.) Was funny that when the chair asked for questions on my course there was silence— [until] finally a question from the chair on prerequisites and one more on why upper level. And I passed 8-0-2; who knows why the abstentions? Now it is up to the students, but I think I have a chance to draw the 20 I need.

Another entry consisted of an article by a female classicist and my arrow pointing out her comments about society not valuing intellectual work, especially in the humanities. Her concluding paragraph could have been written yesterday: "Today we tend to define the American Dream in terms of buying power. But who is 'we'? Who has so defined this dream? Who profits from this definition? Who loses? Isn't it time to decide what things we want to produce and what things we want to dispose of?"

On Valentine's Day, after an accounting of cards received and noting that I had brought cranberry nut bread to the office (such a female offering), I described the latest in a string of strange (and long) faculty meetings. When the chairman had not arrived by 4:10 p.m., one of the longtime faculty members decided to start. Everyone seemed "a bit squeamish," I wrote, but we went ahead with the agenda. Elwood finally came into the room and "immediately took over in mid-stream." No one said a thing. "All went fine until I was called on to give a report on a committee that I did not even realize I chaired. I swear ECK headed it last year. Ugh— one more thing to do!" One bright note was seeing my schedule for [next] fall: 11 and 2 MWF; Monday night; Tuesday 1-3. No early morning class and a "clear" Thursday. One thing about college teaching schedules: They are determined far in advance. But knowing where you would be, say at 10 a.m. on a Wednesday nine months or more in the future, could be disconcerting, too.

The evening before that faculty meeting also fell into the "good news" category. It had occurred to me that a section of the paper about Elias Boudinot I had written for my summer course could be whipped into an article for the journal Journalism History. I immediately tackled that, typed it the next day and mailed it. Repurposing research was important, I came to learn, and could ease the "publish or perish" pressure a bit. It also was important to be persistent with research proposals. One I was working on (topic long forgotten) had been returned for revisions. I wrote about having "a real feeling of accomplishment" after I reworked it. It did mean removing a stipend for myself, however, and "doing it as a real labor of love." I was willing, but not happy about that, simply writing "Ugh."

I also wasn't happy to find that I continued to rehash the same old personal discontents. Somehow I could not seem to grow personally in sync with growing professionally. And even there, twinges of doubt remained.

Reaching for the stars. That's all I've ever seemed to be doing. Nothing wrong with that. Except that under the veneer is a coating of insecurity that I'm not sure anyone has ever realized existed. [Had I bothered to look back at my own journals, I would have seen how wrong I was about that.] I sure know about it, though. I sure wonder how much of me is real and how much is phony. Am I bright or just lucky? Are my thoughts and ideas mine, really, or an amalgam of others? Will I ever know?

Remarkably, the next evening I wrote that "maybe, just maybe, the pieces are starting to fall into place." Late that afternoon the phone had rung in my office. It was "an 'old style' Les call— 'Just wondered how you were.'" I had not had one of those "low key, almost can't hear him, caring calls in a long time. Which I guess means that something in my weekend demeanor must have been disturbing." But even I was surprised by my answer: "OK," I said, "because I've decided I <u>am</u> going to be OK." That night I recounted the conversation during a call to Martha, and my answer still sounded good. "Even better, though, were the 'revelations' of a few minutes ago touched off by a line on a TV show, which was 'Give yourself a chance to be happy.'" I explored that as I continued my journal entry.

> It strikes me that I have not given UWEC much of a chance. I forgot about the adjustment year, which for me stretches (often) beyond that. But I never had a chance. I left after 9 months and set up camp 600 miles away, forcing another mini-adjustment. And when I returned here I seemed only to think about getting away— leaving for "greener pastures" before I really tried anything here. And I never have really given UWEC all of me, in best form, on top of things.
>
> So, BFL, you are here. "Bloom where you are planted." Be thankful for what you've got and enjoy life. It's yours and the only one you are going to get!

The next day I took a chance and left a note for Les summarizing what I had written and pointing out the obvious, "Because you care." I added that I had further decided the answers I was seeking "did not lie in leaving for anywhere." I told him I planned to stay in Eau Claire, "at least for awhile. And am going to do my damndest." In return, he left me this note.

> A big day— my Les is doing HIS paper; I'm introducing Ben Bradlee tonight; and BFL is here. Have you any idea how many of your friends have been concerned about you— here and elsewhere? Your note's encouraging . . . a step needed. We know life alone isn't easy, Barb.

But you have to remember you're NOT alone as long as you have what amounts to an extended family in your life . . . that cares. Let us share. We don't force, you know. But be sure you remain open to folks. . . . You'll find Eau Claire can be liveable . . . yes . . . and likeable. We have good folks and, you know, one doesn't have to stay here 365 days of the year!

I knew as well as anyone that Les spoke from experience, understood me better than I understood myself. He had answered the cry for help I didn't know I had made. Then, at home reading The Christian Science Monitor, it was downright eerie to read a column headlined "'I don't need anybody,' and other illusions." I taped it into my journal. Several sentences are underlined, including these at the end: "Let us admit, in the fine words of John Updike: 'We take our bearings, daily, from others. To be sane is, to a great extent, to be sociable.' And then we can take our beloved liberation from there."

The tea leaves continued to reveal themselves the next day. I was at my desk opening mail when a student from the first Eau Claire class I taught dropped in to talk. I liked Brian, and I had remained his unofficial advisor. He was in the midst of a "sophomore slump." (I suspect I told him about mine!) He questioned his major and was having difficulty being motivated. There were hints of troubles at home. We chatted for an hour, "talking of nothing specific, really, taking a stab at the problem now and then," including my suggestion to visit Counseling Services. I wrote that "if I needed affirmation of my value here, I got it, though certainly I'd not wish it on Brian." Later in the day, I found myself in "a heavy critique session with an editing student who struggled through her [group] project with little help from anyone. It was pretty much a disaster, but she did it." After talking with her, I decided on a grade of C-. "Honestly," I wrote, "the level of work was lower, but I sensed a learning experience. And I may be a bitch of a grader but I'll trust my instincts on this one."

Spring break is a highlight of the semester because it generally provides the last holiday from classes until graduation. On the eve of spring break 1979, I was laughing again, which I found worth writing about. "I feel good about my decision [to stay] and I feel good about me." I looked forward to spending part of the break in Minneapolis.

I was, I hoped, "just going about the business of living my life. And the busyness." I was "hanging loose and glad of it." Luise had a word for my recent "revelation"; she called it an "Aha!" Yes, that concept we freely use now to describe a moment of clarity was then a novelty. "That explains it as good as anything," I wrote, as I continued to focus on the positives coming my way. "There ought to be a safe deposit box in which to salt away an abundance of good things, to be pulled out when times are bad. Perhaps there is no such thing as luck— but when things begin to work out, they do seem to do marvelously— And my life has definitely been on an 'up' lately." To wit:

- ▶ My plans for our first Kappa Tau Alpha honor society initiation gelled and the chancellor had agreed to speak.

- ▶ I was the only departmental faculty member to turn in a subcommittee report on time.

- ▶ I finished my Awards Committee work and had the program planned.

- ▶ The campus-wide Academic Staff Committee document I was helping prepare was taking shape.

"All of which has drawn some [positive] comments from colleagues," I noted. And there was more: I had been successful in lowering the minimum registration for my interim course to 15, which essentially guaranteed that I would teach it. I had agreed to be the first "Professor in the Newsroom" at the La Crosse Tribune. And the editor of Journalism History had informed me that my manuscript would be published in the summer issue. "That takes care of my publishing for the year," I observed.

I could no longer ignore one not-so-small matter on my Ph.D. checklist, however. I was required to demonstrate reading competency in a foreign language, and I had decided Spanish would be easiest. Taking courses didn't make sense to me; I wanted instruction sharply focused on the vocabulary and grammar I needed in order to read and comprehend well enough to pass the standardized test. Fortunately, I found a tutor willing to work with me (she also did freelance writing, so we had something in common). We got started on April 2. My goal was being able to take the exam in the fall, which meant weekly tutoring and nightly homework. A more immediate goal was making peace with being a member of a department "so unwilling to DO things a new way. That becomes more and more apparent. So I guess when J gets tenure he'll fit right in." I was determined "to try not to lose sleep over it, though it bugs me to no end!"

Also annoying was how I had become the department "party planner," as I put it. I knew I was partly at fault because I was good at organizing and getting things done, but it also felt like the men expected the woman to do it. I would not have wanted anyone else to oversee the KTA initiation, of course. The day after that event "I couldn't help but wake up with a grin. Everything came off marvelously. All the faculty showed up; the chairman and the chancellor both spoke well. The champagne [my surprise contribution] was a hit." I am immensely proud that hanging somewhere on campus is the KTA charter I signed.

The departmental convocation I had planned also was a success, and the night before the end of the semester I was in a mellow mood, judging from my journal.

> 10 p.m. Scotch and water. Roberta Flack. Traffic below. I think of Mira in "The Women's Room" and her late-night brandy in the dark.
>
> Today's a benchmark. It was a year ago I left for Mizzou. So much these last 12 months have held. I feel I should be thinking profound thoughts. There are none. Only damp eyes from a TV movie about a May-December romance that didn't end "right," which is to say once again social convention won out over love.
>
> Tomorrow's another benchmark. Classes end. I've only my 8 a.m. And a 4 p.m. department meeting. And the cycle will be complete. At least there have been personal successes. . . . And I've tried to retain my integrity throughout it all, if sometimes naively so. So be it. . . .
>
> Watching spring come, that is the stark black of the trees covered with green soon-to-be leaves, is refreshing— and reassuring.

CHAPTER 18

Another Summer Interlude

I cannot imagine what I was thinking in early May when I wrote that I was concerned about frittering away the few empty weeks in my summer schedule. Professional and personal plans promised to keep me plenty busy. And they did. Just below the surface of the structure they provided, however, swirled my struggles to find myself. Painful as it is to write, alcohol continued to fuel self-doubt. And yet, in a journal entry at the end of August, I judged it to have been "a good summer, perhaps busier than it should have been— but it was a growing summer, too, and more of the building blocks of my life seem to be in place."

My three-week interim course, "Blurred Images: Stereotyping in the Mass Media," started on May 21. I was pleased to have 19 students, especially because the course had faced early cancellation because of low numbers. Interim was a daunting undertaking: teach all morning and prepare all afternoon. (In the evenings, I spent at least an hour on homework from my Spanish tutor.) An advantage, I came to realize, was that I was not trying to teach in three weeks what I ordinarily would teach in a semester. Rather, I had designed the course for this format, a design that I committed to making legitimately worth three credits. Another advantage was that the material engaged me, as I sought to meld concepts and practice in ways that would get students to think differently. The course allowed me to explore ideas I had been involved with since my undergraduate "minority press" days as well as my developing interest in the "isms" (e.g., sexism, racism) in society and in journalism. Sixty percent of students' grades was based on projects that required them to monitor content in newspapers, magazine fiction and ads, TV news, entertainment programming and commercials. For that monitoring, I introduced students to basic content analysis -- a first for the department, I believe. After two weeks, I wrote that the course was going "far better than I ever could have hoped. . . . I've earned my money, for sure— but it has been worth it." At its end, I judged it "successful and rewarding." For me, it proved to be a harbinger of much successful professional work.

The only thing on my calendar for the two "lazy, unwinding" weeks after interim was Phil Polk's commencement, which meant a drive to Lawrence University in Appleton. After that, I would prepare for two glorious weeks back at Arapaho Ranch in Colorado. That would be my real vacation. Even if I brought my Spanish study materials or a writing project, I would be in charge of my time. A creature of habit, I knew that would include plenty of sleeping, reading and exploring with Martha (and, no doubt, Coors).

A midweek telephone call stunned me; Les had taken ill in Pennsylvania. Ruth Anne flew out the next day, and my job became helping to hold down the home front and getting Phil through graduation. I broke the news to John (also at Lawrence) after RA left, but I couldn't reach Phil and left a message. He found me at home that afternoon. By then, all of us were waiting "on the proverbial pins and needles" to hear from RA because we had no idea how serious the situation was. I drove to Appleton on Saturday and had just arrived at John's house when Les called to say they would arrive in Green Bay at 7. We were overjoyed. John, Phil and I enjoyed the afternoon around the pool at my motel, playing foosball and drinking vodka and tonics. Oldest brother Lee and his new wife joined us, until we all "trucked to the airport." The fates must have been with me when I had traded cars with my sister for the weekend; we needed the extra room their Gremlin provided. As it turned out, RA and Les didn't arrive until 8. When the 7:20 flight unloaded without them, we got nervous. "Utter joy and craziness when they arrived. Miraculously, the family is together." Sunday's commencement, "quite the ceremony," was followed by getting Phil moved out, sharing lunch and exchanging goodbyes. Les and RA rode home with me. Finally back in my apartment, I wrote that I was "tired— thankful— rather confounded by the speed of the whole weekend." And even more ready for Colorado.

I drove to Minneapolis to get Martha on June 21, having again swapped Midge for the Gremlin. My nephews had taken to calling the MG "the baby car" and loved to wash it for me. If nothing else, I knew I would return to a clean car. Our drive was uneventful, except for the Gremlin running hot. The only details on our stay are from an end-of-summer journal entry: "We ended up in cabin 10 and we could not have asked for better weather. Saw Tim and Loni [my brother and sister-in-law] twice. Finally made it to Central City— bought my cowboy boots and hat. I have quipped that now that I've fulfilled my childhood fantasies I can begin working on my adult ones." I know I wore the boots and hat to school at least once and explained to my class why it was proper for me to keep the hat on indoors. Whatever was I thinking? Whatever did they think?

After Colorado I had one week back in Eau Claire to get ready for my stint at the La Crosse Tribune. The Tribune was (and is) owned by Lee Enterprises, publisher of daily newspapers in midsize markets in the Midwest, Pacific Northwest and northeastern United States. I didn't know a lot about Lee, but I liked what I heard about the company, especially its commitment to journalistic integrity. I had worked a bit with managing editor Dave Offer and I liked editor Ken Teachout from our first telephone conversation. He confirmed my judgment with the tone of his letter that "will serve to confirm for posterity" that conversation. He wrote that I could expect to split my three weeks between the Metro staff and the copy desk, and I likely would be expected to work one weekend shift of Friday and Saturday nights. I would be paid $250; I would cover my living expenses. (In my evaluation letter to him, I calculated that at most I had "earned" $15 a week.) In addition, we agreed that I would be paid an additional fee plus expenses to spend a fourth week critiquing operations and performance with news staffers and editors. To familiarize me with the paper, "and so that you could determine the good, the bad and the beautiful and provide glaring examples of same," I would get a subscription a month before I arrived.

And so it was that I again found myself living out of a suitcase -- this time in the Ivy motel, close to the office and $20 a night. "An OK place, certainly notches above the Tiger Hole." I didn't write in my journal during that month away. I did keep a diary of my workdays (written in a steno notebook left over from my weeks of reading The Cherokee Phoenix on microfilm) and put my published stories and page designs into a scrapbook. In a file folder labeled "La Crosse Adventure" I found a copy of the article I wrote about my experience. It wasn't published, but the rejections were encouraging. One reaffirmed the approach to storytelling that I hoped to bring to my dissertation and the kind of academic writer I wanted to be: "Your piece was exceptionally well written, and I appreciate its lively, narrative style. I hope you never lose your talent for projecting yourself to the reader."

A PROFESSOR IN THE NEWSROOM

"How'd you find the spelling on Jim Jensen," my editor asked.

My heart fell. I had checked the rest of the names in my story but forgot the man I had called this morning to fill in some gaps. I blushed as I explained my reportorial lapse.

"It's EN," my editor said. I had written ON. I found little consolation as he continued, "Don't feel too bad. It's one of those things you probably wouldn't have found anyway because his name's Albert, although everyone knows him as Jim."

I did feel bad. It was a beginner's error, and I am no beginner. I am a college journalism instructor, and I was doing a three-week stint in the newsroom of the La Crosse (Wis.) Tribune. In real life I teach (news writing and news editing, among other subjects) at the University of Wisconsin-Eau Claire. I spend a lot of time preaching the need for accuracy and checking details. And I had spelled a man's name wrong.

It was a humbling experience.

But I will be a better teacher because of that experience and the others during my brief return to the realities of the newsroom. It is a journey ALL journalism teachers should be required to make periodically.

My opportunity came with a telephone call in March from Tribune editor Kenneth F. Teachout. He explained that Lee Enterprises, Inc., had funded an experimental program for its La Crosse and Corvallis, Oregon, papers. The money was to put a "professor in the newsroom" of each of the newspapers for three weeks during the summer. Was I interested, Teachout asked.

Like many other journalists-turned-teachers, I walk a thin line between my desire to "practice" and my love of "preaching." I jump at any chance to hone my skills, even though such an experience inevitably leaves me with a dilemma: Continue teaching or return to the newsroom? This summer was no different; it was not long before I realized again that there is nothing quite like the thrill of making a daily deadline.

Renewed enthusiasm for my profession, however, is only one of the things I will bring into the classroom from the newsroom. Among other memories:

— Spending seven days as a reporter on the Metro staff during which I seemed to hit brick walls on every story I was assigned. The regulars always have several projects going at once, I recall thinking as I made a mental note to continue to warn future reporters of sure-to-be-encountered frustrations.

Interview a local real estate developer who is a [Jimmy] Carter fund raiser, I was told. "Sorry honey. I'm going to be out of town until late Friday," he told me. A call the next week brought a similar response. Call a 90-year-old man in Illinois who is the only living charter member of the city's Rotary Club. He was seriously ill and hospitalized. Go to Viroqua to interview a visiting African agricultural agent. He proved to be unavailable at least until the end of the week. How about a story on textbook selection for the Back-to-School issue? The necessary school administrator was conducting day-long in-service meetings for the next two weeks.

— Learning first-hand the value of a well-stocked reference shelf and an efficiently-filed morgue, having worked for newspapers with neither. Realizing that my instincts to check the clips first were still there. Realizing that I automatically (almost always) checked names and addresses.

— Hearing the enthusiasm of interns. "I never thought work could be so much fun," one told me. Another said, "Everyone you talk to, you learn so much." We— teachers and employers— benefit from such eagerness.

— Seeing my first Tribune story in print, and remembering the thrill of a byline. I am a copy editor by choice, and I do not see that 10-point boldface much anymore. But there it was, above a "react" after Jimmy Carter's July 15 speech. Thank goodness I had watched, even if half-heartedly. I produced an admittedly routine story whose highlight (for me) was getting our congressman out of the shower to answer my telephone call. Have to admit I was impressed.

— Realizing how GOOD an interview can be when you have a source who is more helpful than you have a right to expect. I finally connected with the school administrator, who said her meetings lasted until 4:15, but if I was willing she would see me after that. That supervisor of curriculum made my job of explaining textbook selection so easy that I found myself writing a story with three sidebars.

It was also during that interview that I picked up on an idea for another story, thus reinforcing my belief that a real reporter comes away from one story with ideas for at least one more.

— Attending the daily news conference and hearing my news feature on gold prices touted for Page 1, where indeed it ended up.

— Catching up with the Zambian agricultural specialist, driving 30 miles to interview him for 45 minutes, returning to the office and "ending" the story on the terminal 75 minutes later.

In my journal, I wrote of the day:

— "If nothing else, it helped reaffirm to me that I can report and write and do it well. In fact, teaching writing has improved my own writing. I find that I automatically work hard on leads and transitions and smooth story development. In the gold prices story, for example, I bothered to explain karat and alloy— and that impressed the Metro editor."

— Moving to the news (copy) desk for eight days, with a chance to do some layout and story selection. Remembering what it is like to be to work early in the morning. Feeling comfortable with the Harris 1500 VDT system after less than a day. A little experience with electronic editing goes a long way, I remember thinking, and we must be careful to continue to teach the basics; the technology is best mastered on-the-job.

Experiencing the rush of approaching deadline and the afternoon "down times." The latter provided plenty of time for discussions with the news editor on philosophy, sloppy AP cutlines, reporters who cannot spell, etc. Scrambling for copy to fill "my" page. Catching a lead that was contradicted well down in a local reporter's story and working with him to clarify it.

— Producing a daily newspaper under ANY conditions. Last day on the desk. Friday. Short-staffed. Slow morning. Deadline approaches. All of a sudden there is a man with a shotgun on a roof somewhere in the county. A few minutes later, word comes that the Tribune has gotten a copy of a local company's offer to its ready-to-strike unions. Out goes the editor's old layout and in comes a new one. And then another, as stories are juggled. I handle the contract story. We are only 15 minutes late. A nice note to end on.

These are more than personal recollections. Some certainly will reinforce old lectures. Others will be grist for new discussions. Now I can talk about one newspaper's commitment to editorial content and how this is reflected in its system for allocating space for news and advertising— a process that starts with the managing editor! And I can explain vividly to struggling copy editors the importance of smooth copy flow from beginning to end in producing a daily paper.

For this journalism teacher, three weeks in the newsroom will be reflected many times over in the classroom.

As for the Tribune editors who had to deal with this "professor" in their midst, their reactions to the program are favorable.

"The experiment was a success," editor Teachout believes. "The Tribune and Barb Luebke benefited in the short run, and the entire profession could benefit in the long haul.

"If there was a drawback, it simply was a case of too short and too little. Two months would be more realistic than three weeks, and more newspapers must participate.

"The purpose, obviously, is to improve professional performance; in effect, to improve the journalistic breed. We're fortunate to be part of an organization which recognizes that, and which makes a commitment to doing something about it.

"The best and brightest students must be attracted to journalism (which we try to do through scholarships and internships), and those students must learn from the best and most professional teachers.

"The Tribune, Lee Enterprises and Barb Luebke have shared in what hopefully will be the first step in achieving that goal."

Managing Editor David B. Offer's and News Editor Merle J. Hill's assessments, while good for my ego, also reassure me that I CAN talk with authority about life in the "real world."

Offer says, "It was great to have Barbara on the staff. She brought some excitement and led some of the staff to ask questions about their own work.

"I remember that last Friday. We were short-staffed— I was filling in on the Metro desk— when those stories broke less than 45 minutes before the final deadline in the composing room.

"There was tremendous pressure on the copy desk. But none of us had to worry about Barbara playing a key role on a major story.

"In her three weeks, she proved that she is the kind of professional who we want teaching journalism students. And I hope that we demonstrated that we are the kind of paper to which she and her colleagues should steer their very best prospects."

Hill gets to the heart of the matter when he says, "It's hard enough for those of us who are here in the newsroom all the time to keep up with technological change these days. Unless teachers of the craft update their knowledge of machines and the people who use them, they will fall hopelessly behind.

"Barb fit in easily and well with us on the copy editing rim and proved at once that she's a pro at this part of the business. The thing that can't be learned from books is pace and timing, the twin heartbeats of copy desk people as they keep an eye on the deadline clock.

"My only regret is that Barb couldn't be here long enough to give her a crack at the slot job. It's pretty hard to learn 'slot' without working it. A few days there would have provided a little additional newsroom insight that would have been helpful to her in the classroom."

All three editors, by the way, can rest assured that I have checked the spellings of their names— twice.

— 30 —

Although I did not mention the week I spent reviewing my critiques with editors and reporters, it was at least as valuable to me and my teaching as it was to the Tribune. The critiques required my close reading and annotation of several weeks' worth of papers, which allowed me to identify tendencies and habits both good and bad. I organized scores of examples and comments for each section. I wrote introductions with my general observations. I assembled everything to share with staff. I must say that when I flipped through those materials recently, I was astounded by what I had compiled. My notes about the critique sessions brought me back to that newsroom. For example, the morning I spent with the Features staff was "the toughest for me to do because it is basically negative." I was "not much impressed" by their product, which quickly became obvious. From my conversations with Dave Offer, I knew I was "reinforcing what he is trying to get out of them," which helped me hold my ground. "They were somewhat defensive (expected) and their laziest reporter (at least that's my ID) is not at all receptive." When I left the conference room I "perceived a chill— and a copy of that critique made it into the newsroom quickly."

Offer knew what was coming for each section because I had begun the week reviewing my findings with him and Teachout. What I didn't know was coming was Offer's assessment of me as "a hell of an editor" who he would "love to lure away." I allowed that I was lureable and we moved on. Before I left the newsroom for the last time, I was surprised to get "a legitimate feeler" from Offer. He said he was waiting for his budget to be approved before he could actually offer me a job. "My requirements: money, leave to research dissertation, copy editor job with open end." I don't know if a job ever was offered, but I know it was not the last time that I would critique a paper led by Offer or the last time he would try to hire me.

For a reason now forgotten, the fall 1979 term started a week later than usual. Not content to rest for the busy semester ahead, I took advantage of La Crosse being a couple of hours closer to Columbia and squeezed in a visit. I stayed with Ruth, which turned out better than I could have imagined when first working for her left me disgruntled. "We had good talks— good food." She organized a party that allowed me to see many friends, and I squeezed in lunches and cocktails with others. Joye had been away, so after visiting Sue in St. Louis I returned to Columbia to spend a day with her before heading north. I summed up the week this way: "I reconnected— and realized how important that is to me. I may be rootless but I've plenty of stems. Strong women who support and inspire me."

CHAPTER 19

Change Is in the Air

The increments of growth, personal or professional, can go unnoticed -- or be ignored -- until change cannot be disputed. After that, only time will tell whether the change was permanent or temporary. Already I had quite a lot of experience with the latter. My journal entry of August 25, 1979, written more than two months after the previous one, ends with a paragraph about change. Reading it perplexed me because it seemed to have come out of the blue. Lacking documentation, I had no choice but to accept its declaration of independence. I am left to speculate that the pieces of my summer coalesced in a way that led me to see myself differently.

> I've come to grips, I think, with my relationship with Les. I no longer feel his advice/approval are essential to my well-being. In fact, I am determined to tell him of La Crosse [job possibility] only after I've decided. And I've decided to [teach] editing the way I feel comfortable with— and that will mean some changes. I don't have to prove myself to him. I am good and I know it— and I'm operating on that basis now!

I want to think that I planned to talk about this with Les, although I realize that would have been out of character for me. Regardless, I didn't get a chance one way or the other. Les, Ruth Anne and Phil were hit by a drunken driver on their drive home from the East Coast. RA and Phil were "more or less okay," but Les' spleen had to be removed and he had a fractured pelvis. Suddenly, the semester ahead looked different. At least in the beginning, in addition to my own classes I would handle

Les' Editing sections and a colleague and I would co-teach Critical Writing. I was having trouble enough getting motivated to return to my Spanish lessons and now my job would require even more of my time.

Les was transferred to an Eau Claire hospital after several days. I saw him for the first time on September 8; he was "quite a sight, in traction and all." My journal entry after my visit was revealing:

> I feel bad that it took me so long to see him, but I just couldn't bring myself to do so. And I'm not even sure why. Was I feeling some kind of guilt because I'd finally felt "free" of him? I don't know. Now he's more family than mentor to please and depend on. I love him in a very special way, still, and always will. But I need to be able to stand and make it on my own.

Typing that today, I am positive that Les wanted nothing less than that for me. To be "family" first, then colleagues on equal footing. It was healthier for all concerned.

Thinking ahead to writing my dissertation, I applied for a grant from the Helene Wurlitzer Foundation in New Mexico. I did so at the urging of Liz Barnes, my Stephens College friend. She thought I might spend time in Taos writing the children's book she recalled me talking about. "DO IT," she wrote. "I am watching." I proposed using two or three months in fall 1980 to complete my Boudinot manuscript and a "historical fiction" account of him written as a young person's book. I was looking for "an environment conducive to writing," I stated in my proposal. Although my application was not successful, there was something magical about presenting myself as a writer.

There was nothing magical about my annual review, which Elwood forwarded to our dean in mid-October. I wasn't deterred by his lukewarm characterization of me "doing a good job in the classroom and rendering a valuable service to the department." I didn't much care that he wrote about "some concern among some of the faculty members and students that her grading policies are tough and she has been criticized for giving low grades." Nor did I foresee becoming "less absolute in this direction once she has taught longer," as he suggested. I did agree with his assessment that I was "fair and can demonstrate this to her critics and her students who inquire into their grades." That was tested when an editing student's mother, concerned about her son's grades, wrote to the academic vice chancellor and Elwood. That student had not talked with me about why he was doing poorly until, apparently, Elwood instructed him to do so. What I find revealing today are sentiments expressed in the chairman's lengthy letter to the mother. He immediately noted that he had had the student in one of his classes and found him "an intelligent, sensitive and hard working student" who "shows the influence of a good home in his conduct. . . ." In his concluding paragraph, he noted that "I do appreciate your concern and as the father of two students currently enrolled in college I know the frustrations a parent often feels." Thankfully, he finished by writing that "we all want the best for [the student] but his final success must be his own effort and achievement."

Because I felt on stronger footing professionally, I wanted the same for my personal life. Nothing new there. Luise remained my steadfast supporter. It is a wonder, I think now, that she never gave up on me. My journal records an intense evening in early September when we talked for almost three hours -- "mostly about me." I described it as "hard, honest talk about alcohol and body (my weight had reached 180!) and needs and fears and thoughts." Luise told me I was too hard on myself, that my expectations about my life were not realistic, that I had trouble realizing my successes and accepting them as successes. "Right-O!" I tossed and turned all night, trying to sort out things. "I know what she says is right; I am chemically dependent on booze. . . . She's been on my back about it for a long time. And in the past, that has always pricked my conscience, but only for a few days. This time _feels_ different." How many times had I thought or written that as I pledged yet again to take it "one day at a time." I only hoped I could do it on my own "because there is that independent streak in me that right now says it's got to be that way." I did tell Luise I was on the verge of seeing a therapist, "if only I could find myself a good feminist." What I _did_ do was join the Y and enroll in Fitness Fantasia, a twice-weekly aerobics class. (To this day, a lively tune whose title I have forgotten takes me back to that class.) I was surprised to learn from my journal that my daily to-do lists ("trying to be both practical and realistic with what I need to do at work and home") date to this period. Perhaps most significant was that a couple of days into my latest effort "it struck me that my struggle to change my lifestyle is really a struggle of liberation. I would not allow my life to be run by another person, and I really don't want it controlled by food or booze, either. The decisions I make must be mine— that will be true liberation." It is ironic that I -- who often had explained that "I would not do drugs because they'd mess with my brain, and my brain is too important to me" -- was stymied by the power of alcohol to do just that.

As the semester moved along, my journal entries became increasingly sporadic -- no doubt because I was so busy *doing*. Or perhaps I had tired of soul-searching through words. Scattered among the pages, however, I found reminders of what tickled my fancy or merited my comment. A sampling:

▶ "Bright colors turn me on lately— clear, sharp, defined colors— in combinations— they seem so vibrant, so alive."

▶ "Paul Hornung, during yesterday's Packers broadcast: 'He's being assisted off the field with help.'"

▶ Helping my brother-in-law replace the roof on the Polks' small screened porch. Fred and I joke about the job to this day, and I believe it was the most difficult physical task I ever attempted. What we didn't know when he volunteered us was that we would have to remove three layers of old shingles. We worked 12 hours, more or less nonstop. Our good-deed day ended with me sporting "band-aids on three blisters and several more that are hopeless." I was "stiff all over; can't even bend over to touch my knees." At the time Martha and I were talking about building our own cabin in the woods, and Fred always reminds me that after our roofing experience I declared that cabin would be completely concrete.

▶ The happy news that Sue was engaged.

▶ A notation on my home calendar to "Buy Tinsel."

▶ Attending Women's Studies and Women in Administration meetings.

▶ Making time for at least a few plays, concerts and movies.

▶ "The fuel oil crunch and skyrocketing prices have me using my fireplace nightly. Cozy and warm, at least for now. And in this my austerity year, I'll try anything to keep from spending money I don't have!"

▶ Taking my nephews to get birthday presents for their mom. "Billy wanted to get a doll but we ended up with a T-shirt she wanted. Nicky got bubblegum that Bo got into. Damn dog!"

▶ Joining a volleyball league at the Y. "Physical exercise agrees with me, and I realize how much I have missed it— and competition— during these sedentary years. . . . I need athletic competition to get it out of my system. Otherwise I 'push' at the wrong things."

▶ A neighbor visiting with Les noted that he collects coats and his mother collects husbands. The neighbor said he has never bought a coat -- but the latest husband (No. 5) is short and chubby "and all I can wear are his ties."

▶ Made my first pie for Thanksgiving, "including the crust because the store didn't have a frozen one."

Life, as I wrote in late October, had "pretty much leveled out." I was "at ease with myself, for the most part— steadily losing about a pound a week" and exercising regularly. I worked diligently for two weeks grading newspaper analyses so I could enjoy a long weekend in Minneapolis with Luise and Martha. I especially looked forward to a play at the famed Guthrie Theater. On Thanksgiving eve, I wrote that "all is well at my house— all is super, in fact." Five days later, my last journal entry of the semester noted that "the Thanksgiving break was peaceful." I did nothing school-related. Dinner with Kris and family was fun, although "I ate way too much. But I also started running." I patted myself on the back for that. I began baking for my Christmas open house. Saved inside the recipe booklet given to me when I left Antigo are lists of what I made for several such parties, including that for 1979.

Christmas 1979

Recipes				
1	4 small loaves	date-nut	(1 Tim, ½ Sue, ½ home, 2 party)
1	6 " "	cran-nut	(1 Tim, 1 Sue, 4 party)
1	3 " "	honey-nut	(½ Tim, ½ Sue, 2 party)
½	2 " "	banana br
2	9½ dozen gingerbread men
2	10½ " white cookies
1	Peanut Clusters - 4 dg
1	62 pieces - Moroccan Coconut fudge
1	1 loaf Bishop's Bread
1	Peanut Cluster #2 - 4 dg
1	Minted Walnuts
1	Choc Fudge — 68 pieces
1	P. Butter Fudge (RA) — 37 pieces
1	Rum Balls - 34
1	Divinity — 100 pieces

Read More (not turn out good)
Long Trib recipe

How did I do it? I recall working every weekend starting with Thanksgiving. I remember being driven -- and exhausted. I also "did a bit of shopping. Read a book. Slept a lot. And on Sunday had a second dinner with Les and Ruth Anne, which was quite enjoyable." I concluded by declaring, "If I'm feeling smug, and there is no doubt that I am, I figure I'm entitled. I've come a long way in these past months and I'm anxious [eager] to keep at it."

A New Decade

In January 1970 I was in my sixth semester as a student at WSU-EC. As I turned my calendar to 1980, I was preparing for my sixth semester of teaching at what was now UWEC. Such serendipity has always fascinated me (as have numerical palindromes). I returned to my journal on New Year's Day, as reflective as ever and with a positive outlook:

And so it is 9:30 a.m. on the first morning of a new year— a new decade about which there has been much written. I find it easier to think about the end of a single year or the end of the holiday season. Both of which are hard to believe. Obviously, my Polk family is glad

384

that the year . . . is over. Joanie [a former Missouri student] called yesterday, and the new year certainly owes her a bit of happiness— though in the back of my mind there has begun to be a gnawing fear that I am being used.

But I have to say that **I'm** starting off on a far better foot this year— and while I care deeply about my friends, right now I'm worrying most about ME for a change. And the fact that I am exercising regularly, have lost 25 pounds and have cut down on booze makes me feel great— and hopeful. So need I say more? Right now I don't feel the need to put words on paper— maybe the creativity will begin to return and I can fill these pages with some worthwhile thoughts.

The call from Joanie once more reminded me of the meaningful connections I had made with many students in my short career. I didn't need old letters to remind me that Sue and I had been confidants almost from the day we became friends. But it was in letters from others -- females and males -- that I continued to find what I craved: being needed. For example, a couple of weeks after her call Joanie wrote to tell me about her new job. She then observed that "it sounds like you feel so much better about yourself" and wondered how I had "learned to enjoy being alone for so long." She asked for pointers on "how to accept casual relations with men and remain unattached." Obviously I did a good job of hiding my bouts of loneliness and insecurities about aloneness. A month into her new job, Joanie wrote again: "Hey, this profession is a damn lonely one. Didn't realize it so much in Columbia, because there were so many others in the same boat." It is clear we had corresponded about how journalists' work schedules can make it difficult to find friends outside the newsroom. She wrote: "I admire you, lady. You take my breath away when you tell me all you've been doing. And your self-confidence seems 100% positive since I saw you in Columbia. Maybe it's contagious; I hope so for my sake."

For once, as near as I could determine, I stayed put during a school break. I wrote about "a pleasant vacation" with lots of sleeping, reading, TV, jogging and "no guilt (or at least not much) about it." A few days before spring semester classes started, I wrote that "my enthusiasm for the coming semester is building." Lunch with Les and Ruth Anne at our favorite restaurant helped; "things seemed to be heading back toward normal."

I anticipated tension and unpleasantness in the department because one of my hapless colleagues had been denied tenure and was challenging the decision. But I found comfort in Les' perspective that "this too shall pass." I was scheduled to teach three sections of News Writing and a section of Editing, all old hat by then and requiring minimal preparation. More challenging would be teaching Mass Media to Native American adults from a nearby reservation; the experimental program meant teaching Friday afternoons and Saturday mornings every other week. Snuck into a journal entry was a reference to "my own restlessness, real or perceived." I would be OK, I wrote, as long as it "doesn't find me making unthinking decisions." Only now do I see the prescience of that concern.

Outside the classroom, the Y played a significant role in my life that semester. When the aerobics class restarted, I wrote: "How GOOD it feels to be able to use my body again. It's a tired body tonight, but I like this kind of fatigue." Familiarity with the routines, the instructors and many participants allowed me to no longer hide in the back row. I also reveled in being back on the volleyball court. Our team was not particularly good, but I was proud "about some nice moves I made" and was "confident that I can hold my own." Later, when my racquetball league was about to resume, I was "so psyched to play" that I dreamed about it. (That I remembered the dream was amazing; I almost never do.) I looked forward to improving my game with two league matches a week and a regular match with Rae, a university friend. The competition left me wistful, though, thinking how nice it would be to be a high school girl post-Title IX. At the same time, I was fascinated by "how vain the young ones are. I was spellbound yesterday as I watched them primp in front of the mirror, combing every hair in place, rolling up their shorts, and complaining that they look awful. You'd think they were at a beauty contest. Now I see the attraction of a Health Club membership: adults!" That observation notwithstanding, I concluded that "if I must be 31 I am glad I've discovered the Y."

By my birthday, life already had returned to its nonstop pace. The year's best gift came from Sue, who asked me to be an attendant in her wedding, scheduled for November in St. Louis. A triple birthday celebration for me, my nephew Nicky and Les was a blast. Good health was an amazing elixir. My journal entry for January 23 began: "In general, my head is in a far better place than 365 days ago. Body is in better shape, with pounds still to lose, but looking in the mirror is fun! And I've [run a total of] six miles in each of the last three weeks and today I am convinced that if I get the right warm-up exercises, I'll soon do my mile regularly and continue to build on that." Equally as important, a couple of days earlier my first thought when I awoke was, "I am going to stay here. This is the kind of teaching I am committed to; there are no other pipe dreams." I shared that with Les during the birthday party and "he didn't seem too surprised." He did, however, again suggest that I take a leave for a year to get experience in the "big-time real world." I wasn't opposed to the idea, but neither did I see a need to do so in the short term. After all, I still had a Ph.D. to earn.

A month later, the "calm times" that engendered just a few journal entries had become unsettled. I do not know why; I only have the words "Life has not been without its downs recently" to signal that something had changed. "I rediscovered how easily I can fall into old behavior patterns. On the weekend it was booze— that restless Saturday afternoon pattern of tv sports and alcohol. Used to be beer; now it was Chablis wine. End result the same, of course." I had thought about "why," I wrote, but came up with no answers. "When I start it just seems like a nice way to spend the afternoon. By the next a.m., with the hangover, there's the old guilt and regret and then I punish myself by sloth and overeating and 12 hours of couching and tv." I speculated that fatigue might be a culprit but was puzzled because "I get plenty of sleep— sound sleep because of the exercise, I'm sure." I ended the entry with the hope that "the fatigue is not an indicator of depression to come" and added that "I'm being careful and cautious of mood changes."

Of March, I can write only how surprised I was to find no journal entries. Thankfully, my calendar's square for the 21st had the notation "Madison." On that Friday, I completed another Ph.D. requirement when I earned a passing score on the standardized language exam measuring my Spanish reading comprehension. I had registered to take the exam mostly to see what it was like and gauge what more I needed from my tutor. I made the three-hour drive to Madison rather nonchalantly. On the way back to Eau Claire, I hooted and hollered and laughed in astonishment about my success. No doubt the vocabulary of the social sciences was a bonus, with enough transliteration to help me intuit meaning. I knew just enough grammar to make sense of passages. I recall that I got perhaps 20 points above the minimum, but as athletes are fond of saying, "A win is a win." Whenever I have told this story over the years, I have ended it by saying that during my drive home I probably forgot 90 percent of the Spanish I had "learned." No matter; I had done what the University of Missouri required.

Tucked inside the blank pages between my February 21 and April 27 journal entries I found two sheets of yellow notebook paper, neatly folded into quarters. Their words speak for themselves.

Easter Sunday 1980 [April 6]
I have just come through perhaps the wildest 24 hours of my life. In some ways I am numb; the enormity of the decisions I have made hasn't quite sunk in. So as I sit in Columbia [Missouri] Regional Airport on yet another leg of the journey, I'm quivering in excitement and expectation, with not an absence of trepidation. Certainly it has something to do with the flight. But this nervousness is more an attempt to remain grounded in reality. The tale unwinds in chronological order:

Monday 3/31— The Convocation brochures are nowhere to be found; [my colleague] seems to have pulled another one of her irresponsible stunts. I am in the office bitching to [the chairman]. The phone rings— it is for me— Daryl [Moen, at the *Missourian*]. I have the call transferred to my office. He wonders if I am interested in the copy desk job— two nights and teaching. Sure, I say— toss my name around. I don't give it another thought.

Tuesday 4/1— Daryl catches me at home, where I'm watching TV soap operas for the afternoon. The dean wants me to come down. I get reservations for Thursday. I call Sue. Change my reservations to include an overnight in St. Louis.

Wednesday 4/2— I have a 1 p.m. meeting. Karen [my Spanish tutor] and Rae are coming for dinner to celebrate the victory over Spanish. The night before, Kris and I had gone shopping so I could find something (a) that fit and (b) was suitable for an interview. I need to hem the sleeves. Need to go to the bank. Need to pack. Need to think. It is in the 60s and gorgeous outside.

Thursday 4/3— It is snowing. At first, it's light, but by the time I'm at the airport it is heavier and wet and gray and foggy. Our plane cannot land because of the weather and because there is a small plane lost somewhere in the area. They tell us a bus will be here to take us to Minneapolis. I am glad I had a 3-hour layover. But the bus does not leave until noon. I have a 2:10 flight. I am doubtful; they say I'll make it. We arrive at 2. I run to the farthest gate and my plane is still there. But it now is full with standbys and I cannot get on. I manage to get a flight to St. Louis but it is leaving 1 hour late and I'll not make my connection to Columbia. The late flight is overbooked. I arrange to rent a car out of St. Louis and call Ruth. A beautiful flight to S.L. The pilot tells us it is 71 degrees. Hertz gives me a big Cougar with power everything and I lurch toward Columbia, arriving about 8. A former student had been in town for the day and stays with Ruth so we all can have dinner. At 11, I'm in bed— exhausted.

Friday 4/4— A day of talks with various faculty members. The sun is out and my light jacket and pants are perfect for the day. The talks go well. They are pretty much formality, it seems. I feel confident and more self-assured than I ever have. I realize how much more I have to offer now than six years ago, and I say so. I tell of my desire to stay in touch with the practical and also to be in the classroom. I am assured of that and encouraged that I'll have a chance to teach a variety of courses.— Time to board —

I didn't finish my narrative about that trip until April 27, when I wrote that "the dean offered me the job at the end of our 45-minute conversation. I'm proudest of myself for negotiating for $1,000 more than he offered; I'll get $21,000! That's $6,000 more than now!!" What is more, "by 24 hours later I had found a 3-bedroom town-house to rent beginning June 1. Accepted the job. Spent a marvelous late-into-the-evening with Ruth, Joye and Jane. Then there was Easter breakfast with Loretta, who unfortunately is off to [a new job in] Boston June 1. [Then] 24 hours with Sue and Charlie. And now, in a month, I'll be leaving." I concluded by wishing I had had a photo of the look on Daryl's face when I told him the dean had offered me the job before I left his office, because it turned out there was at least one candidate yet to be interviewed. Ah, the dean had not changed his stripes.

I had not changed my stripes either, it would seem. Three months after declaring my intention to remain in Eau Claire I had made what some saw as a rash decision to leave. With 40 years of hindsight, I am prone to agree with that assessment. Though in fairness to myself, I believe my openness to new opportunities was not a secret. Up to that point in my career, I had entertained every professional possibility offered and freely acknowledged being ambitious. My growing disillusionment with the Eau Claire Journalism Department was one factor in my latest decision. There was the strong-armed "leadership" of the chairman, mediocre-at-best senior colleagues who never seemed to be held accountable, and mediocre-at-best new colleagues whose hirings baffled me. Another factor was my desire to be recognized as a journalism teacher in my own right, not just Les Polk's protégé. That was complicated because we aligned -- and were in the minority -- on almost every departmental issue.

On the other side of the balance sheet were the family and friends -- not to mention the many students -- who made life in Eau Claire enjoyable. Anticipating goodbyes, however, was made easier because I was leaving for a familiar place. I would not have to start over to find connections; I would be able to add to them. Actually saying goodbye -- over and over and over -- was wrenching, and I didn't always do it well. At the annual Journalism Picnic, the students gave me a wine carafe. There was lunch with the faculty, who gave me an engraved beer mug. I fit in a quick trip home to see my parents and another to Minneapolis to spend time with Luise and Martha. Kris and Fred threw me a going-away party. It didn't require a lot of goodbyes because a couple of days later many of those marvelous friends made light work of moving me out of my apartment (goodbye to high heating bills!). They packed the U-Haul truck in 90 minutes, carrying so many boxes of books that student Brian dubbed it "moving the BFL memorial library." Lots of tears followed; rather than characteristically trying to hold back, I allowed them to flow freely. My sadness was profound. So profound that the next morning I could not bear to speak *goodbye* to Les and Ruth Anne. Could not even bear to see them. I slunk off, barely able to drive because of my sobs. I knew it was a cowardly thing to do, but I couldn't help myself.

Snapshots

Who says college instructors couldn't be silly? Credit my brother-in-law for one of my favorite photos.

My nephew Billy enjoyed washing my MG, sometimes dubbed "the baby car."

I showed off my newly purchased cowboy boots and hat (while holding a Coors beer) during a visit with my brother and then-sister-in-law.

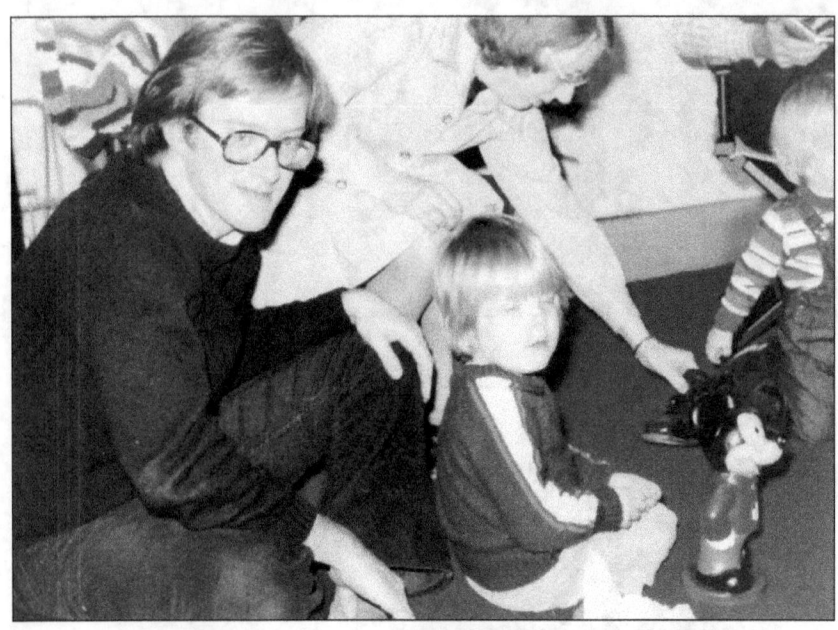

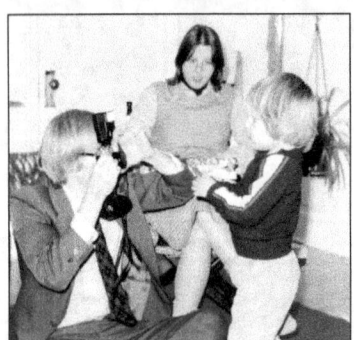

Celebrating Christmas 1978 at my Eau Claire apartment with Les, Ruth Anne, John and Phil (with camera) Polk. My nephews got lots of attention.

CHAPTER 20

Single-minded and Persistent

Getting settled back in Columbia was a breeze. Fred had squeezed his motorcycle into the back of the U-Haul and drove my possessions south. Sue came from St. Louis to help me move in, and we had the house livable in no time. Despite packing for her vacation, Ruth made time to stop over on the weekend. I had dinner with Joye on her first night back in town, followed a couple of nights later by dinner with her and three friends. Martha sent a beautiful plant, and when Jane came for cocktails she brought a plant, too. The greening of BFL's house. Never had I felt so welcome.

Nonetheless, my first journal entry after moving -- dated June 5 -- began with me noting that "I've been in my new house (my new life) for one week and four hours now— and I must confess to being not entirely content." As I had explained to Joye, I thought that was "because my head still does not comprehend the changes that have come so swiftly." I felt I deserved "this lazy week" but was alarmed to find myself "into the Coors Light . . . a sure sign I've not kept myself busy enough." Determined not to revert to my old ways, I pledged to get back to work. *So how do I feel about the move?* I asked myself. My answer: "Ever committed to finishing my degree by May '81 (and scared it can't be done). Glad to be back here. Desperate to be HAPPY. Desperate to be GOOD— to find my niche in Journalism Education at Missouri."

I righted my emotional ship once I wrote my first post-Eau Claire letter to Les and Ruth Anne. I wrote the words I had been unable to speak. I apologized for my behavior on moving-day morning and tried to explain that I didn't know how to handle my pain at leaving them, so rather than try I just left. What I hope I also told them was how awful this behavior made me feel. (What I didn't know was how many years it would be until I learned to stop running away from my feelings.) In a letter dated June 17, Les replied: "Your letter arrived today and it was a relief to have heard from you." They had learned second-hand that I was "okay and had arrived without mishap. Good, I guess." Why the qualifier? he asked, and his explanation perfectly described the dynamic at work.

> Well, I guess it's going to be difficult for the LDP family to know that Bfl is gone, for good. Life's patterns don't repeat themselves; it always moves on and in different ways and the reality of life is that you no longer live here, work here, or will be a part of our daily sorts of lives. Friendship becomes habit, taken sometimes too much for granted when it's here; too little when it isn't. And we must adjust to not seeing you walk by, not having you ring the bell. And we never did get that "last supper at Austin's." And it all seemed to me to be such a damned rush, and blur, and confusion in finals and end of semester and Madison meetings that it never got straight quite [sic], and left me feeling a bit "unsatisfied" about the whole departure number.

Before sharing department news that confirmed my concerns (by November, a former colleague wrote that "working in this place this year is like working in an asylum"), and before the news that confirmed my family status, Les was nostalgic.

> I can always enjoy the satisfaction of knowing you are doing well where you are and that somewhere I might have had a bit of teaching there for that little De Pere girl who had to "eat up" all those classes early on, before they'd developed into what they are now, while they were still my "hunches" about what was right about J ed, and who, with classmates, are some sort of living testimony that just maybe there was something right going on. It's nice.

I read a bit of despair in his observation that "I'm not sure I'll like being here alone." I, on the other hand, at least at that moment, was focused on what was to be, not what had been. When I later despaired about lengthy lapses in our letter-writing, it didn't occur to me (as it does now) that it was us in our own worlds being overwhelmed by our lives and demands and responsibilities. As Les wrote at the end of a missive eight months later: "This is intended to make up for a long-non-intentional silence, Barb. We both think often of you, miss our friend walking by, the light on in the apartment, the occasional Fridays together; the little home things no one else knows of. I'm sure students miss your teaching and trust that what's being done there is fine."

I missed that familiarity, too, but I had no qualms about the unfamiliarity of living on the outskirts of Columbia. My townhouse was spacious. Today, the lower level would be described as "open concept" and the upstairs' three bedrooms allowed one for me, one for a study and one for guests (of which there would be many). The view out my front windows was marvelous at all hours of the day, but never more so than when the sun was low in the sky and made the gold sheen of the field across the road mesmerizing. I loved "watching the waving wheat, if we are lucky enough to have a breeze." I could listen to birds and crickets and "dream a lot." At the back, the sliders from my dining room to a small patio filled the downstairs with light. When the weather cooled, I took to napping on the floor in the warmth of that sunshine. "I feel lucky to be here," I told my journal. "I like my house and my place in life right now— hope I deserve it— hope I do it right."

I had forgotten how hot and humid Columbia could be, and it seemed that summer was off to a miserable start. I might have coped better with inactivity had I been able to sit outside and read, but that was out of the question. The weather also interfered with my running program, such as it was. While I did go out every morning, I didn't seem to have much endurance. "20 minutes is it. Maybe it's the hills— or humidity." Whatever it was, I hoped for better. I had not forgotten about moving's low moments, and the early weeks of this one had a few. But I worked out of them. Watching a crew bale hay in mid-June reminded me of childhood days spent at the farm of friends. The ride there from Lande Street seemed so long, though it was probably just 5 miles or so. "Oh, the multiples of 5 miles I have travelled since," I wrote. "For the most part, though, I think I've enjoyed those miles. They are so right for me!"

I had chosen to not work at the Missourian that summer so I could prepare to take my comprehensive exams -- the last hurdle between me and official ABD (All But Dissertation) status. I hadn't been getting a lot of encouragement or help from my advisor, and I was beginning to resent that. (Perhaps he had been one of those who doubted I would finish my degree after I moved to Eau Claire.) I knew I was "capable of the single-mindedness necessary to achieve my goals," but I needed "some indication it will/can work." I was temporarily thrown into a tizzy when I discovered that I had to be an enrolled student to take the comps. Luckily, because the J-School offered two summer sessions I was able to register for one credit of Research. All would be "legal." Even as I worked at getting those details straightened out, I spent a couple of hours on campus reading, but found "the effort is aimless, wandering— and thus frustrating." I was ready to *not* be a graduate student. On the other hand, I was eager "to actually be researching. I really look forward to the challenge of bringing Boudinot to life" in my dissertation. I had to fight "the urge to be doing that instead of comps studying."

Not working, however, also felt weird. It took me a couple of weeks to come to grips with the toll the move had taken on me, especially combined with inactivity and the inattention from my advisor. I was buoyed when I answered a call and heard, "Want to go swimming?" My heart smiled to have another friend who didn't have to identify herself; it was Joye. That afternoon, when I shared my frustrations, Joye acknowledged that it was an abnormal time to return to Columbia, with many people gone, classes not yet in session and such. She observed how unlike me it was to be "down" (Wow!) and reassured me that coming to grips with what I had been feeling was a big step because now I knew "where you've been and where you need to go." Indeed. I ended that night's journal with a plan: "Tomorrow is comp reading in the a.m. Cherokees in the afternoon. And a bit of comps in the evening. Time to get on with it, BFL!!"

And I did get on with it -- "it" being lots and lots of reading, including a Saturday immersed in frontier journalism history and days revisiting symbolic interactionism and Murray Edelman's contrary views of political science. Next came memorizing outlines for my answers.

I had described the comps process to friends as three days of writing term papers without notes; was it any wonder I was "damn apprehensive"? But just when I was in stress-induced funk, feeling "unloved or unwanted" because of no phone calls or letters, friends reached out in support. "At the next big crossroad in this mad pursuit of academic legitimacy," I reminded myself in my journal, "I have come too far to blow it and am not about to— with God's help and lots of help from caring and loving friends." (For the record, agnostic me cannot explain the God reference.)

On Monday, June 30, in the cool of the early morning and fueled by adrenaline, I jogged farther than I ever had. Then, from 8:30 to noon I settled into a colleague's office, locked the door and "finished 1/3 of my comps. I feel good about it." I got to choose the three questions I answered for my political science professor. Two were ones I had anticipated. Of the remaining two, I "wasn't real comfortable with either but I got daring and challenged the premise of one of them. We'll see." Tuesday would be the journalism history exam from my advisor. "I'm a bit more scared of that one— but at least the process is not unknown now." Sit and write. No hassles. Walk a bit to give the mind a break. Besides, I wrote, "Why shouldn't I be comfortably confident. After all, I did the Spanish, I did the coursework, I can write and think. And I can jog almost two miles. So what's to stop me?"

Nothing did stop me, although having to wait for Loretta's sociology questions delayed me. "The feeling of euphoria about noon [of day two] was overwhelming— as was the feeling of relief." At the same time, there was anticipation of a different sort. As I prepared for my comps I also had been busy planning a research trip to Oklahoma. That explains the last paragraph of my July 2 journal entry: "I hardly can believe I actually am going to travel and do research for my DISSERTATION. Doesn't seem possible that it's come together. The ball really is in my court."

Marking time during the intervening few days was unnerving. I thought I had a lot to do so decided against a trip to St. Louis for the Fourth of July. Then I wrote about being "at such loose ends I don't know what to do with myself, literally." I was read out. I unpacked books until I ran out of shelf space. I cleaned and did laundry. I worried about the heat wave that promised to only get worse as I traveled west. I worried "about me making my way in all these strange places— and eating too much and not exercising and BLOWING IT. I can't leave there with loose ends. I surely will leave there broke. Ugh! It's going to be a trying time. At least the motels should have pools. At least I'll be DOING." And at least I had the good sense to rent a car with air conditioning rather than drive Midge. I cheered myself on: "Let's get up and get out of here, BFL, and things will be OK. You worry too much— a sign of your true self-centeredness. Hang loose. Head to Oklahoma. Do your work. Have a bit of fun. Learn how really self-reliant you are. And it will be OK." I couldn't help but ask, "Promise?"

That mindset led me to record several "firsts" during my 10-day trip. It was good to read of instances where, as I would say today, I successfully functioned out of my comfort zone. Indeed, I could have written about the entire trip being outside that zone. I got started later than expected after I decided to rent the car, and so drove only the 235 miles to Joplin, Missouri. The next morning I was up at 6 to jog around the motel parking lot; it was already 77 degrees. At breakfast, I uncharacteristically found myself conversing with a young guy from Detroit. My destination was Tulsa -- two hours away -- and the Gilcrease Library and Archive. I was eager to get to work, but because I also was determined "that there will be some enjoyment on this trip" I first stopped at the Tulsa information bureau "for lots of pamphlets and helpful directions." The archive was adjacent to the Gilcrease Museum, where I was "overwhelmed by the art and the beauty and the history." I judged the day productive— "with only a break for a 'Les lunch' (yogurt and fruit) from Safeway." After winding down in the pool and venturing out for dinner, I plotted my next day's work. It promised to be a long day, but I was eager.

Next up was the research center at the Oklahoma Historical Society in Oklahoma City. But before that, I stopped at the National Cowboy Hall of Fame (a Columbia friend had insisted I do so). "It was fun. Got postcards for [my nephews]. More Russells and Remmingtons, though I think the Gilcrease was better. Also another Blumenschein, who first caught my attention at Gilcrease with his large, surrealistic, fantasy-of-sort paintings of Indians. I'd like to see more." I worked at the historical society from about 11 to 4, by then accustomed to being allowed only paper and pencil for notetaking. A "<u>super</u> helpful" young research assistant made the experience enjoyable, but I wasn't "sure how much useful stuff I'm getting." Still, the "thoughts and directions of the paper are beginning to form. Boudinot as a journalist really is virgin territory." What more could I ask for? Wasn't a point of research to allow direction to reveal itself? I was eager for a 9-5 day on Friday.

As for my comfort zone:

> [The] cheap motels here were close to the capital but what <u>dumps</u>. So I'm at a Best Western that's an easy hop to the society— but this still obviously is the central city. I was the only white in the Sirloin Stockade where I had dinner tonight, and the only white in the store where I stopped for an expensive 6-pack of Coors Light. The place ironically called Toms!

As I expected, I worked "long and hard" on Friday, but not before I took a tour of the Capitol "with a marvelous 82-year-young man" and saw for myself that there really are working oil wells on the grounds. Dinner that night was at a Dairy Queen "and again only Black faces."

Limited time and money for my research trip were great motivators. Saturday took me to Norman, where I had reserved an $11-a-night room on the University of Oklahoma campus. But I decided "no tv and pool were just too much (or too little)" so I opted for Howard Johnson's at $30 a night. "I will just have to push so I only need three nights here— no regrets, at least now." I needed to crash comfortably. At 6:30 p.m., I was already in bed. Even People magazine was more than my tired eyes could handle. I looked forward to spending Sunday morning around the pool before working in the university library and preparing for a Monday immersed in Special Collections documents. As each day passed, I saw more clearly how the dissertation would develop.

In the end, my time in Norman "was marginally useful" and I "was not much impressed with the city." The Five Civilized Tribes Museum in Muskogee turned up "a few more nuggets." I had hoped to find Boudinot's grave in Tahlequah, capital of the Cherokee Nation, but my search was futile. Before I left the area, though, I nervously decided to attend an evening performance of the "Trail of Tears" at the outdoor

Tsa-La-Gi Amphitheater near Tahlequah. The play, which ran from 1969 to 2005, told the story of the Cherokees' forced removal from the Southeast to Oklahoma. I wrote of my research and that powerful experience:

> My senses are beginning to feel overloaded. To be immersed in all these names and places that once were only secondarily familiar is overwhelming. Topped off tonight by the just completed "Trail of Tears" portrayal. Super. To see the highlights re-enacted. The march scene. The Civil War scene so powerful. The dances. Outdoors under the stars. Hearing them pronounce Boudinot with a hard "t." To watch him come to life (unfortunately post-removal).

The next day I ended a debate I had been having with myself about returning to Tulsa to check on a missionary's diary. I was concerned that "I may have blown it" when I did not stop at the University of Tulsa at the beginning of my trip. But I didn't want to risk a late-return charge for the rental car, so I chose to head home. It was 110 degrees. A few days earlier I had read about 150 heat-related deaths in Missouri; there had been one when I left. "What senseless deaths," I wrote, "and what does it say about the state of things when our old people are so afraid that they die rather than unboard windows for air."

By then, my days had run together. My return trip stood out because I -- so anxious about getting lost -- made my first navigational mistake when I followed US 59 North instead of State 59. I had hoped to pass through a corner of Arkansas so I could tick it off my "states visited" list. I did not drive through any of Arkansas; I did see some pretty country, albeit out of my way. Despite that, I returned the rental car on time. That was good news for my wallet. Even better news was a break in the weather a couple of days later. A morning jog in 65 degrees "was pure joy," as was being able to read outdoors and turning off the air conditioning to "let the breeze blow through the house."

I needed to unwind from the breakneck pace I had maintained to maximize my research. That was not easy and, as I soon came to realize, finishing my dissertation would be even more all-consuming. For a couple of days, however, I enjoyed catching up with friends. Needing to be busy, of course, I also prepared for my delayed sociology comps questions. I was determined to polish off that process so I could begin assembling my course syllabi and learning the Missourian's new VDT (computer) system. I tried to resist resuming my research -- plenty remained -- but I so enjoyed it that I couldn't stop myself from spending time in the library.

Journal entries indicate I struggled to find balance in the waning weeks of summer. "In the quiet of the morning, the refrain running through my head is an unpleasant one: I am the person I least like." Despite all that I was doing, I seemed to see only "laziness, inactivity, sleep, beer, poor meals, no exercise." I am now, as I was then, at a loss to explain myself. "There must be more to it than two months off from the job." One thing was clear: "I have not been denying myself anything lately. I want a 6-pack, I get it (usually two because I know one won't be enough). A yearning for M&Ms, I get 'em. Cookies— I make 'em." It had been almost a year since my first aerobics class. I didn't think I had a subconscious desire to regress, "but I sure seem to be acting that way. I wish I knew what would snap me out of this— I want to like me again!"

After the fact, I characterized the earning of a Ph.D. as a test of persistence. And throughout my life I have been nothing if not doggedly persistent. I discovered a sentence in my journal that requires an amendment to that characterization. "I am obsessed with dissertation, I realize. But feel I must be if I am to do it— and do it well." That preoccupation— noted in mid-August 1980— would only intensify as the school year progressed.

Returning to the classroom and newsroom left me exhausted at the end of the first week, but it felt good. A letter from a former colleague in Eau Claire made me a bit homesick, I wrote, "but I feel so comfortable here. I belong. No doubt in my mind." I taught my first classes on Wednesday "without a single twinge of nervousness, which was a first. Guess as I begin year 7 I finally am a veteran." My confidence was reinforced a couple of weeks later after I lectured in Joye's graduate course on women and the media. My presentation using slides and music was well-received, and Joye later said, "You are a born teacher." I hoped my lecture might result in requests to serve on a couple of master's committees. That would be an important step in my faculty progression.

Sandwiching my first classes was my return to the copydesk on Monday and Thursday. "About 19 hours each from get-up to get-home. Ugh." I picked up the VDT system quickly and loved it — "what it can do, the time that it saves us." I was hooked on technology. I still am.

If Fridays found me running on empty, weekends "with more things to do than there are hours" kept me hopping. Saturdays often found me researching in the library, but my social calendar included lunches and dinners and hikes and movies. And Tigers football. I gladly joined a group of colleagues-now-friends and became a season-ticket holder. It was the heyday of the old Big Eight Conference, and for the first time I experienced big-time college football complete with tailgating and postgame partying. Cheering along with more than 62,000 others helped erase my resentment of working Saturdays during my first years on The Missourian. Screaming out M*I*Z / Z*O*U released a lot of stored-up tension.

Another positive development was the widening circle of Journalism Women. Susan had joined the advertising faculty in 1978 and VJ began teaching photography in 1980. The group's get-togethers remained social but also evolved into an important forum for discussing J-School issues from our point of view, often decidedly different from "the old boys' network." Susan and I bonded over racquetball; VJ and I as advocates for women in the newsroom. Also increasingly important was my friendship with Robin, botanist and wife of colleague George. She had come by for a celebratory drink after I finished my first two comps questions, and before she left (after several hours of conversation) she said how glad she was that we had been given a second chance to know one another. I was, too.

At the end of September, I officially passed my comprehensive exams by orally defending my written answers. At long last I was "a tried and true Ph.D. candidate." I wrote nothing about the experience. Rather, I observed that "the cattle [across the road] were restless last night. Wonder what makes them bellow so in the middle of the morning." I also made note of how "life takes funny twists." A letter from a friend that day mentioned a new book by May Sarton, an author I first encountered a few weeks earlier when Joye loaned me the book I had paged through at her house. After reading the letter, I found that book, "Journal of a Solitude," to continue reading. I randomly opened it to the page for September 29, the current date. All I could write was "Wow." [An aside: Over the years, I read everything Sarton wrote and was lucky to hear her speak twice.]

My few journal entries in November and December focused on writing my dissertation, continuing research for my dissertation, writing my dissertation, inflicting dissertation talk on my friends even when they dragged me away for a couple of hours of fun, writing my dissertation, doing holiday cards with messages centered on my dissertation, writing my dissertation, and never being satisfied with progress on my dissertation. At least I seem to have left "the Big D" in Columbia when I went to St. Louis for Sue's wedding. "Each time I wear my dress or pearls or carry the antique lace bag, I'll remember 11-1-80— and one of the quickest wedding ceremonies I ever heard. Wanted it to be longer so the memory would have more time to sharpen." To this day I treasure the precious gift of deep friendship, first from my college friend Laurel and then from Sue, that includes being a part of their weddings. Remembering their anniversaries has been my way of honoring that gift.

One episode I didn't write about but never have forgotten was supervising the copy desk the night John Lennon was shot. How I wish I could have had a do-over of December 8, 1980. My determination to make deadline clouded my judgment. Likely I was exhausted and eager to go home, but that was no excuse for overruling the TA who argued for redesigning Page 1. He believed we needed to accommodate a larger headline and photo and more story. Instead, I ordered a one-column headline and thumbnail photo; at least it was at the top of the page.

My decision resulted in a teachable moment I frequently referenced, including my acknowledgment that I seriously underestimated the cultural impact of the Beatles.

Dr. Aunt Barbie

My commitment to receiving my degree in May 1981 required meeting deadlines set by the Graduate School, which in turn required self-imposed deadlines. I was determined to make good use of the break between semesters. I had given my advisor the first three chapters on December 1 and had planned to write one more before I went to Wisconsin for a week at Christmas. I assume I did. I was anxious about how those chapters would be received. My desire to write an engaging biography took me to what felt like uncharted dissertation territory. For the introductory Chapter 1 laid out the historical context in traditional academic style. But Chapter 2 signaled that I was going to tell Elias Boudinot's story with anything but dry academic prose. It began:

> Oowatie walked along the Oostanaula River, contemplating the forthcoming birth of his first child. Shortly, he reached his favorite spot, away from the houses and outbuildings of his Cherokee neighbors, under a stand of chestnut trees. Oowatie was a quiet, contemplative man, and it was here that he came when he wanted to be alone, when he wanted to think. This day, with the sun high and warm, he wished to think about his child. He found much pleasure in anticipating all that he would tell his new son, for he had a premonition his first-born child would be a male. And in thinking about the things he would teach that son, he remembered what his father had taught him, and his father before him.

In the new year, I returned to "dissertation central" -- my dining room table with its manual typewriter, stack of typing paper, well-used eraser and the latest edition of Kate Turabian's "A Manual for Writers of Research Papers, Theses, and Dissertations." The floor around the table was littered with index cards color-coded to match source details with my research notes, photocopies of documents and microfilm pages, and piles of library books. I had used the same system of organizing research since my undergraduate days, but never had I needed to make sense of so much information. The system worked! When it came to footnotes and bibliography, I almost always had every bit of information I needed. When I didn't, I cursed my carelessness and added to my library follow-up list.

I pushed through my fatigue. My journal describes the week following Christmas break as "a 60-hour week at the Missourian and equal number of hours on the D— which paid off but left me unready for school. Though I muddled through and even think my lectures are improved." My birthday passed "with no wishes from family" and left me blue. The next afternoon, however, I opened my front door to Robin and George, birthday cake with candles lit while they sang "Happy Birthday." *That was the nicest thing anyone has done for me in a very long time*, I thought. Later, Sue called and we enjoyed a long talk. "So many special people in my life," I wrote. "Sometimes I fail to remember that." I certainly failed to cut myself any slack or figure out how to deal with the pressures I felt. "Something is going on in my psyche I do not grasp. I eat and drink at will and look at the numbers on the scale and almost seem determined to push them higher. At the same time I play the self-hate game in front of the mirror each a.m. It is all quite frightening and leaves me wondering once again how screwed up I really am."

And still I persevered. By February 5 I had proofread Chapter 8 and organized my notes for Chapter 9. I hoped to draft it over the weekend, although I felt a cold coming on and was registered to play in a racquetball tournament. "But there are lots of hours in between if I can resist snuggling in my warm bed and watching TV." On Valentine's Day, I amazed myself when I typed the last entry in my bibliography because I had indeed spent several days in bed battling a "bear of a cold." For most of that, I stared at the TV, the sound low so it wouldn't grate on my nerves. "You never know how good you feel until after a hangover or a cold!"

I had produced 401 pages with nine chapters, seven appendices (including Boudinot's fundraising "An Address to the Whites" and his three "Liberty of the Press" columns), nine illustrations, 840 footnotes and 155 bibliographic entries. I opened a bottle of champagne and wished for "someone here to share with." Absent that, I called Kris and Fred to announce my accomplishment. I also returned to Sarton's "Solitude" and copied a couple of passages. In the moment, I felt such kinship with her. (Eventually, I tired of what I perceived as her wallowing in self-pity. That sentence, as it spilled from my keyboard, left me thinking about pots calling kettles black.) On that long-ago night I found optimism in this passage:

> I feel a bit firmer now. It always comes back to the same necessity: go deep enough and there is a bedrock of truth, however hard. It looks as if I were "meant" to be alone, and that any hope of happiness is not meant. Am I too old to acquire the knack for happiness? Too old, perhaps, ever to take in another's life to share with mine on a permanent basis? If so, I must make do with what I have . . . and what I have is a great richness of friends and a positively ardent love of nature. Not nothing."

I, too, was optimistic that "with the D nearly out of the way, life can move on. I can 'be' again— And I wonder what that will be!?!"

There could not have been many days after that when I wasn't dealing with the dissertation. I would have been "negotiating" issues and changes with my advisor and committee members. I would have worked out the details of getting the manuscript typed to Graduate School specifications. Paper quality, acceptable margins and passing muster with the "format police" vexed every graduate student I knew. I had to identify faculty readers and persuade them to join my committee — no small task because it added to their workload with little reward. My nerves were frayed. Then I discovered that Loretta could not participate from Boston; she had to be present when I defended my work. After I learned she would be in Columbia on March 30, my advisor told me to schedule it. I was left wondering what might yet go wrong. In bed that night, "all I could think about was 'what does one do for an encore?' I feel doomed — that a hitch will develop and all of the grand plans for Dr. BFL on May 9 will be done in by some damn technicality." My anxiety was not groundless. After the scare about Loretta's presence, I got a phone call informing me I had not met the university's residency requirement. It turned out the problem was easily solved, but having to deal with it left me shaky. By that evening, I had confirmed that all my committee members could make a 9:30 a.m. defense on March 30. Everyone had their copies of the dissertation. All that remained was filling the hours until D-Day.

Work didn't keep me busy enough, at least by my standards. One enjoyable task was spending time with "a young woman" interviewing for the Journalism History position. It was the first time I was included in the rotation for a candidate's visit, which was another sign of how my faculty status was different from my first Missouri years. I remember feeling a bit awkward interviewing someone a tad older than me, but Karen List and I hit it off immediately. She had earned her doctorate from the University of Wisconsin, so we easily found common ground. By the time she left my office, I was convinced she was the perfect choice for the job and would be a welcome addition to the faculty -- and to our Journalism Women group.

Increasingly important to me was another circle of women, friends whom Joye had introduced me to and who had welcomed me into their lives. "Such a wonderful group of women— who truly care about one another— who have shared so much— who laugh so well. I feel privileged (and a bit overwhelmed) when I am allowed (word choice?) to be part of them." Their social gatherings had nurtured me through the dissertation months, and I looked forward to celebrating with them. They were among the few people who knew I was to defend on the 30th, and Joye suggested a celebration afterward at her home.

Before that, I had a spring break trip to Eau Claire planned. (I was unusually anxious about seeing Les. We had been out of touch for some time, and when I finally heard from him on March 1, his letter made no mention of my dissertation.) Remarkably, Deb (my sociology colleague and friend from Eau Claire) had landed a job teaching at Missouri. Even more remarkably, she and her husband lived a block away; we could wave to one another from our backyards. Deb and I had decided to drive north for the break that sent sane people south. We would return to Columbia on Saturday, so I would have only one nerve-wracking day before my defense on Monday. The fates had another plan for me, however, and I never got out of Columbia.

In fact, I left my bed and the house only to see a doctor. Diagnosis: probable viral pneumonia. I got sick on the 19th, and whatever it was hit fast and hard. On the 20th it seemed clear I shouldn't travel, but it wasn't until the next morning that I called to tell Deb I *couldn't* travel. "The decision not to go was difficult, but in retrospect even when I made it I don't think I realized how sick I was." A week later, which would have been our return trip, I still was "not very energetic," and my terrible cough remained. It had been "a week in which the days ran together." I had told Susan, colleague and racquetball foe, of my situation so at least one person would know I was in town. Eventually word got around, and a couple of visits and lots of calls minimized my cabin fever. I was "surprisingly content to plant myself in bed, TV on, and read my 800-page book" -- when I wasn't coughing (usually quite violently) or sleeping. I depended on others for deliveries of medicine and food. I remember that about all that tasted good was easy-to-swallow tapioca pudding.

Facing the prospect of a chest X-ray if my horrible cough did not cease, on the 29th I wrote that I had given little conscious thought to "tomorrow . . . one of the most important days in my life." Loretta called to say she was in town. Joye called to wish me luck. Our celebration had to be postponed until Wednesday, but she told me to "stop by right after you finish." *It will be good to share the joy*, I thought. The defense itself was anticlimactic. I had been counseled that a successful defense was akin to a stimulating conversation, and that is how mine transpired. Of course, there was the heart-stopping minute when my advisor instructed me to step outside so the committee could deliberate. Followed by the summons back into the room for one handshake after another, each prefaced with "Congratulations, Dr. Luebke." As of 10:30 a.m., I was official. Martha had more than once told me her professor father said "Dr." was pretentious. I tended to agree. But on March 30, 1981, "and for the next many days it will sound damn good, and I am not stopping anyone from using it." (What the rest of the world would remember of that date was the assassination attempt on President Reagan. It was the second time that momentous presidential news and momentous BFL news intersected!)

Post-defense loose ends meant I had some work left to do, but for the time being I could walk taller and grin wider. I could catch up with Loretta and share lunch with Susan. There was applause and congratulations in the Missourian newsroom; even the dean stopped in to pat me on the back. Once home, I called Martha. I called my sister. My parents called me. Deb stopped over for a drink. I had bought a bottle of champagne, and although most of it bubbled out when I opened it, I didn't care. Later, "while a healthy BFL might have demanded a more outgoing celebration, the-less-than-healthy BFL was quite content to finish a beer, rest in bed, and think ahead to sharing the joy that overflows" with friends and family. "I cannot help but feel so lucky."

I didn't feel lucky a few nights later when I learned that my fifth reader, who had been ill and missed the defense, now was hospitalized. He would not sign my papers; he said he had read only the first chapter. I fretted all weekend despite "knowing inside all would work out." And it did. The Graduate School approved adding a new reader. I just had to find someone. Joye volunteered. I hesitated; it felt like an imposition on an already-too-busy professor. She countered that she wanted to read my dissertation anyway (she certainly had listened to me talk at length about Boudinot), so I agreed -- as long as she agreed to put my dissertation at the bottom of her work pile.

Once I had made the few required corrections and added the official page of signatures certifying my work "worthy of acceptance," I ordered the bound copy required for the library and several for myself. *It's now real,* I thought. I wanted the people I named in my preface to know they had been included and to see the quote I used. I wanted them to know how much they meant to me, so I bought "some real classy notecards," carefully typed the paragraph on them, signed them and dropped them in the mail. After many paragraphs of obligatory thanks, I had concluded my preface with "The Brothers Karamazov" quote I managed to save, find (journal entry dated 3/3/74) and use as planned:

> I am particularly thankful for some special friends who, if they tired of my obsession with Elias Boudinot, never said so. It was their love and caring that supported me -- through good times and bad. To them -- Martha Allen, Jane Clark, Ruth D'Arcy, Luise Forseth, Veita Jo Hampton, Karen Hjemboe, Susan Littell Johnpeter, Robin Kennedy, Deb Lower, Joye Patterson, Rae Schilling-Smets, Susan Stiegemeyer, Loretta Williams -- I offer this: "And even if we are occupied with important things, even if we attain honor or fall into misfortune -- still

let us remember how good it was once here, when we were all to-gether, united by a good and kind feeling which made us . . . better perhaps than we are."

Robin's first words in a call after she got her card let me know that my goal had been met: "You've got a lot of class, Barb Luebke."

Now all that remained were two ceremonies and a party. And end-of-semester chores. The latter included working on The Missou-rian 25 hours out of 33 and grading editing papers "until my eyes hurt." My journal entry from May 5, titled "Snatches," records more-pleasant memories:

- ▶ How nice that on the evening after the Journalism Awards Convo-cation a student for whom I had written a recommendation called to say thanks.

- ▶ Winning two hard racquetball games— coming from behind in one. Grit.

- ▶ The pride in seeing the "D" bound. My book— my sweat— my hard work.

- ▶ An evening with the Journalism Women. An expensive meal but a good time.

I ended by copying two passages from Mary Gordon's "Final Payments," a story about self-reinvention. The first was some dialogue about lone-liness, including ". . . I've stopped thinking of myself as having missed something. I try not to look at my life as a biography. One day at a time it's very satisfying." I suspect I found that aspirational. The second pas-sage ended, "What I had done to myself was not final. . . ." I wrote **YES**, suggesting I found that line inspirational.

Graduation on May 9 was "better than I thought it could be." That's how I started one of my lengthier journal entries ever. It was written a couple of days later, when I needed "to put impressions on paper because already they begin to fade." I didn't want to lose the eupho-ria quite yet. I had experienced other moments of pure joy and exhil-aration, but nothing compared to being called forward so my advisor could drape a Ph.D. hood around my neck. It was the university's main ceremony, held in the cavernous basketball arena. From the stands, my family (*lots* of them) and friends (including Martha and Luise from Minneapolis) hooted and cheered and stomped their feet. I am sure I blushed.

The Journalism School held its own ceremony in the early afternoon in Peace Park. I got about 30 minutes at home before I had to leave for it -- time enough for champagne and a peanut butter sandwich. It had rained in the morning and most of us questioned the dean's decision to hold our ceremony outdoors, but we made it. "Students clapped for me when Taft introduced me. Sue got my pix in front of the Columns. Hugs from faculty— and lots of handshakes. Even somebody's father shook my hand. 'You were one of a kind today,' he said. I thought that was nice." [An Aside: My research for this book determined that I probably was just the seventh woman to earn a Ph.D. in journalism from the University of Missouri. The School of Journalism had awarded its first Ph.D. in 1934 but it wasn't until 1961 that a woman's name appeared among the graduates. Joye was one of two women earning degrees in 1966!]

There was another picture-taking session at my townhouse and then we got down to some heavy-duty partying. I drank copious amounts of champagne -- "out of the bottle! The guests were **super**. And the rain bothered no one." I remember George leafing through my dissertation, spotting a typo or two and teasing me mercilessly. I didn't record what time we gave in to fatigue. I do know all my beds were occupied and so was the living room floor. Sunday morning I joined an assortment of family members at their hotel for breakfast before they left for Wisconsin and Michigan and Ohio. My brother and sister-in-law came back to the house with me. We built a fire, made coffee and greeted weary guests as they awoke. Robin was a lifesaver when she arrived with doughnuts; I sent her home with a giant bowl of potato salad and a plate of raw vegetables. We spent the rest of the day lounging in front of the fire, chatting and picking at leftovers. People departed according to their timetables until it was just me and former student Joanie, who was spending another night. I was happy about that because I didn't think "I could have stood being alone— and we needed a chance to talk." I concluded that "talk— or lack of time for it— was the hardest part of the weekend."

I don't seem to have given much thought to the next stage of my life -- academic or personal -- other than to acknowledge that "it is a new beginning. Time to get on with things." I didn't think the fact that "the long-planned day is over" had sunk in yet. I figured it might take a while. But Dr. Aunt Barbie (as the nameplate from my nephews identified me) was "ready for what is ahead."

Changing Course

I was not expecting the sense of loss I felt in the days immediately following my graduation. I had been single-mindedly pursuing the Ph.D. for so long that I couldn't remember *not* doing so. I knew plenty of rungs remained on the academic ladder (publish, tenure, promotion), but surely I could rest for a bit, maybe even for the entire summer. Or not. By May 15 I already was coping with the fatigue of two nights on the copy desk with new students. All of them were graduate students from my spring editing course and so, I joked with them, "My reputation is on the line." It was like old times to go out for beers at the end of the night -- and then go home to an empty house.

A couple of days later, a new challenge presented itself at lunch with Robin and our friend John. They were planning to hike the Appalachian Trail and suggested I join them. Although I never had done anything of the sort, was again out of shape and putting on weight, I seriously considered the offer. "I think I owe myself the challenge— the physical challenge of hiking and the mental challenge that would accompany it," I wrote. I also thought time on the trail might help me sort out a recent attraction to a new acquaintance that I had acknowledged only to myself. Ultimately, I decided against hiking. A long talk with John and his realistic assessment of the challenges guided me. I told him I thought I *could* do it. But although he suggested there never is a right time for an adventure, one has to make the time, I didn't buy that. "I am physically and mentally tired from the 'D.' I don't need another strain right now. And it is important to me to spend time in Eau

412

Claire and Minneapolis." (Robin and John left the Trail after just a few days, all in torrential rain. Robin hated it and John banged up a knee.)

On the day I made that decision, the crush resolved itself when I spent time with that acquaintance and her roommate, who I had not known about until the day before. "In watching them, the special looks, the love was so obvious. And I realized that it <u>can be</u> and can be good. And in that moment I realized how much I want that! No longer [her]— but someone. I've never been so close to such affection. And now, home, I can't help but wonder at it. It seems so special— so obviously real. The hell with convention!" I had turned a corner; how sharp a turn would reveal itself in the months ahead.

May Sarton had become a touchstone, and on the Saturday in June when I was painfully sad about missing John Polk's wedding in Wisconsin, I was reading her novel "As We Are Now." In my journal I described it as "a compact story masterfully told— overflowing with thoughts worth saving." I chose this passage:

> One day she asked me, "Why didn't you marry, lovely as you are?"
> It was a hard question to answer. How could I tell her, perhaps that I am a failure, couldn't take what it would have cost to give up an authentic being, myself, to take in the stranger? That I failed because I was afraid of losing myself when in fact I might have grown through sharing an equality with another human being. And yet . . . do I really regret not marrying? No, to be quite honest, <u>no</u>.

The following weekend promised to be better, if only because a brief trip to St. Louis for a baseball game on Sunday would be my first time out of Columbia since Christmas. Unfortunately, Major League Baseball went on strike that Friday so Sue, Charlie and I had to make our own fun. We never had difficulty with that. What made the weekend unforgettable, however, was Midge breaking down on my return drive on Monday. I was about 60 miles from home. Stranded on the shoulder of Interstate 70, I was frantically considering my options when a U-Haul truck pulled over and stopped in front of me. The driver offered me a ride to the next service station. Without thinking, I said yes and hopped into the front seat. He talked about how he was moving, was an avid hunter, had all his guns with him. I tried not to panic. Before long,

I saw the sign for an exit and was relieved when he took it. I quickly jumped out of the truck, told him there was no need to wait for me to arrange to have Midge towed, and headed inside the station. All I could think about as I sat there was how stupid I had been. How I had forgotten everything from my long-ago series about self-defense for women. I vowed never again to make myself vulnerable like that.

It took a few weeks to get my car repaired. I wrote more than once about how lucky I was to have friends willing to ferry me about. And how I hated being dependent. I was ready "in my head" to buy a new car but was determined "to go at it intelligently," not impulsively as I had done when I bought the MG. I was more concerned about another round of people moving out of my life. Susan left for a new job in Kansas City. Not only had we lost one of our J-Women, but I lost a valued friend, racquetball partner and the comfort that came from "at 11:55 being able to find someone to lunch with." Kay, my very capable teaching assistant— who had stayed at my house when I went to St. Louis so she would have quiet and cool to study for her comprehensive exams— was off to Washington, D.C., for her master's project. I had not converted her from reporting to editing, and she was genuinely surprised that I had recommended an A+ for her. She had set the bar high for my future TAs. Another student with whom I had become friends was off to do her master's project in Taiwan. My proficient copy desk crew left when their summer session ended in late June, about the same time Robin headed out for the Appalachian Trail. "Why must there be comings and goings in our lives?" I wondered, not for the first time.

I was staying put -- for several days at least. "Vacation. How good it feels. My body is reacting by sleeping— an unbelievable amount. It is clear to me how tired I really am." Yet winding down was not easy. I had "this need to be busy" and plugged away at writing query letters hoping to interest a publisher in a Boudinot book. That's what most new graduates do to get mileage out of their dissertations, and I was confident because the time seemed right for my topic. I also spent time in the library, gathering information for one of two articles I wanted to write while in Colorado. In between, my friend/colleague/neighbor Deb and I regularly enjoyed sun and beers at nearby Cedar Lake.

Once again the plan was for me to meet Martha in Minneapolis;

we would tuck ourselves into her Karmann Ghia for the drive west. I was "really spooked" about making any trip in Midge. Although I knew it was silly to wish for assurances my car was OK, I wasn't ready to be stranded again. "If Midge behaves it will be a marvelous trip," I wrote in anticipation of time in Eau Claire before joining Martha. I was relieved that Midge behaved; time with Les and Ruth Anne renewed me. Our trip across the unbearably hot Plains rewarded Martha and me with crisp mountain air. I always appreciated how well I usually slept at Arapaho Ranch -- never more so than that summer. In part it was "a sign of the fatigue that goes so deep." In part it was "the beer being consumed in quantity." It was comfortable returning to our cabin, where I quickly found myself "doing some soul searching— or at least trying." That was prompted by a visit from my brother and his then-wife, who lived a few hours away at Rabbit Ears Pass in north central Colorado. I wrote that it was "a good visit— what I remember of it."

> [That was] the spooky part. Got damn drunk. I don't remember leaving the restaurant, where I had treated to dinner, and anything after. Never had a blackout so extensive. . . . I am more than a little afraid this has gotten out of hand. Have not had alcohol for 48 hours— and that may be the longest stretch of the summer. I don't think there is any turning back this time.
>
> So I sit by Boulder Creek and watch the water and contemplate. What will it take to effect the "click" of two autumns ago, when I was in a similar state and got myself squared around? Only now to have backslid almost completely. I don't want to go any farther. I really don't.

"Restless" doesn't appear in any of my journal entries written that week, but in rereading them it was the word that came immediately to mind. There was physical restlessness, at odds with the fatigue I felt. I wrote that "this certainly will have been a peculiar month off, with far too much driving" even as I decided to drive to spend another day with my brother. There was intellectual restlessness, if you will, that insisted I work on my writing projects even though without a keyboard I found it difficult to think and more difficult to write. Nonetheless, I kept at it. Finally, there was mental restlessness evident in what I characterized as "serious introspection."

I tried to stay in the moment, and the routines Martha and I had established during our previous Colorado stays were reassuring. Coffee and yesterday's newspapers in the morning along with breakfast fare hardly ever eaten at home: "bacon (rather, Sizzlean), eggs and bread (too lazy to light the oven to broil toast)." Classical music on a Denver radio station. Walks. I wrote of spotting a new color of lily and took delight in hearing a bird I could not identify. Once, in between rain showers, Martha and I took a walk "for some serious flower identification. At least she is serious. I look for new varieties but get impatient with the work of identifying. So I just poke around and try hard to really see the beauty all around me."

I never seemed to get impatient reading, even when I found a book to be poorly written. That was true of "The Killing of Karen Silkwood." What kept me going was that I found the story intriguing, the police dumb and the Kerr McGee workers naïve. "The machinations are incredible, though I guess not surprising. Who among us is spying for whom?" Immediately after finishing it, I started a book of Martha's, written by a young St. Paul, Minnesota, woman. From the first paragraph, I found the writing in "A Romantic Education" to be "so much better than Silkwood." But it was reading two "powerful books" in less than 24 hours that "overwhelmed my sensibilities." The first was Tillie Olson's "Yonnondio," written in the 1930s and first published in 1974. I found her story about the life of a 1920s working-class family "a quick read; skillful even though 'unfinished.'" I was delighted Deb had loaned it to me and was eager to learn about the significance of the poem from which the title came. (Today Google made that easy.)

The second powerful book I referred to was Sarton's "The Small Room." I had come to value her fiction because she wrote "so positively about women— they are central— and the love between and among them is real and beautiful." Here her main characters were students and teachers, and so it was no surprise the book hit close to home. I marked several passages and copied a few into my journal. "A lot more, too long to record" left me exclaiming *Yes!* in my marginal notes. Among the copied are these:

"Is there a life more riddled with self-doubt than that of a woman professor, I wonder?" she asked the evening air.

". . . what people will not understand about our profession as teachers," she said, walking up and down the length of the room, "is that it takes the marrow out of your bones, and something or other has to put it back."

The relationship between teacher and students "is as various, as unpredictable as a love affair."

. . . she wondered [if this is] what you take on if you chose to be a teacher— this, the care of souls.

After a night when my introspection "seemed reflected in dreams that woke me several times, which hardly ever happens," I wondered if the alcohol "being cleansed from my system" explained why. I had come close to drinking a couple of times, but the beers had remained in the refrigerator and I swilled diet soda. "Sure isn't always easy," I wrote. How then to explain that a couple of days later, after my first-ever sober week in Colorado, I was drinking a beer in my room at the Best Western in Canistota, South Dakota? I was on my way to Minneapolis, then perhaps Eau Claire; I had not decided. (I don't remember the details of why I was alone for the return trip. I do know I had put in for a cabin for two weeks in 1982.) The motel's postcard promised "complete rest in a quiet small town," to which I responded, *And ain't it the truth!* I regretted having to send Martha's book home with her; I had read only about a third of it. I made a note about the author quoting "someone who quoted Virginia Woolf: 'Observe perpetually.' Isn't that what a journalist is all about?" I couldn't wait to buy my own copy.

I may have done so during the days I spent with Luise in Minneapolis. I called them "the best days of the month except for those in the mountains." While Luise worked, I enjoyed quiet hours of reading and watching television. In the evenings, there was "talk, racquetball, walks and good food. Me able to articulate what I'd been thinking about. How I'd decided I was ready for some counseling, to be approached as a growth experience." As it turned out, that would not happen for several years. I did stop briefly in Eau Claire, including a short visit to the Journalism Department, after which I thought about how glad I was that I had gotten out. From there I drove to La Crosse, where I enjoyed lunch with David Offer, the Tribune's managing editor. A boost to my ego because he once more tried his best to hire me. Had I known about the difficult months ahead for the J-School, I might have been tempted.

The recession that had crippled the U.S. economy at the beginning of 1980 got a second wind by July 1981 (and continued through most of 1982). The university had cut budgets, frozen hiring and signaled tiny pay raises. Looking ahead to more of the same for the 1981-82 academic year, the chancellor was quoted in The Missourian as saying faculty should be encouraged by the "psychological income" teaching brings. Ha! I returned from vacation to learn that my fall schedule had been changed. "The Budget Crunch hits the copy desk! Along with no raises and no bonuses," I wrote. Perhaps I was channeling the chancellor when, the night before the start of classes, I wrote: "And tomorrow it all begins in earnest— and before we know it, it will be December. The students, we hope, will be a bit more versed in it all and we teachers will have learned a bit, too. And will remain committed to each other."

Snapshots

My Ph.D. hooding.

At the Journalism School ceremony with colleagues Joye Patterson and Bob Humphreys (my landlord).

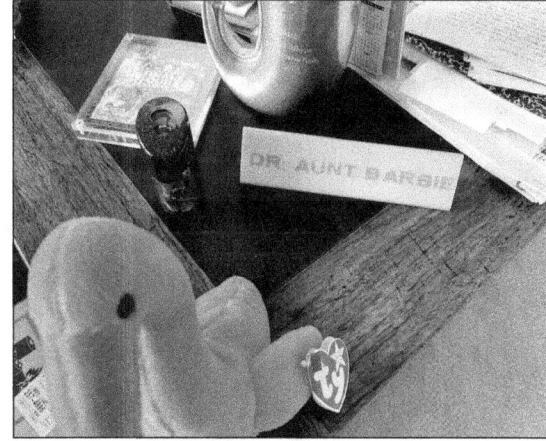

The Dr. Biffle doll and Dr. Aunt Barbie nameplate are treasured mementos.

Celebrating with champagne and posing for one of many photos with family.

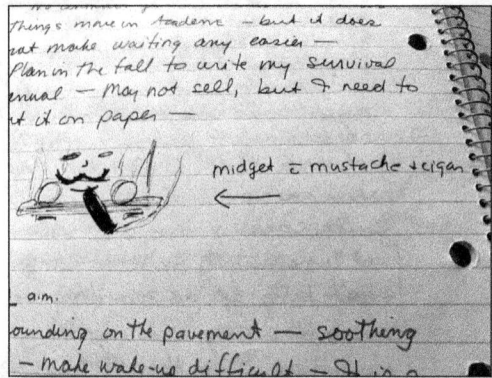

things move in tandem — but it does
not make waiting any easier —
Plan in the fall to write my survival
manual — May not sell, but I need to
get it on paper —

midget c̄ mustache + cigar ←

a.m.
...ounding on the pavement — soothing
— made wake-up difficult — ...

A journal reference to the "survival manual"
I never wrote.

Reading the Missourian and enjoying the sunshine
through my patio doors.

CHAPTER 21

The Power of Words

With the Ph.D. behind me, I approached the new academic year quite differently. "Not much fazes me anymore," I wrote at the end of the first week. My two nights overseeing the copy desk had gone fairly well. I was excited to be teaching Women and the Media along with a section of Introduction to Editing for graduate students. The combination of skills and conceptual courses was my yin and yang. Despite the daunting economic situation, I felt confident enough about my future to consider buying a condominium. I did not, but it was the first time I even entertained the idea of home ownership.

Because I no longer needed every nonworking minute for research and writing, I was able to regularly socialize with colleagues and friends. As I had hoped, Karen List was hired. "How exciting that she is here!" I liked her more each time we talked, and it didn't surprise me that she fit right in with the Journalism Women. Joye and I took her to lunch shortly after classes began, and I suggested she join us a couple of afternoons later to meet the new Women's Studies director at an open house. My newsroom experiences, longtime interest in media stereotyping, and developing commitment to studying women and the media brought me to Women's Studies. The connections with feminists that I began to make at the open house reverberated throughout the rest of my career.

Several journal entries reminded me how woman-centered my world had become. Oh, I managed quite nicely in the male-dominated Missourian newsroom. I was a veteran editor, after all, one who didn't hesitate to call out deadline-challenged city editors or poky reporters.

Although I had become increasingly conscious of the J-School's sexism I remained reluctant to confront it. (When a male colleague asked me at lunch one day, "Will you ever get married?" I was so startled I just stammered, "I don't know; probably not.") It was easier to complain when the Journalism Women got around to the topic, which was whenever we gathered. My social life, too, primarily revolved around female friends. After an early fall get-together of eight of us, I wrote: "How do you write about the good feeling of being among a special group of friends who make you laugh harder than any other people— and isn't that quite a gift." Once, after being with them, I observed "how full my cup is— how special I feel."

Nonetheless, something (someone?) was missing in my life. One night, as I tossed and turned "from 1:30 until forever, it seemed," a thought "came to me and got turned over and over in my mind: Sometimes I desperately need to be held— and to hold!" Completing my dissertation had kept such feelings mostly at bay; there simply was no space for someone else. Now I had begun again to feel a strong need for "embracing— nothing more— just that physical closeness." I made do with the thoughts I put into words and shared only with my journal. "I live quite nicely in the fantasies of my mind," I wrote to end an entry.

Just one day later, I was jolted to my core by words not of my writing: "Barb Luebke is a militant, feminist and, oops, I almost forgot, lesbian." This sentence was among the graffiti in the women's restroom near the newsroom. (Fast-forward to today and it would have been a social-media post, I suspect.) I saw it for the first time on September 10, 1981; I didn't know how long it had been there. I had no choice but to compose myself and return to my office. Thankfully, it was a Thursday and I did not have to spend the night on the copy desk. I preserved the encounter with the graffiti in my journal and noted:

> It has thrown me for quite a loop. I really don't know what to think— who would have written it or why. And how should I react/ respond. That it may be entirely true is neither here nor there. Even if I don't read it as an insult (and I'm just not sure) how is it being read by the others who will see it?
>
> This really has gotten me— definitely am, in Luise's terminology, obsessing on it. And I don't know where to turn.

I had to work the desk on Friday. I avoided that restroom until the evening, when there was no other option. I noticed that it appeared someone had attempted unsuccessfully to rub out the graffiti (which never occurred to me to do). I took some consolation in that but remained depressed about the episode. Each time I thought about telephoning a friend, I couldn't bring myself to do so. I feared how each might respond. I couldn't imagine myself saying what I thought, that "I'm not at all sure I consider it an insult— but I know how many people will see it— and how it will raise questions, etc." *Or am I getting truly paranoid?*

The burden of my mental anguish spilled over into Saturday. It was the first home football game; I didn't want "to deny myself the things I enjoy" and yet I felt "really low. Wanting to be part of pregame festivities— to <u>share</u> in the event." Instead breakfast was beer and an apple fritter! I could have picnicked with Robin and George and their friends "but I would have felt like an intruder." I didn't write anything more about the weekend. More likely than not a hangover was involved. And lots more ruminating.

Monday brought another night on the copy desk. I soldiered on. I caught an error in a 48-point headline and several errors in copy, which I happily had time to explain (that wasn't always the case). We made deadline. Still, I was "plagued by the graffiti" and feared depression. I could tell "by my sighs— the indecision— the listlessness." I didn't want to continue dwelling on the situation, but I needed to figure out the why. Driving home that night "it struck me that perhaps it is the obvious lack of respect that is most injurious. Of all things from students, [respect] is most important. I know I am liked by many, and I am glad. But I would hope <u>all</u> would/could respect me— and I think that is in jeopardy."

My healing began on Wednesday when I met Robin for our weekly lunch. I was determined to share what had happened and I haltingly managed to do so. I was reassured that she did not think my preoccupation with the graffiti was unhealthy. Indeed, she suggested I probably wouldn't be able to forget the incident at least until the semester was over because I would continue to wonder which student was responsible. That certainly had been the case so far. What I chose not to share with Robin was my own "unsureness about my sexuality." I wrote that I thought I *could* share "but I really am not there yet." I finished the entry this way: "I don't think it is sex— but I am drawn to certain women intellectually and emotionally. Even my strong fantasy life does not involve sex."

I chased away more stress with racquetball matches on Thursday. Dinner with Joye followed, and it was a relief to talk with her about the events of the past week. Joye's response was different from Robin's. For one thing, she offered to erase the graffiti, but I would not tell her where it was. More importantly, she told me that what mattered was, "You know who you are. And you know you are a good teacher." I have carried those affirming words with me ever since, and even in that moment could begin to see a way forward.

> I made it clear, I think, that I did not take it as an insult (and I don't). I didn't perceive shock on her part (now I wonder what was going through her mind as I unwound)— at least not shock about what I said but surely anger and shock that I should have to go through this. She made it clear that I must realize this is a person(s) lashing out at me— obviously angry and obviously not knowing any other way to confront me.

There was one more person I needed to share with: Luise. I came home from class the night of September 22 ready to call her. "Her perspective, her knowledge of me, where I have been and am and how I have struggled to get here. For some reason the time was right (ripe?) to talk." I wasn't disappointed. Hers was a perspective of action. "Erase it. Write some absurd response. But DO!" I wasn't sure about that but did see how correct she was in asserting that it was the *old* me that hadn't done anything. My journal entry reminded me it was only to Luise that I said of the graffiti, "It just might be true. So what." It was a "line of thinking I must pursue. [What is it that] allows me to think of the possibility of being a lesbian but not able to talk about it."

During the many twists and turns of my conversation with Luise, I remembered that I had failed to record a line from the latest Sarton journal I had begun reading. I had jotted Joye a note to thank her for dinner and lending me the book, and asked, "Did you jog this morning in the mist and see the sun come up? Beautiful." I had, and I thought of

Sarton saying of herself: "You are well and your depth is there, very easy to touch and in some way exposed and unguarded." *Yes. I am.* Sarton by then had captured my heart. "Here is a woman I could love, I think— a woman I do love— admire— respect at a distance. What a role model she is for living alone— for loving whomever— for growing old. And such a writer." I had yet to read any of her poetry, and when I eventually did I never understood why she considered herself a poet above all else. But "as a journal-ist, I rate her superb— and so brave to be so honest."

[An aside: I always have been a bit uncomfortable when reading another person's copy of a book. To come across someone's marginal notes or underlining is like overhearing a conversation. Were you meant to or was it accidental — and what does it mean? I long to mark up the book myself and return it saying, *See, here's where I found particular meaning.* I now do much of my reading on a Kindle, where the underlining allowed by the technology is that of anonymous readers. The intimate connection I felt with shared books from Les, Joye, Sue and a few others is no more. I am left to muse over whether someone will ask what prompted my Kindle underlinings.]

[Another aside: That Christmas, Joye's gift was "The Small Room," the novel that had made such an impression on me in Colorado. If I did not realize it at the time, when I reread the book recently it was clear to me how deliberate Joye had been in choosing it. More than once I again found my thoughts echoed in a main character's words: "I teach for the singular, for the exceptional. . . . And you forget . . . that teaching is only half my life; my work is still . . . quite extraordinarily absorbing." And more than once I recognized that my struggles mirrored those of the novel's young teacher, Lucy.]

I don't want to leave September without mentioning the juxtaposition of my activities on its last weekend. Friday night included a Holly Near concert with Robin and George; Saturday was football. The timeline on Near's website states that she was touring that year "to save Women's Studies programs." (I don't think I was familiar yet with the concept of "women's music"; I certainly didn't know it would become important in my life.) It was also the year Near was featured in People magazine, "perhaps the first out lesbian to be interviewed in a popular 'supermarket' magazine." I wrote of her, "What a voice!" I described "one real touching moment" when she had the audience singing along to "We Are a Gentle Angry People." Before the refrain "We are gay and lesbian people," she commented how it might be difficult for some audience members to sing that. "But you never know who's sitting next to you." Robin squeezed my arm, and we shared our own private moment.

Three weeks after I first saw the graffiti, I wrote that "obviously I am still bothered. No longer obsessed, but at odd times it will flash into my mind. And of course I wonder— not so much any more about who wrote it but of its truth." Two weeks later I saw that someone had "Flair-ed it out." The more I relearned about that semester, the more I realized how much it represented the Missouri experiences I have carried with me for the last 40-plus years. I *endured* the painful times, but along with certain people it is the many important life- and career-affirming experiences that I have *cherished*.

My appreciation for the natural world blossomed in central Missouri during hikes and quarry swims and picnics along the Missouri River and elsewhere. Drives along back roads and visits to small towns near and far. Always with question-ladened conversations that inevitably led to *I wonder.* . . . musings. We -- the group of women of varied professions I so enjoyed -- all were curious, well read and intellectually engaged. And sometimes incredibly silly. I remember saying once how great it would be to have an encyclopedia with us at all times to get instant answers to our questions. I often think about Joye and Liz and Ruth and others and what they would make of Siri and Google.

It was in that post-Ph.D.-earned fall that I found myself writing more melodically, the kind of creative thoughts that had been rare for too long. For example:

> Fall has arrived with the new month— that <u>crisp</u> feeling early in the morning lingers all day. Tonight's sky so dark, the stars so clearly defined and the sliver of moon. And this morning, before actual sunrise, the clouds and their colors were so magnificent. Sometimes when I go out to get the paper (barefoot but dressed) I am overwhelmed by the beauty of the early day.

One Saturday I wrote about grading papers, listening to a football game and watching "the sky through my northern and southern windows.

Such contrast there was as the storms moved across and around. I find a new pleasure in observing nature. I see more. Wonder why?" Rereading that reminded me of when I began to be captivated by light and shadows.

At last I seemed to be living an adult life. My social circle was larger than it ever had been. Weekend weariness was often ignored to enjoy time out with friends, some of whom were colleagues I saw daily. One such Friday, for example, began with Karen List and I sharing a beer before being joined by her husband, Jay, and Robin and George. Pizza and more beer followed before Robin and I rushed off to a movie. Saturday was "cleaning and shopping and laundry— and napping." I felt a cold coming on and was in bed by 9. Sunday morning was racquetball with Joye (I was teaching her the game) followed by brunch. She shared an extra ticket for a wine and cheese fundraiser for the "can ban" folks that afternoon. I was "feeling pretty ugh" but the "new me" went anyway. It was a dud; I didn't bother staying long. But it sure beat the old days of being home alone on my couch watching TV and drinking beer.

My weekday pace was hectic -- no surprise there. My achy throat and hacking cough reminded me of my bout with pneumonia. I hoped I was wrong about it signaling another; I didn't have time to be sick. In addition to my usual newsroom and classroom responsibilities, I was under the gun to finish the new Missourian Manual for students and faculty. How it had grown since I first used it in 1974. I had not found a publisher for my dissertation, but that week received the good news that Grassroots Editor was going to publish the article I began writing in Colorado. In "Perils of Publishing," I wrote about Elias Boudinot's experiences as a "frontier editor." I also was advising my first master's thesis and serving on the committees for a couple of others.

I finally saw a doctor midweek (which proves just how miserable I was); he diagnosed bronchitis. The worst seemed to be over, he said, but added that since my pneumonia I was susceptible. He recommended lots of sleep. All I could say was, "Ugh." I muddled through the week "but was not in good form at all." I had agreed to meet with Liz's class at Stephens College (the second oldest women's college in the United States) on Friday. "How career-oriented/concerned they were. They asked good questions." I probably should have gone home to bed afterward; instead I ended up "with quite a tableful" of women for beer and shrimp at a favorite restaurant. "A good unwinding. Some good talk. Lots of laughter. I am curious as I come more into contact with this community of single women, who obviously are committed in life-style to 'partners.' Curious, I guess, about how they met the 'other'—because I like what I see and wonder if that is for me. Or am I a loner?"

Our conversations that evening might have included the assassi-nation earlier in the week of Anwar Sadat. Although I spent my days immersed in the news, I seldom wrote about it in my journal. This time I did. I called the murder of the Egyptian president "another shock to the sensibilities." I noted that he was being described most often in news reports "as a man of peace fallen victim to his struggles to unite Egyptians and Israelis. How crazy the world— and how scary." I also referenced one of my favorite writers, Ellen Goodman, whose column cited a poll showing 68 percent of us expect a war in the years ahead. "God help us!" Given the rarity of such entries, I was surprised to find another just a few days later. More surprised by its content, where I questioned my news judgment:

> What a peculiar news day. None. And again we wait for something local that really does not pan out. I struggle about the play on an ERA [Equal Rights Amendment] story and use of photo. I had not even pegged it for Page 1. DM did. I finally made choice to also use the wire photo with it. But certainly did stop to question my "why."

An encounter earlier in the day was on my mind, I suspect. At the end of a conference with one of my Editing graduate students, she said she had one last question -- on a personal note. Then she asked if I were a feminist. She said I came across as such. My first thought was one of concern because "I didn't want politics to interfere with my credibil-ity." Quickly I decided "that it was no problem. I am a feminist and I plan to continue being vocal." I understood the student to be admon-ishing me "to keep doing whatever for equality in the newsroom."

During these weeks, I found little time to read. When I could, I nibbled on a Sarton whose title I did not record. It clearly had a hold on me; I copied several passages into an unusually long journal entry. "And now the fragments of newsprint that marked the pages are gone.

It is not an easy book to return." Sarton seems to have given me permission to be OK with my life. I wrote that "for a brief moment, driving to work, a real feeling of contentment . . . swept over me. I wonder why— because there remain great gaps that I know work can't fulfill." In Sarton's words: "What I have chosen to do here is difficult, but I want to do it. Most of the time I am happy doing it. But there is no doubt that one pays a price in panic for extreme solitude. . . ." Sarton was mourning lost love. I was not, but I could identify with the struggle she described:

> . . . I am beginning a new phase. Perhaps one must always feel absolutely naked and abandoned and desolate to be ready for the inner world to open again. Perhaps one has to dare that. This morning I feel better for having let the woe in, for admitting what I have tried for weeks to admit— loneliness like starvation.

The graffiti certainly had left me feeling that naked vulnerability. But over time I had become convinced that I knew who its author had been. "That student who today commented on some women being forced from the local pool hall/beer joint and told to 'go drink at a queer bar.'" Apparently the women were planning a protest meeting, and that student "out of nowhere said to me, 'They want you to come.' Damn. They have a right to be angry and I share their anger!" I did not name the student I suspected. I wonder why. I don't know if I attended the meeting.

I regularly attended plenty of other meetings. Most involved the Journalism School, but I also chose to be involved in Women's Studies and now and then found myself at a university-wide assembly. It was the price of being a responsible faculty member, I believed. Yes, the discussions/debates could stretch beyond one's tolerance for sitting. Yes, people could be incredibly petty, myopic and self-important. But it was especially useful to know what was going on during this period of reduced resources. And a lot was going on in the Journalism School.

Dean Roy Fisher had told the faculty in late September that he planned to retire effective August 1982 (news I did not record in my journal). I don't remember there being a lot of surprise. He was in his tenth year as dean and more than a few of us were tired of his leadership style. He and the chancellor (a woman) were often at odds, as I recall. His "routine evaluation" had been delayed until he decided if he would seek reappointment, and many believed he was concerned the evaluation would not be positive.

My own standing among the faculty was going well. Having Ph.D. after my name (and assistant professor in front of it) brought a new kind of respect, it seemed to me. I served on the Graduate Studies Committee and the Editorial Department's Curriculum Committee. No longer was I valued just for my journalistic prowess; I was proving my mettle as an academic. Though I wasn't always convinced of that. When I was appointed to a subcommittee to study "our foreign student situation," I wrote that "[the chair] is either testing me or is impressed with what he has seen so far." After I was elected chair of the Editorial Advisory Committee (a position I would hold for three years) I called it "more or less by default." The specifics about that committee's work have faded from memory; my journal did anticipate its significant workload, on top of the rest of my workload. I managed to write a short essay on excellence for the school's newsletter, which garnered "positive comments from a couple students, including one face I know but not name." I did worry about my expectations for student success, as I wrote before returning Editing midterms. "Even when I feel I have lowered my standards a tad I find few attaining the level of performance I seek. Frustrating for them, I am sure. But do they know how it frustrates me?!"

Typically, as the semester wore on I had less and less time for my journal. On the last Monday of October I was home and in bed by 11:30, "a first for the semester." It had been a "smooth, slow night" on the copy desk. Daryl was handling my class Tuesday morning and I relished not having to rush to the office. I wrote a catch-up entry (often, I did my writing in bed after work). Of note was my elation at having seen the "EXQUISITE!" Dance Theater of Harlem, my first professional dance performance (the second would not come until 2019!). The entry continued with an almost breathless accounting of the week.

▶ My brother-in-law called from Eau Claire with news that Elwood Karwand, still the Journalism Department chair, was being investigated for skimming Spectator funds.

- My former colleague David called with the same news. "We're looking for a chairman with a Ph.D.," he said. To which I responded, "You're looking in the wrong place."

- Les Polk did *not* call. "That no longer strikes me as curious. Nor do I much care. I made my amends this summer. I can't hold up the relationship alone."

- I chaired my first Advisory Committee meeting (no details). "Then came home to put antifreeze in Midge in anticipation of 24 degrees. Did it all myself and quite proud of the effort."

- I was at the office by 7:30 a.m. on Friday. When I ran into Karen, we made plans for lunch. By noon, my good mood had disappeared. I would have to do the nightshift on the copy desk because the instructor was ill. I went 16 hours with less than an hour away from an editing terminal. I never did get in my office to work "and it proved the downfall of my weekend."

- Saturday I was up early for the noon kickoff of Missouri vs. Nebraska. Tigers lost 6-0; "great game." No postgame socializing for me; I hurried home to grade papers and eat leftovers. It was the night to set clocks back an hour, "so I in effect go to bed at 7:30 and don't wake up until 8:30 Sunday!" I spent a long day at the office working on the Manual before a chili-in-front-of-the-fire dinner with Robin. By 7 we both were yawning; I was home in bed by 7:30 and asleep before 9.

A week later, sitting in front of my own first fire of the season, I wrote there was no reason to recount the days since my last entry because "they've been much like the previous 'runs' of nights home only to sleep. With a few good moments."

One of those good moments had been a call from a one-time graduate assistant who was looking for "new stars" to fill an opening at the Fort Worth Star-Telegram. I enthusiastically told him about my recent teaching assistant Kay, who was finishing her master's degree at our Washington, D.C., reporting program. Amazingly, a bit later she called to catch up, having received a letter from me. Brian, a favorite student from Eau Claire, regularly wrote for advice and to share gossip and department news, which now included updates on the Karwand situation. Eventually he was charged with stealing at least $26,205 in Spectator advertising revenue since about 1977. His three-year sentence for felony theft was stayed and he was placed on five years' probation. The judge cited the many letters of support, including from his peers and past and current students. I was not among them. I shared my shock and dismay with a Spectator reporter who contacted me for comment. I couldn't get past the fact that "this was the man who taught us ethics."

I couldn't help being curious about which, if any, students in my current classes might join those who stayed in touch. Classroom ties were different from my 1970s newsroom ties. Women and Media included undergraduate and graduate students (maybe even a non-journalism-major). One of those undergrads had talked me into allowing her to take my graduate editing course because of a scheduling conflict. P had talked to me a couple times about a "personal upheaval"; I did a lot of listening and what I termed "head-patting." P reminded me of my early Missouri experiences, I realized, when I was eager "to extend myself to students who bother to seek me out." Put another way, I wanted to be needed and here was someone whose actions spoke volumes about needing *me*. She also reminded me of my undergraduate self (good mind, curious, lots of insecurities). When late in the semester she said, "I wish you weren't my teacher so we could be friends," I likely was thinking of my relationship with Les when I responded, "The two do not have to be mutually exclusive."

Just as a select few had experienced meaningful time with Les outside the classroom, some of my Women and Media students began joining me to continue talking after class ended. By late in the semester, we regularly adjourned to The Heidelberg, a campus restaurant/ watering hole. I can easily picture us seated in a booth or at a big round table. If we had a guest speaker, she usually joined us. Discussions were wide-ranging -- and not always serious. It was good to hear students laugh. I'm sure my fretting over my wardrobe for the Kappa Tau Alpha initiation and dinner brought chuckles as I described my plan for "dress day." The idea of "skirting it" -- going to work in something other than slacks -- was anxiety provoking *and* a recognition of what then was considered "suitable" attire for a professional woman.

One topic I couldn't share with students were the repercussions as I sensed myself "growing more and more 'feminist' in my approach to my job." It left me feeling that I was in a "precarious position." Two episodes stand out. The first occurred as Robin and I were discussing a story headlined "Is there life in Boonville if you are young, single and female?" We didn't understand why the story was only about females. I didn't want "to call wolf too often," however, and had not planned to raise objections to the story. But when Daryl overheard us talking as he passed my office I couldn't resist. He didn't see our point; we agreed to disagree. A couple of days later I wrote about "a bit of a reprimand from Daryl about my continual 'strident' effort to point out our 'sexist mistakes.' He doesn't want me to stop but [thinks I should] point it out to faculty first, then maybe [raise] in class." His chastisement left me speechless. Later I wrote that "I do feel myself continuing to be radicalized. And this sure adds to it." An understatement, to be sure.

It is surprising that I had time to bring up *any* issues of substance. Yet again I was living on caffeine and adrenaline because I was determined to meet my December 1 deadline to finish the Missourian Manual. It was frustrating to have to browbeat colleagues to complete their sections. Without that work, I could not edit, assemble and oversee production. (I was beyond thankful that a student had volunteered to help with pasteup.) Fatigue brought on by too many 16-hour days caught up with me. I was tired of my brain going 100 miles an hour from the moment I woke up (always too early). I experimented with not having alcohol to see if I could sleep through the night. I didn't. One morning it took me just 22 minutes to get up and out of the house (at 7:34). I picked up a biscuit and large coffee from Hardee's. The next thing I knew it was 9:30 p.m. and I was finally home.

I missed time for myself (although the forced break from being self-absorbed with finding my "authentic self" was probably good for me). I missed spending time with Joye, bogged down in her own work, and talking with Karen, out sick for days. I told Robin that I felt "like I'm on the brink and if someone would come up behind me and yell 'boo' I'd go over." Just when I didn't think I could handle another thing, I got a note from George (now the Editorial Department chairman) informing me I had been recommended for a midyear raise. And by the way, he needed my updated *vita* the next morning! He got it. George had explained his process for recommending raises during a faculty meeting I had described as difficult. I wrote that "I admire/envy his strengths— wisdom— ability to do the hard things." I only wished he could have given me a bit more time.

I also needed a bit more time to polish the Manual and approve it for printing. I missed my deadline by three days. I was OK with that. I'm sure my attitude was helped by sharing an enjoyable Thanksgiving with Joye and her longtime friends from Memphis. (I remember word games and being lovingly teased and so much laughter.) On Saturday Robin and I had a leisurely lunch, then she came over and sewed while I baked cookies and breads and made candy for my holiday open house. On my first Sunday at home in six weeks I addressed the envelopes for my Christmas cards and wrote a dozen of them. When I returned to campus on Monday, I was ready to polish off the Manual. I was ready for the end of another semester. I looked forward to no longer being "teacher" to a couple of students with whom I felt a special connection, including P. I wasn't ready for her six one-syllable words: "I have a crush on you."

CHAPTER 22

What Might Have Been

Who hasn't looked back on her life and wondered how different it might have been -- if only? P's simple declarative sentence on December 15, 1981, turned my world upside down and inside out. When I wrote about it, I was thankful to have been sober when she spoke it. My handwritten description of the encounter filled both sides and a margin of a sheet from a legal pad. (I had not gotten around to buying a new journal.) After recording a bit of conversation, I parenthetically added "or words to that effect; my mind's dialogue recorder wasn't in gear. I was trying to focus on her and my feelings simultaneously and not doing too well at it."

I was a few weeks shy of turning 33; she had just turned 21. I was a professor; she was one day removed from being my student. My professional life had never felt more settled, even as I continued to try to sort out personal identity. She was in turmoil over her parents' divorce, a guy who wanted to sleep with her, and uncertainty about her future. Today I understand; then I acted impulsively (much as I had done with car-buying and job-changing). The details of the next days-months-years -- saved in journals with excruciating specificity -- are not important. Suffice it to say that on December 22, I committed these words to paper: "I am, quite simply, head-over-heels in love— and it is being returned. And how wonderful and easy and natural it has felt." Suffice it so say that reckoning with that part of my history revealed incredible highs and agonizing lows from start to finish. And it painfully reminded me that the moral compass I take pride in is not infallible.

I found a piece of paper addressed Dear P and a scribbled note; I think it was the draft of an inscription for a book I gave her that first Christmas.

> I should like to write something so originally clever it would bring to your face that radiant smile I see constantly in my mind's eye. Failing that, I quote [from the text on a serigraf by] the artist Corita Kent: "... I am coming alive, I am living now. I am beginning to feel that love is the most powerful force in the world. You provided the sunshine. There is a song on the radio which says I have been waiting so long to be where I am going in the sunshine of your love."

Forbidden love. Such a cliché. May-December romance. Such a cliché. First love and all its accompanying firsts. Such a cliché. Eventual heartbreak. Such a cliché. Yet the positive personal pieces of my 34 months with P live on in friendships and all that I learned (new music, new poets, new authors and so much more) from some amazing young lesbians (and a few older ones, too). And especially in the life I have lived since. The world was less hospitable back then. I never felt closeted, but I lived secretly. Today I can write openly about my life because of lessons I learned. I can continue telling my story without shame, without the anger I hung onto for decades.

Nonetheless, when taking notes for this book I wrote that "my stomach churned after reading" those late-December 1981 entries. *How did I let myself do that?! I am embarrassed, appalled.* Before I began this chapter, before I determined what I would share, I endured an agonizing struggle to understand. I needed to forgive myself all over again for the decision I wish I never had made. Then, just when I thought I had worked through its repercussions, I had another "aha" moment. For the first time I understood that the self-hate I frequently wrote about had been misdirected. If I were to hate anybody it was someone in my buried past. On that fall Sunday in 2021, I realized I had been raw with vulnerability when P spoke of her crush, and I fell hard. I understood that up until then I had done everything in my power to mask my vulnerability because it scared me. I had shared it only with my journal or during drunken conversations, not realizing how vulnerable the latter actually made me. While I *think* I now grasp the essential truth that to be human requires me to be open to others (and therefore open to hurt), I am not entirely sure how firm my grip.

◇◇◇◇◇

I ended my January 2, 1982, journal entry with a declaration: "I am not a professor. That is what I do, not who I am. I made that realization yesterday, and I think that wall is now permanently down!" I fooled myself about that for a while, but in truth being a professor/journalist was (and is) *who* I am. I make no apologies for that. The Intersession weeks did pause my *doing*, though. While journal entries attest that I was laser-focused on being half of a new couple, I was relieved to read that I did not totally abandon friends and plans made earlier. I had joined friends in buying season tickets for men's basketball, so I attended games (and the women's games that sometimes preceded them). I enjoyed lunches with Robin. I enjoyed a laid-back weekend in St. Louis with Sue and Charlie (the coldest weather in decades, I noted). It was our first time together since Sue had called with the news that I was going to be an "aunt" in July. My journal entry on Les' birthday was another declaration of independence. (Overly harsh, as time would prove.)

> Happy Birthday, Les— I hope your card arrived. I know I sent that one to someone before; was it you? Would you care? It really does not matter much, now. You seem truly to be a part of my past. A good part. But you no longer are a part of my present. And I don't need your approval for ANYTHING anymore. I am legit as a person and journalist and teacher. You helped me get there— in the early stages— and those were struggling times. But I got there on my own— and I think I finally realize that.

There is no denying, however, that I began the spring 1982 semester distracted, a state of being that proved to last too long. For the first time in my adult life I was focused on me and my newfound personal happiness rather than on professional goals. I struggled to solve the calculus of secret love and professional obligations. How to balance what I longed to be doing with the demands of my job. Almost immediately I knew that I needed/wanted to share my news with the people closest to me. My journal doesn't contain the words "coming out," and I have no recollection of thinking in those terms. I had concluded I had more to lose in not sharing than with sharing, but that didn't mean I wasn't wary. (Since then, I seldom have felt the need to say *I am a lesbian*. I simply have lived my life unafraid of personal pronouns.)

I shared first with Joye, in late January when our schedules finally allowed us time for dinner together. As the comfortable evening in her warm and always-welcoming home progressed -- and the wine flowed freely -- I opened up. "She was understanding and supportive (as always)." Lunch with Karen followed. I nervously told her what had been going on in my life. "I know, you dummy," she said. We laughed over that and marveled at how we had become so much more than colleagues in such a short time. A couple of days later, after brunch with her and Jay on my birthday, I wrote how she was "so openly and honestly pleased; generally caring. . . ." Telling Robin was more difficult. Our improbable friendship had us so in sync that she already had detected changes in me and earlier wondered why I wouldn't tell her about my "current involvement." I had reassured her that I wanted to but wasn't quite ready. When I did tell her, she said she had "suspected" it was a woman. I quibbled with her verb and wrote in my journal that "she asked the kind of questions your mother would ask if you could tell her."

A few days before classes started, I learned that I had been awarded a $5,000 raise. (Getting George that revised resumé on short notice had paid off.) Along with classroom duties, I supervised day shifts of Missourian editing students Monday-Wednesday and the usual 3 p.m.-closing on Thursdays. Working just one night was a dream compared with my semesters of three or four. It was nice to be able to write positively: "We [the entire city room] did our jobs so well tonight— four minutes early on what undoubtedly will be our biggest news day of the semester. Gas fires in 24+ houses in Centralia. How good it feels now to sit and think a bit about that accomplishment." Days -- supervising production of the editorial page and advance pages -- generally were uneventful but did allow for more one-on-one time with students. That was immensely rewarding.

I was discouraged that I had not found a publisher interested in Boudinot, but I also had grown weary of him and was eager to take my research and writing in new directions. (By the end of the year I shelved that book project, never imagining I would return to it.) I contributed an essay on editing for stereotypes for a widely used textbook that my colleague Brian was helping to revise. I wrote "Two Polls on Investigative Reporting" for The IRE Journal. (The organization Investigative Reporters and Editors was and is headquartered in the J-School.) I squeezed in library time for preliminary research for a couple of possible articles. In other words, I did what assistant professors working toward tenure do. I also continued to take advantage of the many perks of being on a major university campus and a faculty member in its premier school. Intellectual stimulation was easy to find; lots of notables came to speak and prominent journalists always seemed to be visiting. I loved being asked to judge contests (journalists are notorious for finding ways to pat themselves on the back), including the Inland Daily Press Association public service award, the Penney-Missouri contests, and annual competitions for investigative reporters and business writers. Each made me feel as if I had something to contribute to the profession. Each scratched my itch to continue learning.

In hindsight, I might have been better served learning about how to have a mature adult relationship. When Karen and I next talked, she asked if I would give up my job for "this relationship [with P]." I "confidently answered yes." I didn't record how she responded but wrote of myself: "How peculiar I find that answer and yet how healthy. To care about something/someone beyond job and self. To find oneself deserving of love— desired— and capable at long last of loving— without fear (more or less)— and often with crazy wild abandon." Weirdly, my next day's entry began with an excerpt from the eulogy for a Soviet idealogue: "Sleep peacefully. You have lived a great and glorious life," to which I added, "eulogy we might hope for us all!" It was followed with an accounting of my day, including a pitcher of beer with a student to discuss her thesis and reading an essay by Adrienne Rich that was "both uplifting and challenging, and has given me fodder for my Off Our Backs essay." OOB was a radical feminist newspaper published 1970-2008. It was planning a special issue devoted to education. In March "I took a chance and sent an essay." It was not used; amazingly I could not find a copy in all that I had saved.

I may not have been burning the work candle on both ends as much as in the past, but it didn't take long for my work-personal life balance to get out of whack. A "cold that won't quite burst into full bloom or go away" had me "spending only the time necessary at the office." The extra rest was not enough to ward off "the damn cough, husky voice, runny nose, painful eyes." I self-diagnosed bronchitis (having been warned I was prone to it since my pre-dissertation pneumonia). Somehow I went to the Missourian for my Thursday shift. Thankfully it was slow (even after the computer "ate 90 percent of the stories" in the system). It quickly became apparent that I was in for a difficult night. "It hurt to read at the terminal. I took a long dinner hour and spent most of it lying down with my eyes closed." What's more, at 10 o'clock I did the unprecedented. I left the desk in the care of my teaching assistant and went home to bed. It was early February. My journal entries became more sporadic and the gaps between entries longer. After not writing for almost a month, I observed that ". . . mostly, I suppose, it is a matter of getting out of the habit. Of not feeling inner turmoil of any duration. And of having a partner who talks back, so I 'talk' to her and not journal pages."

When I wrote again, in early April, I chided myself that with the coming of spring I had "an overwhelming need to play— at the expense of just about everything else I have to do." While I reveled in "moving forward" in my relationship, I added, "One of these days, Barbara, you really must prepare your first-ever conference paper!!" (Seeing how I used my full name reminded me of being scolded by my mother.) I had been invited to make a formal presentation in a few weeks at the Conference on American Indian Journalism. A bonus was that the conference was being held at the University of Wisconsin in Madison. Another was that the proceedings would be published, a twofer in the academic world of professional activities. My challenge was to condense all that I knew about Boudinot and leave time for discussion -- and do so in 30 minutes. I quickly concluded that was "barely time to say anything meaningful (and of course so far I have not)." Eventually, I succeeded. I didn't simply read my prepared paper because I always tuned out presenters who did. My session was well-attended and the feedback positive. I also survived separation from P after four months

440

of togetherness. Five days and four nights in a city I treasure, a city where in the 1970s I had experienced the truth of "when everything is bizarre, nothing is bizarre." If only it weren't so darn cold in the winter!

As I was working on that conference paper, I experienced another first when I submitted a question for the master's degree comprehensive exam. Just a few years removed from taking that exam as my Ph.D. qualifier, I couldn't help but feel accomplished. I hoped at least one student would choose to answer my question; five did. I don't know what I asked, but it probably required a consideration of the practical in the context of the theoretical, which has defined my testing approach forever. A few days later there was yet another first: I convened a Journalism Week session. That had forced me to shop for something appropriate to wear. I was back to feeling fat and certainly didn't want to shop, but I also was "tired of corduroys and long-sleeve shirts." A more painful first was a Journalism Women get-together where "I ate too much and drank too much and talked to much. . . . I came home really drunk and more than a little bit embarrassed." It was Easter evening; we had not gathered in such a long time that I felt compelled to go even though an awful day with P had left me in the doldrums. It was the first -- and I believe only -- time when "I didn't have much fun" with that special group of women.

And then, suddenly -- at least in my journal -- the semester wound down toward another graduation. As usual, I had too much to do. That included 150 editing papers to grade. I kept "hauling them home [my place or P's] at night and to the office in the morning (undone)." I was physically tired. I was tired of being "the editing ogre." And I was tired (yet again) of alcohol ruling my life. By the time we got home from a picnic for a visiting professor and her younger partner, for example, I described myself as "that rambling, babbling lost soul that comes out with the booze. How I hate that person. How scared I am of her." If only I could have seen then what I see now, that I was using alcohol to avoid uneasiness about my relationship or to screw up the courage to express my feelings. From its beginning, I believe, there was a part of me that knew life with P was a mistake. Maybe that explains why, when I most needed to communicate, I often could not.

On the one-year anniversary of "earning my sheepskin," I asked and answered:

> Hey, BFL, how do you feel? Legitimate yet? On academic sure-footing? The time really can get away— what have you got to show for the last 365 days?
>
> Well, I've been tending to my personal life. About time, don't you think?" Or is that the hazard? Am I risking more than I admit to in loving— especially a woman— at this point? Or have I realistically said/decided/accepted the risks because the payoff is so great?
>
> Damn, it's hard work, maintaining a relationship, this relationship.

It was about to get more difficult because P would be in my summer-school editing course (although I would not supervise her on the copy desk). There was no way around that, and I was "a bit scared" of those 7½ weeks. "We can make it," I wrote. We did. I cannot explain how because I wrote nothing of those weeks, nor do I remember them.

I do remember going to Springfield, Illinois, in June for a last-gasp ERA rally. More precisely, I remember Midge breaking down -- again -- in a motel parking lot in Hannibal, Missouri. I remember watching the tow truck driver winch my car up onto its back wheels, then drop it! I remember spending an impatient (and expensive) extra day in Hannibal waiting for Midge to be repaired. I remember a nervous drive back to Columbia. I remember sadly concluding that I needed to buy a new car before driving to Colorado for two weeks at Arapaho Ranch. On June 22 I called my new 1982 Toyota Corolla SR5 "nice, sporty." I did "miss Midge a bit but felt secure in travelling again." I did not acknowledge the irony of buying a new Corolla for its dependability after dumping the used Corolla that had stranded me 10 years earlier in Oregon.

I brought "quite a lot" of work to Colorado. My plan was to relax and rejuvenate for the first week, which was for "feeding mind and soul," then tackle my work "rather eagerly." On the way west, I had dipped into my art fund to buy an armload of books at a feminist bookstore in Kansas City. Among them was "The Coming Out Stories," which left me reflecting on life. "There is no turning back now for me— only going forward to learn how to live (and love) proud and free!!" I had learned over my summers at Arapaho that even I had a reading-time limit. I knew I had reached it when restlessness overwhelmed me. On this trip, I described trying to deal with it. "I move outdoors to the picnic table— watching a squirrel, listening to the creek, realizing I have spent no time on 'my' rock in the sun. The mosquitoes drive me in to the silence— only NPR news and the creek." It was time to buckle down and prepare my workshop materials for the Brazilian journalists who were coming to campus shortly after I returned.

I had "grand plans— a long list of projects" for the fall. I hoped to apply for tenure and promotion to associate professor; I felt ready and thought the school would support me. I believed my teaching, scholarship and service had demonstrated my ability to more than ably serve the School of Journalism for decades. I already was working with a growing number of master's degree students, including one for whom I was the advisor. "I just want her to do well— as good as she is capable of," I wrote. Indeed, that is what I wanted for every student.

Leadership at the school remained in flux. After nine months of work, the committee in charge of the search for a new dean had sent five names to the provost. Each eventually withdrew from consideration. Mizzou grad and former ABC News president Elmer Lower was named interim dean. He made a point of announcing his open-door policy when he met the faculty for the first time. That promised to be a refreshing change. He had his hands full with the continuing budget difficulties in the state and on the campus. I skipped the faculty cocktail party that welcomed Lower and kicked off the 1982-83 school year. I had wavered about going; small talk never has been easy for me. My mind was made up after I tried on a pair of slacks I had bought in April and they no longer fit. I found those details in an August 21 journal entry. I did not write again until December 16, the day before P was to graduate. That entry also noted that I had been out of work for two weeks because of another bout of pneumonia "with a sinus infection tossed in for pain" and concluded that I needed to take better care of myself. Another gap in my journal stretched to April 27, 1983. Odds and ends from that entry provided the prompts that helped me fill in few blanks.

I'm not sure when it was that Dean Lower asked to meet with me. I do know that when I walked out of his office, I had agreed to chair the

13-member committee that would plan the School of Journalism's 75th anniversary celebration. I was honored, but I also chuckled as I recalled how I had tired of my "cruise director" days at Eau Claire, when I was the go-to person for planning almost every department event. It didn't take long for the committee to conclude that a gaudy celebration during difficult budgetary times could not happen. (Today we might have explained, *The optics wouldn't be good.*) A yearlong celebration -- from Journalism Week 1983 through Journalism Week 1984 -- would have to be done on the cheap. One of the highlights would be visits throughout the year by distinguished alumni. As described in former Dean Earl English's history of the school, invitees "have been asked to return at their own expense and donate their time and talent as an anniversary gift to their alma mater." Clever, huh? English quoted me as explaining to the faculty: "It's very open-ended. We're trying to tailor each visit to what the speaker, faculty and students want." I did not remember Ted Koppel doing his national "Viewpoint" telecast as a feature of the 1983 J-Week. I did remember the bargain-basement notepads we produced in-house and freely distributed; I still have a couple.

I did apply for tenure. The process was bumpier than anticipated. My "home-grown-Ph.D." status became an issue once my case moved out of the School of Journalism. So did my publication record which, while seen as appropriate for a practitioner of journalism, was deemed insufficient for a scholar. I *had* demonstrated potential, it was said, but to professors from elsewhere on campus that was not enough. The campuswide Promotion and Tenure Committee voted to deny me tenure. At the urging of the Journalism Women and with the backing of my department and the Journalism P&T Committee, I appealed. But I was a mess. For the first time in my professional life things were not going my way. And I wasn't handling it well. "The depth of the hurt. The fear. The anger." On May 1, the appeals committee vote on my case was 3-3, which meant it would go to the provost without a recommendation. I got the news at 7:30 p.m. and was stunned to also learn that two other denials had been overturned. "So now we play the waiting game some more— wait to hear from the provost. His decision is likely to stand. Can't think much beyond that right now."

But wait; there was more.

George had decided to step down as Editorial Department chair at the end of the academic year. His successor was the topic of much speculation. When the Journalism Women gathered we were, as I recall, unanimous in believing the appointment was a done-deal for one of our male colleagues. The "good old boys" network at work. We felt strongly that the dean should have a selection of candidates from which to choose. Joye was our obvious choice, and we were confident she could "win," which would signal significant change. Was any faculty member more respected? She, however, was not interested and we could not argue with her reasons. Joye and the group turned to me. I hesitated. Was I ready? Could I possibly win? Did I want to be pitted against Daryl, who had brought me to DeKalb and then Missouri and then Missouri again? I concluded that I needed to put my money where my mouth was. At worst, I would be the sacrificial lamb to make the point that unilateral decision-making no longer was acceptable at the School of Journalism. At best I would be the first woman to chair the Editorial Department. That didn't happen.

But wait; there was more.

Late one Saturday, during a weekend visit to St. Louis, my car (not even a year old) was T-boned. P was driving when the other car ran a red light and hit the passenger side, where I sat. The car spun and was grazed by a third vehicle. Thankfully, we had been wearing seatbelts and ended up bruised but not broken. (*Thank you, Grandpa Conger.* I was 16 when he died after being pinned under his overturned car. I have insisted on seat belt use ever since; I even wear mine when just backing out of the garage.) My car was not so lucky. Although it was not judged a total loss, it was under repair for several weeks. When I got it back, I once more found myself driving a car that I no longer trusted.

But wait, there was more.

On May 10 I worked my last Tuesday of the semester on the copy desk -- and reminded myself to avoid Tuesdays in the future (too many municipal meetings, I think). That morning I had my annual meeting with my department chair "and it certainly did not go as I had expected." I thought "with all the tenure stuff of late that I had heard it all. Surprise, surprise." George opened by saying he had two points to make and neither was good. *Oh my god, what?!* After a lengthy preface, he said "rumor has it" that I had been or was "emotionally involved" with a person who was a student of mine. Somehow I managed not to flinch. He continued by saying I was not being singled out; that during his years as chair the situation had come up twice before "and I called them in, too." He warned how things can appear to others and said "some students" had suggested I had "an aversion to men." I did not respond to the relationship matter and told him I was most concerned about the other statement. He said he was, too. I was emphatic in declaring it "totally unfounded" and suggesting it might be a reaction to my high standards. The other point he wanted to make concerned my Missourian work. He had asked Daryl for a memo about faculty editors, and Daryl had written that I seemed less enthusiastic and committed, while "of course still performing competently." I told George three factors had taken their toll: burnout, poor students and work that no longer challenged me. Early the next morning I recorded a lengthy reaction to my meeting with George.

So what is the message in all this? My immediate private reaction was to make plans to get out of Dodge. Then fear set in; fear that I would react differently to P— that my from-the-beginning bravado would disappear. Then a question: Have I tossed a secure career down the drain for passion? Then anger that the matters were even raised (although I feel safe in saying George was not comfortable in raising them, though sexual preference was not mentioned).

Now, home after another blockbuster Tuesday, after a strong scotch, I am _____.

I don't know how to fill in the blank. I do know I want to teach and be a good teacher. I want to continue to learn. I want to be an academic.

I do know I want to love P, though I have not done a very good job lately of doing that.

In my heart of hearts, I know I do not need to remain here. I also know I fear leaving here.

But how does the balance sheet end up?

BFL, you now are confronted with really being a lesbian. Can you handle it? Can you function in this place?

I don't know.

I feel on the brink— the edge— and each day I seem pushed closer.

I decided these things [the day before my evaluation]: for

physical health, to exercise daily; for mental health, to drink beer only on Saturdays; for emotional health, to be better to P and to myself.

And now this— BOOM!!!

A week later, I wrote that "my life feels put on hold. Who knows when there will be word on tenure? And what might the repercussions [of my meeting with George] be?" Summer school had begun and I was back on the Missourian. I didn't like it that one night I second-guessed myself about using a story about a Chinese feminist. As an editor "I cannot function like that." Still, on days or nights when the copy desk went well, I had "a great deal of pride and find satisfaction in my work." After one such shift, I crowed: "Why, I even told/made myself be patient with a problem student. Perhaps this is what I really belong doing and to attempt to be an academic is a sham. But I don't think so." Outside the office, my mood had swung to the "never been happier" side of the pendulum. It had been swinging a lot, however, so there was no telling how long optimism about having P in my life would last. Because I didn't write in my journal again until November 7, I was left to mine my memory bank and stash of correspondence for clues. Neither was of much help.

I think it was in the late spring when I learned that I had been awarded tenure and promoted to associate professor. In my mind's eye, I can see myself at a high-top table in a downtown bar celebrating. But I cannot see who was with me. Surely relief mixed with euphoria. After all, tenure is the *sine qua non* of a successful academic career. And I was tallying successes. I was an active member of the Women's Studies Committee and my scholarly interest in media stereotyping morphed into a focus on women in the media. That included a public presentation -- "Reading the Fine Print: Sexism and the Media" -- at the Women's Center. I gained permanent-course status in the journalism curriculum for "Women and the Media." I taught during the first summer session and seem to have spent much of my time after that rendezvousing with P at a point halfway between Columbia and her reporting fellowship. I recall happy times and horrendous times, often within a couple of hours of each other.

I found no evidence that I had shared much with friends, although it is difficult to imagine that those months were without heart-to-hearts with Joye or Karen or Robin. For so many years a prodigious letter writer, I seem to have badly neglected friends and former students in favor of self-absorption. Nonetheless, I noted that my network now had quite a few feminists and lesbians, which provided new perspectives on the world (journalistic and otherwise). I was surprised by a note from a graduate student describing ideas for her thesis proposal and hoping it wouldn't interfere with my ageism scale. I had forgotten the genesis of that project -- which I never did complete and for which I saved a giant folder of materials. I identified with a friend who found it "a bitch being in the same field" as her partner. Another former student reminded me of my Antigo days when she described "slowly coming out of the fog I've been in for the last three months to realize that yes, I am actually in Ardmore (where?) Oklahoma working as lifestyle editor." She shared an observation she had read, "that a woman's mouth can be used for two things— to eat and also to say what she wants" and added that she "was beginning to like that philosophy . . . becoming a little brazen is pretty tempting." Like virtually every former student, she ended by asking me to offer greetings to a list of Journalism School folks. A note from Eau Claire Brian reminded me how small the world could be: His new publisher had been a journalism student during my first Missouri life. Eau Claire Molly wrote from Nebraska, where she had found a reporting job. "Life has been exciting, yet reflective. My mental paralysis [at her previous job] has cost me: nearly five years of experience on a weekly newspaper renders me still roughly equivalent in salary and responsibility" to a recent college grad, she wrote. Her paragraph about what she was reading, doing at the Y and cooking sounded oh so familiar. A card that proclaimed "We miss you and your intellectual stimulation" reminded me I was making an impact on a new group of young women in journalism. That couple mentioned Cathy, and a few days later the mail brought a note from her with a clipping about a guy who temporarily quit coaching so his wife could pursue her career. "Wonderful!" she concluded. A hint to P and me, perhaps?

◇◇◇◇◇

If contentment had been the root cause of previous gaps in my journals, my entry for November 7, 1983, makes clear that could not have been true for the early months of another new school year. Tenure, which promised lifetime employment at the world's greatest school of journalism, did not bring stability to my life. P was now employed 400 miles away. We still talked of a life together; the problem was how to do that. I often sensed that she was trying to pull away and I was desperately hanging on to being half the couple I had longed for since who knew when. Now reading what I wrote that November morning, I hear echoes of so many past entries:

> Perhaps the early morning is the time to do the heavy thinking my life requires. To write before the demands of the day set in. To write early to help release the tensions that have me awake early every day. To focus my brain waves.
>
> To change the pattern.
>
> I need to come to grips with the dangers of the old patterns.
>
> When did I last exercise seriously? Now I am winded by walking up stairs; once I could play three or four competitive games of racquetball.
>
> The drinking. It is a problem. I sense I am losing myself and I fear losing P because of it. And if I am honest I would say that I am scared that I cannot handle it alone. But (again) I am going to try. It no longer is a case of giving up beer for awhile. It is the necessity of not drinking alcohol— PERIOD.
>
> The inability to relax. I have to do something with my time other than work or drink. I need to learn to handle the stress that is an inevitable part of this job.
>
> My job. I need to figure out where I want to be and what I want to be doing.
>
> Mostly, though, it adds up to learning to like **me** again— however I am— and I haven't felt that way for a long time. I want to work to find the me of two years ago. How did I ever let Her get away??

Today I still can feel the pain that oozes out of those sentences.

A letter from Les on November 21 suggests that I had, at long last, filled him in on my personal life over the last two years. "No, Barbara, you are not 'disowned' and never would be," he declared, much to my relief.

> It is and has been simply the press of paper and business. . . . But it's also been a bit difficult to say. I care and want you to be happy. If

you are, good. And I hope you don't think it's a case of stereotyping but I guess I always rather expected such an outcome, even hoped for it for a person I found to be a fine person . . . but lonely in many ways. . . . You've always been so important to our lives, and you will remain so.

Despite that acceptance from afar, I wonder today if it was the power of my anguish that silenced my pen. The last 20 pages of that journal are blank. The first words in a new one were not written until mid-1984. By then I had decided my future.

CHAPTER 23

Falling. Floundering. Finding.

Day after day after day beginning with June 8, 1984 -- often both in the morning and the evening -- I strung together thousands of words about change, pain, disbelief, anguish, doubt, incredulity, despair. I questioned P's love, motives, promises, honesty, sexuality, maturity. I questioned my sanity. But never my love or commitment. Until I finally faced REALITY. It was time to find my way forward. It was time to direct my energy to building a new life. In Hartford, Connecticut. As for why I was there -- and was there without P -- conjure a recipe for an epically messy ending to a relationship (including that trite "I love you but I'm not in love with you"), add a dash of long-distance cowardice, and garnish it with every cliché in the platitude pantry. Serve with a heaping helping of chagrin.

For decades, my explanation for why I had resigned from the University of Missouri went like this: (1) I wanted to live on the East Coast. (2) After orchestrating the School of Journalism's 75th anniversary celebration, I had the daunting thought that I could be around to do it again for the 100th. (3) Because I was very good at my Missourian job, I had trouble imagining a time without those responsibilities. Only a few people knew the *real* explanation, however. (Others might have speculated, I suppose.) I was in love, and the only way for my love and me to live together required us to find a city that would provide jobs for us both.

So when I finally returned to "journaling" (I really hate that word, but. . .) it was a "time of change and stress." Because I had moved often, I felt that "I should know what to expect." But, I wrote, at least two things made this move different. For the first time since arriving in Missouri 10 years earlier, I was leaving for an unknown city. And I was not the only person involved. Something else made the move different, something that did not click for me until an early morning drive in November 2021: The University of Hartford was the first job I got entirely on my own, without "connections."

That June journal re-entry concluded with me writing: "Geographically, I am heading east. Personally I have chosen to follow my heart and love a woman. Professionally I am going to try some 'real' teaching. It all will come together, I hope, in a life that has meaning and gives meaning. I wonder if that is too much to seek." On that day, I knew where I was going (although not where I would be living) and where I would be working. P did not. She used her vacation a couple of weeks later to go job-hunting in and around Hartford. She also found us an apartment.

In January I had applied for a job at the University of Hartford, and by late February it was mine. I was by then a couple of months into the sobriety that I continue to enjoy. (One Sunday morning I had opened the refrigerator and was astounded by how little wine remained in the jug I had bought the day before. *If I keep doing this I am going to die*, I thought. I never took another drink.) I thought I was making decisions with a clear mind. There was evidence to the contrary, however. For starters, there was the fact that I was a well-compensated tenured associate professor soon to be a less-well-compensated untenured assistant professor. And there was this: Although I have no record of exactly when it was, a leisurely drive on a sunny afternoon ended with me buying a new car. That Renault Fuego was sleek and sporty: black with leather interior and a massive sunroof. It definitely was not my significantly repaired, plain Jane, white Toyota sedan! It definitely proved to be an expensive albatross.

My June journal entries also suggest that even as I organized my move I harbored doubts about the future I had committed to.

The halfway mark of the year. I wonder if P and I will finish it to-gether. At this moment I am not so sure. . . . It is so hard for me not to look at Mizzou and feel I have given up so much to follow my heart. And maybe when I am 60 and look back I will do so seeing what a right move it was professionally. That is hard to do now with only UNKNOWN facing me. . . . Is it selfish or unrealistic to expect that she will do her part of what I thought we had agreed to, that is move somewhere where we could set up life together? On the other hand, how good can it be if she is a reluctant partner in the venture. So where does that leave me, her, us? Damned if I know. I believe I want her, but if she does not also want me, I won't put up a fight.

Days later, I wrote:

[P]aying a heavy price for this move— but I must never forget to practice what I preach so easily: to accept responsibility for my de-cision. I wonder if the nagging questions hidden in the corner of my person ever will go away, the "what if this doesn't work out?" Is that a natural feeling? Or is it a question born of a commitment taken too seriously, or perhaps too lightly.

As "a newly sober dyke" (words from my journal; when did I begin referring to myself as a dyke? Why didn't I simply describe myself as newly sober?) in the throes of upheaval, I had a new mantra: "Oh well, in a year it will all be history." I added that I said it "not so much with resignation but in an attempt to remain centered amid upheaval." By June 29, my *home* of four years was quickly becoming a *house*. The sec-ond floor was ready for movers; the garage was filled with junk; and I continued to sort and toss and pack. "If I could put the energy I've put into packing these last three days into something creative, it would be a winner," I wrote. Ironically, that also was the day I learned P had found us an apartment in Hartford, which I expected us to turn into a home. It was the third floor of a six-apartment triple-decker (a term new to me) just 2½ miles from campus.

During the first week of July, I counted down my Mizzou "lasts" and the days until I would leave Columbia. I took note of odds and ends, as I was fond of doing when journal writing was routine.

- Lillian Helman died today; it will be interesting to see what [coverage] that rates in tomorrow's papers. She was something special, and it is sad to think no more of her words will be forthcoming.

- Seen at the car wash this morning— a farmer with his John Deere tractor. It came out such a bright Deere green. [I never would have guessed that one day I would own a Deere riding mower.]

- Looking out my upstairs window, I again marvel at the view, and a glorious sunset. But I think we have western windows in Hartford, so I will not lose sunsets.

- My last Friday night in Columbia and I spend it watching some silly TV movie about a football game between "pigs and freaks." Why are they showing this in 1984?

The last entry I wrote in Columbia (on July 8) referenced an unexpected glitch with boxes of books I was giving away, the Missourian computer system crashing, and a low-key evening with Joye. She told me she saw Hartford as an adventure with lots of possibilities. She did not see the move as out of character, as my friend Sue had described it when she, Charlie and toddler Betsy came for a goodbye dinner.

My first stop on the journey east actually took me north, to visit my family in Wisconsin. From there I was off to spend time with P (which ended up being two weeks). Conveniently, the Society for Historians of the Early American Republic was holding its annual conference in Indianapolis, where I was to present a paper on Elias Boudinot's commentaries. I described myself as being in limbo. "The move and all accompanying changes, of course, but also the rocky road [we] seem to be travelling these days." P worked a lot. I played with our cats, watched a lot of TV and read. I felt like a visitor. We mostly ate out, socialized now and then. We regularly rehashed slights and perceived differences to no conclusion. I was committed; more and more I sensed she was not. I was left "feeling as if I am ready to crash onto a sidewalk, splattered about. I have allowed myself to be vulnerable" and I feared that "pain, real pain, is just around the corner."

It most certainly was.

On August 2, I wrote from Clarion, Pennsylvania: "halfway home." Before I left the Midwest, P and I shook hands(!) on her promise to move to Hartford within two months. On Sunday morning, September 23, I wrote about being "frightened to the very core of my being." Six weeks of back-and-forth, emotion-ladened conversations and letters were lit matches tossed onto the fuel of my doubts about her actually moving. I started that entry with, "Something is very wrong with me. I don't know what it is." At 7:15 that night I wrote again. "No— something wasn't very wrong with me this morning. I was, I believe, feeling P's vibes." Vibes that I no longer had to imagine after our afternoon telephone conversation and one simple declarative sentence.

"I don't want to be with you anymore."

Over the many messy months that followed, before I finally could write that "I feel I have my feet planted firmly on the ground" again, I somehow persevered. The specifics of P's declarations and behaviors -- the sources of gut-wrenching pain I never imagined possible -- are not important. Of my own declarations and behaviors, suffice it to say that I had a *very* difficult time letting go, even after I learned P had begun sleeping with a man six weeks before THE phone call! I choose here to focus on the specifics of how I coped (or didn't). On who and what supported me until my world emerged from darkness to light and I went from hopelessness to a new sort of happiness. Although the story is more than a generation old, I know its lessons remain relevant and worth examining. As Louise Erdrich wrote in "The Sentence," "In love as in death and mayhem, small things start a chain of events which veer so out of control that sooner or later an absurd detail intrudes, bringing the trail of events back for us to ponder."

The Wisdom of Friends

I found it difficult to end the call that shattered my world. The call that sent my emotions careening every which way. *It feels so final*, I thought after I finally hung up. I wanted to be angry, but I was not, "at least not yet." I felt betrayed. I ached with hurt and felt hollow. "Our lives are so entwined— how do we untangle them. All the things a couple share [are] no more. It seems at this moment inconceivable." One thing I didn't feel was "equipped to cope." For once I was smart enough to reach out (time zones and the expense of long-distance telephone calls be damned). I called "our" friends R and J, who as journalism graduate students had lived down the hall from P. They listened, patiently waiting when uncontrollable sobbing interrupted my narrative. I haltingly said I didn't think I could get through this crisis alone, that I probably needed to see a therapist. But how? R promised to "get the network going" to find someone for me. Just two nights later she called to check on me and to give me a name. I promised to call that therapist the next day.

About that same time, I finally caught up with my friend/former colleague Karen List in Columbia. "How I miss her. A straight friend but one who listens and understands." We made plans to talk again the next day, but not before she shared that it had not taken her long to know that the University of Rhode Island (her previous job) was not right for her, and how she set out to change her situation. I wrote, "I don't know yet if [the University of Hartford] is wrong for me, and sorting that out given the circumstance is going to be tough. But I've got to be honest with myself and not be afraid to ask the hard questions— about my professional life and my personal life. I hope I can summon the strength to do that and the courage to deal with the answers." Karen must have told Joye what was up because Joye called me at the office the next day. I was ecstatic to hear her voice. Try as I might, I couldn't stop myself from breaking down. She suggested I visit Columbia to get away from the pressures. I wasn't sure that was an answer, but I was "glad to have the refuge."

I was amazed to discover that my words about that first Hartford year filled more than three volumes. What also jumped out at me was my handwriting: neat, small, precise, controlled. My emotions were all over the place, just as they had been during previous periods of upheaval. But gone were the almost indecipherable words recorded in a haze of alcohol. It's as if I subconsciously concluded that if I were not in control of my life, at least I could control how I wrote about it. After tapping those journals for the sustenance I was wise enough to record, I have settled on those words that when spoken or shared in a letter (or written in a book, because I consider books to be friends) brought perspective and context. The original tiny group of friends who consoled me grew as I shared my change in circumstance (at minimum the fact of finding myself alone in Hartford). After my Christmas correspondence (I sent about 65 cards and wondered how folks would respond) the support continued. I had neglected so many people during the P years and was relieved to reconnect with many of them.

I have tried to convey my roller-coaster ride of emotions by offering those words in the order I received them. But I am compelled to start with a mind-blowing realization that emerged only after many conversations: I was a relationship adolescent! A break-up neophyte! The few *boyfriends* I had over the years never had meant much to me. They had been in my life but not *in* my life, so when they were out of my life it had been no big deal, at least not for long. Besides, I usually had been the one to step away. At age 35, I was totally unprepared for all I would feel after I was discarded by a *girlfriend*.

On to the useful advice:

▶ You need to give P some space. As hard as it may be to face, perhaps you will decide she was not right for you.

▶ P's letter, when you learned you had been the last to know she was sleeping with a man, was appallingly callous. It showed no regard for you. We would be concerned if you weren't angry about it. We think you are coping as well as could be expected.

▶ It's up to you when— or if— you see P again.

▶ I'm calling to check on you, to let you know we are thinking about you.

▶ Someone will love you again.

▶ You were her experiment.

A Thanksgiving Interlude

How smart I had been in October when I finally accepted R and J's invitation to visit them for Thanksgiving. I flew out of Hartford on a beautiful Saturday morning "on a DC-10— so big— don't think I've flown one before." There were just 87 of us on the flight to Chicago, including a group of prep school kids. (That sort of education was new to my world and merited a mention in my journal.) I had the window seat in a row all to myself. I later wrote that "I was reading a new dyke mystery, which [one of the two women] in front of me recognized as she passed by on her way to the restroom. That was fun." I remembered that the last time I had flown out of Hartford (after interviewing), "I was full of excitement. I knew the job was mine if I wanted it and there seemed to be so much promise for P and me." This time "I was flying away to escape the horrors of the breakup, to find some TLC and understanding from two friends who I have come to treasure."

The trip had seemed so far off when it was suggested that night I first called R and J. On the plane I thought about how "time does move on and hurts heal, if ever so slowly." Being with friends, in a city I had not visited since my DeKalb days, and doing new things proved to be an important step. We ate dinner with J's father at an Armenian restaurant on Saturday night. We spent a very cold Sunday on a walking tour of Frank Lloyd Wright buildings in Oak Park. (I found Unity Temple "quite wonderful and peaceful.") Wright's home was the last stop, and by then we were tired, hungry and crabby so we traded the tour for dinner at a Bohemian restaurant. We talked, but because we were in a public place "I had to hold it together." I even managed to joke, in a macabre way, when a good-looking woman caught my eye. "I do want a relationship," I told my friends. "A committed, monogamous, settled-in, loving relationship." I think it was the first time I spoke hopeful words.

From Chicago, we made the 250-mile drive to J and R's home. On Wednesday, while they went grocery shopping I wrote at length in my journal. It took all my energy to not call P's father to leave a happy Thanksgiving message for her. I held back tears until I copied a line from a book I was reading: "You of all people should know tears are emotion and not weakness." I had a difficult time believing that. Always had. But I moved closer to believing it over that holiday, when it became easier to allow myself to cry in front of my friends. And then . . . it was time to return to Hartford, but not before attending a big-time women's college basketball game. And in doing so, I missed Mizzou all over again.

Back to words of wisdom:

- ▶ Do you still really love P, or are you in love with being in love?

- ▶ Trust us, you are healing. But your self-confidence about relationships really has been shot.

- ▶ Forget her!

- ▶ The answers are within *you*. No matter how much we talk about it, it's got to be worked out within you.

- ▶ Get into the community as quickly as you can. Find someone to do things with.

- ▶ A "parentheses" era, as described by John Naisbitt in "Megatrends," catches us between the old and the new as we examine the past and try to figure out the future. He saw it as exciting because it's the only time when there can be real change. *An apt description for this time in my life.*

- ▶ I am really angry with P. Why aren't you?

- ▶ In a box of P's stuff, I found "How To Recover From the Loss of a Love." "Pretty schmaltzy and yet on the mark," I observed. I especially liked this: She asks if seeing me/is a drain./No, not a drain./Seeing you is a sewer.

- ▶ It's probably for the best.

- ▶ *Dear Sweet BFL.* That salutation on the "very accepting" Christmas card from a longtime friend "really got to me."

A Christmas Interlude

My final exam schedule included the last block of time, so I had booked my flight to Green Bay for the 23rd. I didn't mind having a bit of post-grading time to unwind. At the airport, my penchant for remembering "anniversaries" and "meaningful dates" (often unhealthy, I recently realized) put me in a funk after I wrote a short journal entry directed to P.

There's a plane about to leave for St. Louis— but that's not mine. I'm waiting for #235 to Detroit, then on to Green Bay. Because three months ago today you ended US. Oh, the end came more slowly (in fact I'm still fighting it), but it ended that day.

I still don't understand why— or how you so quickly (it seems quickly to me) had no more desire for me in your life. Oh, you want to remain friends, but . . . you say you had been lying to yourself and me for a long time. When I re-read your cards and letters I cannot believe the love and caring were lies— but I guess I have to take your word for it.

Midmorning on Christmas Eve, I was wrapping presents and "trying hard to hold it together." Outside it was 10 degrees and snowing; Mom was at work and Dad had driven to De Pere. I thought about my last Christmas at the farm, with "my friend P." When I had told Mom she wasn't coming to Hartford, I remember her asking if we were still friends. "For the moment," I answered. I had "trusted my gut" and mailed an honest letter to my parents on December 1. Turns out Mom had known almost from the beginning of our relationship. So did my sister and brother. The letter was news only to Dad who, I had been told, was upset about being the last to know. "I think things will be OK," I wrote. "I'm glad the cards are on the table." In hindsight, I don't think it made much of a difference because once in Wisconsin I retreated to my familiar pattern of emotionally shutting down.

Christmas "was pretty joyless— and pretty ordinary." The television was on all day and that, along with reading and napping, pulled me through. I could not escape "a jumbled flood of memories" and concluded that "I did not deserve today." I was withdrawn. When Mom asked about therapy, I answered in monosyllables. I wasn't ready to share— at least not with her. I seemed to be constantly fighting back tears. "I will not break down in front of them. I will not allow that." There was comfort to be had, I am certain, but I could not get beyond being my self-described "rough and tough as nails." Could not get beyond believing that in my parents' house "I am always going to be 'Little Barbie.'" In fact, I wrote about how "I sat last night, a 35-year-old Ph.D. college teacher, and as the family and friends of my parents arrived to share their anniversary dinner, 'Little Barbie' was spotted and greeted. No wonder I cannot figure out my identity here."

I had packed four books for the break. By the day after Christmas, I already had finished two: "Prism," a novel about an older lesbian finding love, and "Woodswoman," nonfiction about a woman who built a cabin in the Adirondacks. A couple of days later, I added Doris Grumbach's "The Ladies." Her novel fictionalized the story of Eleanor Butler and Sarah Ponsonby, well-born Irish women who in the 18th century left Ireland to live as a married couple in a Welsh hamlet. Grumbach wrote, "They had learned the lessons that made living together possible: to bear each other's failings with fortitude and to freely indulge their own without guilt." I wrote, "Yeah!" I was so taken with their story that I decided on the spot that the kittens I planned to get would be named Lady Eleanor and Miss Sarah.

I resented how little privacy I had over the break. Outdoors it was "too damn cold" and snowy for walks; and besides, I didn't have boots. Indoors my space felt confined and haunted by memories. I wasn't sure I could last until January 6. But what would I do differently were I in Hartford? "I need some new memories, but I know I won't find any here this Christmas. This is just a year for getting by." Back-to-back football bowl games and reading got me through New Year's Day. I took time to quote a passage from my latest book, Sandy Boucher's "Heart-women/ An Urban Feminist's Odyssey Home": "Something I find difficult to understand is loss of feeling. Both in oneself for another and coming from someone else -- how you can care one day, and the next all feeling is gone." I got to talk about that book and so much more when I met Rae, an Eau Claire friend and racquetball foe, for lunch. We had not seen one another for almost three years, but we had exchanged long letters. If I had qualms about our reunion, they dissolved when we hugged hello and then talked for more than two hours. A psychologist, she was a good listener. She started out asking about me "and it was tough to turn off. It was so easy to be open." Afterward, I wondered if I had talked too much (a concept generally foreign to me). We caught up on the past and easily moved forward. Book recommendations flew across the table. She asked about good titles for women struggling with their identity. I grabbed hold of her affirmation of how I was handling my situation and took to heart her reminder that I needed to be patient with myself. "Your grieving process really only has just begun," she said. She assured me that not only was it OK to rehash memories, it was necessary. "You have to experience something in order to learn how to deal with it," she explained.

I had a long way to go. The day before my flight "home" to Hartford, I summarized the holiday: "I have left nothing of myself here this trip. Have probably caused Mom and Dad pain. But there is nothing I want to share with them right now. And this place no longer feels like a refuge but rather like a trap. [Or] perhaps I am the trap— confining myself out of confusion and fear."

On to more words of wisdom:

▶ In past conversations, when P and I were friends, I sometimes felt a selfishness in her. When your hurt goes away, I am convinced you will find yourself really lucky to be out of the relationship.

▶ It helps to compare notes on the idiocies of our breakups, the wrongs done us and the behaviors since. I'm so glad you called.

▶ I admired you for making the move in the first place, and now for how you've handled the loss of P. You are in my thoughts daily. "With admiration and affection."

▶ Jane Rule's "engrossing" novel "This Is Not for You" had me reading far too late into the evening.

▶ Happy Birthday to you. I sent P a "kiss-off" letter, by the way.

▶ A late-night call from Texas was so good. "Another connection in my widespread network of dyke journalism students from Missouri."

▶ Audre Lorde's "Zami" struck a chord. The writing compelled me to read on, often late into the night. The final pages, her recounting of a "failed" love, brought me to the edge of tears.

▶ You're a strong kid, kiddo!

The Right Therapist

As I had promised R, I called the therapist; it was just three days after I was dumped. She explained that she was 30 miles away and offered to refer me to someone in Hartford. I wanted to give her a try; I had confidence in "the network" (whoever they were). She couldn't see me for several days, so "all I have to do is make it until then," I wrote. I wondered to myself why I couldn't "seem to get angry and scream and holler." I hoped I was about to find out.

Only after the fact did I understand that *seeking* professional help and finding the *right* help are not the same. I was fortunate that the nameless network I had trusted was spot-on in recommending Jane. I was a broken, nervous woman -- so nervous I did a practice drive to her office in the daytime -- when I first met with her on the evening of October 2, 1984. The day before, I had written about being curious and scared about what lay ahead. "But there is no question that I will survive!" When I wrote about our first night's work, it was to state: "I am amazed how the words poured out of my mouth. Being able to talk to someone. Being honest (I hope). Realizing I'll be OK in my professional life— through this healing process— but wanting also not to lose the personal/human side of me. And wanting to keep growing in that dimension." Months after our last session on April 3, 1985, I sent Jane a barrel cactus with a note that said simply, "I don't think I ever said Thank You." When she called about it, I said I had decided cactus don't need much care, just the right kind of care. Left unspoken was: *I think we are those kind of women.*

Because of my journal, I have plenty of words detailing my journey with Jane. I would willingly share them, but I think most are best saved for a future essay. I will violate the "show, don't tell" maxim for journalists and ask you to trust me when I tell you: I eventually would have found my way out of the post-breakup morass without Jane, but it would have taken much longer. It would have been much more painful. And I would have had much less self-awareness and understanding to bring to my next stage of life. To be totally honest, however, I also must tell you that when, down the road, I strayed from my hard-earned changes I painfully learned about backsliding. Which in an ironic way reinforces the importance of finding the right help, which I would be able to do again because of my time with Jane.

Grit and Determination

In the best of circumstances, the move to Hartford would have challenged me. My minimal experience with the Northeastern United States had come on a drive-through in 1971, when I was a new college graduate. I had never lived in a big city. An urban apartment after a suburban townhouse felt like a step backward. (Not to mention the fact that someone else had chosen it.) I had never taught at a private university. I had never taught in an academic unit without "journalism" in its name. I am pretty sure I never thought much about any of those realities until I began to live them. And that was in the worst of circumstances. But even as my personal crisis dragged on, I wrote hopeful words. I was a productive professional. I proclaimed time and again that "I am a survivor."

I had written my first journal entry from Hartford on August 11; it was relatively brief with few details. I suggested that not writing was "a sign of the relative smoothness of this transition." I remember driving into the city on the cusp of the evening rush hour, frantically trying to follow the directions P had given me from I-84 to our Evergreen Avenue apartment. I met the landlord, Jack, who agreed to pay for my hotel room while he finished repainting. I remember the moving van arriving on an incredibly hot and humid day that felt like Missouri. I remember being impressed by the guys who endured countless trips up and down three flights of stairs. One man so slight, and yet with straps and know-how he effortlessly carried up the heaviest items. The other obviously a day hire just one wrong move away from back strain. I remember that Jack brought them beer and I thought he should have waited until they finished. And I remember the Goodyear Blimp flying overhead (reconnaissance for the upcoming Greater Hartford Open golf tournament, I later learned). My journal noted that it took me only four days to get the apartment in "as good of shape as possible." I added that I had begun going to campus, and that "my mental health is pretty good."

The apartment was not air conditioned. I don't recall if all the windows were screened; there was little choice but to sleep with them at least cracked open. City noises, I shortly learned, were a way of life. On one of my first nights I awoke to a whooshing that seemed to be coming from inside. A bat had found its way into my apartment. I huddled under the sheet and hatched a plan. I would try to get out of the bedroom and close the French doors in order to trap the bat. I would use the bedspread to tuck between the doors and the floor. It worked. I hoped the bat would leave the way it apparently had arrived, but I took no chances; I spent what remained of the night on the living room floor. As soon as the sun was up, I called Jack and insisted he deal with the situation. Although he didn't find a bat, his prompt response suggested he might be an attentive landlord. When I complained about the stove, he brought "the better one" up from the basement, the one with 2½ working burners (he broke the knob for the oven during transport). By winter, I persistently called on him because I couldn't get the apartment warm no matter how high I set the thermostat. (Shades of Eau Claire, only this furnace used natural gas, not oil.) Unfortunately, I learned, attentiveness did not always translate into successful problem solving.

As a first-time city dweller -- one decidedly attuned to all the "bad" things because that's what made the news -- I never felt entirely comfortable in my surroundings. Especially in the beginning, I heard every sound in the night and awoke thinking the worst. In my first week, a neighbor told me his car had been broken into while parked out front. I resigned myself to accepting that "if the bad guys want something" from the Fuego "they'll get it." I missed having a garage. I hated living on a street with odd/even parking, which I came to learn was enforced even if you were sick in bed during a blizzard and shoveling out your car to move it felt life-threatening.

Among my reasons for wanting to write regularly in my journal was "to record the sensations of this new place." To wit:

There is just so much that can assault the senses. In Columbia, on my patio, I'd be occupied by birds and bugs and tiny red things the size of a pin head. Out here [on my porch], today it is the traffic, the pigeons, people walking by three floors below, a couple arguing in the building across the street, a phone ringing somewhere. No music today, but last weekend the punk [rock] played into the night.

Six weeks into life in the Nutmeg State, I had assimilated the economic and social differences across the nearby border between Hartford and West Hartford. During breakfast one morning, I overheard a conversation that included this: "We've decided how to celebrate our 50th anniversary. We're going to take a trip on the Orient Express." My commentary: "Only in West Hartford." I also knew that the "inner city" was a mile or so east of me. I think I was one of just a few in my circle of colleagues with a Hartford address. I also think that had I been the person searching for housing, that would not have been the case. Nonetheless, the location of my apartment came to play a significant role in the first year of my Hartford life. That's because Reader's Feast bookstore and café was around the corner.

When RF, as I referred to it in my journal, opened in 1983 it was the first independent, progressive bookstore in the area. The co-founders, Carolyn Gabel and Tollie Miller, were women's rights and gay rights activists. Their goal was a community bookstore that was inviting, safe and stocked with culturally diverse and politically progressive titles. A café shared the space; it helped finance events such as author readings/signings and musical performances. Volunteers supplemented a tiny staff. I presume I visited RF shortly after I moved in. I know that I recorded "three good things that happened to me" on October 17, and one was that I had volunteered to begin working at the bookstore. I was not new to volunteering; in Columbia, P had talked me into regular shifts at the food co-op. The difference would be that I *loved* books and bookstores, whereas I was not familiar with much of what I sold at the co-op (the worst part was bagging blocks of tofu).

My first RF shift was two hours. I probably unpacked or shelved books. Several days later I volunteered for extra time. Tollie asked what brought me to Hartford and how I liked it. I told her I came for personal and professional reasons, that the personal had fallen apart and the professional was OK. "And she was genuinely concerned." I particularly liked working on Sundays, which typically involved "four busy hours with little time to think about myself." It was when business was slow that P sometimes "snuck into my conscience." Seeing too many pairs of women tugged at my memories. "This would have been a good place for us," I sensed, "and so that must mean it can be a good place for me." It already was. Not long after my first shift, I wrote: "What a bright spot the store has become in my life. A few women know my name. A place to work with them. To joke, and now and then laugh. A place to feel wanted." I was good for RF, too. Eventually I became one of the volunteers entrusted to open or close the store (even after I accidentally walked home one night with the cash register key). By mid-March 1985, when Carolyn and Tollie asked if I were interested in working (for minimum wage) on Friday nights, my affirmative answer was proof of progress. Not at the bookstore, but in my life. "But what happens when I fall in love again?" I joked, with more than a bit of seriousness. And Carolyn sensed that she could answer "Lots of contacts here on a Friday night" without embarrassing me.

While I took my time getting used to Hartford (once I found a laundromat and market), I had to acclimate to the University of Hartford as quickly as possible. Classes would begin after Labor Day and I had much to do. The campus was small, compared with others I had worked on, so finding my way around was a challenge for only a couple of days. The nature of the university itself -- and my department -- proved to be longer-term challenges. The university grew out of the 1957 melding of the Hartford Art School (Harriett Beecher Stowe was among its founders), the Hartt School of Music and Hillyer College. As described on its website in 2021, the result was atypical of private New England colleges because along with liberal arts it included engineering, technology and education. When I started working there, the university had transitioned from a largely commuter school to one with a broader reach. President Stephen Joel Trachtenberg was a skillful fundraiser and there always seemed to be a construction project or two. (I found it pretentious that he always used his full name. He signed it with a flourish not matched until the 45th U.S. president.) I remember meeting with him during my interviews. He clearly had studied my *vita* and I chuckled when he suggested I might study "old women Indian journalists."

University policy required hiring me as an untenured assistant professor. To prove myself worthy, I guessed. But I did get a title:

journalism program director in the Department of Communication. Two things had attracted me to apply for the job, besides location: the opportunity to build a program and the existence of a Women's Studies committee. I was tasked with reviewing courses (a couple existed, taught by a professor who was part-time English and part-time Communications), developing courses and energizing the "track" for students interested in journalism. Other pathways for students were, as I recall, mass communication, organizational communication, interpersonal communication and small-group communication. Fields of study that I knew next to nothing about, by the way.

The faculty was young, but I still felt out of place at the chairman's "welcome" barbecue -- "socializing with seven strangers, including two sets of newlyweds." The other new faculty member was a woman who was scheduled to finish her dissertation in December. "Not familiar with Ms. [magazine]. But I'll try to hold off on my judgments of all until I can be fair, have been here awhile," I wrote. I already was "pretty sure there are no Joyes or Karens in the department," but I was hopeful that "somewhere in the University there must be a professional soulmate" for me.

I felt better after my first official university gatherings. On Tuesday, September 4, I wrote:

> It is hard not to feel good about this place. Yesterday's faculty meeting to hear the president and then a get-acquainted cocktail party. All we newcomers with traditional red carnations. And then an Arts & Sciences cocktail party and buffet. For something that could have been quite awful it was not half bad. But I was exhausted when I got home (and not booze-induced, either). Tired/sleepy again tonight. What will it be like after three back-to-back classes tomorrow?

I didn't write about what that day was like, but after meeting classrooms of new students for three consecutive hours I surely wondered if a sadist had created my schedule. Because I still had not adjusted to living in the Eastern time zone, I imagine *fatigued* would be an appropriate adverb. I did write about my productive Friday and "wanting very much" to use Fridays for research and writing. I was eager to add to my record so I would be ready to apply for promotion and tenure when the time came. I was excited to be able to work at home as well as at the office. One of the first things I had splurged on in August was a personal computer. (An IBM clone, it cost me $1,200 plus $99.60 in interest on the bank loan to pay for it. Talk about the "old days"!) I had become so accustomed to writing and editing on a video terminal that I didn't want to function any other way. Personal computing was only a few years old, but I was fascinated by the technology and had a love/hate relationship with the challenges of learning to use it. That love part never has gone away.

[An aside: One of the first times I used my computer was to type a story I had written during my two weeks at P's. The idea had come to me during a thunderstorm, when I had "this overwhelming need to write a kids' story. I mean, I really feel as if the muse struck. I made a few notes, got out a legal pad and spent the afternoon creating a story. Which seems to have flowed out of the pen. I had the ending in mind and it was like driving; I just set out to get there." At the time, Ms. published a column called "Stories for Free Children" and I thought I might submit mine. It took me until the end of September to prepare the manuscript (the computer ate it at one point) and mail it. "Extra, Extra, Read All About It" was not published, but I still have it, including the handwritten original. **Appendix B**]

On that productive Friday, I put the finishing touches on my content analysis examining news about women offered by the wire services. I had easy access to the wires at Missouri, where I gathered my data. I had presented my preliminary findings at the Midwest Region National Women's Studies Conference in Columbia in April. I turned it into a formal research report, crossed my fingers and mailed it to Journalism Quarterly, then the most important scholarly publication in my field. I hoped the editors would find "News About Women on the 'A' Wire" significant. They did, and eventually it was published in the summer 1985 issue.

That Friday I also returned to a piece I had first worked on in Colorado in the summer of 1982. For my newswriting course at Eau Claire, I had created a speech-writing assignment using the "Sermon on the Mount." The article I wrote about that was intended for an audience of *doers*, not researchers (although it did have a couple of footnotes). I titled it "THE JESUS SPEECH/An Assignment for Beginning Newswriters" and polished it to submit to Journalism Educator. I began this way: "Hamilton," the city editor barks, "a songbird expert from the Audubon Society is speaking to the Midtown Birdwatchers tonight. Give it a shot." The next few paragraphs put newspaper stories about speeches in context, followed by a discussion of how many instructors start by giving beginners the text of a speech to write from. Like those instructors, I once turned to "Vital Speeches of the Day" before I took a gamble on the Sermon. I wrote, "Surprised? So are the students, who once they begin reading the unlabeled text generally react with hoots of, 'I don't believe it' and 'You've got to be kidding.'" The rest of my article explained why I wasn't kidding. It also ended up being published in the summer of 1985. That Friday, I wrote about "feeling I am off to a good and necessary start." Indeed!

I didn't feel as good about my first encounters with students. "What will I do with a student who wants to be an interior decorator? A disc jockey? Or the one who doesn't like to read?!" *You're not in Missouri anymore, Barb.* I also was reminded of that when I got my first paycheck -- after an afternoon spent chasing it down. "The pleasant part was that my take-home is a bit more than Mizzou. And it is better than I thought because my [retirement] is tax-sheltered. So the pay cut doesn't affect me as severely as it could." And I was reminded of it yet again on Rosh Hashana. It was my first semester with a significant number of Jewish students. After arriving to find just four of 12 people in one class, then four of 15 in the next, I wrote "CANCELED" on the board for my third class and went home.

Another difference I quickly noticed was related to the campus' location in a mostly residential area. No more walking a block or two for lunch. (I sorely missed Monday lunches with Joye and Karen, especially after Joye sent me some Missourian clippings along with a brief note: "I hope you know how much you are missed. We'll light a candle for you on Mondays.") Hartford had a room set aside for faculty dining, however, which facilitated meeting colleagues. I had been convinced for years that journalists and sociologists have an affinity for one another, and at Hartford I saw it extended to communications people. I think some of the best conversations occurred at "our" table, which also was popular with younger historians and political scientists. Topics were wide-ranging and I remember lots of laughter. I began to make friends.

The semester was just a few weeks old when I noticed how often complaints about students dominated our lunches -- and our coffees and occasional social get-togethers. *Their cars cost more than we make. They are sooo rude. Too many are unprepared for college.* I swear that sooner or later everyone claimed to have seen a student arrive in a limousine and be moved into a dorm by the driver. My 10 years of teaching had not prepared me for students like the one I wrote about at midterm. I was holding 15-minute conferences with my "Fundamentals of Journalism" students, including "the fluffy young woman who is a junior not sure what she wants to do with her life. But she really would like to do research for the TV program 'Entertainment Tonight' because she really is interested in stars." No wonder I was nostalgic for the high achievers at Missouri and Eau Claire. No wonder I so enjoyed receiving letters from a decade's worth of graduates and interns (with postmarks including cities such as Kansas City, Los Angeles, Fort Worth, Jacksonville, Milwaukee, Seattle, New Orleans, Phoenix, Nashville -- even Hong Kong -- and small towns such as Cumberland, Wisconsin; Conway, Arkansas; Galesburg, Illinois; and Ardmore, Oklahoma). At least by the end of the fall semester, as I prepared for the rush of exams and calculating grades (determined to do that on my computer), I could write: "All things considered, I think the semester has been OK. I have seen progress. And most important, I have a sense of this place and know I need to rethink how I do some things."

CHAPTER 24

Hartford Grows on Me

I returned from my holiday break on a late-night flight. I don't know if I noticed, but there were signs of my life's changes all around. My co-newbie Patricia fetched me at the airport. Our friendship was in its nascent stage, but we already had nurtured it with forthright conversations and more than a little fun. Another friend, a sociologist of course, was leaving for greener pastures and I helped engineer a going-away dinner for her. When I walked into my apartment that January, it was 52 degrees. I handled that by calmly unpacking before putting on long johns and a sweatshirt and climbing into bed. For reading, I chose May Sarton's "Crucial Conversations," a novel about the breakup of a marriage. It did not prompt tears, as it might have months earlier. In a catch-up session with my therapist, she talked about "how determined" I was to move ahead. When I said I didn't want to be the social cripple I felt myself to be, she admonished me to give myself some credit because "cripple" did not apply. I topped my wish list with a house (not least because I would be able to control my physical environment). Before classes resumed, a journal paragraph about one day's activities shouted *ordinary*: a couple of hours at the office handling correspondence, lunch with colleagues, shopping for a rug, stopping at Reader's Feast and being greeted like a friend, buying a book for my nephew Nicky's birthday (delighted that I was eligible for a 40 percent discount), calling the Humane Society about adopting kittens, and making bean soup. [An aside: Books always have been my gift of choice, be it for a newborn, a birthday, a holiday or "just because." In a thank-you note one Christmas, Sue referenced "Anna Bear's Winter," which I sent for her younger daughter. "However do you find books with the girls' names?! (Remember the Betsy books? She [older daughter] adores them yet!) It's a darling book . . . and we are on our 450th reading.")

I faced another horrible class schedule, with Wednesdays being the longest: classes 1:30-2:20, 2:30-3:45 and 7-10. "But it should be a good semester, with Editing again. Media Criticism will be a challenge." I was proud of myself for finally getting the Criticism syllabus organized. *It looks good on paper*, I thought. An early birthday card from the university, signed by the president, didn't impress me because "the students haven't received grades [from the fall] and we have no class lists." *What a way to run a university!* When classes started, I was disappointed to find only a couple of journalism majors in my Fundamentals class. Criticism had 21 students, most of them from our graduate program. One-third of my 18-person Editing class had had an adjunct instructor for Fundamentals the previous semester. "They got A's and know nothing," I discovered. "All they wrote was a fantasy and a fairy tale! And some of them are journalism majors! So I need to deal with the problem. He [the instructor] better not step foot on campus!!" That discovery reinforced for me the enormity of my charge to inject life into the journalism component of the Communications Department. (By late March, with the blessing of my department, I submitted a memo outlining proposed changes and new courses to the Arts and Sciences Curriculum Committee.)

I may have been feeling particularly put out because of my approaching birthday (my 36th). "Maybe if I'm lucky I will have the energy to do something nice for myself. Maybe if I am lucky I won't be in a blue mood. Maybe if I am lucky I will get through the day without tears. But I don't expect a wonderful day. Maybe next year." Adding to the pall was the fact my birthday fell on a Wednesday. At least I was able to hang out in my (chilly) apartment until after lunch. There were no tears; there was applause from my evening class when I told them it was my special day. The heated mattress pad from my parents was the best gift I could have received.

Despite being occasionally frustrated by reminders that UHa was not Mizzou or Eau Claire, I took advantage of several opportunities for professional development. The first had been a conference in early October with the added advantage of it taking place in northern Vermont. There was no way I could have booked two nights in a Burlington-area hotel in that season on my own. Kudos to the New England Newspaper Association; someone knew the leaf-peeping weekend would draw a crowd for its Journalism Education Symposium. My goal was networking, so it was an inconvenience that my business cards were not ready. I don't mingle well but did my best to talk with participants when we had welcome breaks from a very long day of presentations. I hit it off with a woman from a weekly newspaper in northwestern Connecticut, and we shared dinner at a marvelous little restaurant she knew. I judged the symposium average but wrote that it had been good for me to get out of Hartford -- even though the music I chose for the drive sparked sadness and tears.

The web of Mizzou journalism connections, often referred to as the Missouri Mafia, extends around the world. As a university graduate and former School of Journalism professor, I am a member. I was mindful of that each time I connected a job-seeking student with a job opening, for example. A few weeks after I got to Hartford, however, it was me on the receiving end. An assistant managing editor at The Courant had been a student during my mid-'70s Mizzou gig, and I arranged to have lunch with him and the managing editor. I was eager to let them know of my hiring and hoped they (and their staff) would be resources as I developed our journalism program. I must have talked about the research I was doing on "first-women stories." They must have encouraged me to write an op-ed essay for their consideration. Regardless of who initiated it, I sent "'First Woman' Stories Strain for Significance" to the Editorial editor on Monday, November 12. On Friday the 16th a staff member called to say they were going to use it, perhaps as early as Sunday. And indeed that is when it was published. Timing is everything. On Tuesday the 13th the governor had nominated a female Supreme Court justice -- a first -- and the staff member wanted my OK to add that detail to the essay.

My Missouri ties also paid off -- in an unexpected way -- in late January 1985, when I received a call from the Courant's Features editor. I vaguely remembered her, also from my first Mizzou stint. She wondered if I might be interested in some part-time editing. *Would I ever!*

We worked out the details a few days later: Thursdays on the Features copy desk beginning February 21. Ten dollars an hour. "I am vowing that it will go into savings." I didn't ask permission to accept the job. As I had learned, teaching at a private school was different from a state university (at least back then). I was confident that should someone question my "side work," I could easily explain its value in keeping my journalistic skills up to date, which benefited my students and the university as much as me. Truth be told, as I wrote, "It will be good to be in a newsroom, even if I'm doing features— to be in contact with newspaper people." It meant I would do my academic research and writing on weekends, "but for now that is OK." Looking back, I was a bit surprised to see how eagerly I gravitated back to the newsroom/classroom workload that had worn me out in the past. I think that keeping busy was the *sine qua non* powering me through my "being dumped" hangover, which lingered. Besides, my love affair with editing had never waned.

Burying myself in work was nothing new. Having more time to do so *was* new. I struggled with how to reclaim Sundays for myself after ceding them to "couples' stuff" for so long. I still wanted a leisurely morning in bed to enjoy coffee, pastry and a fat newspaper, but what about the long afternoon and evening? Along with bookstore hours and an occasional outing, in the winter of '85 I had two conferences to prepare for -- one related to Native American journalism, the other to my new research on women in the media. That work allowed me to lose myself at the computer; I knew the hours would pass swiftly (something that to this day happens).

Post-dissertation, I had connected with two men at the University of Arkansas at Little Rock who oversaw the American Indian and Alaska Native Periodicals Research Clearinghouse. We corresponded as they were creating the American Native Press Research Association, or ANPRA, which would debut in April 1985 with a session at the annual meeting of the Mid-America American Studies Association. I was excited that there was enough interest to organize ANPRA, excited to be in on the ground floor, excited to be asked to chair that April session. Being involved again with scholars outside the confines of journalism validated my need to be seen as more than a journalist. (As had the *very* formal paper on Boudinot I presented the previous July at the annual conference of the Society for Historians of the Early American Republic.) One other detail about the April meeting buoyed me. It was being held on the campus of the University of Illinois, a mere 300 miles from Columbia. I began plotting how I might visit. If it were accepted, the conference paper I worked on also would be presented to an audience new to me: the Eastern Communication Association. I think all my department colleagues were members, and it seemed logical that I find a way to fit in. Besides, the group's annual meeting would be in nearby Providence, Rhode Island. My plan was to tweak the research I had been doing on first-woman stories.

My journal reminded me that an altogether different sort of writing also occupied me after I re-settled into Hartford. My therapist had me recording my dreams (always a challenge because I so seldom remembered them) and completing exercises from a workbook titled "Making Order Out of Chaos." That explained entries focused on "reviewing your day as if you were a detached observer . . . [who] also had the capacity to see what was happening within." It proved particularly valuable the day after I began, when a telephone call left me "thinking and dreaming." After introducing himself as a faculty member at California State University-Hayward (now Cal State East Bay), the caller surprised me. Their journalism department was looking for a "chairman" and my former Missouri colleague George had given them my name. I was not job hunting, but I'm sure George knew how my circumstances had changed. *Maybe I've been too harsh on him,* I thought. I decided I had "nothing to lose in testing the waters," so that evening I cranked out a *vita* for California. And in my journal, I responded to workbook questions:

> —Who stimulated you? Drained you? "The Cal state guy stimulated me. A couple of students with good questions stimulated me. Everyone else moved in and out of my day with no memorable effect."

> —What moments had the greatest effect on your energy levels? "High energy after the CSU call. Had to tell someone, so took Patricia into my confidence."

> —Which emotions did you carry with you longest? "The 'high' from the CSU call."

I concluded that "I seem to have been carried along on a wave through the day— the impetus for my activities being outside focus."

In rereading my journals, it was at about this point where I realized how my entries had begun to include noticeably fewer words about the painful recent past. During a therapy session, I initiated an assessment of how I was doing and where I was going. Jane smiled when she agreed the time for that was right. Her view: I was better than in September, but Christmas and a birthday card from P were setbacks. Still, she said, "The crisis *is* over." My view: "Sometime I don't feel like the crisis is over. I do know I'm better than in September. Know I need to make some choices but not sure I know what my options are." One thing was clear to me: I needed some new activities. "Books and the TV are escapes from life and I want to <u>live</u> life." Over the next several days, I listed possibilities; today they make me smile. Something with my hands, a craft. (I have tried so many things over the years. LEGO, which I began in early 2021, have engaged me like nothing else ever did.) Puzzles. (Hate jigsaw puzzles. Loved sudoku for a while. Crossword puzzles annoy me because I like words I can use in real life.) Baking bread. (Have enjoyed doing so on and off.) Movies. (Check.) Theaters and concerts. (Check.) Bowling. (Once upon a time.) Assembling models. (See LEGO.) Cross-country skiing. (Hadn't tried yet; after I did I mostly hated it.) Relearn chess. (Nah.) Relearn bridge. (Nah.) Stained glass. (No idea where this came from.) Most important, these journal entries confirmed that I believed it when I wrote, "I am going to be OK."

Forward Progress

Feeling more settled emotionally allowed me to inch back toward the kind of life I had led in Columbia. For example, I welcomed visitors. The first were a couple who had been important in introducing reluctant me to the lesbian scene in Columbia and were among those supporting me through my painful fall. One was a first-rate copy editor, and I had quickly grown fond of her partner, who was a nurse. Although it was difficult to watch them being affectionate during their visit, I discovered that I could "talk about my relationship in the past tense with a fairly calm demeanor." We enjoyed "quite laid back" days with a bit of exploring and a lot of conversation about living as a lesbian. Not surprisingly, after they left, I was aware of how empty my apartment felt.

I also chose to socialize more with colleagues. One Friday, for example, I joined several of them for happy hour, which I later described as "a fun 90 minutes." I didn't feel out of place drinking Diet Coke, and I found myself enjoying the conversations and "some good laughs." What I thought especially important was that "I left when I was ready, when I was feeling I had had enough." But "I left feeling glad that I had gone!" I practiced that "social skill essential to me" -- leaving gracefully -- when I attended Patricia's potluck, centered on watching the film "Terms of Endearment." I had seen it and wasn't keen on watching it again, but I wanted to go to the party. So I made Cuban bread, grabbed a stick of butter, bought Havarti cheese and off I went. I already was proud of myself and felt even more so at the end of the evening. "I managed conversations okay, and surprisingly most enjoyed talking in the kitchen [with two men], which was an out from the movie. That also made it possible for me to leave when I was ready." I concluded that I had "a long way to go until I feel comfortable, but I'm doing better and feeling good about it."

I began to rediscover "creative observations" that I recorded with an eye toward some future writing project. After frequently seeing the neighborhood "bag lady" it struck me that "The Bag Lady Wears a Mink Coat" was a great title for a short story. "Or maybe I'll save it for my recounting of my Hartford experience," I noted before adding, "Oh yes, our bag lady really does wear mink and her dog has a coat, too!" (Sadly, I never used that title. Happily, I still have time. And most unconventionally, I still tend to begin a writing project with a title or the idea of a title.)

The confident woman who, in order to make a point, dared run for department chair at Missouri had been missing in action at UHa. Thus I saw it as a sign of progress when I first took a stand during a department meeting. I argued against a proposal that would have us evaluating each other and ranking each other for raises. "I may be alone, but I figure that's what [the department chairman] is getting paid for," I said. When it came time to prepare a *vita* and highlight my accomplishments, I decided I "had a good year. And they don't even know the stress under which I have operated."

Over the years, I had proved myself a willing listener with big shoulders always ready to be leaned on. That woman, too, had retreated for months; I was happy when she began to re-emerge. When a UHa friend was feeling blue on her birthday, it felt good to be the person she turned to, the person who suggested coffee and conversation. When a former student from Missouri wrote about the boyfriend who would not commit, it felt good to focus on someone else and useful to empathize from experience. When an Eau Claire grad agonized over a long-distance relationship, it felt good to be the person she turned to for "words of wisdom." And it was rewarding to accept a "consulting job" from an unhappy Hartford graduate I didn't know. A reporter at a small paper, she had shared her work with an editor elsewhere in hopes of moving up. She wasn't happy with his evaluation, so I agreed to review her work and recommend a course of action.

Playing out in the background was the Cal State search. Even today I question whether sending my *vita* was a remnant of unhappiness that fed restlessness or a sign pointing to progress in understanding I had options. I certainly hoped to be invited for an interview. A couple of weeks after their initial inquiry, the search committee called "unofficially" to say they were interested in me (and thus see if I were still interested in them). It took another week for them to officially invite me for a visit. I was psyched. "Hope it holds potential. I sense they are really interested in me. And I have nothing to lose, so I'm going with my mind open— I hope." I shared the news with two West Coast friends and was able to arrange to spend a day with Carol (graduate assistant from the Missourian People desk), who lived in San Jose with her physician husband. I shared the news with Missouri friends; all thought my going for the interview was a good move. Although I wasn't obligated to share the news with my chairman I did because I believed I owed it to the department "to be open about what was going on." I thought he was surprised. I also thought "he clearly wants to keep me, so an offer . . . may help me, even if I should choose not to accept it." (With a tinge of bitterness, I remembered that Missouri had not made me a counteroffer when I informed them I was leaving.)

My transparency did lead to some awkwardness -- and a lesson about university hiring practices. My colleague Roger dropped by my office the day before I was to leave for California. Turned out he had applied for the job and "would kill for it" because he was eager to return to his home state. He could not understand how it was the school was bringing me out because the search did not even close for a few more days. I told him I didn't know about the timing, that they had approached me. He seemed surprised by that "and considering the size of his ego, somehow put out. I got a kick out of that." In retrospect, I wish I had seen the "red flag" evidenced by that flaunting of their deadline. At least I saw one with the retiring Hayward chairman, who referred to women as ladies, as in: "I want you to spend some time with the ladies in the office" and "I can arrange for you to meet the lady from Women's Studies." And I didn't need 20-20 vision to see the biggest red flag of all: No one was present to meet me at the airport! That search committee member apparently had forgotten his assignment. Then, when finally I reached someone who could arrange for someone to fetch me, I learned we would go to dinner before I was taken to my hotel. Yowza! I had just flown across the country. My body was operating on Eastern time and already wanted nothing more than to sleep. And even if I had been hungry, a 7 p.m. California-time meal was the last thing I wanted.

I can't write about how my interview day went because I don't remember it (beyond being exhausted) and I didn't include specifics in my journal. I did take note of "wall-to-wall people, incredible traffic, green about to turn brown when the rains end, and what appears to be a pretty average campus." Happily, I do have specific memories of spending the next day with Carol, who ensured that I experienced the hairpin turns of Lombard Street, saw the Golden Gate Bridge, shopped at the Ghirardelli Chocolate Co. and savored lunch at Alice Waters' Chez Panisse. I wrote about how it had been fun to see women holding hands in Berkeley, to see the Pacific Ocean crashing against the shoreline, and to be warm. I wrote that "I really wanted to like California -- both the state and the job. I don't think I like either. Not sure it is the place for the kid from De Pere who has grown into the 36-year-old me." I continued: "So much to sort out and sort through. How little I learned in 72 hours and how much. And now I must make sense of it." I was told they were interviewing two others, which in my experience was typical, but I didn't know when. I hoped to be offered the job because then the "choice is mine; the other way is no choice for me, although it would be easier, I guess."

I arrived back on the UHa campus to the news I would get a $1,500 raise for the next academic year. Jane's admonition to "give yourself credit" was beginning to sink in. "I do feel good about [how far] I have come and I am challenged by where I am yet to go." On March 30, I finally got the call: Cal State-Hayward had offered the job to someone else. (I came to believe I was interviewed as the token woman candidate.) The call came the day after I got back a manuscript and was told it needed major revisions. "Feels like two rejections, something I'm not used to," I wrote. "The sting is deep, I suppose because so much of my image of myself is wrapped up in the professional me." I told myself it was time to take inventory. "Who are you, really, in 1985?!" My written response was:

> Feels like rejection even though the manuscript, in a slightly different form, will be presented at a conference in May. Feels like rejection even though I had decided that California, at least Hayward now, was not right for me.
>
> So chin up, Barb. There were 62 applicants for the job and you were one of three interviewed. Doesn't that say something positive about your work? And you don't want to publish mediocre stuff, so do with it what you can/want and move on.

Season of Rebirth and Renewal

My friend Martha's Easter/spring words, first shared a decade earlier on the porch of her Columbia apartment, rang true with the semester winding down. I drew on them as I "spoke" in this brief journal entry:

First day of spring

When you told me you were bailing out, it had just become fall. It passed, and now winter, too. And it is the season of rebirth and renewal. It can be for me, too, if I want it. And I do. If I let it. And I want to try. I want to do better than cope. I want to live again. To love and be loved. I need to love and be loved.

I drew on them when I described my fears about getting involved with someone again and told Jane I felt like I was in junior high school. "You are," she responded, "but you won't stay there long." I drew on them when I ticked off examples of what I had been doing in my work and socially to meet my needs. I drew on them when I thought about how appropriate it was that I began reading "Annapurna," a story of the marvelous courage of women who climbed that Nepalese mountain, on the day I claimed the courage and strength I had discovered in the last six months. Finally, I drew on them in my lengthy journal entry, as fitting a coda to this section as any words I might write today.

I want to "talk" tonight with the person who had the good day today, OK?

Q Who did have the good day?

A The professional Barb— who had an office to go to and work to do even though it is break.

Q Is she separate from the Barb who had a rather down weekend— at least a very subdued weekend?

A Not completely. This Barb had to fight an urge to come home after only an hour when it looked like she might have to eat lunch alone. So there was part of the Barb who easily retreats into her shell.

Q Why didn't she go home?

A She realized she wouldn't get much work done if she went home. Would probably just watch soap operas. She felt a strong urge to finish one of the tasks on her list. And she did. She was able to cross off one task, finished on Sunday, and two done today.

Q What did she do about lunch?

A Well, she stopped at the bank and then bought a Times at the bookstore, so she had something to read, and went to the cafeteria. And ended up eating with a colleague from History, who joined her at her table.

Q How did that go?

A It was OK. He's a rather stuffed shirt, but the conversation was okay

Q What else went on today?

A Got a call from a former Missouri Ph.D. who is interested in our job opening, so I found myself trying to "sell" the school. That was weird. Came home about 3:30 and graded obits— another task done. Got my federal tax refund, so I can send $1,000 to my money market and pay Missouri taxes and pay off charges. That feels real good. And I did a couple of things for myself: getting a haircut tomorrow; made an appointment for a screening at the HMO; made dinner and ate at the table; didn't eat a cookie at lunch.

Q So can you talk about why today felt better than the weekend?

A I felt useful (as opposed to slothful). I took charge of my day and didn't let it take charge of me (unlike yesterday, which I just sort of floated through, doing only the "easy").

Q Any ideas about how you might change the pattern of your weekends being so hard for you?

A I'm not sure. I have tried to be busy, e.g. doing a stint at RF or baking here, but that doesn't seem to help much. I could work but I really don't want to. I don't know that it won't feel better until there are some more people in my life. Opportunities to do. So if I choose not to do, it will be a choice and not default.

Q Why can't you do alone?

A I can [and did], but that hasn't been much fun. I guess I end up feeling sorry for myself.

Q So what's the answer?

A I've got to get myself into some situations where I might meet people and I have to take advantage of them, not go into my shell!

Closing Out the School Year

It was March 30, and three 8-week-old kittens were asleep on the bed in my guest room. I imagined that they couldn't figure out what had happened, only that they had been taken from their mother and familiar surroundings. After enduring a car ride tucked into a laundry basket covered by a towel, they were in a strange new house. The two females were mine; I was babysitting the other until a bookstore friend returned to town to take him. (I hoped we would be able to tell the boy from the girls!) As planned, I had named mine Eleanor and Sarah, "my ladies," and I looked forward to many years with them. So far the story sounds a lot like me arriving in Hartford. One of the kittens had shit on the cover of my new journal, which led me to write like an expectant parent (or a new love):

> I've thought a lot about what it means to be a cat owner— my respon-sibility to another living thing(s). Will I know when they are sick? When they need something from me? To recognize their moods? Will I be patient when their behavior doesn't match my needs/expecta-tions? Can I accept them for what they are? And how many ways will they change my life?

Not surprisingly, I turned to a book for guidance; it was the same book P had bought when we got our cats, Emma (in honor of Emma Gold-man) and Nikita Banana (my fanciful riff on the name-brand fruit). I hated that I would have to leave the kittens after only a week (the book emphasized how susceptible they were to stress) but I was eager to fly to Columbia for a visit before I headed to my conference in Illinois.

I compiled a lengthy list of expectations for Missouri. "I expect to find support— love— caring— sympathy maybe." I also expected to confront lots of memories— "most of them good"— so "I'll need some time for reflection." I expected to feel some regret, sadness and lone-liness, which also would require time for reflection. I most definitely expected to have some fun. Then there were my hopes, chief among them to hear some "we miss you; wish you were here." I also hoped "to be able to be me." The visit didn't disappoint. It was "non-stop peo-ple— friends backed up and stacked up as I moved from one to an-other." Rather than sapping my energy, as I had feared, the days gave me strength.

It did feel strange to be a visitor to Columbia, but staying with Joye and immediately talking with Karen (a new mom) ensured that I was not treated like a visitor. Yet again I realized how "Joye has made such a nest here for herself— so comfortable. It is what I hope for myself."

How nice it was to wake up to quiet piano music, hot coffee and her "Good morning." How nice it was to share a bit of conversation before starting our days in earnest. On visits to the Journalism School and Missourian, I enjoyed "lots of ego stroking." Everyone said how good I looked. More than a few people asked when I was coming back. I sat with Daryl one noon "and was glad he greeted me warmly and that we had a good hour together." My *real* lunch with Joye and Karen was just like the old days; we even went back to Karen's office to consult about a thesis. I was pleased to be asked to review a book for the journal published by the group Investigative Reporters and Editors. (I had served as its managing editor the year before I left Mizzou.) On the last day of my stay, I had Lunch 1 with a former graduate student, Lunch 2 with my former copy desk colleague Brian, then "real lunch" with Robin. We spent a wonderful afternoon together, including dropping in to see George. *Nice that there are no hard feelings. Nice that Robin and I found our way back to deep friendship after my coming out.* I dropped by the Women's Center before meeting another graduate student for a drink. Dinner was with Joye and two friends. Breakfast the next morning was with Joye and a friend, then I was on my way to Illinois. I got out of town without tears. I wrote that I didn't think it was because "I was trying to be tough. Rather, I was/am feeling strong. [I have] a new confidence in myself."

I arrived on the Illinois campus in the late afternoon. My hotel was connected to the student union, so after unwinding for a while I headed off to dinner in its dining room. "I put on the clothes I wanted to, took a book, and held my head high as I ate a leisurely meal." My remarks for the next day were written; I looked forward to the session I was chairing. And amazingly I looked forward to going *home*. Our Sunday-morning session -- the last on the conference schedule -- guaranteed a small audience (I knew from experience), but I never expected it would be just two! Luckily the Arkansas guys and I had handled our business over breakfast, so I got out of town early. I was excited about what we were doing and glad to be involved. As I sat in the St. Louis airport waiting for my direct flight to Hartford, I wrote about the need "to unwind and come back down to earth. For now, let me record that I feel good about the trip and good about me." I was happy that I had a therapy session on Tuesday so I could "do some rehashing and reflecting -- and then move on."

Move on I did, with days and weeks often as busy as my time in Columbia. The kittens were a handful, but there was no denying I enjoyed them. They appeared frequently in my journal, where I recorded their antics. One evening, when I wanted to climb into bed and read, I delayed doing so because "I feel guilty when I go in there. The kittens look sad when I keep them out, but they are in their chase mode now and I need peace." At the end of April, it clicked with me that "I have been here long enough to do spring cleaning." That inspired me to move my desk and computer equipment into the guest room, replacing them with its single bed. I covered that with a spread and pillows to create a sort-of couch. The kittens loved the new arrangement. I wrote how they "are so cute. They have taken over the rocker and its afghan, but they can't quite figure out why the rocker moves." After I cleaned out my back entryway, Eleanor and Sarah "got their first extended view of the outside world. How tentatively they crept toward what heretofore has been forbidden territory. But now they are glued to the screen door, probably dealing with sensory overload." *Who was this woman?* I wonder now.

I wrote less about teaching than I did the cats, and then it was generally to express frustration. I struggled to meet my students "where they were" because I found most to be far below my standards for minimum performance. After I spent an evening preparing progress reports for my Fundamentals class, for example, I concluded that "I doubt they will appreciate it, but I am glad I did it." Another time I wrote about having "to dress down four students" in that class. I "hauled them into my office and laid down some rules [about behavior]. The first [rule] to be broken gets them thrown out." I didn't want to have to do that, I told them, but I would "for the sake of the class." I found being *the* department disciplinarian (I was convinced no one else was) "was tough. If I wanted to deal with these sorts of problems I'd be a high school teacher." It was not that my students at Missouri and Eau Claire were all driven to excel, but almost all my journalism majors there had been committed to the profession. At UHa I found too many students unprepared for the "pay your dues" career path common in journalism as well as the rigors of my classroom.

Outside the classroom, I continued to grow more comfortable with my Communication Department colleagues. An interesting test of that came at the ECA conference in Providence, where I chaired a session and presented my paper, "Where Are the 'Second Woman' Stories?" In order to save money, four of us shared an $88-a-night room at The Biltmore ("quite the hotel"). After all, we didn't figure to spend much time in it. I found it "strange to be sharing a bed" with a married woman and so didn't sleep well. On the other hand, she and I had plenty of time to talk, and I enjoyed that. It was rewarding to have several people tell me they enjoyed my paper, but I had no interest in the rest of the conference, so I left early. (In fact, I had not even registered for it!) The high point of Providence was spending a couple of hours with Harry Williams, a buddy from the Missourian copy desk who had left to pursue a Ph.D. at Brown. We reminisced about our collaborative work on media stereotyping and he took me to dinner at a classic rib house in a part of the city I never would have found on my own.

My conference paper signaled an end to my scholarly obligations for the time being. I was eager for the semester to end and, more important, for a summer with few professional commitments. I was determined to make the most of that time. It seemed everyone talked about Cape Cod and how people flocked there during the summer. I lucked into renting a cottage on a dune above the Bay in East Sandwich and had immediately invited R and J to join me there in July. Lakeside-cottage vacations had been a staple of my childhood, and I hoped to do that, too. When I saw a classified ad in the New York Times for one in Vermont I checked it out, then rented it for two weeks in August. (I remember my phone call to the owners; one of my questions was, "Is it safe for a woman there alone?")

Among the myriad late-spring milestones (feeling that way to me, at least, because I still couldn't believe my personal crisis had passed), three stand out: I bought a new car. I ended therapy. A woman I met at Readers Feast asked for my telephone number. Each shows bits of the "old me" co-existing with the still-in-development "new me."

Car tale: The Fuego tried my patience from the moment I drove it off the lot. Niggling electrical problems required service almost as often as my MG, but I always was assured the issue had been corrected. Silly me to believe that over and over. In late October, I missed a speech by NPR's Susan Stamberg when I discovered I had no interior lights -- and no brake lights. I felt lucky to have made it home the night before, when I must have driven on the interstate with no taillights. Fuse replaced. Two nights later I had to cancel therapy because I again discovered there were no lights. I fumed! A couple of days later, I had lights -- on one side only. I vowed to make my rescheduled therapy appointment. I did. A week later, the car died as I was exiting the interstate some 25 miles from home. Luckily there was a service station at the bottom of the exit ramp; luckier still the car coasted into its lot. That would have been the last straw, but I was then in such a fragile state I barely could manage the decision-making needed to get it repaired. So it was that the Fuego and I limped along until it required repairs for the umpteenth time. "That cracks it," I wrote. "I'm getting rid of this thing before it goes off warranty." That was a reasonable move; the one I made next was not. Commencement was May 19. I was my usual end-of-the-semester exhausted but was contractually obligated to attend. The next afternoon, the old impulsive me bought a car. After listening to the sales pitch and test-driving a Toyota MR2 sports car, I made a $2,000 down payment. By the time I got back to my office, I knew I had made a mistake. I was apprehensive about the salesman's assurances he could sell the Fuego privately (for much more than the $2,900 the dealership offered) and besides, I didn't need to own a $13,000 car. Back to making a reasonable move, I called and unbought the car. Five days later I bought "a practical and dependable Subaru hatchback." The only question mark was how financially damaging the transaction would be. It hurt! (As my friend Sue put it recently, "I guess I am just now processing how cars are your kryptonite.")

Therapy ends: To paraphrase T.S. Eliot, the end came not with a bang but with quiet acknowledgement that it was time. The idea had been broached a couple of weeks earlier, but I was not quite ready. I needed time to think about how I would function without our "conversations." At our late-June session, Jane reminded me that in September I said the one thing I wanted out of therapy was to not lose touch with my feelings. She judged that I now was routinely acknowledging them, evaluating and deciding. "So, onward and upward," I wrote later. "Life does move along. And there's so much growing to do." I knew I would miss the woman who had been a regular fixture in my weeks for the last eight months. On my drive home, I wondered if I had said thank you. "I hope so, but I can't remember. Would a card be appropriate?"

Baby steps: In late April, a bookstore friend told me she had been playing matchmaker, so it wasn't totally unexpected when a fellow volunteer asked me if I wanted to hear a women's duo perform after work. Still, it seemed sudden and I needed time to process the turn of events. I asked for a rain check and we exchanged phone numbers. That night I wrote that "a movie and coffee, with time for talk, sound attractive to me." I also noted the scant details about her I had learned, including that she grew up in Wisconsin and, even more important, she was "age appropriate." Six days later we went to dinner. As I got ready for that date, I had more than a few anxious moments. After all, my only history was the "lightning bolt" that was P. "How do I behave tonight? How much do I want to tell? I don't want to scare her off and yet I have an overwhelming need to be up front about where I'm at right now. And that alone is probably enough to scare off anyone." I didn't scare her off. The starts and stops, twists and turns, ups and downs of "us" accounts for much of what I wrote through the summer of 1985 and beyond.

CHAPTER 25

Summer in the City

Despite the creature (dis)comforts of living in a third-floor walkup during Hartford's too-frequent heat and humidity (at times as awful as Columbia), I did enjoy moments of pure delight on Evergreen Avenue. On days like the laid-back Saturday after graduation, during a string of warm, sunny days and cool nights, I spent as much time as I could on my porch. That Saturday I started out there with my morning coffee and the newspaper. "It was remarkably quiet. Watching the neighborhood come awake. Making up stories to go with the people. Like the gay guy across the street who walked one lover to his car and not too long after met another guy. I saw them later in RF for breakfast. Or all day watching a couple fight, coming and going, she always screaming at him."

It was delightful to have unfocused days, even if they usually left me restless by the afternoon. I read whatever I wanted. I clipped stories from newspapers and magazines; some were for my future use, many got sent with letters as I returned to being a faithful correspondent. Sometimes I included a tidbit from the TV news, such as this quote from an investigator after an $8 million Wells Fargo robbery in New York: "It looks like a professional job, but when we catch them I doubt that they'll be Rhodes Scholars." I laughed aloud for at least 30 seconds after that. Other days were busy. I continued my shifts at RF, where I was doing something called shortlisting, a seemingly endless task that I described "not unlike dogpaddling in mud." One of my newspaper days went like this: Left the apartment at 8:15 to get gas and go to the post office. Courant at 9. Left at 12:45 for lunch meeting at UHa. Back to Courant 2-5:30. Home to feed kittens and change clothes. Colleague called and we talked until I had to leave for 7 p.m. appointment. Back to Hartford. Out for a late bite with NW, my date from the bookstore.

Summer-school classes were popular with young UHa faculty because they were a lucrative way to supplement one's salary. My department favored four-day, 9-5 workshops on a timely topic sure to attract significant enrollment. They were team-taught by whoever wanted to participate. In 1985 (and again in 1986) we offered "Communication Problem Solving in the Workplace: Case Studies." I jumped at the chance to join the team; my role was to examine the relationships among the press and organizations. I very much enjoyed teaching students how to deal with the news media during crises such as the Tylenol poisoning deaths in 1982. It was the first time I studied the journalism/ public relations roles in depth, and preparing my lectures broadened my own knowledge base. I advocated transparency and truth-telling, concepts that remain foreign today in many circles. (I didn't know that eventually my career would bring me back to public relations.) In addition to that workshop, I also agreed to offer "Perspectives on Journalism," a decision I regretted when I got my class list. "I must be doing something wrong because my seminar of two turns out to be two of the worst students I can imagine. One started the course in the fall and dropped; the other is one of the troublemakers from this spring's Fundamentals class. Ugh! It will be a long six weeks." I didn't mince words a couple of days later, either. "I don't want to teach Perspectives to those two jerks. I can't see us filling three hours with engaging discussion." At the time I was reading James Agee's "Let Us Now Praise Famous Men," one of the books we would study.

An unexpected bonus of being in Hartford that summer was the opportunity to spend time with Les and Ruth Anne. As soon as I got the note from Les saying they would be in Ogunquit, Maine, the first two weeks of June, I made plans to visit. The timing was perfect; I badly needed some R&R. "My sign is Aquarius, but I never have thought much about that until yesterday morning, walking the beach at Ogunquit in the fog. The tug was so strong. Wading in the cold surf— just looking— thinking— feeling content and at home." We three spent important time in "good, honest talk." Les and I walked the mile-long Marginal Way path along the coast to Perkins Cove. I ate my first clam chowder and my first swordfish. I enjoyed my best night's sleep in weeks at a gay-operated bed and breakfast. I returned to the Marginal Way to search for two rocks to use as bookends. (Most recently they were in a border in one of my gardens.) I didn't want to leave, but I had tickets for a women's music concert that evening. The drive proved effortless and I arrived home "convinced that my Subaru decision was the right one."

Even as mixed signals after numerous dates with NW coupled with my own "neediness" continued to perplex and challenge the "new me," I made numerous decisions that made the summer enjoyable. Being in the city allowed innumerable new experiences, many shared with friends and others alone. There was dinner and the ballet with my colleague Patricia (whose long-distance boyfriend left her lots of free time). There was an outing to the shore for seafood with an RF pal. There was shopping (at long last) for a stereo to replace the one stolen in Columbia. Patricia and I welcomed summer with dinner at a vegetarian restaurant (where I ate "curry something" for the first time), after which we drove into Hartford for a modern-dance program (another first for me). The next day we headed out of the city to a lake where Patricia could sailboard. We were joined later by some friends. I couldn't remember ever going to the beach with a group of friends, and I liked it. Although I did get too much sun and returned home with "a bit of burn" and a headache. The next morning I awoke to find myself "bright pink and prickly" and longing for a second set of hands to get lotion on the far reaches of my back. Eventually I went out to buy the Times and a one-pound bag of M&Ms before spending "a decadent afternoon reading, watching the Red Sox on TV and napping." Best of all, I "did not feel slothful."

Equating relaxation with slothfulness has dogged me throughout adulthood. It was nice to find journal entries reflecting how often I shed such guilt over that summer. On July 26 I put a "Gone Fishing" sign on my office door; I did not plan to return until September. Without my journal, I would not remember the many afternoons I spent lounging around the outdoor pool at UHa. It was a favorite destination on hot afternoons. I was content simply to be outside and in the sun. If only the cloudy days had been Courant days. I was glad to have that gig, but on the rare days I went to the newsroom only to learn there was no work for me, I didn't complain, other than to once mention how a day of editing would have paid for the $102 worth of books I had bought.

It also is only because of my journal that I know about my first Gay Pride Festival. In 1985, the festival was still considered "daring" for conservative Hartford (the first festival had been in 1982). My participation started with leaving a party at Patricia's before it really got going because I wanted to see the new documentary "The Times of Harvey Milk." Even though I went alone, "I wasn't alone in the auditorium; I was among an audience of 'my' people." I was proud of myself for finding the auditorium at Trinity College. I knew that "not too long ago I would have opted to stay home rather than venture out alone." I wanted "to remember how good it feels to do what I want, regardless." The next day, "with a great deal of lesbian pride," I helped set up the RF booth, which gave me "a feeling of belonging and contributing," then returned to the store so others could join the rally and march. Later I was able to return to the festival, "too late to get a T-shirt so I settled for a 'You Ain't Seen Nothing Yet' button."

Not long after the festival, it was time for the quick visit from J (half of the couple who had hosted me at Thanksgiving), who was on her way to a workshop in Maine. It wasn't just the comfort of spending time with an old friend with whom I could be tearfully honest about the NW situation. It wasn't just her sage advice about rebound relationships and admonishing me to be careful that I wasn't being used to fill someone's lonely times. It was the fact that she helped me shop for an air conditioner *and installed it*. Goodbye, 85-degree apartment! Over the weeks I also benefitted from Patricia's "listening, prodding, teasing, accepting." Equally important was how easily she and I "played" that summer. Topping my memory list is the free outdoor concert by Roberta Flack, among my favorite performers. We packed a picnic dinner and nonalcoholic wine, found a spot for our blanket and soaked it all in. At that moment, I thought how good it felt to be living in Hartford, how good I felt about how I was handling my life. That pride in self was bolstered after a conversation with NW during which I asked the difficult question that had been on my mind: "Why don't you think something serious could likely happen between us?" Her answer is not important; the fact that I asked meant I wasn't wrong about "liking the me I am becoming."

Summer 1985, on the rocky beach below my Cape Cod rental.

I already liked the me who over the years had generously shared my spaces with friends (and sometimes strangers who were friends of friends). In 1985, I shared August. First was the Cape, where the days with R and J left us each content in our own ways. Lazy days on the beach, just steps outside the back door, made losing track of time inevitable. I quickly concluded that I could easily spend two weeks, despite the cottage's smallness and dank-basement shower. (In fact, I did so for several years after that first stay.) I tried to enjoy our first trip to Provincetown, "but all around me and with me I saw pairs of women— and I wanted that too." We returned to P'town when a rainy day made the cottage feel even smaller. Incredibly, we ran into two women that R and J knew from Missouri. Our late-night drive back to East Sandwich was harrowing because of a gas gauge on E and not an open service station to be found. Thankfully, our nightmare vision of curling up and sleeping in the car did not come true. On our last night, I was in a mellow mood as I sat outside with my coffee to watch night come. "Haze on the water. Hard to tell the water from the early evening sky as gray-blue washes into gray-blue. Only if I look hard can I discern the outline of the water that, if we allowed it, would take us into open ocean. Someday. . . ."

A week later, I was writing from the screened porch of a cottage overlooking Lake Dunmore, in central Vermont. "Night sounds and quiet music on the stereo. Wonderful." That's how I started the entry detailing that trip. I arrived midafternoon (later than planned) and it was "a bit weird" because Tollie (from the bookstore) and a friend arrived a couple of hours later. I expected two more bookstore folks after they were to leave, but in between I would have part of a day to myself. "I'm glad I can share what I am lucky enough to have. And I'm trying hard not to get weirded out by the situation I have created. I make space for myself as needed."

One way I did that had me feeling like a kid again, and in my mind's eye I saw the black and white photo of my sister and me proudly displaying our catch at Lake Archibald. In between guests, I used the cottage's rowboat to go fishing. After three hours on the water, I had 10 fish in the freezer -- "several probably too small to bother with, and I won't from now on. But I feel pretty proud of myself for getting the boat out and in the water alone. For dealing with swallowed hooks and cleaning fish on instinct and distant memory." There had been "enough action to prevent boredom," and I fished until I didn't want to. I did think "an anchor would be nice," suggesting there had been logistical challenges. (When my parents called, I checked on my fish-cleaning technique, which Dad assured me was correct.) I continued to fish over my two-week stay; I thought it would be fun to have a "cottage party" when I got back to Hartford. I did admit to being unsure about what kind of fish I had in the freezer, and I found the Department of Conservation booklet's "what fish is it section" decidedly unhelpful. I therefore suspected I had "numerous illegals [too small]." I fervently hoped not to see any rangers.

I did hope to see more sun. My first week was marked by more than a bit of overcast. On one such day, I wrote that "today looks to be one of those days parents must dread— cloudy and gray and a shower. What do you do with the kids? Of course, I'm not so sure what to do with this adult. Maybe a walk— football or baseball on TV— read." It also had been cooler than I would have liked, and "right chilly" overnight. I wasn't brave enough to fire up the woodstove, until after a couple of days I just had to get the chill out of the cottage -- and me. On the

Monday of my second week, it was raining "not hard, but persistently, and the gray sky seems to promise a day of it." I was ready to be outdoors, but fishing in the rain didn't interest me. Boredom was preferrable to being cold and wet. At least the inclement weather gave me time to finish the novel "Civil Wars" by Rosellen Brown. Begun on the Cape, it had "the look now of a well-read book. No doubt sand and saltwater stains somewhere within its 419 pages (in paperback)." My review: "Quite a story and so well written. Almost too full to fully comprehend." I was "glad to have read it, and glad now to have finished it."

Finished just in time to welcome my last guest, the nurse who had been jilted by my former editing student. Remembering how she had been an understanding confidant, I immediately had invited her to get away from Virginia and join me in Vermont. The quiet and the rest would do her good, I knew. She arrived with horrendous circles under her eyes, her past week fraught with confrontations. During our five days together, we talked "intensely and in long spurts." We covered all the bases: life and love and like and lost and loving and all points in between. Our conversations seemed good for her and felt good to me. "My broad shoulders always have been good for listening," and I now had "some experience to draw on so my advice rings less hollow." Her presence gave the week a different shape than I expected, but before we left I told her how very glad I was that she had come. That I had enjoyed her "and the week would have been diminished without her."

And then it was September. (For the record, I left Vermont a day earlier than planned after I woke up and decided I wanted to see NW.) My second year in Hartford was under way. It started not with a personal crisis but with plenty of uncertainty. In the spirit of a favorite greeting card drawn by Mary Engelbreit, I wrote these words in my journal: "Life is beginning to feel like a chair of bowlies again."

Snapshots

There were numerous conversations with NW during my two weeks in Vermont in August 1985.

Sarah and Eleanor made themselves at home in Hartford.

CHAPTER 26

Hartford's Life Lessons

"Goddess willing [NW and I] will be together tomorrow and continue this process of growing in— like or lust or love or whatever." That was the last sentence I wrote in Vermont. And the last sentence I wrote before the "crazy, intense" two weeks without journal entries that followed. Next came the inevitable return to reality, to the world that required very different things of each of us. I did not realize how much of myself I had set aside; if ever a person had willed a relationship to be, that was me. At the time, however, I did not see that. My longing to be needed, wanted and loved blinded me to what others might have seen: two women rebounding into a couple. I only saw a couple. Until I heard the mixed signals in her words. "I care for you; you matter to me. I don't want to lose you from my life. But developmentally I'm not in a place for exclusivity or commitment, which would be real easy to do with you."

Words. Always it comes back to words. I didn't know where *I* was "developmentally." Some part of me sensed a change, though. I wrote: "I don't like the insecurities and fears that [have] surfaced— and oh that moment sitting at my typewriter, the sky crystal blue, a crisp fall day. And I was overwhelmed by the feeling that it was last fall. I was taken aback. And down." On Friday the 13th (how appropriate; how cliché) it seemed to me that I had no control over the "situation," and I didn't like the way I was handling that. The good news, I see now, was that I at least knew I was feeling something (desperation, uncertainty) and acknowledged it, if only to myself. My public response was a familiar one; I threw myself into my work.

I can write only sparingly about that work, however, because my journal once more became excruciatingly focused on my personal life. I had classes to teach, of course. I tried to be optimistic about finding a serious student or two or three on whom to focus my energies. I would do the best I could with the rest. At least my courses required less preparation because I had cycled through them. In May I had learned that I was selected to be a Humanities Center Faculty Fellow for 1985-86, so I had a project to work on. I had proposed examining images of women in Connecticut newspapers through a content analysis of published photographs. Because I was new to campus, I thought my application was a longshot. I was excited to have been wrong. The fellowship paid me a small stipend and released me from teaching one course in spring 1986. "Whoopee for me!"

I also spent time in the fall of 1985 in what I like to think of as the "academic two-step" -- the back-and-forth negotiating between editor and writer before a research article is published. It goes like this: (1) Faculty member submits her article to a carefully selected journal, along with a letter making the case for why it belongs there. I had sent an essay based on my "first women" stories research to Women's Studies in Communication. (2) Journal editor sends the article to reviewers for a "thumbs up" or "thumbs down," along with comments and suggestions. (3) Faculty member anxiously awaits a letter from the editor. Mine came August 9, 1985. She wanted to publish my essay in the spring 1986 issue, but the two reviewers thought some revisions were in order. One didn't like the title; the other thought the "purpose paragraph could be more-clearly worded and the writing tightened throughout." (4) Faculty member thinks things over. Eventually she responds to the editor. I did so with a letter on September 3. I argued that the title was "appropriate and does not contradict the point of the essay." I added that "If you want to change it, I think that is an editor's prerogative." I also sent a slightly revised conclusion. Lastly, I took issue with the second reviewer's editing. "I do not mean to seem obstinate, but I take offense at changes that, rather than correcting error, are of the 'I'd have written it this way' variety." (Something I regularly cautioned my students against doing.) I stood by my revised manuscript, but again conceded it was the editor's prerogative to make minor editing changes. (5) Faculty member eagerly waits to see her essay in print.

499

Thankfully, fewer steps were involved when I was invited to write profiles of several Native American periodicals for the multivolume historical reference guide being compiled by my colleagues in Arkansas. I had begun work on my assignments in Missouri, and writing about the two Navajo newspapers in my master's thesis was easy. But trying to track down other publications put my pre-Google reporting and researching skills to the test. I didn't always succeed. For a couple, I even reached out to the woman who had coordinated the weekend program for adult Indians I taught in at Eau Claire. She provided me some leads. Sadly, she also told me her program had run out of money and enthusiasm from students and faculty and no longer was operating. Professionally, I was happy to remain active and visible as a scholar of Native American journalism, although increasingly my focus was on women's issues. It was at Hartford that I began to identify primarily as a feminist scholar.

One of my early connections with like-minded scholars at UHa was Sherry, an art historian. She welcomed me into the Women's Studies fold; equally important, when I decided to move out of my Evergreen Avenue apartment, she alerted me to a vacancy in the Whitney Street house next to hers. The kittens and I happily took that first-floor apartment, a decided upgrade from our climate-uncontrolled space. We were a few blocks closer to campus -- and a couple of blocks up the street from NW. The spacious living area required more than my recliner and bed-couch, but shopping for furniture would have to wait. Shortly after settling in, I was off to Reston, Virginia, for a weeklong seminar at the American Press Institute. In those days, API described itself as a nonprofit center for the continuing education and career development of newspaper people. As I read through my stash of letters, I was surprised to learn how many of my former students had over the years attended API. Its three dozen or so annual seminars included one designed to keep journalism teachers up to date on the industry. I didn't feel out of date but had nothing to lose when I applied to attend. Its contributions to my efforts to build a journalism program were modest, but I learned something important about myself: I could drive the Northeast corridor and navigate the Beltway around Washington, D.C. Even then there was nothing fun about that route. (Driving into Hartford from Missouri, for example, had taught me to cringe when I saw a New York license plate in my rearview mirror.)

Shortly after returning from Reston, I stood in line among the preteens waiting to get their ears pierced at J.C. Penney. I already had gotten a "softer" perm, and shopping for clothes and furniture was on my "to do" list. NW definitely inspired me to dress better, and she helped me see how to do it. She cleaned up my language, too. She made it clear that I dropped the f-bomb much too often and she did not like it. I was uneasy about these changes, according to the infrequent journal entries I wrote in the late fall of '85. I vacillated between eschewing expectations and justifying them. I had not expected to become so involved with the first woman I actually dated. I was determined "not to lose myself again." At the same time, I felt more comfortable every day with the possibility of long-term with NW. Until I didn't. My therapist had assured me my junior-high school stage would be short-lived. I now think it lasted much longer than I realized. I had yet to learn how naïve romanticism might cloud my thinking. If I believed what I wrote, at least I had learned that "it can only be good between us if we communicate."

Lucky for me, I was not at all naïve about what UHa needed to shape up its journalism program. (Time would suggest I *was* naïve about the likelihood of succeeding.) The fall of my arrival, the university's Observer devoted an issue to the Department of Communication. The headline over the story about me was, "For aspiring journalists there is a very tough row to hoe." It started this way:

> A journalist's lot is not an easy one.
>
> The hours are horrendous. There is constant deadline pressure. Reporters often drink too much, eat too much and smoke too much. Some of the writing, such as obits and weddings -- which every fledgling reporter has to do -- is deadly dull. Relationships are strained, as are eyes that have spent too many hours in front of the video display screen.
>
> That's what journalism is actually like, says Barbara F. Luebke....
>
> Nevertheless, young people with stars in their eyes and visions of instant celebrity still aspire to be reporters.

> Luebke ... will help these young people on their way, while
> warning that "it's not a glamour job. There's a lot of drudgework that
> goes on behind the scenes."

The story went on to quote me about hoping to create "a program that will prepare reporters and editors for the print media" as well as provide "a grounding in the basics" for students interested in public relations and magazine careers. Students were writing their news stories in longhand, and the Observer mentioned my hope for a classroom with a typewriter for every student. By fall 1985, I had managed to get my reporting class scheduled into a classroom with computers! Thinking and composing at a keyboard is different than taking pen to paper, and having students in that environment allowed me to provide feedback while they wrote, not just after they had written. Helping students make that transition was challenging. Grading their papers was a lot easier. I found the Macintosh computers easier to master than my PC and before long I was an Apple convert. That is one decision I have never second-guessed.

I do wish I had not abandoned my journal after November 15; I did not write again until January 10, 1986. And then only to write that NW and I were "working to figure it out." A single monthly entry continued until the last, written April 15. Discovering that, I wondered why I had stopped writing. I wondered how it was that I was back to linking my happiness to another person. Here is what I learned from those paltry journal entries.

▸ 1985 was "an awful financial year," I concluded after doing my taxes. I "took a bath on the car, the furniture and now this— my taxable income almost double from last year and little to show for it." The mention of furniture referred to the Scandinavian-design living room set I had ordered from a store in Northampton, Massachusetts. Foolishly paid for in advance. The store declared bankruptcy shortly after my purchases. I never was informed of that. After promised delivery dates passed and numerous phone calls went unanswered, I became a reporter in search of answers. (Had Google existed, it would have saved me a lot of time and headaches.) I ultimately joined a long list of creditors and angry customers who, at best, might get 1 percent of their money back in bankruptcy court. I did not. Another lesson learned the hard way.

► I was promoted to associate professor, thereby returning to my rank when I left Missouri. It was still too soon to apply for tenure.

► I was working regularly at the Courant and therefore subject to evaluation. It was highly positive. My status also made me eligible for a year-end bonus, which at the time could be as much as six weeks' salary. The amount depended on how well the paper had fared financially, and in those days the country's oldest continuously published newspaper was doing very well. For me, it was like found money (and definitely more welcome than DeKalb's Christmas ham). Being in the office the day the bonus was revealed was like being in a room of lottery winners. Ah, the good old days.

► As much as I enjoyed the comforts of my new apartment, as the months wore on I spent less and less time there. I didn't neglect the cats, but Sarah and Eleanor didn't get the attention from me that they deserved. They frequently demonstrated their unhappiness by unspooling the roll of toilet paper throughout the apartment. In April I wrote that I would move in with NW "this minute— but maybe that's because I virtually have." With clever understatement, I explained that "I pay $505 a month for a two-bedroom cat house!"

To complete the story of my Hartford years, I relied on prompts from the dry recitation of facts and dates that comprise my *vita*, calendars, a variety of documents, and letters and cards from friends who did not give up on me even if I wrote less frequently than they were accustomed to. Those prompts proved amazingly effective in loosening shards of memory from which details emerged. Although there is in what follows an absence of the reportorial accuracy my written words have provided elsewhere, I am confident in the overall veracity of what I share.

My University Life

This is as good a spot as any to explain why I use UHa as shorthand for the University of Hartford. Quite simply, the faculty friends I hung around with did not hold our workplace in particularly high regard; saying and writing UHa (instead of the then-preferred UofH; today it is UHart) was a minor act of rebellion.

I couldn't complain about the professional support I enjoyed at UHa, and I contributed my share of university service. I coordinated the department's writing award and increased the amount the winning student received. I was elected or appointed to several committees, including the advisory group overseeing students applying for a semester in Washington. My favorites were the Women's Studies Steering Committee and the Arts and Sciences Committee on Academic Standing, the latter because of its role in upholding standards.

My Humanities Center fellowship required me to participate in the center's spring-semester symposium, "Sexuality and Culture." Of the nine presentations, mine was one of three by "locals"; the others included scholars from New York University, Yale and Southern Methodist University, and the author Carolyn Chute. (Her then-popular first novel, "The Beans of Egypt, Maine," had been published in 1985.) I offered a slide show to supplement my academic remarks, "Out of Focus: Images of Women and Men in Newspaper Photographs." Rereading those remarks in 2021, I couldn't help but wonder how much change I would find if I replicated that study today.

It was that fellowship project that prompted me to apply to be a Scholar in Residence at the Women's Research Institute at Hartford College for Women for the 1986-87 school year. (HCW was at the time a private two-year college. It merged into UHa in 1991 but kept its campus and all-women status. In 2003 UHa announced it was closing the campus and moving HCW programs to its College of Arts & Sciences.) I was disappointed to be wait-listed but couldn't argue with the reason: The selection committee believed I would be able to complete my project without their support, whereas two other "strong applicants" probably would not. I was encouraged to read that committee members were familiar with my scholarship, "which is very good." Ultimately, I was the beneficiary when one of those applicants dropped out.

As a "scholar," I received office space, library privileges and staff support for my latest project, "Images of Women and Men in Eight Connecticut Newspapers." Somehow I worked around my teaching and Courant schedules to block out time for my most extensive content analysis since my master's degree project. I enjoyed getting away to my quiet cubbyhole on the HCW campus, where I could work without interruption. Ruler in hand, I spent hours measuring and categorizing newspaper photographs. It was tedious but important work, I thought, gathering the data to prove the obvious: Newspapers mostly ignored women and often stereotyped those who made their way onto the printed page.

In February 1987, HCW sponsored a panel discussion on "Women in the Media: The Rise to the Top." One of four panelists, I was charged with discussing "Journalism: A New 'Pink Collar' Ghetto?" With more and more women in newsrooms, the issue of their impact (or lack of) was being widely discussed at the time. My "scholar" designation also caught the attention of the host of a community-run cable television program, who invited me to join a panel discussion about women and media. It was my first (and I think only) TV appearance. I would have been more nervous about it, but I knew how few people were likely to watch.

Although I was writing more about women and media, I had not abandoned Native American journalism. As planned, the ANPRA held its second meeting in February 1986 in Little Rock, Arkansas. As secretary/treasurer of the organization, I kept busy with correspondence and program-planning. I had not yet become jaded about attending professional meetings and was eager for that one because my trip would allow me to visit Mary Jo Meade, a Missouri student-turned-friend. One of the funniest people I have known, she was a faithful correspondent whose letters always made me laugh. The conference also would allow me to catch up with one of my graduate advisees, Dean Nelson, who was presenting a paper based on his thesis research. (He was then a new faculty member at Point Loma Nazarene College in San Diego; I had suggested that a presentation would be good for his *vita*.) What I most remember about that weekend is deplaning to a big hug from Mary Jo immediately followed by her breathless question, "Do you know who you were flying with?" I didn't have a clue. I probably didn't even know Bill Clinton was the governor.

There was one professional experience I could have done without. On June 3, 1986, I spoke to the journalism and mass communication classes at Portland (Connecticut) High School. In the letter inviting me, I had been told to expect 25 to 30 students. The teacher hoped I would "talk about newspaper editorials, specifically how topics are chosen, how a newspaper decides on a stand on an issue, and strategies, if any, are utilized by newspapers to assure fairness in dealing with the selected topic." Whew! "Additionally, we would like you to be able to talk about headline writing and editing. Because you are closely involved with these processes, you will be able to give students a 'first hand' knowledge of these newspaper processes." I would have about 40 minutes, by the way.

Since I gave my first newspaper tour to a group of Scouts in 1973, I have understood the importance of community outreach. The most-asked question may have been "How much does that roll of newsprint weigh?" but any opportunity to convey a love of journalism and its importance to democracy was worth taking. Portland came close to disabusing me of that notion. The students had no interest in what I had to say; they were there only because it was required. From the start, they ignored me, chatted (not quietly) among themselves, and behaved obnoxiously. The teachers waited painfully long before trying to control them and ultimately shooing them from the room. A letter dated the following day and signed by the students (but clearly written by an administrator or teacher) asked that I not judge the school based "on the behavior of a few" and hoped that I would "return to our school again under better circumstances." *Never!* Besides, they always misspelled my last name.

Whatever professional satisfaction I felt wasn't enough to override my steadily increasing dissatisfaction with teaching at UHa. I wasn't alone; hardly a lunch hour went by without someone griping about a student or students in general. As a private university, we were tuition-driven, so enrollment ruled the day. I recall being reminded at an all-university faculty meeting that the loss of 100 students meant $1 million less in the coffers. Whatever the numbers, lunch-table chatter involved all manner of opinions about quality being sacrificed in the interest of financial stability. Many of us simply could see no other reason for the full-tuition "pre-college" unit that we characterized as "grade 13." [An aside: To be fair, there was the fall semester that was delayed two weeks so a dormitory could be completed. Faculty were not expected to be on campus and were paid, which I cannot imagine happening at a public school. That delay allowed NW and I to visit Acadia National Park after Labor Day, a decided advantage vis-á-vis crowds and cost.]

Although infrequent, there were teaching moments inside and outside the classroom that provided me satisfaction and intellectual stimulation. A few students were as stellar as any undergraduates I ever taught, and their names elicit memories. We corresponded for varying periods after they graduated; as I had become accustomed to over the years, they sought advice and shared news of their careers and lives. For example, one wrote to thank me "for all your support, guidance and instruction. You really helped me define my career goals by sharpening my journalism skills and demonstrating how women really can get ahead in the newspaper industry." While letters such as that were reminders of one of the joys of being a teacher, there simply weren't enough such students. Eau Claire and Missouri (especially Missouri) had spoiled me.

There *was* satisfaction in teaching the summer workshops, especially the one my Political Science friend Victor D'Lugin and I designed. Victor was a lunch buddy before I really got to know him through his participation in Women's Studies. First we were on a panel that "debated" pornography, then he and I joined two other faculty members to present an intense two-hour program on date rape (for fraternity and sorority members, I think). In 1987, that topic was new; the first academic studies of sexual assault and rape on campuses had been conducted just a couple of years earlier. Eventually Victor and I collaborated on the summer course "Pluralism: Living With Diversity," another example of us being on the leading edge of a relevant topic, I think now. It was a tough sell to the committees that had to approve it. Our first challenge was persuading some committee members that we were qualified to teach it. Another was its cross-disciplinary nature, and a third was our proposed title. We obviously were onto something, because not only was the course successful but we later were selected to present a paper about it at the 1990 Senior Year Experience conference in Atlanta. And for that, we used our original title: "Celebrating Diversity."

As the deadline to apply for tenure grew closer during that 1986-87 academic year, I knew I did not want a lifetime position at the University of Hartford. My choice was to seek tenure anyway, knowing full well I would at some point leave, or give notice that I wasn't going to apply for tenure, which would trigger a terminal contract for the following year. I don't remember the decision being difficult. Although not applying for tenure was professionally risky, it wasn't the first time I chose an unconventional (dare I say exceedingly rare) path. By the spring of 1987, everyone knew what I had decided. The next academic year, my fourth at the University of Hartford, would be my last.

Interlude

By the time I decided my UHa fate, I already had made another major life decision. Instead of renewing my lease in the fall of 1986, I moved down the street to share NW's apartment. We had decided we were a couple, figured one rent was better than two, and chose her apartment over mine. (I have no idea why.) Our decision required me to solve two problems: what to do with my furniture (including some less than a month old) and what to do with my cats. The furniture went into storage; that was easy. The cats went to the Humane Society, my fingers crossed that they would be adopted. Abandoning them ranks among the most difficult things I've ever done.

Life as a couple who actually lived together was good -- and busy, as my calendars reminded me. I had my job, she had hers; both of us were less than satisfied at work. (I, at least, continued to be happy editing at the Courant. I lunched regularly with the deputy editor of the paper's Sunday magazine who, amazingly, was the "star" copy editor from my very first semester at Missouri. (Do an internet search on Jan Winburn to read about her incredible career.) Outside of work, there were concerts and movies, lunches and dinners with friends (gay and straight), parties and more. I remember a December trip to New York City to hear the Paul Winter Consort at the magnificent Cathedral of St. John the Divine. I think we ate at a hole-in-the-wall Hungarian restaurant. I know the New Age music bored me by intermission. And New York City still made me nervous. NW introduced me to cross-country skiing, which I tried to enjoy but seldom did. I did, however, enjoy reading in front of roaring fires at the Maine and Vermont inns where we became regulars.

Kay (the A+ Missouri copy editor committed to being a reporter) wrote in mid-May, and in response to my 1986 Christmas card stated: "You just sounded 'plain happy,' as if life were in balance and your most crucial expectations met. Carry on!" A couple of weeks later, my father suffered a stroke -- in bed after my mother had left for work. She found him when she returned to their dream retirement home in the woods north of Abrams and some 35 miles from the nearest hospital. (I never have been able to erase my thought about the terror he must have felt all those hours.) I didn't learn of the situation for a couple of days because NW and I were house-sitting (no cellphones, remember). When I finally spoke with my mother, she advised me to wait to come home until Dad left the hospital. That's why NW and I kept our reservation for Ogunquit a week later -- and why I let my family know how to reach me. I was floating on my back in the pool at the Anchorage resort when the call came that my father had suffered a second, even-more-debilitating stroke. Eventually my mother insisted on taking him home. On my flight to Green Bay to help her do that, I told myself I was about to do the most difficult thing I ever had done. I told myself I was strong enough to do it. And for the next week I tried to do as much as I could to get my father and mother settled into their new reality.

NW and I confronted another sort of reality: too many nights of our downstairs neighbor falling into a drunken sleep while his stereo's bass boomed. We began house-dreaming. By the time my terminal UHa year officially began, we were house-hunting. I had to tell my department chairman because I knew our employers would be contacted during credit checks. I didn't want him to lie about the fact I might be unemployed by the next summer; I did ask him not to volunteer that information. He agreed. Eventually we found a house "in the country" about 30 miles southeast of Hartford. Our offer was accepted in early October. NW withdrew her down-payment money from an investment account shortly after that. Just before Black Monday on October 19, 1987. Talk about timing.

An early November trip to Columbia provided me with a break from fretting about all that had to happen before the raised ranch with in-ground pool could become ours. The Science Journalism Center at Mizzou was hosting its Gatekeepers Conference for editors and writers, and Joye had arranged for me to discuss "When Science Crosses the Copy Desk." (I never failed to appreciate how strong my School of Journalism ties remained.) Best of all, it meant a free trip with time to visit friends. "Will be much fun having you here! 'Your' room is ready," Joye wrote. The conference challenged me to reflect on how my editing philosophy applied to an area of news with which I had limited experience. In preparation for my session, I tried to be more conscious of what I was doing and why as I edited stories for the Courant's Health and Science section. The result, I think, was among my best (and best-received) practical presentations.

I returned to Hartford energized by my trip. We closed on the house November 23rd (a Tuesday) and spent the weekend prepping it for the movers. That included a long Thanksgiving that left us beyond exhausted and happy to have a late-day dinner reservation at an inn near Hartford. We were not exactly appropriately dressed for the upscale dining room, but we didn't care. Home-owning readers won't be surprised that settling in was hard work, full of surprises that would continue for months. One of the first unpleasant tasks was stripping off black velvety wallpaper in what must have been a teenage boy's room filled with posters. By the time we finished spackling the holes, we were pros. So busy were we making the house ours that I did something I had promised myself I never would: I wrote a Christmas letter instead of crafting personalized messages in the six dozen or so cards I mailed. Sadly, I don't have a copy; it probably lived on a computer disc long since inaccesible.

Among our early guests at the house were a few of NW's coworkers, including Tony and his partner. Tony had volunteered to help me when I moved my furniture into storage, and I remember thinking at the time that he did not look well. I didn't think a lot about it, however, because he seemed to effortlessly carry heavy and awkward pieces of furniture. Not long after that we learned he had been diagnosed with HIV. He was the first person I knew to die of AIDS. The second came in 1996: my friend Victor, at age 51. I have unusually clear memories of three personal moments with Victor. (1) It was not unusual for him to drop into my office to chat, but this time he asked to close the door. He quietly said he wanted to tell me how much he admired me for *the way you just live your life, not "out" or loud but also not in the closet*. He said I inspired him to do the same. Until then I thought he was gay but was waiting for him to share. (2) NW and I hosted a birthday party for Victor, and I couldn't wait to give him my gift: a reproduction of an old advertising sign for poultry with Gay Cock in huge letters. He blushed as the rest of us laughed until we cried. (3) Victor came for Thanksgiving dinner in 1988, and before we sat down to our feast, he shared with me and NW that he had learned he was HIV positive. He didn't want to spoil our get-together, he said, but he needed us to know. I was thankful that he entrusted us with that devastating news. When I hugged him, I didn't want to let go. [An aside: A recent post about Victor in the "Hartford on the Brain" blog reminded me of his numerous accomplishments "both in terms of legislative victories and philosophical changes to the state of activism in Connecticut." The 1991 speech in which he came out publicly as HIV positive and his testimony to legislators, many believe, were "instrumental to the passing of Connecticut's gay rights bill" that year.]

A UHa Surprise

Throughout my final year at UHa, I was confident that I would find a job and not be without a paycheck for long; after all, I always had done so. As a homeowner responsible for half a mortgage, however, I felt added pressure. Fortunately, there were universities within commuting range that had journalism programs. Fortunately, a few were searching for a faculty member. Fortunately, I possessed credentials that were difficult to ignore, and so I was invited for interviews. Unfortunately, none was a good match. Within several minutes of meeting the faculty at one, I knew that I wasn't interested. Another seemed more promising, until I sensed they really were not interested in my ideas. After a miserable drive to a third, which I had suspected was too far away, I had decided "no way" by the time I found a parking space. Perhaps that is why I failed to stop myself from dropping an f-bomb, for which I immediately apologized by saying it was just that I felt so comfortable there!

Then, sometime in spring 1988, came a surprise offer. I had tried to not pay attention to the search for my replacement, but it was difficult. I didn't know the details but did know it hadn't gone well. The dean suggested that the department chair ask me if I would be interested in staying another year if he could get my appointment approved. With no job and no more teaching prospects, I said yes. The administration did too, but made it crystal clear in my highly unusual appointment letter that 1988-89 really would be my last year as a University of Hartford faculty member.

Out of necessity, I turn to my Christmas letters of 1988 and 1989 to end this chapter because they are the primary sources for most of what I can document about that stage of me. I was emboldened by what Les wrote after receiving one: "You write a great Christmas letter that belies all the bitching about them we have heard in various columns and articles over the years. I feel I am a part of the Luebke family and all the goings-on as a result of that. It just plain demonstrates that you are a writer-editor-journalist, after all, doesn't it?" Perhaps, I think now, that was the ultimate lesson Hartford taught me.

[An aside: I am immensely proud to have played a small role in Les' move to the University of Kansas in 1986. I alerted him to the opening for an experienced editing teacher and encouraged him to consider applying. Later we discussed it at length when he and Ruth Anne were vacationing in Ogunquit. I think I wrote a letter on his behalf. When he called to tell me of his hiring, I was overjoyed. He deserved to teach in a first-rate journalism school at a first-rate university (even if it was Mizzou's archrival in athletics). It felt like a circle closing, from his earliest encouragement of college-sophomore me, to his years of personal and professional advice, to us commiserating as colleagues, to accomplished-professor me encouraging *him* to spread his wings.]

December 1988

Season's Greetings, Friends:

From Lebanon, Connecticut, comes my sincere wish for a joyful holiday and a peaceful new year for you and your loved ones. I

512

treasure this time of year, not the least for the chance to renew friendships; each of you enriches my life.

*   *   *

I first tried my hand (my computer, actually) at a Christmas letter last year, when I was overwhelmed by settling into a new (and first) house. This year we have gone through the seasons on Goshen Hill Road, and house-owning veterans say there will be fewer surprises. I hope so.

New Year's Day 1988 ended with a non-functioning water pump. (Here that means NO water -- never mind enough for flushing; just ask our overnight guests.) Ever tried to find a plumber on a holiday weekend? Super Bowl Sunday found us mopping dishwasher water off the kitchen floor. Oh well, we were saved from watching all those Redskins TDs! The rest of winter was manageable (only had to have the driveway plowed five times), and spring found us marveling at how beautiful our yard is at that time of year. Of course, to get it looking good and to keep it looking good, we started most Saturdays and Sundays with trips to the hardware store. (And you should see me on the John Deere riding mower!!) We learned something about concrete and "easy-to-assemble" toys when we installed my NBA basketball backboard. And we learned something about digging up sod when our "hired hand" proved to be less than adept at rototilling new gardens.

Late spring found us opening the pool, and for 10 days or so we were the dispirited owners of a 20,000-gallon algae farm -- until a new filter could be installed. I learned a lot about better living through chemicals as I slowly coaxed the murky water back to inviting, sparkling blue. Now if only we can figure out what makes the belching noise! That noise didn't stop us -- and a whole lot of friends -- from enjoying the pool, however. I swam every day in August save for three rainy ones, and I took my last dip in mid-September.

While my partner, [NW], reads seed catalogs this winter, I'll be reading pool-accessory catalogs in search of a solar cover or solar water-heating system. I intend to have the longest swimming season in New England. I don't know what [NW] intends -- except to double the size of the garden. I'm not sure why; by late August breakfast was my favorite meal because I didn't feel compelled to eat tomatoes.

Our October burglars didn't, either. They climbed in the kitchen window and knocked a row of late-ripening orbs into the sink. Then they helped themselves to all our jewelry, some camera equipment, the VCR and tape deck. We live only 30 miles from the Insurance City, but we are still waiting for our checks.

Shortly after the break-in we marked the end of our first year here, with the furnace displaying a mind of its own. The repairman, squeezed into our tiny furnace room, just looked about in wonder -- and somehow undid the mess a previous do-it-yourselfer had created.

Does all this sound like Money Pit II? I didn't see the film and I don't plan to; I've lived it. Maybe we should have held out for a 250-year-old saltbox after all.

* * *

Lest that chronology leave you despairing that my 1988 was a disaster, I offer these tidbits:

I found gainful employment -- another year at the University of Hartford. . . . and I am in the midst of job-hunting again. Quite fortuitously, the University of Rhode Island is looking for a journalism department chair and the University of Connecticut is adding a journalism faculty member, so I at least have teaching jobs to apply for. Wish me luck.

Our household grew by one on August 1, when we adopted 2-month-old Katie -- a golden retriever/Samoyed. She's good-tempered and smart -- and full of puppy spunk. So far, so good. (If only she could catch moles, not just sniff them out; we have the New York subway system under our yard.)

Tried X-country skiing again last winter; this winter I decide whether I like it or not! It took me only a week on Cape Cod in 1985 to decide I love it there. This year's stay did include one week of rain, which limited my beach time. Went to Maine and Acadia National Park after Labor Day, and was smitten by a two-hour sail on a three-masted schooner. I'm ready to go for a week -- I think.

I had a scholarly article ["Out of Focus: Images of Women and Men in Newspaper Photographs"] accepted by the journal Sex Roles, and the only change asked for required me merely to add one sentence.

And so it went here in 1988. I am banking on 1989 -- the year of my 40th birthday -- to be equally full. No sympathy cards or black balloons for me. I expect it to be a Fab 40!!!!!

*   *   *

Of the cards I received that December, two stood out. UHa student Mindy's included this: "I've done it! In a few weeks, I'll receive my Bachelors. Thank you for helping me realize this dream. There was a lot of struggle and pain, but I believe I'm better because of it. Good luck to you. I hope you'll decide to continue teaching -- somewhere. You're a great teacher." Peggy, a Missouri graduate with a wicked sense of humor (I could make a bundle publishing her and Mary Jo's letters to me), started as a high school teacher before going to work for Hallmark. I did a double take when I saw that she was credited with the words on the front of the card she sent. And the sentiments written in three *serious* cards she included were hers, too. I couldn't have been prouder.

<u>Christmas 1989</u>

Dear friends:

Holiday greetings from Lebanon, Conn. As another year winds down, I am glad to have the excuse to share a few words with you. I hope this letter, my third seasonal communication, finds you well, happy and ready for the '90s.

I began drafting this letter on Thanksgiving weekend, when the whole Luebke gang got together for the first time since my Ph.D. party in 1981. We (brother Tim in from Denver; [NW] and I from Connecticut; Kris, Fred, their three boys and 72-pound yellow Labrador, and Grandma Conger from Oshkosh) created quite a full house for my mom and dad up in the woods of Northern Wisconsin, but I don't think they minded too much. We joked about mom's 30-pound turkey, but by the time we all left on Sunday, there weren't many leftovers. There were lots of other laughs that weekend as we reminisced about adolescent antics mom apparently had wisely forgotten -- or never known about. Needless to say, the cliched good time was had by all. The cherry on the sundae: watching three quarters of the Packers-Vikings game and then listening to the victory enroute to the airport. Tim, [NW] and I -- who must be content to cheer on our Packers from afar -- were in pig heaven.

1989 turned out to be quite a family year for [NW] and I. We drove to Wisconsin after my five-year penance at the University of Hartford ended in May and spent a week. My hands will never be the same after raking the oak leaves that seemed to take forever to rake down the hill and then haul away from mom and dad's Crivitz yard. After they left on a Fishing Has No Boundaries trip, we headed to Kris and Fred's [in Oshkosh] for a couple of nights on the sofa/sleeper. (Later in the year, I was happy for them when they bought their dream house; I was happier for me when Kris told me she had sold that sofa.) Somehow during the course of our visit we invited my 12-year-old nephew, Nick, to come East after school was out. And he did. Whew! We showed him as much of New England as we could in 10 days, and Kris never has forgiven me for introducing him to the L-word (lobster). I think he had a memorable visit; I know I will never forget watching him in the Atlantic off the coast of Maine in mid-June and wondering why he didn't turn blue.

We played tour guide again in September, when my parents and two aunts came to visit for a week. Because my dad won't fly, and because of his health, we were not sure they would ever be able to drive the 1,200 miles east. So it was a real treat to have them. It also prompted us to do some things in the house we had talked about for two years: new lighting fixtures, repairing the plumbing in the downstairs bathroom and painting over the black woodwork in the spare bedroom. We rented a van and the six of us toured northeastern Connecticut and then, when it was obvious Hurricane Hugo was going to miss us, we headed north to Vermont. (By the way, the northeast is banning my mother; last time she was here she brought Hurricane Gloria, which did not miss us.)

Other visitors this summer (ahh, the pool!!) included my friend Karen Small, up from Tennessee, and our friends D and C from Philadelphia. They were in the house-hunting phase and went home with all our horror stories -- and sunburns -- and promptly found themselves an abode. Already they have horror stories of their own. Ain't adulthood grand?!

*   *   *

I am happy to report that I found gainful employment -- and not as a fast-food counterperson. Since July 1 I have been chairwoman of the Department of Journalism at the University of Rhode Island. I am working harder than I have in years, and mostly loving it. The challenges of the job are exciting and rejuvenating. We have 265 majors and six full-time faculty. I am reminded of my own undergraduate days at Eau Claire, and I feel as if I have returned home. My proudest accomplishment so far is getting us a $176,000 grant to refurbish our reporting/writing lab. I can't wait for the new year, when the planning and buying gets in high gear. That's got to be more fun than the "begging" was.

*   *   *

I turned 40 without too much trauma. And with 41 just around the corner, I figure I am safe until The Big 50. That one does sound scary. I find that with teaching I have trouble marking time. Weeks and months fly by and I am never sure where they have gone. For the past 15 years, I have spent most of my time with people whose faces change but whose ages don't; so why should mine? Oh well, as the bumper sticker says: I may grow old but I'll never grow up! (I wore red Chuck Converse sneakers to my birthday bash.)

*   *   *

In the spring I started working on a young adult's book, and I have three chapters pretty well in hand. Even took an adult education class to learn some of the ropes of book publishing, and hired nephew Nick as my first reader. Haven't given him much to do lately, but I hope to change that. I'd like to be able to include order forms with next year's letter!!

*   *   *

Katie the pooch turned 1 in June, and off we went to dog school. Barb, the reluctant dog owner, got the privilege, given her "not working" status at the time. What fun; I'll stick to people school, thank you. Katie's attention span proved to be close to non-existent and my ability to issue commands in dog-appropriate tones was the same.

Then there was the rain. Dog school was on Wednesdays, which proved to be this spring's Designated Rain Day. Eight weeks of school stretched into 9, 10. . . . Class got smaller and smaller, until one night just Katie and I showed up. Forty-five minutes in the spotlight was just too much. On the way home, I asked Katie if she wanted to go for the last two classes. She said no, so we didn't.

*　*　*

And that was the year that was. Or at least some of it. I could tell you about having to drain water <u>out</u> of the pool several times because we had such a wet summer. I could tell you about how [NW] doubled the garden and seemed to thus double the critters, who got more of the produce than we did. I could tell you about failing to get all 210 bulbs planted before winter set in and searching in vain for a way to salvage them. I could tell you about the stuffed penguins in the front yard, the little one stolen by some Neanderthal. I could tell you about a dozen different kinds of birds at the feeders in winter. I could tell you about terrific sunrises and sunsets seen commuting an hour to and from work. I could tell you about the pleasures of being a captive audience for "All Things Considered" during those commutes. But I won't. I'll simply close by telling you that at various points during my year, you pop into my thoughts. And I treasure those moments, even as I treasure the various shapes our friendships take.

CHAPTER 27

Moving On, Moving Up

My Christmas 1989 summary was upbeat, and the paragraph about my new job accurately conveyed my professional enthusiasm. The summary was also incomplete; personal turmoil did not belong in a holiday letter. It was brewing, but I was unwilling to acknowledge any discomfort at home. I had for months denied the stresses of potential unemployment, home ownership and family issues -- not to mention ghosts of relationships past. I slowly but steadily retreated to behaviors I had worked hard to change. Professionally, words flowed freely as I wrote and talked my way to the University of Rhode Island. Personally, I disregarded my feelings and clammed up. Eventually I paid the price; so did NW.

My "bonus" year at UHa is best described as weird. The lame-duck year that preceded it had been more awkward than I expected. In fact, after our first department meeting in September 1987 I stewed a bit before deciding to go "on the record" with a letter to the department chairman about my concerns. I explained that "like my fellow lame duck, Ronald Reagan, I continue to take the responsibilities 'of the office' seriously. I had hoped that whatever expertise I brought to the department three years ago would continue to be valued." I felt it was not. I was upset to have first learned about two developments directly impacting the journalism program at the department meeting. To have not been told about them, I wrote, was "a serious breach of professional courtesy." To have not been consulted about them "felt like an insult." Particularly galling was the creation of a media writing course for spring, something I had been suggesting for more than a year. I did not understand why I was not involved in planning the course. I concluded my letter by writing, "If my decision to leave the university, based on considerations important to me, means I no longer am considered an active member of this department, so be it. But I prefer that this not be the case, because I think the department is the loser in that scenario."

Speaking out seems to have made an impression. When the search for my successor resumed a year later, my "lamer duck" status found me somehow involved, although the details are long lost. Les noted in a letter that he had seen a reference to me in a professional newsletter that prompted him to ask, "What are you doing? Leading the search for your own replacement? That's different if that's it." And then he asked if I was having "any luck with other positions." He was not alone in wondering, and when my spirits flagged, the mail seemed to magically bring a message of support. One that moves me still came from Ursula Runions, the mother of my University of Oregon friend Brenda Ann (and our spring break host way back in 1972). "Let us know if you change positions," she wrote. "Must keep track of my girls. Made me proud of you to think it was not that easy to replace you, and you were asked to stay."

Just a few months later, having been hired to chair the Journalism Department at the University of Rhode Island, I was the proud one. Also the relieved one. The excited one. The eager one. The confident one. How lucky was I to find a position just a 50-mile commute away? A position that was a step up -- not lateral or down? Nonetheless, I don't remember thinking of URI as my forever job. For one thing, I was aware that Karen List, my Missouri friend who had since moved to the University of Massachusetts, had not been happy there. But I thought it was the perfect job for me at the time.

I exuded competence and confidence in my application letter. Given my experience and accomplishments, I would have been surprised not to make the first cut (a telephone interview). I was amused by being able to sit at the dining room table in pajamas, the cord stretched from the wall phone in the kitchen, as the search committee chair quizzed me. When I eventually was invited to campus for a formal interview, it was time to shop. I was determined to dress for success. With NW's help, I settled on two suits (in case there would be a follow-up interview): one double-breasted, black-and-white pin-striped, the other purple. Those proved to be the last skirts I ever bought.

[An aside: That wall phone was my physical lifeline, its coiled cord so often stretched to the maximum that it slowly lost shape. It kept me connected to the people *who really mattered*: family and the friends I reached out to -- and who reached out to me -- in good times and bad. To this day I can picture myself receiving two particular calls. The first was from Joye, calling in early 1989 to tell me she was getting married on March 18! The ceremony would be for family only, but she hoped I could come for the celebration afterward. It took me a minute to process her news; my profuse congratulations followed. Sadly, I was unable to make the trip to Columbia. The second unforgettable call came in early February 1990. My longtime friend David Gunderson was the bearer of its bad news: Les Polk had died (he was just 61). After we hung up, I called fellow Eau Claire friend Laurel Walker, who was getting ready to call me with the news, which she had seen in a wire-service transmission. Sadly, I was unable to make the trip for Les' funeral. Afterward, Ruth Anne wrote that although "I owe you more than this card," she wanted to thank me "so much for the beautiful flowers . . . and for your call and writing to the boys." *It wasn't enough*, I knew. *I could never do enough to show my love.*]

I allowed plenty of time for my first trip to Kingston, Rhode Island. Good decision, because I was more nervous than expected and made a navigational error that took a few miles to correct. That proved to be the day's only hiccup. I was accustomed to the university routine of tightly scheduled interviews, which for this job included search committee, department members, some students, two associate deans, the dean and the provost, with a working lunch that ensured I had no time to relax. I found the faculty and students on edge. The department only recently had averted a merger with the Communication Department. They were rightfully proud of being the only stand-alone journalism program in the state and were bruised from the fight to remain independent. The dean was not convinced that was the right decision, I thought. (Indeed, he had appointed a woman from English as interim chair.) I concluded that if the new "chairman" failed, the department would, too. I took advantage of every opportunity to make clear my commitment to *journalism* and to educating *journalists*, i.e., reporters and editors, and my philosophy about how best to do that. I also was

521

adamant that the classroom/lab equipped with electric typewriters was woefully outdated and had to go.

I was particularly appreciative of a letter to the search committee written by my UHa colleague John Roderick (ironically, a Rhode Island resident). John had been on the committee that hired me; he held a joint appointment in English and Communication, and taught journalism courses. He explained that my extensive practical experience at Missouri had suggested I was "the ideal candidate to get our job done. She was." In one paragraph, he captured my five years of hard work at UHa: "Single-handedly, she developed a half dozen new courses, ushered them through the difficult maze of college and university curriculum committees, and began to teach them in the newly fashioned journalism program. She was instrumental in moving the University to support an entire lab for computerized instruction in print journalism." Of my teaching, he observed: "In a word, she is excellent. . . . If her students ever have a complaint, it usually comes early in the semester when they initially encounter the rigors of her expectations. All come to appreciate the attention to detail and caring that ultimately mark her courses." John's description of how he experienced my leadership style was reassuring. "She knows her discipline well enough to provide the kind of quiet leadership that engenders respect. She listens to the viewpoints of others; she has a keen sense of fair-play; and she knows instinctively that a team effort can accomplish more than solitary performance while she nevertheless permits each team member to run with his or her particular strengths."

Eventually I was offered a position as an associate professor of journalism with tenure, along with a three-year appointment as department chair. I had lobbied for full professor, which I believed my 15 years in higher education warranted, but I made peace with the fact that URI wanted me to prove myself there. Academic-career-wise, my credentials would be the same as those I had left Missouri with five years earlier. Oh well. At least tenure guaranteed me employment. But before I told the dean yes, I raised one concern.

On April 10, the New York Times had reported that the U.S. Department of Labor cited the university for acting unfairly when it did not promote two female associate professors. Shortcomings in pay equity, job assignments and maternity leave for six other women also were found. The dean echoed the president, who was quoted as blaming "procedural errors" and saying there was "no clear and concise proof of any pattern of discrimination." The president of the faculty union was quoted as saying university officials "haven't unlearned their former practices" since a sex discrimination lawsuit the school settled for $1.3 million in 1985. I couldn't help a momentary pause to wonder what might lie ahead for a feminist lesbian department chair fond of red high-top sneakers. Then I accepted the job.

I officially began work on July 1, 1989, but I had gone to campus a couple of times before that. Once was in mid-April, after my appointment was made public, when I made an unannounced visit to attend a symposium organized by a journalism faculty member. I remember being greeted warmly by my soon-to-be colleagues, students about to graduate, other students I would get to know, and several alums who had been instrumental in protesting the proposed merger. But what I most remember is the flamboyant faculty member from the English Department who greeted me with "I absolutely *love* your shoes." I didn't wear those red pumps nearly as often as my red high-tops, but I thought of John Leo every time I did. My second pre-job trip was to show the campus to Joye, who had stopped in Connecticut for a visit. We enjoyed lunch in a small commercial area adjacent to the campus and then, odd as it seems to me now, searched in vain for the town we knew must be nearby. I had not yet learned how URI is unlike other campuses I knew. There is no off-campus student "ghetto." After a year in a dorm, most students choose to live "down the line" near the beach in rentals available in the off-season. Wakefield, that nearby town, is about 4 miles from campus; its livelihood does not revolve around the university.

No stranger to a new job in an unfamiliar setting, I was prepared for a period of uneasiness as I learned my way around yet another campus. One thing was decidedly different: I had a secretary. More accurately, the department had a secretary. She considered me first among equals, however, although I seldom played that card. I was used to preparing my own correspondence, for example, and she never could understand why I continued to do so. Even though I found only a clunky manual typewriter in my office when I arrived (she had an electric), it made no sense to me to write a letter in longhand so she could type it. (It didn't take me long to realize that in doing so I had cut off the flow of "inside" information she was accustomed to.) I also could not get used to her opening my mail; eventually I asked her not to. (Thus eliminating another source of her information.) I had much to learn about being "a boss."

[An aside: My office was the most spacious of my career. One of its doors was off the hallway; I used the other one, which took me through the secretary's space. My "open door" policy meant the door between us was seldom closed to her eavesdropping. The furnishings struck me as having been chosen by a male business executive: large desk, couch and chair of faux leather, credenza, small round table and filing cabinets. One morning, just a few weeks into the job, I arrived at 8:25 and when I unlocked the door into my office I was startled to find a custodian asleep on the couch. *This will never happen again!* I commanded as I ushered out bleary-eyed Jim. Many months later, after my office was burglarized for its computer equipment, the credenza came in handy. I had it moved to block the door from the hallway.]

More familiar was working under a micromanaging dean. This one, for example, expected us to be on campus from 8:30 to 4:30 and was known to call to check on faculty. I had not experienced that kind of oversight in some time, and it didn't take me long to remember every irritating habit of Roy Fisher at Missouri. But monitored office time was a moot point because I had more to do than there were hours in the day. And besides, I was a workaholic prone to putting my job ahead of all else. I did, however, try to leave campus at 4:30 to be home for dinner. Commuting thus kept me from attending most evening and weekend programs, which over time didn't sit well with me.

The dean allowed a "research day," when I could have worked at home, but I quickly excused myself from any expectations of research/ writing for a year. At institutions such as URI, faculty are evaluated on three contributions: teaching, research (scholarship) and service. The "publish or perish" cliché reflects the common belief that research is most important, and I was aware I would be expected to do more of that if I were to be promoted. Nonetheless, my first priority was helping the department do everything necessary to solidify its independent place in the College of Arts and Sciences. My second priority was teaching. And although I was eager to be involved on campus, that too would have to wait -- with one exception. During my interview with the dean, I told him of my desire to be a part of the interdisciplinary Women's Studies program. I broached the topic again early in the summer, and he suggested I meet with the program's director when she returned from a sabbatical in Ireland. More on that fateful encounter later.

The summer of 1989 was unlike my most recent summers, which had been generally carefree and focused on maximum pool time. Instead, I faced a summerlong initiation into what exactly it meant to be a department chair at URI. As I came to learn, the job involved pushing a lot of paper, running interference between faculty and administrators, advocating for the department's needs even as all the other chairs were doing the same, and often having to say no. Having worked with department heads for 15 years proved to be necessary but not sufficient training for the role.

I wasn't naive about bureaucratic tasks, but I was idealistic about leading colleagues to do great (or at least good) things. I wasn't naive about faculty members prone to self-absorption and abstraction. I wasn't naive about lip service paid to students by jaded colleagues unwilling to change. I *was* naive about an institution's ability to bog itself down in committees, meetings and dust-collecting studies. And I was idealistic in believing things could be different and incredibly excited to be doing what I had been longing to do: help build a better journalism program *at a school that cared.*

I was immediately consumed by the work of doing that. I wish I had been keeping a journal then. Absent such a record, I grasped at bits of information in a frustrating effort to re-create that summer and my first academic semester at URI. I know I wrote (and spoke) thousands of words in memos, evaluations, position papers, proposals and the like. Without a doubt, the most important were those that resulted in funding for a contemporary writing/editing classroom for our students.

I had hoped we might find financial support from the Providence Journal, then privately owned and the most significant news outlet in the state. I quickly learned that with two private schools (Brown and Providence College) in the city, and with New Englanders' penchant for valuing private education over public, we should not count on the newspaper for much of anything. Kingston was only 30 miles from Providence, but in tiny Rhode Island they were worlds apart. (Rhode Islanders, the joke goes, pack a lunch for a trip to South County, the common designation for the southern part of the state.) Thankfully, during my interview with the provost he had mentioned a foundation that annually funded a few URI projects. It was the Champlin Foundations (sic) that ultimately ensured that URI journalism graduates would have the computer skills increasingly necessary to compete for jobs.

My proposal to modernize the classroom with networked computers, printers and such was among several "asks" from around campus; it made the cut and was one of those the president agreed to support. To prepare it, I had worked for weeks with salesmen from Apple and IBM to define our needs/wants and test products. Personal computing was in its infancy, and choosing one platform over the other had significant financial and educational implications. I also worked with furniture suppliers, university computing technicians and networking specialists, a university project manager and more. Every encounter was a learning experience. What finally emerged was a proposal for 20 Apple Macintosh workstations et al. that would require $176,000! (That's $369,705 in today's dollars; think of the technology that could buy.) Next came tweaks to the proposal and rehearsals with university administrators, all designed to increase our likelihood of funding.

I don't remember anything about the day I made my pitch (I do have a photo of me dressed for success), but I'll never forget the euphoria when I learned our work had paid off. I'll also never forget the work that followed as I managed my first grant. So many decisions, so many hours, so many phone calls, so many purchase orders and invoices to track, and every expenditure to account for. That high school bookkeeping class my father had insisted I take came in handy. I am hard-pressed to think of anything else I did for the department that was as important and personally rewarding as opening that game-changing classroom in the fall of 1990. By then, much also had changed for me personally.

Late in the spring 1990 semester, I was forced to confront the reality that life with NW no longer was working for me, a reality I had ignored for a long time. I was relatively new to the joke about lesbians bringing a U-Haul to their second date because they were ready to move in together. For months I had behaved like the old me, afraid to acknowledge my feelings, let alone talk about them. Or as my new therapist would later observe: "Someone said you should meet this woman. You did. And you married her." I thought that was a bit simplistic but wrote that "in general that is how it was. And in that context it sounds pretty weak— which it was. A foundation of fear and insecurity, which is <u>not</u> a foundation at all." Ironically, during a workshop at a Women's Studies conference in April 1990 I had gone so far as to write in a *private* response to a prompt that I was most proud of my almost-5-year-old relationship. Talk about denial! (I wasn't just hiding my feelings from NW. In what proved to be his last letter to me, dated December 19, 1989, Les had written: "I'm happy for you in your new job. You seem contented and much more satisfied. It will be interesting to see what you and [NW] decide to do with the house thing. That would involve her moving her job, wouldn't it? That could be a big move, too.")

Several weeks after that conference I started a new journal, which speaks volumes about my state of mind. *Wrestle with life by writing about it.* I opened by exploring the roots of my recent behavior. (Its entries, I see now, were almost exclusively personal.) I had found it impossible to admit to NW that we were in trouble because "this wasn't supposed to happen, and so it couldn't be, right? But I'm tired of denial <u>by both of us</u>. And finally I put the wall back up, as high and strong as ever." When that wall became too much to maintain, I acknowledged there were problems and agreed to couple's counseling. A few days later, not yet able to say *I don't love you*, I did say that "I don't think I want to work at [fixing our relationship]." I was scared of being P, who had deserted me, and of causing NW "that degree of hurt." It wasn't just that I wanted out, however. I *needed* out. I had concluded that "this relationship is not forever. I wanted it to be. Mandated it. How foolish. Will I ever learn?" I wrote optimistically that I was "working on . . . honesty— on the ability to speak my feelings and not be afraid that doing so will have hurtful consequences— and learning how to deal with those consequences if they <u>are</u> hurtful." I was taking it one day at a time. I wrote those words a lot over the ensuing months.

Today, rereading those journal entries, I see how little space there was between my being jettisoned from one relationship and falling into the intensity of another. Let me just write that the third time was indeed the charm. On August 11, 1990, on a hill above the old Marconi station at the Cape Cod National Seashore, Mary Ellen Reilly and I exchanged "Celtic Band" rings as a symbol of love and promise. Surrounded by beach roses, we promised to give ourselves "time to make sure that being together is healthy and nurturing for each of us and for us— and if so, as we believe it will be, we will 'join hearts' in hopes of forever." Our story, which began after she returned from her sabbatical and we met to talk about the URI Women's Studies Program she directed, continues. I detailed its latest chapter in my 2020 book, "Dementia's Unexpected Gifts: A memoir of falling into caregiving, then learning to live my best life."

[An aside: When I was wrestling with this section, I happened to glance at the back cover of that newest journal (a gift from Mary Ellen) and saw that the Chinese character *kai* on the front means "to open and explore." The accompanying explanation was that the symbol "presents the image of opening new doors" and came from an ancient pictogram. I no doubt was aware of that in May 1990, when I committed to therapy and opening my own doors.]

The months between the day I found the courage to leave my Connecticut life and that joyous day in August were tumultuous. All I wanted from the couple's therapy NW had arranged was to exit "with grace and civility." I was smart enough to find myself a therapist in Rhode Island. My hope was she would help me "to sort things out— learn— grow— find peace— and the strength to move forward." At just our second session the secret I had been carrying since high school spilled out of me. The words came haltingly, and I suspect I never made eye contact with Beverly. But at some level I knew that unburdening was a key to moving forward.

My secret: I had been sexually abused by a high school teacher.

It had taken me a quarter century to frame what had been done to me as sexual abuse. During those years -- and for a couple decades since -- that teacher/newspaper advisor had been an uninvited ghost intruding on my life. It took me countless hours of therapy to understand and accept that I had been a victim. It took writing this book for me to finally understand how profoundly his actions had affected my life. To finally understand my alcohol abuse, my inability to trust, my inability to commit. To understand how large my insecurities loomed, how I turned things around to see myself at fault, as unworthy of love. To understand why I walled off my emotions, why I feared my feelings (if I even knew I had them), and why I so seldom could talk about *me*. Or why, when I did, I avoided eye contact. (I have vivid memories of my college friend and DeKalb colleague Dave Hass insisting again and again that I look at him when we were talking. And those were "ordinary" conversations. When I backslide, I still think of him.)

One Sunday morning in November 2021, as hot water washed over me in the shower, I broke down in tears. My morning reading, Louise Erdich's "The Sentence," had awakened a long-buried feeling. My eyes were closed; my heart was shouting.

> *I acknowledge I loved you from afar, many of you, none more than* [*name omitted*]. *I was fated to fall into ME because she so reminded me of you. Her look. Her gentleness. Her mind. Her kindness. ME, you weren't just a surrogate . . . however. I loved you. I love you. I hope you knew that. Know that. I hope I honor you. And our love.*

I opened my eyes and spoke more words:

> *I wish I had realized that all the self-hate I had was misdirected. Why did it take me so long to know that it was "the creep"* [as I had come to refer to my abuser] *who deserved my hate, not me?*

I screamed: *I hate him! I hate him! I hate him!* I let the water wash over my pain. Anguish in my voice, barely above a whisper, I acknowledged my shame. My embarrassment. My regrets. My pain. *I want to let them go.* And so I did. I allowed them to wash down the drain, then hugged myself as Weight Watchers had taught me. To embrace what was, what is, whatever might be.

Until I wrote "Dementia's Unexpected Gifts," I had shared the story of my abuse only with my therapist and Mary Ellen. Except, that is, for the words I used to tell "One Story" (without identifying information). I wrote it for Mary Ellen to use at a workshop she conducted in December 1990 for Northport, New York, schools. While I never have wanted that chapter of my life to overshadow all the others, I *almost* shared it during the #MeToo movement that started after an October 5, 2017, New York Times story. I am braver now and have included "One Story" as **Appendix C**. In doing so, I also acknowledge that there are related incidents and images seared into my memory whose words I cannot yet speak aloud or commit to paper. A line of dialogue from Kathy Reich's novel "Death Du Jour" resonates: "The brain is an amazing archive."

Stubborn, Resilient and Optimistic

In the throes of personal turmoil, I compartmentalized my work life, which no doubt was easier because I had not yet developed friends on campus. I rarely shared what was going on for me personally; when I did it was with a few women from my earlier lives. For all the socializing NW and I had done, the Hartford network was essentially hers. No one missed me when I withdrew, I am sure. I didn't miss them, either, but I did miss a couple of UHa pals. Chief among them was Victor, and I looked forward to us going to Atlanta in March 1990 to present a paper on our "Celebrating Diversity" course. That did not work out, however, and I attended the Senior Year Experience conference alone. It was my first academic presentation as a URI faculty member. Given the hoops Victor and I had jumped through to offer our course, including my own department not supporting it, I was tickled to receive $400 from the URI Faculty Development Fund to support my travel.

I remain immensely proud of that course; Victor and I were ahead of the times in seeing the importance of our topic. As we wrote in our paper: "The roots of [the] course have at least three branches: (a) intolerance as represented by actual experience, (b) the growing evidence of diversity in the workplace as a real issue and (c) the role of the university as a mechanism for responding to both of these phenomena." We explained that as educators, "We could see that the time was right for a course that would help students make the connections around the issue of diversity to eventually see that what is important is not tolerance for a particular group of people who are different but a positive affirmation of those differences."

Now, more than 30 years later, it saddens me to know the course would likely be challenged and criticized even more than it was. But at least we would be able to find the kinds of teaching materials that did not then exist. And rereading our paper reminded me how, since my first days of teaching, I have understood the need for an "open" classroom. In summarizing our experiences, we wrote:

> [W]hat emerged, and emerged early [in the course], was a very safe environment for a classroom (vs. a dormitory room, for example). Students were able to ask any questions and felt comfortable honestly reacting and responding to the material. [T]he luck of the draw [of students who enrolled] may have had something to do with this. But we also believe that a contributing factor to this safe environment was us. Although we share a core set of values, there are things about which we disagree strongly. In the classroom, we are comfortable talking about our differences. So we presented the students an image or model of appropriate kinds of disagreement, several times showing that there are things about which one can seriously disagree and that such disagreement leads to greater variety and understanding.

Closer to home, I had another opportunity to share my scholarship when the New England Women's Studies Association held its annual conference at URI in April. I had joined the Women's Studies Committee at its first meeting in the fall, but my only role at the conference was staffing the registration table for an hour. NW and her friend Susan joined me in Kingston, which felt awkward and made me uncharacteristically nervous. (Now I understand that subconsciously I had begun disengaging.) My session, "Making News: A Strategy for Challenging the Media," focused on practical ways to combat media sexism. Then, as now, I argued for thinking less about *the media* and more about the individual newspapers, broadcast stations, magazines and the like that one uses. Rather than criticizing with a broad brush (such as current railing at the "mainstream media" or "the elite media") most of us can be more effective challenging sexism locally.

May's commencement marked the end of my 16th year of university teaching. Referencing the ceremony was the first time I wrote in my new journal about school. I noted that several students had greeted me during the processional "and that felt good." I also wrote that the only line I remembered from all the speeches was "the old guy from the Board of Governors who advised his graduating grandson, 'Don't get interested in a girl whose father calls her princess. She probably already figures she is one.'" I thought of the many such "girls" I had dealt with at UHa and felt lucky to have landed where I was sure I was meant to be: a state university. I didn't mind that I would work much of the summer. I had rented a small house in Narragansett starting June 1 and I looked forward to getting settled before my sister and youngest nephew visited for 10 days. I looked forward to a week on Cape Cod and a couple of days in Maine. I planned to travel to Wisconsin for a family reunion and party for Grandma Conger's 87th birthday. It would be, I imagined, the kind of summer schedule I would have for the foreseeable future: a healthy mix of work and play.

Until now my story has moved forward with its own momentum, but at this point I got stuck. I could have simply written that URI turned out to be my forever job, just as Mary Ellen is my forever partner. But those were not facts in the summer of 1990, and I spent a lot of time thinking about ways to bring my story to the present. I decided to organize "The URI Years" like a play, with a prologue (the year just described), two acts and an intermission.

CHAPTER 28

Act I

Summer 1990–June 1998

Once upon a time, I was told that the Chinese refer to copy editors as "polishers," which I regularly work into my discussions about editing. As I thought about these URI years, I saw my career stops to date as "rough cuts" bringing out facets of a stone. It was at URI that the polished gem eventually emerged to reveal more than I expected. No other period in my life brought as much professional growth and satisfaction as these eight years, something I realized only as I reflected on them for this book. Forgotten bits and pieces continued to surface for weeks (often at odd moments that left me scrambling for a way to make note of them). Life outside of work also was rich with new people, places and experiences, not to mention a few difficulties.

Well on my way to establishing myself as a successful department chair after only a year, I steadily grew into a go-to faculty member able and willing to accept a variety of campus positions. Leadership skills I knew I possessed -- and had demonstrated elsewhere -- blossomed. I worked hard with my new therapist, who I credit with helping me to heal and grow personally, to find my professional voice, to manage my fear of criticism. Confronting ghosts and finding confidence in my "authentic self" propelled me forward professionally. Numerous accomplishments stand out for me, especially the following:

Uncomfortable Decisions

Curriculum development was the easy part of my job. I loved drawing on my experiences elsewhere, reading widely and thinking broadly about what was happening in journalism education, talking with colleagues and students, and crafting revisions designed to strengthen our program. Sometimes such revisions required uncomfortable personnel decisions. I had not given much thought to managing people until I attended a workshop for new department chairs. I had looked forward to that weekend at the University of New Hampshire's conference center with new chairs from around New England. It was eye-opening to learn how varied our job descriptions were, from "petty bureaucrats doing the administration's bidding" (and thus a job few faculty want) to "departmental leaders standing up for faculty" (a job many academics are not suited for). Accordingly, our roles in personnel matters varied, but the consensus among attendees was nervousness about supervising our peers.

My first personnel decisions came after the department's initial round of curriculum changes. It was clear that two full-time adjunct instructors no longer could teach what we needed taught, and it was up to me to tell them their contracts would not be renewed. Neither took it well, and I had a sleepless night after I met with them. Some years later, when a tenure-track faculty member's record was deficient, I made the case for his terminal contract. He caused me sleepless nights when he lodged an affirmative action complaint (unsubstantiated) against me. Yet another time I removed an instructor just before his contract was to be renewed after I learned about his persistent harassment of another faculty member.

Decisions relating to students were another sort of personnel issue. With those, at least, I had lots of experience as a teacher and advisor. There were plenty of occasions to give good news, but as chairwoman, being the bearer of bad news seemed to predominate. Most challenging were those times when I had to disabuse students of their "dream job" when it was clear that they were not suited to journalism. Offering bad news never was pleasant. Reactions ranged from stoic acceptance to nastiness to tears, and I always had a box of tissues nearby. While the criers made me most uncomfortable, interfering parents were the most difficult to deal with. In my undergraduate days, after all, we fended for ourselves; never would we have expected Mom or Dad to call on our behalf. [An aside: Although the term "helicopter parents" apparently dates to a 1969 book about parents and teenagers, it wasn't until the late 1990s that I began to see a steady stream of parental involvement in my students' campus lives.]

By far the messiest personnel decision I was involved with was building the case to rid us of our secretary. To say I was unprepared for how that scenario played out is an understatement. I was, however, prepared to do whatever was necessary to deal with the toxic environment that had developed around her. I kept detailed notes about her performance, problematic behaviors and our other concerns, so I had the specifics needed to write a persuasive memo demanding her removal. By then she was an icy presence at her desk. She seldom spoke with me and I could not depend on her to do even the simplest task. The last straw was a very public shouting match she initiated with a faculty member.

I never doubted my decision to have her removed from the department. I certainly never expected her husband to storm into my office in hopes of changing my mind. He was a longtime professor in another department; I guess he thought that gave him the right to close my door and demand I listen to him "explain" his wife. When I told him how inappropriate it was for him to be there, he berated me at length. I did not respond, other than to tell him to leave. Eventually he did. To this day I am certain that had I been a man, he never would have confronted me that way. I didn't enjoy having to fire that secretary, but I was proud of myself for doing so. After the fact, I learned that previous supervisors had had problems with her too, but no one ever bothered to document them and her union always supported her. My penchant for documenting and saving "evidence" paid off, just as it would time and again when I was able to write *positively* on behalf of faculty members, students and others.

Professional Development

I was fortunate to be selected for a number of workshops that allowed me to stretch my wings. In June 1992, for example, I spent a week participating in the annual Leadership Institute for Journalism and Mass Communication Educators. Sponsored by the Freedom Forum Media Studies Center, then located on the campus of Columbia University, it took me out of my personal and professional comfort zones. Before I even applied for the institute, I had to make peace with my dislike of New York City and, even more important, my anxiety over the prospect of traveling there alone.

I don't remember the train ride to Penn Station or the taxi ride to the Salisbury Hotel, across from Carnegie Hall. I do know I clutched a paper on which I had written out what exactly I should say to the taxi driver (which I had copied from something I read in New York magazine). I don't remember anything about the institute except for meeting a couple of "big names" in journalism education. I do remember bravely walking from the hotel around the block, I think, to go to a bookstore. I remember our group dining at the Harvard Club. I remember summoning a taxi back to Penn Station at the end of the week. Remarkably, tucked in the back of the last journal I seem to have kept (its final entry a short one on September 29, 1991), I found a page from a stenographer's notepad. It is dated Friday 6/26/92 Penn Station NY.

> I cannot help but feel distressed— Exiting the city seemed the last great hurdle and we are delayed 1 1/2 hours— which means departure about 3:30 instead of 2:05— So I am stuck sitting, an overloaded briefcase strapped over my shoulder and impeding movement— My stuffed garment bag on the floor— I obsess over not having gone to Providence— that might have meant I could have gotten on the train that did leave— at 1— But I'm not even sure it stopped at Prov— and it is all a moot point— So why do I feel bad— Fear and anxiety that I have controlled all week are just under the surface, ready to erupt and overtake me— All the successes of the past days momentarily forgotten— I want to be on my train— even if it sits— I would feel safe— in control— I would have gotten myself where I need to be— Now all is unsureness— Please let this happen before rush hour— so I will

find my way— not be crushed by hundreds and hundreds who <u>know</u> where they are going— I can and will do this— I will be OK— And it might be fun— I've a Club Car ticket— Mary Ellen thinks that is "first class" for trains— So let me put this "found" time to good use— flip to a clean sheet of paper and sort out the week— So I reframe this from disaster to opportunity— And I choose to make the best of it—

At the risk of using *gobsmacked* one too many times in this book, I can think of no other word that more accurately captures my reaction to reading that. I heard myself acknowledging feelings and figuring out how to deal with them, to reframe them in a positive way. I honestly thought my ability to do so didn't come until much later. I also saw myself through the lens of someone who in the ensuing 30 years frequently traveled alone to unfamiliar cities and managed in her own way to thrive despite various degrees of anxiety.

A couple of years after New York, I was selected for the American Press Institute's weeklong Journalism Educators Seminar, held on the campus of the University of Nevada-Reno. What luck to be active when journalism organizations were flush with cash and invested in education. The seminar no doubt was professionally valuable but is memorable for other reasons. (1) Still an uncomfortable flier, I had only recently allowed myself on 50-passenger planes (because they allowed me to fly into Oshkosh, Wisconsin, where my parents then lived). The trip west was direct to San Francisco (probably directly over Reno), where I boarded a plane with considerably fewer than 50 seats for the bumpy ride back over the Sierras. (2) The casinos of the so-called "Biggest Little City in the World" were just a couple of blocks walk from my lodging. I played slot machines for the first time. And I saw firsthand how little space there was between the glitz and the seamier side of Reno. (3) I got a personal tour of the residential glitz outside the city from the new dean of the School of Journalism. Jimmy (as I knew him) Gentry had been director of the Business Journalism Program at Missouri during my second stint there. Before going to Nevada, he spent seven years as journalism dean at the University of Kansas. (4) Late one afternoon, we seminar participants were loaded onto a bus for the drive to Lake Tahoe, where we enjoyed incredible scenery and even more-incredible food. I know both were provided by Gar Woods Grill

& Pier (which was still operating as I wrote this) because I have the matchbox I filched as a souvenir.

Campus Leadership

My first exposure to campus governance had come during my college journalism days, when I sometimes reported on the Faculty Senate and its committees. Once I began teaching, I participated on such committees, although I never stayed anywhere long enough to become entrenched in "the system." That began to change almost immediately at Rhode Island. It was rare, I learned, for a department chair to be hired from another institution, so perhaps my newcomer status earned me immediate credibility. Just as likely, I suspect, I was viewed as "easy pickings" not yet jaded enough to say "no."

Near the end of my first year, the provost named me to the advisory committee that would lead the search for a new dean of Arts and Sciences. In other words, I helped identify candidates to replace the man who had hired me. That didn't feel nearly as awkward as helping find my replacement at Hartford, but it presented its own complication. Mary Ellen also had been named to the committee, which required our professional discipline in order to not give away our nascent personal relationship. [An aside: I think she was the faculty union's appointee to the committee. Having been at URI since 1973, she was among the most respected individuals on campus. I have never known a faculty member who contributed as significantly to a campus as she did to URI; among her notable achievements was the role she played in the successful 1985 sex-discrimination lawsuit I mentioned earlier. I certainly never would have known as many people from offices around the campus or met so many significant feminists were it not for her.]

Mary Ellen and I supported the female finalist and were disappointed -- but not surprised -- when the deanship went to a man, Steffen Rogers. He was a personable dean, not prone to micromanaging, and I enjoyed working with him. Years later, he was named president of Bucknell University in Lewisburg, Pennsylvania. I include that detail because it was there in 2003 that Mary Ellen and I caught up with him and his wife, Athena. We were on our way to a nephew's wedding in Pittsburgh, and Lewisburg was our overnight stop. We arranged to have dinner with them, and it proved a most enjoyable evening, one interrupted frequently by people stopping at our table to greet Stef. He obviously had found his niche, one neither Mary Ellen nor I would have predicted, I daresay. [An aside: We had found refuge in Lewisburg on our way home from the Women's Final Four basketball tournament in April 1997. The weather turned nasty, and after we watched a semitruck fishtail across a high bridge we decided to take the next exit and find a motel for the night. The next morning, we learned that the April Fool's Day blizzard had closed Interstate 80 just a few miles away, trapping drivers overnight. Although April 2 was sunny and dry in Lewisburg, we didn't want to drive into that mess. We were able to keep our room for another night, then enjoyed a day exploring the area, including the Bucknell campus.]

It was my election to the University College/General Education Committee for 1990-1993 that started my transformation from reticent participant to active leader. The committee, with its oversight of the basic course requirements for most students regardless of major, was right up my interest alley. I don't know of a campus where that type of program is not controversial, which made the committee's work more interesting than many others. I remember the defining moment for me this way: Committee members were seated around a big conference table in Bliss Hall, then home to the Engineering dean's office. Whatever was being debated had me mulling responses, but a couple of overbearing, loquacious faculty caused me to remain silent. Until I no longer could and so I spoke my piece. I don't know what followed, only that I left that meeting thinking, *Thank you, (therapist) Beverly. I spoke up and the world didn't end. Watch out, world.* It wasn't quite that easy, of course. Insecure me still regularly surfaced, but I silenced myself less and less -- and that made all the difference.

In January 1992, the College of Arts and Sciences appointed me to fill a three-semester vacancy on the Faculty Senate. Much to my surprise, when the slate of officers for the following year was being assembled later that semester, I was asked to run for vice chair. I chuckled when Senate coordinator Sheila Black Grubman called to ask. "I never win elections," I told her, "but go ahead and count me in." I was the most surprised person in the room when the ballots were tallied and I won. (Turns out I was on a roll; college faculty elected me to my own Senate seat in May 1993.) The apocryphal curse, "May you live in interesting times," without a doubt is appropriate to my service during Act I of my URI life.

The backstory, briefly: In 1991, the university welcomed a new president, Robert L. Carothers, who frequently was described as "a poet, lawyer, scholar, administrator." At 49, he was twenty-one years younger than the outgoing president. It was a generational changing of the guard; think John F. Kennedy succeeding Dwight D. Eisenhower. When he stepped down 18 years later, he was credited with "strengthening the university's structure, infrastructure and curriculum." His tough-love stance on alcohol use on campus (The Princeton Review college guide calling URI the top party school had been embarrassing) was widely applauded.

But Carothers' presidency was controversial almost from the beginning, due in no small measure to his impatience and his penchant for ignoring (some would say belittling) faculty concerns. The staunchly independent faculty (academicians know that description is redundant) resisted his plans for revamping curriculum and scoffed at his allegiance to Total Quality Management. The Rhode Island economy forced painful budget cuts and belt-tightening. Bashing "ivory tower obstructionists" was all too common. The Faculty Senate provided me with more than a front-row seat to the unfolding dramas. When I was elected chairwoman for the 1993-94 school year, I became the faculty's official spokeswoman. I didn't always have an easy time of it, either. But a year later I was nominated without an opponent and re-elected by acclimation.

Back to my story: I learned the Senate ropes during my year as vice chair. My tutor, Leonard Kahn, was a physics professor absolutely committed to faculty governance and the independent role state law defined for us. He was thoughtful, deliberate and precise in his analysis. He was not afraid to challenge the president and regularly remind him that the faculty, not the president, controlled the curriculum. I admired Leonard's mastery of meeting protocol and his ability to quickly and appropriately respond to senators' questions and comments. *I wish I was that quick on my feet*, I regularly thought. Often, the "right words" came to me only after I had ruminated for hours.

It was that self-evaluation that caused me to hesitate when I was approached about running for Senate chair. Could I handle the often contentious Senate meetings? Leonard assured me that I could. I knew I would need thick skin to deflect criticism, which came with the position, and I wasn't sure I had it. On the other hand, I saw myself as a consensus-builder and was confident that I could work effectively with the president. After I was elected in May 1993, one of the first actions I took was to plan a series of summer "kaffeeklatsches" with senators. I not only wanted us to get acquainted but I believed it was important to gauge where people stood on the issues the Senate was dealing with.

One thing I did not expect to deal with -- a debilitating case of Lyme disease -- upended those plans. In July, Mary Ellen and I rented a vacation house in Provincetown; we shared the week with two couples, each in their own rental. As we all were walking on a beach early in the week, ME noticed a nasty red spot behind my left knee. I thought it was a green-fly bite. After I passed out at the house the next day, she insisted I get checked at an urgent care clinic. I offhandedly raised the possibility of Lyme, but the diagnosis was urinary tract infection, and I was sent home with an antibiotic. (Lyme occurred to me because it was much in the news in New England.) After a miserable night of fever and chills, I returned to the clinic. They did a test for Lyme, which came back negative, and I was told to continue with the antibiotic. We carried on with our vacation, but I was sluggish and out of sorts. On the drive home on Saturday, after stopping for lunch, I told Mary Ellen she had to drive a while. I would not drive again for six or seven months. I had indeed been bitten -- by a deer tick -- and a second test confirmed Lyme. Bless my own doctor, who said, "If it walks like a duck and sounds like a duck, we'll assume it's a duck" and began treating me for Lyme while waiting for test results. My numbers were off the charts. She prescribed three weeks of an IV-delivered antibiotic, which I was taught to administer. I could barely think straight and I was responsible for doing that. Scary! I was so weak that I could brush my teeth or comb my hair, but not both. When I wrote the check for that first doctor's visit, I couldn't remember how to make a 4. An MRI of my head, I guess to make sure nothing else was causing cognitive impairment, did provide an unexpected bonus: I have pictures of my brain!

News of my illness alarmed my mother, who could not be dissuaded from her belief a tick bite had caused my father's stroke. It took every ounce of my almost-nonexistent energy to persuade her not to rush to Rhode Island. Eventually, we paid for her to visit, which proved good for all of us. In her thank you note, she called it "a vacation that was relaxing to body, soul and mind." The time away from day-to-day care of my father meant as much to her, I think, as her relief at seeing me and knowing I was recovering. But that recovery was agonizingly slow. "We didn't want to tell you, but you were very, very sick," someone in the doctor's office told me late in the ordeal. "I sort of figured that out," I replied.

It also had not taken me long to figure out I couldn't hold my get-togethers with senators. I was close to tears when I called the Senate coordinator to tell her what was going on. I was worried about the fall semester but was too miserable to think that far ahead. I also should mention two other factors at work during my early weeks of illness: (1) Mary Ellen's mother was not doing well and ME spent most of her time driving in order to be a caregiver for her in Massachusetts and for me at home. (2) Mary Ellen and I were working on a book.

Eventually, I began to feel a bit better; I could actually shower and brush my teeth before collapsing back in bed. I had the department's first-generation Mac laptop at home, so I pecked away at the book whenever I had spurts of energy. I was determined to meet my fall-semester responsibilities to the Journalism Department and the Senate, and to stop being a burden on my partner. Stubbornness, resilience and optimism worked in my favor. So did a rejiggered schedule that relieved me of teaching and minimized the time I absolutely had to be on campus. I never missed a meeting of any substance. I handled most of my department tasks and was thankful for colleagues who pitched in whenever I asked. Mary Ellen continued as my driver; I hated that but accepted that it was necessary.

Following the final Senate meeting of the semester on December 9, I wrote what I believe was the first holiday letter from a chair to senators. I thought it was important to acknowledge what we had done together and to thank the principal players. I had another motive, too.

With the letter, I conveyed my conviction that together we *would* accomplish some of what the president wanted -- but on our terms. We already had held nine meetings; originally 10 had been scheduled for the entire year. Five were special meetings devoted exclusively to consideration of the president's Strategic Plan proposals. Determined to lead the Senate to make decisions in "real time," I wrote:

> I believe the Senate's willingness to grapple expeditiously with those proposals by allowing senators and others every opportunity to express themselves about the matters under consideration reflects our commitment to support curricula changes -- but only after the faculty has had the opportunity to shape them. That shaping is under way, of course, and when our committees and colleges return to the floor of the Senate with their proposals, we once again will be challenged. In the meantime, I urge you to channel your ideas and concerns to the appropriate committees now. Further, I urge you to make clear to your faculty colleagues and constituency that now is the time for them to communicate their concerns and ideas. Nothing has been decided yet.

Our work continued throughout the spring semester, and I was re-elected by acclamation for a second term. I had the president's trust, I think. More important to me, I had begun meeting regularly with newly appointed Provost Beverly Swan, an ally of the faculty. I looked to her for perspective; over time she became a mentor. (Her association with URI began as a student, and as an English Department faculty member she had chaired the Senate.)

Until I unearthed a stash of materials from this period, I had forgotten about a project I began on Commencement Day, May 22, 1994. I labeled the first page in my handwritten notebook "A Professor's Year." The five-page entry began with an explanation of my undertaking:

> [A] rather microscopic examination of a year in my life as an academician— We are bashed so often— and what we do so misunderstood— that I have on more than one occasion suggested that we, like lawyers, should keep track of our work in billable hours— charting our days in 15-minute increments— Now I want to try— as well as to record commentary.

Regrettably, I made it only to June 24. I suspect my fondness for trying to capture my world by *writing* and *reflecting* was superseded by the demands of my work. I enjoyed rereading the 15-minute notations, but it was that initial entry that carried me back to my reporting days; its concrete descriptions and details could have come from one of my reporter's notebooks. It also reminded me of the controversy over the president's decision to override the Honorary Degree Committee's recommendation of Patricia Ireland, National Organization for Women president, as commencement speaker. The uproar that ensued eventually forced his hand.

I love commencement— one of the few ceremonies I "do"— Today was flawless— It had been cold and rainy all week, but Saturday and Sunday were warm and clear blue — My day started about 10:30 with brunch at the President's [house]— always nice— no budget worries evident here— tables ladened with food, including smoked salmon, quiche, tons of pastries— I managed to mingle a lot (for me)— getting pretty good at going up to someone and introducing myself as chair of the Faculty Senate— Had a long chat with [the president's assistant], who seems genuinely concerned about his not consulting and listening and has the noble goal of working on that this summer— Good luck.

At noon it was over to Carlotti [the administration building] to robe and eventually line up— I avoided the governor, who in the paper on Saturday was quoted as calling the faculty "immature" and more for its meeting and resolution opposing a plan to cut another 1.3 [million dollars] from academic affairs next year— Some of my colleagues Sunday took to calling me the Head Brat!— I only knew I was not interested in introducing myself to Bruce [Sundlun, the governor].

On the way out to line up, I patted the president on the back and wished him a good afternoon— and learned he had on his bulletproof vest— The Patricia Ireland flap had everyone worried— and we seemed to prepare for any eventuality— But there had been no protesters outside the brunch (at least none I noticed)— and I saw only one on my walk to Carlotti— selling NOT NOW stickers— I didn't see many on grads.

The processional started a few minutes late— about 12:40 I

think— Ireland made it and marched in— plans had been just to walk her up to the platform— she seemed a lot less worried than URI— I didn't hear the bagpipes— one of my favorite moments— I did notice that students seemed unusually orderly— URI graduations had deteriorated to almost total chaos by 1992— a real effort was made and last year was much better— This year, we all noted at its end, was fabulous— no beachballs— no visible booze— students sober— no rowdiness— I did see a grad in the back go out for pizza! And there was a bit of milling about— But when all was said and done, not a thing to be chagrined about!

And commencement itself— about an hr. and 10 min— WOW! Ireland's speech both short and also meaningful— She didn't skirt the controversy but talked about how we need to respect one another, even when we don't agree— Only incident was a plane overhead with a "Life, what a beautiful choice" banner— There had been a flurry of activity (though I suspect unnoticed by most) when [a staff member] spotted a person on top of Ranger Hall— I caught this out of the corner of my eye— she couldn't get Security's attention— when I looked at Ranger and saw it was a woman, I wasn't much worried (naïve, aren't I?!) —

. . . [D]uring the brief wait to march on stage [for the Arts & Sciences ceremony], a colleague was telling me he had heard my name being taken in vain by a student at a party the night before — Seems I had given her a B+ and thus was being held responsible for her missing graduating with honors by some hundredths of a point — He said he suggested to her that she think about all her courses over 4 years —

4 p.m. — Reception for Patricia Ireland— private— arranged by the folks who had originally arranged to bring her after her rejection as speaker— Was glad to see a lot of faculty colleagues— And particularly pleased that the provost came by for a half hour or so —

About 5:45— off to a party for a local Honorary Degree recipient who Mary Ellen knows well— President and Provost there— Also the Athletics biggies—

About 7— it's over— I'm ready to put my feet up— in anticipation of four days in Ogunquit— What a good idea we had last October when we made these reservations— I am taking no work, even though our book is due back to the production editor on 6/3! I/we need a break— and I know the work will get done— Tops on my agenda is finishing the "alphabet" mystery I started reading at [our niece's] Roger Williams University commencement on Saturday.

My Senate years taught me much, which always has been how I measure/judge experiences. I learned that I could do productive work even when I wasn't 100 percent healthy. I didn't need a parliamentarian's grasp of the minutiae of "Robert's Rules of Order" to run successful meetings. I certainly didn't need to fear senators who knew that book from cover to cover -- or behaved as if they did. Clever comebacks weren't nearly as valuable as respectful listening. Learning people's names (always a challenge for me) and calling on them as Senator So-and-so was subtly affirming. Patiently allowing certain people to have their say -- and then have it again, and maybe even again after that -- made it easy to finally (and forcefully) cut them off.

Scholars do not make the best legislators; we are trained to be skeptical, independent thinkers with a narrow focus on our own specialties. We are deliberate and loathe to act until all possibilities have been considered from every angle. Seeing the "big picture" doesn't come easy to many of us. I came to understand how that created a naturally adversarial relationship with administrators, whose jobs require big-picture thinking and real-time decision-making. Too many faculty members are cynics. Changing an institution from within the governance structure is usually more successful than attacking it from the outside -- and a lot more work. Participating in faculty governance is vital if one is to be a good citizen in the campus community, and ought to be recognized as such.

Creative Activities

As my career progressed, I developed a love/hate relationship with traditional scholarship. I never had been the least bit interested in racking up published articles for the sake of meeting an artificial standard that was a hurdle to be cleared on the way to promotion. Put another way: Just as I resist speaking up unless I have something to add, I am unwilling to do research for the sake of research. (I went so far as to write a commentary for the Newspaper Research Journal titled "No

More Content Analyses." In it I reflected on how little had changed with the portrayal of women in the news media despite a growing body of evidence from the research, including mine.) So, if I were going to write a book, it had to be useful. That's how I ended up co-authoring "Women's Studies Graduates: The First Generation" with Mary Ellen. All in all, it was a good experience despite me being slowed midstream by Lyme. Once we had real books in hand (in 1995) we kept our promise to celebrate at the historic -- since 1673 -- White Horse Tavern in Newport. Here's how we got there:

To craft our proposal, I used my notes from the adult education course on book publishing I had taken in Connecticut. Mary Ellen used her connections to get that proposal into the hands of a member of the editorial board for the Athene series at Teachers College Press. They were impressed. We got a contract. We got small grants to help with our research. I balked at having to submit our questionnaire to the research office for "human subjects" review. *I'm a journalist. We can ask anyone anything. They don't have to answer, but we don't need permission to ask.* Mary Ellen, a feminist sociologist recognized for her research on sexual harassment, prevailed. It was enormously rewarding to hear from so many Women's Studies graduates, including a couple I knew from Missouri days. It was enormously rewarding to provide answers to the oft-asked question, "What can you do with a Women's Studies major?" It was enormously rewarding to share the experience with the woman who, as I wrote in my dedication, "daily renews my faith in goodness and who constantly dazzles me with her brilliance."

[An aside: As I came to realize when I sorted Mary Ellen's papers, our research interests overlapped long before we knew one another. For example, at the same time Victor and I were developing our summer diversity course (and as I continued to explore stereotyping in the media), Mary Ellen was proposing a project titled "Confronting Stereotypes-Recognizing Diversity." It was intended to pilot a general education course for freshmen, with subject areas including racism, sexism, ethnocentrism and heterosexism.]

Funding for the Journalism Department's computer lab had included money to provide faculty members with personal computers. I think I was more excited by that than my colleagues; I had been lost without a computer in my office. The more I learned, the more ideas I had about how I might make creative use of the hardware and software now at our disposal, not just in my teaching but also for the department. But my first creative project was a labor of love. I surprised Mary Ellen with a simple book of her mother's poems, designed and produced (complete with a cover illustration) on an Apple Macintosh. It was my first desktop publishing project, and I have never looked back.

I consider myself systems-oriented, and I enjoyed devising creative ways to simplify departmental work. The computer allowed me to design an easily updatable advising checklist to help students track their progress toward graduation. We printed it on pink paper, and it wasn't long before our advising appointments began, "Do you have your pink worksheet?" I encouraged the department to be a campus leader in developing course outcomes and student assessments. Once we finished that work, I developed, wrote and produced our first Student Handbook, another significant advising aid made easier by a computer. I took pride in our being one of the first URI departments to have a presence on the World Wide Web. It was fun to revisit that history, but what seemed groundbreaking then feels (and looks) ancient today.

The spring semester of 1997 found me enjoying a sabbatical. Such a paid leave of absence (time away for scholarly pursuits -- and renewal) typically comes every seven years or so. My first, and what would prove to be my only, came during my 23rd year of teaching! I concentrated on renewal, and afterward privately quipped that I had used my sabbatical to play a lot of video games on my Nintendo. (I credit Mario Golf with teaching me how to think my way around a course.) I forget what I had proposed to use my sabbatical for, but my unofficial scholarly activity was teaching myself HTML, which at the time was the primary code used to create documents for what we called The Web. I quickly was hooked. The coding used to tell the computer what to do reminded me of marking up text for newspaper typesetters, which I had been doing since my undergraduate years. I enjoyed the challenges of conceptualizing how a page would look and be read on a computer screen, which generally was different from how it looked on paper. I enjoyed the challenges of finding the coding errors when what I got didn't match what

I thought I had done. In short, creating for The Web reignited my creative juices.

That summer I hired a computer engineering student to help me develop the department's website and function as its first webmaster. (I was the second.) Eventually, I also designed my own website. And even though I wasn't able to secure funding in 1993 to study "interactive news," my application supported my self-characterization as forward-thinking. My proposal asked for a modest $1,700 to attend the four-day Interactive News course at the Center for Creative Imaging in Maine. I described my goals as "simple":

> (1) to begin to acquire the tools necessary to understand the principles of interactive media -- and to begin to learn how to do it; (2) to be able to help my colleagues see and understand the importance of these technological advances, particularly as they relate to curricular needs; (3) to be able to help my colleagues take full advantage of our facilities; and (4) to begin exposing journalism students to the world of interactive media and the news, because this is the world in which they will be doing journalism.

[An aside: I was familiar with the center because I had tried to surprise Mary Ellen for her 50th birthday with a week at the Maine Photographic Workshops in Rockport. The staff's letter-of-acceptance *to her* ruined the surprise, and as it turned out Mary Ellen the perfectionist hated just about every aspect of the experience. I, on the other hand, enjoyed my time in Rockport, especially an afternoon sail on a three-masted schooner.]

[Another aside: Years later I was unsuccessful when I applied for a second sabbatical. It merits mentioning, I think, because of my topic: I proposed to study what I believed had been "a marked increase in first-person journalism" in recent years. More significantly, I believed "there has been a qualitative change in the nature of the first-person story; it increasingly comes more from a posture of revealing than of telling." I suspected "a link between the increase in the number of women reporters and the emergence of what I am labeling The Journalism of Self-Disclosure." I suggested that my work had "the potential to expand professional conversations about the role of the contemporary reporter/writer." I was on to something, don't you think?!

Teaching

I was accustomed to using technology in the classroom. (I got my start in high school, when I was trained to operate the movie projector to show health films to the girls' physical education classes.) At Eau Claire, for example, I had mimeographed a newspaper-like document for my news writing students. Called THE GOOD, THE BAD AND THE UGLY, it promised "The facts and the phosphorescence" in sharing examples from students' work. Over time, my website became central to my teaching, and along with that came significant changes in how I approached my courses. One thing that didn't change: I brought my "hard-ass grader" approach with me, as a review of gradebooks from my first two years at URI reminded me. I had negotiated to teach just one course each semester in my first year. I had 18 students in my fall Editing class: One B+, one B, one B-, seven C+, six C, one D+ and one F. In the spring I had 14 students, including one A-. No Editing student in the 1990-91 school year earned an A. In fairness, grades are not perfect predictors of professional performance, and the students I most remember are not necessarily the ones who earned the top grades. What is important to me is that throughout my career -- no matter the school, the course or my approach to teaching the content -- I reserved A's for excellence and remained true to the "honest C."

It was not easy to reconstruct the evolution of my teaching, nor do I feel compelled to spend a lot of words on it. What I most remember is working hard (struggling?) to replicate in my classrooms the kinds of experiences my undergraduate years had provided for me -- intellectual growth and practical preparation for real-world journalism. How could I innovate? How could I motivate? How could I adapt to changes in students' attitudes, behaviors, work ethics? Each course -- be it one I had taught numerous times, one previously taught by a colleague, or a new one I had designed -- brought its own challenges. Because curricular change was at the heart of what I did the first several years at URI, my array of teaching assignments regularly changed.

It was fun to discover a stack of 4-by-6-inch index cards for "The First 'Barbie' Awards for JOR 321 Accomplishments," dated May 2, 1994. I had forgotten about that attempt to recognize the efforts of my feature writing students. I had purchased small rubber "statues" of some sort to go along with my citations, which included:

- ▶ "For a body of work demonstrating that there is a plethora of health-related stories at URI just begging to be written"
- ▶ "For going to the greatest lengths (to Chicago) to get a story"
- ▶ "For finding a story subject who goes to the greatest lengths -- outer space -- for her work using the Hubble telescope"
- ▶ "For capturing the spirit of winter surfers and 2 a.m. in a donut shop with a keen eye for description and a keen ear for quotes"
- ▶ "For working hard -- and always with a smile -- to conquer the tough task of describing focused story ideas. And for a nicely done profile of a young hockey player"
- ▶ "For the most story ideas -- but mostly for her growth as a reporter/ writer over the last four months"
- ▶ "For writing the first URI People story to make me go 'Wow!' and the only 'How To' story requiring no revisions."

That last citation reminded me that this was the semester the student newspaper agreed to my proposal that it publish several of our stories in a special section of profiles we produced.

Another time, I led five students in a special seminar to prepare a critique of The Newport Daily News. Editor Dave Offer and I reconnected shortly after he was hired, and over dinner one evening we talked about my month as "professor in the newsroom" and the critique I had done for him in La Crosse. That led to him wondering if I could do the same for his new paper, and I suggested including a few of our best students. What better way to have them think critically about news and its presentation? The result of our analysis was a written report for Dave and a workshop for his staff.

Restless Ambition

A letdown after my two years as Senate chair seemed inevitable. One day I was a significant participant in fascinating, consequential work. The next I was a "former." But I was fortunate to not lose whatever influence I had earned over those two years. For one thing, I continued to be part of the president's ad hoc Advisory Committee that was developing a new financial planning tool. That work had begun under the radar, and once it became public it was controversial. A positive phrase from a newspaper story and a derisive adjective attached to us were even memorialized on a tee-shirt, which my sister preserved on a quilt.

I believed having a faculty member involved in that work was better than the alternative and so never blinked when, still Senate chair, I had been invited to participate. At a "ceremony" we held for ourselves at the end of the committee's work, I received "the Conductor Award for Keeping Everyone on Track." Not a bad legacy.

Our efforts garnered national attention, and the vice president for research was asked to discuss news coverage of the project at the annual meeting of the American Association for the Advancement of

Science in February 1997. When he wasn't able to attend, I was asked to pinch hit to discuss "Accuracy in Science News Reporting." I was happy to do so, not least for the free trip to Seattle (although it did mean I was not home for Valentine's Day). Being on a panel at AAAS was a big deal; so was the chance to see Sarah, an old friend and one-time summer houseguest in Columbia. And although I didn't visit the Space Needle, I made sure to walk through the Pike Place Market to watch fish being tossed about and to eat in a restaurant overlooking Puget Sound.

After the Senate, I also arranged to be a half-time special assistant to Provost M. Beverly Swan, a position I held from September 1995 to December 1996. I had made the case that my Senate experience, combined with leadership training I had received, could be put to good use in her office. Thankfully she agreed. My Senate work had provided some relief from teaching; I wasn't eager to resume spending more time in the classroom. I assured the provost that I could continue to do the department's work, which I still enjoyed. Once the details were worked out, I informed my colleagues. They may not have been happy, but over those 15 months I never gave them cause to complain that I neglected them or the department. Being a workaholic suited me, despite my declarations to the contrary. I was happy to tackle whatever job the provost assigned. Several times that involved drafting remarks or a memo on her behalf. It was not easy because she was renowned for being a clever wordsmith. Once I got the hang of writing in her distinctive voice, however, I decided I could have enjoyed being a ghost writer.

I credit the provost for the training I cited when lobbying to work in her office. She had forwarded a brochure for the HERS Leadership Institute to me after I first was elected Senate chair. Its monthlong summer program, held at Bryn Mawr College in Pennsylvania, intrigued me. I had come to see myself as so much more than a journalism teacher/administrator, and with each passing year I grew restless to do something new. I was approaching a personal record for years spent in one place, too. I knew myself well enough to realize that if I weren't professionally challenged, I couldn't be personally happy. The more I learned about the program, the more I wanted to apply. I thought it would be ideal preparation for moving into an administrative position. I hoped that could be at URI.

I was excited to be accepted by HERS, then disappointed when Lyme disease forced me to defer participation until the following summer. Mary Ellen -- who abhorred change as much as I seem to need it -- wasn't excited about me being away for a month. I wanted to soak up everything the institute, the beautiful campus and the area had to offer (including spending time with my old friend and Vermont guest Desiree, now living in Philadelphia). Reluctantly, I agreed to come home for a weekend at the midpoint. In the pre-cellphone environment, I tried to be an attentive partner, talking with Mary Ellen daily and regularly sending notes. On a rare "unstructured day" during my first week away, I wrote to reassure her.

> I've been reflecting— thinking. My foundation premise is that I love you and above all else want to spend my life with you! I am committed to the energy and growing and learning and adopting that requires. The bottom line, then, is that I choose to put my person and personal life above all else. I see us standing side by side, arms entwined, working out our future and futures, direction and directions, together. That will/does require of me more negotiating than in the past (my past lives). It is a process I am eager to embrace.

A couple of weeks into the institute, I explained to Mary Ellen how I found "something very exciting about this learning environment of women. I suspect you found that at The Elms [her undergraduate college], but it is new to me." I remained committed to public education, "but can imagine real value to this experience of small and private." (I might have added female and elite, because my experiences at small and private UHa were so different.) "We [Institute participants] are rather removed from the world, and I can see how one might have to fight that tendency— but for a few weeks it feels rather grand— certainly idyllic— and to be part of such talent!"

Perhaps the most important lesson I learned from HERS was that I did *not* want to be a university president. Whatever such aspirations I might have harbored were dashed on our first day. Exhausted, I fell into the single bed in my spartan dorm room that night wondering if the organizers had planned the nonstop schedule (from early morning to late evening) to impress upon us the stamina required of high-level

554

administrators. If so, it worked for me, still struggling to get up to speed after Lyme. I was unwilling to consider any job where 16-hour days were the norm. The personal toll would be too much, as I knew from experience. Reflecting on that, I see how that attitude was a positive development for me. I might have left my partner for a few weeks so I could meet *my* needs, but there was a limit to how much I would sacrifice.

Perhaps the most important contribution I made to HERS was challenging the status quo during a panel discussion late in our month together. I had volunteered for the career panel "after much thought and with considerable trepidation" because I believed "there are important things to be said that have not been dealt with aloud yet." I hoped my colleagues would remember two thoughts: (1) Trying to live an "authentic" life is a continuous struggle fraught with potholes; and (2) It is not enough to be inclusive in theory and word -- it requires action, too -- "and a level of consciousness and sensitivity most of us have not yet developed." I came out to the group (**Appendix D**). I was proud of myself. When I told Mary Ellen what I had done, she was furious. She believed that I should have consulted her beforehand because sharing that I am a lesbian meant I had outed her, too. *But none of those women know you*, I countered. "Would that I were as easy going as you are," she later wrote in a card explaining her hurt and anger.

When I drove away from Bryn Mawr on Friday, July 22, I was more determined than ever to follow a career path to academic administration. I had a cleverly illustrated plan. Until I could make that happen, I would have to find ways to continue to grow professionally.

Life Away from Campus

I choose to sparingly share the love story I experienced in Rhode Island. In my author's note for "Dementia's Unexpected Gifts," I wrote how "more than most, my 'well' partner was hypersensitive about keeping the personal private." I wondered then how I could tell an honest story "while showing respect for my partner's essential self?" As I write now, my perspective has been altered only slightly by the recognition that I cannot tell *my* story without including something of *our* story because they have co-existed for more than three decades. I cannot parse the changes in me without references to her. But to the extent I can, I focus on *my* thoughts, actions, behaviors, decisions. I wrote far fewer words recording details of these than for other periods in my life, however. To the extent that makes my story incomplete or frustrating, well . . . it sometimes feels that way to me, too. Looking back, I think it was a wonder that we overcame our pasts to create a life together. What I eventually concluded while working on this book was that when all is said and done, the only thing that matters is we remain together. I did not abandon her (as she feared I would) and she did not give up on me (when I periodically gave her every reason to).

Despite the paucity of written words, I was fortunate to discover a treasure-trove of photographs for the years comprising this Act I. Having prints -- as opposed to digitally preserved images -- is somewhat like having letters, I realized. Organizing them by year and viewing them alongside the few written documents I found brought me to these conclusions: Life, although not without rocky moments, was generally good. Building a life together challenged each of us, and not always at the same time. Promising to change isn't always followed by lasting change. Work and play often co-mingled. Family responsibilities were ever-present, often exhausting, often tension-producing -- and very often joyful. The eight-year difference in our ages did not matter much -- until it did.

By the time I moved to Rhode Island I had managed once again to lose weight, and a few more pounds melted away as I coped with the upheavals I had created. Of one photo of myself, I wrote in my notes "young and svelte." NW had encouraged me to dress more professionally and my vision of what an administrator should look like found me paying even more attention to my attire. Like so many professional women of the time, I believed I would be taken seriously if I looked serious: in suits and blouses with feminine ties, and pumps with sensible heels. I was initially more resistant to changes Mary Ellen suggested because I was determined to never again lose me in order to please another person. I wanted to be acceptable and accepted; at the same time, I feared criticism and rejection. As I would come to understand over the years, her suggestions came from the heart and, more important, were usually spot-on.

Mary Ellen was not particularly fond of my gelled, spikey hair; I thought she should be happy it wasn't the tightly permed "afro" I had sported for years. Mary Ellen also told me I would be more attractive if the space between my top front teeth (which I never thought about) could be eliminated, and she cajoled me into going to a dentist for the first time in 20 years or so. (That avoidance came from fear based in the reality of the horrid experience a visiting cousin had with our family dentist.) Lucky for me I agreed to an appointment with Mary Ellen's dentist, a woman who proved to be understanding, nonjudgmental, gentle and a skilled practitioner. Remarkably, I had no cavities! I did have periodontal disease, which would require attention before any orthodontic work. I took Dr. Benoit's recommendations for specialists and never looked back. The fixes were costly but proved to be worth every penny.

By the time I was ready for braces, I thought I might write about the experience from an adult's point of view, so I have a diary of the early days of that ordeal. (It was 1992, and orthodontics was still primarily for kids.) I noted that my braces would be in place for my 43rd birthday and that my 20th birthday also "had been dictated by dental matters." All four of my wisdom teeth were pulled just before that so my parents' health insurance would cover the procedure. When I finished rereading my "braces" notes, which ended after just a few weeks, I wondered if I had gotten bored or too busy to continue. *I really should have written that article*, I think today. Here is what I would have shared with readers about January 20:

A dusting of snow as I drive to the office . . . arrive 15 minutes early for my 2 p.m. appointment . . . woman and young boy in waiting area . . . "You're too big for braces," he announces. I am glad the waiting room isn't more crowded. I tell him I'm not, but I wonder if he is right. Sandy, the receptionist, has a video for us to watch. I'd rather read People [magazine], but I dutifully pay attention and see what I'm about to go through. They talk about foods to avoid, including raw vegetables. The boy thinks braces are a great idea; he won't have to eat vegetables. A second video tells me how to take care of the appliances I am about to acquire. Sandy's timing is great; she must have watched/heard these things more times than she would care to count.

I'm beckoned. Doc and I chit chat about the upcoming URI-University of Massachusetts basketball game, about a couple of well-known people he'd like to get in the chair. What you see depends on where you sit. The spacers come out. What a great feeling. We're done now, right, I quip. Ha Ha. First the spaced teeth get fitted with what I come to call my anchors. I help customize them by biting down, over and over and over, on command. Just when I think they are in, they are out, then glued in!

A brief break. My chair is made upright. I'm allowed to rinse out the foul-tasting adhesive leftovers. But nobody tells me how you rinse with metal jutting out in four corners of one's mouth. I'm beginning to get a sense of what I have gotten myself into.

Back to the chair, down we go. How come we always need to be upside down, I ask doc. It's either you or me, he replies. A good straight man! The tedious part of installation is the brackets attached to each tooth. Some bizarre plastic things hold my mouth open and keep things out of the way. My teeth are cleaned and dried. Doc and his assistant, who never speaks, have this routine down. He picks up the tin bracket, reaches across me with it, she glues it, he dips it in something, and puts it on its tooth, then fine-tunes his placement. XX times.

After he finishes, it's time to rinse again.

The last step. It gets progressively faster and easier, he tells me as he loops wires through hooks and clamps things into place. I have yet to see what it all looks like; all I know is it FEELS awkward. Finally, at about one hour forty, the job is done. Well, not quite. There's the no-no food list to go over: written for children, but applicable to adults, too. And the directions for brushing and flossing.

In my car, I immediately check things out in my rearview mirror. I've got braces.

Dinner time. I'm prepared. I think. Four rounds of periodontal surgery over the summer taught me about soft foods and sore teeth. This night, though, the problem was not so much sore teeth as it was a mouth full of metal that seemed to defy chewing. Macaroni and cheese slid down nicely.

Although I did not write the article about my experience, I shared freely with my students. I swapped stories with several and sought their advice as the process moved along. After discovering that colored bands were available, I began showing off my choices. *As long as I am enduring this I might as well have fun*, I explained more than once. Maybe that attitude helped soften my "hard-ass professor" image just a bit.

Mary Ellen the professor was more approachable than I, and she was a much-admired teacher. One trait we shared was our workaholic natures. I still wonder sometimes how we managed to grow a relationship, let alone nurture it, when we both were consumed by professional responsibilities. Often the professional crossed over to include the personal, including some of our travels and many of our social activities. Particularly in our formative years, those were linked to Women's Studies-related programs. There were potlucks for faculty and students at the end of every semester (my lasagna was a hit). There were speaker series and film series and programs addressing issues local, national and international. There was a trip to Chicago for two days of interviews with 18 candidates for a joint Women's Studies/English position. (We already had sifted through 200 applications.) It took place at the annual meeting of the Modern Language Association: 10,000 English professors in one place! To this day I remain amazed by how I navigated our rental car from O'Hare airport to our downtown hotel in a snowstorm.

When we finished our work, we drove to Oshkosh to surprise my parents for their 42nd anniversary on December 30. Thus it was that we greeted 1991 in Wisconsin, and my oldest nephew greeted me with the news that Rhode Island's governor, just a few minutes after his inauguration, had closed dozens of banks and credit unions. *Surely not mine*, I thought. On the day we were to fly home, that rental car balked at the subfreezing temperatures and refused to start. We did a Keystone Cops-like routine to get a new one in time to make our flight. The plane was somewhere over Middle America, I wrote in my Christmas letter for that year, "when I saw a photograph in the Chicago Tribune of my credit union being guarded by nattily dressed state troopers. Uh oh. No time to panic, though. There was a house to pack as we prepared for our January 8 move. It snowed that day, too. My credit union also reopened; I was one of the lucky ones because there are lots of people who still do not have their money." The financial crisis did have an impact on us. Again, I turn to my Christmas letter, where I described how "we and other state employees decided to help Rhode Island out of its financial mess by giving up 10 percent of our pay for 58 weeks. 'Hello; come work for us and, by the way, you will immediately get your pay cut. But not to worry. You will get it back when you leave state employment.' There's lots of healthy skepticism around about that one!" We groused about the state of the state, then got on with living in it.

After a couple of years, as I spread my wings on campus, Journalism Department events and lots of athletics joined the mix of activities that filled our lives. It takes my breath away when I think of the people, places and events we shared. My life was incredibly enriched by this aspect of us. In "My Bucket," a short essay I wrote after retiring, I admitted that I do not have a Bucket List. "I've always been more of a 'play it as it lies' sort of gal -- taking life as it comes to me," I explained. But in the wake of the "The Bucket List" movie, "I started an accounting of my experiences. That was followed by this realization: Although I don't have a Bucket List, I do have My Bucket." I could have added that it already had overflowed.

More than a few of the items in that Bucket are connected to family milestones. We have been incredibly fortunate that, from the beginning, each of our families accepted *us* (however they defined us). We had been together only a few weeks when my sister and youngest nephew visited me in Narragansett. It was Mary Ellen who drove us to Boston to meet their plane. And it was I who countered that harrowing trip 10 days later by putting Kris and Mitch (who turned 6 during their stay) on a bus back to Logan airport. A couple of months later Mary Ellen's youngest nephew and niece spent a weekend with us. I found Billy more conversant on current affairs than some of my students; Kassie was overnighting away from home for the first time and not happy about it. From then on, the holidays, birthdays, graduations (high school and college), visits, illnesses, parties, weddings and eventually funerals accumulated. I almost never wrote about these. I *lived* them, which on reflection was a positive development. And yet. . . .

My first journal of the Us Years was similar to many of my earlier volumes as I recorded in exacting detail my personal struggles, shortcomings and successes. That stopped with the second journal, sporadic entries giving way to no entries. Much as a nursing mother seldom knows "this was the last time I breastfed her," I didn't know my entry dated "29 Sept 91 Sunday 11 a.m." ended my journaling. (Nor could I know I would return to such wordsmithing more than 20 years later.) As much progress as I made in figuring out who I was and what I wanted, eventually I stumbled when it came to communicating with my partner. I was loathe to dispel her characterizations of me as strong, steady, kind and easy going -- adjectives she frequently used in cards to me. When I resented how much of our precious free time she used to care for her mother, I told her I admired her devotion and volunteered to stay home and tend to chores (especially my growing number of flower gardens). When I felt invisible because I thought all her energies in Massachusetts were focused on her steadily declining mother, I said nothing. When I secretly rejoiced at having a weekend to myself, I tucked a "missing you" card into her purse (and played *lots* of golf). If she begged off a trip to Wisconsin with me, I hid my relief at not having to deal with her travel anxieties. I held my tongue because I knew her vulnerabilities and could not bear the thought of hurting her, of causing her more pain than she already had endured in her life. She knew me equally well, I believe, so after almost a decade together she might have been dismayed but she was not surprised by what came next.

CHAPTER 29

Intermission

Following Head and Heart

I may have tried, but I could not hide my growing professional dissatisfaction. (Was that why I had put on so much weight? Again!) In my 1996 birthday card, Mary Ellen wrote, "I hope that the year ahead will bring you the fulfillment that you crave and the challenges that you want." In another card, she acknowledged that "I know you are restless." When I bought a red Thunderbird in June of that year, she called it my "midlife reward." I had been naively hopeful about finding an administrative home at URI. In 1998 I wrote Mary Ellen that there had been "plenty of opportunity for [the provost or the president] over the last couple of years to say 'there will be something for you here,' and for whatever reasons they did not." I also wrote about disenchantment with my department, feeling "so little support for what I was trying to do." Yes, we made significant changes, but too often it seemed I was the only one committed to them. Had we truly collaborated to reach consensus or had I worn down my colleagues until they agreed to do it my way? Sadly, I once again chose to clam up; my fear of rejection remained strong. For example, when the provost was going to appoint an interim dean for Arts and Sciences, I offhandedly asked her to keep me in mind. I was profoundly disappointed when she announced her choice. I don't know if she even considered me because I never asked.

I quietly began to search for an administrative job. Geographic proximity was a must. An advertisement in the March 13, 1998,

Chronicle of Higher Education caught my eye. Where, I wondered, was Fitchburg, Massachusetts; the state college there was searching for a dean of undergraduate studies. It is about 100 miles north of Wakefield, I learned. Proximity, I decided, is relative. Mary Ellen -- who frequently drove 330 miles roundtrip in a day to check on her mother -- wasn't so sure. I wanted to apply for the job and so I did. I think my three-page application letter was the best I ever wrote. Not only did I incorporate lessons from HERS, but I had read hundreds of such letters and was well-schooled in the bad as well as the good. (My experience chairing what I generously described as "the messy" search for a vice president for business and finance at URI -- an assignment usually given to another vice president -- proved to be worth every aggravation.)

Eventually I was invited to Fitchburg State College for the range of interviews I was well-acquainted with, including dinner the night before with the search committee chair. I was as prepared as I could be the next day, though I was surprised by how compact the campus was. Dressed for success in a new Evan Picone pantsuit, I confidently shook a lot of hands and answered a lot of questions. I made my requirements clear with the two questions I asked of everyone: *Does the president leave Academic Affairs alone to do its work? Does the vice president for academic affairs make decisions?* I think my last interview was with the VPAA, Patricia ("Call me Pat") Spakes. She had come to FSC the year before and was responsible for the major reorganization that created the position for which I was interviewing. All services related to undergraduate students -- day, evening, on-campus and off-campus -- were being moved into a single administrative unit. Similarly, a dean of graduate studies also was being hired for her Academic Affairs team.

Pat and I hit it off immediately, not least because she earned her Ph.D. from UW-Madison, so we could "talk Wisconsin." The interview was more like a collegial conversation. When near the end she asked what I thought my biggest challenge would be were I to be hired, I paused before answering. I knew I could do the job, but I was less sure if my relationship could survive it. So my honest response to her was "the personal adjustments it would require." On the drive home, about all I could think about was how much I wanted the job. The college's size felt right for a first-time administrator (about 3,400 undergraduates in the "day" school and another 900 in its continuing-education program; about 200 full-time and 150 part-time faculty). I was ready to tackle *everything* the dean would be tasked with doing.

[An aside: Much has been written about the connection between smells and memories. I vividly recall that happening in a most unusual way in the administration building at FSC. The first time I used a restroom there, I noticed the pleasant odor of the liquid soap. I didn't think much about it until a subsequent visit (too much coffee), when the smell seemed stronger. I suddenly realized it reminded me of Grandma and Grandpa Conger's little house in Ridgeville, Ohio. *I am destined to work here*, I thought.]

Back home, I was eager to hear from Fitchburg and anxious about what it would mean to be hired or passed over. Mary Ellen's anxiety topped mine, though, because the time had come to move her mother to a nursing home. The money to provide the 24-7 care her dementia demanded was gone. We powered through our weeks, neither of us able to emotionally support the other as well as, I believe, we wanted. When I came home one afternoon and shared that the provost had talked with Pat Spakes and concluded that "they are very serious about you," Mary Ellen said she feared she was losing me. I had to temper my excitement and assure her that we could find a way to make it work.

A couple days later, Pat called to offer me the job. She explained that they could match my salary but couldn't go higher. That was acceptable, I said, and so I became a dean. (Actually, the 12-month FSC salary was a pay cut because my URI nine-month salary was supplemented by my summer earnings. But I was a dean, and that's all that mattered.) I was buoyed by a congratulatory note from Joye in Columbia, who wrote: "Takes a certain temperament to be a good administrator— and you have those traits." And I shared the sentiments in Mary Ellen's card: "I will miss our day-to-day life together but we'll find a way to grow and thrive together from a distance."

Before I submitted my resignation to URI, Mary Ellen convinced me to instead apply for a "leave without pay," which would give me a year to make sure I liked the job and living arrangements. Yet again, she was the wiser of us. Nonetheless, when I moved out of my URI office I was certain that I was finished teaching. I joyfully cleaned out filing cabinets, desk drawers and the credenza whose presence had always puzzled me. I tossed almost everything, including lecture notes, teaching materials, files of clippings and stacks of textbooks. It felt great! Cleaning out Mary Ellen's mother's house didn't feel good at all. Over a couple of incredibly hot May days we, along with her sister-in-law Caryl, worked tirelessly. I seldom have been as exhausted. I don't think I ever saw Mary Ellen look as dejected as she did in the last photo we took there. On all our subsequent trips to Pittsfield to visit her mother, we never drove past her longtime home.

I started my new job on July 1 without a place to live during the workweek, which was unsettling but temporary. I soon rented a condo in a converted apartment complex in Shrewsbury. Mary Ellen helped me shop for furniture -- just enough to make me comfortable -- and a few household goods. I lived like a 1970s career girl just starting out. Muffin and coffee in hand, I left Wakefield by 6 a.m. on Mondays and drove to Fitchburg. On Friday afternoons, I tried to get away in time to beat rush hour in Worcester. In between, the condo's proximity to the highway left me a generally easy 30-mile drive to work. (Except in winter ice or snow, when my rear-wheel drive Thunderbird and the hilly terrain did not get along.)

I quickly got caught up with trying to get settled, and in a rare card I apologized to Mary Ellen for being "so thoughtless about [not] writing." I added that it "sure is not related to lack of thinking about you— I do. A LOT." Instead of letters, I had been relying on email and phone calls "to feel immediate connections." In the card I described "trying to balance the excitement over my job, which makes my days go by quickly, and adjusting to the different life it requires." I admitted to being "scared sometimes that it won't work." But "having been away from journalism just a few weeks, I am real clear on how **good** that feels." Nevertheless, I hated "this rhythm of work, eat, sleep, kill time at the apartment etc. etc. And I miss you. I worry about you."

I had reason to worry. On one of my first afternoons on the job, when I still was in the "not-much-to-do" stage, I had gotten a call from a friend saying Mary Ellen was in the hospital. *Damn!* I thought. *Why now?* The friend assured me that she was OK. She had feared a "cardiac event," but it was not; it probably was stress related. I said I would be home as soon as possible. Selfishly, I wondered if Mary Ellen's health scare was a sign that my days-old job was doomed. One consequence of that incident was my quiet affirmation to a few new colleagues that my "housemate," as I had referred to her, was more than a roommate. Happily, our relationship never was an issue; indeed, over time I introduced Mary Ellen to a number of FSC folks.

Also happily, I had no issues with my secretaries. I inherited Dan, whose clerical-work gig was temporary. He patiently trained me in FSC's procedures, expertly handled paperwork, and skillfully ran interference with faculty and students. A recent chemistry graduate, he saddened me with his announcement that he was leaving for a job with a Boston-area company (developing an artificial skin compound, as I recall). His departure, however, gave me the opportunity to tailor a new job description to match my needs. Sorting through a few dozen resumés, I quickly picked out a couple of possibilities. After interviews, Carolyn Poirier topped my list. She proved to be a first-rate hire -- anywhere, any job!

The relative quiet of summer on a small college campus was a welcome environment for this new administrator. The so-called learning curve was steep, but I steadily adapted. I arranged individual meetings with the heads of all undergraduate programs. One of my first responsibilities was to help departments develop assessment plans, and that work had to get started. But mostly I listened; I wanted the faculty leaders to describe their programs' strengths and weaknesses. I made no commitments beyond the assurance that I would work *with* them, and if my office door was open they were welcome to drop in. The governance structure at FSC was different from what I was used to, but I was glad to have a role on the policymaking All College Committee. Also new to me was that the dean had little role in the tenure and promotion process, which was codified in the faculty's contract. On the other hand, the dean was solely responsible for deciding academic appeals from students; I was used to a committee doing that.

The job and I were a good match. I was thrown into the deep end of the pool, so to speak, with unexpected challenges/opportunities. It was imperative that I be a quick study about areas that were new to me, such as nursing-program accreditation reports and overseeing a Board of Higher Education-mandated review of the Technology

Education Program. Day in and day out, my journalistic skills -- gather information, make sense of it, communicate it clearly -- proved invaluable. Ditto for my ability to meet deadlines and an uncommon comfort level with ambiguity (in daily journalism, after all, there is no telling what the next minute might bring). By far, most memorable was the furor that accompanied release of the results of Massachusetts' first teacher-certification exam.

It was mid-July, and I was barely settled into my sparsely furnished temporary office when the state education department announced that as many as 59 percent of all the April test takers had failed. The brouhaha that followed was widely reported, with most news stories pointing out that the two-part exam tested literacy skills and subject-area competency at the eighth- to 10th-grade level. At FSC, there was shock and embarrassment; the school had been founded in 1894 as Fitchburg Normal School and its education programs were well-regarded. The trustees were not happy. The president was livid, ranting at Education administrators and faculty, as well as all of us in Academic Affairs, including the newbie deans. He demanded the impossible: an instant fix, whatever it would take to get our graduates passed. One of my early assignments was to parse the data for our graduates to see if I could find *anything* to help us figure out what that fix might be.

The fallout from that teachers' test eventually revealed (unleashed?) a president less hands off with Academic Affairs than had been described to me during my interviews. Evidence mounted over the months as he increasingly gave only lip-service to teamwork and shared decision-making. Clashes with his vice president for academic affairs were inevitable. I admired how Pat stood her ground, how she supported faculty, how she remained a consensus-builder, how she continued to thoughtfully make decisions in the best interest of the college even as the president worked to undercut her. She mentored her new deans with her actions as well as her words. Pat listened to us and encouraged us to try things. That was incredibly valuable. I am especially proud of four projects: my proposal for a committee to hear academic appeals, my proposal to change the standard for academic suspension, creation of a Dean's Fund To Support Undergraduate Research, and sponsoring a celebration of faculty scholarship.

567

I was not successful in legislating the appeals committee; faculty did not want the responsibility. I could live with that. More important to me was the new academic standard, which *was* adopted. At the end of a semester, I was required to notify students whose grades put them on probation or required their suspension. They could appeal. Those appeals were eye-opening. FSC students were primarily first-generation college; many were minority and/or economically disadvantaged. *Life gets in the way of life*, I told more than one student after hearing of their multiple jobs, commutes from the Boston area with a clunky car, substandard housing, family responsibilities and the like. I offered a second chance whenever I could, and made sure students connected with the appropriate college services. For the life of me, however, I could not understand someone appealing a 0.00 GPA. I argued that such students were not ready for college, and it was a disservice to readmit them. After some debate, the All College Committee approved my proposal for immediate suspension without appeal.

Because I controlled a modest budget, I was able to create the fund to help students doing research. I thought that would be useful in growing our honors program. Organizing the celebration of faculty -- a first for the college -- was fun. It had not taken me long to begin describing FSC faculty as the hardest-working faculty I ever knew. The usual teaching load was four courses a semester; many taught a fifth to supplement their salary *and* taught summer school, too. On the campus, research was less important than teaching, but many chose to be active scholars, too. I thought it was important for morale to recognize people's publications, creative activities and conference presentations. I tapped into my budget again, and Carolyn and I planned a party. I asked faculty to share their accomplishments and from that compiled and printed a program for "A Community of Scholars" reception. I planned to make it an annual gathering.

I never got the chance.

In January, Mary Ellen had thrown a party to celebrate my 50th birthday. Photographs show that I was all smiles as I chatted with friends from URI (including the provost), the neighborhood and our small social circle. On the surface, it seemed all was going well for our dual-career, two-city relationship. We were proving that I could have the career I wanted, the life I wanted. I thought I had managed to be true to love as I had described it years earlier in a journal entry about Mary Ellen. "What do I mean when I say I love you? It is a question I must ask myself, because I need to be sure I'm not just using words— And I know I am not." My lengthy enumeration included:

I mean that you are essential to my life.
I mean that I want to take care of you.
I mean that I want to protect you.
I mean that I am there for you— regardless.
I mean that you can trust me with your life.
I mean that I will be faithful to you.
I mean that we can tell one another anything.
I mean that I support the you that you were— are— and are becoming.

I know I felt good enough about the future to raise the possibility of us buying a second home in Fitchburg. Mary Ellen was only a few years from retirement, at which time we could move to Massachusetts. In the meantime, we would have a "get-away" that would allow me to live near my workplace. She agreed to look; I found a real estate agent. The search took a while, but finally turned up a suitable condo.

Four days away from signing the purchase and sales agreement, I went home for the weekend. We had company, so there wasn't much time for us to talk. But as I sat on the edge of the bed on Sunday afternoon, I no longer could ignore the unsettling thoughts I had kept to myself for weeks. I knew in my gut that Mary Ellen was not happy about us buying the condo and was afraid it was another step toward me abandoning us. I wondered if I really was withdrawing, beginning to "uncouple" -- and the condo would make it easier. And in that moment I listened to my heart and chose not to go through with the purchase. And in the next moment I yelled to Mary Ellen to come upstairs. I tearfully told her I had decided to resign my deanship. She didn't try to talk me out of that, other than to ask if I was sure.

On the morning of May 11, 1999, with a lump in my throat and tears threatening, I told Pat that I was resigning. The second sentence of my official notice explained that "I have enjoyed my work here immensely, but the environment created by the president is not one in which I want to work." The last straw, I think, had been walking out of an all-college meeting and having a fellow administrator say, "I counted [some number] of lies [by the president]. How many did you catch?" By then, with him undermining Academic Affairs on a daily basis, the future was not promising. I believed people had described the president honestly and accurately during my interviews but, I told a former URI colleague, he had "changed dramatically in words and deed."

Pat shared my resignation memo with the president, who was spending a lot of time in his office behind closed doors. I don't remember him speaking to me again; if he did, I probably paid little attention. In her memo to the faculty, Pat's summary of my contributions included those I took most pride in.

> While Dr. Luebke was with us for a short time, she very quickly became an integral part of the Academic Affairs "team" and demonstrated a strong commitment to academic quality and standards. She also made significant contributions to the College in her work with departments on program reviews and outcomes assessment.

I was gratified by the outpouring of support I received from around the campus. Unlike the other times when I was a "lame duck," my opinions continued to matter, and I was counted on for leadership and guidance. I had pledged "to work for the academic good of the College through my final day in the office" and I did. In fact, I agreed to stay in a Fitchburg hotel for a few days after that to complete a project.

After the movers emptied my Shrewsbury rental, they picked up my roll-top desk and a few boxes from my office. I hugged Carolyn goodbye, left the administration building without fanfare, climbed into my red Thunderbird and drove away from the campus. I cried as I headed home. I was disappointed, dejected and disillusioned. After I had notified my department that I was returning to my tenured professorship at the end of my leave, the response was anything but welcoming. I was angry. I wasn't prepared for how much worse I would feel in the months ahead.

CHAPTER 30

Act II

Back to the Future

I moped my way through the summer of '99, dreading the start of my 26th academic year. Readjusting to being home full time with Mary Ellen was not always easy -- for either of us -- but it *was* where I belonged. Yet I couldn't seem to stop myself from second-guessing. *Had the leave of absence made it too easy for me to abandon Fitchburg? Was resigning another one of my impulsive career moves?* I clung to my FSC ties. Pat had been at a meeting the day I left, so after she returned, we met for lunch halfway between Fitchburg and Wakefield. I gave her a thank-you gift: a hand-crafted kaleidoscope chosen because, I told her, "I admire your ability to see many ways to look at a situation." She gave me the inside scoop on what others had described to me as the president's increasingly bizarre behavior. (Shortly after I had left for good, Pat was preparing for vacation and emailed me: "Say prayers or do some protective rituals on behalf of Academic Affairs while I'm gone!") She also shared her doubts that the internal search for a suitable interim dean would be successful. It helped me to know that -- for yet another time in my career -- I was not easy to replace. More helpful were her assurances that she understood my reasons for leaving and the decision was the right one.

[An aside: After another year, the Graduate Studies dean hired with me moved on. Pat, who served at the pleasure of the president, returned from a Thanksgiving break to learn she was fired. She landed on her feet, going first to Shippensburg University as provost and then to the University of Washington-Tacoma as chancellor. Mary Ellen and I, along with my Fitchburg colleague Shirley Wagner, visited Pat in Pennsylvania in October 2002. (Our trip occurred during the three weeks that the "D.C. snipers" were terrorizing motorists; I remember nervously pumping gas.) It was homecoming, and I still have the little souvenir football I caught at the game. In another small-world moment, I served on NCAA committees during the leadership of Mark Emmert, the former University of Washington president who in announcing Pat's hiring referred to her as "someone with fresh perspectives and innovative ideas." I couldn't agree more.]

I had good reason to believe at least one of my journalism colleagues would be less than thrilled with my return. Someone had confided in me that that faculty member once told a group of students my initials stood for "Big Fat Lesbian." Unwilling to try to confirm that story, I had remained silent. Cognizant of the expiration date on my leave, I had promptly notified the acting department chair about my plans. Hoping to "retool," I asked to be assigned two courses instead of three for the fall. I was "deeply disappointed" by his response and didn't hold back in a follow-up memo. (I have always written outrage better than I verbalize it.) For one thing, I was "appalled that you chose not to advocate on my behalf [for two courses] -- or were ineffective in doing so." I challenged his outrageous assertion that I did not teach enough when I was chair by pointing out that "an examination of the record would show a number of semesters when I carried a course load beyond that specified in my letter of hire."

A second bone of contention was his suggestion that the specifics of my teaching assignment required the dean's approval. "That is unprecedented in my 25 years in higher education," I wrote (playing my "experience" card). I pointed out that teaching assignments "always have been negotiated by faculty member and chair." Which led to my third and most strenuous objection: that he had not consulted me about that teaching assignment.

> At the least, common courtesy -- not to mention department culture -- dictates such collaboration. Your behavior flies in the face of how I treated you every semester and the countless accommodations

I made for you. Do not misunderstand this anger; I know that options are limited. . . . But I also know which courses were listed in the scheduling booklet as "staff." And I have preferences! Keep in mind, too, that I was away on an approved leave of absence. My decision about returning . . . was not required by the university until 30 May. If you did not take that into account when planning for fall, that is your problem.

If the chair had any doubts about the attitude I was returning with, I made it clear with my closing paragraph: "I have resigned from an administration position I love because I will not work for a president who only gives lip service to teamwork and shared decision-making. Rest assured that I will not tolerate that in a department chair either."

Once back in Rhode Island, I was determined to spend as little time on campus as possible. In a faculty-sized office for the first time since Hartford, I wanted minimal furnishings. I got the institutional metal desk and filing cabinet (I had few files, remember) removed. The movers delivered my roll-top desk and Missouri-era rocking chair from Fitchburg, and I bought myself a small wooden bookcase. A simple stand held a computer and printer. I hung a couple of posters and taped my schedule to the door (with only as many official office hours

as expected by the university). Then I stayed away until I was contractually obligated to be on campus.

Photos reminded me that there was some fun that summer. Mary Ellen and I visited family in Atlantic City. I accompanied her to Albuquerque, where she presented a paper at the annual meeting of the National Women's Studies Association. I lobbied to rent a convertible, which proved to be expensive and, given the heat, quite foolish. Driving historic Route 66 with the top *up* was not what I had dreamed. I also was disappointed to not love New Mexico, which I found oh-so beige. The saving grace was a visit to Santa Fe and the Georgia O'Keeffe Museum. For a real vacation, we spent a week in a rustic cottage on Lieutenant's Island off Wellfleet, Massachusetts, where our comings and goings were determined by the tides and the causeway to the mainland. I relaxed at last.

When the semester got under way after Labor Day, I promised myself I would be the best teacher I could be and I would not shortchange students. But I had no intention of doing more than the minimum required. I had every intention of returning to higher education administration as soon as possible. I wanted to be home at night, but beyond that I was open to any sort of job and every sort of institution. I was confident in what I had to offer. I was confident that given the opportunity, my references and I could explain Fitchburg. For 18 months or so, there were just enough jobs advertised to keep me on tenterhooks. Search committees could take weeks (even months) to respond to applicants. Finally, for the sake of my mental health and my relationship, I chided myself: *Stop looking! Stop torturing yourself! Accept that you are going to teach at URI until you can retire.* And just as I had quit smoking and drinking cold turkey, I gave up my dream of an administrative position. For what turned out to be 10 years, I figured out how to teach on my terms. Way back in 1974, when I was still dreaming about a possible teaching career, Les Polk reflected in a letter how after just a few years his teaching was already different from what I had experienced. "Maturity changes teaching," he observed. I now understood how that might be true of me. I found ways to challenge myself, to grow professionally and to contribute meaningfully. It took a few years, but I finally came to characterize my year at Fitchburg as a professional development year. I drew on my experiences there for the rest of my career.

Eventually I took advantage of a required performance review to reflect on my *new* work at URI. Although there was a time when promotion to professor was the last time faculty members were evaluated, those times were disappearing around the country. No longer was productivity assumed (or lack of it ignored); we had to prove ourselves again and again. At URI we now had "levels," with Full III being the ultimate rank. Along with it came a sizable raise. When it was time for that mandatory review, I stuffed three giant binders with evidence supporting my sustained excellence in teaching, research and service. Having to do so offended me. But in the first paragraph of my personal statement, I concluded that "if I had known 30 years ago . . . that I would be required to publicly review [my] career, especially the last several years of it, to demonstrate my continued productivity, I can honestly write that I would have done little differently." I flooded my reviewers with documents and words, including a list of 20 areas where I had provided leadership in my lone year at Fitchburg. *No way will you deny me Full III,* I smugly thought.

Rereading my Statement on Teaching, I was surprised by how it foreshadowed the landscape of the present I am now writing in. It encapsulated a philosophy of journalism education that I proudly stand by today:

> I believe that the most important gift we give journalism majors is an appreciation for the centrality of **content** in news media. This is as true for the student who wants to be a public affairs reporter as it is for the broadcast journalism student, the web-design student or the future sportswriter. It is not enough to satisfy students' voracious appetites for "media" technology. Instead, we must help them become critical producers -- as well as consumers -- of the news. We must help them develop ethically so they can thrive in a wonderfully diverse world where words and images are used as easily to deceive and destroy as to inform and enlighten. Thus it is imperative that every course -- "skills" or "conceptual" -- centers on developing critical thinkers. In addition, we must foster students who can work independently and as members of a team, who appreciate the history and

traditions of our profession as well as its contemporary issues and challenges. They must learn to be comfortable with deadlines, ambiguity and uncertainty. They must learn to be assertive and willing to challenge authority.

Designing my courses to do those things and developing each into a performance-based experience engaged me intellectually. That engagement energized me, and in addition to reengineering courses I tweaked them and experimented with new materials each semester.

Nowhere was that more apparent than with editing, which I had been teaching *forever*. I had come to believe the traditional approach was neither the most effective nor the most efficient. I also was desperate to minimize the repetitive, mind-numbing grading that bored me. So I devised a competency-based course that allowed students to work on basic skills such as grammar, Associated Press Style and math until they mastered them. I offered them several ways to demonstrate copy-editing competency. I was a resource, but students had to take responsibility for their own learning. They could work at their own speed. Course grades were linked to the degree to which competencies were achieved. For example, "A" work meant the student could edit as an entry-level professional. As in all my classes, students were required to keep a portfolio of their work and write "Reflections" on it at the end of the semester. I tapped their portfolios for future lessons and mined their reflections to help me improve the course.

Dismayed by too many editing students who paid too little attention to the news (and whose gaps in general knowledge hindered their ability to edit), I began giving weekly general knowledge quizzes. I enjoyed creating these as much as students groused about taking them. For example, one required students to quickly identify public figures from recent newspaper photographs. After they passed the photos to the next student, they were to check their spelling of the name and add a short statement describing why the person had been in the news. The instructions for another quiz explained, "Sports terminology has crept into everyday usage more than we might imagine. For each term below, give the sport and the meaning of the sports term and describe a more general use." As an example, I used "home stretch = from racing, indicates nearing the end of the race; might be used to describe the last days of a political race." Yet another began with the premise that news and feature writers often draw on fiction, and rely on readers' familiarity with characters, dialogue or plots to make their point. "Consider, for example, the sportswriter whose story included this sentence: 'Frankly, coach, we don't give a damn,' the frustrated players seemed to be telling Shula. The editor who recalls what Rhett said to Scarlett in 'Gone With the Wind,' and the context will be able to judge the effectiveness of the writer's approach. The editor who is in the dark will not. She/he also will not be able to ensure that the writer has been true to her/his source."

Commenting on my Full III dossier, one of my colleagues called me "an institution builder," which I think accurately captured my professional persona. She described how I had begun to familiarize myself with the technology used by broadcast majors "and has taken on the rather intimidating world of digital technology, fearlessly, indulging in hours of self-training on the equipment. I believe it's her desire to be a life-long learner; she handles modern changes with little trepidation." I will go so far as to say that "technology" saved me from boredom, one of my great fears. Before I went to Fitchburg I had been invested in the department taking full advantage of our computerized lab. One of my undertakings had been creating The Source, which I envisioned as an online news service offering the best student-written stories to Rhode Island newspapers. A journalism student with interest and web proficiency came along just as I was ready to implement the grant I received for The Source. Together we got it going -- ever so slowly. Then I left and it languished, and although I later worked to rebuild it, The Source proved to be my dream more than the department's. Another project for which I had high hopes was Ram ScOpe, a magazine (named by a student) I created to showcase students' work. Its inaugural issue was devoted to the projects of students in the Coastal Institute fellowship program. The stories were written by Feature Writing students and the design was completed by advanced-editing students. Again, no one carried on that work in my absence, nor could I muster enthusiasm for it when I returned. Instead, I focused on the evolving array of online tools and resources that could help me prepare students for success as 21st-century journalists.

[An aside: When I inventoried my URI decades, topping my list was students, which came as no surprise. The constant in my life since 1974 has been the young women and men who chose to study journalism. Their well-being and success were at the root of the projects I undertook, projects that also broadened the scope of my accomplishments and regularly reminded me why I had chosen education as a career. I had quickly learned when I was the department chairwoman that our relationships would be different. They never could be just students in my courses because I was not just their teacher. I had additional responsibilities and authorities to make decisions directly affecting their progress toward graduation. I was friendly, but I could not be their friend. (That I had aged out of that role was coupled with the changes in the environment of higher education since my Missouri days, too.) I came to miss those one-on-one relationships that highlighted my previous jobs. To some extent, I found them again after I returned to URI and settled into my faculty-only role. Just recently I finally felt comfortable becoming Facebook friends with a number of those graduates, although over the years I had kept up to date on many thanks to my friend and colleague Linda Lotridge Levin. (I never have told her about being a tad envious of her "beloved" status with so many students.)]

I immersed myself in software and drooled over the latest hardware. Among other things, I taught myself page-design software so I could incorporate it into my new publication design course. That course also required me to think beyond newspaper design to satisfy the needs of students interested in magazines and public relations. (And when it was time for a Journalism faculty member to oversee the public relations major, I volunteered!) I continued to hone my web-design skills by learning software such as Dreamweaver. Doing that allowed me to offer a special course on writing, editing and producing stories for online news sites. It also prepared me to enhance the department's website (and my own). I didn't succeed in bringing my colleagues into the online fold as much as I wanted, but at least I offered opportunities to my students. And I had fun!

Especially rewarding was the "A Day in the Life of the University of Rhode Island Project" produced in 2005 by the 14 students in my Online Journalism course. I had wanted to do a "Day in the Life" project for a long time, inspired by Life magazine's primarily photographic

"One Day in the Life of America" in 1974. The students volunteered for time slots, which began at 12:01 a.m., and then spent an unseasonably warm spring day (and night) capturing the sights and sounds of campus life. They used digital cameras to take photos. Their stories were written and edited and posted online within a couple of days. The university news bureau wrote a story about our efforts. I could not have been prouder of those students.

To bring attention to their writing and research, as well as to inspire their peers, I also posted exemplary projects from my other courses. Among them: a guide for students wanting to make the transition from journalism to writing fiction; an annotated bibliography on New Journalism; an exploration of the field of sports and entertainment law, and how a journalism major is good preparation for that profession; an annotated bibliography of resources and references for fashion journalism. I was so impressed by the student who snagged an interview with Anne Garrels, NPR journalist and author of "Naked in Baghdad," that I posted her project. And then there was Amanda Selvidio, who uncovered the wonderful story of reporter Emma Shaw Colcleugh when I devoted Perspectives on Reporting to the study of female journalists. I posted much of those students' research online, and nominated Colcleugh for the Rhode Island Press Association Hall of Fame. She was inducted in November 2002, with Amanda present to receive well-deserved kudos.

[An aside: Upon reflection, I am struck by how Perspectives, which I usually describe as a *literature of journalism* course, brought the undergraduate me full circle. I had started college as an English major because I loved to read, and within a semester was a journalism major because I also loved to write. Perspectives exposed students and me to long-form reporting, usually book-length, usually newly published, always topical. Reading a book a week challenged students. So did being given responsibility for leading/guiding our discussion of one of those books. They almost always rose to the occasion, and I left most classes energized rather than depleted. I loved reading end-of-the semester confessions about never having read a complete book, let alone *so many*, in a semester. I loved sharing my "dirty little secret" when I was reading a particular book for the first time along with them, because I enjoyed how that altered the nature of the discussion.]

Just as my fascination with using technology rescued me from classroom boredom, so too my involvement with URI athletics provided me a new arena for leadership. An avowed sports junkie (to this day I read the Sports section of a newspaper first), I had been delighted to discover that Mary Ellen enjoyed attending URI volleyball matches and women's basketball games. We did a lot of that in Act I, and in the mid-1990s I had been one of the "super fans" coach Linda Ziemke asked to form a Women's Basketball Booster Club. I enjoyed a peek into coaching and got a firsthand look at how coaches are teachers, too. I was invited to be an honorary coach for a game, which found me sitting at the end of the bench, joining time-out huddles and delivering postgame comments in the locker room. Unfortunately, the team lost. Unfortunately, Mary Ellen had been unable to attend the game.

More memorable than that experience, however, was being in the room with the team for Selection Day, when participants for the 1996 women's basketball tournament were announced. URI had enjoyed its best season in program history and hopes were high. As the brackets were revealed, tension mounted. With just two empty spots remaining on the board, everyone in our room seemed to be holding their breath. The 63rd school's name was called. Now only one chance remained to hear "University of Rhode Island." We did, and the room erupted into elation. In a stroke of luck, URI was to play Oklahoma State in Athens, Georgia, at the start of our spring break trip to Hilton Head. We'd have tickets and a hotel room if we could get to Athens. I drove to the Providence airport so I could speak in person to a ticket agent in hopes of changing our itinerary. And when I explained to her why I *really needed* to do so, she got us new flights and waived extra costs! We were unsure if we would drive back to Athens if URI advanced to play a second game. They did not. But of all my basketball experiences -- including attending several women's Final Fours -- it is that opening round game I treasure the most. (The week on our beloved Hilton Head was pretty sweet, too.)

Even during my year at Fitchburg, Mary Ellen and I managed to attend several URI women's basketball games. By then, there was a new coach with a very famous volunteer assistant: the legendary Boston Celtics player and coach, K.C. Jones. He provided another priceless basketball moment when he serenaded me with "Happy Birthday" after a fellow booster pointed out the day's significance. When I returned to URI, I resumed publishing Sidelines, the boosters' newsletter I had created to fill the gap left by the absence of women's basketball news in the local press. I played with its design, wrote two columns ("Inside ScOOps" with brief items and "The Rhody Way," a series of lessons "to enhance your understanding of Lady Rams basketball"), reported news and wrote feature stories. If anyone questioned the time I spent working on it, I called it professional development or community service. Privately, I called it salvation.

After a few years of resisting campus involvement, I also returned to the Senate (even serving a term as vice chair). Among other committees, I served on and then chaired the Curricular Affairs Committee, where I earned a reputation for efficient meetings that produced results. By far my favorite assignment was the Athletics Advisory Board, which is the Senate's policy review board for all athletic programs. It brought together my love of athletics and my commitment to academic standards and athletes' success. After AAB chair Yngve Ramstad's illness forced him to resign, I replaced him. Yngve had also served as the university's Faculty Athletic Representative to the NCAA, and I successfully lobbied the president for that appointment. It felt like a role I had been born for, and the timing couldn't have been better. I was ready to be out of the classroom; in truth, I was ready (but not quite financially able) to join Mary Ellen in retirement. I drafted a formal job description for the FAR, with reduced teaching and guaranteed support for travel, which the president agreed to. I *loved* being the FAR. I *loved* that it was a gateway into NCAA committee work, which meant travel, new challenges and new people (one "old" link, too; the Committee on Academic Performance was chaired by Walter Harrison, president of the University of Hartford). I *loved* that the national work allowed me to contribute to enhanced academic standards for athletes, to strengthened monitoring of Title IX mandates, and to accreditation for athletic programs on par with longstanding ones for academics. It is easy today to fault the organization for the many ways it has failed or faltered, but I remain proud of the work done by the groups I gladly joined and reluctantly left. And I am proud that after I took my leave, President Harrison wrote to "celebrate what a great member you have been. Thoughtful, analytic, highly principled. Everything any chair could ask for."

[An aside: Yngve and I had served on the Senate Executive Committee together. His wife, Alexa Albert, was a sociologist and longtime colleague of Mary Ellen's. She also taught several hundred students in Introduction to Sociology and when she brought her class to a women's basketball game, attendance swelled. We four occasionally socialized. Before we knew of Yngve's diagnosis, Alexa was enduring a recurrence of breast cancer. One afternoon in late 2006 she called to ask if Mary Ellen and I would drop by their house. That is when Yngve shared his amyotrophic lateral sclerosis diagnosis, and Alexa wondered if Mary Ellen could help them navigate university bureaucracy and such. They may not have known then that they would depend on her for so much more, but I knew she would do whatever they needed. And she did. Alexa died on May 2, 2007. That fall, I helped organize a charity Walk Around the Quad as part of the statewide Walk to D'Feet ALS. Yngve watched from his wheelchair as hundreds of "Ramstad's Rams" -- student-athletes, students, administrators, staff and faculty -- walked in his honor. And raised more than $10,000 for ALS research. Yngve's decline was rapid, but he planned to attend the June 2008 "Evening of Hope" at which he was to be honored with the Courage Award. I agreed to produce a video biography to be shown that night. It turned out to be several minutes longer than the organizers wanted, but I didn't care. I was saddened that Yngve was unable to attend the gala. I know he would have enjoyed meeting football legend Jim Brown. I certainly did,

and the photo of him, me and Mary Ellen earned a prominent spot in my office. When Yngve died on July 5, I lost my best friend on the faculty. Preparing remarks for his memorial service a month later left me without words until the last minute.]

On the Homefront

If the early months of URI ACT II were unsettled, the new millennium thankfully did not deliver the chaos some predicted. A review of our activities confirms that in the ensuing months we settled back into our patterns of work and play, except I focused on play and Mary Ellen on work. She grew increasingly exhausted from the physical and mental strains of Women's Studies responsibilities and overseeing the care of her mother, first at home and then in the nursing home. [An aside: Many months after releasing "Dementia's Unexpected Gifts," I found something Mary Ellen had written in 1992, after we had visited my Grandma Conger: "Nursing homes are so hard for me. I hope that we can keep my mother at home until she is no longer aware of anything. As for me, I don't want to live this way when the time comes." Sigh.] On June 29, 2001, we were in Atlantic City for the ShopRite LPGA golf tournament when Mary Ellen got a call that her mother was dying. We quickly repacked the car and I drove us through 275 miles of Friday afternoon traffic to Pittsfield, Massachusetts. Ten days of "death watch" (my first such experience) followed. We camped out in a hotel, with me making a one-day roundtrip home to do laundry and tend to things. I remember watching the Pittsfield Fourth of July parade and choking back tears when a band's military march brought to mind my oldest nephew, a naval aviator then deployed on a carrier bound for the Persian Gulf. I remember not feeling well on Sunday the 8th and dropping off Mary Ellen at the nursing home with the promise to return by dinner. I awoke suddenly from a nap that afternoon and my first thought was *I need to go back now*. I did, and not long afterward Dorothy Dowd Reilly died.

The surreal experience of seeing someone draw her last breath was a first for me. As I write, that remains true. When my father died on December 9, 2002, my sister and I were driving back from the Milwaukee airport, our brother had left the nursing home for a bit, and Mom had stepped out of Dad's room. (We talked later about how he had waited for us all to leave before dying. We were certain he wanted to protect us from the experience.) My words to him when I reluctantly went into his room afterward were simple. *I love you. Thank you for being my Dad.* When my mother died unexpectedly on December 28, 2009, she was in Colorado, having spent the holidays with my brother and niece. I don't expect to ever forget my primal scream when I got the news. I had spoken with her on Sunday and wished her a good flight home. I was dumbfounded when my brother called about lunch time Monday to say she had been hospitalized. Someone held the phone to her ear late that afternoon so I could say goodbye. *I love you. Thank you for being my mother.*

Such sadness was remarkably rare for me and remarkably common for Mary Ellen -- at least that is how I remember the Act II years. But then, as the "glass half full" partner, I can be excused for focusing on the rich variety of places, people and experiences that our life afforded us. I would be remiss, however, if I overlooked my health scare that began shortly before the death of Mary Ellen's mother.

In early June 2001, what I thought was a routine mammogram -- until I got called back for "more pictures" (even then I thought the film had been messed up) -- had turned up microcalcifications. Mary Ellen's connections got me an almost-immediate appointment for a second opinion from one of the preeminent experts in the country. After a sterotactic core biopsy (a truly weird procedure) was judged inconclusive, it was decided I needed a surgical biopsy. On August 2, 2001, Mary Ellen wrote about being "in a hospital waiting room again. . . . We thought that the summer of 1993 was bad [my Lyme, her mother's hospitalization] but this one will be etched forever in our memories." My surgical biopsy also proved inconclusive, which was confirmed by another second opinion, but my surgeon was confident the cells were *not* pre-cancerous. We got that news while eating breakfast in a favorite restaurant in East Sandwich; we were on our way to a well-deserved vacation in Wellfleet, Massachusetts. Our tears were of joy and relief.

Mary Ellen retired in 2003; she probably was ready earlier but she waited to make sure. (And even then she was, as I observed, a reluctant retiree. She didn't know what she would do with her time, which for as long as I had known her centered on her mother and her job.) I would have gone then, too, but needed several more years to maximize the health-care benefits that finally were in our contract. Mary Ellen had played a significant role in the effort to get the state to treat us like other state employees, who enjoyed benefits we did not. I was livid several years later when the faculty union bargained away those benefits, and angrily resigned from the union. I was lucky a couple of years after that when the university offered a package of perks to induce faculty considering retirement to do it. I already had privately decided to retire at the end of the 2011-2012 school year but had not done any paperwork. Our financial advisor had demonstrated that I could live to age 99 and not run out of money; the early retirement plan would (among other benefits) take me to Medicare. I skipped around the house shouting "Yippee!"

My last official day as Barbara F. Luebke, Professor of Journalism, was June 30, 2012. I had emptied my office by then, and when I left Chafee Hall for the final time I never looked back. Barbara F. Luebke, now Professor Emerita of Journalism, was ready for new adventures.

Snapshots

Ready to leave home for my interview at URI. Spring 1989.

Shortly after I moved to Rhode Island, Kris and Mitch flew out for a visit. Here we are at Narragansett Beach.

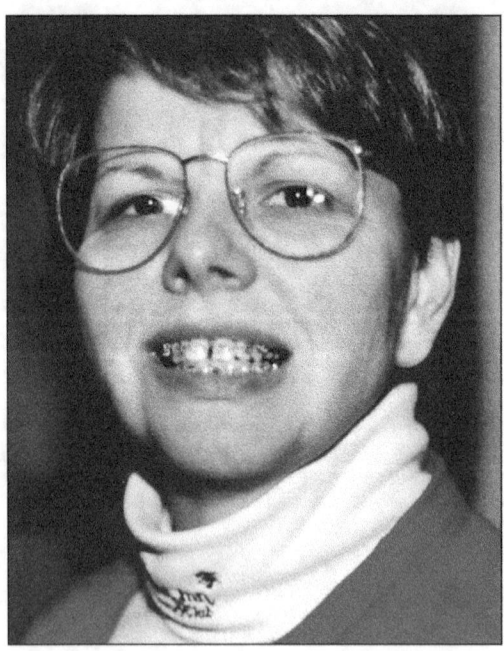

For a few weeks in 1992, I kept a diary of my ordeal with braces.

My first major accomplishment as Journalism Department chair was creating a computer lab for reporting and editing classes.

Three of Mary Ellen's nieces look through the poetry "book" I created for their grandmother. Christmas 1990.

At a Women's Studies dinner for Maggie Kuhn, founder of the Gray Panthers movement, who I first met at Eau Claire.

At a reception for CNN's Christiane Amanpour (a URI alumna) and journalism students in 1995, when she was awarded an honorary degree.

As NCAA Faculty Athletics Representative, I had many memorable moments -- none more picturesque than visiting the U.S. Military Academy for an Army-URI football game.

Assisting Provost Beverly Swan in hooding James Carey, longtime journalism dean and scholar. I nominated the Rhode Island native for an honorary degree in 1998. Twenty years later I discovered that a woman in my golf league was his sister.

I was immensely proud when the Athletics Department honored me (third from left) as a Rhody Role Model in 2013.

BFL has left the office

September 1974 - June 30, 2012

Dear You -- In September 1974, I sat in my office at the Columbia Missourian and watched a horde of new reporting and editing students pour in to the newsroom. I wondered what I had gotten myself into. On April 26, I taught my last class: Sports Journalism at the University of Rhode Island. In between there were stints at UW-Eau Claire, Missouri again and the University of Hartford. There was even a year (how I wish it had been longer) as Dean of Undergraduate Studies at Fitchburg (Mass.) State College. I have been a URI Ram since 1989, and have had the privilege of being the NCAA Faculty Athletics Representative for the last six years. All in all, it has been quite a ride. You were a part of my professional -- and personal -- journey; many of you still are. Because retirement brings with it frequent moments of reflection, you are in my thoughts a lot these days. The fond memories are too numerous to mention, but late nights in the Missourian newsroom (and the Heidelberg), Christmas tree-decorating parties and holiday meals come to mind. Everyone asks what I have planned; the answer, for now, is nothing. I look forward to allowing life to continue to reveal itself, day by day. Though rest assured that there are golf, books, travel with ME and Packers games in the mix.   Do stay in touch (bfluebke@me.com).

Cheers. -- BFL / Barb / Barbara / Dr. Luebke / Aunt Barb / Barb Teyze

CHAPTER 31

Turning a Page

<u>Monday 10/15/1990 7:23 a.m.</u>

Leonard Bernstein died last night— Five days or so ago he announced he was retiring— I don't want just 5 days— Selfish? I don't think so— If this relationship works (and even if it does not) I want years to do with my lover/friend/partner— We will have <u>worked</u> for years— we will deserve time to do as we please— So many people don't get that— Mom and Dad did not— But I <u>do not</u> want my work to be my entire life— And I <u>do</u> want to be able to put it behind me when the time is right.

I was 41 when I wrote that journal entry, just a few months into my relationship with Mary Ellen. I was 63+ when I retired. In the intervening years, I had spent a lot of time thinking about myself and what I wanted out of the rest of my life. Shortly after my 42nd birthday, I wrote that "more today than yesterday . . . is not a cliché and we must not let it become one. Rather it is a statement reflective of how we approach our relationship." I resisted whenever I was asked, "Will you marry me?" I feared a loss of independence. Still, I wrote:

> I do believe in forever (and very much <u>want</u> forever)— but . . . the [kind of] forever that creeps up on you— until one day you realize it has been. The statement also reflects how I'm working to get better at living and loving— More in charge of myself— More aware of my essence, my needs and wants— I struggle to figure those things out— I want/need to know who I <u>really</u> am.

My therapist assured me that despite doubts such as those I have a strong sense of self. I wrote about knowing "that is vital to my survival— Each time I am able to feel and express/acknowledge, I have success. Each time I can break a destructive pattern, I succeed." I enumerated some of those successes, "small things— big things. I am living differently in ways that count— I am proud of myself for taking care of M.E. this week without resentment— I am proud of myself for being able to say 'this is what I need'— I am proud of myself for consciously noticing how we are different and how we react to things or handle things differently AND letting that be OK."

Although I never was as successful as I might have been in defining myself beyond my work, I was successful in letting go of my job. Still, I remained at heart a journalist, an observer, a creator, an editor and a wordsmith who is happiest when she is *doing*. And one thing I had been doing during Act II was applying my journalistic skills to a range of personal projects. Words (mine and others') were at the heart of most of them, but I also became adept at visual storytelling. I was familiar with photo editing because I came of age when photography (taking pictures, developing film and printing photos) was a staple of journalism education. As a news editor and editing teacher, I had lots of experience choosing newsworthy shots and preparing them for publication. The gift I created for my sister's 50th birthday in 2000 was my first large-scale photo project. It was made possible by the Mac computer Mary Ellen and I bought after we won $1,200 at a slot machine in Atlantic City. (It was 1997 and we were on our way to Annapolis, Maryland, for my nephew Bill's Naval Academy graduation.) My birthday magazine, complete with a cover mimicking Time, felt like a major accomplishment. Today it looks amateurish, and yet the love that produced it remains evident -- making it a success.

That "BFL Publication" remained a singular achievement until 2004. By that time we had an iMac that allowed for importing video as well as photographs, and burning CDs and DVDs. I bought a video camera to document Bill's wedding in August and planned to make a "movie" for their Christmas present. "Shelly & Bill Got Hitched" debuted as a "Red Fish" production, the moniker I continue to use. The project emboldened me to tackle "North to Alaska," a movie about our (me, Kris, Mom and Mary Ellen) trip in late spring 2006. My ambition got the better of me, sad to say, and the finished movie (complete with background music and a script to be narrated using the professional mic kit I bought) was too long for one DVD. Then a corrupted file prevented editing to shorten it. (I do have the script and the raw video; all I need is the will to try again). Almost a dozen photo books and video projects followed before my retirement; others came after. **Appendix E**

Frequently asked -- and what retiree is not? -- what I planned to do with my time, I parroted the cliché "Whatever I want." My reflective self did not let me rest for long, however. In the Preface to my book "MUSINGS of a newly retired professor," I explained:

> The ideas for these musings (I first thought they would be essays, but that is not the shape they took) emerged on morning walks in the weeks before and after my official retirement day. . . . I jotted notes and working titles on the back of an envelope. Sometimes an opening sentence formed in my subconscious overnight and bloomed on a walk. Other times a word or two was all I had -- until days later they were shaped into an idea. . . .
>
> Eventually, what started as a project to satisfy a selfish desire to commit memories to paper so they might survive had a larger purpose. From where I sit, there was an inner me yearning to be shared.

I shared "MUSINGS" with family and a few friends for Christmas 2012. When I pull it from the shelf today, I see a work of art built on words.

"MUSINGS" brought retired me back to my roots -- writing and editing. I pulled out the project I had begun some 30 years earlier and decided to finish my young adult's biography of Cherokee editor Elias Boudinot. I found a few new books with potentially useful information and brought them along for our spring 2013 trip to Hilton Head. I then spent rainy summer days writing, and Mary Ellen served as my first reader. She seemed to labor over the task, but I didn't think much about that until after she was diagnosed with mild cognitive impairment later that year. I set my work aside to edit my friend Sue Johnpeter's manuscript, eventually published as "No Ordinary Life/Memoir of a World War II Bombardier." After I finished writing my Boudinot story, I used the design and layout skills I had developed beginning as an undergraduate and took advantage of a variety of new technologies that allowed me to self-publish. Not because I feared outside judgment but because I valued the freedom of controlling my product. Six more books of my own and two edited for others followed. Working on several of them provided me important space for myself as Mary Ellen's dementia progressed. Writing "Gifts" (a couple of years after I moved her to a nursing home) was one way I reclaimed me, honored her and offered hope to others.

[An aside: In 2021, in search of a hobby, I assembled my first LEGO project (a bouquet of flowers). I was hooked. Learning to follow instructions without words has proved to be enormously satisfying. When a friend judged my projects "not creative" because I am merely following directions, I said I was OK with being "the engineer, not the architect." Recently, as I was extolling the advantages of self-publishing, something clicked: *When I write, and edit, and design interior pages, and create a cover I get to be both architect and engineer!*]

I might have described my books as the significant accomplishments of my first decade of retirement. And without a doubt each is an accomplishment, and all are significant to me. But the truly significant accomplishments are those I most recently wrote about in "Dementia's Unexpected Gifts," with its academic-length subtitle: *A memoir of stumbling into caregiving, then learning to live my best life.* I didn't know it on July 1, 2012 -- when I woke up retired and without a plan for retirement -- but I already had entered a Twilight Zone of undetermined length. The disease creating it was not mine, but it would test me in ways I never imagined and teach me character-defining lessons. It still is.

◇◇◇◇◇

Endings. So important. Who gets the last word?

I miss a lot of endings these days because I fall asleep at the wrong time. Common with older folks (and if I must, I can admit to being one), common with busy folks (I remain one), common with early risers (I still wish I weren't one). Luckily I no longer care all that much about which beach house the cranky couple bought, or how the mediocre movie with hackneyed plot concluded, or even how the Packers game played out. And when I do care, I generally remain alert (or I later Google). With books, on the other hand, I choose when to read and when to pause, and I almost always get to the ending. Fiction or non, I am satisfied even if that ending was not.

What I came to realize while I wrote this book is that daily life is filled with endings -- most of which we tend not to absorb. Until and unless we reflect, review, seek to connect the dots only to find the resulting line twisting and turning and crossing over itself again and again. Each dot an ending and a beginning! Six separations among people? Perhaps. But how about six separations among places, dates, experiences and more? Or is it just my beloved *serendipity* at work. And why is it certain words, phrases, sentences remain with me?

Heed the need.
You have spatulate fingers.
My, but you have a talent for this work.
Collage.
Pooh Bear.
Muffy.

Writing this book gave me a rare opportunity to reconnect -- indirectly and occasionally directly -- with people from throughout my life, especially students and colleagues from my 38 years of teaching. Each name encountered in telling my story gave -- gives -- me pause, brought -- brings -- a memory or more. The ache of remembering once-important-to-me individuals now deceased and discovering that others have died. Letting go of reconnections attempted and not made. The satisfaction of reading about so much success by former students (the earliest now retired themselves) and thinking back to all the potential seeping through their words in letters and cards. *I knew you when.* . . . The euphoric joy of being welcomed back by the adult version of my long-ago bonus "little brother" John. Reveling in the precious few friendships that continue to grow with me. Being immensely grateful that I am lovingly accepted by family -- mine and Mary Ellen's.

Now it is time to cease chronicling. It is time to write the words for my final sentence:

This book is ending, which means yet another beginning for its author.

Epilogue

This is not an epilogue I expected to write. That sentence came to me in the early days of tumultuous change -- change I precipitated during my winter 2022 stay in Florida. It was an odd thought; I had several chapters yet to write, had not written a word in weeks and was not thinking much about writing. Furthermore, I was not even sure I would write an epilogue. Here is the explanation for why I have.

After Covid-19 concerns prompted Kris and me to skip Florida in 2021, we were eager to return to Punta Gorda in January 2022. Being together in the sunshine and warmth suits us. I had ended up isolating there alone in March and April 2019, time I put to good use by almost finishing my draft of "Dementia's Unexpected Gifts." This trip, Kris planned a short visit back to Wisconsin in late January so I brought a fat printout of draft chapters of my current project that I might edit -- or not. I also brought some source materials in case I might be motivated to write. Just like last time, Kris ended up being away longer than expected and I got more book work finished than expected. It seemed I was well on my way to meeting my self-imposed deadline: publishing before the end of the year.

In quiet moments on the lanai I had found myself pondering why -- beyond the weather -- I so enjoyed the condo. I realized that its size suited me. Even more significant was the joy I found in not being responsible for it. Owning and maintaining a four-bedroom house by myself had become a chore. I primarily lived in the den and study, only slept in the primary bedroom, infrequently cooked in the kitchen, and used the dining room table as a LEGO workspace. As for the many gardens, I had observed for years that "I wish the 40-year-old gardener had thought about the 65-year-old gardener" (now 73)! I was ready to sell the house. I reached another important conclusion while Kris was away: I didn't want to move away and start over somewhere new. I didn't want to have to find new doctors, a new hairdresser, a new market, etc. I wanted to remain in Wakefield, where I am near Mary Ellen's nursing home.

During phone calls before Kris returned, I shared my thoughts. When she was back and we resumed our twice-daily walks, I bounced ideas off her. I was adamant about not wanting to own again (not even a condo). We hashed that over; as she correctly observed, I had been working up to selling for a couple of years. I had done some looking and knew there wasn't much senior housing near me to choose from. The "memory care" unit where Mary Ellen lived briefly before the nursing home was part of a larger community with independent living and assisted living wings of apartments. I thought moving there might be the answer. We hashed that over, and Kris offered two more important observations: (1) Doing so would give me a place to live after the sale that (2) didn't mean a "forever" commitment. The more it felt as if I had a plan, the more eager I became. I called Brightview Commons to make an appointment to visit just three days after my arrival back in Rhode Island; I didn't want to be able to put off moving forward. I got pricing information and rethought two bedrooms; I decided I could make do with one bedroom and a den. I couldn't wrap my head around the price tag, but every time I came close to canceling the visit Kris talked me out of it. I followed the Brightview website, and every time I told Kris I wasn't sure I would "fit in" she talked me off the ledge. When I said I would find a way to give it my best shot for a year and then reassess, she applauded.

Week 1

I arrived home on Saturday, April 16. I knew I needed probate court permission to sell the house (because Mary Ellen and I owned it jointly and I was her legal guardian). On Monday I called my lawyer about that and arranged to meet her on Friday. I visited Brightview on Tuesday and nothing I heard or saw dissuaded me. No apartment in my preferred floorplan was available, however, and we agreed to touch base every 10 days or so. That was OK; I envisioned making it all happen before I returned to Florida in January 2023. I was surprised to learn from my lawyer that I needed a signed purchase and sales agreement (and an independent appraisal) *before* we went to court. I had imagined the opposite. And because probate court in our town meets only once a month, we were not far from the filing deadline for the June 16 meeting. I didn't see any way that would happen, which was fine with me.

Week 2

At least I had the wherewithal to ask my lawyer if she could suggest a Realtor and an appraiser, and the good sense to contact them immediately and hire them. I met the Realtor who, as luck would have it, lived in my neighborhood, on April 26. Before she left she took exterior photos for a listing and asked when I could have the interior ready for photos. Ever the journalist, I answered, "Give me a deadline and I will be ready." She offered May 5. About the same time as that meeting, I heard from Brightview. A one bedroom with den was going to be available soon. It was on the second floor and also met my other criterion: outdoor space (a balcony). I arranged to see it on April 29. I brought along details about furniture I might move and a measuring tape. Before I left that Friday afternoon, I had made a down payment -- I didn't want to risk losing the apartment -- and agreed to move in before the end of May! On April 27 I had begun clearing off the flat surfaces and removing art from the walls in the house. Now I began to sort and separate and pack my possessions. I would have been overwhelmed if my move were months away. Realizing it was just a few weeks away, I was OVERWHELMED!

Week 3

The week was a blur. My golf league started, but I didn't play. I met the deadline for the interior photos by filling closets and much of the basement and garage. And closing the door to the study, which would not be photographed. I couldn't get over how empty the house already looked. Or how the cosmetic work I knew it needed jumped out at me. I couldn't get over how exhausted I was. And I remained overwhelmed by the work ahead. I tried my best each day to quit when my achy body said quit, and to get up each morning determined to do as much as I could and be satisfied. I got an official move-in date of May 25 from Brightview and made arrangements for that.

Week 4

My Realtor had scheduled a block of time on Wednesday, May 11, to show the house. Mortgage rates had recently gone up, but based on how crazy the market had been she would show it only by appointment. She had one caller, who asked to see it Friday. My heart sank at that news. She also had scheduled a traditional open house for Saturday. I tried not to be pessimistic when she called to say six groups had stopped by, one of them from the neighborhood. When she called again about 8 p.m. to say she had received an offer, I was stunned and asked only if it were "a serious offer." She assured me it was, and we agreed to meet the next morning. I was so tired (I may even have been asleep when the phone rang) that I didn't want any details to ruminate over. I wanted a good night's sleep and a clear head for Sunday.

Week 5

I was astounded to hear that the offer was $2,000 above the asking price, which I had set on the high side, with room for negotiation if necessary. My agent called it a "very clean" offer. I accepted it. Amazingly, we were on track to meet that probate court filing deadline, and more amazingly I got the necessary paperwork signed with my lawyer on Monday. Despite facing a mountain of work to get myself moved out and empty the house (tentative closing date July 15), I headed off on Tuesday for the three nights in Ogunquit, Maine, which I had booked the previous fall. I tried to leave my worries in Rhode Island.

Week 6

The week was filled with appointments: eye doctor, golf (skipped again), inspection, veterans' group pick-up of donations, bank appraiser and more. While eating lunch on Monday, I had heard a noise from the garage but figured a box had fallen over. If only. A cable on the garage door had snapped. Luckily my car was outside. Unluckily, I couldn't get a repair person until Thursday and the movers were coming Wednesday morning. All the boxes and items I had carried into the garage so they would have a straight shot into their truck had to be carried back through the house. (Thankfully, by strong, young men.) The move went off without a hitch. So did delivery of the stressless recliner I had bought for myself. On May 25, I became an independent-living resident of Brightview Commons, where I spent each night: eating the dinner my fee included and dozing in my chair until bedtime. I was out the door daily -- often as early as 7 -- to resume dealing with all that remained at the house, and dragged myself "home" about 4. Day after day after day. Because I had been more than ready to downsize, the process was less emotional than it could have been. It did mean discarding most of the artifacts that made this parts of this book possible, but not before I photographed many of them. Some, like my childhood teddy bear, earned a tearful *Thank you!*

Weeks 7-13

Probate court was a breeze on June 16. A mandatory waiting period followed, but it was all systems go for the closing. I donated as much as I could locally. I was thankful for the veterans' group that accepted donations of almost anything and, most important, picked up weekly. I was thankful for Goodwill, especially because they accept holiday decorations year-round. And because they unloaded my stuffed car. My nephew Bill and family arrived from Virginia on June 20 to help continue the cleanout. As much progress as I had made -- and I will pat myself on the back and say my efforts had been herculean -- so much remained to be done. Shelly, Bill's wife, proved to be the focused, driven, dispassionate help I needed, and what we did together in four days would have taken me *much, much* longer. Xavier, Max and Connor sorted Packers memorabilia, disassembled LEGO creations and helped out however we asked. My heart smiles to know that the family rolltop desk has found a home in Xavier's room. My heart smiles to know we made one last set of family memories at Barb Teyze's house in Rhode Island.

On Thursday, July 7, the guys I had hired to cart away everything remaining in the house did just that. On Sunday the 10th, the single mom I hired to clean did her thing. I returned to the house early Monday morning, did a quick walk through and said my goodbyes. I thanked the house for all the good years, told the gardens they had brought us much joy, and said I hoped the new owner would enjoy living there as much as Mary Ellen and I had. (It continues to amuse me that I had repeatedly said *This house needs a family* and its buyer was a single woman.)

I was able to sign my paperwork on the 14th, so I didn't attend the closing the next morning. Instead I visited Mary Ellen at the nursing home. I told her about the sale, even though all she probably heard were meaningless sounds. (Only I know that had she not become ill, we most likely never would have left the house that she had designed for resale. Its sale price would have astounded her, I am sure.) My lawyer called while I was driving to a celebratory lunch. Surprising us both, the deed already had been recorded and so she could release the checks to me. At the office, she told me the buyer raved more than once about how clean the house was. I couldn't stop laughing.

As I enjoyed a lobster roll and craft NA beer, I felt the weight of the last several years -- and especially the last three months -- begin to lift. I was reminded that my downsizing had required the single-mindedness I brought to completing my master's degree in nine months and successfully navigating the sometimes rocky road to my Ph.D. Credit my stubborn persistence and focused determination for pulling off the improbable in all three instances. But as this book -- like "Dementia's Unexpected Gifts" -- has chronicled, I am a significantly different person now than I was, and that is making all the difference!

Afterword

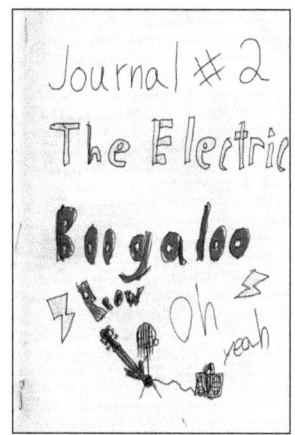

Created by Max Parmentier

<u>14 Sept 2022 / 6:45 p.m.</u> -- I begin writing exactly 2 hours after my dear ME found peace and freedom from her horrible disease— I was with her, and that something I so fear provided a last moment of intimacy— The window open, a pleasant breeze, the western sun shining onto her, that spot on her arm warm while the hand I held was so cold— Her last breaths— face not exactly serene but her mouth relaxed and closed for the first time in days— After the nurse checked and "called it" I closed the door and spent a last couple minutes with her— my eyes the last to see her— As I had been doing over the last days, I talked of our love— Thanked her for her years with me— Assured her we all would be OK and she would live on in our hearts and lives— Then I pulled the sheet up to give her privacy, gathered my things and left— to begin making calls (most can wait until tomorrow) but not before a big hug from the receptionist, who assured me I should have no regrets; I had been wonderful to her— That I know— I did not run away— I did not abandon her— These last years are my proudest accomplishment— I want to honor ME until the day I die and I want to live the best life I can!!

In Gratitude

I start each day by looking outside and speaking: *Good morning, world. Thank you for the day. Thank you for yesterday.* I follow with a recitation of at least three specific gifts: as "ordinary" as the happiness elicited by spotting a redwing blackbird; as uncommon as sleeping through the night; as grand as joy sparked by good news. Since September 15, 2022, I have ended with thanks for 32 years of loving Mary Ellen and being loved by her. As I contemplated writing a traditional Acknowledgments, I gravitated toward the unconventional. Unlike an author with the usual suspects to thank for guiding her book to fruition, I have little need to do so. After all, I am my own agent, publicist, marketer, personal assistant and whatnot. I trust that the team at Mayfly Design knows how much I value their professionalism. I asked much of dear friends Sue Johnpeter and Karen Small, who know how much I appreciate their keen editing of my manuscript. And my families know how much I love them. I thus have chosen to keep it simple: I express my **profoundest gratitude** for every person, place, experience, disappointment and achievement that have brought me to this moment in life.

Appendix A

Barbara Luebke
1-8-71
a new consciousness

If dogs run free/why not we/across the swooping plains/...The best
is always yet to come/That's what they explain to me/Just do your
thing/and you'll be king/if dogs run free....

Bob Dylan

When I climbed the steps of the bus that sunny Sunday morning and
handed the ticket to the driver, I had only one thought on my mind--to
try to forget the long ride ahead which would take me home for a Christmas holiday. And a holiday it was to be. School would not exist. Nor
required reading. Nor heavy thoughts.

But then, somewhere between Cadott and Boyd(two of the one-minute,
seemingly unending milk-run stops ~~the bus had~~ we were to make)that damn dog ran
in front of the bus. And those lyrics from Bob Dylan ran through my
mind. They were to haunt me for the next 15 days.

I had with me the September 26 issue of New Yorker, ~~######~~ which
contained a good portion of Charles Reich's new book, "The Greening of A-
merica." I had a vague idea of what it was about, and I thought the Yale
law professor might serve to reinforce some of the opinions I was sure to
have to defend while home. I was wrong.

Because stretched out in my seat(for the first time in a couple of
dozen such trips sharing it only with myself)I was challenged. Reich's
theory of revolution fascinated me, and for some unknown reason Reich
and Dylan made me wonder...Would the folks at home buy this:

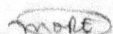

"There is a revolution under way. It is not like revolutions of the past. It has originated with the individual and with culture, and if it succeeds it will change the political structure only as its final act. It will not require violence to succeed, and it cannot be successfully resisted by violence. It is now spreading with amazing rapidity...Its ultimate creation could be a higher reason, a more human community, and a new and liberated individual....At the heart of everything is what must be called a change of consciousness. This means a new way of living--almost a new man. This is what the new generation has been searching for, and what it has started to achieve."

As mile after mile of woods and fields and farms and an occasional small town rolled by at 50 miles an hour, doubt creeped into my mind. I wondered whether Reich's revolution was, or could be, spreading as fast as he implied.
Does
~~And~~ it, in the form he presented, even really exist? And if it ~~did~~ does
it permeate the entire younger generation or only select portions of it?

There were two women sitting behind me for much of the ride, and perhaps it was psychic, or perhaps just luck, but their conversation provided some of the factual data Reich failed to provide ~~for me~~ in his book. I was ecstatic.
samples --
I had my own ~~(~~Consciousness I and Consciousness II ~~samples of whom Reich had~~ in Reich's terminology - Of them he
wrote:
~~written:~~

Consciousness I "is unable to accept the reality of an interdependedt society that requires collective responsibility" and Consciousnees II "understands the realities of organization life but does not see that organizations and their policies are, by themselves, inhuman."

I had to put down ~~the magazine,~~ Reich fake sleep and listen as they talked. The older one was on her way to spend Christmas with her "youngsters," grown, married, working and living a long way from home. The world had left her behind, and her primary concern, after the electricity shortage predicted

more

in the latest Reader's Digest, seemed to be dying and not being found for
several days. The younger woman was going to visit her mother, nursing-homed
by a paralyzing stroke. The cost of living got her down, as did the younger
generation, and she remarked of her children that she "ofetn has to put the
skids on them--they just always can't do what they want. After all, their
father and I have been around longer and do know the world a little better."
And wasn't it to bad that soandso got laid off and was forced to take a job
with a pay cut. They "actually had to sell a car and not buy a third
snowmobile."

But Consciousness III, the younger generation, my generation, is supposed to be looking at such things differently, to be restoring humanity
to an inhuman world. Reich theorized that the revolution of Con. III "is not
directed against other people, but against an impersonal system. And its objective is to place that system under a mind--to reassert values where none
are now recognized."

I thought of the people I had gone to high school with and those who were
there now. Do they know about this reassertion of values? Are they aware
of this revolution "expressed all around us by the bloom of renewed life.
Faces...gentle and more beautiful. People...better with each other...more
smiles, more love." I wanted to know, figuring that if they were I could
find Reich's assumptions more plausible. For to examine a societal change
such as he was purporting, I thought it necessary for one to look at more than the
Berkelys, San Frans, Bostons and New York Citys. One must also consider the hundreds of thousands of young people, Consciousness III people if
you will, living in towns the size of small colleges or large high schools.
De Pere is such a city.

Located on the eastern edge of Wisconsin, it is a city of about 10,000
inhabitants. Its history dates back to the fur trading and logging days,

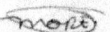

and its two paper mills are major sources of employment today. (I can remember grade school and high school days, when if your father didn't work
at "the mill" (Nicolet) or farm, you were an odd duck. I was an odd duck.) Physically,
the city hasn't changed too drastically since my ~~F~~ high school days, the ~~last~~
last time I had spent ~~any amount of~~ extended time in the city. The downtown area has
been revamped ~~and~~ there are ~~many~~ several new stores and the residential sections, like
those most everywhere, have spread out in all directions. But a lot of the
                                                    has moved in
old ~~sto~~res have disappeared, and ~~there's been~~ little new industry. (The ex-
mayor's industrial park is still very much a pi~~p~~e dream.) ~~The mill is still~~
~~most important.~~

The Fox River, very polluted by ~~that~~ the mill ~~s~~ and ~~//////~~ others upstream,
divides the city--East and West. Though the Milwaukee Journal (and some would
                                     doesn't
add the local weekly) ~~does not~~ admit West De Pere exists, it has its own post
office, its own ~~//////////~~ school system, and perhaps most importantly, its
own special kind of economy.

The east has the money, the big houses and two-stall garages, the kids
in exclusive colleges, Miss De Pere, the mayor (the last several, really),
city hall, the fire and police station, the industrial park/ and 30/year mortgages. The west has the Oneida Indians, the farmers, the government subsi-
dized 235 housing project and the mill. The rivalry which exists between high
schools on the football field and basket ball court (I learned it "West is Best
                        is ingrained in
and East is Least") runs deeper, ~~permeating~~ local politics and business.

The city is basically Catholic (settled in the 1600s by a French missionary).
~~///////////////some major churches~~
There are Saturday masses and an occasional contemporary service with guitars ⊗
They   the   of the settled citizens⊗
~~to~~ raise ~~eyebrows~~ "I never will understand what's so special about a guitar
                                          C
in church." The city is home for St. Norbert ~~C~~ollege, a private, liberal arts
                                    He has liberalized it, but
Catholic school with its first lay president. ~~At one time an all male school,~~

is faced with mounting /
~~it is becoming more liberal and suffering~~ financial problems. There's also
a public library, one movie theater, a couple of pizza *s* pots and drive-ins.
On the other ~~side~~ side of the city limits sign is an 18-year-old bar.

De Pere is not an isolated city, but is part of the large metropolitan
area surrounding Green Bay. Milwaukee is only two hours away. *madison less⊗)* ~~It could,~~
conceivably, have a pleasant combination of small *town* atomosphere and proximity to culture. It does not. For many(if not most) De Pere residents,
+ Madison are)
Milwaukee ~~is~~ foreign territory. And Green Bay's cultural life, outside of
football, is nil. Though there are three theaters, good films are usually a
long time coming. There is no bookstore, to speak, unless you venture to
new University of Wisconsin-Green Bay campus.   *few people venture ⊗)*
the ~~university (UWGB)~~ It's out in the sticks and ~~i haven't ventured.~~

That's where the Wisconsin-Michigan coach was taking me. ~~////////////~~
~~///////////////////////////////////~~ I was prejudiced, of course. But
I strongly believed that my years of growing up there and the experiences I
had had since leaving would allow me to judge what $\frac{i}{2}$ would find. I was curious
if Consciousness III ~~#~~ existed in De Pere.

I hit Green Bay in the early evening, ~~#####~~ greeted by a bus depot of
noisy, jostling holiday ~~#~~ travellers. My search for revolution began then.
It was to be silent(much listening and subtle ~~#########~~ control (of conversations). It was to be anonymous. The quest for information was on, but only
i was to know it.

I wasn't really sure how to go about my search for Consciousness III.
I had lost contact with the people in the city, both St. Norbert and UWGB
were recessed, and if there was a "community" anywhere I didn't know about
it. But a couple of leads and a bit of instinct were enough to give
direction to the search.

more

For the most part, what I found did not suprise me. I learned a lot
though, and I'm still trying to sort it out in my mind. I'm not really sure
what it all means, and I doubt if at this point in history such an assess-
metn is possible. But I do think what I saw, what ~~~~ I heard, what I
felt ~~~~~~~~~~~~~~~~~~~~~~~ enables one to put Reich into some
perspective.

My first full day was spent christmas shopping. The opportunity to observe people was at its best, and the first thing I attacked was Reich's
thoughts on the clothes of Consciouness III--the jeans, the bell bottoms, the
unisex ~~~~ "...the also nudge the wearer with deeper questions of identity
that have rarely been posed in Consciousness I and II society because their
very freedom reminds him that he does have choice....The new clothers
express profoundly democratic values. There are no distinctions of wealth
or status, no elitism; people confront each other shorn of these distinctions....The new clothes deny the importance of hierarchy, status, authority,
position, and they reject competition."

I was unable to substantiate these thoughts. Oh, there are bell
bottomed jeans ~~in Denver~~--plenty of them. But more times than not they were
topped with respectable $65 maxicoats or White Stagg or Pendleton. There
were complimenting scarves and leather boots. There was seldom the scruffy,
grubby, total army surplus look of Minneapolis' Cedar Aveenue or Milwaukee's
east side. It looked instead if parents had conceded to jeans(and an occasional workshirt)but overall "decent" prevailed.

Why do you wear what you do? "I like it." "Bells are more dressy than
jeans. And besides, they're in." "My girlfriend bought them for me." "I
just do....I don't know why."

There were no questions of identity, especially deep ones. And
there was status in what was worn, whether purchased from Id, the shop for
Saturday hippies,) from the local discount store or ~~from~~ one of the exclusive mens
or womens store. The clothes themselves were status, were important, for
none of the kids "wanted to be out of it." Like the junior high ~~aged~~ boy
who was chided because his pants had cuffs ~~on them.~~

But there is more to Consciousness III than clothes, much more. I
wondered about this new humanity. Was it overflowing? ~~Was~~ Is it a liberated
younger generation calling this ~~the~~ city home? Not really. No one ~~was~~ is preaching
Thoreau and "~~Walden Pond.~~" Walden The ~~individuality,~~ unwillingess to get involved,
~~It~~ is similar to any really big city. ~~Witness the letters to the editor~~
There is no movement toward humanization that unites the young people. The uniting factor is the
~~about the "vandalizing teenagers," the irresponsible boys who wouldn't stop~~
desire "to get out of school, got some money and a car and
not get drafted." ~~to help" etc.~~

I asked kids about their plans for the future. Were they going into
professions of public service or were they after the quick buck? "I'd really
like to help, but after college I can't see two years in the Peace Corps or
Vista." "It's a tough world. If I want to make good I'm going to have to
work hard. No one's going to help me and I can't see why I should go out of
my way to help." "I just wanted to get married, have fo(ty) or five kids (and
a husband who can make a good life for us." "I'll go to Vocational school
and then get a job." "Going to try to make the family farm go."

Disastisfaction with these kinds of answeres led to the other major part
of my search...the "head shops." There ~~were~~ now, unbelievabley, two in Green
The only visible means of telling that a subculture does exist
Bay. But the experiences the one was having only served to ~~further~~ exemplify
what Conscious III was up against.

The Chute, which sells ~~sold~~ underground newspapers, incense, posters, arm
patches, peace flags and the such, has ~~had~~ been forced ~~out of its rented location~~
to move
after ~~when~~ a local group of "peace loving" and "loyal citizens" calling themselves

Eagle went to scare tactics. They claimed ~~that~~ there was drug trafficking going on in the shop, and said that unless the people were evicted there would be damages to the realator's other holdings. The Post Office is investigating(because the threats were made through the mails)but no one seems to know who the Eagle is, how widespread, how representative.

~~proprietors of the other shop are a bit paranoid and the possibilities~~ of being forced to move make them cautious. They have a good selection of pipes, but they are reluctant to talk about them. It's more a case of caveatt emptor.

/////Like/most places today, the city is paranoid about drugs. There was a/big/bust lately, and it scared some of the people. But the attitude of a/fffff/ keystone cop game are also present--how long can one escape getting fffff/

I ran into a few consciousness III people, a few who are living their own life, trying to find sanity in a mad corporate world. But they are, ~~there at least~~ few and far between. (I think, from my own experiences, much of it has to do with lack of exposure to a sub-culture(assuming it does exist). For many, "that communist paper" Fox Valley Kaleidescpoe is "the other culture".)

In the end, I was ~~forced~~ inclined to agree with a reviewer in The Village Voice who said of consciousness III: "That it is a state worth striving for I have no doubt; it's beautiful. But if the revolution hinges on great masses achieving it, then I have great doubts about the revolution. Maybe what is happening, contrary to Reich, is that only a small number of people are wholly converted to the New Consciousness, and a much larger number are partially converted, while retaining ties to New Property. But since the essence of Consciousness III is ~~////////////~~ eliminating the duality between work and play, being partially Consciousness III is not being III at all, but only a high speicies of II. #

612

now that you've read the paper, id like to add a couple of other thoughts.
i was not pleased with it, basically. i think, for what it was to be, i
bit off more than i could chew(cliche)...it doesnt have enought substance,
enough fact...im afraid it might come off sounding like advocacy j..and i
didnt, dont, want that...its in ff two parts, and im afraid the style of the
first ½ doesnt carry through...and i really worked at that first half..im
not sure if i like it...
the paper bothers me, it bothers me to turn it in(but that is a reality of
being a student)...i think i let myself down with it and i d know its not
up to your expectations...
if there is anything in it worth pursuing, tho, i want to pursue it...i dont
want to let it hang, because it really is, to mep more than just an assignement,
and id like to finish waht ive started, if ive started...
this is not meant as an apology of any sort, and thats why its at the end of
the paper...but maybe it will get across what all your damn courses have
developed in me--a trying to be aware of my own failings, of not being content
with the mediocre, a willingness to try again...thanx

I didn't think Women's libbers, the revolutionists, whatever did that.

You sell yourself short. If this is mediocre, Hello, Hemingway.
Advocacy journalism, no. It's you, that's all. It's alive. It responds
to your eye. You admit your prejudices. At times /////// it is possible
they are even more than a little evident. So what, don't apologize.
I'm prejudiced now. That's why I'm being so hard. ??? Facts, you say.
Perhaps somewhat short, as you say, but is it not possible that too many
more might destroy the real intent, might actually hurt the paper.

It's tight. It's close. But more than that, it is extremely
readable. It's heavy, but its not going to give me a hernia trying to
pick it up; it's not going to knock me out. Because of it's interest
factor, it sort of sneaks up on you. You find it there when you're done.
You aren't forced to digest it paragraph by paragraph, word by word.
Slowly, methodically. Never.

I read it, reread it. Put it down. Picked it back up and
again and wanted to read it again. Criticisms, hell, no, although I'm
sure you want some and so does someone else who probably wnats to see
if we can analytically analyze, criticize, destroy, whatever someone's
(it said all in good fun—I was in a good mood at the time)
paper. Well, I suppose I probably could. I do it enough with my own
in my own mind or with other stuff I've read which I find fault with.
But, here, I'm sorry, I don't want to. It seems a little foolish.
Besides, you've been hard enough on yourself already, it seems, so
you can tell me what's wrong with it. I don't want to look for it.
I enjoyed it.

How about Consciousness III expanded, however, Like Milwaukee,
or even Eau Claire--other things you are familiar. You might find something
different. Having been through all, I'm sure DePere has its own
idiosyncracies, attitudes different from somewhere else.

To anyone, I would simply say read it, Enjoy it, digest it. To do anything else
would be to destroy it.

614

Appendix B

First page of handwritten draft

Typed draft

EXTRA, EXTRA, READ ALL ABOUT IT

RE·SPON·SI·BIL·I·TY

[I need simple def here]

Shannon ~~[crossed out]~~ studied her word-a-day calendar. It was Tuesday, July 23. She was dressed & ready to go downstairs for breakfast w/ her mother & her aunt, visiting for a few days. But first she memorized today's word & its ~~[crossed out]~~ definition. Shannon loved words, loved learning ~~[crossed out]~~ new ones. "A reporter needs to know lots of words," her Aunt Karen had told her two Christmases ago, after Shannon had opened ~~[crossed out]~~ the package from Aunt Karen. Shannon hoped they'd keep making word-a-day calendars, & she hoped her aunt always would include one in her Xmas box. AK was a reporter for the Indiapolis News (the India-no-place News, her [mom] ~~[crossed out]~~ called it), & S dreamed of the day when she could be a reporter, too. "Every day is different," AK told her, & S ~~[crossed out]~~ thought ~~[crossed out]~~ it sounded exciting. Maybe some day, she would get to interview Michael Jackson. "You never know," AK said.

~~[crossed out]~~,

"What's today's word, Shan?" asked her mother as she poured Shannon's juice. "And you want granola or yogurt?"

"Responsibility. Yogurt. [def]"

~~[crossed out]~~ "How about a sentence," AK asked.

"Uhh — Everyone should take responsibility for themselves."

"Good. But it's 'herself.' Everyone should take responsibility for herself."

"Or himself," mom chimed in.

"Everyone is a singular [noun]," AK expl to Shannon, "so the pronoun needs to be singular too."

"Right," Shannon nodded. "Sometimes I forget."

"So do some of my colleagues," AK said. ~~[crossed out]~~ And they are

615

'EXTRA, EXTRA, READ ALL ABOUT IT"

RE*SPON*SI*BIL*I*TY

Shannon studied her word-a-day calendar. It was Tuesday, July 23.

She was dressed and ready for breakfast with her mother and ~~her~~ Aunt

Karen, in town for her summer visit. But first she memorized today's

word and its definition. Shannon loved words.

"A reporter needs to know lots of words," AK had told her two

Christmases ago after Shannon had opened the package with her first

word-a-day calendar. ~~Shannon hoped they would keep making the calendars,~~

~~and she hoped AK would always include one in her Christmas box.~~

Aunt Karen was a reporter for the Indianapolis News (the

India-no-place News, Shannon's mother called it), and Shannon dreamed of the

day when she could be a reporter, too. "Every day is different,"

AK told her, and Shannon thought that sounded exciting. Maybe some

day she would get to interview Micheal Jackson or Boy George. "You

never know," AK said.

"What's today's word, Shan?" asked her mother as she poured

Shannon's juice. "You want granola or yoghurt?"

"Responsibility. Yoghurt."

"How about a sentence," AK asked.

"Uhhh --- Everyone should take responsiblility for themselves."

"Good, but it's 'herself.' Everyone should take responsibility for herself."

"Or himself," Mom chimed in.

"Everyone is a singular noun," AK explained to Shannon, "so the pronoun needs to be singular, too."

"Right," Shannon nodded. "Sometimes I forget."

"So do some of my col·leagues," AK chuckled, "and they are supposed to know better. I sure hope you learn grammar in your English classes, Shan."

AK went back to reading the front page (of The Gazette). Shannon picked up the sports section and picked at her yoghurt. "The Brewers lost again," Mom said.

"Go Sox," her mother teased. She had followed the Boston Red Sox since a visit to her grandparents as a child, and she and Shannon compared notes on their teams each morning. Both read the sports pages first, including the box scores. It was a habit AK could not understand.

"Games. Boy's games," she said, devouring the front page word by word.

617

"You working today Mom?" Shannon asked.

"No. Karen and I are going to the gallery and then to lunch."

"May I use the computer?"

"Sure."

Shannon's mother, an ~~an accountant~~ AC·count·ANT, did much of her work at home on ~~her~~ a personal computer, which she had taught Shannon to use. Shannon could sit for hours making up stories and typing them onto the screen, moving ~~sentences and~~ words and paragraphs with the push of a button. Today, though, Shannon had other plans. It was ~~an~~ almost time for another issue of The ~~Neighborhood~~ Gnus ~~Shannon's monthly collection of neighborhood news.~~

The Gnus _____ had been AK's idea last summer. "You're bored? Why don't you put out your own newspaper." And ~~by the end of the afternoon~~ so the Gnus _____ was born. AK suggested the name. She called it a pun. "You say it "news" but it's really an Afarcan antelope."

Although Peggy and RacÞel her friends, soon had ~~s~~ tired of the project (Racel's into boys and Peggy would rather watch MTV," Shannon told her mother), Shannon ~~reveled~~ reveled in it. She found an old gray fedora at a garage sale and printed a card that said PRESS, which she tucked into the hat band.

[left margin handwritten: Need to better tie Gnus to the Park?]
[left margin handwritten: need better transition]
[right margin handwritten: ? how is this handled?]

"You belong in the comics with Brenda Starr," AK told her, but

she admitted it was fun watching Shannon scour the neighborhood each

week and then plan how each story would fit onto the page. All too

soon, however, AK was gone, summer was over, and Shannon was too busy for the

Gnus.

When summer vacation came around again, Shannon eagerly pulled

the fedora from the back of her closet, wandered the neighborhood and in

early Jane she had (25) copies of Volume 2 Number 1 to sell for ten cents.

She had sold two garage sale ads for a dollar each and Johnny

Malone paid her fifty cents to tell everyone he was big and strong and

willing to mow lawns and wash cars to earn money for a basketball

backboard.

"You don't go into journalism for the money," she had hear AK

say. Shannon didn't care. She felt good when

Johnny told her he had two new lawn jobs. She felt even better when

Mrs. Mercer stopped her at the drugstore to say how much she enjoyed

reading about Mrs. Ferguson's garden and wasn't it "refreshing to see a

child doing something worthwhile" and when was the next issue coming out.

Well, Shannon thought, on Tuesday the next issue will be out soon. Just a few

more blocks of the neighborhood to canvas. She hoped she would find

619

something <u>really</u> interesting for her front page. Right now she wasn't

sure whether to use the story about Evergreen Street being closed for

repairs next week (a tip from Mr. Jones, who worked for the city) or her

interview with the exchange student from Holland who is living with the

Rubensteins.

"Need some hot news," she thought to herself as she ~~set out from~~ left home.

First stop: Mrs. Ferguson's garden. Mrs. Ferguson leaned on her

hoe, pushed back her giant straw sun hat and proudly told Shannon that

~~she~~ just yesterday won first prize in the garden show ~~with her gladiolas.~~ her gladiolas No

biggie, Shannon thought, ~~saying politely,~~ she said "I'll be glad to include it."

~~xkikexxxdesterxgeingxfremxpmiientxtep~~

Next stop: Ferd's ~~corner~~ market. The day's special, the outdoor

chalkboard proclaimed, was fresh melons. "Here, try a slice," Ferd said. Watkins

The market was empty, so ~~Ferd Watkins~~ he was eager to chat. He had been in

the neighborhood forever and knew everybody -- and everybody's

business. But the best piece of news he had today was that little Becky

Andersen was painting her tree house ("bright ~~lavender,~~ LAV·EN·DER pray tell") and

fell and broke her ~~harm~~ arm. Nothing to stop the presses for, Shannon thought as she headed toward Woodruff Place. Maybe I'll get Mom to do

something artsy on the computer and use that on the front page.

Woodruff Place, with its big old houses set back off the street,

among giant oak trees, was one of Shannon's favorite streets in the

neighborhood. There weren't many kids there, though, she knew only

a few families. But She had been leaving the gnus in all the

mailboxes, and she hoped somebody might be out working in the yard. She

had on her PRESS hat, which helped give her the courage to talk to people.

About halfway up the street, Shannon noticed a strange odor. She

stopped, sniffed. But she couldn't quite put her finger on the smell,

so she continued on. A few houses away, Mr. Kalish was pulling weeds.

Shannon's mother kept the books for Mr. Kalish's hardware store, and Shannon

had talked with him often. He tended to be, what was the word ---

CON*DE*SCEND*ING --- toward her. Treated her as if she was just playing

reporter. Still, she knew from her mother that he was an important person

in town, so she put up with him.

"Hi, Mr. Kalish. You on vacation?"

"Yeah --- some vacation. Just look at this yard."

"Going anyplace interesting?"

621

"Just to see my daughter in Kansas City. You gonna put me in your paper?"

"Well .... I am collecting news. Got any scoops?"

"Only ice cream. Ha ha!"

Shannon wasn't amused.

"Well, I've got to be going. Say, do you smell something weird?"

"Got sinus trouble. Can't smell a thing."

"Well, bye Mr. Kalish Kalish."

Shannon turned for home. "Street closing or Death student?" she mused. The foul odor nagged at her. It was really strong in front of 107 -- a cute bungalow that looked out of place on Woodruff Place. Shannon stoped. O*DOR*IF*ER*OUS. The calendar word from Saturday flashed through her mind. something clicked. Gas. She was smelling gas. And they make it smell so bad because it's dangerous. Shannon had read an ad about that in the paper last winter. She was panicky "What do I do?" She remembered the ad. Shannon hollered to Mr. Kalish, now pruning the roses he couldn't smell.

"Call 9-1-1. I smell gas."

"What?" He was caught up in his roses. we create word picture

Yelled again

EX*AS*PER*A*TED, Shannon repeated. "Call 9-1-1. I smell gas."

~~At the same instant,~~ she knocked on the door at 107. An elderly woman

peeked out. "Quick," Shannon said, "I smell gas. Get out."

Shannon repeated the warning at 105 and 109, and soon a knot of

people was gathered outside. ~~As~~ fire trucks roared up ~~&~~ the odor was

stronger. "We'd better get farther away," Shannon said. Mr. Kalish

agreed, and the group moved across the street.

The crowd grew, drawn by the sirens. Kids on bikes weaved in and

Adults shouted at them.

out. A baby cried. Firefighters jumped from their trucks and roped off

the street. The crowd was pushed back even farther. The odor of danger

matched the odor of the gas.

Shannon ~~was taking it all in.~~ took it all in. She ~~talked~~ stopped to talk with the woman from

107, who clung to her wildly barking ~~Pekingese~~ PEKINGESE. "You've created

quite a stir, young lady. But I'm ~~sure glad~~ thankful you've got a good nose.

Her Majesty ~~has been~~ has been barking all morning, but I couldn't figure out why.

Guess she smelled it, too."

"You didn't smell anything?" Shannon asked.

"No. I lost most of my sense of smell years ago.

Who'd of thought it would matter so much. Just can't taste my food much."

Out of the corner of one eye, Shannon saw the Channel 6 TV crew

pull up in their brightly painted van. Right behind them was a station wagon from The Gazette. Shannon edged ~~(n)~~er near them, intent on watching

the reporters.

One of the first people the reporters stumbled on was Mr. Kalish,

who was explainin~~t~~ᵍ the situation to a fire captain. "Here's the person

you should talk to," he said, pointing to Shannon. "She smelled it and got

the p~~o~~eple out of their houses.

Suddenly, Shannon was in the spotlight. As the fire captian

shook her hand, the reporters ~~fired~~ (spit) out their questions.

"How did you ~~t~~know it was gas,?" one asked.

"What did you do when you smelled it?" asked another.

"Shake hands again," a photographer commanded.

"How old are you?" "Where do you live?" "Where do you go to school?"

Then the Gazette~~s~~ reporter spotted the PRES~~S~~ card in Shannon's hat.

"What's this?" ~~And~~ as the reporter~~s~~ scribbled notes, Shanno~ⁿ~t told her

about the   Gnus   and AK and ~~other own reporting~~ (her mother + Mrs Ferguson + Ferd ⊗)

~~Her questions~~

"Did your aunt ever tell you what a sidebar is," the reporter asked.

"No."

"Well," the reporter explained, "it's a little story that's

related to a big story. (kind of like its cousin⊗) How ~~w~~would you like to come down to the Gazette with me and write your story as a sidebar to my story about the gas

leak?"

I: She remembered AK saying

      Shannon was speechless --- but only for a moment.

      "Sorry," she said as she rolled her wheelchair toward home. "I finally

got a real scoop for my front page."

      "And it's not ice cream, Mr. Kalish!."

      THE END

Appendix C

"One Story"

You should know there is little about which I can write with certainty.

I am certain however, that as a high school student I was a victim of what is now defined as sexual harassment.

Over time, that sexual harassment became ongoing sexual assault.

I remain its victim today. But I have finally named it what it was and I am healing.

*   *   *

Mr. B was a popular teacher who had been at the high school for years. Boys liked him because he had been a coach of some sort and talked their language. Girls liked him because he was charming. He had a reputation for being tough and for screaming at the lazy or the inattentive in his classroom.

In 1964-65 I was in his sophomore Latin class. I also worked for the student newspaper, for which he served as adviser. He encouraged my participation. And he began to cast a spell over me -- a spell of special attention, privilege and status. He masterfully manipulated me, as I am sure he manipulated girls before me and after me.

I developed a schoolgirl crush. Over time, he took advantage of that. He told me I was smart; he treated me like an adult. He told me I was more talented than the senior girl who was editor of the paper. I remember a staff meeting where he humiliated her in front of us all. I probably thought how much I did not <u>ever</u> want him to do that to me. Eventually he told me I was pretty.

I turned 16 in January 1965.

His name began to appear regularly in my diary. It is my memory. It tells me he regularly gave me rides home from school. That he telephoned me at home. That he asked for my help on projects. It also helps me see how he cleverly lured me. By spring he was "teasingly" ordering me to dance with him at a dance he was going to chaperone: "As long as I have to be there I might as well do something enjoyable." Or complimenting a dress I had made and then observing, "Looks like pajamas." Or asking if I was angry with him: "Don't be; I need you too much."

In April 1965 he introduced me to his wife. To his dog. I liked them both. They had no children; I felt like an only child. He gave me a trinket for my birthday; "they" gave me a green sweater for Christmas.

Summer came. He said they would invite me to their cottage. He helped me find a volunteer job. I spent a lot of time waiting for phone calls that did not come.

Sometime in August we talked for 1 1/2 hours; that "was heaven— I learned a lot about him." Was it then that he told me he and his wife had separate bedrooms?

About this time he gave me a driving lesson. His car had manual transmission. He held my hand on the gearshift to teach me how to use it.

When school started, he appointed me editor-in-chief of the newspaper. He got me a hall pass so I could move freely about the school. The darkroom -- across from his classroom -- became my "office." At first I spent an occasional study hall there. Soon I was there daily. He knew my schedule; I recognized his footsteps. I worked for his approval in all that I did -- inside and outside the classroom. He seemed to care about me.

Some of my friends also had "special" teachers. So Mr. B's attention did not feel that unusual. By the time the sexual assaults began, I was convinced that he loved me. I think it was early in the fall of my junior year.

I became secretive, sneaking about. He no longer drove me all the way home; instead, he would drop me off a block away. I suspect he made me promise not to tell anyone about "us." By November my diary entries end with WLAK (?? with love and kisses??). They are also elusive. "I wish I could write all . . . maybe in a year. . . ." In April 1966, I wrote, "He is my life." And for months I had been jealous of another girl who seemed to be getting his attention. He toyed with those emotions. He told off a boy who was pursing me: "I think I am rid of him."

The summer before my senior year, he created a paying job for me on a federal reading program he was administering. That gave him lots of reasons to call me, to see me, to have me with him. I also was to be editor again my senior year, so I kept my "office."

Did people suspect? Know? My diary tells me my mother intervened on a couple of occasions. Said I was not to accept any more rides home. Said I was not to work on the newspaper with him on weekends. A poem I wrote suggests to me that the guidance counselor suspected. I can't help but think that some of his teaching buddies had to wonder. And how could his wife have been blind to his behaviors?

Ironically, I remain in the dark about most of the details of what went on in that darkroom 25 years ago, except for the repeated incidents of what I now know as second-degree sexual assault. I cannot recall much about the summer of '66, or of my senior year, except for one particular sexual assault. I do not know when it all stopped.

I do know that the after-effects continue and perhaps always will. I struggle to reclaim the adolescent me, to learn to love with trust. I had every right to trust Mr. B; he had **no** right to abuse that trust!

Appendix D

HERS panel presentation

Transcribed as hand-written

I am at heart a private person, too serious for my own good, and I volunteered for this panel only after much thought and with considerable trepidation. I did so because I believe there are important things to be said that have not been dealt with aloud yet. But these 10 minutes feel real risky to me.

With Adrian's admonition about audience memories in mind, let me start by saying I hope you'll remember the following 2 thoughts:

1. borrowed from Judith = AUTHENTICITY – Trying to live an "authentic" life is a continuous struggle fraught with potholes

2. Inclusiveness – it is not enough to be inclusive in theory and word – it requires our action, too – and a level of consciousness & sensitivity most of us have not yet developed

So, here's my story:

45 years old – Midwesterner by birth – working class – 1st generation college – product of public HE – BA to MS to reporter to editor to teacher (1974) – PhD – Moving up the ranks & moving around – Eventually earning tenure at the world's oldest school of journalism – Gave up tenure to come East and try private HE – Bad fit – URI opportunity – w/a career map

For the first 10 years of my HE career, I was driven to succeed. Every choice I faced was made in favor of my professional self. I finally listened to my heart when I moved to Connecticut, and that proved to be a personal disaster and professional mistake. Ultimately, I found new challenges being offered to me: come rescue this department. Professional concerns prevailed. I once again was driven – and driving, too (at first commuting two hours a day).

Today, the conflicts and tensions that arise between my professional & personal lives are not unlike those my colleagues spoke about: I am ½ of a dual-career couple. I have aging parents with serious medical conditions -- 1500 miles away. My Signif Other has a parent who requires 24 hr care a few hours away. My mobility is restricted right now, & thus professional choices are constrained by personal commitments.

It also is true that I am a lesbian. Thus my attempts to live a coherent life, with the personal and professional in some balance, to make choices, to live and work in ways that are true to myself – all are enmeshed – and complicated by – this one fact.

I live in a world that is not hospitable to me. I work on a campus that is not hospitable. Though both – like the Institute – often spend a great deal of time in conversation about diversity (inclusiveness) in theory – in practice I am rendered invisible in a myriad of ways because those with whom I spend the bulk of my hours make it all too clear to me – by their deeds, seldom by their words – that I do not belong. It is not necessarily a hostile world – but it is not hospitable.

Dare I host the party to recognize the accomplishments of a colleague? How do I explain I need to go w/my SO to tend to her mother for a few days? Do I even bother to look at ads in the Chronicle? When I get an "and guest" invitation, do I bring my SO? Each decision I make has an added complication – often requiring me to confront my own internalized homophobia.

My strategies? I'm not sure I have many or the best ones – a scary thought, but . . .

- I count on my significant other for wise counsel, support . . . .

- I try to live my life w/out apology. While I am not "out" on my campus, in that I have not used the L word, neither do I hide.

632

- I count on my therapist to help me find perspective.

- I count on a small circle of friends, all of whom are professional women, for honest conversation – & fun.

- A serious bout w/Lyme disease was a powerful reminder about smelling the roses. I try to remember its lessons each day – and I've taken to growing roses.

Appendix E

The story of my Red Fish "imprint" is this: I don't know when I began sending my nephews Swedish fish candy from Sweenor's Chocolates in Wakefield, only that it remains a custom. When Bill, the oldest, was first deployed as a Naval Flight Officer in 2001, I included them in Care packages. (They were just heading into the Gulf when 9/11 occurred.) He would share them -- sparingly -- with his pilot on their long missions. (To this day he can make a stash of the red, chewy candy last longer than any other family member.) For their 2004 wedding, Bill and Michelle used small bags of Swedish fish -- from Sweenor's -- as table favors. And when I began producing projects, choosing Red Fish as my label was a no-brainer.

Books

Island Bark/Hilton Head Discoveries (Essay and photos). 2010. Published on Blurb. 7 inches square; 44 pages.

Mayo and More/An Irish Holiday. 2011. Published on Blurb. 9.5 x 8 inches; 136 pages.

Musings of a newly retired professor. 2012. Published on Blurb. 5 x 8 inches; 78 pages.

An Alphabet for Max. Christmas 2012. Published on Blurb (by Barb Teyze, Turkish for Aunt Barb and what my grandnephews call me). Hardcover; 10 x 8 inches; 30 pages.

Cherokee Editor/The life and times of Elias Boudinot, father of American Indian Journalism. 2014. Published using Amazon's CreateSpace. 6 x 9 inches; 168 pages.

My Peruvian Adventure/A whirlwind trip to Lima and beyond (photos). 2015. Published on Shutterfly. Hardcover; 8 inches square; 20 pages.

Summer 2015 (photos and text). Published on Shutterfly. Hardover; 8 inches square; 20 pages.

I Will Build You a Song, 2nd edition. *The Collected Poems of Dorothy M. Reilly with Photographs by her daughter, Mary Ellen Reilly*. Christmas 2018. Published on Shutterfly. Hardcover, 10 inches square, 30 pages. ". . . to honor Mary Ellen and to give her family and friends a tangible memory of the spirit and creativity she shares with her mother."

Dementia's Unexpected Gifts/A memoir of stumbling into caregiving, then learning to live my best life. 2020. Published using Amazon's CreateSpace. 6 x 9 inches; 268 pages.

Video Creations

"Shelly & Bill Got Hitched" -- story of their August 28, 2004 wedding.

"B Loves ME/A Valentine from My Heart" -- 2005.

"Christmases Past/A Family Story" -- for Mary Ellen's brother and sister-in-law, Mike and Caryl Reilly).

"S is for Sargolini/A Children's Alphabet" -- Christmas 2006 (Kim Reilly Sargolini is Mary Ellen's oldest niece).

"Stories for Alyssa" -- Christmas 2006 (for my only niece, then almost 5 and living in Colorado; family members videotaped their reading her stories, which I assembled).

"Summer Gardens" -- July 2007.

"Scenes from a Wedding" -- Karrie Reilly and Chris Sadler, July 26, 2007.

"Yngve Ramstad/A Man of Courage" -- June 2008.

"Parmentier Pomp/Circumstances Worth Celebrating" -- 2 parts -- Christmas 2008 (stories of my sister's graduation from the University of Wisconsin-Oshkosh and my youngest nephew's completion of Officer Candidate School).

"40 & Counting/Celebrating Kris & Fred" -- October 2011 (for a surprise anniversary party).

"Dad & Daughter/A Photographic Journey -- Christmas 2011 (for my brother and niece).

Editing for Others

No Ordinary Life/Memoir of a World War II Bombardier by Sue Johnpeter, 2014.

Hope. Healing. Spirit. Strength, Solace and Self-Advocacy for the Bipolar Community by Dr. Kay Bernard, 2016. (Published using CreateSpace. Editing, cover design, interior design.)

First People/Stories of the Indigenous Nations of North America by Lorne Pollard, 2017. (Published using CreateSpace. Editing, cover design, interior design.)

Appendix F

Transcribed exactly as written and edited. Slug was "women's softball-humor goody." I don't know when it was written, but today I would call it "Ode to My First Love."

"Coach, what are your plans now that the female softball season is over?"

"After a couple of weeks, I'll put the team on their off-season training program."

"I imagine that means calisthenics, jogging."

"No, it means limited smoking, drinking and playing around."

"Babies have got to come before May 30. We can't afford losing our players in the middle of the season."

"Were you pleased with the team's play this year?"

"Oh yes. They played hard, they played to win, and by the end of the season the number of balls going past the outfielders was only about 65 per cent -- down from 100 per cent."

"Could you pick out any particular player as a start?"

"Our bench warmers batted beautifully -- 633 for 633. They sure know how to swat mosquitoes. Seriously, they all tried hard and did their best.

"I would holler 'snap those wrists' and 'show 'em where you live.'" And they did. But, with the fence to the east and my players from the west, well, we kept the opposing catchers in shape catching foul balls.

"And they could rally snap those wrists -- we broke three this year."

"What about your running game, coach?"

"We couldn't keep up with the younger teams -- our average age is

35 and four kids -- but I think I've solved the problem. I found a good deal on spiked roller skates."

"How about fielding?"

"We really shined here. The infielders always got the ground balls by the fifth or sixth bounce, and when the ball was in the air, we had everybody going for it."

"But, did they catch it?"

"What counts is that you get 'em going after it -- you can always pick the ball up after somebody's head has stopped it."

"Would you change anything you did this year?"

"Only one thing. I should have ordered two gross of tranquilizers instead of one."

"Your girls really must get butterflies."

"No, the pills were for me."

"What about spring?"

"We take off for Miami and two weeks in March. After we return, we will go into our rigorous training period -- absolutely no smoking, no drinking, no sex. Then too, we have our famous two-a-week practices and grass drills."

"Like in football?"

"No, the team does a lot of early lawn cutting, with push mowers, to get their legs in shape. Then, once the season begins, it's games every Tuesday, practice on Thursday and a team 'meeting' every third Tuesday night."

"Team meeting?"

"Sorry, can't answer any more questions. My harem is calling me to the bar. It must be my turn to buy. Come on girls, snap those wrists; you want to drop those bottles?"

640

About the Author

Barbara F. Luebke (*Please, call me Barb*) doesn't care that the widely used quotation "Growing old is mandatory; growing up is optional" is probably apocryphal because she embraces it as her guiding aphorism. Her goals include keeping all her own body parts and continuing to spend winters in Florida. A retired educator, she currently lives (adverb used because who knows what the future holds) in Oshkosh, Wisconsin, where she keeps busy writing, playing golf, reading, building LEGO and sharing adventures with her sister and brother-in-law. She also revels in being Aunt Barb to her niece (Alyssa), her nephews and their wives (Bill and Shelly, Nick and Jenny, Mitch and Gabby), and Barb Teyze to her "grands" (Xavier, Max, Connor, Hawker, Cru, Leo and Finnian). You can email golf tips, book critiques, questions or comments to rhodydoc@gmail.com.

www.ingramcontent.com/pod-product-compliance
Lightning Source LLC
Chambersburg PA
CBHW071130130626
46553CB00004B/1319